The New Political Economy of Globalisation
Volume II

Wherever possible, the articles in these volumes have been reproduced as originally published using facsimile reproduction, inclusive of footnotes and pagination to facilitate ease of reference.

For a list of all Edward Elgar published titles visit our site on the World Wide Web at
http://www.e-elgar.co.uk

The New Political Economy of Globalisation
Volume II

Edited by

Richard Higgott

Professor of International Political Economy,
University of Warwick, UK

and

Anthony Payne

Professor of Politics,
University of Sheffield, UK

An Elgar Reference Collection
Cheltenham, UK • Northampton, MA, USA

Published by
Edward Elgar Publishing Limited
Glensanda House
Montpellier Parade
Cheltenham
Glos GL50 1UA
UK

Edward Elgar Publishing, Inc.
136 West Street
Suite 202
Northampton
Massachusetts 01060
USA

A catalogue record for this book is available from the British Library.

Library of Congress Cataloguing in Publication Data

The new political economy of globalisation / edited by Richard Higgott and Anthony Payne
        p. cm. – (Elgar mini series)
    Includes bibliographical references and index.
    1. International economic relations. 2. International economic integration. 3. Globalization—Economic aspects. 4. Globalization—Social aspects. I. Higgott, Richard A. II. Payne, Anthony. III. Series.

    HF1359 .N482 2001
    337—dc21   00–062291

ISBN   1 84064 056 1 (2 volume set)

Printed and bound in Great Britain by MPG Books Ltd, Bodmin, Cornwall

Contents

Acknowledgements

The editors and publishers wish to thank the authors and the following publishers who have kindly given permission for the use of copyright material.

Blackwell Publishers Ltd for articles: Gary Marks, Liesbet Hooghe and Kermit Blank (1996), 'European Integration from the 1980s: State-Centric v. Multi-level Governance', *Journal of Common Market Studies*, **34** (3), September, 341–78; Richard Devetak and Richard Higgott (1999), 'Justice Unbound? Globalization, States and the Transformation of the Social Bond', *International Affairs*, **75** (3), July, 483–98; Paul Taylor (1999), 'The United Nations in the 1990s: Proactive Cosmopolitanism and the Issue of Sovereignty', *Political Studies*, **XLVII**, 538–65.

Cambridge University Press for articles: David Held and Anthony McGrew (1998), 'The End of the Old Order? Globalization and the Prospects for World Order', *Review of International Studies*, **24**, Special Issue, 219–43; Robert W. Cox (1999), 'Civil Society at the Turn of the Millennium: Prospects for an Alternative World Order', *Review of International Studies*, **25** (1), January, 3–28.

Council on Foreign Relations, Inc. for articles: Jessica T. Mathews (1997), 'Power Shift', *Foreign Affairs*, **76** (1), January/February, 50–66; Anne-Marie Slaughter (1997), 'The Real New World Order', *Foreign Affairs*, **76** (5), September/October, 183–97.

Gordon and Breach Publishers for article: Saskia Sassen (1995), 'The State and the Global City: Notes Towards a Conception of Place-Centered Governance', *Competition and Change*, **1** (1), 31–50.

Millennium: Journal of International Studies for articles: Lorraine Eden (1991), 'Bringing the Firm Back In: Multinationals in International Political Economy', *Millennium: Journal of International Studies*, **20** (2), Summer, 197–224; A. Claire Cutler (1995), 'Global Capitalism and Liberal Myths: Dispute Settlement in Private International Trade Relations', *Millennium: Journal of International Studies*, **24** (3), Winter, 377–97; Andrew Hurrell and Ngaire Woods (1995), 'Globalisation and Inequality', *Millennium: Journal of International Studies*, **24** (3), Winter, 447–70.

MIT Press Journals for articles: John Gerard Ruggie (1993), 'Territoriality and Beyond: Problematizing Modernity in International Relations', *International Organization*, **47** (1), Winter, 139–74; Kathryn Sikkink (1993), 'Human Rights, Principled Issue-Networks, and Sovereignty in Latin America', *International Organization*, **47** (3), Summer, 411–41; Louis W. Pauly and Simon Reich (1997), 'National Structures and Multinational Corporate Behavior: Enduring Differences in the Age of Globalization', *International Organization*, **51** (1), Winter, 1–30.

New Left Review Ltd for article: Robert Wade (1996), 'Japan, the World Bank, and the Art of Paradigm Maintenance: *The East Asian Miracle* in Political Perspective', *New Left Review*, **217**, 3–36.

Lynne Rienner Publishers for articles: James N. Rosenau (1995), 'Governance in the Twenty-first Century', *Global Governance*, **1** (1), Winter, 13–43; Ronnie D. Lipschutz (1997), 'From Place to Planet: Local Knowledge and Global Environmental Governance', *Global Governance*, **3** (1), January–April, 83–102; Cecelia Lynch (1998), 'Social Movements and the Problem of Globalization', *Alternatives*, **23** (2), April–June, 149–73.

Routledge, Taylor and Francis Books Ltd for excerpt: Jan Aart Scholte (2000), '"In the Foothills": Relations between the IMF and Civil Society', in Richard A. Higgott, Geoffrey R.D. Underhill and Andreas Bieler (eds), *Non-State Actors and Authority in the Global System*, 256–73.

Timothy J. Sinclair for his own article: (1994), 'Passing Judgement: Credit Rating Processes as Regulatory Mechanisms of Governance in the Emerging World Order', *Review of International Political Economy*, **1** (1), Spring, 133–59.

Taylor and Francis Ltd for articles: Leon Gordenker and Thomas G. Weiss (1995), 'NGO Participation in the International Policy Process', *Third World Quarterly*, **16** (3), 543–55; James Anderson and James Goodman (1995), 'Regions, States and the European Union: Modernist Reaction or Postmodern Adaptation?', *Review of International Political Economy*, **2** (4), Autumn, 600–31; Richard Falk (1998), 'Global Civil Society: Perspectives, Initiatives, Movements', *Oxford Development Studies*, **26** (1), February, 99–110; John H. Dunning, 'An Overview of Relations with National Governments', Leslie Sklair, 'TNCs As Political Actors' and Andrew Walter, 'Do They Really Rule the World?' in Ankie Hoogvelt *et al.* (1988), 'Debate: Transnational Corporations', *New Political Economy*, **3** (2), July, 280–92.

In addition the publishers wish to thank the Library of the London School of Economics and Political Science, the Marshall Library of Economics, Cambridge University and B & N Microfilm, London for their assistance in obtaining these articles.

The editors acknowledge the support of the ESRC Centre for the Study of Globalisation and Regionalisation at the University of Warwick for research assistance in the compilation of these essays. Thanks to Jane Booth for initial support.

Part I
New Modes of Governance

[1]

Territoriality and beyond: problematizing modernity in international relations
John Gerard Ruggie

We shall not cease from exploration
And the end of all our exploring
Will be to arrive where we started
And know the place for the first time.

—T. S. Eliot, *Little Gidding*

The year 1989 has already become a convenient historical marker: it has been invoked by commentators to indicate the end of the postwar era. An era is characterized by the passage not merely of time but also of the distinguishing attributes *of a time,* attributes that structure expectations and imbue daily events with meaning for the members of any given social collectivity. In that sense, what the journalist Theordore H. White observed in 1945 is true once again: the world, he wrote, is "fluid and about to be remade."[1] Arguments will continue for many years to come about the determinants of the collapse of the old postwar order and the contours of the new post-postwar order. But even among diverse theoretical traditions there exists a shared vocabulary describing "the world" that has become fluid and is being remade: in its simplest, irreducible terms, it is the world of strategic bipolarity.

The same cannot be said of another "world" that also may be fluid and in the process of being remade: the modern system of states. This world exists on a deeper and more extended temporal plane, and its remaking involves a shift not in the play of power politics but of the stage on which that play is

An earlier draft of this article was presented at the British Social Science Research Council Conference on Nation-States and the International Order, Emmanuel College, Cambridge, 4–6 September 1991. I am grateful to Barry Buzan, Caroline Bynum, Ernst Haas, Andreas Huyssen, Stephen Krasner, Hendrik Spruyt, Tracy Strong, and Alexander Wendt for their comments and to David Auerswald for research assistance.

1. Theodore H. White, *In Seach of History: A Personal Adventure* (New York: Harper & Row, 1978), p. 224.

International Organization 47, 1, Winter 1993
© 1993 by the World Peace Foundation and the Massachusetts Institute of Technology

performed.[2] Here, no shared vocabulary exists in the literature to depict change and continuity. Indeed, little vocabulary for it exists at all.

Take efforts to express the emerging architecture of the European Community (EC) as a case in point. "It is a negative characteristic which first imposes itself," the Marxist theorist Etienne Balibar concedes. "The state today in Europe is *neither national nor supranational,* and this ambiguity does not slacken but only grows deeper over time."[3] From the other side of the political spectrum, *The Economist* agrees and gropes for metaphor: in place of older federative visions, it sees "a Europe of many spires," a European "Mont Saint Michel."[4] For their part, Eurocrats speak of overlapping layers of European economic and political "spaces," tied together, in the words of EC Commission President Jacques Delors, by the community's "spiderlike strategy to organize the architecture of a Greater Europe."[5]

These formulations are not terribly precise or definitive. Still, they are improvements over the treatment Europe typically receives in the standard academic literatures. In Kenneth Waltz's classic neorealist treatise, the EC earned only a few fleeting references, and then only to argue that it would never amount to much in the "international structure" unless it took on the form of a unified state.[6] In the instrumental rationality of game theory and transactions cost analysis, macrostructures are either taken for granted or treated as relatively unproblematic consequences of the interplay of micromotives, and hence generate little interest as independent social facts.[7] And, regional integration theory long ago acknowledged its own obsolescence in the face of the new European reality.[8] In none of these theoretical perspectives is there so much as a hint that the institutional, juridical, and spatial complexes associated with the community may constitute nothing less than the emergence of the first truly postmodern international political form.

---

2. For a specification of the ontological and epistemological differences among incremental, conjunctural, and secular or epochal time frames, see John Gerard Ruggie, "Social Time and International Policy," in Margaret P. Karns, ed., *Persistent Patterns and Emergent Structures in a Waning Century* (New York: Praeger, 1986), pp. 211–36. Within that typology, the "normal politics" studied by much of the international relations field falls into the incremental category, the cold war exemplifies the conjunctural, and the modern system of states the epochal time frames.

3. Etienne Balibar, "*Es Gibt Keinen Staat in Europa:* Racism and Politics in Europe Today," *New Left Review* 186 (March/April 1991), p. 16, emphasis original.

4. "Many-spired Europe," *The Economist,* 18 May 1991, p. 16. Some twenty years ago, I suggested that integration theory move from the model of a "tree" (in graph-theoretic terms) to depict the institutional end-point of the integration process to one of a semi-lattice—the definition of which sounds very much like a formal representation of *The Economist's* European Mont Saint Michel. See John Gerard Ruggie, "The Structure of International Organization: Contingency, Complexity, and Postmodern Form," Peace Research Society (International) *Papers,* no. 18, 1972.

5. "Inner Space," *The Economist,* 18 May 1991. Delors is cited in Alan Riding, "Europeans in Accord to Create Vastly Extended Trading Bloc," *New York Times,* 23 October 1991, p. A1.

6. See Kenneth Waltz, *Theory of International Politics* (Reading, Mass.: Addison-Wesley, 1979).

7. See, for example, Geoffrey Garrett, "International Cooperation and Institutional Choice: The European Community's Internal Market," *International Organization* 46 (Spring 1992), pp. 531–60.

8. See Ernst B. Haas, *The Obsolescence of Regional Integration Theory,* Research Mongraph no. 25 (Berkeley: Institute of International Studies, University of California, 1976).

Prevailing perspectives may have difficulty describing and explaining the process of European transformation, but none suggests that it is not occurring. At the level of the global economy, in contrast, the phenomenon of transformation not only strains the available vocabulary but on some accounts, its very occurrence remains in doubt.

There has been a remarkable growth in transnational microeconomic links over the past thirty years or so, comprising markets and production facilities that are designated by the awkward term "offshore"—as though they existed in some ethereal space waiting to be reconceived by an economic equivalent of relativity theory. In this offshore area, sourcing, production, and marketing are organized within "global factories,"[9] in some instances "global offices,"[10] and most recently the "global lab"[11]—real-time transnational information flows being the raw material of all three. Financial transactions take place in various "Euro" facilities, which may be *housed* in Tokyo, New York, and European financial centers but which are considered to *exist* in an extranational realm.[12] Cross-investment among the leading firms or other means of forging transnationalized intercorporate alliances increasingly are the norm.[13] Trade is made up disproportionately of intrafirm transactions as opposed to the conventional arms-length exchange that is the staple of economic models and policy.[14] And, the financial sector, which historically (and in theory) is assumed to follow and service the "real" sector, now dwarfs it completely.[15]

Furthermore, the largest share of the "goods" that are "traded" in this offshore world actually are "services."[16] *The Economist* magazine, with tongue

9. For a description of global factories, see Joseph Grunwald and Kenneth Flamm, *The Global Factory: Foreign Assembly in International Trade* (Washington, D.C.: The Brookings Institution, 1985).

10. Steve Lohr, "The Growth of the 'Global Office'," *New York Times,* 18 October 1988. For example, Citibank does some of its financial data processing in Jamaica; American Airlines processes ticket stubs in Barbados and the Dominican Republic; and New York Life processes claims and McGraw-Hill, magazine subscription renewals, in Ireland.

11. The term is drawn from Pollack: "Just as they once moved manufacturing plants overseas, American companies are now spreading their research and product development around the world, helping to turn the creation of technology into an activity that transcends national borders." See Andrew Pollack, "Technology Without Borders Raises Big Questions for U.S.," *New York Times,* 1 January 1992, p. A1.

12. Joan E. Spero, "Guiding Global Finance," *Foreign Policy* 73 (Winter 1988–89), pp. 114–34.

13. See Robert B. Reich, *The Work of Nations* (New York: Knopf, 1991).

14. Some 40 percent of U.S. trade is of the intrafirm variety, a ratio that increases to close to two-thirds if more relaxed definitions of "related party" are used. Moreover, intrafirm trade has been growing more rapidly than the standard stuff, and it is less sensitive to such macroeconomic factors as exchange rates. For evidence, see Jane Sneddon Little, "Intra-firm Trade: An Update," *New England Economic Review* (May/June 1987), pp. 46–51; and the earlier but still useful study by Gerald C. Helleiner, *Intra-firm Trade and the Developing Countries* (London: Macmillan, 1981).

15. International trade amounts to some $2.5 to $3 trillion per year; international capital markets turn over at least $75 trillion, and foreign exchange transactions now amount to approximately $1 trillion per day.

16. Definitions are so bad that the balance of world services imports and exports routinely is off by as much as $100 billion per annum—a margin of error equivalent to fully one-fifth of all traded services; see Ronald K. Shelp, "Trade in Services," *Foreign Policy* 65 (Winter 1986–87). Bhagwati suggests several creative definitional distinctions but ends up recommending that the term "trade in services" be abandoned in favor of "international service transactions"; see Jagdish Bhagwati,

only half-in-cheek, has proposed defining services as "things which can be bought and sold but which you cannot drop on your foot,"—acknowledging the difficulty of devising a more rigorous definition.[17] Nor is it entirely clear what it means to say that services are traded. In merchandise trade, factors of production stand still and goods move across borders; in traded services, typically the factors of production do the moving while the good (service) stands still: it is produced for the consumer on the spot. What is called trade, therefore, is really "investment," or at the least "right of establishment," baffling trade theorists and negotiators alike.[18]

The orthodox liberal position that these developments somehow imply the growing irrelevance of states is, as Janice Thomson and Stephen Krasner suggest, "fundamentally misplaced."[19] Indeed, states are anything but irrelevant even in the ever more integrated EC. Nevertheless, the standard realist ground for rejecting the transformational potential of these developments is equally misplaced. A leading realist journal of opinion recently offered a particularly egregious illustration in response to Robert Reich's probing question about the new world of transnationalized production networks, "Who is 'Us'?"[20] Reich sought to voice the conceptual complexities entailed in determining whether something is an American product any longer and whether the legal designation, "an American corporation," still describes the same economic entity, with the same consequences for domestic employment and economic growth, that it did in the 1950s and 1960s. The response to Reich was a baffling and bizarre—but not atypical—string of non sequiturs, for example: "Only the state can defend corporate interests in international negotiations over trade, investment, and market access. . . . If the existence of the state is in doubt, just ask the depositors of BCCI in some fifty countries who

---

"Trade in Services and the Multilateral Trade Negotiations," *The World Bank Economic Review,* voi. 1, no. 1, 1987. See also Dorothy I. Riddle, *Service-Led Growth* (New York: Praeger, 1986); Orio Giarini, ed., *The Emerging Service Economy* (London: Pergamon Press, 1987); Terrence G. Berg, "Trade in Services," *Harvard International Law Journal* 28 (Winter 1987); and Mario A. Kakabadse, *International Trade in Services* (London: Croom Helm for the Atlantic Institute for International Affairs, 1987).

17. "A Gatt for Services," *The Economist,* 12 October 1985, p. 20. See also "Netting the Future: A Survey of Telecommunications," *The Economist,* 19 March 1990; and "A Question of Definition: A Survey of International Banking," *The Economist,* 7 April 1990.

18. At the time of this writing, indications are that the Uruguay Round will bring into the General Agreement on Tariffs and Trade (GATT) framework that portion of international services which fits the conventional understanding of international trade. However, that portion is relatively small compared with the whole, and numerous highly disputatious issues lurk beyond the conventional framework. See "GATT Brief: Centre Stage for Services?" *The Economist,* 5 May 1990, pp. 88–89; and "GATT and Services: Second Best," *The Economist,* 3 August 1991.

19. Janice E. Thomson and Stephen D. Krasner, "Global Transactions and the Consolidation of Sovereignty," in Ernst-Otto Czempiel and James N. Rosenau, eds., *Global Changes and Theoretical Challenges* (Lexington, Mass.: Lexington Books, 1989), p. 198. See also Stephen D. Krasner, "Global Communications and National Power: Life on the Pareto Frontier," *World Politics* 43 (April 1991), pp. 336–66.

20. See Ethan B. Kapstein, "*We* are US: The Myth of the Multinational," *The National Interest* 26 (Winter 1991/92), pp. 55–62. The full exposition of Reich's argument is in *The Work of Nations,* the final chapter of which is entitled "Who is 'US'?"

woke up one morning in July to find their accounts frozen. . . . If the United States wanted to prevent the gathering or transmission of information by satellite, it could easily do so by shooting the satellite down."[21] And thus the conclusion, in the title of the essay, that *"We are US."*

There is an extraordinarily impoverished mind-set at work here, one that is able to visualize long-term challenges to the system of states only in terms of entities that are institutionally substitutable for the state. Since global markets and transnationalized corporate structures (not to mention communications satellites) are not in the business of replacing states, they are assumed to entail no potential for fundamental international change, Q.E.D. The theoretical or historical warrant for that premise has never been mooted, let alone defended.

Illustrations of analytical problems of this sort can be multiplied many times over in other issue-areas. The global ecological implosion inherently invites epochal thinking, yet analytically informed empirical studies of "ozone diplomacy" or of attempts to save the Mediterranean invariably focus on negotiation processes and the dynamics of regime construction, as opposed to exploring the possibility of fundamental institutional discontinuity in the system of states.[22] They do so because, among other reasons, prevailing modes of analytical discourse simply lack the requisite vocabulary.

The worst offender by far is the American field of security studies. Notwithstanding its alleged renaissance, no epochal thought has been expressed by any serious specialist in that field since 1957, when John Herz published his essay, "Rise and Demise of the Territorial State"—and this despite the fact that changes in military technology and in the relations of force are widely acknowledged to have been driving factors of political transformation throughout human history.[23]

The long and the short of it is, then, that we are not very good as a discipline at studying the possibility of fundamental discontinuity in the international

21. Kapstein, *"We are US,"* pp. 56 and 61.

22. See Richard Elliot Benedick, *Ozone Diplomacy* (Cambridge, Mass.: Harvard University Press, 1991); Lynton Keith Caldwell, *International Environmental Policy* (Durham, N.C.: Duke University Press, 1984); Oran R. Young, *International Cooperation: Building Regimes for Natural Resources and the Environment* (Ithaca, N.Y.: Cornell University Press, 1989); and Peter Haas, *Saving the Mediterranean* (New York: Columbia University Press, 1990).

23. On the field's alleged "renaissance," see Stephen M. Walt, "The Renaissance of Security Studies," *International Studies Quarterly* 35 (June 1991), pp. 211–39. For John Herz's view, see his articles "Rise and Demise of the Territorial States," *World Politics* 9 (July 1957), pp. 473–93, and "The Territorial State Revisited—Reflections on the Future of the Nation-State," *Polity* 1 (Fall 1968), pp. 11–34, in which he elaborated and modified some of his earlier ideas. The recent interest in the "obsolescence" of war among democracies was not initiated by international security specialists—see, for example, John Mueller, *Retreat from Doomsday: The Obsolescence of Major War* (New York: Basic Books, 1989)—though it has now attracted serious attention from some. For examples see Bruce Bueno de Mesquita, Robert W. Jackman, and Randolph M. Siverson, eds., *Democracy and Foreign Policy: Community and Constraint,* special issue, *Journal of Conflict Resolution* 35 (June 1991). A partial exception to my characterization of the security studies literature is Robert Jarvis, *The Meaning of the Nuclear Revolution* (Ithaca, N.Y.: Cornell University Press, 1989). On the historical relation between military changes and political transformation, see William H. McNeill, *The Pursuit of Power* (Chicago: University of Chicago Press, 1982); and Charles Tilly, *Coercion, Capital, and European States AD 990–1990* (Cambridge, Mass.: Basil Blackwell, 1990).

system; that is, at addressing the question of whether the modern system of states may be yielding in some instances to postmodern forms of configuring political space.[24] We lack even an adequate vocabulary; and what we cannot describe, we cannot explain. It is the purpose of this article, in Clifford Geertz's apt phrase, to help us "find our feet" in this terrain, which is the necessary first step of any scientific endeavor, no matter how hard or soft the science.[25]

In the next section, I summarize briefly the major features of the lively debate about postmodernism that has been taking place in the humanities. It is suggestive in many respects, but it does not solve our problem entirely because the modern state and system of states barely figure in it. The bulk of this article therefore is devoted to a relatively modest and pretheoretical task: to search for a vocabulary and for the dimensions of a research agenda by means of which we can start to ask systematic questions about the possibility of fundamental international transformation today. The central attribute of modernity in international politics has been a peculiar and historically unique configuration of territorial space. Hence, I shall proceed by re-examining the transformation whereby this configuration of territorial space first came to be.

The ends of modernity

The concept of postmodernity suggests a periodizing hypothesis, an epochal threshold, the end of "an historical project."[26] That much is clear. But, what is the universe of discourse and practices to which it pertains? To that question numerous possible answers exist, not all of which are of equal interest for present purposes.

When the term "postmodernity" first gained currency in the 1970s and 1980s, it referred largely to recent developments in the realm of aesthetics or style: the nostalgic eclecticism in architectural forms, the prevalence of pastiche and abrupt juxtapositions of imagery in art, the deconstructivist impulse in literature. Simultaneity and superimposition replaced sequence; the subject was decentered, dismembered, and dispersed; and language was made to turn in on itself to create a void of infinite signification where the quest for meaning had previously unfolded.[27] In the field of international relations, these expressions of postmodernity have been symptomatic at best; as Pauline Rosenau has shown, they are preoccupied with style and method and offer only limited substantive insight.[28]

---

24. One recent attempt to correct this shortcoming, to which I return below, is James N. Rosenau, *Turbulence in World Politics* (Princeton, N.J.: Princeton University Press, 1990).

25. Clifford Geertz, *The Interpretation of Cultures* (New York: Basic Books, 1973), p. 13.

26. The term is due to Albrecht Wellmer, "On the Dialectic of Modernism and Postmodernism," *Praxis International* 4 (January 1985), p. 337.

27. Ihab Hassan, *The Postmodern Turn* (Columbus: Ohio State University Press, 1987), especially chap. 4, which presents a widely used schema differentiating modern from postmodern aesthetic practices.

28. Attempts to relate the postmodern reading of texts to issues in international relations may be found in James Der Derian and Michael J. Shapiro, eds., *International/Intertextual Relations*

It was not long, however, before postmodernity came to be associated not merely with matters of style but with a historical condition, indicating, according to Andreas Huyssen, a "slowly emerging cultural transformation in Western societies."[29] This transformation concerns the fate of what Jürgen Habermas calls the "project" of modernity, first formulated by the eighteenth-century philosophers of the European Enlightenment; i.e., systematic efforts "to develop objective science, universal morality and law, and autonomous art, according to their inner logic."[30] The Enlightenment was animated by the desire to demystify and secularize, to subject natural forces to rational explanation and control, as well as by the expectation that doing so would promote social welfare, moral progress, and human happiness. The optimism, certitude, and categorical fixity of this project were shattered—by Nietzsche, Freud, Wittgenstein; Darwin, Einstein, Heisenberg; Braque, Picasso, Duchamp; Joyce, Proust, Becket; Schoenberg, Berg, Bartok; two world wars, a Great Depression, Nazi death camps, Stalin's Gulags, Hiroshima, and Nagasaki—long before Lyotard, Foucault, and Derrida pronounced and celebrated its demise.

Although the terrain is high culture, the subsequent battle between "Frankfurters and French fries," as Rainer Nägele has described it irreverently, has been fought largely on political grounds. Habermas has endeavored to hold on to the *intentions* of the Enlightenment in order to complete its project.[31] According to Huyssen, Habermas "tries to salvage the emancipatory potential of enlightened reason which to him is the *sine qua non* of political democracy. Habermas defends a substantive notion of communicative rationality, especially against those who will collapse reason with domination, believing that by abandoning reason they free themselves from domination."[32] Lyotard is hostile to the very thought: "We have paid a high enough price for the nostalgia of the whole and the one," he shouts. "Let us wage a war on totality; let us be witnesses to the unpresentable; let us activate the differences."[33] Even Habermas's admirers express doubts about the viability of his quest.[34] Nevertheless, the Paul de Man saga, especially the shameful defense of de Man by several leading deconstructivists, shows poignantly how deleterious the politi-

---

(Lexington, Mass.: Lexington/Heath, 1989). For a sympathetic yet critical review of this literature, see Pauline Rosenau, "Once Again into the Fray: International Relations Confronts the Humanities," *Millenium* 19 (Spring 1990), pp. 83–110.

29. Andreas Huyssen, "Mapping the Postmodern," *New German Critique* 33 (Fall 1984), p. 8.

30. Jürgen Habermas, "Modernity and Postmodernity," *New German Critique* 22 (Winter 1981), p. 9.

31. These are Habermas's terms; see ibid.

32. Huyssen, "Mapping the Postmodern," p. 31.

33. Jean-Francois Lyotard, *The Postmodern Condition* (Minneapolis: University of Minnesota Press, 1984), pp. 81–82.

34. See Huyssen, "Mapping the Postmodern"; and Martin Jay, "Habermas and Modernism," in Richard J. Berstein, ed., *Habermas and Modernity* (Cambridge, Mass.: MIT Press, 1985), pp. 125–39.

cal consequences can be that follow from the moral vacuum—if not moral vacuity—the French fries would have us inhabit.[35]

The two distinctively modern programs for mastering international relations are deeply implicated in this project of modernity: realist balance-of-power thinking and idealist institutionalism, both of which have their origins in the eighteenth century. On the realist side, the Treaty of Utrecht (1713) enshrined the notion of a self-regulating equilibrium as a core feature of European society together with the idea that the defense of that equilibrium should be of concern to one and all.[36] For realist theorists of the day, "the sovereign states followed their ordered paths in a harmony of mutual attraction and repulsion like the gravitational law that swings planets in their orbits."[37] On the idealist side, the eighteenth century opened with the Abbé de Saint-Pierre's institutionalist plan to secure a *"Perpetual Peace,"* and closed with Kant's.[38] Post–World War II realism and liberal internationalism are but the latest incarnations of realist and idealist thought, and neither, as I suggested above, has much to say about fundamental transformation today.[39]

The concept of postmodernity also has been projected beyond the cultural realm, into the political economy, initially by Marxist analysts. Frederic Jameson led the way.[40] For Jameson, postmodernism depicts "the third great original expansion of capitalism around the globe (after the earlier expansions of the national market and the older imperialist system)." The production and manipulation of signs, images, and information are the raw materials of this new "mode of production" as well as the means by which its expansion is achieved. But this is an expansion, Jameson suggests, that in effect "internalizes": just as the Bonaventure Hotel in Los Angeles or the Eaton Center in Toronto seeks to internalize its exterior, aspiring "to be a total space, a complete world, a kind of miniature city," so too does global capitalism today internalize within its own institutional forms relationships that previously took place among distinct national capitals. This results in a "postmodern hyperspace," as

35. See David Lehman, *Signs of the Times: Deconstruction and the Fall of Paul de Man* (New York: Poseidon Press, 1991).

36. See M.S. Anderson, *Europe in the Eighteenth Century, 1713–1783* (London: Longmans, 1963).

37. Martin Wight, "The Balance of Power and International Order," in Alan James, ed., *The Bases of International Order* (London: Oxford University Press, 1973), p. 98.

38. F. H. Hinsley, *Power and the Pursuit of Peace* (London: Cambridge University Press, 1963), chaps. 2 and 4.

39. In a certain sense, James Rosenau's recent book touches on this cultural category of the postmodernist debate. The major driving force of international transformation today, Rosenau contends, consists of new sensibilities and capacities of individuals: "with their analytical skills enlarged and their orientations toward authority more self-conscious, today's persons-in-the street are no longer as uninvolved, ignorant, and manipulable with respect to world affairs as were their forebears. . . . [T]he enlargements of the capacities of citizens is the primary prerequisite for global turbulence." See Rosenau, *Turbulence in World Politics*, pp. 13 and 15.

40. See Frederic Jameson, "Postmodernism, or the Cultural Logic of Late Capitalism," *New Left Review* 146 (July/August 1984), pp. 53–92; and "Marxism and Postmodernism," *New Left Review* 176 (July/August 1989), pp. 31–45.

Jameson terms it, a heteronomy of fragments which nevertheless remains unified by virtue of expressing the logic of late capitalism.[41]

Several other works of this genre have elaborated on Jameson's notions of a postmodern capitalist mode of production and its consequences.[42] They resonate at a superficial level with the brief description of global microeconomic changes at the outset of this article, as well as with the images of spaceship earth, global warming, nuclear winters, and the like, by means of which the ecosphere is popularly visualized. But, they remain silent on the issue of the state and the system of states, which in the end is not surprising in light of the fact that they are cast in a modes-of-production framework.

Nevertheless, these works are suggestive at a deeper level in their emphasis on the space-time implosion experienced by advanced capitalist societies. Harvey notes that "space and time are basic categories of human existence. Yet we rarely debate their meanings; we tend to take them for granted, and give them common-sense or self-evident attributions."[43] Ultimately, he contends, the current transformation in capitalist production relations is merely one specific expression of a reconfiguration in social space-time experiences to a degree not witnessed since the Renaissance. Harvey concurs with Jameson, however, that "we do not yet possess the perceptual equipment to match this new hyperspace, . . . in part because our perceptual habits were formed in that older kind of space I have called the space of high modernism."[44]

And so the postmodernist debate has shifted in barely two decades from the domain of aesthetics, to culture more broadly, to political economy. Correspondingly, the meaning of "modern" in "postmodern" has shifted from what it is in modern art, the modern novel, or modern architecture, first, to the so-called age of Enlightenment; next, to the structure of capitalist production relations; and then to the very epoch in Western history that was initiated by the Renaissance. It is the last of these space-time frames that concerns me here, because it also marks the transformation that produced the modern mode of organizing political space: the system of territorial states. However, since no perceptual equipment exists, as Jameson remarks, through

41. The quotations are from Jameson, "Postmodernism, or The Cultural Logic of Late Capitalism," pp. 80 and 81.

42. The most comprehensive work is David Harvey, *The Condition of Postmodernity* (Oxford: Basil Blackwell, 1989). For a detailed empirical study of the relationship between global capital and the reconfiguration of urban spaces, see Manuel Castells, *The Informational City* (Oxford: Basil Blackwell, 1989). Marxist theorists of postmodernity encounter an inherent contradiction, to borrow their term, by the very nature of the enterprise. One of the features of postmodernity on which virtually all other schools of thought agree is that it invalidates the possibility of producing metanarratives, or *metarécits*, more fashionably—that "totalizing" and "logocentric" practice of modernity on which Lyotard urges us to wage war. Of course, few narratives are more "meta" than Marxism. Jameson's somewhat feeble response, in "Marxism and Postmodernism," is that a system that produces fragments is still a system.

43. Harvey, *The Condition of Postmodernity,* p. 201.

44. Ibid.

which to grasp what he calls "global hyperspace," I hope to advance our understanding of the possible rearticulation of international political space by looking for clues to the past to discover how the modern political form itself was produced.

Modern territoriality

Historically, the self-conscious use of the term "modern" to denote "now" dates from the sixteenth century.[45] The epochal sense of modern to denote "modernity" dates from the eighteenth century, when the threshold demarcating its beginning was put at roughly 1500.[46] Writing in the eighteenth century, Lord Bolinbroke defined an epoch by the chain of events being so broken "as to have little or no real or visible connexion with that which we see continue. . . . [T]he end of the fifteenth century seems to be just such a period as I have been describing, for those who live in the eighteenth, and who inhabit the western parts of Europe."[47]

One of the chains in which visible connection to the past was ruptured was the organization of political space. The fact of that rupture is well enough known. But, what, if any, categories and modes of analysis does it suggest for the study of international transformation more generally? To that, the main task of this article, I now turn.

Differentiation

Let us begin at the very beginning: politics is about rule. Adapting a formulation by Anthony Giddens, we can define the most generic attribute of any system of rule as comprising legitimate dominion over a spatial extension.[48] I use the term "spatial extension" advisedly, to drive home the point that it need not assume the form of territorial states. The social facticity of any spatial extension in turn implies some mode of differentiating human collectivities from one another. By this I do not mean the progressive structural differentiation that was long a staple of macrosociological theorizing and which is now thoroughly discredited.[49] Instead, I mean the notion of differentiation that John Locke had in mind when he asked "how men might come to have a

45. Raymond Williams, "When was Modernism?" *New Left Review* 175 (May/June 1989), pp. 48–52.
46. Reinhart Koselleck, *Futures Past: On the Semantics of Historical Time*, trans. Keith Tribe (Cambridge, Mass.: MIT Press, 1985), p. 243.
47. Cited in Martin Wight, *Systems of States* (Leicester, England: Leicester University Press, 1977), p. 111.
48. Anthony Giddens, *A Contemporary Critique of Historical Materialism*, vol. 1 (Berkeley: University of California Press, 1981), p. 45.
49. See, for instance, Charles Tilly, *Big Structures, Large Processes, Huge Comparisons* (New York: Russell Sage, 1985).

property in several parts of that which God gave to mankind in common."[50] There are at least three ways in which prior or other systems of rule have differed in this regard from the modern territorial state.

First, systems of rule need not be territorial at all. That is to say, the basis on which the human species is socially individuated and individuals, in turn, are bound together into collectivities can take (and historically has taken) forms other than territoriality. For example, anthropologists quaintly used to characterize as "primitive government" those systems of rule wherein the spatial extension was demarcated on the basis of kinship. Moreover, they held that a critical stage in societal evolution was precisely the shift from consanguinity to contiguity as the relevant spatial parameter.[51] To be sure, territory was *occupied* in kin-based systems, but it did not *define* them.

Second, systems of rule need not be territorially fixed. Owen Lattimore's work on nomadic property rights is of relevance here.[52] Writing of Mongol tribes, Lattimore pointed out that no single pasture would have had much value for them because it soon would have become exhausted. Hence, driven by what Lattimore called the "the sovereign importance of movement," the tribes wandered, herding their livestock. But, they did not wander haphazardly: "They laid claim to definite pastures and to the control of routes of migration between these pastures."[53] Accordingly, "the right to move prevailed over the right to camp. Ownership meant, in effect, the title to a cycle of migration."[54] The cycle was tribally owned and administered by the prince.

Third, even where systems of rule are territorial, and even where territoriality is relatively fixed, the prevailing concept of territory need not entail mutual exclusion. The archetype of nonexclusive territorial rule, of course, is medieval Europe, with its "patchwork of overlapping and incomplete rights of government,"[55] which were "inextricably superimposed and tangled," and in which "different juridical instances were geographically interwoven and stratified, and plural allegiances, asymmetrical suzerainties and anomalous enclaves

---

50. John Locke, "On Property," in the second of the *Two Treatises of Government*, sec. 2.25, Thomas I. Cook, ed. (New York: Hafner, 1947), p. 134. Luhman has developed a nonteleological formulation of differentiation that I have found useful in which he distinguishes among segmentation, functional differentiation, and stratification, with segmentation having an obvious temporal priority. See Niklas Luhman, *The Differentiation of Society*, trans. Stephen Holmes and Charles Larmore (New York: Columbia University Press, 1982). I use the term here in the sense of segmentation.

51. The classic statement of the traditional anthropological view is found in Lewis Henry Morgan, *Ancient Society*, first published in 1877; a reprinted edition was edited by Eleanor Leacock (Gloucester, Mass.: Peter Smith, 1963). For a contemporary discussion, see Jonathan Haas, *The Evolution of the Prehistoric State* (New York: Columbia University Press, 1982).

52. See Owen Lattimore's works *Inner Asian Frontiers of China* (London: Oxford University Press, 1940) and *Studies in Frontier History* (London: Oxford University Press, 1962).

53. Lattimore, *Studies in Frontier History*, p. 535.

54. Lattimore, *Inner Asian Frontiers of China*, p. 66.

55. Joseph R. Strayer and Dana C. Munro, *The Middle Ages* (New York: Appleton-Century-Crofts, 1959), p. 115. See also Joseph R. Strayer, *On the Medieval Origins of the Modern State* (Princeton, N.J.: Princeton University Press, 1970), passim.

abounded."[56] The difference between the medieval and modern worlds is striking in this respect.[57]

Briefly put, the spatial extension of the medieval system of rule was structured by a nonexclusive form of territoriality, in which authority was both personalized and parcelized within and across territorial formations and for which inclusive bases of legitimation prevailed. The notion of firm boundary lines between the major territorial formations did not take hold until the thirteenth century; prior to that date, there were only "frontiers," or large zones of transition.[58] The medieval ruling class was mobile in a manner not dreamed of since, able to assume governance from one end of the continent to the other without hesitation or difficulty because "public territories formed a continuum with private estates."[59] In this connection, Georges Duby writes, wryly, of Henry Plantagenet: "This was Henry, count of Anjou on his father's side, duke of Normandy on his mother's, duke of Aquitaine by marriage, and for good measure—but only for good measure—king of England, although this was of no concern to the country in which he spent the best part of his time."[60] In addition, the medieval system of rule was legitimated by common bodies of law, religion, and custom expressing inclusive natural rights. Nevertheless, these inclusive legitimations posed no threat to the integrity of the constituent political units because these units viewed themselves as municipal embodiments of a universal moral community.[61] Hence the "heteronomous shackles," in Friedrich Meinecke's words, on the autonomy—indeed, on the very ability of thinkers to formulate the concept—of the state.[62]

56. The quotations are from Perry Anderson, *Lineages of the Absolutist State* (London: New Left Books, 1974), pp. 37 and 37–38, respectively.

57. I have explored these differences at greater length in John Gerard Ruggie, "Continuity and Transformation in the World Polity: Toward a Neorealist Synthesis," *World Politics* 35 (January 1983), pp. 261–85. Markus Fischer has recently claimed that I and other theorists who find fault with neorealism's inability to capture the phenomenon of transformation "imply" or "would expect" medieval life to have been more harmonious and less conflictual than modern international relations. Certainly in my case the claim is entirely fictitious, backed only by Fischer citing a sentence in my article that had nothing to do with this point and linking it to what he "would expect" me to have said. See Markus Fischer, "Feudal Europe, 800–1300: Communal Discourse and Conflictual Practices," *International Organization* 46 (Spring 1992), pp. 427–66; the questionable reference is cited in his footnote 12.

58. According to Edouard Perroy, as paraphrased by Wallerstein, this was "the 'fundamental change' in the political structure of Europe." See Immanuel Wallerstein, *The Modern World System*, vol. 1 (New York: Academic Press, 1974), p. 32. An extended discussion of the difference between borders and frontier zones may be found in Lattimore, *Studies in Frontier History*. See also Friedrich Kratochwil, "Of Systems, Boundaries and Territoriality," *World Politics* 34 (October 1986), pp. 27–52.

59. Anderson, *Lineages of the Absolutist State*, p. 32.

60. Georges Duby, *The Three Orders: Feudal Society Imagined*, trans. Arthur Goldhammer (Chicago: University of Chicago Press, 1980), p. 286.

61. Garrett Mattingly, *Renaissance Diplomacy* (Baltimore, Md.: Penguin Books, 1964), p. 41 and passim.

62. Friedrich Meinecke, *Machiavellism*, trans. Douglas Scott (New Haven, Conn.: Yale University Press, 1957). The term is attributed to Meinecke by Scott in his introduction to the book, which was first published in 1924.

The antonym of Meinecke's term is "homonomous."[63] The distinctive
signature of the modern—homonomous—variant of structuring territorial
space is the familiar world of territorially disjoint, mutually exclusive, functionally similar, sovereign states.

The chief characteristic of the modern system of territorial rule is the
consolidation of all parcelized and personalized authority into one public
realm. This consolidation entailed two fundamental spatial demarcations:
between public and private realms and between internal and external realms.[64]
The public sphere was constituted by the monopolization on the part of central
authorities of the legitimate use of force. Internally, this monopolization was
expressed through the progressive imposition of what was called the "king's
peace," or the sole right of the king's authority to enforce the law. As Norbert
Elias notes, this idea was "very novel in a society in which originally a whole
class of people could use weapons and physical violence according to their
means and inclinations."[65] Externally, the monopolization of the legitimate use
of force was expressed in the sovereign right to make war. Philippe Contamine
has put it well: " 'The king's war' and 'the kingdom's war' must, in the end, be
identical."[66] Finally, the inclusive bases of legitimation that had prevailed in the
medieval world, articulated in divine and natural law, yielded to the doctrine of
sovereignty, and *jus gentium* slowly gave way to *jus inter gentes.*

To summarize, politics is about rule. And, the distinctive feature of the
modern system of rule is that it has differentiated its subject collectivity into
territorially defined, fixed, and mutually exclusive enclaves of legitimate
dominion. As such, it appears to be unique in human history.[67] Without the

---

63. The term "heteronomous" refers to systems wherein the parts are subject to different
biological laws or modes of growth and "homonomous" to systems wherein they are subject to the
same laws or modes of growth; see *The Oxford English Dictionary,* 2d ed. s.v. "heteronomous" and
"homonomous." In the original, biological sense of the terms, the fingers on a hand would exhibit
homonomous growth—for a current international relations meaning, read "all states are
functionally alike"—and the heart and hands of the same body heteronomous growth—read "all
states are functionally different."

64. According to Perry Anderson, "the age in which 'Absolutist' public authority was imposed
was also simultaneously the age in which 'absolute' private property was progressively consolidated";
see Anderson, *Lineages of the Absolutist State,* p. 429. Eric Jones reaches a similar conclusion via a
different route: "Productive activities that had been subject to collective controls were becoming
individualized. This is a staple of the textbooks. But that Europe moved from the guilds and the
common fields toward *laissez-faire* is only half the story. The missing half is that just when production was
becoming fully privatised, services were becoming more of a collective concern, or where they were
already communal, now the government was being involved." See E. L. Jones, *The European Miracle:
Environments, Economics, and Geopolitics in the History of Europe and Asia* (Cambridge: Cambridge
University Press, 1981), p. 147. Jones is referring to the provision of such services as internal pacification,
internal colonization of uncultivated lands, disaster management, and the like. The gradual differentiation between internal and external, as seen through the lens of changing norms and practices of diplomatic
representation, is portrayed brilliantly by Mattingly in *Renaissance Diplomacy.*

65. Norbert Elias, *Power and Civility* (New York: Pantheon, 1983), p. 202.

66. Philippe Contamine, *War in the Middle Ages,* trans. Michael Jones (New York: Basil
Blackwell, 1984), p. 169.

67. For a sophisticated survey, see Robert David Sack, *Human Territoriality: Its Theory and
History* (New York: Cambridge University Press, 1986).

concept of differentiation, then, it is impossible to define the structure of modernity in international politics—modes of differentiation are nothing less than the focus of the epochal study of rule. Hence the supreme irony of Waltz's continued insistence that the dimension of differentiation "drops out" from the neorealist model of international structure.[68]

The obvious next issue to address is how one accounts for this peculiar form of sociopolitical individuation. Now, providing an account of things in contemporary international relations research typically means specifying their causes. That in turn requires that we have a theory—in this case, a theory of international transformation. But we have no such theory. As I have suggested, we can barely even describe transformation in the international polity. Hence, I mean something far less ambitious by the phrase "providing an account of." The modern system of states is socially constructed. The issue I mean to address is simply what were the raw materials that people used and drew upon in constructing it? I find that developments in three dimensions of European collective experience were particularly salient, and that the three dimensions are irreducible to one another: namely, material environments, strategic behavior, and social epistemology.

Material environments

The study of the *longue durée* has become a special province of the *Annales* school of historiography.[69] The starting point of the *Annales* approach is the "ecodemographic" dimension of human collectivities, on the premise that it poses the biggest long-term challenge for social structures. It then moves on to various constructed environments and patterns of routine social practices. If we were to view the emergence of the modern mode of structuring territorial space from the vantage point of this perspective, what sorts of developments would catch our eye?

Consider the material side of life throughout the thirteenth and into the fourteenth century: human ecology, the relations of production, and the relations of force. Climatologically, the early phase of the period remained favored by the so-called little optimum of the early Middle Ages.[70] Population grew markedly. Land clearing, draining, and diking progressed rapidly, increasing the size of the cultivated area and breaking down barriers to

---

68. Waltz, inexplicably, views the differentiation of a collectivity into its constituent units to be an attribute of the units rather than of the collectivity. His original argument is in *Theory of International Politics*, chap. 5; and a defense of his position can be found in Kenneth Waltz, "Reflections on *Theory of International Politics*: A Response to My Critics," in Robert O. Keohane, ed., *Neorealism and Its Critics* (New York: Columbia University Press, 1986).

69. The exemplar of this school, of course, is Fernand Braudel; his general approach is discussed in Braudel, *On History*, trans. Sarah Matthews (Chicago: University of Chicago Press, 1980).

70. David Herlihy, "Ecological Conditions and Demographic Change," in Richard L. De Molen, ed., *One Thousand Years: Western Europe in the Middle Ages* (Boston: Houghton Mifflin, 1974), p. 13. See also Emmanuel Le Roy Ladurie's classic study, *Times of Feast, Times of Famine: A History of Climate Since the Year 1000*, trans. Barbara Bray (Garden City, N.Y.: Doubleday, 1971).

communication within territorial formations while expanding their external frontiers.[71] Although the overwhelming proportion of the population continued to live in rural areas, medieval cities grew, and some (Milan, Paris, Venice) may have reached 150,000 inhabitants.[72]

A sustained economic expansion took place as well. Productivity increased; more and more goods were produced for sale or exchange; and trade revived, not merely in luxury goods but increasingly in staples. That last point is crucial. In the words of Eric Jones, "the peculiarities of European trade arose because of the opportunities of the environment. Climate, geology and soils varied greatly from place to place. The portfolio of resources was extensive, but not everything was found in the same place."[73] Moreover, economic relations became increasingly monetized, and developments in "invisibles," including the great fairs, shipping, insurance, and financial services, further lubricated commerce and helped to create a European-wide market.[74]

In the realm of force, the feudal cavalry was coming to be undermined by the longbow, pike, and crossbow and the feudal castle, subsequently, by gunpowder.[75] The monetization of economic relations, together with the commutation of feudal services into money payments, made it possible for territorial rulers to retain mercenaries. Generating revenue through taxation augmented the trend toward standing armies. The more effective internal pacification produced thereby provided a more secure economic environment, which in turn increased both private and public returns.[76]

Nevertheless, territorially defined, territorially fixed, and mutually exclusive state formations did not emerge at this point. It was not that simple. What happened instead was that this period of expansion and diversification was arrested suddenly and ferociously in the mid-fourteenth century. Famines, wars, and plagues decimated the population of Europe, reducing it by at least one-third and probably more. Entire localities disappeared; deserted lands reverted to heaths and swamps. The economy went into a deep and seemingly permanent depression and pillaging, robbing, and civil unrest again became endemic. Recovery did not return until the second half of the fifteenth century.[77]

71. Jones, The *European Miracle*, chap. 4.
72. According to Herlihy, even in the most densely populated areas, northern Italy and Flanders, three out of four people continued to live in the countryside; elsewhere this proportion was roughly nine out of ten. See Herlihy, "Ecological Conditions and Demographic Change," p. 30. For a more elaborate discussion of the structures and functions of towns in premodern Europe, see Paul M. Hohenberg and Lynn Hollen Lees, *The Making of Urban Europe, 1000–1950* (Cambridge, Mass.: Harvard University Press, 1985), chaps. 1–3.
73. Jones, *The European Miracle*, p. 90.
74. See ibid, chap. 5; Herlihy, "Ecological Conditions and Demographic Change"; and Elias, *Power and Civility*. Elias explores the importance of monetization not only for economic but also for political development.
75. McNeill, *The Pursuit of Power*, chap. 3.
76. See ibid.; Elias, *Power and Civility;* and Jones, *The European Miracle*, chap. 7.
77. Surely the most readable account of this period is Barbara Tuchman, *A Distant Mirror: The Calamitous 14th Century* (New York: Ballantine, 1978). For a standard history, see Denys Hays, *Europe in the Fourteenth and Fifteenth Centuries*, 2d ed. (London: Longman, 1989).

These changes in the material world, both positive and negative, were so profound, however, that existing social arrangements were strained to the point of collapse.

Strategic behavior

Indeed, economic growth and diversification from the thirteenth to the fourteenth century had encountered institutional limits well before they were snuffed out by the Black Death and the Hundred Years' War. These limits included the feudal structure of property rights and forms of labor control; inadequate investment, especially in agriculture; the maze of secular and ecclesiastical jurisdictional constraints that pervaded medieval society; and the socially parasitic nature of the multiplicity of territorial rulers. One way to characterize the impact of the material changes discussed above on the prevailing institutional order is to say that they altered the matrix of constraints and opportunities for social actors, giving rise to different situations of strategic interaction among them. This is the subject matter of the "new economic history."[78] Consider the following illustrations.

First, the drastic demographic declines of the fourteenth century affected relative factor prices, favoring agricultural workers and industrial producers while disadvantaging the land-owning class—the very basis of feudal society.

Second, as Jones has argued, the fourteenth-century calamities created opportunities for "entrepreneurial politicians" to prove their social utility by providing a variety of social services, ranging from disaster relief to more effective institutional arrangements for the conduct of commerce. According to Jones, the forces favoring institutional change responded more imaginatively to the calamities than the forces that sought to impede it.[79]

A third example involves the relationship between medieval juridical authorities and the trade fairs—a relationship that in some respects resembles that between the transnational economy and national jurisdictions today. The medieval trade fairs were encouraged by local lords; some took place only a stone's throw from the feudal castle. The fairs were favored for the simple reason that they generated revenue. In the case of the famous Champagne fairs, O. Verlinden writes that revenues were gained from "taxes on the

---

78. For the purposes of the present discussion, the pathbreaking work is the brief book by Douglass C. North and Robert Paul Thomas, *The Rise of the Western World: A New Economic History* (Cambridge: Cambridge University Press, 1973).

79. See Jones, *The European Miracle,* chap. 7. Perhaps the drollest illustration cited by Jones, but nonetheless a significant one, actually comes from a later century, when the Austrian Hapsburgs built a *cordon sanitaire* some 1,000 miles long, promising to shut out the plague that persisted in the Ottoman empire. Their feat had little epidemiological effect, but it called forth considerable administrative effort and social mobilization and contributed, thereby, to statebuilding. Douglass North and his colleagues have produced a fascinating formulation of the process whereby innovations in contracts were created and enforced; see Paul R. Milgrom, Douglass C. North, and Barry R. Weingast, "The Role of Institutions in the Revival of Trade: The Law Merchant, Private Judges, and the Champagne Fairs," *Economics and Politics* 2 (March 1990), pp. 1–23.

residences and stalls of the merchants, entry and exit tolls, levies on sales and purchases, dues upon weights and measures, justice and safe-conduct charges upon the Italians and Jews."[80] Moreover, local lords at any time could have closed down a fair in their domain—much as states today can close down offshore markets or even shoot down communication satellites—though other lords in other places probably would have been only too pleased to provide alternatives sites.

In no sense could the medieval trade fairs have become substituts for the institutions of feudal rule. Yet, the fairs contributed significantly to the demise of feudal authority relations. They did so because the new wealth they produced, the new instruments of economic transactions they generated, the new ethos of commerce they spread, the new regulatory arrangements they required, and the expansion of cognitive horizons they effected all helped undermine the personalistic ties and the modes of reasoning on which feudal authority rested. As Marvin Becker has put it, the medieval trade fairs were a place in which "the exchange system was freed from rules and rituals."[81] Like the exchange system, the system of governance also ultimately became unraveled. Once momentum shifted from fairs to towns, greater institutional substitutability did come to exist because, in the words of a medieval maxim, "Town air brings freedom"—that is to say, the towns actually exercised jurisdiction over and evoked the allegiance of their new inhabitants.[82]

Fourth and finally, Hendrik Spruyt recently has shown that the erosion of the medieval system of rule, the growth of trade, and the rise of the towns triggered new coalitional possibilities among kings, the aristocracy, and the towns. Indeed, Spruyt explains the pattern in political forms that succeeded medieval rule—territorial states in some places, city-states in others, and city-leagues elsewhere still—by the specific nature of the coalitions that formed.[83] In short, the exogenous shocks of the fourteenth century fundamentally strained the existing social order and created a new matrix of constraints and opportunities for social actors.

Some of the new economic historians want to go further, however, to imply

80. O. Verlinden, "Markets and Fairs," *Cambridge Economic History of Europe*, vol. 3 (Cambridge: Cambridge University Press, 1963), p. 127. Verlinden also points out another possible analogue to the present situation, namely that "from the middle of the thirteenth century onwards, money-changing [in the fairs] begins to take precedence over trade" (see p. 133). Also see Robert-Henri Bautier, *The Economic Development of Medieval Europe*, trans. Heather Karolyi (London: Harcourt Brace Jovanovich, 1971), chap. 4.

81. Marvin B. Becker, *Medieval Italy: Constraints and Creativity* (Bloomington: Indiana University Press, 1981), p. 15. See also the excellent review article of Becker's book by Janet Coleman, "The Civic Culture of Contracts and Credit," *Comparative Study of Society and History* 28 (October 1986), pp. 778–84.

82. The original quotation is "Stadtluft macht frei," and is found in Fritz Rorig, *The Medieval Town* (Berkeley: University of California Press, 1967), p. 27. See also Jacques Le Goff, "The Town as an Agent of Civilization," in Carlo M. Cipolla, ed. *The Middle Ages* (London: Harvester Press, 1976).

83. Hendrik Spruyt, "The Sovereign State and Its Competitors: An Analysis of Systems Change," Ph.D. diss., Department of Political Science, University of California, San Diego, 1991.

that the modern system of states resulted *directly* from this process because the state represented the optimal size of political units that was required to provide efficient property rights and physical security. Smaller units simply "had to grow," Douglass North and Robert Thomas contend.[84] In the economic realm, this drive for juridical expansion is said to have come, on the demand side, from a desire for efficient property rights, which would reduce the discrepancy between private and social rates of return. On the supply side, expansion, they argue, was driven by the fiscal interests of rulers for higher revenues.[85] In the security realm, new weapons technology and a shift in advantage to the offense allegedly drove the desire for larger and fiscally more capable political formations.[86]

The theory that the modern state was functionally determined in this manner has at least two serious shortcomings. First, its retrodictive value is severely limited: centralizing monarchies emerged in the west, to be sure; but city-states were consolidating in Italy and principalities as well as city-leagues in Germany, thus preventing their formation into larger (and by the logic of the new economic history, presumably more efficient) political units. Meanwhile, eastern Europe merely sank back into the somnambulance of another round of serfdom. Moreover, as Spruyt demonstrates, two other successor forms to the medieval system of rule, the Italian city-states and the Hanse, in fact were viable political alternatives to the territorial state, fully able to levy taxes and raise armies, for the better part of two centuries.[87] In social life, two centuries is no mere time lag.

Second, there is a substantial logical and empirical gap between the existence of some functional pressure for political units to grow, and their blossoming specifically into a system of territorially defined, territorially fixed, and mutually exclusive state formations. To assert that the specificities of the modern state system *also* were functionally determined entails a claim of staggering historical and intellectual proportions, which the new economic history cannot vindicate. We shall now see why.

---

84. North and Thomas, *The Rise of the Western World*, p. 17.
85. See ibid; and Jones, *The European Miracle*.
86. See McNeill, *The Pursuit of Power*.
87. For a more elaborate summary of prevailing patterns of state forms, see Charles Tilly, "Reflections on the History of European State-making," in Charles Tilly, ed., *The Formation of National States in Western Europe* (Princeton, N.J.: Prinston University Press, 1975), pp. 3–83. Tilly points out a methodological problem that the "new economic historians" gloss over: there are many more failures than successes in the history of European state building. "The disproportionate distribution of success and failure puts us in the unpleasant situation of dealing with an experience in which most of the cases are negative, while only the positive cases are well-documented" (p. 39). Tilly explores a greater variety of state-building experiences in his most recent work, *Coercion, Capital, and European States, AD 990–1990*. Spruyt's methodological critique is even more damning, however. He points out that because successor forms to the medieval system of rule other than territorial states have been systematically excluded from consideration, there is no fundamental variation in units on the dependent-variable side in theories of state building. See Spruyt, "The Sovereign State and its Competitors."

Social epistemes

Michael Walzer points the way. "The state," he once wrote, "is invisible; it must be personified before it can be seen, symbolized before it can be loved, imagined before it can be conceived."[88] The process whereby a society first comes to imagine itself, to conceive of appropriate orders of rule and exchange, to symbolize identities, and to propagate norms and doctrines is neither materially determined, as vulgar Marxists used to claim, nor simply a matter of instrumental rationality, as the irrepressible utilitarians would have it.

German social theorists in a line from Max Weber to Jürgen Habermas have viewed society as comprising webs of meaning and signification. In the French tradition, from Durkheim to Foucault, there has been a continuing exploration of *mentalités collectives*. No single concept captures both sets of concerns, the one being more semiotic, the other more structural. For lack of a better term, I shall refer to their combination as expressing the "epistemic" dimension of social life, and to any prevailing configuration of its constituent elements as a "social episteme."[89] The demise of the medieval system of rule and the rise of the modern resulted in part from a transformation in social epistemology. Put simply, the mental equipment that people drew upon in imagining and symbolizing forms of political community itself underwent fundamental change.

At the doctrinal level, students of international law and organization have long noted the impact on the concept of sovereignty of the novel religious principle *cujus regio ejus religio,* which placed the choice between Protestantism and Catholicism in the hands of local rulers, and the corresponding secular principle *Rex in regno suo est Imperator regni sui,* which stipulated that the political standing of territorial rulers in their domains was identical to that of the Emperor in his.[90] Sir Ernest Barker exclaimed that in these two phrases "we may hear the cracking of the Middle Ages."[91] Moreover, the rediscovery of the concept of absolute and exclusive private property from Roman law no doubt aided in formulating the concept of absolute and exclusive sovereignty.[92]

At the deeper level of political metaphysics, historians of political thought have long noted the impact on the emerging self-image held by European territorial rulers of a new model of social order: a view of society as a collection

88. Michael Walzer, "On the Role of Symbolism in Political Thought," *Political Science Quarterly* 82 (June 1967), p. 194.

89. With due apologies, I adapt the latter term from Michel Foucault, *The Order of Things* (New York: Random House, 1970).

90. See, for example, Leo Gross, "The Peace of Westphalia, 1648–1948," in Richard A. Falk and Wolfram Hanrieder, eds., *International Law and Organization* (Philadelphia, Penn.: Lippincott, 1968); and F. H. Hinsley, "The Concept of Sovereignty and the Relations between States," *Journal of International Affairs,* vol. 21, no. 2, 1967, pp. 242–52.

91. Cited by Gross, "The Peace of Westphalia," pp. 56–57.

92. Berki writes that " 'private' . . . refers not so much to the nature of the entity that owns, but to the fact that it is an entity, a unit whose ownership of nature . . . signifies the exclusion of others from this ownership." See R. N. Berki, "On Marxian Thought and the Problem of International Relations," *World Politics* 24 (October 1971), pp. 80–105. On the relationship between private property and sovereignty, see Ruggie, "Continuity and Transformation in the World Polity."

of atomistic and autonomous bodies-in-motion in a field of forces energized solely by scarcity and ambition. This is a view within which such distinctively modern theorists as Machiavelli and subsequently Hobbes framed their thinking.[93]

It may be possible to claim, though I think hard to vindicate, that both the doctrinal and perhaps even the metaphysical changes were determined by power and greed, or by "efficiency" considerations, to use the more clinical term favored in the literature today. However, the new forms of spatial differentiation on which the novel political doctrines and metaphysics were constructed are another matter: their specifically political expressions mirrored a much broader transformation in social epistemology that reached well beyond the domains of political and economic life.

Consider, for example, analogous changes in the linguistic realm, such as the growing use of vernaculars, and the coming to dominance of the "I-form" of speech—which Franz Borkenau described as "the sharpest contradistinction between I and you, between me and the world."[94] Consider analogous changes in interpersonal sensibilities, as in new notions of individual subjectivity and new meanings of personal delicacy and shame. These changes, among other effects, led to a spatial reconfiguration of households, from palaces to manor houses to the dwellings of the urban well-to-do, which more rigorously demarcated and separated private from public spheres and functions.[95]

93. See Walzer, "On the Role of Symbolism in Political Thought"; Sheldon Wolin, *Politics and Vision* (Boston: Little, Brown, 1960); C. B. Macpherson, *The Political Theory of Possessive Individualism* (New York: Oxford University Press, 1962); and J. G. A. Pocock, *The Machiavellian Moment* (Princeton, N.J.; Princeton University Press, 1975).

94. On the use of vernacular, see Lucien Febvre and Henri-Jean Martin, *The Coming of the Book*, trans. David Gerard, and Geoffrey Nowell-Smith and David Wootton, eds. (London: Verso, 1984), especially chapter 8, which contains interesting statistics on books in print by subject and language. On the I-form of speech, see Franz Borkenau, *End and Beginning: On the Generations of Cultures and the Origins of the West*, Richard Lowenthal, ed. (New York: Columbia University Press, 1981).

95. Changing sensibilities are illustrated and analyzed at length by Norbert Elias, *The Civilizing Process* (New York: Urizen Books, 1978). To illustrate only one aspect of medieval household organization as late as the fourteenth century, consider the following excerpts from Tuchman, *A Distant Mirror:* "Even kings and popes received ambassadors sitting on beds furnished with elaborate curtains and spreads" (p. 161); "Even in greater homes guests slept in the same room with host and hostess" (p. 161), and often servants and children did too (p. 39); "Never was man less alone. . . . Except for hermits and recluses, privacy was unknown" (p. 39). See also David Herlihy, *Medieval Households* (Cambridge, Mass.: Harvard University Press, 1985); and Georges Duby, ed., *A History of Private Life*, vol. 2, *Revelations of the Medieval World*, trans. Arthur Goldhammer (Cambridge, Mass.: Belknap, 1988). Martines documents that "Francesco di Giorgio Martini (1439–1502)—the Sienese engineer, architect, painter, sculptor, and writer—was one of the first observers to urge that the houses of merchants and small tradesmen be constructed with a clean separation between the rooms intended for family use and those for the conduct of business." See Lauro Martines, *Power and Imagination: City-States in Renaissance Italy* (New York: Vintage Books, 1979), p. 271. Finally, the differentiation between person and office also evolved during this period. As Strong notes, "the possibility that one human being could separately be both a human being and a king—a notion on which our conception of office depends—is first elaborated by Hobbes in his distinction between natural and artificial beings in the Leviathan." See Tracy Strong, "Dramaturgical Discourse and Political Enactments: Toward an Artistic Foundation for Political Space," in Stanley Lyman and Richard Brown, eds., *Structure, Consciousness, and History* (New York: Cambridge University Press, 1974), p. 240.

Arguably, the single most important of those developments occurred in the visual arts: the invention of single-point perspective. Previous visual representation exhibited two spatial characteristics. First, artists rendered their subjects from different sides and angles "rather than from a single, overall vantage."[96] Second, variation in figure scale was determined by the symbolic or social importance of the person or object represented and "not by any principle of optical inversion."[97] As Harold Osborne explains, in single-point perspective (the invention of which is generally credited to Filippo Brunelleschi about 1425) "the pictorial surface is regarded as a transparent vertical screen, placed between the artist and his subject, on which he traces the outlines [of the visual field] *as they appear from a single fixed viewpoint.*"[98] The corollary to the fixed viewpoint, from which the world is seen, is the horizon vanishing point, at which objects recede out of view.

By virtue of this development, precision and perspective became prized; Brunelleschi, for example, also made major contributions to optics and cartography. But of greatest significance is the fact that this was precision and perspective from a particular point of view: a *single* point of view, the point of view of a *single* subjectivity, from which all other subjectivities were differentiated and against which all other subjectivities were plotted in diminishing size and depth toward the vanishing point.

If there is one common element in the various expressions of differentiation that we have been discussing, this novel perspectival form surely is it. Every civilization tends to have its own particular perspective, Edgerton concludes in his classic study, its own dominant symbolic form for conceiving and perceiving space, and single-point perspective "was the peculiar answer of the Renaissance."[99] What was true in the visual arts was equally true in politics: political space came to be defined *as it appeared from a single fixed viewpoint.* The concept of sovereignty, then, was merely the doctrinal counterpart of the application of single-point perspectival forms to the spatial organization of politics.[100]

This transformation in the spatial organization of politics was so profound—literally mind-boggling—that contemporaries had great difficulty grasping its full implications for many years to come. Mattingly, for example, recounts the

96. Samuel Y. Edgerton, Jr., *The Renaissance Rediscovery of Linear Perspective* (New York: Basic Books, 1975), p. 9.

97. John White, *The Birth and Rebirth of Pictorial Space* (Boston: Faber and Faber, 1987), p. 103.

98. Harold Osborne, *Oxford Companion to Art* (New York: Oxford University Press, 1970), p. 840, emphasis added.

99. Edgerton, *The Renaissance Rediscovery of Linear Perspective*, p. 158.

100. Marshall McLuhan made several offhand remarks in *The Gutenberg Galaxy* (Toronto: University of Toronto Press, 1962) about an alleged parallel between single-point perspective and nationalism. He thereby misdated the advent of nationalism by several centuries, however. Moreover, he was less concerned with developing the parallel than with attributing its cause to the cognitive impact of the medium of movable print. Nevertheless, I have found McLuhan's thinking enormously suggestive. The relationship between changing perspectival forms and the organization of cities and towns is explored extensively in the literature; see, among other works, Martines, *Power and Imagination;* and Giulio C. Argan, *The Renaissance City* (New York: George Braziller, 1969).

efforts of Francis I as late as 1547 to reform the apparatus of the French state by fixing the number of *secretaires d'Etat* at four. Rather than separating their duties according to the logical distinction, by modern standards, between domestic and foreign relations, each of the four was assigned one quadrant of France *and* the relations with all contiguous and outlying states.[101]

To conclude, material changes may have awakened both a need and a desire for this broad transformation in the prevailing social episteme, which produced fundamentally new spatial forms. And entrepreneurial rulers could and did try to exploit those new images and ideas to advance their interests. Nevertheless, the breadth and depth of these changes argue, at the very least, in favor of a relative autonomy for the realm of social epistemology. Walzer has put it well: "If symbolization does not by itself create unity (that is the function of political practice as well as of symbolic activity), it does create *units*—units of discourse which are fundamental to all thinking and doing, units of feeling around which emotions of loyalty and assurance can cluster."[102]

Accordingly, I turn next to the domain of social practice, wherein the new unity was achieved. I highlight two aspects of it in particular: the process of social empowerment, which facilitated the consolidation of territorial rule; and the process of "unbundling" territoriality, which made it possible for the new territorial states, who viewed their individual subjectivity as constituting a self-sufficient moral and political field, to form a society of states.

Social empowerment

The disarticulation of the medieval system of rule meant that parametric conditions would have to be fixed at three levels in the newly formed social aggregations of power: the domestic social structure, the territorial formation, and the collectivity of territorial units. In each case, the relative success of the contending parties was shaped not simply by the material power they possessed or the interests they pursued but also by a process of social empowerment that reflected the ongoing transformation of social epistemes. I focus below on the territorial state and its collectivity.[103]

---

101. Mattingly, *Renaissance Diplomacy*, p. 195.
102. Walzer, "On the Role of Symbolism in Political Thought," pp. 194–95, emphasis original.
103. For a rich and provocative discussion of the process of social empowerment domestically, see Albert O. Hirschman, *The Passions and the Interests: Political Arguments for Capitalism Before Its Triumph* (Princeton, N.J.: Princeton University Press, 1977). As Hirschman puts it: "Weber claims that capitalist behavior and activities were the indirect (and originally unintended) result of a desperate *search for individual salvation.* My claim is that the diffusion of capitalist forms owed much to an equally desperate search for a way of *avoiding society's ruin,* permanently threatening at the time because of precarious arrangements for internal and external order" (p. 130, emphasis original). Thus, according to Hirschman, the ultimate social power of the bourgeoisie benefited from a shift in social values whereby commerce became socially more highly regarded—not because of any perceived intrinsic merit or interest in commerce but for the discipline and the restraint it was thought to impose on social behavior in a period of severe turbulence and grave uncertainty. Cf. Max Weber, *The Protestant Ethic and the Spirit of Capitalism,* trans. Talcott Parsons (New

At the level of territorial state formations, the key parametric condition to be fixed was precisely where in society (i.e., around which power aggregation) the right to rule would crystallize. Let us return for a moment to the western European monarchies around the middle of the fifteenth century. Their future looked bleak. In Castile, whose king sometimes claimed the title Emperor, the crown was among the weakest in all of Europe; the towns were dominant. In Aragon, the towns were weak and the nobility was in control, pledging allegiance to their king with this unimpressive oath: "We, who are as good as you, swear to you, who are no better than we, to accept you as our king and sovereign lord, provided you observe all our liberties and laws: but if not, not."[104] In France, the monarchy had to be saved in 1429 by a farmer's daughter who was guided in her quest by visions and voices from "higher" sources; but not even that intervention helped, and when the Hundred Years' War finally ground to a halt more than two decades later, the country lay in ruins. England, already weak and divided, became further torn by the deadly Wars of the Roses. And so it went.

The turn came suddenly. By the end of the century, strong centralized administration had "almost completely transformed the political life of western and west-central Europe," in Johnson and Percy's words.[105] The new political units had become a palpable reality, no longer simply an aspiration, a trend, or a struggle. In France, moreover, a weak central monarchy ended up absorbing a stronger duchy of Burgundy in the process.

How can this shift be explained? One way to put it is that central rulers became more powerful *because of* their state-building mission. A fundamental shift was occurring in the purposes for which power could be deployed by rulers and be regarded as socially legitimate by their subjects. Internally, legitimate power became fused with the provision of public order, steadily discrediting its deployment for primitive extraction and accumulation. Externally, legitimate power became fused with statecraft, steadily discrediting its deployment for primitive expansion and aggrandizement.[106]

This process of empowerment also helps to account for the geographical pattern of successful centralizing efforts noted above. The monarchs in the west tended to hitch their fate to those new objectives, and large-scale exclusive state formations emerged. West-central Europe and Italy, on the other hand, still had to cope with those meddlesome remnants of heteronomy, the Holy Roman Empire and the Papacy. While they lacked the power to prevail, so long

---

York: Scribners, 1958). Additional support for Hirschman's argument may be found in Pocock, *The Machiavellian Moment:* "It looks, then, as if Machiavelli was in search of social means whereby men's natures might be transformed to the point where they became capable of citizenship" (p. 193).

104. Jerah Johnson and William Percy, *The Age of Recovery: The Fifteenth Century* (Ithaca, N.Y.: Cornell University Press, 1970), p. 56.

105. Ibid., p. 73.

106. See Pocock, *The Machiavellian Moment;* and Bernard Guenee, *States and Rulers in Later Medieval Europe,* trans. Juliet Vale (New York: Basil Blackwell, 1985).

as they retained some degree of social efficacy it remained difficult to formulate clearly the concept, let alone create the institution, of an exclusive state formation. Here city-states and principalities became the expression of homonomous territoriality. In the east, these social changes never took hold in the first place. One should not exaggerate the ease with which these processes took hold even in the western kingdoms. As Charles Tilly points out, the leaders of prior institutions and even ordinary people "fought the claims of central states for centuries," right into the seventeenth century.[107] Over time, however, the issue at stake increasingly became the *terms* of central rule, not the fact of it.

At the level of the collectivity of states, the critical parameter to fix concerned the right to act as a constitutive unit of the new collective political order. The issue here was not who had how much power, but who could be designated *as* a power.[108] Such a designation inherently is a collective act. It involved the mutual recognition of the new constitutive principle of sovereignty. Martin Wight points out that "it would be impossible to have a society of sovereign states unless each state, while claiming sovereignty for itself, recognized that every other state had the right to claim and enjoy its own sovereignty as well."[109] Reciprocal sovereignty thus became the basis of the new international order.

To be sure, the new organizing principle of reciprocal sovereignty was challenged in and hammered home by wars; but even in the evolution of European wars we can see signs of that new principle of international legitimacy taking hold. As already noted, private wars ceased to be tolerated, and war making came to be universally recognized as an attribute of sovereignty. Even more interesting, European warfare thereafter seems to exhibit a progression in the dominant forms of war.[110]

The first form we might call "constitutive" war. Here the very ontology of the units—that is to say, what kind of units they would be—was still at issue. The Wars of Religion are the prime instance. As characterized by Reinhart Koselleck, the Peace of Augsburg (1555) "meant that the fronts of religious civil war were to be shut down, frozen in situ."[111] It also produced a moral compromise. As described by Koselleck: "The compromise, born of necessity, concealed within itself a new principle, that of 'politics,' which was to set itself

---

107. Tilly, "Reflections on the History of European State-making," p. 22.
108. Richard K. Ashley, "The Poverty of Neorealism," *International Organization* 38 (Spring 1984), especially pp. 259 and 272–73.
109. Wight, *Systems of States*, p. 135.
110. Kaiser points out that all wars throughout the period I am here discussing had specific political and economic objectives, but that prior to the eighteenth century they also exhibited very complex overlays of other dimensions that have not been seen since. See David Kaiser, *Politics and War: European Conflict from Philip II to Hitler* (Cambridge, Mass.: Harvard University Press, 1990), chap. 1. I am here attempting to capture and give expression to these other dimensions.
111. Koselllek, *Futures Past,* p. 8.

in motion in the following century."[112] Still, an international politics morally autonomous from the realm of religion did not become firmly established until the Peace of Westphalia (1648), ending the Thirty Years' War.

This first phase was followed by warfare in which the nature of the units was accepted but their territorial configuration remained contested. We might call these "configurative" wars. The Wars of Succession of the early eighteenth century—Spanish, Polish, and Austrian—and the Seven Years' War (1756–63) illustrate this form. Among other factors, these conflicts revolved around the principles of territorial contiguity versus transterritorial dynastic claims as the basis for a viable balance of power. In the end, territorial contiguity won out, at least in the European core.[113]

The third phase in the evolving form of warfare consists of the familiar strategic and tactical wars ever since, wars that we might call "positional"— interrupted by periodic quests for universal empire, which have been successfully repulsed on each occasion.[114]

Finally, when the concept of state sovereignty expanded to become the concept of national sovereignty, the use of mercenaries in warfare declined and ultimately was eliminated altogether. Armed forces subsequently became an expression of the nation.[115]

The critical threshold in this transition was the passage from constitutive to configurative wars, for it first acknowledged the principle of reciprocal sovereignty. When all was said and done, Europe ended up with a great many not-so-powerful states, including the nearly two hundred German principalities, which could not possibly have vindicated their right to exist by means of material power, but which were socially empowered by the collectivity of states to act as its constitutive units.[116]

Thus, the process of social empowerment was part of the means by which the new units of political discourse were inscribed in social life to produce new units of political order.

112. Ibid.

113. See Anderson, *Europe in the Eighteenth Century, 1713–1783;* and Kaiser, *Politics and War.*

114. Ludwig Dehio, *The Precarious Balance* (New York: Knopf, 1962). What Gilpin calls the cycle of hegemonic wars does not contradict my point. As defined by Gilpin, a "hegemonic war" concerns which power will be able to extract greater resources from and exercise greater control over the system of states; neither the nature of the units nor the nature of the system, for that matter, is at issue. In fact, Gilpin's description of the calculus of would-be hegemons suggests that hegemonic wars fit well into my generic category of positional wars. See Robert Gilpin, *War and Change in World Politics* (New York: Cambridge University Press, 1981).

115. For a good discussion of this development, see Janice E. Thomson, "State Practices, International Norms, and the Decline of Mercenarism," *International Studies Quarterly* 34 (March 1990), pp. 23–47. On the emergence of national sovereignty, see Benedict Arnold, *Imagined Communities: Reflections on the Origins and Spread of Nationalism* (London: Verso, 1983).

116. Strang has demonstrated the impact of reciprocal sovereignty for the entire history of European expansion into non-European territories since 1415. He finds that polities that were recognized as sovereign have fared much better than those that were not. See David Strang, "Anomaly and Commonplace in European Political Expansion: Realist and Institutionalist Accounts," *International Organization* 45 (Spring 1991), pp. 143–62.

The paradox of absolute individuation

Our story ends in a paradox. Having established territorially fixed state formations, having insisted that these territorial domains were disjoint and mutually exclusive, and having accepted these conditions as the constitutive bases of international society, what means were left to the new territorial rulers for dealing with problems of that society that could not be reduced to territorial solution?

This issue arose in connection with common spaces, such as contiguous and transborder waterways as well as the oceans: how does one possess something one does not own? And, still more problematic, how does one exclude others from it? Inland waterways could be split down the middle and typically were, though often not until other and more violent means had been exhausted. Ocean space beyond defendable coastal areas posed a more substantial problem. Spain and Portugal tried a bilateral deal whereby Spain claimed a monopoly of western ocean trade routes to the Far East and Portugal the eastern, but they failed to make their deal stick. At the request of the Dutch East India Company, a young lawyer by the name of Hugo Grotius launched a distinguished career by penning a pamphlet entitled, and proclaiming the contrary doctrine of, *Mare Liberum,* which did stick.[117]

The really serious problem arose not in the commons, however, but right in the heart of the mutually exclusive territorial state formations: no space was left within which to anchor even so basic a task as the conduct of diplomatic representation without fear of relentless disturbance, arbitrary interference, and severed lines of communication.

In medieval Europe, the right of embassy was a method of formal and privileged communication that could be admitted or denied depending upon the social status and roles of the parties involved and the business at hand.[118] Ambassadors had specific missions, for which they enjoyed specific immunities. For a variety of misdeeds and crimes, however, ambassadors were tried and sentenced by the prince to whom they were accredited, as though they were a

---

117. Grotius's immediate aim was to establish the principle of freedom to conduct trade *on* the seas, but in order to establish that principle he had first to formulate some doctrine regarding the medium through which ships passed as they engaged in long-distance trade. The principle he enunciated, and which states came to adopt, defined an oceans regime in two parts: a territorial sea under exclusive state control, which custom set at three miles because that was the range of land-based cannons at the time, and the open seas beyond, available for common use but owned by none. See Aster Institute, *International Law: The Grotian Heritage* (The Hague: Aster Institute, 1985).

118. The following discussion is based on Mattingly, *Renaissance Diplomacy.* Note Mattingly's summary of medieval practice, and contrast it with what we know to be the case for the modern world: "Kings made treaties with their own vassals and with the vassals of their neighbors. They received embassies from their own subjects and from the subjects of other princes, and sometimes sent agents who were in fact ambassadors in return. Subject cities negotiated with one another without reference to their respective sovereigns. Such behavior might arouse specific objection, but never on general grounds" (p. 23).

subject of that prince. This solution ceased to be acceptable, however, once the right of embassy became a sign of sovereign recognition and ambassadors were in place permanently. The short-term response was to grant more and more specific immunities to resident ambassadors as the situation demanded. During the century or so of religious strife, however, that option too came to be undermined by, among other factors, the so-called embassy chapel question.

As the term implies, this had to do with the services celebrated in an ambassador's chapel, at which compatriots were welcome, when the religions of the home and host sovereigns differed. For example, Edward VI insisted that the new English prayer book be used in all his embassies; Charles V would tolerate no such heresy at his court. It was not uncommon for diplomatic relations to be broken over the issue in the short run. In the long run, however, that proved too costly a solution; the need for continuous and reliable communication among rulers was too great. A doctrinal solution was found instead. Rather than contemplate the heresy of a Protestant service at a Catholic court and vice versa, it proved easier to pretend that the service was not taking place in the host country at all but on the soil of the homeland of the ambassador. And so it gradually became with other dimensions of the activities and precincts of embassy. A fictitious space, designated "extraterritoriality," was invented. Mattingly has put the paradox well: "By arrogating to themselves supreme power over men's consciences, the new states had achieved absolute sovereignty. Having done so, they found they could only communicate with one another by tolerating within themselves little islands of alien sovereignty."[119] These islands of alien sovereignty were seen, Adda Bozeman adds, "not only as the foreign arm of each separate government, but also as the nucleus of the collective system of ... states ... outside of which no sovereign could survive."[120]

What we might call an "unbundling" of territoriality (of which the doctrine of extraterritoriality was the first and most enduring instantiation) over time has become a generic contrivance used by states to attenuate the paradox of absolute individuation.[121] Various types of functional regimes, common markets, political communities, and the like constitute additional forms whereby territoriality has become unbundled. Thus, in the modern international polity an institutional *negation* of exclusive territoriality serves as the means of situating and dealing with those dimensions of collective existence that territorial rulers recognize to be irreducibly transterritorial in character. Nonterritorial functional space is the place wherein international society is anchored.

---

119. Ibid, p. 244. See also Adda B. Bozeman, *Politics and Culture in International History* (Princeton, N.J.: Princeton University Press, 1960), pp. 479–80.

120. Bozeman, *Politics and Culture in International History*, pp. 482–83.

121. I adapt this notion from the discussion of unbundling sovereign rights in Kratochwil, "Of Systems, Boundaries and Territoriality."

Patterns of change

Mattingly, in his magisterial study, acknowledges that "the taproots of the modern state may be followed as far back as one likes in Western history [even] to the cities of antiquity whereof the hazy images continued to provide some statesmen in every medieval century with an ideal model of authority and order."[122] But, he shows persuasively, the modern state did not *evolve* from these earlier experiences; rather, it was *invented* by the early modern Europeans. Indeed, it was invented by them twice, once in the leading cities of the Italian Renaissance and once again in the kingdoms north of the Alps sometime thereafter. This suggests a final issue for consideration: the patterns exhibited by epochal change. Three are indicated by the medieval-to-modern transformation.

First, unanticipated consequences played a major role in determining the ultimate outcomes of long-term changes. The Crusades were not designed to suggest new modes of raising revenues for territorial rulers, but they ended up doing so.[123] The modern state was not logically entailed in the medieval papacy; yet, according to Strayer, by the example of effective administration it set, "the Gregorian concept of the Church almost demanded the invention of the concept of the State."[124] Society did not vote for capitalism when it endorsed the civilizing impulses of commerce; but the bourgeoisie, the social carriers of commerce, embodied it. Later, monarchs did not set out to weaken their constitutional powers by selling offices or convening assemblies to raise taxes; they sought only to increase their revenues.[125] In short, the reasons for which things were done often had very little to do with what actually ended up being done or what was made possible by those deeds.[126]

Second, fundamental transformation may have had long-standing sources, but when it came, it came quickly by historical standards. Moreover, it came amid crisis and disintegration of the previous order—amid a generalized loss of predictability and understanding of, in Tracy Strong's words, "what might

122. Mattingly, *Renaissance Diplomacy,* pp. 105–6.
123. Ronald C. Finucane, *Soldiers of the Faith* (New York: St. Martin's, 1983).
124. Strayer, *On the Medieval Origins of the Modern State,* p. 22.
125. North and Weingast demonstrate this very nicely, both formally and empirically, in the case of seventeenth-century England—except for the overall logic they attribute to the process, which "interprets the institutional changes on the basis of the goals of the *winners.*" See Douglass C. North and Barry R. Weingast, "Constitutions and Commitment: The Evolution of Institutions Governing Public Choice in Seventeenth-century England," *Journal of Economic History* 49 (December 1989), p. 803, emphasis added. The problem with their interpretation is that the goals of the *losers*—the insatiable quest for revenues on the part of rulers—not of the winners, drove the process that ultimately made possible the imposition of constitutional constraints on the prerogatives of monarchs.
126. Discussing a biological parallel, Stephen Jay Gould contends that avian limbs became useful for flying once they were fully developed into wings, but they probably evolved for so commonplace a purpose as keeping birds warm. See Gould, "Not Necessarily Wings," *Natural History* 10/85.

count as politics, of what counts as evidence and what as fact, and of what is contentious and what might appear secure."[127] Once the system of modern states was consolidated, however, the process of fundamental transformation ceased: "[states] have all remained recognizably of the same species up to our own time," Tilly concludes, though their substantive forms and individual trajectories of course have differed substantially over time.[128] Paleontologists describe this pattern of change—stable structures, rupture, new stable structures—as "punctuated equilibrium."[129]

Finally, change has never been complete or all-encompassing. As Spruyt makes clear, the medieval system of rule in the first instance was succeeded by several viable forms of territorial governance: large-scale territorial states, city-states, and city-leagues. And the process that ultimately selected out the territorial state embodied a different logic than the process that produced both the state and its alternative forms.[130] Moreover, keep in mind that the formal demise of the Holy Roman Empire (1806)—a relic of medievaldom that historians insist never was holy, nor Roman, nor an empire—actually is closer in time to the birth of the European Community (EC) than to the Peace of Westphalia, the usual marker of the inception of modern international relations. Finally, sociopolitical collectivities of very long historical standing remain vital today without being contained in territorial states.[131] In short, the coexistence of different historical forms is not unusual. Designating dominant historical forms, therefore, is a matter of balance: of judging ascendancy and decline, relevance and spurious signification. Nonetheless, it is the case that the modern state has succeeded in driving out substitutable alternatives more effectively than any other prior form.

127. Strong, "Dramaturgical Discourse and Political Enactments," p. 245.
128. Tilly, "Reflections on the History of European State-making" p. 31. For a suggestive typology of different substantive state forms, see Michael Mann, *States, War, and Capitalism* (New York: Basil Blackwell, 1988), chap. 1.
129. See Niles Eldredge and Ian Tattersall, *The Myths of Human Evolution* (New York: Columbia University Press, 1982). Eldredge, in a personal conversation, attributed the basic insight for the punctuated equilibrium model to the historian Frederick Teggart—which is ironic in the light of the influence that the Darwinian model of human evolution has had on social thinking, including historiography! See Frederick J. Teggart, *Theory of History* (New Haven, Conn.: Yale University Press, 1925). Bock has described large-scale social change in similar terms: "In place of a continuous process of sociocultural change, the records clearly indicate long periods of relative inactivity among peoples, punctuated by occasional spurts of action. Rather than slow and gradual change, significant alterations in peoples' experiences have appeared suddenly, moved swiftly, and stopped abruptly"; see Kenneth Bock, *Human Nature and History: A Response to Sociobiology* (New York: Columbia University Press, 1980), p. 165. Excellent discussions of punctuated equilibrium and path dependency in the origins of the modern state may be found in two articles by Stephen D. Krasner: "Approaches to the State: Alternative Conceptions and Historical Dynamics," *Comparative Politics* 16 (January 1984), pp. 223–46; and "Sovereignty: An Institutional Perspective," *Comparative Political Studies* 21 (April 1988), pp. 66–94.
130. See Spruyt, "The Sovereign State and its Competitors."
131. The so-called Arab nation is a case in point; see Albert Hourani, *A History of the Arab Peoples* (Cambridge, Mass.: Belknap Press, 1991).

Historicizing postmodernity

At the close of the fifteenth century, Europe stood poised to reach out to and then conquer the globe. By the beginning of the twentieth century, this "Columbian epoch," as Sir Halford Mackinder characterized it in 1904, was coming to an end.[132] In his seminal essay, Mackinder addressed two distinct dimensions of the new "global" epoch. The first has attracted the most attention but is the less important for present concerns: the strategic consequences of the essential unity of the world's oceans, which gave rise to the great heartland/rimland and land-power/sea-power debates that became the stuff of geopolitics, right down to the postwar theory of containment. The second, which subsequent commentators have largely ignored, concerned the spatial and temporal implosion of the globe: the integration of separate and coexisting world systems, each enjoying a relatively autonomous social facticity and expressing its own laws of historicity, into a singular post-Columbian world system.[133]

In this essay, I have looked for a vocabulary and the dimensions of analysis that would allow us to ask sensible questions about possible postmodern tendencies in the world polity. I have done so by unpacking the process whereby the most distinct feature of modernity in international politics came to be: a particular form of territoriality—disjoint, fixed, and mutually exclusive—as the basis for organizing political life. In conclusion, I summarize briefly the main findings of this endeavor and point toward some methodological as well as substantive implications for future research.

To summarize, the concept of differentiation was the key that allowed us to uncover the historically specific and salient characteristics of modern territoriality. Accepting that the international polity, by definition, is an anarchy, that is, a segmented realm, on what basis is it segmented? On what basis are its units individuated? What drove the peculiarly modern form of individuation? And what were its implications for the international collectivity? The mode of differentiation within any collectivity, I suggested, is nothing less than the central focus of the epochal study of rule.

The modern mode of differentiation resulted from changes in several domains of social life, which are irreducible to one another. These domains included material environments (ecodemographics, relations of production, relations of force); the matrix of constraints and opportunities within which social actors interacted (the structure of property rights, divergences between

132. See H. J. Mackinder, "The Geographical Pivot of History," *Geographical Journal* 23 (April 1904).
133. As Mackinder predicted, "Every explosion of social forces, instead of being dissipated in a surrounding circuit of unknown space and barbaric chaos, will be sharply re-echoed from the far side of the globe, and weak elements in the political and economic organism of the world will be shattered in consequence." See ibid, p. 421.

private and social rates of return, coalitional possibilities among major social actors); and social epistemes (political doctrines, political metaphysics, spatial constructs). Each was undergoing change in accordance with its own endogenous logic. But these changes also interacted, sometimes sequentially, sometimes functionally, sometimes simply via the mechanism of diffusion, that is, of conscious and unconscious borrowing. Whereas individual strands of change can be traced back almost at will, at a certain point the new forms crystallized fairly quickly and shaped all subsequent developments.

The domain of social epistemes, the mental equipment by means of which people reimagined their collective existence, played a critical role.[134] The specificity of modern territoriality is closely linked to the specificity of single-point perspective. Social epistemes did not, however, act as some ethereal *Zeitgeist* but through specific social carriers and practices. Social epistemes affected outcomes via the mechanisms of social empowerment and delegitimation and by informing such doctrinal contrivances as extraterritoriality, on which the society of territorial state formations came to rest.

Our case offers some methodological implications for the study of transformation today. One methodological point follows directly from the relative autonomy of the diverse domains wherein past change occurred. Clearly, different bodies of contemporary international relations theory are better equipped to elucidate different domains of contemporary change and continuity. Neorealism is very good on the endogenous logics of the relations of force, but it is even more reductionist than most modern Marxisms when it comes to appreciating the role of social epistemology. The microeconomics of institutions provides great insight into strategic behavior, but it is silent on the origins of the social preferences that give it substantive meaning. Cultural theories are virtually alone in addressing the role of spatial imageries, but typically they neglect the effect of micromotives, and so on. Each, therefore, can become a "grand theory" only by discounting or ignoring altogether the integrity of those domains of social life that its premises do not encompass. Nor are the various bodies of extant theory in any sense additive, so that we could arrive at a grand theory by steps. In short, while there may be law-like generalizations *in* the medieval-to-modern transformation, there are none *of* it. Accordingly, understanding that transformation—and presumably any analogous shift that may be taking place today—requires an epistemological posture that is quite different from the imperious claims of most current bodies of international relations theory. It requires, as Quentin Skinner characterizes it, "a willingness to emphasize the local and the contingent, a desire to underline the extent to which our own concepts and attitude have been shaped by particular historical

---

134. There is no adequate English translation of Duby's notion *l'imaginaire sociale*, which I draw on here; his translator renders it as "collective imaginings." See Duby, *The Three Orders*, p. vii.

circumstances, and a correspondingly strong dislike ... of all overarching theories and singular schemes of explanation."[135]

A second methodological point follows directly from the first. If it is true that the intellectual apparatus by which we study fundamental change is itself implicated in a world that may be changing, how valid and viable is that intellectual quest to begin with? This is particularly vexing in attempts to understand the prospects of postmodernity, insofar as prevailing scientific approaches are part and parcel of the very definition of modernity.[136] Not being a philosopher of science, my answer perforce remains somewhat unschooled. Nevertheless, I find fault with the postmodernist epistemologues and the dominant positivists alike.

For the postmodernists, modern scientific method represents either force or farce. In its stead, they retreat into a fettishistic parent(he[re]tical) obscurantism that they impute to poststructuralist/postmodernist method.[137] But their "move"—to borrow one of their "privileged" terms—is deeply misguided, as a simple example will show. In discussions of cultural transformations toward postmodern forms, few insights are accorded greater significance than Einstein's theories of relativity. This is because relativity shattered one of the fixed and even absolute pillars of modernist thought by revolutionizing human understanding of space and time. Yet Einstein's theories were soon confirmed: the special theory by laboratory experiments and the general theory during the eclipse of 1919, all in accordance with fairly straightforward scientific methods. What Einstein did was to formulate an entirely new and different *ontology* of the physical world. Indeed, he never even accepted the implications for *epistemology* that others drew from his work, as illustrated by his often-cited rejoinder to the uncertainty principle, that God does not play dice with the universe. Hence, it is entirely possible to say things of importance about postmodernity, and even to have contributed to the historical condition of postmodernity, without degenerating into what passes for postmodernist method.

As for the dominant positivist posture in our field, it is reposed in deep Newtonian slumber wherein method rules, epistemology is often confused with method, and the term "ontology" typically draws either blank stares or bemused smiles. I choose the Newtonian analogy deliberately and with care. Gerald Feinberg's depiction helps to show why it is useful: "Newtonian mechanics by itself did not attempt to explain what forces might exist in nature, but rather described how motion occurred *when the force was known*."[138]

135. Quentin Skinner, *The Return of Grand Theory in the Human Sciences* (New York: Cambridge University Press, 1985), p. 12.

136. For a superb discussion of these issues, see Seyla Benhabib, "Epistemologies of Postmodernism: A Rejoinder to Jean-Francois Lyotard," *New German Critique* 33 (Fall 1984), pp. 103–26.

137. For examples, consult the extensive bibliography in Pauline Rosenau, "Once Again into the Fray."

138. Gerald Feinberg, *What is the World Made Of? Atoms, Leptons, Quarks, and Other Tantalizing Particles* (Garden City, N.Y.: Anchor Books, 1978), p. 9, emphasis added.

Merely by substituting "structures" or "preferences" for "forces" in that sentence, one obtains an apt rendering of prevailing international relations theories today.[139] They describe how "motion" occurs—*given* a set of structures or preferences. Accordingly, these theories cannot, ontologically, apprehend fundamental transformation, for the issue of "what forces [structures/preferences] might exist in nature" is precisely what the study of transformation is all about.[140]

Our examination of the emergence of modern territoriality also has substantive implications for the study of potential transformation in the international system today. A full application of the historically grounded conceptual framework sketched out here is well beyond the scope of this article. Nevertheless, I close with an overall analytical lead, as well as some working hypotheses about each of the illustrative cases with which I began.

The preceding analysis suggests that the unbundling of territoriality is a productive venue for the exploration of contemporary international transformation. Historically, as we have seen, this is the institutional means through which the collectivity of sovereigns has sought to compensate for the "social defects" that inhere in the modern construct of territoriality.[141] This negation of the exclusive territorial form has been the locale in which international sociality throughout the modern era has been embedded. The terrain of unbundled territoriality, therefore, is the place wherein a rearticulation of international political space would be occurring today.

Take first the EC, in which the process of unbundling territoriality has gone further than anywhere else. Neorealism ascribes its origins to strategic bipolarity; microeconomic institutionalism examines how the national interests and policy preferences of the major European states are reflected in patterns of EC collaboration; and neofunctionalism anticipated the emergence of a supranational statism. Each contains a partial truth. From the vantage of the

---

139. Using Kratochwil's typology, mainstream international relations theory traffics mostly in "the world of brute facts," or the palpable here and now; it discounts "the world of intention and meaning"; and it largely ignores altogether "the world of institutional facts." See Friedrich Kratochwil, *Rules, Norms, and Decisions* (New York: Cambridge University Press, 1989), chap. 1.

140. Structurationist theory is one recent attempt to formulate an ontology of international relations that is predicated on the need to endogenize the origins of structures and preferences, if transformation is to be understood. See Alexander Wendt, "The Agent-Structure Problem in International Relations Theory," *International Organization* 41 (Summer 1987), pp. 335–70; David Dessler, "What's at Stake in the Agent-Structure Debate?" *International Organization* 43 (Summer 1989), pp. 441–73; John Gerard Ruggie, "International Structure and International Transformation: Space, Time, and Method," in Czempiel and Rosenau, *Global Changes and Theoretical Challenges*, pp. 21–35; Alexander Wendt and Raymond Duvall, "Institutions and International Order," in ibid., pp. 51–73; and Alexander Wendt, "Anarchy is What States Make of It: The Social Construction of Power Politics," *International Organization* 46 (Spring 1992), pp. 391–425.

141. Once again, I have in mind a Lockean understanding, namely those "Inconveniences which disorder Mens properties in the state of Nature," the avoidance of which is said to drive "Men [to] unite into Societies." See Locke, *Two Treatises of Government*, sec. 2.136. These "social defects" thus may be thought of as the generic form of international "collective action problems," of which various types of externalities, public goods, and dilemmas of strategic interaction are but specific manifestations.

present analysis, however, a very different attribute of the EC comes into view: it may constitute the first "multiperspectival polity" to emerge since the advent of the modern era. That is to say, it is increasingly difficult to visualize the conduct of international politics among community members, and to a considerable measure even domestic politics, as though it took place from a starting point of twelve separate, single, fixed viewpoints. Nor can models of strategic interaction do justice to this particular feature of the EC, since the collectivity of members as a singularity, in addition to the central institutional apparatus of the EC, has become party to the strategic interaction game. To put it differently, the constitutive processes whereby each of the twelve defines its own identity—and identities are logically prior to preferences—increasingly endogenize the existence of the other eleven. Within this framework, European leaders may be thought of as entrepreneurs of alternative political identities—EC Commission President Delors, for example, is at this very moment exploiting the tension between community widening and community deepening so as to catalyze the further reimagining of European collective existence.[142] There is no indication, however, that this reimagining will result in a federal state of Europe—which would merely replicate on a larger scale the typical modern political form.

The concept of multiperspectival institutional forms offers a lens through which to view other possible instances of international transformation today. Consider the global system of transnationalized microeconomic links. Perhaps the best way to describe it, when seen from our vantage point, is that these links have created a nonterritorial "region" in the world economy—a decentered yet integrated space-of-flows, operating in real time, which exists alongside the spaces-of-places that we call national economies. These conventional spaces-of-places continue to engage in external economic relations with one another, which we continue to call trade, foreign investment, and the like, and which are more or less effectively mediated by the state. In the nonterritorial global economic region, however, the conventional distinctions between internal and external once again are exceedingly problematic, and any given state is but one constraint in corporate global strategic calculations. This is the world in which IBM is Japan's largest computer exporter, and Sony is the largest exporter of television sets from the United States. It is the world in which Brothers Industries, a Japanese concern assembling typewriters in Bartlett, Tennessee, brings an antidumping case before the U.S. International Trade Commission against Smith Corona, an American firm that imports typewriters into the United States from its offshore facilities in Singapore and Indonesia. It is the world in which even the U.S. Pentagon is baffled by the problem of how to maintain the national identity of "its" defense-industrial base.[143] This nonterri-

---

142. This process is by no means free of controversy or resistance, as a recent London front-page headline ("Delors Plan to Rule Europe,") makes clear—but historical change never has been. See *Sunday Telegraph*, 3 May 1992, p. 1.

143. At the time of writing, the Pentagon is considering, among other options, a "reconstitution" model for the U.S. defense-industrial base, now that large and long-term procurement runs are

torial global economic region is a world, in short, that is premised on what Lattimore described as the "sovereign importance of movement," not of place. The long-term significance of this region, much like that of the medieval trade fairs, may reside in its novel behavioral and institutional forms and in the novel space-time constructs that these forms embody, not in any direct challenge that it poses as a potential substitute for the existing system of rule.

Consider also the transformative potential of global ecology. The human environment is of central importance for future planetary politics from many perspectives. Central among them is its potential to comprise a new and very different social episteme—a new set of spatial, metaphysical, and doctrinal constructs through which the visualization of collective existence on the planet is shaped. This episteme would differ in form from modern territoriality and its accoutrements insofar as the underlying structural premise of ecology is holism and mutual dependence of parts. The difficulty is in tapping this social epistemological dimension empirically. Nonetheless, it may be possible to infer from state behavior whether and to what extent it is coming to express new and different principles of international legitimacy, for example. The concept of international custodianship is an obvious candidate for closer scrutiny. Under it, no other agency competes with or attempts to substitute for the state, but the state itself acts in a manner that expresses not merely its own interests and preferences but also its role as the embodiment and enforcer of community norms—a multiperspectival role, in short, somewhat in the manner of medieval rulers vis-à-vis cosmopolitan bodies of religion and law.[144] Another possible approach is to examine the impact of real or simulated environmental catastrophes on the thinking of policymakers and on the popular imagination at large: Chernobyl, the Antarctic ozone hole, and global warming scenarios come to mind.[145]

Finally, this analysis also potentially enriches the field of international security studies. To cite but one example, despite the severe dislocations that have accompanied the collapse of the Soviet Union's East European empire and then of the Soviet Union itself, no one in any position of authority anywhere in Europe to date has advocated, or is quietly preparing for, a return to a system of competitive bilateral alliances. Thus far, all of the options on the table concerning the external mechanisms for achieving security in Europe,

---

unlikely to persist widely. It has proved extraordinarily difficult, however, to decide whether what should be available for reconstitution should be defined by ownership, locale, commitment to the economy, nationality of researchers, or what have you—the divergence between those indicators of national identity being increasingly pronounced—and to determine whether, once defined, such units will actually exist and be available for reconstitution when needed.

144. Allott considers several provisions of the maritime Exclusive Economic Zone to exhibit "delegated powers," under which coastal states act "not only in the mystical composite personage of the international legislator but also in performing the function of the executive branch of their own self-government." See Philip Allott, "Power Sharing in the Law of the Sea," *American Journal of International Law 77* (January 1983), p. 24.

145. On the epistemic import of the Antarctic ozone hole, see Karen Therese Litfin, "Power and Knowledge in International Environmental Politics: The Case of Stratospheric Ozone Depletion," Ph.D. diss., Department of Political Science, University of California, Los Angeles, 1992.

East and West, have been multilateral in form.[146] These mechanisms include NATO reaching out institutionally to the EC via the West European Union on one side; and, on the other side, to the East European states via the newly created North Atlantic Cooperation Council, comprising the membership of the two formerly adversarial alliances, as well as to the Conference on Security and Cooperation in Europe.[147] This development suggests a hypothesis for further exploration. Within the industrialized world, and partially beyond, we may be witnessing emerging fragments of international security communities— alongside the traditional war system that continues elsewhere. These security communities are not integrated in the sense that the ill-fated European Defense Community would have been, but they are more extensively institution- alized than the "pluralistic security communities" of integration studies in the 1950s.[148] Once more the term "multiperspectival" seems appropriate. Within the scope of these security communities the imbalances of advantage that animated positional wars throughout the modern era now are resolved by more communitarian mechanisms instead. Such mechanisms do not imply the abolition of the use of force; they do imply, however, that the use of force is subject to greater collective legitimation.

It is truly astonishing that the concept of territoriality has been so little studied by students of international politics; its neglect is akin to never looking at the ground that one is walking on. I have argued that disjoint, mutually exclusive, and fixed territoriality most distinctively defines modernity in international politics and that changes in few other factors can so powerfully transform the modern international polity. What is more, I have tried to show that unbundled territoriality is a useful terrain for exploring the condition of postmodernity in international politics, and I have suggested some ways in which that might be done. The emergence of multiperspectival institutional forms was identified as a key dimension in understanding the possibility of postmodernity.

On reflection, though, the reason territoriality is taken for granted is not hard to guess. Samuel Becket put it well in *Endgame*: "You're on earth, there's no cure for that." Unbundled territoriality is not located some place else; but it is becoming another place.

---

146. John Gerard Ruggie, "Multilateralism: The Anatomy of an Institution," *International Organization* 46 (Summer 1992), pp. 561–98. Waltz distinguishes between internal and external balancing mechanisms in *Theory of International Politics*.

147. Based on personal interviews at NATO headquarters, Brussels, May 1992. Japan has undertaken a slow but systematic process of its own to normalize its security relations by means of multilateralization: through the postministeral conferences of the Association of South East Nations, for example, as well as through the recent legistation permitting Japan to participate in United Nations peacekeeping forces (based on personal interviews at the Ministry of Foreign Affairs, Tokyo, May 1992).

148. The classic study is Karl W. Deutsch et al., *Political Community and the North Atlantic Area* (Princeton, N.J.: Princeton University Press, 1957).

Global Governance 1 (1995), 13–43

Governance in the Twenty-first Century

——————— ⊕ ———————

James N. Rosenau

To anticipate the prospects for global governance in the decades ahead is to discern powerful tensions, profound contradictions, and perplexing paradoxes. It is to search for order in disorder, for coherence in contradiction, and for continuity in change. It is to confront processes that mask both growth and decay. It is to look for authorities that are obscure, boundaries that are in flux, and systems of rule that are emergent. And it is to experience hope embedded in despair.

This is not to imply that the task is impossible. Quite to the contrary, one can discern patterns of governance that are likely to proliferate, others that are likely to attenuate, and still others that are likely to endure as they always have. No, the task is not so much impossible as it is a challenge to one's appreciation of nuance and one's tolerance of ambiguity.

Conceptual Nuances

In order to grasp the complexities that pervade world politics, we need to start by drawing a nuanced set of distinctions among the numerous processes and structures that fall within the purview of global governance. Perhaps most important, it is necessary to clarify that global governance refers to more than the formal institutions and organizations through which the management of international affairs is or is not sustained. The United Nations system and national governments are surely central to the conduct of global governance, but they are only part of the full picture. Or at least in this analysis global governance is conceived to include systems of rule at all levels of human activity—from the family to the international organization—in which the pursuit of goals through the exercise of control has transnational repercussions. The reason for this broad formulation is simple: in an ever more interdependent world where what happens in one corner or at one level may have consequences for what occurs at every other corner and level, it seems a mistake to adhere to a narrow definition in which only formal institutions at the national and international levels are considered relevant. In the words of the Council of Rome,

14   *Governance in the Twenty-first Century*

> We use the term governance to denote the command mechanism of a so-
> cial system and its actions that endeavor to provide security, prosperity,
> coherence, order and continuity to the system. . . . Taken broadly, the
> concept of governance should not be restricted to the national and inter-
> national systems but should be used in relation to regional, provincial and
> local governments as well as to other social systems such as education
> and the military, to private enterprises and even to the microcosm of the
> family.[1]

Governance, in other words, encompasses the activities of governments, but
it also includes the many other channels through which "commands" flow
in the form of goals framed, directives issued, and policies pursued.

Command and Control

But the concept of commands can be misleading. It implies that hierarchy,
perhaps even authoritarian rule, characterizes governance systems. Such an
implication may be descriptive of many forms of governance, but hierarchy
is certainly not a necessary prerequisite to the framing of goals, the issuing
of directives, and the pursuit of policies. Indeed, a central theme of this
analysis is that often the practices and institutions of governance can and do
evolve in such a way as to be minimally dependent on hierarchical, com-
mand-based arrangements. Accordingly, while preserving the core of the
Council of Rome formulation, here we shall replace the notion of command
mechanisms with the concept of *control* or *steering* mechanisms, terms that
highlight the purposeful nature of governance without presuming the presence of hierarchy. They are terms, moreover, informed by the etymologi-
cal roots of *governance:* the term "derives from the Greek 'kybenan' and
'kybernetes' which means 'to steer' and 'pilot or helmsman' respectively
(the same Greek root from which 'cybernetics' is derived). The process of
governance is the process whereby an organization or society steers itself,
and the dynamics of communication and control are central to that process."[2]

To grasp the concept of control one has to appreciate that it consists of
relational phenomena that, taken holistically, constitute systems of rule.
Some actors, the controllers, seek to modify the behavior and/or orientations of other actors, the controllees, and the resulting patterns of interaction between the former and the latter can properly be viewed as a system
of rule sustained by one or another form of control. It does not matter
whether the controllees resist or comply with the efforts of controllers; in
either event, attempts at control have been undertaken. But it is not until
the attempts become increasingly successful and compliance with them increasingly patterned that a system of rule founded on mechanisms of control can be said to have evolved. Rule systems and control mechanisms, in
other words, are founded on a modicum of regularity, a form of recurrent

behavior that systematically links the efforts of controllers to the compliance of controllees through either formal or informal channels.[3]

It follows that systems of rule can be maintained and their controls successfully and consistently exerted even in the absence of established legal or political authority. The evolution of intersubjective consensuses based on shared fates and common histories, the possession of information and knowledge, the pressure of active or mobilizable publics, and/or the use of careful planning, good timing, clever manipulation, and hard bargaining can—either separately or in combination—foster control mechanisms that sustain governance without government.[4]

Interdependence and Proliferation

Implicit in the broad conception of governance as control mechanisms is a premise that interdependence involves not only flows of control, consequence, and causation within systems, but that it also sustains flows across systems. These micro-macro processes—the dynamics whereby values and behaviors at one level get converted into outcomes at more encompassing levels, outcomes that in turn get converted into still other consequences at still more encompassing levels—suggest that global governance knows no boundaries—geographic, social, cultural, economic, or political. If major changes occur in the structure of families, if individual greed proliferates at the expense of social consciences, if people become more analytically skillful, if crime grips neighborhoods, if schools fail to provoke the curiosity of children, if racial or religious prejudices become pervasive, if the drug trade starts distributing its illicit goods through licit channels, if defiance comes to vie with compliance as characteristic responses to authority, if new trading partners are established, if labor and environmental groups in different countries form cross-border coalitions, if cities begin to conduct their own foreign commercial policies—to mention only some of the more conspicuous present-day dynamics—then the consequences of such developments will ripple across and fan out within provincial, regional, national, and international levels as well as across and within local communities. Such is the crazy-quilt nature of modern interdependence. And such is the staggering challenge of global governance.

The challenge continues to intensify as control mechanisms proliferate at a breathtaking rate. For not only has the number of UN members risen from 51 in 1945 to 184 a half-century later, but the density of nongovernmental organizations (NGOs) has increased at a comparable pace. More accurately, it has increased at a rate comparable to the continuing growth of the world's population beyond five billion and a projected eight billion in 2025. More and more people, that is, need to concert their actions to cope with the challenges and opportunities of daily life, thus giving rise to more

16   *Governance in the Twenty-first Century*

and more organizations to satisfy their needs and wants. Indeed, since the needs and wants of people are most effectively expressed through organized action, the organizational explosion of our time is no less consequential than the population explosion. Hastened by dynamic technologies that have shrunk social, economic, political, and geographic distances and thereby rendered the world ever more interdependent, expanded by the advent of new global challenges such as those posed by a deteriorating environment, an AIDS epidemic, and drug trafficking, and further stimulated by widespread authority crises within existing governance mechanisms, the proliferation of organizations is pervasive at and across all levels of human activity—from neighborhood organizations, community groups, regional networks, national states, and transnational regimes to international systems.

Not only is global life marked by a density of populations, it is also dense with organized activities, thereby complicating and extending the processes of global governance. For while organizations provide decision points through which the steering mechanisms of governance can be carried forward, so may they operate as sources of opposition to any institutions and policies designed to facilitate governance. Put in still another way, if it is the case, as many (including myself) argue, that global life late in the twentieth century is more complex than ever before in history, it is because the world is host to ever greater numbers of organizations in all walks of life and in every corner of every continent. And it is this complexity, along with the competitive impulses that lead some organizations to defy steerage and resort to violence, that makes the tasks of governance at once so difficult and so daunting.

Disaggregation and Innovation

An obvious but major conceptual premise follows from the foregoing: There is no single organizing principle on which global governance rests, no emergent order around which communities and nations are likely to converge. Global governance is the sum of myriad—literally millions of—control mechanisms driven by different histories, goals, structures, and processes. Perhaps every mechanism shares a history, culture, and structure with a few others, but there are no characteristics or attributes common to all mechanisms. This means that any attempt to assess the dynamics of global governance will perforce have multiple dimensions, that any effort to trace a hierarchical structure of authority that loosely links disparate sources of governance to each other is bound to fail. In terms of governance, the world is too disaggregated for grand logics that postulate a measure of global coherence.

Put differently, the continuing disaggregation that has followed the end of the Cold War suggests a further extension of the anarchic structures that have long pervaded world politics. If it was possible to presume that the absence of hierarchy and an ultimate authority signified the presence of anarchy during the era of hegemonic leadership and superpower competition, such a characterization of global governance is all the more pertinent today. Indeed, it might well be observed that a new form of anarchy has evolved in the current period—one that involves not only the absence of a highest authority but that also encompasses such an extensive disaggregation of authority as to allow for much greater flexibility, innovation, and experimentation in the development and application of new control mechanisms.

In sum, while politicians and pundits may speak confidently or longingly about establishing a new world order, such a concept is meaningful only as it relates to the prevention or containment of large-scale violence and war. It is not a concept that can be used synonomously with global governance if by the latter is meant the vast numbers of rule systems that have been caught up in the proliferating networks of an ever more interdependent world.

Emergence and Evolution

Underlying the growing complexity and continuing disaggregation of modern governance are the obvious but often ignored dynamics of change wherein control mechanisms emerge out of path-dependent conditions and then pass through lengthy processes of either evolution and maturation or decline and demise. In order to acquire the legitimacy and support they need to endure, successful mechanisms of governance are more likely to evolve out of bottom-up than top-down processes. As such, as mechanisms that manage to evoke the consent of the governed, they are self-organizing systems, steering arrangements that develop through the shared needs of groups and the presence of developments that conduce to the generation and acceptance of shared instruments of control.

But there is no magic in the dynamics of self-organization. Governance does not just suddenly happen. Circumstances have to be suitable, people have to be amenable to collective decisions being made, tendencies toward organization have to develop, habits of cooperation have to evolve, and a readiness not to impede the processes of emergence and evolution has to persist. The proliferation of organizations and their ever greater interdependence may stimulate felt needs for new forms of governance, but the transformation of those needs into established and institutionalized control mechanisms is never automatic and can be marked by a volatility that consumes long stretches of time. Yet at each stage of the transformation, some form of governance can be said to exist, with a preponderance of the control

18   *Governance in the Twenty-first Century*

mechanisms at any moment evolving somewhere in the middle of a continuum that runs from nascent to fully institutionalized mechanisms, from informal modes of framing goals, issuing directives, and pursuing policies to formal instruments of decisionmaking, conflict resolution, and resource allocation.

In other words, no matter how institutionalized rule systems may be, governance is not a constant in these turbulent and disaggregated times. It is, rather, in a continuous process of evolution, a becoming that fluctuates between order and disorder as conditions change and emergent properties consolidate and solidify. To analyze governance by freezing it in time is to ensure failure in comprehending its nature and vagaries.

The Relocation of Authority

Notwithstanding the evolutionary dynamics of control mechanisms and the absence of an overall structural order, it is possible to identify pockets of coherence operating at different levels and in different parts of the world that can serve as bases for assessing the contours of global governance in the future. It may be the case that "processes of governance at the global level are inherently more fragile, contingent, and unevenly experienced than is the case within most national political systems,"[5] but this is not to deny the presence of central tendencies. One such tendency involves an "upsurge in the collective capacity to govern": despite the rapid pace of ever greater complexity and decentralization—and to some extent because of their exponential dynamics—the world is undergoing "a remarkable expansion of collective power," an expansion that is highly disaggregated and unfolds unevenly but that nevertheless amounts to a development of rule systems "that have become 1) more intensive in their permeation of daily life, 2) more permanent over time, 3) more extensive over space, 4) larger in size, 5) wider in functional scope, 6) more constitutionally differentiated, and 7) more bureaucratic."[6] Global governance in the twenty-first century may not take the form of a single world order, but it will not be lacking in activities designed to bring a measure of coherence to the multitude of jurisdictions that is proliferating on the world stage.

Perhaps even more important, a pervasive tendency can be identified in which major shifts in the location of authority and the site of control mechanisms are under way on every continent and in every country, shifts that are as pronounced in economic and social systems as they are in political systems. Indeed, in some cases the shifts have transferred authority away from the political realm and into the economic and social realms even as in still other instances the shifts occur in the opposite direction.

Partly these shifts have been facilitated by the end of the Cold War and the lifting of the constraints inherent in its bipolar global structure of superpower competition. Partly they have been driven by a search for new, more effective forms of political organization better suited to the turbulent circumstances that have evolved with the shrinking of the world by dynamic technologies. Partly they have been driven by the skill revolution that has enabled citizens to identify more clearly their needs and wants as well as to empower them more thoroughly to engage in collective action. Partly they have been stimulated and sustained by "subgroupism"—the fragmenting and coalescing of groups into new organizational entities—that has created innumerable new sites from which authority can emerge and toward which it can gravitate. Partly they have been driven by the continuing globalization of national and local economies that has undermined long-established ways of sustaining commercial and financial relations. And, no less, the shifts have been accelerated by the advent of interdependence issues—such as environmental pollution, AIDS, monetary crises, and the drug trade—that have fostered new and intensified forms of transnational collaboration as well as new social movements that are serving as transnational voices for change.

In short, the numerous shifts in the loci of governance stem from interactive tensions whereby processes of globalization and localization are simultaneously unfolding on a worldwide scale. In some situations these foregoing dynamics are fostering control mechanisms that extend beyond national boundaries, and in others the need for the psychological comfort of neighborhood or ethnic attachments is leading to the diminution of national entities and the formation or extension of local mechanisms. The combined effect of the simultaneity of these contradictory trends is that of lessening the capacities for governance located at the level of sovereign states and national societies. Much governance will doubtless continue to be sustained by states and their governments initiating and implementing policies in the context of their legal frameworks—and in some instances national governments are likely to work out arrangements for joint governance with rule systems at other levels—but the effectiveness of their policies is likely to be undermined by the proliferation of emergent control mechanisms both within and outside their jurisdictions. In the words of one analyst, "The very high levels of interdependence and vulnerability stimulated by technological change now necessitate new forms of global political authority and even governance."[7]

Put more emphatically, perhaps the most significant pattern discernible in the crisscrossing flow of transformed authority involves processes of bifurcation whereby control mechanisms at national levels are, in varying degrees, yielding space to both more encompassing and narrower, less comprehensive forms of governance. For analytic purposes, we shall refer to the former as transnational governance mechanisms and the latter as subnational governance mechanisms, terms that do not preclude institutionalized governmental mechanisms but that allow for the large degree to which our concern is with dynamic and evolving processes rather than with the routinized procedures of national governments.

While transnational and subnational mechanisms differ in the extent of their links across national boundaries—all the former are by definition boundary-spanning forms of control, while some of the latter may not extend beyond the jurisdiction of their states—both types must face the same challenges to governance. Both must deal with a rapidly changing, ever more complex world in which people, information, goods, and ideas are in continuous motion and thus endlessly reconfiguring social, economic, and political horizons. Both are confronted with the instabilities and disorder that derive from resource shortages, budgetary constraints, ethnic rivalries, unemployment, and incipient or real inflation. Both must contend with the ever greater relevance of scientific findings and the epistemic communities that form around those findings. Both are subject to the continuous tensions that spring from the inroads of corrupt practices, organized crime, and restless publics that have little use for politics and politicians. Both must cope with pressures for further fragmentation of subgroups on the one hand and for more extensive transnational links on the other. Both types of mechanisms, in short, have severe adaptive problems and, given the fragility of their legal status and the lack of long-standing habits of support for them, many of both types may fail to maintain their essential structures intact. Global governance, it seems reasonable to anticipate, is likely to consist of proliferating mechanisms that fluctuate between bare survival and increasing institutionalization, between considerable chaos and widening degrees of order.

Mechanisms of Global Governance

Steering mechanisms are spurred into existence through several channels: through the sponsorship of states, through the efforts of actors other than states at the transnational or subnational levels, or through states and other types of actors jointly sponsoring the formation of rule systems. They can also be differentiated by their location on the aforementioned continuum that ranges from full institutionalization on the one hand to nascent processes of rule making and compliance on the other. Although extremes on a continuum, the institutionalized and nascent types of control mechanisms can be causally linked through evolutionary processes. It is possible to trace at least two generic routes that link the degree to which transnational governance mechanisms are institutionalized and the sources that sponsor those developments. One route is the direct, top-down process wherein states create new institutional structures and impose them on the course of events.

A second is much more circuitous and involves an indirect, bottom-up process of evolutionary stages wherein nascent dynamics of rule making are sponsored by publics or economies that experience a need for repeated interactions that foster habits and attitudes of cooperation, which in turn generate organizational activities that eventually get transformed into institutionalized control mechanisms. Stated more generally, whatever their sponsorship, the institutionalized mechanisms tend to be marked by explicit hierarchical structures, whereas those at the nascent end of the continuum develop more subtly as a consequence of emergent interaction patterns which, unintentionally, culminate in fledgling control mechanisms for newly formed or transformed systems.

Table 1 offers examples of the rule systems derivable from a combination of the several types of sponsors and the two extremes on the continuum, a matrix that suggests the considerable variety and complexity out of which the processes of global governance evolve. In the table, moreover, are hints of the developmental processes whereby nascent mechanisms become institutionalized: as indicated by the arrows, some of the control mechanisms located in the right-hand cells have their origins in the corresponding left-hand cells as interdependence issues that generate pressures from the nongovernmental world for intergovernmental cooperation which, in turn, lead to the formation of issue-based transnational institutions. The history of more than a few control mechanisms charged with addressing environmental problems exemplifies how this subtle evolutionary path can be traversed.

However they originate, and at whatever pace they evolve, transnational governance mechanisms tend to be essentially forward-looking. They may be propelled by dissatisfactions over existing (national or subnational) arrangements, but their evolution is likely to be marked less by despair over the past and present than by hope for the future, by expectations that an expansion beyond existing boundaries will draw upon cooperative impulses that may serve to meet challenges and fill lacunae that would otherwise be left unattended. To be sure, globalizing dynamics tend to create resistance and opposition, since any expansion of governance is bound to be detrimental to those who have a stake in the status quo. Whether they are explicitly and formally designed or subtly and informally constructed, however, transnational systems of governance tend on balance to evolve in a context of hope and progress, a sense of breakthrough, an appreciation that old problems can be circumvented and moved toward either the verge of resolution or the edge of obsolescence. But relatively speaking, subnational mechanisms are usually (though not always) energized by despair, by frustration with existing systems that seems best offset by contracting the scope of governance, by a sense that large-scale cooperation has not worked and that new subgroup arrangements are bound to be more satisfying. That

22   *Governance in the Twenty-first Century*

Table 1   The Sponsorship and Institutionalization of Control Mechanisms

	Nascent	Institutionalized
Not State-Sponsored Transnational	• nongovernmental organizations • social movements • epistemic communities • multinational corporations	• internet • European Environmental Bureau • credit rating agencies
Subnational	• ethnic minorities • microregions • cities	• American Jewish Congress • the Greek lobby • crime syndicates
State-Sponsored	• macroregions • European community • GATT	• United Nations System • European Union • World Trade Organization
Jointly Sponsored	• cross-border coalitions • issue regimes	• election monitoring • human-rights regime

distinction between transnational and subnational governance mechanisms can, of course, be overstated, but it does suggest that the delicacies of global governance at subnational levels may be greater than those at transnational levels.

To highlight the variety of forms transnational governance may take in the twenty-first century, the following discussion focuses on examples listed in Table 1. Due to space limitations, only some of the listed examples are subjected to analysis, and even the discussion of those is far from exhaustive. But hopefully both the table and its elaboration convey a sense of the degree to which global governance is likely to become increasingly pervasive and disaggregated in the years ahead.

Transnational Nascent Control Mechanisms

Private volunteer and profit-making organizations.   Irrespective of whether they are volunteer or profit-making organizations, and quite apart from whether their structures are confined to one country or span several, NGOs may serve as the basis for, or actually become, nascent forms of transnational governance. Why? Because in an ever more interdependent world, the need for control mechanisms outstrips the capacity or readiness of national governments to provide them. There are various types of situations in which governments fear involvement will be counterproductive, or where they lack the will or ability to intrude their presence. (And, as noted below, there are also numerous circumstances where governments find it expedient to participate in rule systems jointly with organizations from the private sector.)

Put more specifically, just as at the local level "community associations are taking over more of the functions of municipal governments,"[8] and just as in diplomatic situations distinguished individuals from the private sector are called upon when assessments are made that assert, in effect, that "I don't think any governments wanted to get involved in this,"[9] so are NGOs of all kinds to be found as the central actors in the deliberations of control mechanisms relevant to their spheres of activity. Whether the deliberations involve the generation and allocation of relief supplies in disaster situations around the world or the framing of norms of conduct for trade relationships—to mention only two of the more conspicuous spheres in which transnational governance occurs—volunteer associations or business corporations may make the crucial decisions. In the case of alliances fashioned within and among multinational corporations, for example, it has been found that "transnational actors, unlike purely domestic ones, have the organizational and informational resources necessary to construct private alternatives to governmental accords."[10] And even if only a small proportion of NGOs preside over steering mechanisms, their contribution to global governance looms as substantial when it is appreciated that more than 17,000 international nongovernmental organizations (INGOs) in the non-profit sector were active in the mid 1980s and that in excess of 35,000 transnational corporations with some 150,000 foreign subsidiaries were operating in 1990.[11]

Furthermore, in their activities both volunteer and profit-making organizations are not unmindful of their role in nascent control mechanisms. That can be discerned in the charters of the former and in the public pronouncements of the latter. An especially clear-cut expression along this line was made by the chairman and CEO of the Coca-Cola Company: "four prevailing forces—the preeminence of democratic capitalism, the desire for self-determination, the shift in influence from regulation to investment, and the success of institutions which meet the needs of people—reinforced by today's worldwide communications and dramatic television images, . . . all point to a fundamental shift in global power. To be candid, I believe this shift will lead to a future in which the institutions with the most influence by-and-large will be businesses."[12]

Social movements.   Much less structured but no less important, social movements have evolved as wellsprings of global governance in recent decades. Indeed, they are perhaps the quintessential case of nascent control mechanisms that have the potential to develop into institutionalized instruments of governance. Their nascency is conspicuous: they have no definite memberships or authority structures; they consist of as many people, as much territory, and as many issues as seem appropriate to the people involved; they have no central headquarters and are spread across numerous locales; and they are all-inclusive, excluding no one and embracing anyone who wishes to be part of the movement. More often than not, social movements are organized around a salient set of issues—like those that highlight the concerns of feminists, environmentalists, or peace activists—and as such they serve transnational needs that cannot be filled by national governments, organized domestic groups, or private firms. Social movements are thus constituent parts of the globalizing process. They contribute importantly to the noneconomic fabric of ties facilitated by the new communications and transportation technologies. They pick up the pieces, so to speak, that states and businesses leave in their wake by their boundary-crossing activities. Just as the peace movement focuses on the consequences of state interactions, for example, so has the ecological movement become preoccupied with the developmental excesses of transnational corporations. Put even more strongly, "The point about these antisystemic movements is that they often elude the traditional categories of nation, state, and class. They articulate new ways of experiencing life, a new attitude to time and space, a new sense of history and identity."[13]

Despite the lack of structural constraints that allow for their growth, however, social movements may not remain permanently inchoate and nascent. At those times when the issues of concern to their members climb high on the global agenda, they may begin to evolve at least temporary organizational arrangements through which to move toward their goals. The International Nestlé Boycott Committee is illustrative in this regard: it organized a seven-year international boycott of Nestlé products and then was dismantled when the Nestlé Company complied with its demands. In some instances, moreover, the organizational expression of a movement's aspirations can develop enduring features. Fearful that the development of organizational structures might curb their spontaneity, some movement members might be aghast at the prospect of formalized procedures, explicit rules, and specific role assignments, but clearly the march toward goals requires organizational coherence at some point. Thus have transnational social movement organizations (TSMOs) begun to dot the global landscape. Oxfam and Amnesty International are two examples among many that could be cited of movement spinoffs that have evolved toward the institutionalized extreme of the continuum. The European Environmental Bureau (EEB), founded in 1974, has moved less rapidly toward that extreme, but it now has a full-time staff quartered in a Brussels office and shows signs of becoming permanent as the environmental movement matures.[14]

Subnational Nascent Mechanisms: Cities and Microregions

The concept of regions, both the macro and micro variety, has become increasingly relevant to the processes of global governance. Although originally connotative of territorial space, it is a concept that has evolved as a residual category encompassing those new patterns of interaction that span established political boundaries and at the same time remain within a delimited geographic space. If that space embraces two or more national economies, it can be called a macroregion, whereas a space that spans two or more subnational economies constitutes a microregion.[15] As can be inferred from Table 1, both types of regions can emerge out of bottom-up processes and thus evolve out of economic foundations into political institutions. This evolutionary potential makes it "difficult to work with precise definitions. We cannot define regions because they define themselves by evolving from objective, but dormant, to subjective, active existence."[16]

Abstract and elusive as it may be, however, the notion of micro- and macroregions as residual categories for control mechanisms that span conventional boundaries serves to highlight important features of transnational governance. In the case of microregions, it calls attention to the emergent role of certain cities and "natural" economic zones as subtle and nascent forms of transnational rule systems that are not sponsored by states and that, instead, emerge out of the activities of other types of actors—which at least initially may foster a relocation of authority from the political to the economic realm. To be sure, some microregions may span conventional boundaries within a single state and thus be more logically treated as instances of subnational control mechanisms, but such a distinction is not drawn here because many such regions are, as noted in the ensuing paragraphs, transnational in scope. Indeed, since they "are interlinked processes,"[17] it is conceivable that the evolution of microregions contributes to the emergence of macroregions, and vice versa.

An insightful example along these lines is provided by the developments that have flowed from the success of a cooperation pact signed in 1988 by Lyon, Milan, Stuttgart, and Barcelona, developments that have led one analyst to observe that "a resurrection of 'city states' and regions is quietly transforming Europe's political and economic landscape, diminishing the influence of national governments and redrawing the continental map of power for the 21st century."[18] All four cities and their surrounding regions have an infrastructure and location that are more suited to the changes at work in Europe. They are attracting huge investment and enjoying a prosperity that has led to new demands for greater autonomy. Some argue that, as a result, the emerging urban centers and economies are fostering "a new historical dynamism that will ultimately transform the political structure of Europe by creating a new kind of 'Hanseatic League' that consists of thriving city-states."[19] One specialist forecasts that there will be nineteen cities with at least twenty million people in the greater metropolitan area by the year 2000, with the result that "cities, not nations, will become the principal identity for most people in the world."[20] Others offer similar interpretations, anticipating that these identity shifts will have profound implications for nationhood and traditional state boundaries.[21]

And what unit is evolving in the place of the nation-state as a natural unit for organizing activity within the economic realm? Again the data point to emergence of control mechanisms that are regional in scope. These regional control mechanisms are not governmentally imposed but "are drawn by the deft but invisible hand of the global market for goods and services."[22] This is not to say, however, that region states are lacking in structure. On the contrary, since they make "effective points of entry into the global economy because the very characteristics that define them are shaped by the demands of that economy."[23] Needless to say, since the borders of regional states are determined by the "naturalness" of their economic zones and thus rarely coincide with the boundaries of political units, the clash between the incentives induced by markets and the authority of governments is central to the emergence of transnational governance mechanisms. Indeed, it is arguable that a prime change at work in world politics today is a shift in the balance between those two forces, with political authorities finding it increasingly expedient to yield to economic realities. In some instances, moreover, political authorities do not even get to choose to yield, as "regional economic interdependencies are now more important than political boundaries."[24] Put differently, "The implications of region states are not welcome news to established seats of political power, be they politicians or lobbyists. Nation states by definition require a domestic political focus, while region states are ensconced in the global economy."[25]

This potential clash, however, need not necessarily turn adversarial. Much depends on whether the political authorities welcome and encourage foreign capital investment or whether they insist on protecting their non-competitive local industries. If they are open to foreign inputs, their economies are more likely to prosper than if they insist on a rigorous maintenance of their political autonomy. But if they do insist on drawing tight lines around their authoritative realms, they are likely to lose out.

It seems clear, in short, that cities and microregions are likely to be major control mechanisms in the world politics of the twenty-first century. Even if the various expectations that they replace states as centers of power prove to be exaggerated, they seem destined to emerge as either partners or adversaries of states as their crucial role becomes more widely recognized and they thereby move from an objective to an intersubjective existence.

State-Sponsored Mechanisms

Although largely nursed into being through the actions of states, macroregions may be no less nascent than cities and microregions. And like their micro counterparts, the macroregions, which span two or more states, are deeply ensconced in a developmental process that may, in some instances, move steadily toward institutionalization, while in others the evolutionary process may either move slowly or fall short of culminating in formal institutions. Movement toward institutionalization—or in Hettne's felicitous term, "regionness"—occurs the more a region is marked by "economic interdependence, communication, cultural homogeneity, coherence, capacity to act and, in particular, capacity to resolve conflicts."[26]

Whatever their pace or outcome, those processes have come to be known as the "new" regionalism, which is conceived to be different from the "old" regionalism in several ways. While the latter was a product of Cold War bipolarity, the former has come into being in the context of present-day multipolarity. The old regionalism was, in effect, created on a top-down basis from the outside by the superpowers. The new regionalism, on the other hand, consists of more spontaneous processes from within that unfold largely on a bottom-up basis as the constituent states find common cause in a deepening interdependence. As one observer puts it,

> The process of regionalization from within can be compared with the historical formation of nations states with the important difference that a coercive centre is lacking in processes of regionalization which presuppose a shared intention among the potential members. . . . The difference between regionalism and the infinite process of spontaneous integration is that there is a politically defined limit to the former process. The limitation, however, is a historical outcome of attempts to find a transnational level of governance which includes certain shared values and minimizes certain shared perceptions of danger. Like the formation of ethnic and national identities, the regional identity is dependent on historical context and shaped by conflicts. And like nations and ethnies, regional formations which have a subjective quality . . . [are] "imagined communities." . . . Despite enormous historical, structural, and contextual differences, there is an underlying logic behind contemporary processes of regionalization.[27]

Currently, of course, the various new regions of the world are at very different stages of development, with some already having evolved the rudiments of control mechanisms while others are still at earlier stages in the process. As noted below, Europe has advanced the most toward institutionalized steering mechanisms, but the decline of hegemons, the advent of democracies, and the demise of governmentally managed economies throughout the world has fostered the conditions under which the new regionalism can begin to flourish. Pronounced movements in this direction are discernible in the Nordic region, in the Caribbean, in the Andean Group, and in the Southern Cone of South America. Lesser degrees of regionness are evident in the three Asia-Pacific regions—East Asia, Southeast Asia, and the European Pacific—and the former Soviet Union, while the regionalization process has yet to become readily recognizable in South Asia, the Middle East, and Africa.

Whatever the degree to which the new regionalism has taken hold in various parts of the world, however, it seems clear that this macrophenomenon is increasingly a central feature of global governance. Indeed, the dynamics of macroregions can be closely linked to those of microregions in the sense that as the former shift authority away from national states, so do they open up space for the latter to evolve their own autonomous control mechanisms. "This can be seen all over Europe today."[28] The dynamics of globalization and localization are intimately tied to each other.

Jointly Sponsored Mechanisms

Issue regimes. Despite a mushrooming of literature around the concept of international regimes—as the rules, norms, principles, and procedures that constitute the control mechanisms through which order and governance in particular issue areas are sustained—there has been little convergence around a precise and shared notion of the essential attributes of regimes. Indeed, "scholars have fallen into using the term regime so disparately and with such little precision that it ranges from an umbrella for all international relations to little more than a synonym for international organizations."[29] Notwithstanding this conceptual disarray, however, the conception of governance used here as steering mechanisms that are located on a nascent-to-institutionalized continuum serves to highlight regimes as important sources of global governance. Most notably, since they allow for the evolution of a variety of arrangements whereby nongovernmental as well as governmental actors may frame goals and pursue policies in particular issue areas, regimes meet the need for "a wider view" that includes not only states, international organizations, and international law "but also the often implicit understandings between a whole range of actors, some of which [are] not states, which [serve] to structure their cooperation in the face of common problems."[30] In some instances the control mechanisms of issue areas may be informal, disorganized, conflictual, and often ineffective in concentrating authority—that is, so rudimentary and nascent that governance is spasmodic and weak. In other cases the control mechanisms may be formalized, well organized, and capable of effectively exercising authority—that is, so fully institutionalized that governance is consistent and strong. But in all regimes, regardless of their stage of development, "the interaction between the parties is not unconstrained or is not based on independent decision making."[31] All regimes, that is, have control mechanisms to which their participants feel obliged to accede even if they do not do so repeatedly and systematically.

It is important to stress that whether they are nascent or institutionalized, the control mechanisms of all regimes are sustained by the joint efforts of governmental and nongovernmental actors. This shared responsibility is all too often overlooked in the regime literature. More accurately, although the early work on regimes allowed for the participation of NGOs, subsequent inquiries slipped into treating regimes as if they consisted exclusively of states that were more or less responsive to advice and pressures from the nongovernmental sector. However, from a global governance perspective in which states are only the most formalized control mechanisms, the original conception of regime membership as open to all types of actors again becomes compelling. And viewed in that way, it immediately becomes clear that issue regimes evolve through the joint sponsorship of state and nonstate actors. To be sure, as regimes evolve from the nascent toward the institutionalized extreme of the continuum, the more intergovernmental organizations will acquire the formal authority to make decisions; but movement in that direction is likely to be accompanied by preservation of the joint sponsorship of state and nonstate actors through arrangements that accord formal advisory roles to the relevant NGOs. No issue regime, it

30   *Governance in the Twenty-first Century*

seems reasonable to assert, can prosper without control mechanisms that allow for some form of participation by all the interested parties. As one observer puts it with respect to several specific issue regimes,

> Increasingly, this transnationalization of civic participation is redefining the terms of governance in North America, not only in the commercial arena but also on issues such as the environment, human rights, and immigration. Nongovernmental organizations, particularly grassroots groups, located throughout these societies are playing a growing role in setting the parameters of the North American agenda, limiting the ability of public officials to manage their relationship on a strict government-to-government basis, and setting the stage for a much more complete process of interaction.[32]

As indicated in Table 1, it follows that not all the steering mechanisms of issue regimes are located at the nascent end of the continuum. Some move persistently toward institutionalization—as was recently the case in the human rights regime when the United Nations created a high commissioner for human rights—while others may be stalemated in an underdeveloped state for considerable periods of time. However, given the ever greater interdependence of global life, it seems doubtful whether any issue area that gains access to the global agenda can avoid evolving at least a rudimentary control mechanism. Once the problems encompassed by an issue area become widely recognized as requiring attention and amelioration, it can hardly remain long without entering at least the first stage of the evolutionary process toward governance. On the other hand, given the disaggregated nature of the global system, it also seems doubtful whether any regime can ever become so fully institutionalized that its rule system evolves a hierarchy through which its top leadership acquires binding legal authority over all its participants. Rather, once a regime acquires a sufficient degree of centralized authority to engage in a modicum of regulatory activities, it undergoes transformation into an international organization, as is suggested in Table 1 by the evolution of GATT into the World Trade Organization.

How many issue regimes are there? Endless numbers, if it is recalled that issue areas are essentially a conglomeration of related smaller issues and that each of the latter evolves identifiable mechanisms for governance that are at some variance with other issues in the same area. The global agenda is conceived in terms of large-issue areas only because those are more easily grasped and debated, but it is on the smaller issues that particularistic activities requiring special governance arrangements focus.

Cross-border coalitions. Some issue regimes, moreover, are so disaggregated as to encompass what have been called "cross-border coalitions."[33] These can be usefully set aside for separate analysis as instances of jointly sponsored, nascent control mechanisms. The emphasis here is on the notion of coalitions, on networks of organizations. As previously noted, INGOs are by definition cross-border organizations, but their spanning of boundaries tends to occur largely through like-minded people from different countries who either share membership in the same transnational organization or who belong to national organizations that are brought together under umbrella organizations that are transnational in scope. Cross-border coalitions, on the other hand, consist of organizations that coalesce for common purposes but do not do so under the aegis of an umbrella organization. Some of these may form umbrella INGOs as they move on from the nascent stage of development, but at present most of the new coalitions are still in the earliest stage of formation. They are networks rather than organizations, networks that have been facilitated by the advent of information technologies such as E-mail and electronic conferencing and that thus place their members in continuous touch with each other even though they may only come together in face-to-face meetings on rare occasions. Put more dramatically, "rather than be represented by a building that people enter, these actors may be located on electronic networks and exist as 'virtual communities' that have no precise physical address."[34]

It is noteworthy that some cross-border coalitions may involve local governments located near national boundaries that find it more expedient on a variety of issues to form coalitions with counterparts across the border than to work with their own provincial or national governments. Such coalitions may even be formed deliberately in order to avoid drawing "unnecessary or premature attention from central authorities to local solutions of some local problems by means of informal contacts and 'good neighborhood' networks. Often it [is] not a deliberate deception, just an avoidance of unnecessary complications."[35]

That cross-border coalitions are a nascent form of issue regimes is indicated by the fact that they usually form around problems high on the agendas of their communities. During the 1993 debate over the North American Free Trade Agreement (NAFTA), for example, a number of advocacy groups concerned with environmental, human rights, labor, and immigration issues linked up with their counterparts across the U.S.-Mexican boundary, and in some instances the networks spanned the sectoral issue areas as the implications of NAFTA were discovered to have common consequences for otherwise disparate groups. This is not to say that the advent of cross-border coalitions reduced the degree of conflict over the question of NAFTA's approval. As can be readily expected whenever a control mechanism is at stake, coalitions on one side of the issue generated opposing coalitions.

In short, "the new local and cross-border NGO movements are a potential wild card. They may be proactive or reactive in a variety of ways, sometimes working with, sometimes against, state and market actors who are not accustomed to regarding civil society as an independent actor."[36]

Transnational Institutionalized Control Mechanisms: Credit Rating Agencies

Turning now to transnational control mechanisms that are located more toward the institutionalized extreme of the governance continuum, the dimension of the global capital markets in which risk is assessed and creditworthiness legitimated offers examples of both discernible rule systems that came into being through the sponsorship of states and others that evolved historically out of the private sector.[37] The International Monetary Fund (IMF) and the World Bank are illustrative of the former type of mechanism, while Moody's Investors Service and Standard & Poor's Ratings Group (S&P) dominate the ratings market in the private sector. Although the difference between the two types is in some ways considerable—unlike the agencies in the private sector, the IMF and the World Bank derive much of their capacity for governance from the sponsorship and funding by the state system that founded them—they are in one important respect quite similar: in both cases their authority derives at least partially from the specialized knowledge on which their judgments are based and the respect they have earned for adhering to explicit and consistent standards for reaching their conclusions as to the creditworthiness of enterprises, governments, and countries. And in both cases the judgments they render are authoritative in the sense that the capital markets acquiesce to and conduct themselves on the basis of their ratings. To be sure, fierce debates do break out over the appropriateness of the standards employed to make the risk assessments of debt security, but the credibility of the private rating agencies has not been so effectively challenged as to diminish their status as control mechanisms.

That the private agencies are transnational in scope is indicated by the fact that both Moody's and S&P have branches in London, Paris, Frankfurt, Tokyo, and Sydney. Most of the other agencies in this trillion-dollar market are domestically focused and confine their assessments to the creditworthiness of borrowers in the countries where they are located, albeit there are signs that a Europewide agency is in the process of evolving.

In sum, the private ratings agencies are a means through which key parts of national and transnational economies are, relatively speaking, insulated from politics. By presiding over that insulation, the agencies have become, in effect, control mechanisms. Put differently, "rating agencies seem to be contributing to a system of rule in which an intersubjective framework is created in which social forces will be self-regulating in accord with the limits of the system."[38]

Subnational Institutionalized Mechanisms:
Crime Syndicates

It is a measure of the globalization of governance that crime syndicates have evolved institutional forms on a transnational scale, that they can properly be called "transnational criminal organizations" (TCOs). Their conduct, of course, violates all the norms that are considered to undergird the proper exercise of authority, but their centrality to the course of events is too conspicuous not to note briefly their role among the diverse control mechanisms that now constitute global governance. Indeed, upon reflection it seems clear that, "with the globalization of trade and growing consumer demands for leisure products, it is only natural that criminal organizations should become increasingly transnational in character," that they have been "both contributors to, and beneficiaries of, . . . a great increase in transactions across national boundaries that are neither initiated nor controlled by states,"[39] and that

> not only is transnational activity as open to criminal groups as it is to legitimate multinational corporations, but the character of criminal organizations also makes them particularly suited to exploit these new opportunities. Since criminal groups are used to operating outside the rules, norms and laws of domestic jurisdictions, they have few qualms about crossing national boundaries illegally. In many respects, therefore, TCOs are transnational organizations *par excellence*. They operate outside the existing structures of authority and power in world politics and have developed sophisticated strategies for circumventing law enforcement in individual states and in the global community of states.[40]

A good measure of how new opportunities have facilitated the explosiveness of TCOs in the present era is provided by the pattern of criminal activities that has evolved in the former Soviet Union since the collapse of the Soviet empire. "More than 4,000 criminal formations comprising an estimated 100,000 members now operate in Russia alone," and of these, some "150 to 200 . . . have international ties."[41]

While TCOs operate outside the realm of established norms, and while they are marked by considerable diversity in size, structure, goals, and membership, they are nevertheless institutionalized in the sense that they control their affairs in patterned ways that often involve strategic alliances between themselves and national and local criminal organizations, alliances that "permit them to cooperate with, rather than compete against, indigenously entrenched criminal organizations."[42] Yet TCOs have not succumbed to excessive bureaucratization. On the contrary, "they are highly mobile and adaptable and able to operate across national borders with great ease . . . partly because of their emphasis on networks rather than formal organizations."[43] It is interesting and indicative of the dynamics of globalization that legitimate multinational corporations have recently come to resemble TCOs in two ways: first, by developing more fluid and flexible network structures that enable them to take advantage of local conditions and, second, by resorting to strategic alliances that facilitate development on a global scale.

State-Sponsored Mechanisms

The United Nations system. The United Nations is an obvious case of a steering mechanism that was sponsored by states and that took an institutional form from its founding. To be sure, its processes of institutionalization have continued to evolve since 1945 to the point where it is now a complex system of numerous associate agencies and subunits that, collectively, address all the issues on the global agenda and that amount to a vast bureaucracy. The institutional histories of the various agencies differ in a number of respects, but taken as a whole they have become a major center of global governance. They have been a main source of problem identification, information, innovation, and constructive policies in the fields of health, environment, education, agriculture, labor, family, and a number of other issues that are global in scope.

This is not to say that the collective history of the United Nations depicts a straight-line trajectory toward ever greater effectiveness. Quite to the contrary, not only have its many agencies matured enough to be severely and properly criticized for excessive and often misguided bureaucratic practices, but also—and even more important—its primary executive and legislative agencies (the secretary-general, the General Assembly, and the Security Council) have compiled a checkered history with respect to the UN's primary functions of preventive diplomacy, peacekeeping, and peacemaking under Chapter VII of its charter. For the first four decades, its record was that of a peripheral player in the Cold War, an era in which it served as a debating arena for major conflicts, especially those that divided the two nuclear superpowers, but accomplished little by way of creating a new world order that provided states security through the aggregation of their collective strength. Then, at the end of the Cold War, the United Nations underwent both a qualitative and quantitative transformation, one that placed it at the very heart of global governance as states turned to the Security Council for action in a number of the major humanitarian and conflict situations that broke out with the end of superpower competition. The inclination to rely on the United Nations, to centralize in it the responsibility for global governance, reached a peak in 1991 with the successful multilateral effort under UN auspices to undo Iraq's conquest of Kuwait.

It is not difficult to demonstrate the quantitative dimensions of the UN's transformation at the end of the Cold War. In 1987, the United

Nations had assigned some ten thousand peacekeepers—mostly troops in blue helmets who were supposed to resort to force only if attacked—to five operations around the world on an annual budget of about $233 million. Seven years later the number of troops had risen to seventy-two thousand in eighteen different situations at an annual cost of more than $3 billion. Similarly, whereas the Security Council used to meet once a month, by 1994 its schedule involved meeting every day, and often twice a day. Put differently, during the first forty-four years of its history, the Security Council passed only six resolutions under Chapter VII in which "threats to the peace, breaches of the peace, acts of aggression" were determined to exist. Between 1990 and 1992, on the other hand, the Security Council adopted thirty-three such resolutions on Iraq (twenty-one), the former Yugoslavia (eight), Somalia (two), Liberia (one), and Libya (one).

Even more impressive are the qualitative changes that underlay the UN's transformation: as the cold war wound down and ended, two remarkable developments became readily discernible. One was the advent of a new consensus among the five permanent members of the Security Council with respect to the desirability of the United Nations's involvement in peacekeeping activities, and the other was the extension of that consensus to the nonpermanent members, including virtually all of the nonaligned states elected to the council. These changes are evident in the fact that the number of unanimously adopted Security Council resolutions jumped from 61 percent (72 of 119) in 1980–1985 to 84 percent in 1986–1992 (184 of 219). In 1993 alone, the Security Council passed more than 181 resolutions and statements, all of which high-mindedly addressed peacekeeping issues (such as a demand for the end of ethnic cleansing in the former Yugoslavia).

Furthermore, those transformations rendered the United Nations into a control mechanism in the military sense of the term. The organization's operations in both Somalia and Bosnia found the secretary-general conducting himself as commanding general and making the final decisions having to do with the application of air power, the disposition of ground forces, and the dismissal of commanding officers.

Despite those transformations in its role and orientations, in its performances the United Nations has not lived up to the surge of high hopes for it that immediately followed the end of the Cold War. Rather than sustaining movement toward effective global governance, it foundered in Somalia, dawdled in Bosnia, and cumulatively suffered a decline in the esteem with which it is held by both governments and publics. The reasons for this decline are numerous—ranging from a lack of money to a lack of will, from governments that delay paying their dues to publics that resist the commitment of troops to battle—but they add up to a clear-cut inability to carry out and enforce the resolutions of the Security Council. Consensus has evolved on the desirability of the UN's intervening in humanitarian situations, but there is a long distance between agreement on goals and a shared perspective on the provision of the necessary means: the readiness to implement multilateral goals and thereby enhance the UN's authority so as to achieve effective governance is woefully lacking, leading one analyst to describe the organization's activities in the peacekeeping area as "faint-hearted multilateralism."[44]

But the checkered history of the UN's institutionalization suggests that its present limitations may undergo change yet again. The organization continues to occupy a valued and critical position in the complex array of global control mechanisms. The need for collective action in volatile situations is bound to continue, so that it is likely that the world will seek to fill this vacuum by again and again turning to the United Nations as the best available means of achieving a modicum of governance. And in the processes of doing so, conceivably circumstances will arise that swing faint-hearted commitments back in the direction of a more steadfast form of multilateralism.

The European Union.   Much more so than the United Nations, the history of the European Union (EU) is a record of the evolutionary route to institutionalization. Even a brief account of this history is beyond the scope of this analysis, but suffice it to say that it is one macroregion that has passed through various stages of growth to its present status as an elaborately institutionalized instrument of governance for the (increasing number of) countries within its jurisdiction. Sure, it was states that formalized the institutionalization, but they did so as a consequence of transformations that culminated in the member countries holding referenda wherein the establishment of the EU was approved by citizenries. In this sense the EU offers a paradigmatic example of the dynamics that propel evolutionary processes from nascent to institutionalized steering mechanisms. As one observer puts it, this transformation occurred through "the gradual blurring of the distinction made between the 'Community' and the 'nation-states' which agreed to form that community in the first place. . . . Although the two are by no means linked as tightly as are subnational units to the center in the traditional state, the Community-state entanglement is such that the Community is very far from being a traditional regional organization."[45] Indeed, such is the evolution of the European Union that it

> is now better conceptualized as a union of states rather than as an organization. The international law doctrine that actors are either states or organizations has become unrealistic. . . . In [a 1992] decision the Court of Justice established that Community law within its sphere is equal in status to national law. Further, the court has successfully maintained that, because law should be uniform, Community law must take precedence over conflicting national law.[46]

In short, while the EU does not have "federal law because Community legislation suffers from the defect that its statutes are not legitimized by a democratic legislature,"[47] it does have a rule system in the combination of its executive and judicial institutions.

Jointly Sponsored Institutionalized Mechanisms

A good illustration of how control mechanisms can evolve toward the institutionalized end of the governance continuum through the sponsorship of both states and NGOs is provided by the emergence of clear-cut patterns wherein it has become established practice for external actors to monitor the conduct of domestic elections in the developing world. Indeed, the monitoring process has become quite elaborate and standardized, with lengthy instructional booklets now available for newcomers to follow when they enter the host country and shoulder their responsibilities as monitors. And no less indicative of the degree of institutionalization is that some of the monitors, such as the United Nations or the National Democratic Institute, send representatives to observe virtually all elections in which outside monitors are present.

But does external monitoring constitute a control mechanism? Most certainly. Whatever hesitations the host countries may have about the presence of outsiders who judge the fairness and propriety of their election procedures, and irrespective of their attempts to circumvent the monitors and load the electoral outcome, now they yield both to the pressure for external monitoring and to the judgments the outsiders make during and after election day. Elections have been postponed because of irregularities in voter lists detected by the external monitors, "dirty tricks" uncovered during the balloting have been terminated at the insistence of monitors, and the verdict of outsiders that the final tallies were fraudulent has resulted in the holding of new elections. To be sure, a few countries still adamantly refuse admission to outside monitors or do not allow them to be present on a scale sufficient to allow for legitimation of the electoral outcome, but the monitoring process has become so fully institutionalized that normally the host countries overcome their reluctance as they begin to recognize the problems they cause for·themselves by refusing to acquiesce to the monitoring process. Put differently, the advent of established procedures for the external monitoring of elections demonstrates the large extent to which control mechanisms derive their effectiveness from information and reputation even if their actions are not backed up by constitutional authority. It might even be said that governance in an ever more complex and interdependent world depends less on the issuance of authoritative directives and more on the release of reliable information and the legitimacy inherent in its detail.

As for the presence of both state and NGO actors, the spreading norm that the establishment of democracy justifies the international community's involvement in domestic elections attracts both official and unofficial groups to train and send monitors. Whatever organizations may have led the negotiations that result in the acceptance of outside observers, a number of others (such as the Organization of American States [OAS], the Socialist International, and the Latin American Studies Association in the case of Paraguay's 1993 election) find reasons important to their memberships to be present, and there are few precedents for denying admission to some monitoring teams while accepting others. Although the monitoring process may not be free of friction and competition among the numerous teams, the more procedures have been institutionalized, the greater has been the collaboration among the teams. It is not stretching matters to conclude that not only does the international community turn out in force for domestic elections in distant countries, but it does so with representatives from many of its diverse segments. In the 1990 Nicaraguan election, for example, 2,578 accredited observers from 278 organizations were present on election day.[48]

Continuing and Changing Forms of Governance

The above observations suggest that a full picture of what are likely to be the contours of global governance in the decades ahead requires attention to the dynamics of localization and how they are in part responses to the dynamics of globalization, responses that give rise to what can be called "distant proximities" that may well become systems of rule with diverse types of control mechanisms. Although some localizing dynamics are initiated by national governments—as when France decided to decentralize its steering apparatus and reduce Paris's control over policy and administrative issues—perhaps the preponderance of them are generated at subnational levels, some with the help and approval of national agencies but many in opposition to national policies, which then extend their scope abroad. The tendencies toward strengthened ethnic subgroups that have surfaced since the end of the Cold War are a case in point. Even though these actors may not have direct ties to supporters in other countries, their activities on the local scene can foster repercussions abroad that thereby transform them into aspects of global governance. The recent struggles in Bosnia, Somalia, and Rwanda are examples. Similarly, since so many of the world's resource, water, and air quality problems originate in subnational communities, and since this level is marked by a proliferation of both governmental and nongovernmental agencies that seek to control these problems within their jurisdiction and to do so through cooperative efforts with transnational counterparts, the environmental area offers another array of local issues that are central to the conduct of global governance.

The emphasis here on transnational and subnational mechanisms is not, of course, to imply that national governments and states are no longer central loci of control in the processes of global governance; they are very central indeed. No account of the global system can ignore them or give them other than a prominent place in the scheme of things. Nevertheless, states have lost some of their earlier dominance of the governance system, as well as their ability to evoke compliance and to govern effectively. This change is in part due to the growing relevance and potential of control mechanisms sustained by transnational and subnational systems of rule.

Governance in the Twenty-first Century

If the analysis were deemed complete here, the reader, like the author, would likely feel let down, as if the final chapter of this story of a disaggregated and fragmenting global system of governance has yet to be written. It is an unfinished story, one's need for closure would assert. It needs a conclusion, a drawing together of the "big picture," a sweeping assessment that offers some hope that somehow the world can muddle through and evolve techniques of cooperation that will bridge its multitude of disaggregated parts and achieve a measure of coherence that enables future generations to live in peace, achieve sustainable development, and maintain a modicum of creative order. Assess the overall balance, one's training cries out, show how the various emergent centers of power form a multipolar system of states that will manage to cope with the challenges of war within and among its members. Yes, that's it—depict the overall system as polyarchical and indicate how such an arrangement can generate multilateral institutions of control that effectively address the huge issues that clutter the global agenda. Or, perhaps better, indicate how a hegemon will emerge out of the disaggregation and have enough clout to foster both progress and stability. At the very least, one's analytic impulses demand, suggest how worldwide tendencies toward disaggregation and localization may be offset by no less powerful tendencies toward aggregation and globalization.

Compelling as these alternative interpretations may be, however, they do not quell a sense that it is only a short step from polyarchy to Pollyanna and that one's commitment to responsible analysis must be served by not taking that step. The world is clearly on a path-dependent course, and some of its present outlines can be discerned if, as noted at the outset, allowance is made for nuance and ambiguity. Still, in this time of continuing and profound transformations, too much remains murky to project beyond the immediate present and anticipate long-term trajectories. All one can conclude with confidence is that in the twenty-first century the paths to governance will lead in many directions, some that will emerge into sunlit clearings and others that will descend into dense jungles. ⊕

Notes

James N. Rosenau is University Professor of International Affairs at George Washington University. He is the author or editor of numerous publications, including, *Global Voices: Dialogues in International Relations* (1993), *The United Nations in a Turbulent World* (1992), *Governance Without Government* (1992), and *Turbulence in World Politics: A Theory of Change and Continuity* (1990).

The author is grateful to Walter Truett Anderson and Hongying Wang for their reactions to an early draft of this article.

1. Alexander King and Bertrand Schneider, *The First Global Revolution: A Report of the Council of Rome* (New York: Pantheon Books, 1991), pp. 181–182 (italics added). For other inquiries that support the inclusion of small, seemingly local systems of rule in a broad analytic framework, see John Friedmann, *Empowerment: The Politics of Alternative Development* (Cambridge, Mass.: Blackwell, 1992), and Robert Huckfeldt, Eric Plutzer, and John Sprague, "Alternative Contexts of Political Behavior: Churches, Neighborhoods, and Individuals," *Journal of Politics* 55 (May 1993): 365–381.

2. Steven A. Rosell et al., *Governing in an Information Society* (Montreal: Institute for Research on Public Policy, 1992), p. 21.

3. Rule systems have much in common with what has come to be called the "new institutionalism." See, for example, Robert O. Keohane, "International Institutions: Two Approaches," *International Studies Quarterly* 32 (December 1988): 379–396; James G. March and Johan P. Olsen, "The New Institutionalism: Organizational Factors in Political Life," *American Political Science Review* 78 (September 1984): 734–749; and Oran R. Young, "International Regimes: Toward a New Theory of Institutions," *World Politics* 39 (October 1986): 104–122. For an extended discussion of how the concept of control is especially suited to the analysis of both formal and informal political phenomena, see James N. Rosenau, *Calculated Control as a Unifying Concept in the Study of International Politics and Foreign Policy*, Research Monograph No. 15 (Princeton: Center of International Studies, Princeton University, 1963).

4. Cf. Rosenau and Ernst-Otto Czempiel, eds., *Governance Without Government: Order and Change in World Politics* (Cambridge: Cambridge University Press, 1992). Also see the formulations in Peter Mayer, Volker Rittberger, and Michael Zurn, "Regime Theory: State of the Art and Perspectives," in Volker Rittberger, ed., *Regime Theory and International Relations* (New York: Oxford University Press, 1993), and Timothy J. Sinclair, "Financial Knowledge as Governance," a paper presented at the Annual Meeting of the International Studies Association, Acapulco, 23–27 March 1993.

5. Anthony G. McGrew, "Global Politics in a Transitional Era," in Anthony G. McGrew, Paul G. Lewis, et al., eds., *Global Politics: Globalization and the Nation-State* (Cambridge: Polity Press, 1992), p. 318.

6. Martin Hewson, "The Media of Political Globalization," a paper presented at the Annual Meeting of the International Studies Association, Washington, D.C., March 1994, p. 2.

7. John Vogler, "Regimes and the Global Commons: Space, Atmosphere and Oceans," in McGrew, Lewis, et al., *Global Politics*, p. 118.

8. Diana Jean Schemo, "Rebuilding of Suburban Dreams," *New York Times*, 4 May 1994, p. A11.

9. Steven Greenhouse, "Kissinger Will Help Mediate Dispute Over Zulu Homeland," *New York Times*, 12 April 1994, p. A8.

10. Peter B. Evans, "Building an Integrative Approach to International and Domestic Politics: Reflections and Projections," in Peter B. Evans, Harold K. Jacobson, and Robert D. Putnam, eds., *Double-Edged Diplomacy: International Bargaining and Domestic Politics* (Berkeley: University of California Press, 1993), p. 419. For interesting accounts of how multinational corporations are increasingly inclined to form transnational alliances, see "The Global Firm: R.I.P.," *Economist*, 6 February 1993, p. 69, and "The Fall of Big Business," *Economist*, 17 April 1993, p. 13.

11. Jan Aart Scholte, *International Relations of Social Change* (Philadelphia: Open University Press, 1993), pp. 44–45.

12. Roberto C. Goizueta, "The Challenges of Getting What You Wished For," remarks presented to the Arthur Page Society, Amelia Island, Florida, 21 September 1992.

13. Joseph A. Camilleri, "Rethinking Sovereignty in a Shrinking, Fragmented World," in R.B.J. Walker and Saul H. Mendlovitz, eds., *Contending Sovereignties: Redefining Political Community* (Boulder: Lynne Rienner, 1990), p. 35.

14. Janie Leatherman, Ron Pagnucco, and Jackie Smith, "International Institutions and Transnational Social Movement Organizations: Challenging the State in a Three-Level Game of Global Transformation," a paper presented at the Annual Meeting of the International Studies Association, Washington, D.C., March 1994, p. 20..

15. Robert W. Cox, "Global Perestroika," in Ralph Milband and Leo Panitch, eds., *Socialist Register* (London: Merlin Press, 1992), p. 34.

16. Björn Hettne, "The New Regionalism: Implications for Development and Peace," in Björn Hettne and Andras Inotai, eds., *The New Regionalism: Implications for Global Development and International Security* (Helsinki: UNU World Institute for Development Economics Research, 1994), p. 2.

17. Hettne, "The New Regionalism," p. 6.

18. William Drozdiak, "Revving Up Europe's 'Four Moters,'" *Washington Post*, 27 March 1994, p. C3.

19. Ibid.

20. Pascal Maragall, quoted in ibid. For extensive inquiries that posit the transnational roles of cities as increasingly central to the processes of global governance, see Saskia Sassen, *The Global City: New York, London, Tokyo* (Princeton: Princeton University Press, 1991), and Earl H. Fry, Lee H. Radebaugh, and Panayotis Soldatos, eds., *The New International Cities Era: The Global Activities of North American Municipal Governments* (Provo, Utah: Brigham Young University Press, 1989).

21. See, for example, Thomas P. Rohlem, "Cosmopolitan Cities and Nation States: A 'Mediterranean' Model for Asian Regionalism," a paper presented at the Conference on Asian Regionalism, Maui, 17–19 December 1993; Ricardo Petrilla, as quoted in Drozdiak, "Revving Up Europe's 'Four Moters,'" p. C3. For an analysis by the same author that indicates concern over the trend to citylike states, see Petrilla, "Techno-racism: The City-States of the Global Market Will Create a 'New Apartheid,'" *Toronto Star*, 9 August 1992; and Kenichi Ohmae, "The Rise of the Region State," *Foreign Affairs* 72 (Spring 1993): 78.

22. Ohmae, "The Rise of the Region State," pp. 78–79.

23. Ibid., p. 80.

24. Michael Clough and David Doerge, *Global Changes and Domestic Transformations: New Possibilities for American Foreign Policy: Report of a Vantage Conference* (Muscatine, Iowa: The Stanley Foundation, 1992), p. 9. For indicators

that a similar process is occurring in the Southwest without the approval of Washington, D.C., or Mexico City, see Cathryn L. Thorup, *Redefining Governance in North America: The Impact of Cross-Border Networks and Coalitions on Mexican Immigration into the United States* (Santa Monica: The Rand Corporation, 1993). Although using a different label ("tribes"), a broader discussion of regional states can be found in Joel Kotkin, *Tribes: How Race, Religion and Identity Determine Success in the New Global Economy* (New York: Random House, 1993).

25. Ohmae, "The Rise of the Region State," p. 83.

26. Hettne, "The New Regionalism," p. 7.

27. Ibid., pp. 2–3. For another formulation that also differentiates between the old and new regionalism, see Kaisa Lahteenmaki and Jyrki Kakonen, "Regionalization and Its Impact on the Theory of International Relations," paper presented at the Annual Meeting of the International Studies Association, Washington, D.C., March 1994, p. 9. For a contrary perspective, see Stephen D. Krasner, "Regional Economic Blocs and the End of the Cold War," paper presented at the International Colloqium on Regional Economic Integration, University of São Paulo, December 1991.

28. Hettne, "The New Regionalism," p. 11.

29. Arthur Stein, "Coordination and Collaboration: Regimes in an Anarchic World," in David A. Baldwin, ed., *Neorealism and Neoliberalism: The Contemporary Debate* (New York: Columbia University Press, 1993), p. 29.

30. Vogler, "Regimes and the Global Commons," p. 123.

31. Stein, "Coordination and Collaboration," p. 31.

32. Cathryn L. Thorup, "Redefining Governance in North America: Citizen Diplomacy and Cross-Border Coalitions," *Enfoque* (Spring 1993): 1, 12.

33. For a valuable attempt to explore this concept theoretically and empirically, see Thorup, "The Politics of Free Trade and the Dynamics of Cross-Border Coalitions in U.S-Mexican Relations," *Columbia Journal of World Business* 26 (Summer 1991): 12–26

34. David Ronfeldt and Cathryn L. Thorup, "North America in the Era of Citizen Networks: State, Society, and Security," (Santa Monica: RAND 1993), p. 22.

35. Ivo D. Duchachek, "The International Dimension of Subnational Government," *Publius* 14 (Fall 1984): 25.

36. Ronfeldt and Thorup, "North America in the Era of Citizen Networks," p. 24.

37. This brief discussion of the credit rating agencies in the private sector is based on Timothy J. Sinclair, "The Mobility of Capital and the Dynamics of Global Governance: Credit Risk Assessment in the Emerging World Order," a paper presented at the Annual Meeting of the International Studies Association, Washington, D.C., March 1994, and Sinclair, "Passing Judgment: Credit Rating Processes as Regulatory Mechanisms of Governance in the Emerging World Order," *Review of International Political Economy* (April 1994).

38. Sinclair, "The Mobility of Capital and the Dynamics of Global Governance," p. 16.

39. Phil Williams, "Transnational Criminal Organizations and International Security," *Survival* 36 (Spring 1994): 97. See also Williams, "International Drug Trafficking: An Industry Analysis," *Low Intensity Conflict and Law Enforcement* 2 (Winter 1993): 397–420. For another dimension of transnational criminality, see Victor T. Levine, "Transnational Aspects of Political Corruption," in Arnold J. Heidenheimer, Michael Johnston, and Victor T. LeVine, eds., *Political Corruption: A Handbook* (New Brunswick, N.J.: Transaction, 1989), pp. 685–699.

40. Williams, "Transnational Criminal Organizations and International Security," p. 100.

41. Rensselaer W. Lee III, "Post-Soviet Organized Crime and Western Security Interests," testimony submitted to the Subcommittee on Terrorism, Narcotics and International Operations, Senate Committee on Foreign Relations, Washington, D.C., 21 April 1994.

42. Williams, "Transnational Criminal Organizations and International Security," p. 106.

43. Ibid., p. 105.

44. Thomas Risse-Kappen, "Faint-Hearted Multilateralism: The Re-Emergence of the United Nations in World Politics," a paper presented at the Annual Meeting of the International Studies Association, Washington, D.C., March 1994.

45. Alberta Sbragia, "From 'Nation-State' to 'Member-State': The Evolution of the European Community," a paper presented at the Europe After Maastrict Symposium, Washington University, Saint Louis, 1–3 October 1993, pp. 1–2.

46. Christopher Brewin, "The European Community: A Union of States Without Unity of Government," in Friedrich Kratochwil and Edward D. Mansfield, eds., *International Organization: A Reader,* (New York: HarperCollins, 1994), pp. 301–302.

47. Ibid., p. 302.

48. Of these, 278 organizations were present on election day, with 435 observers fielded by the OAS visiting 3,064 voting sites (some 70 percent of the total) and 237 UN monitors visiting 2,155 sites. In addition, some 1,500 members of the international press corps were on the scene. Cf. Robert A. Pastor, "Nicaragua's Choice," in Carl Kaysen, Robert A. Pastor, and Laura W. Reed, eds., *Collective Responses to Regional Problems: The Case of Latin America and the Caribbean* (Cambridge: American Academy of Arts and Sciences, 1994), pp. 18, 21.

[3]

Political Studies (1999), XLVII, 538–565

The United Nations in the 1990s: Proactive Cosmopolitanism and the Issue of Sovereignty

PAUL TAYLOR

Introduction

During the Cold War sovereignty was usually interpreted by United Nations members in the manner of traditional hard-line realists. The Charter was understood to mean that the rule of non-intervention was to be rigidly applied, and that what happened within states was no concern of outsiders. In the wording of the key paragraph, Article 2, para. 7, the word *essentially* was mostly overlooked as this would weaken the assertion of state exclusiveness. 'Nothing contained in the present Charter shall authorize the United Nations to intervene in matters which are *essentially* within the jurisdiction of any state or shall require the Members to submit such matters to settlement under the present Charter.' (author's italics) The predominant view of governments was that sovereignty was a private world into which the outside world was not permitted to enter. The only exception was operations under Chapter VII: 'this principle [exclusive domestic jurisdiction] shall not prejudice the application of enforcement measures under Chapter VII'. (Article 2 para. 7) Almost always the Security Council justified intervening within a state only when there was a threat to international peace and security, even when there had been gross infringements of human rights.[1]

But there was a contrasting notion of sovereignty: that it could be envisaged as having a licence from the international community to practice as an independent government in a particular territory. Such a licence could be granted by the act of recognition of that government by other states, and a consensus amongst them that this should be done could be interpreted as an expression of the will of the international community. After the end of the Cold War, however, more governments were prepared to demand that those amongst them whose internal policies were not up to international standards should change their ways, and those accused, however defiant, found it difficult to avoid making concessions to international pressure so that policies could at least be given a patina of respectability. The standards by which they were measured were increasingly those of the liberal democratic states.

There were also developments in the concept of the *international community*: in the earlier years of the United Nations the international community and its authority were seen as weak and discountable, but by the late 1990s they had become more substantial and hard to ignore. There were, therefore, two

---

[1] See J. Mayall (ed.), *The New Interventionism* (Cambridge University Press, 1996).

PAUL TAYLOR 539

contrasting notions of sovereignty: that it was a private world, with weak international authority, and that it was an international licence to operate as an independent government, granted by the collectivity of states, which, it is argued here, formed the international community. This essay examines the interplay between these two notions and argues that there was a discernible move to the latter after the end of the Cold War. It sees no prospect for the abandonment of sovereignty but seeks to understand its adaptation to new circumstances.[2]

Traditionally a 'state' was held to be sovereign when there was no authority which had precedence over it: outside actors therefore had no right to be involved in its internal affairs. And sovereignty was an absolute unaffected by the circumstances of the time. But theorists such as Bodin held that there was indeed a superior authority – God. In a number of writings this notion took substantial form in the assertion of a general requirement for civilized behaviour as part of the divine order.[3] In more recent times the idea that there was something above the state was encompassed in the idea of the will of the international community, and, after the end of the Cold War, this was increasingly acknowledged, if not obeyed. There were also very few states that could avoid involvements from outside themselves through which pressures were channelled which could not be resisted by the actors targeted. What is proposed in this essay is that there was after the end of the Cold War an expression in more utilitarian and secular terms of the ancient qualification of sovereignty as an absolute: there was a stronger form of the international community which was a modern equivalent of the divine order.

Sovereignty cannot be considered in exclusively theoretical or philosophical terms, but always needs to be related to the current circumstances of the state, including prevailing expectations about its emerging role. The changing circumstances after the end of the Cold War included, first, developments in the way in which international organizations sought to protect international peace and security; second the further evolution of a system in which laws made outside the state required compliance within it, especially in the world of business and commerce – they imposed upon the state (in this the European Union was the most advanced illustration of a general development); third was the extension of the range of mutual involvements through which common standards, such as democratization, were promoted; fourth, a rudimentary global watch – a full time system of surveillance of states – to identify crisis points, linked with the development of mechanisms for more rapid response, was being set up; and, fifth, the international community had set about establishing mechanisms for rehabilitating and restoring states that had failed.

These various developments reflected and promoted moral interdependence. For instance the idea of increasing international surveillance to detect incipient crises assumed that obligations to assist extended beyond the state, and that there was moral solidarity which took precedence over a community's right to privacy. This implied that efforts to deal with collapsed states, Somalia,

---

[2] The essay is entirely consistent with the arguments in defence of sovereignty which are well developed in M. R. Fowler and J. M. Bunck, *Law, Power and the Sovereign State: The Evolution and Application of the Concept of Sovereignty* (University Park, Pennsylvania State University Press, 1995).

[3] A. Murphy, 'The Sovereign State as Political-Territorial Ideal', in T. Biersteker and C. Weber (eds), *State Sovereignty as Social Construct* (Cambridge, Cambridge University Press, 1996), pp. 81–120.

Cambodia, Bosnia, etc. were not *just* a series of special cases, reflecting the special interests of the Great Powers, but were also expressions of the evolving norms. Discussion of these various circumstances runs through the primary framework of the essay which is chronological.

Before turning to this discussion it is necessary to explain *proactive cosmopolitanism*. There were two contrasting views about how a cosmopolitan community might arise: first that it could emerge from what was imminent and general, as was the case with the realization of Kantian categorical imperatives or the principles of natural law; and secondly, in a positivist fashion, that it was the approximation of the values and behaviour of diverse groups to the values and behaviour of a particular group. In the latter view a cosmopolitan community was established either by conversion, as, for instance, in conversion to Christianity or Islam or to the principles of western liberal democracy; or by empowering those who shared the preferred values and behaviour in the diverse communities.[4] In this view it was argued that there was in different communities a sufficient mutuality as to agree about what such notions as *fairness, justice* and *liberal* meant with regard to behaviour. These notions were not confined to particular communities, and, on the contrary, were universal – there were always people who understood them and reflected them in their behaviour, whatever the religion or ideology – and what was needed to create the cosmopolitan community was practical measures to increase the influence of such people.

The term proactive cosmopolitanism as used in this essay therefore has two components: a deliberate attempt to create a consensus about values and behaviour – a cosmopolitan community – among diverse communities; and the reflection and promotion of cosmopolitan values through specific new activities in international organizations such as the United Nations. This was a modern version of the Kantian strategy of encouraging the specific instruments of hospitality and commerce as well as the actualization of moral imperatives.[5] What it excluded was the imposition of such values from outside. However the United Nations and the European Union, with increasing energy and openness, increasingly pushed the civil and political values of Western Liberal states[6] in other parts of the world. In terms of the moral interdependence concept of Donelly there emerged a greater tendency to do something about the practices of other peoples, publics and elites, which seemed abhorrent, but also to promote western liberal values.[7] But this tendency was linked with the increasing penetration of the state by international instruments which were often

---

[4] See R. J. Vincent, *Human Rights and International Relations* (Cambridge, Cambridge University Press, 1986), especially pp. 37–57.

[5] See the excellent examination of the Kantian approach to peace in F. H. Hinsley, *Power and the Pursuit of Peace: Theory and Practice in the History of Relations between States* (Cambridge, Cambridge University Press, 1963), ch. 4.

[6] In the 1990s the Security Council regularly included in its mandates for peace-keeping operation proposals to advance liberal democratic solutions to internal conflicts and promote Western standards of governance worldwide; the Chinese went along with this! See P. Guillot, 'Human Rights, Democracy, and the Multidimensional Peace Operations of the United Nations', in Mortimer Sellers (ed.), *The New World: Sovereignty, Human Rights and the Self Determination of Peoples* (Oxford, Berg, 1996), pp. 273–304.

[7] See J. Donnelly, 'State Sovereignty and International Intervention: The Case of Human Rights', in G. Lyons and M. Mastanduno (eds), *Beyond Westphalia? State Sovereignty and International Intervention* (Baltimore, The Johns Hopkins Press, 1995), pp. 115–146.

organized through institutions like the United Nations, and such instruments could be regarded as the modern instruments of the Kantian strategy.

In a first section the development of the system with regard to peace and security arrangements is considered. The stress is upon both the way in which they increasingly involved intervening in the state and the changing norms which this reflected. (Parallel changes are also reflected in human rights arrangements, though these are not considered here.) In a second section attention is focussed upon reflections of cosmopolitanism in the expanding agenda of the United Nations regarding the maintenance of international order after the Cold War. In a third section the implications of the developments for sovereignty are discussed and proposals for taking forward the arrangements of proactive cosmopolitanism in the late 1990s are set out; this illustrates the direction of evolution of the agenda.

The Evolution of the System
The Changing Role of the UN and Peace Maintenance

A primary element in the circumstances of sovereignty in the 1990s was the emerging practice of the United Nations with regards to peace maintenance. It is necessary to give some space to discussing its development. Its scale and nature had greatly altered by the 1990s compared with its earlier forms and the changes were themselves symptomatic of deeper changes in the role of the UN. The rules of traditional forms of peace-keeping had emerged by the late 1950s.[8] They included the need for the approval of the host state for the location of the forces, and the requirement that the forces should be lightly armed; and that they should not be proactive in their use, but respond only if attacked first. They were to be placed under the command of the United Nations, with the Secretary General himself as their supreme commander, and UN field command, with the advice of a committee of the contributing states. And the forces would normally not come from any of the major powers. The various examples of peace-keeping before the late 1980s showed a number of variations with regard to these principles, but they were the norm.

The essential condition of all uses of peace-keeping was that they be placed between the forces of the parties to a dispute to encourage diplomacy between them. The indispensable assumption was that a compromise was possible. They were also intended during the Cold War period to help to exclude the super-powers from the conflict, though this was usually a cover for covert involvement by the United States. Without the support of the latter in materials and finance it is doubtful that much peace-keeping would have been done. Nevertheless the Soviet Union found it convenient to ignore this subterfuge and all but the first peace-keeping venture, in Suez in November 1956, derived from a Security Council mandate which necessarily required the approval of the five veto-holding powers. Suez was the exception in that it was set up by the General Assembly.

After 1989 – the end of the Cold War – peace-keeping forces were used more frequently and for a number of tasks that led them to face problems of a different order from those met earlier. As of early 1998, the time of writing,

[8] A useful overview of the development of peace-keeping is J. Sutterlin, *The United Nations and Maintenance of International Security: A Challenge to be Met* (Westport, Praeger, 1995).

about the same number of instances of their use – about twenty – had occurred since 1989 as in the entire period since their first use in November 1956, and at their peak the forces included around 75,000 troops compared with an average of under 10,000 in the 1980s. But these new instances were generally in circumstances that were even more difficult. They involved complex humanitarian crises, in which there were serious infringements of human rights and shortages of food and medicine, and, in addition, major security problems – usually in the context of civil war – with the accompanying intractable political disagreements. In these circumstances the security forces found themselves performing new tasks, especially helping to provide the essentials of life in the face of active opposition, and often they were of necessity more heavily armed, and given a mandate to be more proactive in the use of arms in order to get help through to the ill and starving. This meant that they were much more likely to attract the active opposition of the parties to the dispute. It was much more difficult for them to maintain the position of neutrality which they had sought on earlier occasions – though even then it had not always been possible, as with the experience of the United Nations Interim Force in the Lebanon (UNIFIL) in southern Lebanon after the Israeli invasion in 1982.[9] The forces also now often came from the great powers and even from the superpowers. The USA provided a major force for the operation in Somalia in December 1992, and later was involved in the operation in ex-Yugoslavia to police the Dayton agreement.[10] Major powers such as Britain and France became regular contributors to the forces, and Germany and Japan also became more involved, though not in the front line.

In these circumstances by 1998 peace-keeping forces had experienced a number of new problems. Because of the difficulty of maintaining their neutrality in the eyes of the combatants, the number of casualties was much greater, and contributing countries became much more reluctant to hand over command and control of the forces to the UN without reservation. The US President indicated this in a Presidential Directive, and there were a number of instances of participating forces double-checking with their own governments about whether or not they should follow instructions from UN officers. States also began more frequently to impose limitations on the uses to which their forces could be put by UN commanders. Command and control became an area of contention and too often led to uncertainty about who was in charge, with often damaging consequences, and escalating costs coincided with the reluctance of some states, principally the USA, to pay their allotted share. This led to a massive short-fall in contributions for peace-keeping, as well as on the regular assessed budget.[11]

A further problem concerned the supervision of the forces by the Security Council. Too frequently the original mandate of the Security Council, on which the role of the forces was based, was unclear about ends and means, and was also expanded without sufficient consideration, a process which became known as *mission creep*. There was a degree of ad hocery about Security Council

[9] A. James, *Peacekeeping in International Politics* (London, Macmillan, 1990), pp. 122–130.
[10] See Economides and Taylor, and Lewis and Mayall in Mayall, *The New Interventionism*, pp. 59–93.
[11] For a comprehensive account of these problems as they stood in 1997 see P. Taylor, S. Daws and U. Adamczick-Gerteis (eds), *Documents on Reform of the United Nations* (Aldershot, Dartmouth, 1997), Part II, pp. 65–169.

decision making: commitments were made without thinking through the strategic and logistic implications. The classic example of this was the decision to create the safe areas in ex-Yugoslavia, which led to populations being falsely assured that they were secure in UN protection.

The difficulties of the new peace-keeping were such that a few authorities, including Secretary General Boutros Boutros Gahli, were led by the mid-1990s to the conclusion that the more active form of peace-keeping was unsustainable. This was probably a premature conclusion. After the end of the Cold War it was necessary to find an alternative principle to the superpower standoff for the maintenance of international peace and security, and a more active form of peace-keeping was one of the options. But conditions which had to be met before the regular use of more active forms of peace-keeping was conceivable had to be identified and evaluated. It was necessary to sort out the financial arrangements; it was necessary to develop a system for the more rational development of Security Council mandates and to avoid 'mission creep,' it was necessary to ensure that Security Council mandates were clear and capable of being applied on the ground, and attention had to be given to the tactical imperatives of military operations: if there was the possibility of hot war UN personnel should not be located where they were likely to be taken hostage and used as human shields. It was also necessary to establish clear chains of command and control. These were difficult conditions to meet, but the costs of dealing with them were no greater than the costs likely to arise from keeping the mechanisms for maintaining international peace and security in a kind of time warp, and new peace-keeping was more in keeping with the pattern of the long term development of international society than would be a return to *ad hoc* balances of power, or spheres of influence, be they regional or global.[12]

Peace Maintenance in Longer Perspective

The development of peace-keeping was necessary because it coincided with the logic of the current phase of the development of the relationship between the global institutions and the state. The new peace-keeping was just one manifestation of a wider range of involvements within the state, and reflected a new concern to strengthen the state so that it was more capable of carrying out the necessary functions of statehood in modern international society. The new activism could be enhanced without compromising the traditional norms of intervention[13]: that it should not be directed at imposing an order founded on principles that were foreign to that state. It was, however, adding a new ingredient in implying that such a process of internal maturation need not be violent, but could take place within a framework of internal order under

---

[12] For a balanced evaluation of these problems, see A. Roberts, *Humanitarian Action in War*, Adelphi Paper 305 (London, The International Institute for Strategic Studies, 1996). Roberts concluded that 'The most promising approach to the role of the military in relation to humanitarian efforts is likely to be pragmatic one. While not denying a role for the UN peace-keeping forces, or for full-scale "humanitarian intervention" in cases of extreme emergency, such an approach also stress the importance of other forms of military protection and assistance. ... future attempts ...need to avoid the elements of ambiguity, verging on dishonesty, that have characterized many such efforts ...' p. 87.

[13] For an excellent examination of the concept of intervention and its variations see O. Ramsbotham, 'Humanitarian intervention, 1990–95: a need to reconceptualize?', *Review of International Studies*, 23 (1997), 445–468.

international supervision. It was possible for the international community to use greater degrees of compulsion in holding the ring within a state without compromising neutrality and without constituting intervention in the technical sense of seeking to impose precise forms of outcome from outside.

Just as a police force could remain impartial when using duress within the state, so long as the laws were generally known, and as long as the response of the police was proportional to the scale of the offence, so an active international peace-keeping force could appear neutral as long as the rules of engagement were clear to the parties to a dispute, and no partiality was shown in applying them. Being proactive in the use of force by peace-keeping forces need not jeopardize the principle of neutrality. It was, however, absolutely necessary that adequate means for upholding the rules were available, and could be seen to be available, so that the forces of order were not brought into disrepute by the observation of incapacity. It was also necessary that there should be an efficient and effective United Nations command and control system over such forces. This seemed impossible with enforcement, and the experience of more active forms of peace-keeping had not been encouraging. But some countries, such as Canada, were not as averse as others to accepting such international command, and it was not clear whether the problems hitherto had been ones of principle. The doubts were arguably more to do with a lack of confidence in the United Nations' procedures in this context in the 1990s, and such procedures could be improved. Trends would suggest that this was the preferable course: the difficulties, though serious, were by no means insuperable, and there were strong practical and moral arguments for tackling them.

The background was a trend towards a more general involvement of the UN system in the rescuing of failing states, as was reflected in the new mechanisms for providing assistance in humanitarian crises. But it also fitted into the pattern of the longer term evolution of the state, which had passed through a number of phases since the emergence of a primitive state system out of Medieval Christendom after the Thirty Years War in the early seventeenth century. The fact of this progression was itself evidence of the impossibility of staying with the arrangements as they had emerged in the Cold War and it underlined the point that the new forms of activity were as much about evolving norms as national interests.

- Before the Treaties of Westphalia in 1648 medieval Christendom had been a system of shifting and permeable territories under a variety of Princes, who continuously intervened in each others realms and were challenged by the Church's claims to secular power.
- Between 1648 and 1815 the state in Europe gradually consolidated its internal arrangements and established internal monopolies of force, taxation and administration. At the same time elements of international society emerged, such as a distinctive system of international law, and a body of less formal rules which applied to relations between states and the practice of diplomacy in international society. This was the period of the emergence of an international society more strictly defined as a set of actors – the states – which accepted a range of conventions of behaviour in their mutual relations.
- In the period after the defeat of Napoleon until well after the Second World War, the predominant concept of the state which emerged was that

of a national welfare state, with increasingly formal prohibitions on intervention internally. This was a natural corollary of the extension to the nations of sentiments of attachment which had been previously confined to relations between family members. The notion that such intervention was an infringement of a moral right to domestic privacy was reinforced: this development was linked with the positivist view of cultural relativity, sometimes called communitarianism. The right to privacy reached its high point in the period after the Second World War, and in particular in the insistence in the 1960 Declaration on Decolonization that the right to independence of peoples in states was unconditional.

- This period arguably extended into the mid-1980s and the first indications of change were the new approach by Soviet President Gorbachev and the resulting *entente* among the five permanent members of the Security Council initiated by the British. This was the basis of a growing international intrusiveness in the internal affairs of the UN member states.[14] The relationship between the state and international order was again altered as the idea of cosmopolitanism re-emerged. It was not that the state was challenged, but that its claim as a moral absolute was challenged. McCorquodale pointed out that 'a commitment to applying international human rights law to the right of self-determination reinforces the acknowledgement of states that their sovereignty is not absolute at least as far as the treatment of persons and groups on their territory is concerned'.[15] The challenge to cultural relativism and the re-emergence of cosmopolitanism was associated with the view that what went on within states was indeed of general concern.

A point that needs to be stressed, however, was that accepting obligations to citizens globally had to go along with acquiring a right to judge the behaviour of those citizens, and governments which claimed to speak for them: an increasing preparedness to undertake international humanitarian actions, and the linked use of proactive peace-keeping forces, was necessarily associated with the assertion of the right to judge. The new forms of peace-keeping had to be evaluated in the context of this new cosmopolitanism. The old kind was appropriate to the communitarian approach to inter-state relations: the new kind was a necessary adjunct of the new cosmopolitanism.

Peace-keeping forces were part of a spectrum of involvements in failing states each of which arguably reflected a degree of moral solidarity. This spectrum could be divided into four interrelated stages. First was the stage of using the forces to ensure that food was provided and disease controlled. At this stage the forces might be required to use force to get food through. Second was a stage at which the forces were involved in various kinds of pacification. Such activities had by the late 1990s been identified in a number of categories, including establishing safe areas, corridors of tranquillity, green lines, and the rehabilitation and resettlement of refugees. Activities at this stage might also include restraining the availability of arms to a civilian population and collecting and guarding heavy weapons. In a third stage the forces might be required to provide

---

[14] This argument is borrowed from D. Malone, 'The UN Security Council in the post-Cold War world: 1987–97', *Security Dialogue*, 28 (1997), 393–408.

[15] R. McCorquodale, 'Human Rights and Self-determination', in Sellers, *The New World Order*, p. 26.

back-up support for a range of activities related to the restoration of civil society. These included establishing an administration, civilian police forces, and supervising elections, activities which were becoming a regular feature of the business of the system. They might also involve helping to encourage the establishment of organizations such as forms of representation for workers and political parties – the process of democratization. A final category of activity was found throughout the spectrum and involved attempting to keep apart the armies of the parties to a conflict, and promoting negotiation.

There were of course dangers and difficulties which were typical of each of these activities. There was the risk that help might be diverted to help the warring factions and thereby prolong the conflict. This was a serious argument against humanitarian assistance. But it could not be regarded as a fatal impediment in the way of the development of a more moral community. Evidence from the violence in the Great Lakes area of Africa in the late 1990s was that although this had certainly been a problem in the refugee camps, it had become less so over time. Clearly every precaution needed to be taken to prevent this happening and to encourage the handing-in of weapons. Second, the question arose of whether such investment was worth while when it might lead to the hardening of the lines of division between communities as with the green line in Cyprus. The only response to this was that such a green line was very much cheaper than the prolongation of active war.

In any case the justification for extending the role of peace-keeping was part of a wider process of enhanced involvement in failing states, which derived from the characteristics of the present stage of evolution of international society. It is not here argued that these activities were merely an expression of the need to do good. That they reflected interest in the sense that the active states had specific and general gains – raw materials and security – was undeniable. But there was an admixture of moral imperative: governments could not tolerate undue suffering for a number of complex reasons, including the natural sympathy of their electors with the victims. That it occasionally had outcomes which were difficult to accept as a settlement or solution to a problem, and involved continuing commitment of money and resources by the international community, was no reason for refusing such involvement. It was part of a process of active order maintenance which was relevant to international society, as well as the individual states, which could best be described as pacific engagement. There were moral grounds for such activity, which were an aspect of the development of a cosmopolitan moral community, as well as more utilitarian calculations of costs and benefits.

The UN Agenda after the End of the Cold War

Attention is now focussed upon the evolving practices, and perceptions of new problems, in the 1990s. These are seen as reflections of cosmopolitanism, as well as responses to particular problems.

The New UN and Crisis Response

The skills of the UN in maintaining peace and security and providing humanitarian assistance were much improved in the late 1980s and 1990s in two main

PAUL TAYLOR   547

respects: information gathering and analysis and increasing capacity for speedy response. Again it is useful to place this account in the context of the overall development of the system for promoting peace and security through a global international organization.

- The first example of this was of course the League of Nations. In the original design its executive committee, the League Council was to be convened if a crisis was reported: it was not intended to be in permanent session. And the mechanisms for gathering information were primitive: they depended on ad hoc procedures such as whether states had noticed a crisis and were prepared to convene the Council. It was as if the fire brigade had to be put together when someone happened to notice a fire in the neighbourhood. In the first years more peace maintaining was actually carried out by the representatives of the powers that had been victorious in the 1914–18 war, acting outside the League framework, but this was not part of the design. The League also had no machinery either for setting up or for commanding military forces on a collective basis, though a number of efforts were made without success to correct this deficiency.
- The United Nations was a development from the League in that the Security Council was indeed·a permanent institution which functioned continuously and not just when called into session, with special responsibility for maintaining international peace and security. The fire brigade was now on permanent standby, and the alarm could be sounded either by the member states or by the Secretary-General. The latter was given a new role in the Charter: he was asked in Article 99 to bring any dispute, which, in his opinion, might threaten the maintenance of international peace and security, to the attention of the Security Council. He could report the outbreak of fire anywhere in the world: the watch tower was permanently manned, and the response could be much more rapid. Article 99 proved far more important than it appeared at first sight as it was the legal basis for the gradual expansion of the Secretary-General's role with regard to investigating emerging threats to the peace and mediating between the parties. In order to evaluate the increased range of information a department was created in the Secretariat for the analysis of the information available to it. This was the Department of Political Affairs which worked alongside the Department of Peace-keeping Operations.
- Through the 1980s and 1990s a third phase of development of the global institution was observable. In the preceding phase, despite the enhancement of the United Nations' information collection and analysis capacity, there remained a random quality to the engagement of the Secretary General or states. In the new phase, however, the institution began what became known as a *global watch*. Its information gathering machinery was greatly enhanced, professionalized and on permanent duty, despite the difficulties made by some states.[16] It was not, as had earlier been the case,

[16] Perez de Cuellar set up an Office for Research and the Collection of Information (ORCI) which was abolished by Boutros Boutros-Ghali, its functions being then assigned to the new Departments of Political Affairs (DPA) and of Peace-keeping (DPK). Boutros-Ghali stated 'That Department ... is now organized to follow political developments worldwide, so that it can provide early warning of impending conflicts and analyse possibilities for preventive action ...' (A/50/60 – 1995/1, 3 January 1995, Para. 26).

that the organization surveyed the horizon in search of fire and then acted, but rather that increasingly a whole range of factors which were likely to encourage fire was regularly reported and analysed. Some of this was done in cooperation with the intelligence services of the great powers, but more was done through the United Nations' own resources, and there were advantages in working this way. A beginning was made with the use of satellite and computer technology, and information from local officers in various organizations was systematically collected. A special case of this was the creation of the arms registry, which collected data on the movement of arms around the world, of which a surprising amount was readily available in the public realm, in newspapers and specialist journals.[17] In the late 1990s the next step was to require that both governments and manufacturers should fully disclose the range of their wares and the customers they served.

This information was a help in identifying possible trouble spots. Troop movements could also be more easily spotted, and it was now more likely that a potential malefactor would be aware that his or her misdeeds would be known. The certainty of being found out was likely to be itself a deterrent: the intelligence services of the world's main military powers had the capacity to do this for years but there were advantages in going beyond this to a discrete UN capacity in this area. Information was less likely to be sensitive to political interest and more likely to be generally available in fact and to be believed to be available. Sophisticated information about a developing crisis would be placed firmly in the common realm. In this third phase it was as if the streets of the international neighbourhood were under constant surveillance by video cameras.

There were however two further difficulties in the way of using the information. The first concerned the capacity to respond quickly and to sustain that response. The second was how to bring the attention of the Security Council to a problem after the relevant information had been collected and evaluated by experts in or outside the Secretariat. With regards to the first difficulty there were a number of significant developments in the early 1990s. These included the professionalization of the Department of Peace-keeping Operations. The number of its staff was increased, and included more specialist military and political advisors. It was closely involved in the new system for information gathering. And it was placed on 24 hours operation. A great deal had been achieved, even though more needed to be done.[18]

With regard to the second difficulty there were in the late 1990s a number of proposals. It had been noted that the Security Council had been slow to focus on the Somalia crisis in 1992, and, later, on the crisis in Rwanda and Burundi. Some argued that the Secretary-General had deliberately contrived a row at the London Conference on Yugoslavia in London in the summer of 1992 in order to

---

[17] The United Nations Registry of Conventional Arms was created by the General Assembly in December 1991. Members states were required to provide data for the previous year on imports and exports of battle tanks, armored combat vehicles, artillery, combat aircraft, attack helicopters, warships and missiles and missile launchers, as of 30 April 1993. See J. Tessitore and S. Woolfson (eds), *A Global Agenda: Issues Before the 48th General Assembly of the United Nations* (Lanham, University Press of American, 1993), pp. 141–142.

[18] See *Command and Control of United Nations Peacekeeping Operations: Report of the Secretary-General*, GA, A/49/681, 21 November 1994.

attract attention away from the first world crisis to the worsening Third World crisis in Somalia.[19] There were many other reasons why attention might not be engaged with a crisis, including various kinds of fatigue or a shortage of resources. But the problem was that information about a developing crisis was not itself a guarantee that it would engage the Security Council's attention. One proposal was that a committee of high level experts should be set up alongside the Security Council which would help the Secretary-General to get an item onto the agenda, and advise about the realism of the response. At the time of writing this remained, however, a problem area.[20]

A parallel capacity had also been developed in the United Nations' arrangements for dealing with humanitarian assistance especially the DHA. It had set up a Humanitarian Early Warning System which drew upon the various early-warning mechanisms of other United Nations and non-United Nations organizations – including non-governmental organizations – and used computerized and satellite technology. It also collected information from officers in the field especially those working with the UNDP. A group had been set up to consider the further enhancement of this capacity. It was possible for it to predict from geographical, climatological and social indicators where crises were likely to arise. In the case of humanitarian action capacity to respond quickly, though not always adequately, had been developed. The DHA established teams of assessors from its own staff and other UN bodies, which were like the American DART teams, to go out to a threatened area quickly to assess the scale of a crisis and the response needed. 'These missions have been fundamental, first, in drawing the attention of the international community to the plight of affected populations, and, secondly, in assessing the needs of vulnerable groups for the subsequent planning, elaboration and implementation of humanitarian programmes' (A/51/172 Para 80).

Such teams also existed to assess natural disasters. With regard to so-called sudden-onset disasters the DHA was assisted by the United Nations Disaster Assessment and Coordination Team, with the participation of 18 Member States. In 1995 the DHA had provided assistance to 55 member states to support their efforts to cope with the impact of 82 sudden-onset natural disasters and environmental emergencies. The DHA did, however, point out that although 'each new catastrophe typically triggers close attention to mitigation measures, at least for the disaster type in question, such attention is often localized and short-lived and, as a result, the global socio-economic impact of disasters, measured in terms of the number of people affected by disaster, has continued to increase by about 6% per year' (A/51/172 para 87).

The DHA helped countries to properly assess their full spectrum of risks, to prescribe, on the basis of global experience, the most cost-effective disaster reduction measures, to coordinate external guidance, where needed, on how to apply those measures in the most vulnerable areas, and to stimulate wider

---

[19] See P. Taylor, 'Options for Reform' in John Harris, (ed.), *The Politics of Humanitarian Intervention* (London, Pinter and Save the Children, 1995), pp. 91–144, especially p. 96.

[20] For a useful account of the problems in the way of more effective peace-keeping see G. Evans, *Cooperation for Peace: The Global Agenda for the 1990s and Beyond* (St. Leonards, NSW, Allen and Unwin, 1993), pp. 70–80 and *passim*.

involvement and closer cooperation among the numerous international agencies with relevant technical and managerial expertise. Such risk assessment documents were on the same lines as the Country Strategy Notes developed by the UNDP. The WFP attempted to strengthen local capacities for disaster mitigation with field level vulnerability exercises. (A/51/172 para 59) Some individual countries, including Sweden and Britain, had also set up teams which could be called out at very short notice to evaluate the disaster in the field.

Under Resolution 46/182 the General Assembly had also established a Central Emergency Revolving Fund of $50 million which could help to finance the first efforts of the Agencies to help with a crisis. This fund was not without its difficulties, in particular that the money had to be repaid and could only be provided to assist with the financing of efforts partly funded from elsewhere, and it was too small. DHA also utilized *flash appeals* to ensure timely response to critical first phase emergency needs (A/51/172 para 46). A number of the Agencies had also agreed so-called service packages with governments and other organizations through which military and civil defence assets could be called on at times when the emergency response required reinforcement. UNHCR had such packages. And WFP had eight such logistic service packages in mid 1996 UNICEF was in the process of developing such arrangements. (A/51/172 Para 35)

One of the features of the evolution of UN arrangements in the 1990s was an increasing professionalization of work in a wide range of different fields including peace-keeping and humanitarian activities. A number of countries, led by Canada had started to train military personnel for such activities, and indeed Canada had set up a research institute on peace-keeping. There had also been a complex emergency training initiative led by the DHA and the UNDP, and a UN Staff College was established in Turin under the ILO. Warehouses for the storage of emergency supplies to help peace-keeping forces and humanitarian activities had also been established. The most important of these was at Pisa. In 1997 some functions developed within the DHA were to be located in other institutions, according to the plan outlined by the new Secretary General in July. But the achievement of DHA in this regard remained.

The picture which emerged from this discussion was that the United Nations system had gone through a period of astonishing change in the 1990s with regard to information collecting and evaluating and with regard to the enhancement of its capacity to respond quickly to crisis. The machinery had become more professional despite the continuing shortage of resources and the increase in the number and type of problems with which it had to deal. It is hard to see how the emergence of an enhanced moral solidarity could be excluded from an explanation of its development; this was an aspect of changing views about the proper relationship between the international community and states which was justified primarily in terms of the welfare of individuals. Of course some target states objected, but the increasing capacity to respond and to respond quickly was generally expected and generally required. This was no special plot of the Great Powers, but rather a product of collective obligation. But this was not anti-state: indeed, precisely the opposite – it was focussed upon strengthening the state. The international community could now be dimly discerned as a discrete agent of change, embodying an increasing cosmopolitanism, and enlarging the area of consensus about the norms which were appropriate within states.

New Types of Security Threat

In the late 1990s two patterns of involvement from outside were likely to interact in the state, one from legitimate and another from illegitimate agencies. The former was the increasing involvement of international organization, more evident in the Third World. The latter was a threat to the security of individuals, more often in the first world, from the new dangerous non-governmental organizations of international crime and state-sponsored terrorism. This was becoming increasingly visible, and was beyond the reach of either peace-keeping forces or enforcement procedures from outside the state, and from conventional police forces from within the state. Examples included the various Mafias of the old kind, and new kinds such as those from Russia and the Far East, which were often linked with the trade in illegal substances, but were increasingly operating in a more diverse range of areas, some legitimate. Another new illustration was the appearance of private mercenary armies, such as Executive Outcomes, which in the late 1990s had been hired by some governments in Africa to deal with internal military threats which they could not handle with their own armies.[21]

These various enterprises challenged the state's monopoly of force and were capable of enforcing codes of behaviour, and systems of private taxation, which were alongside or hostile to those of the state. They clearly challenged the security of individuals and threatened order within the states, and had an obvious international dimension. It was a special form of warfare: in some cases states orchestrated the use of violence in other states through groups or individuals which had been infiltrated into the territory of another state. Modern technology and sophisticated skills in evading recognition could make it very difficult for the target state to identify such individuals. The impact of such forces on the civil order, and life and property, in the target state could be very serious, and for the initiating state it would have the effect of war without the need to acknowledge responsibility. Of course comparable developments had occurred in earlier periods, such as the infiltration of Soviet Communist elements into capitalist countries which actively pursued the goal of fermenting revolution and the overthrow of the government. But the new practices were different in that they involved a preparedness to use deadly force in the pursuit of private gain and influence on a scale not seen before.

The nature of these problems indicated the need for strengthening international cooperation between police forces, and setting up unified transnational command structures if the problem required this. States and their individual police forces, assuming they themselves were not a part of the scam, were likely to find dealing with them separately and individually impossible precisely because they were transnational. The organizations were capable of withdrawing from one state and regrouping in others only to be reactivated in the target state later. It was also difficult for police forces in particular states to gain access to the command and control structures of the organizations in other states without themselves transgressing the rules of exclusive national jurisdiction. There were also some kinds of such operations, which were closely linked with government officials, or members of business or political elites in

---

[21] A similar organization was Sandlines which caused embarrassment to the British Foreign Office in 1998 because of its involvement in the war in Sierra Leone and the allegation that it had procured and supplied arms to the ousted government in defiance of UN sanctions.

another state, which needed the weight of an extra-territorial authority to be effective. In an extreme form, when they were directly controlled by another government, doing something about them which was effective could lead to war, either because the controlling government, when found out, reacted with more direct violence, or because the scale of the intervention was such that it could not be coped with except by attacking the source government. This was a problem which, therefore, raised the question of the civil order within states as well as that of maintaining peace and security. It was on a continuum extending from the problems of disorder within the state, and those dealt with by new forms of peace-keeping, to those security problems of a more traditional kind.

The appropriate form of such a force would include the capacity to deploy a range of specialist forces, which could be asked to operate in more open combat or in situations where SAS type skills were more appropriate. But the forces also needed to be linked with sophisticated investigative techniques which could work on an international basis, and which could if necessary demand answers from individuals who were close to governments. An effective arrangement for dealing with such problems therefore also assumed a range of features in the participating state. They would need to be prepared to tolerate the incursion of a transnational police force into their domestic arrangements, and to be open enough at least to accept this.

The European Union was one group of states where advanced police cooperation existed and in which a further enhancement of regional trans-national capacity was being actively sought in the late 1990s: the ability to create forces which were likely to be effective depended on the civil order within the state, but a variety of different forms of liberal domestic order could tolerate the kind of arrangement that was emerging in Europe.[22] But some states – generally those with intolerant and precarious regimes, quite probably at risk of internal humanitarian crisis – would not, and were likely to play the sovereignty card to avoid cooperation. The well-founded state sought after by the international community in the late 1990s was, therefore, also desirable from the alternative perspective of dealing effectively with new kinds of non-governmental threats to individual security. The problem clearly had an international dimension: it suggested the need to confederalize the mechanisms for protecting national civil orders. It was therefore a feature of international society after the Cold War that the range of conceivable force deployments to maintain order had been considerably broadened, compared with the earlier phases of international society, and that the earlier distinctions between national and international security had been blurred.

This implied in the late 1990s something quite startling: that the direction of development of the use of police and military was positively linked with the development of cosmopolitanism – that new peace-keeping was a step towards enhanced international civilian police capacity, and that this was only possible if the civil values of communities around the world become more similar and more liberal. The step beyond that would be a transnational cosmopolitanism linked with advanced forms of police cooperation dealing with crimes over a very wide

[22] According to the new Title VI of the Treaty on European Union. Andrew Duff concluded: 'For all the difficulties what emerges is a picture, in five years time, of an extensive and sophisticated web of police coordination throughout the European Union', A. Duff (ed.), *The Treaty of Amsterdam: Text and Commentary* (London, Federal Trust for Education and Science, 1997), p. 42.

spectrum. Like business and ideology, crime was also likely to become more transnational and to demand transnational response, and to create difficulties in deciding what kinds of crime were local, and the exclusive responsibility of national police forces, and which were transnational and therefore the proper responsibility of a higher police authority.

But at the other end of the scale there were in the late 1990s much stronger grounds to be fearful of rogue governments such as that of Saddam Hussein. It had become possible for a government to adopt an effective international criminal strategy on a scale that had never before been possible. Modern technology could give them the means of global destruction for relatively modest outlay. The dangers posed by such states to international society, to the citizens of the world as well as to governments, were sufficiently appalling to justify firm action against them. Such action could become an imperative if the government appeared to have nuclear, chemical or bacteriological weapons.

The scale of the problem was illustrated in the late 1990s by the response to Saddam Hussein's attempts to evade the UN inspectors appointed to locate and destroy his more dangerous weapons. The international community initially hesitated but eventually accepted the need for a firm response, though disagreement about whether or not to use force remained. One report was that the USA had been prepared to use a specialized nuclear device to penetrate and destroy bacteriological weapons bunkers and their contents. As never before the world could be held to ransom by irresponsible, corrupt or plain mad regimes possessed of such weapons. Once again the case for a strong transnational authority equipped to act appropriately to deal with such regimes was apparent. For the first time technology and custom had reached the point at which the removal of a dangerous government was justifiable simply because of the degree of damage which it could do. There was, of course, the need for satisfactory ways of licensing such action. But this was a revolutionary qualification of the concept of statehood, which happily coincided with the preponderance of the liberal states in the post-Cold War period. It demanded solidarity but it also supported the drive to achieve it.

Democratization and Globalization

In the mid-1990s the trend towards economic globalization had major implications for the circumstances of sovereignty. Globalization was in part a self-serving agenda for the economic forces of the developed world, and went along with the agenda of deregulation, and making the world free for multinational corporations.[23] The prevailing image was of a world which was becoming more interdependent, and more dominated by multinational corporations and global economic forces, such as more widely distributed direct foreign investment. This was seen by many as a positive development, and, in contrast, local attempts to impose conditions upon mutual involvement were seen as setting unacceptable limits upon the development of the common good. Furthermore, it was thought, they were unlikely to succeed: globalization was inevitable.

The opposite view, reflected in the arguments of the G77, the Non-Aligned, and the proponents of social democracy, was that the common good was not

---

[23] For an incisive critique of economic globalization see P. Hirst and G. Thompson, *Globalization in Question* (Cambridge, Polity, 1996).

© Political Studies Association, 1999

served if deregulation was pushed beyond certain limits: certainly it was mistaken to see deregulation, and exposure to market forces in an open world economy, as necessarily beneficial. Liberal internationalism now risked rule by organizations which were hard to control by democratic forms of government and often led to the exploitation of the disadvantaged. Even for developed states like the members of the European Union globalization was an impediment in the way of pursuing social goals such as full employment. It was local organizations, in the state or region, that were more likely to pursue social purposes successfully; at least it was unlikely that global corporations would do this, since the more global they were the more it was likely that their inherent drive to profit would be untroubled by social purpose.

Global corporations were likely to pursue profit maximizing strategies at the expense of high levels of employment, effective welfare provision, and the promotion of democracy. The 'dynamics of globalization are gradually disembedding the domestic social contract between the state and society, which had become integral to the programme of welfare capitalism and social democracy,' and 'the state has itself been "globalized" or "internationalized", that is the policy orientation of the state has ben pulled away from its territorial constituencies and shifted outwards, with state action characteristically operating as an instrumental agent on behalf of non-territorial regional and global market forces, as manipulated by transnational corporations and banks, and increasingly also by financial traders.'[24]

A greater degree of deregulation of economic forces worked to the advantage of core regions, and within them of richer individuals and institutions, and perpetuated the disadvantage of peripheries and poorer elements within them – whether they were in the European Union or at the global level – unless deliberate measures were adopted to shape the global forces to local needs. In pre-democratic countries multinational corporations had no motivation for strengthening legitimate national controls, by tolerating or encouraging trade unions, or other forms of local participation in their decision-making. They were likely to be tolerant of non-democratic forms of organization, as long as they produced stability in the short term – the corporation's first political priority – and would circumvent democratic processes by helping to restrict the expression of opinions which did not reflect their interests, or trying to control host country leaders. There were of course exceptions to these generalizations, but the experience of business attitudes towards democratization in Hong Kong in the late 1980s and 1990s suggested that when successful multinational business faced a choice it preferred a comfortable authoritarianism to a challenging democracy.

Since the late 1980s, however, the UN had become more directly involved in helping the emergence of democracy. A letter from the European Union to the Secretary-General picked up a theme which was increasingly visible in UN and UN-related documents, namely support for enhancing the role of the UN in helping the development of a *civil society* in states that had experienced internal crisis.[25] The use of the term 'civil society' was striking: it was now often found in UN documents, but had rarely been found before the late 1980s. It appeared in

---

[24] R. Falk, 'State of siege: will globalism win out', *International Affairs*, 73 (1997), p. 131.
[25] Letter from the Presidency of the EU, at the Permanent Mission of Ireland to the United Nations, to the Secretary General, 16 October, 1996, Para. 21.

this case in the context of support for the recovery of states in which there had been serious humanitarian crisis, but it often had a wider reference: support for a proactive strategy on the part of the international community in promoting democracy.

In the late 1990s an unprecedented commitment emerged to the promotion of liberal pluralist arrangements as a condition of development on the part of the major players, the World Bank, the UN system and the EU: it encompassed the elements of a well founded civil society and democratization as well as such changes as improved credit and insurance arrangements. The head of UNDP stated in 1998 that 40% of the resources of his organization now went on governance improving activities. There was increasing evidence of UN agencies, 'and other international organizations' helping governments to strengthen democratic forms. Cases mentioned in the mid-1990s included Niger and Guatemala, where UNDP had adopted a more political role in supporting government reform. The point was made that in Latin America the UNDP was an active factor in democratization. This was a remarkable alteration in stress and its significance should not be underestimated: for the first time in the history of the United Nations the organization was directly addressing core structures in the state and even in the difficult continent – Africa – illiberal practices were increasingly being delegitimized. The Security Council's authorization in July 1994 (SC940) of armed intervention in Haiti to restore a democratically elected government was particularly striking: there had been no credible threat to international peace and security.[26] This surely contributed to the de facto dilution of the concept of sovereignty as earlier understood in the Council and elsewhere. UNICEF's strategy had also been rededicated: the new approach was to be 'rights based', meaning that it was to be derived from the Rights of the Child Convention.

The EU urged the adoption of a comprehensive approach in respect of non-military aspects of peace operations (including tasks such as democratization, police training, institution building, capacity building and delivery of humanitarian assistance), to help with the 'transition from humanitarian relief to long term planning, including in the context of support for *civil society*'.[27] The EU had also begun to impose *multiple conditionality* in its relations with the ACP countries: strings were attached to economic support which included democratization.[28] The change in this direction could be traced from the mid-1980s when Margaret Thatcher became the first European leader to attempt to build human rights conditions into provisions for European Community aid to African, Caribbean and Pacific (ACP) countries under the Lome Conventions. 'Although that attempt was initially rejected by ACP leaders as an unwarranted infringement on their domestic sovereignty, by the time of the Lome IV convention of 1990 an explicit reference to human rights in the context of EC aid could no longer be avoided.'[29] In fact the EU programme was broadened to include a requirement for a whole range of internal adjustments to promote

---

[26] D. Malone, 'Haiti and the international community: a case study', *Survival*, 39 (1997), 126–146.

[27] EU letter, p. 8.

[28] See J. Matheson, Multiple Conditionality and the EU, London School of Economics and Political Science, PhD. Thesis, 1997, unpublished.

[29] N. Wickramasinghe, 'From Human Rights to Good Governance: The Aid Regime in the 1990s' in Sellers, *The New World Order*, p. 311.

greater transparency and efficiency in using their aid. Although the mechanisms for dealing with human rights infringements in the international legal system remained flawed it was undeniable that in a number of ways the intrusions of the international community to promote minimum acceptable standards had been extended. The start made upon the setting up of an International Criminal Court in 1998 was an aspect of this. The revolutionary proposal was to bring international criminals to account, including the leaders of states.

The argument emerges that the promotion of well-founded states, which was now seen as essential for international order, was the appropriate counter-strategy to globalization. The weight of evidence in the late 1990s suggested that the assumption was false that development, democratization and globalization were positively connected. Globalization as an economic process contained elements which were corrosive of international order. It was a happy coincidence that its apparent progress coincided with the choice by a number of major actors of a deliberate strategy of democratization. By the late 1990s it was necessary, therefore, to have an agenda of statism, which was now a condition and a consequence of cosmopolitanism. It was necessary to make the world safe for sovereignty.

Changes in the way development was managed were also relevant to the process of democratization. For instance, funds now often went directly to programmes, rather than going through governments, who were thereby reduced in their ability to syphon off money for their own special reasons, the purchase of arms and other forms of indulgence. Since the late 1980s there had been a considerable enhancement of the role of the UN system with regard to the rehabilitation of failing states. The EU document mentioned above recognized and supported this involvement.

Similar arguments related to the proposal for a Multilateral Investment Agreement (MIA) made in the mid 1990s to the World Trade Organization by the EU, Canada and Japan, which was seen by the G77 as a way of guaranteeing the unrestrained right of multinationals to invest with minimum conditionality in their states. In the view of Southern economists, it was unlikely to benefit locals, and was more likely to lead to a further draining of resources to the richer parts of the world. 'Experience in the globalization episode of the last century does not really make out a case of laissez faire and free capital flows having promoted development. Rather it shows uneven global development associated with such flows'; the 'entire argument rests on the existence of efficiency enhancing effects of undistorted price signals – an assumption that draws theoretical support from the welfare principles of unregulated markets. "But" such an assumption is challenged by the reality that there exist market failures of one type or another'. Thus, *there are equally strong theoretical grounds that argue against unregulated markets*'. [my stress][30]

It was pointed out that only seven of the leading 20 host countries for FDI between 1985 and 1995 were developing countries, and that with the exception of China all were middle income countries with rapid growth. This pointed to the important conclusion that FDI was more likely to help a developing economy *once growth was well under way*, but that the usual range of benefits ascribed to FDI-technology transfer, strengthening local industries etc. – were

[30] Third World Network, *North South Development Monitor*, Interpress Service and South Centre, 28 October, 1996, pp. 2–5.

unlikely to accrue until take off had started. Thus it could be important for the poorest states to find a means of imposing conditions on multinationals who proposed investing in their territory, and of deciding what such conditions should be. To do this they needed allies in the international system. In the late 1990s one form of this was the reformed mechanisms of the UN's economic and social organizations. For instance the Country Strategy Notes were the first attempt at an authoritative definition of country specific policies and approaches for economic management and development, involving, as they did, inputs from the range of UN organizations involved in development, with advice from donor officials, and the participation and consent of the host countries and bilateral contributors.

In the late 1990s there was a fundamental opposition, not only between globalization and democratization, but also between development and globalization. The three primary agendas contained damaging contradictions which could only be overcome by an alliance between liberal developed states, acting within international organizations like the EU and the UN, to promote liberal and democratic social and political agendas. This implied in turn not only an active policy of building states which met these conditions, but also a strengthening of the arrangements between them.

But these are mere hints at underlying problems and their solution. State enhancement to counter the threat to international order posed by economic globalization was needed, and a beginning had to be made in the UN system on various new initiatives to achieve this. Proactive cosmopolitanism and state-enhancement were coincident and necessary to protect the international order against the corrosive effects of globalization.

Sovereignty and Cosmopolitanism in the Late 1990s: a Neo-Westphalian System?

The main themes identified in the introduction have now been discussed, with the exception of the development of a legal system within which laws made outside the state increasingly imposed within it. This has been discussed at length elsewhere, and in this essay it is more useful to give space to its implications, which is done below. But the development of mechanisms to protect international peace and security, the extension of the range of involvements to promote common standards, such as democratization, and the emergence of a global watch and more speedy response, have been discussed in their main phases. It is apparent, however, that under these headings only a selection of new interventions and involvements have been considered. Kant had proposed a strategy which stressed the importance of international discourse, commerce and hospitality.[31] By the late 1990s there had emerged countless illustrations of a modern equivalent of this strategy in the work of international institutions, in particular those of the UN system, of which Kant would doubtless have approved.

The point should be stressed again that the involvements and interventions were to consolidate the state, to protect its position and not to weaken or remove it. But by the late 1990s the international community, working through the United Nations system, and other international organizations, seemed to have considerably enhanced its authority compared with the period of the Cold

[31] Hinsley, *Power and the Pursuit of Peace*, pp. 65–7.

War. There was now a sense in which sovereign states were legitimized and sustained by such an authority to which they were in general terms accountable.[32] This accountability was the condition of states being regarded as ultimately responsible on particular matters, and their right to an exclusive domestic jurisdiction was increasingly questioned if their performance fell short in an expanding range of specific practical arrangements. This could be seen as a filling out, and translation into secular terms, of a feature of the Westphalian system: that even princes were subjects of a divine order. In the late twentieth century, however, such a higher authority could only exist in the context of the new cosmopolitanism.

Some reformulation of the act of creating sovereignty seemed to be indicated to reflect the expanding role of the international community in monitoring internal circumstances and rescuing failing states. Indeed there was a case for granting the United Nations primary responsibility for conferring sovereignty through the recognition process – i.e. multilateralizing the process – and for removing that right from states to act individually and separately. If states were to be monitored and rescued multilaterally should they not also be licenced multilaterally? Sovereignty was a goal of the international community deserving recognition in its procedures as well as its constitutive principle.

Popular support of statehood had often been looked for in earlier times as a condition of recognition, but publics and other states were coming to regard this as a starting point. The range of 'sovereignty creating acts' was in effect being expanded from seeing that territory was controlled with some reference to popular support at the time of recognition to a more comprehensive concern with the details of internal arrangements, so that the support would endure. A new condition of sovereignty was therefore now discernible, in addition to the traditional one that a territory should be controlled by a government: that the state was well-founded in the light of the standards of the international community. The terms of the granting of the licence to practice statehood were in the process of being enlarged and giving responsibility for awarding the accolade of recognition to the United Nations was a concomitant of this.

The recognition as states of the territories which had formed Yugoslavia was a fairly *ad hoc* business with unintended and disastrous consequences, driven by the interests of Germany, and imperfectly monitored by the Batinder Commission set up under the authority of the Commission on Yugoslavia;[33] it was unreasonable that the recognition process should be left to states individually and separately, but, as was increasingly happening, the UN[34] be left to pick up the pieces. The obligation of states to the international community to maintain acceptable internal standards needed to be underlined as their poor performance could lead to major costs for other states; there was a straightforward utilitarian justification.

The *ad hoc* character of the recognition of states, was matched by a corresponding 'ad hocery' about their derecognition, the removal of the acknowledgement of sovereignty. The lack of any general procedure for derecognition

---

[32] The elements of continuity in the state system are discussed in R. Jackson and A. James, *States in a Changing World: a Contemporary Analysis* (Oxford, Clarendon, 1993).
[33] Economides and Taylor, in Mayall, *The New Interventionism*, p. 91.
[34] See the excellent discussion of the issues raised here, including recognition by the UN, in J. Dugard, *Recognition and the United Nations* (Cambridge, Grotius, 1987).

PAUL TAYLOR 559

increased the difficulty of intervening – meaning an involvement using force – as the states which separately continued to recognize a state were more likely to argue that the sovereignty of that state should not be breached. But as the cosmopolitan moral community was strengthened sovereignty would be weakened as an impediment in the way of intervention. Indeed the earlier relationship between intervention and sovereignty would be reversed: weight would increasingly be placed on the question of the justice of the state's claim to sovereignty rather than upon the nature of the justification for intervention. The question of which *precise* justification of intervention was proposed, be it a threat to international security under Chapter VII, or a gross infringement of human rights, (whichever happened to fit in with the prevailing interpretation of the Charter) would be of lesser significance as a liberal interpretation of either would suit the case. The logic of the situation was, however, that derecognition should also be a matter for the United Nations, with appropriate safeguard procedures, given the changing character of its role in maintaining international order. It should be done as a single multilateral act under the authority of the UN. This would clarify the point that sovereignty had a relationship with being well-founded, and that when intervention by the international community was judged necessary, a state entity could not be sovereign.

Sovereignty could be interpreted as being ultimately responsible – the buck stops with the sovereign, though paradoxically – as was argued above – being ultimately responsible could come to be the result of an enabling act from the international community. But sovereignty also meant having the right to do certain things: it involved having a role with regard to a range of specific functions. The question was whether this role had been affected by the changing circumstances of sovereignty. New problems in the way of legitimizing states by granting them sovereignty were matched by new problems about deciding what states should be able to do in order to remain sovereign.

Having a role, and doing something, involved being granted a *competence*, and was not the same as being ultimately responsible. In recent years the analytical distinction between these two questions – who was ultimately responsible and who had competence to act – was more frequently reflected in the practice of states and international organizations: the question of which body was ultimately responsible, was increasingly separated from that of which body was allowed competence.[35] The exercise of exclusive control over certain key functions, such as foreign policy and defence, used to be regarded as being central to sovereignty, and could not be allocated to other centres. But in the late 1990s the member states of the European Union could accept that the Union should have a role in their harmonized foreign policy, and that it might increase its involvement in the common defence. There was a majority for this among the Union's citizens, even in cautious states such as the UK. The question of taking decisions in these areas by qualified majority vote had even entered the agenda. This was an astonishing development which seemed to remove the dilemma, discussed *inter alia* by Rousseau, that responsibility for maintaining the peace could not be allocated to a higher, federal authority without fatally damaging the entity which it was designed to protect, namely the state itself.

---

[35] This issue is discussed by the author in his *The European Union in the 1990s* (Oxford, Oxford University Press, 1996), ch. 2.

Ultimate responsibility remained with the sovereign states, as a condition of their sovereignty, as long as they retained reserve powers, including the power to recover the competences, even though the grant of the right to exercise that responsibility came from the international community. Public opinion and governments could accept that such a transfer of responsibility for foreign policy and defence was not an infringement of sovereignty as long as the reserve power was kept! Something remarkable had happened: sovereignty was now a condition, even a form, of participation, in the larger entity. What was stressed in the role taken on by being sovereign was the right to be involved, to participate in the mechanisms of international society, and to represent there the interests of the state. It was even possible to imagine states which were sovereign but which normally exercised no exclusive competences.

The expectation was that the chances of the reserve powers' being utilized would be progressively reduced. Outside the European Union it was unusual for issues of foreign policy or defence to involve supranational authority. But it was common for other questions, previously regarded as essential to the exercise of national sovereignty, especially in the economic, social and other technical areas, to be handled elsewhere in whole or in part. The transfer did not always go smoothly and states were sometimes surprised by what they learned they had given away. For instance in the late 1990s individuals in the US Administration and members of Congress reacted with horror to judgements against the US made by the World Trade Organization. The general trend, however, was for issues to become less sensitive with regard to sovereignty: competences were now routinely exercised by international agencies in areas which would have been sacred to sovereignty in earlier times. But paradoxically the state's survival rested on the assumption that this transfer could not be guaranteed: the competences could still be recalled in principle even if this in practice was unlikely.

If the status of the international community was to be protected it would be necessary to avoid situations in which the reserve powers would have be used. The key to successful diplomacy was the avoidance of policies which could lead to having to make a choice between national interest and courses of action indicated by the agenda of cosmopolitanism, as in this case national interest would have to come first. This was the nature of international society and the state. A policy competence would have to be renationalized if, for instance, a state's ability to provide for the welfare of its citizens was likely to be damaged. The skilled diplomat would increasingly require a sophisticated grasp of paradox. But in a community of well-founded states it would be less likely that a choice would have to be made to repatriate a competence, as the interests of all states would be informed by the cosmopolitan ideology.

Lurking behind these points was another more important one: the dialectical relationship between the state and the international community, as it had emerged by the late 1990s, increasingly demanded that states should be acceptable as proper participants in the international civil order. There was increasingly the perception that unless they met certain conditions of probity and internal welfare they could not be full members. One illustration of this was that members of governments which fell short were more often regarded amongst the community of diplomats as unsuited to the exercise of public office in the institutions of the international community. If this tendency-norm were to evolve into a practice-rule it would be hard to deny that in this key area states had become unequal as citizens of the international community, and that this had grave implications for the question of whether they could be regarded as equal and, therefore, sovereign.

In effect: changes in the circumstances of sovereignty in the late 1990s suggested that it could come to depend upon being recognized as a fit member of international society. It could be ultimately responsible, exercise competences on behalf of its citizens, and play a full part in the community that sanctioned this, only if it complied with the conditions of both the international and the domestic community. It was a short step to seeing the unfit as the unsovereign.

The significance of the above can be underlined by a sketch of conceivable next steps. What was on the agenda of the reform of international organization and its relation with the state in the late 1990s. Where was the system headed? These items give a preliminary indication of a possible route. There were proposals which aimed at enhancing the accountability of governments to the international community; proposals for requiring qualifications of individuals and institutions as a condition of allowing them to operate international instruments (institutional development); and proposals which were aimed directly at improving the lot of individuals within states independently of the proposals aimed at national or international agencies. The proposals in normal type are those which appeared frequently in the literature in the late 1990s:[36] they amounted to expectations about next steps, which were as realistic a measure of what had been obtained by the late 1990s as a discussion of actual attainment. They were the other side of the line represented by the word 'now'. Subsequent steps linked with the proposals might also be entering the discourse and are placed in *italics*: this enhances the sense of the direction of movement.

Proposals under these various headings were:

A. Government accountability
Under this heading proposals appearing on agendas in the 1990s included:

1. Strengthen the War Crimes Tribunal and set up an International Criminal Court.
   A certificate of good housekeeping to be provided at the end of a government's period of office in all states by a designated agency of the UN as representative of the international community, with the power to freeze and sequestrate the assets of malefactors.
2. Tighten up the arms register arrangements and agree an international code for the supply of arms with effective policing. Make it compulsory to register and to apply an international code of manufacture and supply, *with direct access to manufacturers inventories and production facilities for the international arms authority.*
3. *A code of proper behaviour for political leaders to be agreed by the General Assembly linked with the publication of a register of corrupt governments by*

---

[36] The list draws on the wide range of reports on reform of the United Nations which were current in the late 1990s. Particular use was made of The Commission on Global Governance, *Our Global Neighbourhood* (Oxford, Oxford University Press, 1995); *A Report of the Independent Working Group on the Future of the United Nations*, appended to K. Huefner (ed.), *Agenda for Change: New Tasks for the United Nations* (Opladen, Leske & Budrich, 1995); G. de Marco and M. Bartolo, *A Second Generation of United Nations: For Peace in Freedom in the 21st Century* (London, Kegan Paul, 1997), especially ch. 10 and Annexe 1, Summary of previous proposals.

the UN. An index of governments rated with regard to corruption to be published by the General Assembly.

4. More liberal formal procedures for intervention – based on the interests of peoples – Chapter 1, Article 1(3) in contrast to Chapter VII. *A code for the use of force (military or economic), as in Haiti, to restore democracy in the event of military take-over.*

B. Institutional development
Items included:

1. Judicial review by the International Court of Justice of the decisions of the Security Council.
2. Enhancement of the powers of the Security Council to include more sectors eg. Environment and human rights. The capacity to achieve cross-sector coherence in its decisions would be enhanced. *The ICJ could then be granted power to require that such coherence be maintained by the Security Council within and across sectors.*
3. The ICJ to become active in resolving conflicts between acts of international legislation such as that between World Trade Organization rules and Multilateral Environment Agreements. (In 1998 WTO rules required that trade liberalization codes override tighter environmental requirements in the MEAs; there was often a straight contradiction between the two with no formal process of reconciliation.)
4. A Commission of Experts to be created to bring the attention of the Security Council to new crises and recommend an appropriate response: *such a commission could also develop a role in determining the adequacy of resources with regard to SC mandates and their strategic and other implications for peace-keeping. It could be empowered to require that SC resolutions were technically efficient.*[37]
5. *Responsibility for the recognition and de-recognition of states to be transferred to the UN and exercised under a special procedure.*
6. *Exclusion of governments with a low index rating, as determined in the procedure in A4. above, from executive positions in international institutions including the UN – and from voting, or new memberships in international organizations in the UN system.*
   (In the Treaty of Amsterdam in the European Union states agreed that if a member was found guilty of offences against human rights it could be punished by having its voting rights in the Council of Ministers suspended.)[38]

C. Cosmopolitanism and citizens
Items included:

1. All diplomatic relations and diplomacy to be linked to the promotion of human rights.

---

[37] The Report of the Independent Working Group, reproduced in Huefner, *Agenda for Change*, calls this a Security Assessment Staff.
[38] New Article F 1. Clause 2. Referred to the Council's right to 'suspend certain rights ... including the voting rights' ... of a member state found to be in serious and persistent breach of the principles ... (including respect for human rights [Article F]).

2. *All states to have formal constitutions subject to international approval by a designated agency (see C3) which guaranteed civil rights and respect for minorities.*

3. A Commission for Constitutionalism and Due Process to be set up. The UN Human Rights Conventions to be incorporated into all national constitutions under its supervision on the model of the European Convention of Human Rights. (In 1998 the British government was considering such incorporation.)

4. States to be required to pursue a *civil rights first* strategy involving a range of obligations intended to maintain and promote civilized internal orders. These would include an obligation to avoid infringements of internationally recognized civil liberties. *The obligation could be extended to include an obligation to avoid excessive income differentials – mean income – not average – and exclude privileged access to social services, such as health, police, and education. Indicators of civilized society could rate poorer societies more highly than rich countries with, for instance, wider income differentials and uneven social service access.*

5. Removal of prohibitions on direct appeal to international courts and forums by individuals against governments.

6. *Instigation of rules requiring that development and investment strategies promote human rights, equity and environmental considerations.*

7. *The making of a list of recognized NGOs that could operate within all states as of right i.e. without requiring the explicit permission of governments.*

8. More 'mixed' representation in international institutions i.e. by individual, group, region as well as governments.[39]

9. Limiting certain new collateral effects of war upon individuals: e.g. by limiting the use of land mines, *and* damage to health from lack of proper precautions in testing, developing or storing chemical, bacteriological or nuclear weapons. An international mechanism for identifying and destroying redundant weapons.

Two kinds of implications of the changing circumstances of sovereignty were discussed in this section. First was the change in views about the implications of being sovereign, and ways of becoming sovereign. Second was the proposal for future developments which had become conceivable in the late 1990s because of those changes. Such proposals only acquired a veneer of credibility in the light of the changes in views about sovereignty.

Conclusions

The definition of sovereignty always had to take account of the circumstances of the time and of the place. It was an absolute which had to be constantly reinterpreted in the light of the actual limitations placed on state behaviour, and this produced continuous controversy and a steady stream of dissertations – which was hardly surprising in view of the logical impossibility of qualifying an absolute.

---

[39] See the excellent consideration of this question in D. Held, *Democracy and the Global Order: From the Modern State to Cosmopolitan Governance* (Cambridge, Polity, 1995).

One reason for this was that the traditional discussion of sovereignty worked from the state-actor, and its claims to sovereignty, to the compromises with the principle which resulted from membership of international society. This reconciliation was always unconvincing. Changes in the work of the United Nations since the end of the Cold War, and the implications of membership in the European Union, extended the list of anomalies with regard to the traditional view to breaking point: how could a 'state' be sovereign in the traditional sense when its people could appeal to a superior court, such as the European Court of Human Rights or the European Court of Justice, against its own government and when laws made outside the state apparently prevailed over those made within, as in the European Union? One response to the difficulties was to reinterpret the principle as a reflection of the constitutive role of the international community *as well as* an acknowledgement of the innate need of people for self-determination. In the past sovereignty had been seen as being made by the sub-systems, the states; a stronger appreciation was needed of the way in which the international community could constitute the state and express its sovereignty.

Developments in the work of United Nations system in the 1990s, and attitudes towards it, made it possible to identify somewhat more clearly this dialectical quality in sovereignty.

Aspects of this dialectic are brought out in the following summation:

- Sovereignty increasingly defined a unit of participation, and established a right to participate in the institutions and arrangements of the international community. Having the right to participate in the management of common arrangements with other states was a much more important consideration in sovereignty than the traditional right to exclusive management of any single function, even defence and foreign policy. (Luxembourg, but not Quebec, was a sovereign state in the 1990s, not because the former did more alone than the latter – arguably Quebec had more functional independence in Canada than Luxembourg in the European Union. It was rather that Luxembourg had the right to participate in the range of international forums with state members, whereas Quebec did not; and Luxembourg retained the reserve powers mentioned below to limit the competence of external agencies.)
- But: sovereignty increasingly came to be seen as conferring on states the obligation of being accountable to the international community. Being licenced to practice as a state carried with it the condition of its government's being prepared to demonstrate, to the satisfaction of the international community, continued adherence to the terms under which it held the licence i.e. being well-founded in the varying senses discussed above. The sovereign was the entity which was accountable to the higher unit, and states which evaded this obligation were increasingly seen as falling short of the standards expected in the state-citizens of international society.
- Sovereignty identified (a) the locus of responsibility in the state and (b) the focus of popular perceptions about which authority was ultimately responsible. The rights and obligations of sovereignty were vested in a government which was the ultimate guardian of the popular interest and

which could not renounce that interest because it was sovereign. It was the focus of popular hopes and expectations.
- And: it was an embodiment of interest: its government, embodying the sovereignty of the state, had the right to determine a collective interest according to accepted procedures in the state.
- But: with regard to competence:
  a. Sovereignty embodied a grant to the state from the international community of the right to act on its own account in international society.
  b. It was also a grant of the right to extend competence to act to other entities such as international institutions, other states, or private organizations, within its territory or on its behalf in international society.
  c. Conversely the sovereignty of states meant that the system of which they were members necessarily left them with the right to limit that competence. By the late 1990s no form of majority voting in international institutions had limited this right. This was the equivalent in the circumstances of the late 1990s of the traditional right to exclusive domestic jurisdiction. It had, therefore, become less useful to see states as having exclusive domestic jurisdiction and more useful to see them as having reserved the right to limit the effects of legislation made outside. This was because of the development of an increasing capacity for making rules, with direct implications within states, in international institutions; the prime example of this, but by no means the only one, was the European Union.
- Sovereignty also carried the implication of a grant of the right to privacy for citizens. This was the perception that their behaviour among themselves was no business of others. But the limitations of this right included the requirement that practices should have general approval within the state and that they did not compromise the privacy of the citizens of other states. This right did not exclude the rights of others to argue against practices which they found abhorrent, and to promote intervention if a practice was contrary to a clear internationally held standard. But the assumption had to be made that any practice which turned one section of a community into the victims of another was necessarily abhorrent.

These perceptions of sovereignty arose in the context of the late 1990s. They included, in particular, extensions of the role of international institutions, especially the United Nations and the European Union, and the emergence of a more proactive cosmopolitanism which stressed an overlay on diverse cultures of universalizing values. All of this was in the process of *becoming*: it was a consequence of the happy coincidence that the end of the Cold War left the democratic liberal states in a position to push their values.

The entrenchment of cosmopolitanism, based on such liberal values, confirmed the right of outsiders to judge internal arrangements, and to act to ensure that acceptable standards were maintained. This was the essential condition of the grand underlying dialectic: the sovereignty of states obliged them to meet the norms of the international community but the norms of the international community were a product of the sovereignty of states.

Robert Wade

Japan, the World Bank, and the Art of Paradigm Maintenance: *The East Asian Miracle* in Political Perspective

To what extent is the World Bank an actor, an 'autonomous variable' in the international system?[1] Or to what extent are its objectives and approaches the mere manifestations of competition and compromise among its member states? Several writers have argued that the Bank has a relatively large amount of autonomy—from the state interests of its overseers, and that its staff have some autonomy from the senior management. They have traced this autonomy to variables such as 'lack of clarity of the priorities of organizational objectives', 'the difficulty and complexity of accomplishing the organization's mandate', 'bureaucratized structure' and 'professionalism of staff'.[2] But there is something strangely bloodless about this approach. It manages to discuss autonomy without conveying anything of the political and economic substance of the field of forces in which the Bank operates. By focusing only on morphological variables like 'professionalism' and the 'complexity of accomplishing the organization's mandate', it misses other variables like 'correspondence of organizational actions with the interests of the US state'. If the Bank is propelled by its

budgetary, staffing and incentive structures to act in line with those interests, the US state need not intervene in ways that would provide evidence
of 'lack of autonomy'; yet the Bank's autonomy is clearly questionable.

This paper describes an episode in Japan's attempts over the 1980s and
1990s to assert itself on the world stage, to move beyond the constraints of
dependency in a US-centred world economic system. The episode involves
a Japanese challenge to the World Bank and its core ideas about the role of
the state in the strategy for economic development. Over the 1980s Japan
poured aid and investment into East and Southeast Asia, using its strong
domestic capacity to' strengthen its external reach. In doing so, Japan
endorsed a market-guiding role for the state in recipient countries, and
justified this role by pointing to its success in the development of Japan,
Taiwan, and South Korea. The World Bank found Japan's prescriptions
inconsistent with its own programmatic ideas about the role of the state,
which emphasized the need for thoroughgoing liberalization and privatization. Since the Bank's ideas are themselves derived from largely
American interests in and ideas about free markets, Japan's challenge to
the Bank was also a challenge to the US state—the Bank being an important instrument by which the US state seeks to project a powerful external
reach, while having a much weaker domestic capacity than Japan's.

In the early 1980s, when the Bank started to champion liberalization
and the private sector, the Bank and the Japanese government proceeded
along independent paths. But growing tension reached a head in the late
1980s when the Bank criticized Japanese aid programmes, for undermining the aims of the Bank and the International Monetary Fund. In
response, the Japanese government set out to change the Bank's core
ideas about the role of the state in development strategy. It did so by
inducing the Bank to pay more attention to East Asian development
experience, so perhaps the Bank would change its mind, see more validity in the Japanese principles, and enhance Japan's role as a leader in
development thinking. Japan's influence inside and outside the Bank
would then grow. Specifically, the Japanese government persuaded the
Bank to make a special study of East and Southeast Asia, focusing on why
this region has become rich and what other countries should learn from
the experience. The study was published in September 1993 as *The East
Asian Miracle: Economic Growth and Public Policy*.

In this paper we examine, first, the build-up of tension between Japan and
the Bank; second, the process by which the study was written inside the

[1] In addition to the cited sources, this paper is based on interviews with officials in Tokyo
and Washington, DC, who prefer anonymity, and on my own experience as a World Bank
economist in 1984–88. I thank Ngaire Woods, Linda Weiss, Ronald Dore, Devesh Kapur,
Chalmers Johnson, Thomas Biersteker, Manfred Bienefeld, Wendy Law-Yone and Toru
Yanagihara for comments. The paper can be read as a companion to my 'Selective Industrial Policies in East Asia: Is *The East Asian Miracle* Right?', in Albert Fishlow et al., eds,
Miracle or Design? Lessons from the East Asian Experience, Washington, DC, 1994. The theoretical ideas behind the critique are set out in my *Governing the Market: Economic Theory and
the Role of Government in East Asian Industrialization*, Princeton 1990.
[2] Stephen Krasner, 'Regimes and the Limits of Realism: Regimes as Autonomous
Variables', *International Organization*, no. 36, Spring 1982; William Ascher, 'New Development Approaches and the Adaptability of International Agencies: The Case of the
World Bank', *International Organization*, no. 37, Summer 1983.

4

Bank; and third, the resulting text. We shall ask whether Japan's attempt to get the Bank to change its mind was successful. We shall see how the final document reflects an attempt at compromise between the well-established World Bank view and the newly-powerful Japanese view. The result is heavily weighted towards the Bank's established position, and legitimizes the Bank's continuing advice to low-income countries to follow the 'market-friendly' policies apparently vindicated by East Asia's success. But the document also contains enough pro-industrial policy statements to allow the Japanese to claim a measure of success. Taken together with other Bank studies prompted by Japan at the same time, it provides a number of 'attractor points' for research and prescriptions more in line with Japanese views. Although the Bank emerges with its traditional paradigm largely unscathed, this particular episode may even be looked back on as an early landmark in the intellectual ascendancy, in East and Southeast Asia if not in the West, of Japanese views about the role of the state. Finally, we shall come back to the issue raised in the first paragraph—the autonomy of the World Bank, and the extent to which it can be regarded as an 'actor' with objectives and approaches that are not simply the vector of the interests of its member states.

I. The World Bank's Position in the Development Debate

The World Bank enjoys a unique position as a generator of ideas about economic development. Around the world, debates on development issues tend to be framed in terms of 'pro or anti' World Bank positions. The Bank's ability to frame the debate rests on, 1) its ability to influence the terms on which low-income countries gain access to international capital markets, 2) a research and policy-design budget far larger than that of any other development organization, and 3) its ability to attract global media coverage of its major reports.

In the early 1980s the Bank swung into line with a US-led consensus about the needs of the world economy and appropriate economic policies for developing countries. Reflecting the demise of Keynesianism and the ascendancy of supply-side economics in the US and some parts of Europe, the consensus—the 'Washington consensus', as it has been called—was based on the twin ideas of the state as the provider of a regulatory framework for private-sector exchanges (but not as a *director* of those exchanges), and of the world economy as open to movements of goods, services, and capital, if not labour. The Bank's new Structural Adjustment Loans applied conditions conforming to these ideas, such that borrowers had to shrink the state and open the economy to international transactions. Its annual *World Development Reports* have provided the conceptual framework and evidence to justify these conditions. In particular, the *World Development Report 1987*, entitled *Trade and Industrialization*, articulated a strong 'free-market' or neo-liberal argument about the appropriate development approach.[3]

---

[3] Note that 'trade' comes before 'industrialization' in the title. Anglo-American economists see trade and free-trade policy as the motor of industrialization, Japanese economists see trade and managed-trade policy as a subordinate part of industrialization and industrial strategy. See further Robert Wade, 'Managing Trade: Taiwan and South Korea as a Challenge to Economics and Political Science', *Comparative Politics*, vol. 25, no. 2 (1993), pp. 147–68.

The central problem of developing countries, in the Bank's view, is the weakness of their 'enabling environment' for private-sector growth. The enabling environment consists of infrastructure, a well-educated work force, macroeconomic stability, free trade, and a regulatory framework favouring private-sector investment and competition. Policies to secure such an environment are collectively called 'market-friendly'. The 'market-friendly' approach is not the same as laissez faire, the Bank is at pains to say, for there are areas where the market fails, in infrastructure and education, and where the government should step in with public spending.[4] On the other hand, the approach warns against intervention beyond these limits, especially against sectoral industrial policies designed to promote growth in some industries more than others. Market-friendly policies—neither complete laissez faire nor interventionism—are optimal for growth and income distribution, says the Bank. This set of ideas is broadly consistent with US demands that its trading partners—Japan in particular—change their domestic institutions in order to create a 'level playing field' for free and fair trade.

In the late 1980s the Bank paid particular attention to financial sector reform. A Bank Task Force on Financial Sector Operations met to formulate policy on financial system reform, later to be put in the form of a mandatory Operational Directive. The Task Force championed a policy of far-reaching financial deregulation for developing countries, urging removal of all interest rate controls and all directed credit programmes. *The World Development Report 1989*, entitled *Financial Systems and Development* took a somewhat less extreme view. Written by a team that worked at the same time as the Task Force on Financial Sector Operations, it emphasized that private financial markets do make mistakes, particularly because of information problems and externalities—although these mistakes last for a *shorter time* than those of public financial agents. Where supervision and monitoring is effective, directed credit can work. Governments should, however, deregulate, but gradually. In August 1989, one month after the *World Development Report 1989* was published, the Bank issued the Report of the Task Force on Financial Sector Operations—known as the Levy Report, after its chief author, Fred Levy. As noted, it took a strong view against government intervention in financial markets. The later Bank policy directive on financial sector operations took this report, not the *World Development Report 1989*, as its foundation.

II. The Japanese Challenge

Throughout the 1980s the Japanese state has hugely strengthened its external reach through aid programmes and foreign investment. By the early 1980s it was already the principal co-financier of World Bank loans, the number two shareholder in IDA—the Bank's soft loan facility—and the biggest source of bilateral aid for Asia. In 1984 it became the second biggest shareholder in the World Bank (IBRD) after the US. By 1989 it had the biggest bilateral aid programme in the world. In 1990 it became the second biggest shareholder in the

---

[4] See especially World Bank, *World Development Report 1991. The Challenge of Development*, Washington DC 1991.

International Finance Corporation—the Bank's affiliate for private-sector lending. In 1992 it became the second biggest shareholder—equal to Germany—in the International Monetary Fund. By the early 1990s Japan passed the US to become the world's biggest manufacturing economy; it accounted for half of the developed world's total net savings—US savings accounted for 5 per cent; and it became the world's biggest source of foreign investment. For all these reasons, Japan has come to matter for international financial institutions as never before—and also for the US state, whose deficits it has been financing.

The Japanese government has encouraged its recipient governments— the US aside—to think more strategically and in more interventionist terms than can be accommodated by World Bank ideas. In particular, it has sanctioned attempts by low-income states to go beyond the conventional neoclassical tasks of providing a property-rights framework and moderating market failures due to public goods, externalities and monopolies. It has encouraged aid recipients to articulate national objectives and policy choices, to catalyze market agents, and to assist some industries more than others. The Japanese government claims that the potential benefits of the state's directional thrust are illustrated by the actual benefits from the sectoral industrial policies of pre- and post-war Japan, and more recently, of Taiwan and South Korea. A regulated, 'non-liberalized' financial system capable of delivering concessional credit to priority uses, according to the Japanese, was a vital part of the organizational infrastructure of these policies.

In line with this thinking, in 1987 the Ministry of International Trade and Industry (MITI) published *The New Asian Industries Development Plan*, setting out a regional strategy of industrialization for Southeast Asian countries.[5] Responding to the appreciation of the Japanese yen in the mid-1980s and the resulting need to transfer more Japanese production offshore, the plan outlined the ways that Japanese firms making location decisions consistent with the plan would benefit from various kinds of aid for infrastructure, finance, market access, and so on. Officials were explicit that 'Japan will increasingly use its aid... as seed money to attract Japanese manufacturers or other industrial concerns with an attractive investment environment'.[6]

The Dispute over Directed Credit

'Directed' credit—meaning subsidized and targeted or earmarked credit

---

[5] The plan has not been translated into English but for a brief description in English, see Japan Economic Institute, report No. 22A, 18 June 1993, p. 9. The empirical and analytic underpinnings of the plan were put in place by studies of natural resources, trade and industrialization in Southeast Asian economies, over the 1970s and 1980s, by MITI economists and Japanese academics. The plan and its history illustrate the long-term nature of Japanese planning, and the coordination between government and firms. The contrast with the unstrategic nature of British and American aid and FDI policies is pronounced. One sees the results of the plan in the simultaneous spurt of Japanese FDI and aid to Thailand in 1988. Much of the aid was for the construction of industrial estates reserved for Japanese companies. The companies were exiting from Japan to escape quota restrictions on Japanese imports to OECD countries and environmental standards for industrial production, and to tap cheap Thai labour.
[6] Tadao Chino, then vice-minister, Ministry of Finance, in 1991, cited in Edward Lincoln, *Japan's New Global Role*, Washington DC 1993, p. 124.

—was to be a key instrument of this strategy. In the late 1980s Japan's Ministry of Finance (MOF) established the ASEAN-Japan Development Fund, which offered directed credit to support private-sector development. The fund was administered by OECF, Japan's largest aid agency. Unhappy at these developments, Bank officials expressed their reservations to Japanese officials informally—to no effect.

In June 1989, a new Executive Director for Japan, Masaki Shiratori, arrived at the World Bank. As a senior MOF official, he had helped steer Japan's relations with international financial organizations for many years. Between 1981 and 1984, he played a central role in the strategy to raise Japan's shareholding in the IBRD from number five to number two.[7] More persuasive in English than his predecessors, he was concerned to shift Japan's role from cheque-writer to leader—'no taxation without representation', some Japanese comment wryly—and to make the Bank drop its blanket opposition to directed credit policies.

By this time, both the World Bank and the Japanese government had well-articulated development strategies in place, the Bank emphasizing free markets, including nearly free financial markets, the Japanese government emphasizing guided markets, including guided financial markets. Japan was by then the second ranking shareholder in the World Bank after the US. And it had a new, articulate and forceful Executive Director, determined to make the Bank pay more attention to the East Asian experience and to rethink directed credit policies.

In September 1989 the dispute between the Bank and Japan's OECF over credit policies became explicit. Citing the case of the Philippines, a senior vice-president of the Bank wrote to the president of OECF—in charge of the ASEAN-Japan Development Fund —asking him to reconsider the policy of subsidized targeted loans: passing these funds to the banks and final beneficiaries at below market interest rates 'could have an adverse impact on development of the financial sector' and hence '*would create unnecessary distortions and set back the financial sector reforms*' which had been supported by the IMF's Extended Fund Facility and the Bank's Financial Sector Adjustment Loan.[8] The dispute highlighted the underlying differences of

---

[7] Masaki Shiratori was born in 1936, graduated from Tokyo University Law Faculty (1956–60), joined the Ministry of Finance in 1960, studied economics at Columbia University (1964–66), and was director of Coordination Division, International Finance Bureau (1984–85): after two more moves (1985-88), he became Senior Deputy Director-General of International Finance Bureau, then Executive Director for Japan, World Bank (1989–92), after which vice-president of the OECF (1992–). As chief of the International Financial Institutions division of the International Finance Bureau in 1981–84, in addition to raising Japan's rank in the IBRD, his second main goal was to get China accepted as a member of the Asian Development Bank, also successfully accomplished.

[8] Emphasis added. The letter was signed by senior operational vice-president Moeen Qureshi. The Bank's interpretation is as follows: the story began in 1986 when the Bank agreed to help the government of the Philippines restructure two major public-sector banks—including the Development Bank of the Philippines. The banks were both bankrupt, partly because they had become patronage pots—with directed credit as the primary means of patronage. Their restructuring involved eliminating directed credit. Then along came the Japan-ASEAN Fund offering directed credit with a substantial subsidy element for narrowly earmarked purposes—the same instrument the banks had been using to dispense patronage. This was very difficult for the Bank to swallow. 'I remember many heated meetings in Tokyo and here in Washington', said a Bank official closely involved.

8

view, the Japanese arguing that financial policies should be designed to advance a wider industrial strategy, the Bank insisting that credit should always and everywhere be at 'market' or non-subsidized rates.[9]

Japan's Executive Director made strong protests to the Bank's senior management and to the Board of Executive Directors from member governments. Many Executive Directors from developing countries agreed with the Japanese position, but to no avail; Bank management refused to back down. Japan's Ministry of Finance and its OECF began to fight back. A key figure was Isao Kubota, a senior MOF official then on loan to OECF as managing director of the pivotal Coordination Department.[10] He did two things. First, he established a team to write a paper setting out the broad principles of the Japanese government's understanding of structural adjustment. Second, he had discussions with Shiratori about how to get the Bank to pay more attention to the Japanese and wider East Asian development experience. This was the genesis of the *Miracle* study.

Meanwhile tensions were growing between Japan and the US as well. From May 1989 through to 1992, the two states were negotiating over market access—the Structural Impediments Initiative. The US tried to make the Japanese undertake domestic reforms of such features as the retail distribution system and the cross-ownership of firms, so making it more like the 'free market' or American system. The Japanese mostly resisted and in turn urged reform of US institutions. An American business executive in Tokyo later said about the wider relationship between Japan, on the one hand, and the US and Europe, on the other: 'The tired old technique of US and European leaders is to beat the Japanese with a piece of two by four. Not surprisingly, they resent it. They may be less cocky now that the economy is in recession, but there is a deep and growing and potentially damaging distrust of the West in the Tokyo corridors of power'.[11] Also during this period, Tokyo was flirting with membership in the Malaysian-sponsored East Asian Economic Caucus, from which the United States was excluded, while remaining cool to the American-endorsed Asia-Pacific Economic Cooperation forum.[12] This underlined Japan's new willingness to pursue a course apart from, and even opposed to, that of the US.

---

[9] On the contrast between the Japanese and American approaches to these issues, see Hidenobu Okuda, 'Japanese Two Step Loans: The Japanese Approach to Development Finance', *Hitotsubashi Journal of Economics*, no. 34, 1993, pp. 67–85. See also Isao Kubota, 'The East Asian Miracle—Major Arguments on Recent Economic Development Policy', *Finance* (MOF's monthly journal), December 1993 (in Japanese).

[10] Kubota graduated from Tokyo University Law Faculty in 1966, joining MOF immediately. He undertook a BPhil in Economics, Oxford University, 1967–69. In 1985 he became director of the International Organization division of the International Finance Bureau of MOF. Seven years and four postings later, he became Senior Deputy Director General of the International Finance Bureau, the same job Shiratori had had before going as Executive Director to the World Bank.

[11] Quoted in Kevin Rafferty, 'Sun Sets Upon Japanese Miracle', *The Guardian*, 15 January 1994, p.10. On the SII see Kozo Yamamura, ed., *Japan's Economic Structure: Should it Change?*, Society for Japanese Studies, 1990.

[12] See Chalmers Johnson, 'History Restarted: Japanese-American Relations at the End of the Century', in R. Higgott, R. Leaver, and J. Ravenhill, eds, *Pacific Economic Relations in the 1990s: Conflict or Cooperation?*, Boulder, CO 1993, pp. 39–61. And see his 'Wake up America!', *Critical Intelligence*, vol. 2, no. 8 (1994), for pungent views on a whole range of issues to do with Japan, Southeast Asia, and the US.

Back at the Bank, Lawrence Summers, a Harvard economist, joined as chief economist and vice-president in January 1991. Not noted for tact, he openly held the view that Japanese economists are 'second rate'. From January to June 1991, drafts of the Bank's *World Development Report 1991: The Challenge of Development*, underwent discussion within the Bank and the Board. Written under the leadership of a Chicago-trained economist, the report restated a largely free-market view of appropriate public policy for development, under the label 'market-friendly'. The term was coined by Summers who exerted influence at this late stage of the report to moderate the extreme free-market position of the earlier drafts, but in Japanese eyes it still remained extreme.

Blueprint for Development

Then in October 1991 the OECF—whose main parent ministry is the Ministry of Finance—issued the paper initiated by Kubota, entitled 'Issues Related to the World Bank's Approach to a Structural Adjustment: Proposal from a Major Partner'.[13] Its main points are as follows:

1) For a developing country to attain sustainable growth, the government must adopt 'measures aiming "directly" at promoting investment'.
2) These measures should be part of an explicit industrial strategy to promote the leading industries of the future.
3) Directed and subsidized credit has a key role in promoting these industries because of 'extensive failures in developing countries' financial markets.
4) Decisions about ownership arrangements, including privatization, should relate to actual economic, political and social conditions in the country concerned, not to the universal desirability of privatizing public enterprises. For example, there may be legitimate national sentiments about the desirability of foreign ownership.
5) 'Japanese fiscal and monetary policies in the post-war era may be worthy of consideration. These were centred on preferential tax treatment and development finance institutions' lendings.'[14]

---

[13] This is the OECF's *first* Occasional Paper, thirty years after its foundation in 1961.

[14] OECF, 'Issues Related to the World Bank's Approach to a Structural Adjustment: Proposal from a Major Partner', pp. 5–6. Isao Kubota was the chief promoter of the paper, supported by the president of the OECF, Mr. Nishigaki. They aimed to have the paper circulated widely at the Annual Meeting of the World Bank and the IMF in October 1991. Preparation was entrusted to Yasutami Shimamura, director of the Economic Analysis Department of OECF. In addition to drawing on the ideas of OECF people (notably Kubota and Kazumi Goto, a division chief in the Coordination Department), Shimamura also assembled a team of outside academic economists. They included professors Yanagihara (Hosei), Horiuchi (Tokyo), Horiuchi (JDB), Okuda (Hitotsubashi), Urata (Waseda). This group met once a month for five months. They 'found it very difficult to make a consensus' on the content of the Japanese critique, said a participant. Some of them saw little to criticize in the neoclassical paradigm, and others who were sceptical of it were hesitant to openly criticize the World Bank at this time. Eventually, with time before the Annual Meeting getting short, Shimamura wrote a draft, presented it to the research team, modified it to take account of reactions, and then presented it to the Board of OECF, even though some members of the research team were not happy with the result. The OECF Board approved release of the paper in time for it to be circulated at the Annual Meeting. The haste—and the overriding of the rule of consensus—came from the knowledge that if they missed the October deadline they would have to wait a year until the next Annual Meeting. The paper is very short (fourteen generously spaced pages in the English typescript) and the quality of the argumentation leaves much to be desired. It is published (in Japanese) in *OECF Research Quarterly*, no. 73, 1991.

Also in October 1991, at the Annual Meeting of the Board of Governors of the World Bank and the IMF, Yasushi Mieno, head of the Bank of Japan, the central bank,[15] said, 'Experience in Asia has shown that although development strategies require a healthy respect for market mechanisms, the role of the government cannot be forgotten. I would like to see the World Bank and the IMF take the lead in a wide-ranging study that would define the theoretical underpinnings of this approach and clarify the areas in which it can be successfully applied to other parts of the globe.'[16] Mieno's statement was prepared by the International Finance Bureau of the MOF. Isao Kubota—by now transferred back from OECF to a senior position in this same bureau, and drafter of Mieno's statement—later made the point more vividly to reporters: 'It's really incredible. They think their economic framework is perfect. I think they're wrong.'[17]

---

[14] (*cont.*)

Shimamura has a bachelor's degree in economics from Keio University (1960–63), and an MBA from Colombia University (1968–70). He is currently professor of economics at Saitama University. His father is Osamu Shimamura, the celebrated author of the Income Doubling Plan (and PhD in economics from Tohoku University). Kubota has elaborated his views in 'The Case for Two Step Loans', and 'Reflections on Recent Trends in Development Aid Policy', both read at a biannual meeting between the World Bank and the OECF/J-EXIM, in May and November 1991, respectively; and also in 'The Role of Domestic Saving and Macroeconomic Stability in the Development Process', Economic Society of Australia, *Economic Papers*, vol. 10, no. 2, (1991) pp. 34–42. Masaki Shiratori's views are set out in 'Development Assistance to Developing Countries: Japanese Model More Relevant than Simple Marketism', *Nihon Keizai Shimbun*, 20 May 1992 (in Japanese). Kazumi Goto gives his opinion in 'Japan Loan Aid in Perspective: Alice's Adventures in OECF-Land', OECF, London Office, 3 December 1993. See also the views of Akiyoshi Horiuchi (professor of economics, Tokyo University) in, 'Comments on OECF Occasional Paper Number 1', *OECF Research Quarterly 74*, 1992 (in Japanese).

[15] He was deputizing for the Finance Minister, who is the Governor of the Board for Japan.

[16] World Bank, press release no. 16, 15 October 1991, cited in Chalmers Johnson, 'Comparative Capitalism: The Japanese Difference', *California Management Review*, Summer 1993, pp. 51–67.

[17] Quoted in 'Japan Wants Strings on Aid: At Odds with us, Tokyo Urges Managed Economics', International Herald Tribune, 2 March 1992. Around this time, another event illustrated the divergence between the us and the Japanese position, and the Japanese willingness to challenge Bank management. In November 1991 the top management of the Bank and some key Western executive directors opposed publication of a study of World Bank support for industrialization in a number of industrializing countries (World Bank Support for Industrialization in Korea, India, and Indonesia, Washington, dc 1992). The study had been made by Sanjaya Lall, an Oxford economist, for the Operations Evaluation Department (OECD) of the Bank. It concluded that the Bank had failed to draw lessons from successful government intervention in Asian economies for the benefit of its lending practices elsewhere. One of the main lessons was that 'Industrial success at the national level depends on the interplay of three sets of factors: incentives, capabilities, and institutions...Just one set of factors by itself cannot lead to industrial development...Each of the three determinants of industrialization may suffer from market failure...Industrial strategy should address all these interrelated issues.' (ibid., pp. iv, v) The Bank, it said, has unwarrantedly discounted the positive role of industrial strategy, relying too heavily on incentives while underplaying the building up of capabilities and institutions. And it 'has only partially fulfilled the function of correctly analyzing Korea's experience with industrialization.' (p. vii) The report urged the Bank 'to help governments design industrial policies', and to 'adopt a more differentiated, nuanced approach to recommending policy packages to individual governments' (pp. 54, 55). The top management called for the report not to be made available outside the Bank until its conclusions had been suitably revised, on the grounds that it gave 'too strong an endorsement of government intervention...Even if the causes of government failure could be identified and minimized, the report calls for the impossible: fine-tuning an array of trade and industrial interventions to deal with real or perceived market failures is generally not feasible.' The report, says the

By late 1991 tension between Japan and both the Bank and the US was running high. Articles based on interviews with Japanese officials began appearing in the American and Japanese press with titles like 'Japan–US Clash Looms on World Bank Strategy'. The anonymous Japanese officials called the Bank's approach 'simple minded', resting on 'outmoded Western concepts that fail to take account of the successful strategy pursued by Japan and some of its Asian neighbours in developing their economies'.[18] Privately, those officials accused Bank economists of gross arrogance, of presuming to lecture them on why the Japanese government was doing the wrong things while at the same time asking for more Japanese money.

Another statement of Japanese principles came out in April 1992, in the form of MITI's blueprint for economic reconstruction and development in Russia. '*Western* industrial countries', it said, 'can make many suggestions to help Russia with its economic reform. This paper...focuses on what Russia can learn from *Japan's* experience...' It described its approach as being in 'stark contrast' to that of the IMF, presented in a report on Russia earlier the same year. 'Market mechanisms cannot be almighty', it claimed, expressing doubts about whether 'macroeconomic approaches', such as those advocated by the IMF, were sufficient to meet the chief need of revitalizing production. Japan's post-war economic renaissance could be used to formulate appropriate policies in, for example, the design of emergency measures to halt the plunge in output, and of 'priority production programmes' to ensure the supply of essential industrial goods. 'The worst choice would be to diversify investment in an all-out manner, because... what is now most needed is focus on specific sectors of particular importance as a way to increase overall production.'[19] In other words, Russia must as a matter of urgency have a *sector-specific* industrial policy.

III. Why the Japanese Challenge?

As the Japanese government greatly increased its capital contribution

---

[17] (*cont.*)
Bank, offers an approach that 'is at variance with best practices as we know them, and would therefore be very counter-productive to the country dialogues'. It would open the way for governments 'to point out that the Bank's own evaluation department has concluded that the Bank's current approach is incorrect'. (This text is taken from a memorandum sent from a senior vice-president to the chairman of the Joint Audit Committee, who was also the American Executive Director, 11 November 1991. The Joint Audit Committee, made up of representatives from the Board of Directors of the Bank—none from management—is the body to which the Operations Evaluation department reports, which is why the senior vice-president was unable to squash the report himself). Several executive directors, mostly from borrowing countries but including, crucially, Japan's, pressed the Bank to publish the study as is. They prevailed and the study was published.
[18] The title and quote come from an article by Rich Miller in the *Journal of Commerce*, 11 December 1991, p. 1a. See also 'Free Market Theory not Practical in Third World: Interview with Masaki Shiratori', *EIR*, 27 March 1992. And 'Japan Challenges World Bank Orthodoxy', *Far Eastern Economic Review*, 12 March 1992, p. 49; 'Japan Presses World Bank on Lending: Nation Begins Asserting Independent Voice in Global Forum', *The Nikkei Weekly*, 12 March 1992, p. 3.
[19] The plan was not formally a MITI document. It came out of the MITI Research Institute. See Fusae Ota, Hiroya Tanikawa, Tasuke Otani, 'Russia's Economic Reform and Japan's Industrial Policy', MITI Research Institute, typescript, n.d. (April 1992), emphasis added. For a summary, see Anthony Rowley, 'To Russia with Pride: Japan Offers Economic Model', *Far Eastern Economic Review*, 13 August 1992, pp. 59–60.

to the Bank, it wished, not surprisingly, to see its views more fully
reflected in Bank thinking. But why present itself as a champion of 'anti-
paradigmatic' views? As it becomes more powerful, why does it not endorse
free trade and obscure the mercantilist elements in its own history?

There are at least four possible reasons. The first is ideological conviction.
The senior officials in those parts of the government leading the challenge
genuinely believe that interventionist policies can be more effective than
the Bank's 'market-friendly' set of policies. They emphasize the role of
interventionist policies in Japan's own development—the ways in which
selective interventions can help Japanese aid be more effective. Being able
to demonstrate aid effectiveness is especially important when official
development assistance (ODA) has been largely exempt from the government's budget cuts. With many Japanese policy-makers disgruntled
about the amount of aid, the Finance Ministry is under constant pressure to
show it being well used. Indeed, said MOF officials, they have been criticized by other government agencies for being too focused upon aid effectiveness, for not paying enough attention to Japan's national interest.
Their reply is that making best use of aid money helps to stabilize the
world economy, which is also in Japan's national interest. Ideological conviction is especially intense on financial issues. The phrases, the 'moneymaking culture' and the 'thing-making culture', are in common use in
Japan, representing a widespread sense—as in Islamic condemnations of
usury—that making goods and providing services is intrinsically a more
worthy activity than making money by financial dealings, and that the
financial sector should be industry's servant.

The second reason for the challenge is organizational interest. The
Bank's criticism of Japan's concessional and directed aid schemes in
Southeast Asia were aimed at what MOF considered its greatest post-war
achievement. Directed credit was its principal industrial policy instrument in the post-war renaissance of Japan; effective use of directed credit
is the foundation of its claim to have played a major role in the 'miracle'.
The claim is reflected in the OECF's mandate to provide directed and concessional credit as part of the Japanese aid strategy. No wonder MOF—
and when we speak of 'Japan–World Bank' relations we mean MOF–
World Bank relations, for MOF jealously guards its monopoly—resents
hearing the Bank announce to the world that directed and concessional
credit can never be effective, all the more so since the Bank's claim rests
on near total ignorance of directed credit in North-east Asia.

The third reason is national material interest. Building a powerful market position across East and Southeast Asia is a top Japanese government
objective. Interventionist policies can potentially help Japanese firms
and the Japanese government consolidate profits and influence in the
region—enabling the Malaysian government, say, to give special support
to the Malaysian joint-venture partner of a Japanese firm, or to the
Japanese firm directly through targeted loans and protection.[20] Getting
the World Bank to admit the potential desirability of selective industrial

---

[20] The *Economist* gives its own gloss to this point. Talking about foreign car makers coming into Asian countries, it says, 'Once in, the foreigners have a nasty habit of becoming as
protectionist as any local. Their aim is to persuade Asian governments not to open up
their car markets or allow in new investors until their local operations have grown big
enough to become competitive' (15 October 1994, p. 81).

promotion would help to advance this agenda. But why might the Japanese government, or a part of it, wish to *advertise* the fact that it was playing by different rules in its aid programme? The answer may lie in the fact that the Bank had already strongly criticized Japan for doing so. This put the burden on Japan to show that playing by different rules could yield development outcomes better than those of the Bank—or to get the Bank to rethink.

The fourth reason is nationalism, the desire to overcome a sense of being judged inferior by representatives of other states—or in this case, multilateral financial institutions. This sentiment is caught in the phrase often heard in and about Japan, 'economic superpower and political pygmy', or in Ichiro Ozawa's likening of Japan to a dinosaur with a huge body but a tiny brain.[21] In response to the perception of being judged inferior, Japan adopted a state strategy of channelling economic activities so as to achieve independence from, leverage over, and respect in the eyes of other states, rather than to achieve consumer utility, private wealth, or freedom of society from government. As it has become during the 1980s a 'mature' economy with a very large role in the international economy, it has also frequently been criticized for lacking the leadership on the world stage befitting its economic might. There is a growing urge among Japanese officials, politicians and the general public for Japan to set this right. But how?

Japan cannot constantly bow to foreign—that is, US—pressure. It needs to be seen asserting its own views on appropriate rules for the international economy. These cannot be free-trade rules, for the free-trade ideology is already led by the US. It can differentiate its principles from those of the US by basing them on its own experience of economic nationalism, presenting them as general principles confirmed by other East Asian experience and as sources of meta-policies for developing countries today. On these grounds, it can present itself as the champion of developing countries in the governing councils of the international financial institutions. At the same time, its principles also stay away from the dangerous idea of Japanese uniqueness. No country has come to exercise a leadership role in the world system without claiming to represent a universalistic ideology. In short, the Japanese challenge to the World Bank can be seen as part of a wider attempt by the Japanese elite to develop an ideology that goes beyond Japanese uniqueness and yet remains distinct from free trade and orthodox liberalism.[22]

IV. The Bank's Resistance

Bank managers saw the Japanese ideas about the role of the state—

---

[21] Ichiro Ozawa, Nihon Kaizo Keikaku, p.17, cited in Chalmers Johnson, 'The Foundations of Japan's Wealth and Power and Why they Baffle the United States', typescript, UCSD 1993.

[22] What of the relative importance of the four reasons? One might proceed by comparing what the Japanese want for the World Bank and what they do in the Asian Development Bank. From the beginning they have had much more influence in the ADB than in the World Bank—from which one can infer that the pattern of ADB lending gives a close reflection of their principles. Relations between the Japanese President and the US Executive Director have been strained over the past several years, in connection with lending priorities and the need to raise the ADB's capital stock.

the emphasis on directed credit and the more general argument linking the appropriate role of the state to the amount of state 'capacity'[23] —as a serious threat. Why? First, because concessional credit from the Japanese aid budget makes World Bank credit less attractive. The Bank especially needs to find borrowers in East and Southeast Asia, where Japanese aid is concentrated, to raise the average quality of its loan portfolio. Second, the Japanese emphasis on directed credit as an instrument of the industrial policy of recipient governments runs flatly contrary to the Bank's emphasis on financial system deregulation, a central thrust of its macroeconomic reform formula through the 1980s. Third, if the Bank were to embrace the interventionist role of the state wanted by the Japanese government it would, in the eyes of its managers, risk its ability to borrow at the best rates on world money markets —and so face lower demand for its now more expensive funds. It would also risk its second most valuable asset after its government guarantees—its reputation as a country-rating agency, a kind of international Standard and Poors that signals to private investors where they should put their money.[24] Why would such dire consequences follow? Because the Bank's ability to borrow at the best rates and to act as a country-rating agency depends on its reputation among financial capitalists, which in turn depends on its manifest commitment to *their* version of 'sound' public policies. Their version is based on the premise that only one set of rules should apply to all participants in the international economy and that those rules should express a non-nationalistic role of the state.[25] If this premise constitutes an imperative from the Bank's point of view, it is because any change of mind could be very costly.

Fourth, if the Bank were to embrace the Japanese view, it would run against the strategic and diplomatic power of the US, which has used the Bank as an instrument of its own external infrastructural power to a greater degree than any other state. And the Bank would delegitimize itself in the eyes of American academic economics, with its belief in the overwhelming virtues of markets and its political agenda of deregulation—an agenda endorsed by those who do well out of free markets. The President of the Bank has always been an American; Americans are greatly over-represented at professional levels in the Bank relative to the US's shareholding; some two thirds of World Bank

---

[23] Max Weber, of course, would have agreed, and also Gunnar Myrdal.

[24] Standard and Poors is one of the two main US investment rating agencies.

[25] This, at least, is how Bank officials often state the matter. The truth is more complicated. The Bank's top-grade credit rating primarily depends upon its non-borrowing governments' guarantees and its first claimant status for borrowing governments—this status being enforced by knowledge that a non-repaying government will get no more aid from a World Bank-affiliated government. So the Bank's top-grade credit rating does not depend on financial markets' evaluation of the quality of its loan portfolio. Rather, the link between its credit rating and its reputation for 'sound' lending conditions comes via the legislatures of the non-borrowing governments. The decision to honour the guarantees would not, in practice, be automatic. The US Congress, in particular, would have to authorize the expenditure, and has a long history of delaying authorization of foreign appropriations. If it held a low opinion of the Bank, it might delay authorization of the guarantee expenditures for a long time. Whether it holds the Bank in disrepute depends on the Bank's reputation in the eyes of financial markets. Much of what the Bank says in its flagship publications is vetted with this in mind; see especially the two recent *World Development Reports* that have provided a broad overview of development experience and theory, those for 1987 and 1991.

economists are certified by US universities—and 80 per cent by North American or British universities.[26]

Fifth, the Bank's constitution requires it to be 'apolitical', and the single meta-policy, sanctioned as it claims to be by a transcendent and apolitical 'economic rationality', helps the Bank preserve the claim of 'political impartiality'. One of the most important conceptual contributions of the Bretton Woods conference—which created the World Bank and the IMF—was the idea of equal treatment of all members of the new financial order. It was intended to avoid the politicization of the 1920s international rescue operations. There would be no 'favourites', but a community of states supporting each other at times of difficulty by means of a universalistic set of rules. To now admit the potential efficacy of sector-specific industrial policies would require the Bank to discriminate between countries in terms of such factors as government capacity and corruption, on the quite reasonable grounds that industrial policies are unlikely to be effective in states whose governments are thoroughly corrupt. But doing so would expose it to the charge of being 'political', and open it to pressure from *borrowers* saying, 'You urged/allowed country X to do A, why can't we?'[27]

Sixth, commitment to the Bank's meta-policy allows the organization to act quickly and concertedly. The meta-policy is derived from neoclassical economics and receives the endorsement of most US- and UK-trained economists who took control of the Bank from top to bottom over the 1980s; technical specialists—engineers, agronomists, health specialists, and so forth—were removed from operational management positions or not replaced when they retired.[28] The common commitment to the neoclassical meta-policy by the Bank's management cadre helps senior management to overcome the 'agency' problem of subordinates exercising discretion in ways they do not like. It keeps the whole management spine in proper alignment. It also allows country departments to be efficient advice givers. Policies seen to be inconsistent with neoclassical normative theory are excluded from the start. Of course, the Bank's lending practices on the ground have often differed from what the recipe calls for. But the case-by-case modifications come from the need to adjust pragmatically to 'political realities', not from a belief that the *economics* of the meta-policy might be less than universal. (So China, with one of the most interventionist, price-distorting governments of all, was the Bank's

[26] This is based on the staff of the research complex (PRE) in 1991. Of the total 465 Higher Level Staff, 290 had graduate degrees from US universities, 74 from the UK, 10 from Canada, and none from Japan. I thank Devesh Kapur for this information.

[27] In fact, since the early 1990s, the Bank *has* begun to talk more overtly about politics, but warily and in the reassuringly technical language of governance—'accountability', 'transparency', 'predictability', and so on. Even this has generated unease and opposition within the Bank and the Board, on the grounds that it risks being inconsistent with the charter. The issue came to a head in a Board discussion about a research department study, three years in the making, entitled 'Bureaucrats in Business', in July 1995, when some Executive Directors argued strongly that the Bank should not be talking about these issues—the French Executive Director in particular, perhaps with governance in ex-French Sub-Saharan African countries in mind.

[28] Nick Stern, 'The Bank as an Intellectual Actor', paper for World Bank History project, London School of Economics, 1993. See also John Markoff and Veronica Montecinos, 'The Ubiquitous Rise of Economists', *Journal of Public Policy*, vol. 13, no. 1 (1993), pp. 37–68.

fastest growing borrower over the 1980s. The Bank and China need each other—China to get finance and intellectual help, the Bank to lend to a big absorber with little debt.) At the level of principles, the neoclassical and largely free-market meta-policy is insulated from particular modifications.

Seventh, the Bank sees the Japanese position as posing a threat not only to itself but to its borrowers. The Japanese position requires the low-income country state to play a *strategic* role in governing the integration with the world economy—maintaining the relative separation of the domestic and international spheres for policy making—not just the role of transmission belt from the 'realities' of the world economy to the national economy. Such a strategic role, says the Bank, generally *lowers* national welfare. Even if some evidence suggests that some governments some of the time have played this role effectively, 90 per cent of governments have been unable to. Notwithstanding this, the vested interests pushing governments to intervene in counter-productive ways are so powerful that governments will go on doing so unless hindered by some impartial and powerful agency—the World Bank and the IMF, for example. The Japanese views, says the Bank, give unwelcome legitimacy to such interventionist impulses.

Finally, even if such policies raise national welfare in a single case, they can do so only by 'free riding' on the restraint of others—promoting industries to compete in US markets while closing the domestic market to US exports, for example. So the Japanese principles cannot be practised by all at the same time, and in that sense pose a *systemic* threat.

These eight reasons radically over-determine the Bank's reaction of alarm and denial to the pro-interventionist views of its second biggest shareholder. But the danger could be diffused and confrontation contained as long as the Bank did not have to deal explicitly with the causes of East Asia's economic success; in dealing with other regions or with 'development-in-general', it could simply ignore Japanese ideas about development strategy. On the other hand, if it did have to examine in depth the causes of this success, a more or less explicit statement about the validity of apparently very different views would have to be made. Given Japan's power, that resolution would have to make some concession to Japanese views, for otherwise the number two shareholder would lose too much face and become less cooperative. The Japanese MOF decided to force the issue.

V. Making the Miracle: Stage One

To recap: in 1989 the Bank made a strong criticism of the Japanese aid agency, OECF, for its credit policies in Southeast Asia. In response, senior MOF officials considered how to get the Bank to be more 'pragmatic' and heed the experience of Japan and other East Asian economies.

In 1991, soon after the arrival of Lewis Preston as the new president of the World Bank, the Japanese MOF pressed the Bank to make a thorough study of East Asian development experience. The Bank's senior management was reluctant to permit the study, but agreed for two reasons. First, the Japanese would pay for it, the Bank having to bear only the time cost of its own staff.[29] Second, in return for the Bank's concession, the Japanese agreed to drop their opposition to the draft Operational Directive on Financial Sector Operations, which urged full-scale financial deregulation.[30] In January 1992 the study got under way, with a budget of $1.2 million from the Japanese trust fund. It was to be written over eighteen months for publication at the time of the Annual Meeting in September 1993.[31]

The core study, giving the overall analysis and conclusions, was to be based in the Bank's research complex under Lawrence Summers and Nancy Birdsall (the director of the research department, an American). They appointed John Page (DPhil in economics from Oxford, undergraduate in economics at Stanford, another American) to head the study. Page put together a team of six people, all with PhDs in economics, all but one from American universities.[32] None had adult experience of living and working in Asia.

There were also to be a number of case-studies of countries organized by the Bank's East Asia vice-presidency; some to be written by authors inside the Bank, others by outside consultants. The outsiders were offered $10,000 per case-study, and required to submit drafts in six

---

[29] The money came from Japan's amply endowed Policy and Human Resource Development trust fund for the World Bank. Many rich country members of the Bank have trust funds which are controlled jointly by the member country and the Bank to cover jointly agreed operational expenses of the Bank. 20 per cent of the Bank's operational budget is now met from trust funds. The great advantage of this arrangement from the rich countries' view is that each government has a direct say in how 'its' money is used. If, at the same time, these countries squeeze the regular budget, they are able to gain pleasing *bilateral* influence over the Bank. In the late 1980s, the Bank had similarly got the governments which had been voicing concern about the impact of structural adjustment programmes on vulnerable groups—the 'soft' northern governments—to finance much of the Bank's work on the design of anti-poverty programmes.

[30] It emerged as Operational Directive 8.30, Financial Sector Operations, February 1992. It was largely the work of those who had earlier written the Levy Report. The Japanese were its main opponents in the Board.

[31] The Bank's staff costs were about $800,000 ($150,000/year × 1.5 years × 3.5 persons). The Bank provided another $200,000 for miscellaneous costs. This brought the total *Miracle* budget to $2.2 million, about the same as for a *World Development Report*.

[32] Other Bank staff included Ed Campos (Filipino, US PhD in the social sciences but de facto in economics, from Caltech, working on institutional issues), Marylou Uy (Filipina, US PhD in economics from UCLA, working on financial issues). Page, Campos and Uy worked full-time on the study; Birdsall worked half-time. The main consultants included Max Corden (Australian, trade economist, working on macroeconomics); Joseph Stiglitz (American, economic theorist, working on finance); Howard Pack (American, development economist, University of Pennsylvania, working on tests of the effectiveness of selective industrial policy); Richard Sabot (American, development economist, Williams College, working on human capital). Nancy Birdsall also worked with Sabot on human capital. A commentator on an earlier draft, who helped to manage the study, queried my presentation of the personnel: 'Why do you emphasize the fact of so many Americans? It seems you are implying that because we are Americans we had pre-determined conclusions. In fact, we were eager to find a story that would be new. Anyway, you are misleading because the team's composition was about average for World Bank economists.' It is true that the Bank employs very few East Asian economists—but a lot of US-or UK-certified South Asian economists. Experience of employing Japanese economists has been disappointing, perhaps because the Bank is unwilling to hire in groups.

months—so their research had to be largely off-the-shelf. In addition, several background papers on Japan were commissioned from Japanese scholars.

Although it got the country studies, the East Asia vice-presidency felt passed over. The vice-president for East Asia, Gautam Kaji, first heard of the study at a board meeting. Asked by an executive director for his views about the proposed study, he confessed not to know about it. Summers bypassed the East Asia vice-presidency, aware that its senior managers and economists held views towards the free market extreme of the Bank's range. The rivalry between the core team in the research complex and the East Asia vice-presidency was to shape the arguments of the study.

At the same time, a parallel and complementary project was initiated, again with Japanese funding, to examine the effect of directed credit in Japan. This was undertaken on behalf of the Bank by the Japan Development Bank, reviewing its own programmes. Its conclusions were to feed into the *Miracle* study.[33] A third Japanese-funded study about Japan, 'The Evolution, Character and Structure of the Japanese Civil Service, and its Role in Shaping the Interrelationships between the Government and the Private Sector', was undertaken by the Bank's educational arm, the Economic Development Institute (EDI), for use in World Bank teaching courses. Suddenly the Bank was paying a lot more research attention to Japan than ever before, thanks to Japanese initiative and Japanese money.[34]

From early 1992 to early 1993, the first drafts of the *Miracle* chapters were written and discussed within the core group. John Page was given a free hand by senior managers, with no hint of the expected conclusions. Lawrence Summers urged him to think in new ways, to listen carefully to the Japanese arguments. 'We were eager to find a story that would be new, all the more so because the Bank's standard "market-friendly" story had already been told in *World Development Report 1991*', said Page later. Indeed, Summers' reaction to Page's proposed names for the team was: 'Too neoclassical, you will be seen as trying to force East Asian data into a neoclassical strait-jacket'. Page responded that for the report to have an impact in the Bank, it had to use the language of neoclassical economics: the team stayed as he proposed.

The team members accepted that East Asian governments implemented policies at substantial variance from the Bank's orthodoxy, but they found it difficult to unearth clear evidence about the causal impact of these non-orthodox policies on economic growth. Wrestling with this issue for many months, they eventually concluded: 'It is possible that some of these non-orthodox policies helped some of the time, but, with some exceptions, we can't show it'.

Also at this time, this version of the 'institutional basis' chapter was

---

[33] The JDB's data were also made available to two American economists for independent econometric assessment of the effectiveness of the credit policies.
[34] There was also a comparative study of tax systems in Japan, Taiwan, Korea, and India. The additional studies had a combined budget of $1.8 million from the Japanese Trust Fund.

restructured. This version had taken as its main question, 'What features of East Asian institutions enabled these economies to avoid the costs that befall equally interventionist and authoritarian states elsewhere; or why did their many strategic interventions not lead to massive rent-seeking?' It presented government–business consultative councils, for example, as an institutional device that reduced the authoritarian character of East Asian political regimes by providing an institutionalized channel of feedback from the people directly affected by business policies. Birdsall and Page thought this might be interpreted as sanctioning authoritarianism and interventionism—as saying, 'If you have institutional features X, Y, and Z you can avoid the expected costs of authoritarianism and interventionism'. In the rewriting, this theme was much diluted. The chapter was brought into line with the report's larger argument that East Asian states are more successful because they are *less* interventionist, and the implication that some authoritarianisms are better than others was removed.

VI. Making the Miracle: Stage Two

Around March 1993 the second stage of the production process began with rounds of discussion at successively higher levels of the approval hierarchy. A full-time editor, Lawrence MacDonald, was hired from the *Asia Wall St. Journal*.[35] Over the next several months he and Page sent material back and forth, the editor revising the drafts in line with comments, Page commenting on the editor's revisions, the editor taking on board Page's comments and resubmitting to Page. The editor was the only person on the project with work experience in Asia. He attempted to inject some discussion of cultural propensities to save and educate, and of the role of the overseas Chinese. The team rejected these suggestions, the former for being too difficult to pin down with evidence, the second for being too liable to be taken as racist.

To discuss the drafts, many meetings were held with people from the East Asia vice-presidency which had something close to a veto over the study being approved for sending to the Board—and thence for public release. The East Asia staff attacked the work for excessive emphasis on government intervention. 'Where is the *evidence* for what you are saying?', they demanded. The East Asia vice-presidency was well versed in demolishing arguments about the efficacy of industrial policy, its chief economist having just co-authored a book reiterating a largely free-market interpretation of East Asian economic success;[36] its vice-president, still smarting from being excluded from the study's initiation, provided support for such challenges. Its representatives badgered the team about 'strategy'—as in the working subtitle, 'Strategies for Rapid Growth' and phrases like 'a strategic approach to growth'. Such phrases could be misconstrued to mean that East Asian growth was due primarily to 'strategic' interventions in industrial policy, or even to sanction the idea of an alternative East Asian type of capitalism. The East Asia

[35] MacDonald, also an American, worked intensively on the drafts and redrafts from March to September 1993.
[36] Ramgopal Agarwala and Vinod Thomas, *Sustaining Rapid Growth in East Asia and the Pacific*, World Bank Publications, Washington DC 1993.

representatives also argued, more generally, that the Bank had an interest in getting the market-friendly approach, as set out in the *World Development Report 1991*, accepted as the correct approach to economic policy in all developing countries, and it would look odd if the study of East Asia, of all regions, did not embrace it too. Not coincidentally, the *World Development Report 1991* was written by a team headed by the man who was then chief economist for East Asia.

The spectacle of the East Asia vice-presidency evacuating upon the draft convinced Page and Birdsall of the need to make concessions if the draft was to proceed up the approval hierarchy. What could they concede? First, they recognized that 'strategy' and 'strategic' implied—at least to the East Asia vice-presidency—a stronger argument about the efficacy of industrial policy than they wished to make, and were distracting attention from the substance of the argument about market failures. All references to strategy were therefore deleted, being replaced, where necessary, with the innocuous 'functional', as in 'a functional approach to growth'.[37] Second, they praised the market-friendly approach in several places. Lewis Preston's preface was made more explicit: 'The authors conclude that rapid growth in each economy was primarily due to the application of a set of common, market-friendly economic policies'.[38] At this late stage, the editor was asked to write a box summarizing the ideas and evidence for the market-friendly approach.[39] He wrote, 'In the past twenty years a consensus has emerged among economists on the best approach to economic development... These ideas have crystallized into what is now called the "market-friendly" approach.'

By making these concessions, Page and Birdsall hoped to protect two key ideas in what they had earlier called 'strategy'. One was that growth is a function of three sets of policies—those to foster accumulation, efficient allocation, and growth in productivity. Whereas the standard, market-friendly neoclassical argument stresses the need for good performance on all of four dimensions—macroeconomic stability, trade openness, human capital, and a rule-based system hospitable to the private sector—Page and Birdsall thought that there is some substitutability between the policies for accumulation, allocation, and productivity. Hence it is conceptually possible that costs in allocative efficiency (due to distorting industrial policies) are more than offset by gains in productivity (due to learning). The second idea is that markets—effective coordinating mechanisms for private agents in many contexts—may not work well for large and uneven investments in the early stages of development; for these, other mechanisms are needed, such as 'deliberative councils'. But how to stop deliberative councils from becoming cosy havens for sharing out rents? Through contests between selected firms competing within tight rules and under the watchful eye of the government as referee.[40]

---

[37] *The East Asian Miracle: Economic Growth and Public Policy*, p. 88, figure 2.1.
[38] Ibid., p. vi.
[39] Ibid., box 2.1, p. 85.
[40] 'Government as referee' has a powerful resonance in neoclassical economics, and the link to contests takes it towards East Asian realities; but it obscures the point that the government sometimes acts as both referee and player at the same time.

Other parts of the report also came in for strong criticism from elsewhere in the Bank—all the more so now that Summers had left[41]—but in the final version they appeared little changed. The section on directed credit and financial repression was attacked for making too many concessions to the view that these instruments could sometimes work. Page countered that the section did not, as the critics contended, repudiate the Bank line: it clearly stated that there is no *proof* that directed credit worked in Japan and Korea but also that the normal adverse effects of directed credit are *not* seen in those countries. Similarly on the wider question of financial repression, Page countered trenchant internal criticism by urging the critics to read carefully what the text actually said. While admitting the fact of financial repression in Japan and Korea, the text's explanation for why the normal adverse effects on growth are not observed was not out-of-line with established Bank thinking: these effects are not apparent because the degree of repression has been *moderate*—thanks to macroeconomic balance and only slightly concessional interest rates for priority uses. This section of the report was of greatest interest to its Japanese sponsors. Its credibility was bolstered by the pre-eminent status in the American economics profession of its main author, Joseph Stiglitz, winner of the John Bates Clark medal for outstanding work by an economist under the age of forty. In the event, despite all the criticism, the section was left largely unchanged.

The 'institutional basis' chapter, though already diluted, was attacked as the document proceeded up the hierarchy of approval. Many critics called for references to authoritarianism to be dropped. Birdsall and Page defended the chapter successfully, managing to retain oblique references to authoritarianism.[42]

As the deadline loomed, intense effort was made to present a consistent message.[43] The Bank's senior in-house editor was called in. He pasted each chapter page by page along the wall of a conference room. Together with several members of the team, he took a bird's-eye view, suggesting how to bring the messages up front. He paid special attention to the headings, on the presumption that many readers do not go beyond them. Headings should themselves give the argument, he urged. Parts of the draft were revised to emphasize the neoclassical 'fundamentals'. Results of the econometric tests of the effectiveness of selective industrial policy were rephrased to make them more clearly contra than in the original draft.

Page later explained his principle for responding to criticism: if he agreed that the evidence was not strong enough to support a certain proposition, he toned down the statement, regardless of whether it

---

[41] To be Under Secretary to the Treasury for International Affairs in the new Clinton administration.

[42] See for example, *The East Asian Miracle*, p.188.

[43] The draft was also debated in a Singapore round-table discussion (including senior or ex-senior government officials from Singapore, Malaysia and Indonesia) and in Tokyo—three meetings with individual senior officials who gave detailed comments on the first draft: Kubota (MOF), Tsukuda (number two in the OECF), and Ogata (Deputy Governor, Bank of Japan). Individual chapters were presented by members of the Bank team to academic seminars in Singapore, Indonesia, and Korea.

was Bank orthodoxy or not. At the same time, he had to recognize that this was a World Bank document with an 'anonymous' author that sets out a 'Bank' position. So it should steer between the extremes, never straying outside the range of views represented within the Bank. Yet the team members were also anxious not simply to repeat the Bank's standard line, and saw themselves as a vanguard pushing out the frontiers of debate. They were also well aware of the importance of Japan to the World Bank and of Japan's interest in the conclusions. A senior manager later remarked: 'Without the strong leadership of Larry Summers, Nancy Birdsall, and John Page, the report would not have moved anything like as far [from Bank orthodoxy] as it did.'

VII. Argument and Evidence

The final document bears traces of the three-way tussle between Japan, the research vice-presidency, and the East Asian vice-presidency. It concedes for the first time in a major Bank publication the *fact* of extensive government intervention in most of East Asia. It also grants the argument that some of these interventions, in the areas of exports and credit, *may* have fostered growth and equity in some parts of East Asia. Further, the report states that 'More selective interventions—forced savings, tax policies to promote (sometimes very specific) investments, sharing risk, restricting capital outflow, and repressing interest rates also *appear to have succeeded* in some HPAEs [High Performing Asian Economies], especially Japan, Korea, Singapore, and Taiwan, China.'[44] And again: 'Our evidence leads us to conclude that credit programmes directed at exports yielded high social returns and, in the cases of Japan and Korea, other directed-credit programmes also *may have increased investment and generated important spill-overs*.'[45]

Lewis Preston's preface is significant because it is the President who ultimately must keep the main shareholders happy, and in this case the number two shareholder evidently needed to be made less unhappy. The preface was written within the core team and did not have to fight its way past the East Asian vice-presidency. It says, for example, 'This diversity of [East Asian] experience reinforces the view that economic policies and policy advice must be country-specific, if they are to be effective …The report also breaks some new ground. It concludes that in some economies, mainly those in Northeast Asia, *some selective interventions contributed to growth*, and it advances our understanding of the conditions required for interventions to succeed…These prerequisites suggest that the institutional context within which policies are implemented is as important to their success or failure as the policies themselves.'[46] These are Japanese-style statements. Despite all the pressures for the Bank not to admit it has been wrong, the President of the Bank here hints at just that. The preface does not even use the normal protective cover; it says 'some selective interventions contributed to growth', without the 'may have'. A cynic might say that the 'some selective interventions

---

[44] *The East Asian Miracle*, p. 242, emphasis added.
[45] Ibid., p. 356, emphasis added.
[46] Ibid., p. vi, emphasis added.

contributed to growth' statement by Preston, plus the line in the text on page 356 ('other directed-credit programmes also may have increased investment and generated important spill-overs') are the nuggets for which the Japanese paid $1.2 million.

The rest of the text takes a much stronger anti-industrial policy line. The flavour of the overall document is expressed in statements like 'industrial policies were largely ineffective', and 'We conclude that promotion of specific industries generally did not work and therefore holds little promise for other developing economies'.[47] It is not surprising that the bulk of the report gives a strong endorsement of established World Bank ideas. We saw earlier why the Japanese ideas constitute a serious threat. But the Bank cannot credibly reject ideas just because they are a threat. It has to claim to reject them on the evidence—of which the *Miracle* provides lots for its anti-industrial policy arguments.

The trouble, as several analysts have shown, is that most of the evidence does not survive serious scrutiny.[48] Here are three examples:

1) The key proposition that more open economies grow faster than closed ones is based on the finding that indicators of openness are positively correlated with growth in the basic growth regression. One indicator of openness is an index constructed by David Dollar. As Dani Rodrik argues, the index is really a measure of real exchange rate divergence, not of openness.[49] But if used as an index of openness, Dollar's own published results reveal that Japan and Taiwan were *less open* during 1976–85 than Argentina, Brazil, India, Mexico, the Philippines, and Turkey—a result ignored by the *Miracle* study. Rodrik concludes that the evidence presented for the proposition that more open economies grow faster is simply not relevant. To the extent that it is, it points the other way. And here as throughout, had China been included, the evidence would have pointed still more strongly the other way.[50] Since the early 1980s, China has been outperforming most developing countries, yet it has remained —while liberalizing—much less liberal than most, with extensive controls on finance, trade and industry.

2) The report says that 'price distortions were mild', or that 'East Asia's relative prices of traded goods were closer on average to international

[47] Ibid., pp. 312, 354.
[48] See the papers by Rodrik, Wade and Haggard in Fishlow et al, eds, *Miracle or Design?*; Ajit Singh, 'How did East Asia Grow so Fast? Slow Progress Towards an Analytical Consensus', UNCTAD Discussion Paper no. 97, 1995; Alice Amsden, 'Why Isn't the Whole World Experimenting with the East Asian Model to Develop? Review of *The East Asian Miracle*', *World Development*, vol. 22, no. 4, (1994) pp. 627–34; Sanjay Lall, 'The *East Asian Miracle*: Does the Bell Toll for Industrial Strategy?', *World Development*, vol. 22, no. 4, (1994) pp. 645–54; Aadne Cappelan and Jan Fagerberg, 'East Asian Growth: A Critical Assessment', *Forum for Development Studies*, no. 2, 1995. See further, Michael Hirsh, 'The State Strikes Back', *Institutional Investor*, September 1992, pp. 82–92 (for which I was a prime source).
[49] Dani Rodrik, 'King Kong Meets Godzilla: The World Bank and the East Asian Miracle', in *Miracle or Design?*, pp. 35–9.
[50] The set of High Performing Asian Economies includes Japan, Taiwan, South Korea, Hong Kong, Singapore, Thailand, Malaysia, Indonesia; not China and not the Philippines.

24

prices than other developing areas'.[51] This generalization is important
for the argument that, while industrial policies existed in East Asia, their
magnitude was slight. But the report also acknowledges that the relative
prices of Japan, Korea, and Taiwan deviated *more* from international
prices than those of such notorious interventionists as India, Pakistan,
Brazil, Mexico, and Venezuela in 1976-85, another finding it does not
comment upon.[52] How does it reach the vital conclusion about low average price distortions? By averaging the price distortion scores of all eight
East Asian cases, including the Hong Kong and Singapore minnows.

3) One of the tests of the effectiveness or otherwise of sector-specific
industrial promotion uses the correlation between growth in output or
value added by different industries, and the level of wages or value added
per worker in the same industries.[53] If sectoral industrial policies made a
difference, the argument goes, we expect a positive correlation, because
industrial policies aim to favour capital- and technology-intensive
industries and these factor intensities are proxied by high wages. So if industries that grow faster also have higher wages, this means that the
more capital- or technology-intensive industries are growing faster, and
industrial policies can be declared successful. Conversely, if the correlation is negative we have grounds for concluding that structural change is
driven not by industrial policy but by market forces. It can be argued
that the test is mis-specified.[54] But the problem is with what the report
does with its own evidence. The results for several time periods yield
mostly positive correlations (pro-industrial policy) for Hong Kong, and
Japan, and mostly negative ones (pro-free-market forces) for Taiwan and
Korea. But none of the results is statistically significant—except the
negative correlations for Korea. The report still concludes that these
results confirm the *ineffectiveness* of industrial policy in East Asia.

The Middle Road

Once such standards of inference are allowed to leak into what we call
'evidence', confirming results can be pumped out like bilge water.[55] It is
a fine irony that when the one member of the team with work experience
in Asia suggested some discussion of cultural propensities to save and
educate, he was told the matter could not be discussed because of lack of
evidence. The weakness of evidence notwithstanding, the argument
sweeps to its paradigm-protecting conclusions on the strength of several
rhetorical techniques. One is to structure an argument as a triptych with
two extremes and a middle, our confidence in the middle being elevated
by the foolishness of what flanks it. In the *Miracle* we are shown two
cartoonish interpretations of East Asian success—laissez faire and government intervention—and then the sensible market-friendly approach
in between. This was, however, a late addition. Together with the
removal of 'strategy' and 'strategic', it was part of the price of acquiescence from the East Asian vice-presidency, and the means by which the

---

[51] *The East Asian Miracle*, pp. 24, 301.
[52] Ibid., p. 301.
[53] Ibid., table A6.2.
[54] As does Rodrik in 'King Kong Meets Godzilla'.
[55] There are many other examples of dubious evidence in the report; see the papers by
Rodrik, Wade and Haggard in *Miracle or Design?*, and the references cited therein.

chief economist of the East Asia region could propel the conclusions of his *World Development Report 1991* to the forefront of the Bank's thinking on development. The report also seeks to persuade by ignoring serious alternative explanations of East Asian economic success. The main alternatives to such ideas as 'market-friendly policies plus export-push policies yield export-led growth' are not 'laissez faire' or 'government intervention'. Indeed, no serious scholar has argued that the difference between East Asia and elsewhere is to be explained mainly in terms of government intervention.

The main alternative, rather, is 'favourable initial conditions—especially human capital and infrastructure—plus investment-led growth'. The causality runs from higher investment to faster technical change and higher imports, and from these to higher exports—these exports being more a result than a cause.[56] Certainly, export growth helped to maintain the key driving force—high rates of return on accumulation (by permitting economies of scale), but so, too, did rising skill levels and an array of government policies designed to boost productivity and keep the lid on income inequality. Sectoral industrial policies enter the explanation as an important cause of high rates of *aggregate* investment as well as a cause of the structure of that investment, helping East Asia to move quickly from the 'factor-cost' driven stage of competitiveness to the 'investment' driven stage.[57] Of course the report notes the fact of unusually high investment in East Asia, but sees it as more a *result* of market-friendly policies and export-push than as being itself the primary proximate driver—though without doing the econometric tests to examine the causality. As for the fast growth of Southeast Asia—Thailand, Malaysia, Indonesia—the report assumes the causes to lie in domestic factors, and fails to examine the extent to which their growth can be explained in terms of spill-over effects from the fast growth of the more nationally focused, governed-market economies of East Asia.

Furthermore, the report tries to persuade by employing asymmetrical standards of evidence. As the drafts progressed, the many critics who asked 'what exactly is your evidence?' were concerned only with the pro-intervention propositions. They took for granted that if the evidence was not compelling it should be discounted, but did not apply the same scrutiny to propositions in favour of the free market. The market is innocent until proven guilty, the government is guilty until proven innocent.

---

[56]Indeed, Irene Trella and John Whalley go so far as to conclude, from their own quantitative analysis and that of others, that 'outward-oriented policies in Korea have little significance in driving growth'. Trella and Whalley, 'The Role of Tax Policy in Korea's Economic Growth', in T. Ito and A. Krueger, eds, *The Political Economy of Tax Reform*, Chicago 1992. See also Colin Bradford, 'From Trade-Driven Growth to Growth-Driven Trade: Reappraising the East Asian Development Experience', OECD Development Center, 1992; Dani Rodrik, 'Getting Interventions Right: How South Korea and Taiwan Grew Rich', mimeo, Economics Department, Columbia University, 1994; UNCTAD, 'The Visible Hand and the Industrialization of East Asia', *Trade and Development Report*, 1994; and Robert Wade, *Governing the Market*, pp. 47–8, chapters 6 and 9. Nor does the report examine what many analysts, though few economists, consider to be central to East Asia's economic success: the 'informal sector', the skeins of relational networks that operate behind the apparently formal institutions of finance, business and government across the region.
[57] M.E. Porter, *The Competitive Advantage of Nations*, New York 1990, ch. 10.

Finally, the report fails to make explicit some key distinctions, with the effect of allowing readers more scope for interpreting the results in line with their preconceptions. The striking case in point concerns credit. The Japanese were especially interested in getting the Bank to admit that directed credit—targeted at particular sectors—had worked in Japan and elsewhere in East Asia. But the Bank is deeply committed to the view that selective industrial promotion cannot raise national welfare, and so needs to conclude that it did not do so in East Asia. Since directed credit is, it would seem, simply one instrument of selective industrial policy, the two propositions—Japan's directed credit, the Bank's selective industrial policy—cannot both be true at the same time. Yet the report manages to imply that they are. It does so by classifying interventions into three ostensibly non-overlapping categories: selective industrial policies, directed credit policies, and export-push policies. It concludes that the first failed, the third worked, and as for the second— the focus of Japanese interest—it states, as we have seen, 'that credit programmes directed at exports yielded high social returns, and, in the cases of Japan and Korea, other directed credit programmes also may have increased investment and generated important spill-overs'.[58] On the face of it, this says that for Japan and Korea directed credit may have been *effective* as an instrument of sectoral industrial policy, though the report also claims that sectoral industrial policy did *not* work. Dani Rodrik writes that 'It is difficult to fathom how [such a logical inconsistency] found its way into the report (and as a major conclusion, to boot).'[59]

Part of the reason was an editorial failure to make a clear distinction between two types of 'directed' or 'selective' policies: 'functional' and 'sectoral', where 'functional' refers to a non-sector-specific function, like R&D or exports, and 'sectoral' refers to specific sectors—chemicals or machine tools, for example. When the text talks of 'selective' industrial policy it means 'sectoral' or 'sector-specific'; when it talks of 'selective' or 'directed' credit policy, however, it means 'functional'. Its only evidence on directed credit for other than exports comes from a study of the effects of subsidized R&D credit in Japan—that is, a study of a functionally-directed, not sectorally-directed credit policy. On the basis of this study, the report says that (functionally) directed credit worked in Japan in the sense that it had higher social returns than private returns, made a net addition to R&D investment rather than substituting for more expensive commercial credit, and was cut off when no longer needed. So the Bank's conclusion about directed or selective credit applies to functionally-selective policy, while its conclusion about selective industrial policy applies to sectorally-selective policy. Why was such an obvious source of confusion allowed to persist? The effect of fudging the distinction between functional and sectoral was to allow those sympathetic to the Japanese position on credit to infer a greater agreement with that position than was actually the case.

VIII. Responses

In August 1993 the World Bank executive directors (EDs, the represen-

---

[58] *The East Asian Miracle*, p. 356.
[59] Rodrik, 'King Kong Meets Godzilla', p. 28.

tatives of member states who act as overseers) considered the final draft. Their reactions showed nothing like consensus. The US ED gave a glowing endorsement of what he took to be the free-market message of the report. (Some of the core team were disturbed to hear how he spin-doctored all their qualifications away.) The newly arrived Japanese ED was cautiously complimentary. The Argentinian ED said, angrily, that the whole report was an apologia for interventionism. The Indian ED came close to saying that the report's anti-interventionist conclusions were fixed in advance and the evidence tailored to fit. Few changes were made in response to the Board's comments. If one is being attacked from all sides, Page later explains, the argument must be about right. Indeed, unknown to the EDs, the document had already been typeset by the time of the Board discussion to ensure readiness for the Annual Meetings. It could not have been changed even if the EDs agreed on changes.[60] The incident illustrates the independence of the Bank staff from the Board, despite the Board's status as the supervisory body representing member countries.

On September 26, 1993, exactly on time, *The East Asia Miracle: Economic Growth and Public Policy* was launched at the Annual Meetings of the World Bank and IMF. There was a press conference, a press release, and a seminar for Annual Meeting participants. The report 'sells itself', because of outside interest. The diversity of views among the EDs was a microcosm of reactions outside the Bank. In the press, for example, some journalists (mainly Japanese) said that the study confirmed the effectiveness and replicability of East Asia's government interventions. Others (mainly American and British) said that it confirmed their ineffectiveness and unreplicability. The London *Financial Times* led its review of the report with, '*Industrial policies to promote particular sectors or companies have been a failure in East Asia* and do not explain the region's rapid growth in recent decades, according to a World Bank study'. The *Nihon Keizai Shimbun*, Japan's leading business paper, said 'the report cites the accumulation of high-grade human and physical capital as a motivating force and *highly evaluates the effects of government intervention...*'[61]

MOF officials celebrated the fact that the Bank had at last admitted that state intervention can be useful, but were also critical of some of the conclusions. In December 1993 former executive director Masaki Shiratori, now posted to the OECF, delivered a hard-hitting critique at a seminar in Tokyo. He argued that 'Comparative advantage should be regarded as a

---

[60] The version sent to the Board had been revised in the month between being sent to the Board and actually being discussed by it. Many of the revisions addressed issues that the Board brought up, and were subsequently reported to the Board as being made *in response to* Board suggestions.

[61] *Financial Times*, 27 September 1993, p. 16. *Nihon Keizai Shimbun*, 26 September 1993, p. 7, emphases added. The *Far Eastern Economic Review* (owned by the American firm Dow Jones) concludes from the study that 'today the price of growth is eternal vigilance against sometimes well-intentioned efforts to "help" selected industries or otherwise substitute bureaucratic preferences for the millions of individual decisions that each day constitute the wisdom of the marketplace.' (21 October 1993, p. 5) The *Daily Yomiuri* begins its report, 'Economic policies that fuelled East Asia's dynamic economic growth over the past thirty years can also work in other developing regions of the world, according to a new World Bank study...' (27 September 1993, p. 7)

dynamic notion rather a static one...It is theoretically right to pick and nurture specific promising industries which do not have comparative advantage now. Many developing countries desperately need to get rid of the monoculture in such commodities as coffee, cocoa, copper and tin, which resulted from static comparative advantage..A latecomer to industrialization can not afford to leave everything to the market mechanism. The trial and error inherent in market-driven industrialization is too risky and expensive considering the scarcity of resources.' He went on to make a number of theoretical and technical points against the Total Factor Productivity test of the effectiveness of selective industrial policy, concluding, 'In view of these theoretical and technical problems in the Report's analysis of industrial policy, I hope further studies will be made within and outside the World Bank. In the meantime, I sincerely wish that the Bank will adopt "pragmatic flexibility" in prescribing policy advice to developing countries'.[62] Isao Kubota concluded his remarks at the same seminar, saying: 'Perhaps the best lesson could be that policy makers and policy advisers, including those in the World Bank, should not be dogmatic but be pragmatic. For that purpose *modesty, not arrogance, and a sincere attitude* toward finding the right policy measures, are essential'.[63]

A senior MOF official close to the *Miracle* study characterized MOF and MITI reactions as follows: 'MOF people consider this a good step forward, although they are not fully satisfied with the study's negative assessment on industrial policy. The reaction of the MITI people is mixed: they share the MOF view, on the one hand, but they are afraid to be accused of excessive intervention *now* in the course of negotiations with the US and the EC'. He referred to MITI concerns as expressed by, for example, Makoto Kuroda, MITI's best known hard-line negotiator with the US: 'We must not provide a dangerous basis for the argument that says Japan conducts itself by a different set of rules and must be treated differently...For some time I have repeatedly stated that we should avoid expressions such as "Japanese-style practices".'[64]

Opinion about the *Miracle* study within MITI differed between the two key bureaux, the International Trade Bureau and the Industrial Policy Bureau. The former is preoccupied with maintaining access to the *American* market, for which avowed commitment to 'free-market' and 'level playing field' symbols is important; people from this bureau tended to be enthusiastic about the study's conclusion that selective industrial

---

[62] Masaki Shiratori, 'The Role of Government in Economic Development: Comments on the "East Asian Miracle" Study', paper presented to OECF seminar on the *East Asian Miracle*, Tokyo, 3 December 1993.

[63] Isao Kubota, 'On the "Asian Miracle"', mimeo, Ministry of Finance 1993, his emphasis. An American source close to the Bank, who has talked at length to senior MOF officials about the report, characterizes their reaction as follows: 'We feel intellectually vindicated, because the report does recognize that selective credit has worked effectively in Japan and Korea. We are now beginning to find our intellectual voice on development issues, even if our voice does not yet match the size of our financial contribution. We regard the *Miracle* study as a start. We will now wait, regroup, and exert quiet pressure on the Bank to be more pragmatic in its policy advice.'

[64] Chalmers Johnson, 'History Restarted: Japanese-American relations at the End of the Century', in R. Higgott, R. Leaver, and J. Ravenhill, eds, *Pacific Economic Relations in the 1990s: Conflict or Cooperation?*, 1993, p. 59.

policy has, by and large, been ineffective in East Asia. The Industrial Policy Bureau, by contrast, is committed to boosting the idea of MITI's successful steerage of the Japanese economy, and people from this bureau tended to be more critical of the study. MOF's critical stance may reflect its concerns to maintain a strategic aid programme using directed credit and other infant industry incentives. The two agendas—that of the International Trade Bureau of MITI and that of MOF—may reflect a single higher-level strategy: to maintain access to the American market over the five-year middle-run, while building up a dense presence in the Southeast Asian and China markets for the ten-year longer run, at the end of which these markets are expected to be more important than the American.[65]

Within the Board of the Bank, Shiratori's successor as Japan's executive director was less active. He did not push the concerns that lay behind Japan's promotion of the *Miracle* study. This may reflect a high-level decision in Tokyo to calm relations with the World Bank in order to avoid causing even more turbulence in Japan's relations with the US. As part of this calming strategy, the Japanese government agreed with the Bank that Japan's directed credit programmes, though they continue, will not use *narrow* earmarking (will not define beneficiaries narrowly) and will not have a *big* subsidy element (not more than one or two percentage points below the market rate).

As for the Bank's response, a top manager said 'We simply cannot afford to take a more custom-tailored approach to lending conditions, as the Japanese have been urging. If we were to say to the Philippines, "It is OK for Malaysia to do this but not for you", we could be accused of violating the political impartiality condition of our charter.'[66]

No follow-up research has been planned. The director of the research department explained that 'the real issue is the relevance of the East Asian experience for other developing countries...*Now the East Asian study is completed, the research agenda lies more in Africa and other developing countries than it does in East Asia.*'[67] He took for granted that 'the East Asian experience' is the experience as interpreted in the *East Asian Miracle*.

IX. The Art of Paradigm Maintenance—and Change

Our story raises a more general question. How does the World Bank— a large institution, with some four thousand professional staff drawn

---

[65] Indeed, a watershed has already been reached in Japan's trade: for the first time, the surplus with Asia exceeded the surplus with the US in the fiscal year 1993–94.

[66] This is from an American source close to senior levels of the Bank (and himself a former senior official), who asked the most senior manager for his view of the report.

[67] See Lyn Squire, remarks in *Proceedings of the Symposium on the East Asian Miracle*, Tokyo 1993, emphasis added. The Bank may have continued to do a little more, on the research side, if any of the three main protagonists, Summers, Birdsall, and Page, had remained in or close to their positions; but they all moved far from where they could influence the follow-up. Nancy Birdsall went on to be executive vice-president of the Inter-American Development Bank, John Page became Chief Economist for the Bank's Middle East region, and Lawrence Summers, as we have seen, joined the Clinton administration.

30

from many countries,[68] producing dozens of public reports a year—manage to deliver what the outside world hears as a single central message? The art of paradigm maintenance begins with the choice of staff. As noted, about 80 per cent of Bank economists are North American or British trained, and all but a few share the preconceptions of mainstream Anglo-American economics.[69] If they were to show sympathy for other ideas—if they were to argue that sectoral industrial policies can in some circumstances be effective, for example—they would be unlikely to be selected for the Bank, on grounds of incompetence. The organization's few non-economist social scientists are employed on marginal issues like resettlement and participation, like anthropologists by colonial administrations before them.

But within the staff there remains a range of views that command some following. The second technique of paradigm maintenance is the internal review process. A document goes through rounds of discussions at successively higher levels of the hierarchy, each level being a filter that narrows the range of views espoused by 'the Bank'. It is not just that higher levels are more concerned with the Bank's and the system's integrity than with the integrity of the research. It is also that promotion criteria select people for the higher levels who make decisions quickly and with closure, using 'facts' selectively to support pre-conceived patterns and convictions. Such people tend to be intolerant of those who do not share the conclusions to which they leap.[70]

Thirdly, the legions of Bank editors, some in-house, some employed as consultants, are a part of the maintenance mechanism. Their continued employment depends not only upon their ability to write clear English but also on their ability to write copy that, being in line with 'Bank thinking', will not attract criticism.

This is the review and editing mechanism. The criteria applied are partly formal and partly substantive. The formal criteria relate particularly to the need for a clear 'message'. Great emphasis is placed on having a clear message, on minimizing 'on the one hand, on the other hand' statements which are thought confusing to the intended audience of policy-makers. (Indeed, the early meetings of the writing team are often taken up with discussion of 'What are going to be the key messages of this report?', before the research is done.) The message is to consist not of a setting out of possible alternatives and conditions in which they make more or less sense, and still less of acknowledgement that the evidence is mixed or insufficient, but is to consist of the best policy for the 'typical' developing country. This makes for 'clarity'.

---

[68] In Bank parlance, Higher Level Staff. Total staff, including temporaries, in Financial Year 1994 was just over eight thousand.

[69] Bruno Frey et al, 'Consensus and Dissensus Among Economists: An Empirical Inquiry', *American Economic Review*, vol. 74, no. 1, (1984).

[70] This is based on the Myers-Briggs personality inventory, administered to over 1,000 Bank managers in the early to mid-1990s. The results show that over two-thirds of Bank managers (directors, division chiefs, task managers) are 'TJs'; and that among directors (just below vice-presidents) 70 per cent process information in an 'Intuitive' (patterns, linkages) rather than 'Sensing' (detailed) kind of way, compared to 58 per cent of division chiefs.

The need for a clear and consistent message for policy-makers has implications for the content of the message. The members of the team, partly propelled by professional norms, may be concerned to speak the truth as they see it. But at the higher levels reviewers are sensitive to the more 'systemic' pressures for paradigm maintenance discussed earlier—the need not to upset capital markets, and the self-perception of the Bank as a bulwark against the vested interests that push governments to intervene in socially counter-productive ways. Their comments page by page are unlikely to allude directly to these systemic pressures. Rather, they insist that everything should fit the overall message.

This is the mechanism for conformity. All prominent Bank documents go through it. But what issues get onto the Bank's agenda in the first place? On the whole, the Bank has been a reactive rather than proactive organization, taking its lead from outside. The Bank ensures its own expansion and centrality by launching bids for expert status on some of the issues at the top of the current agenda of development debate, proposing market solutions with compensatory or mitigating elements, creating a consensus around its position, and marginalizing more radical alternatives.[71] Outside the Bank, the debate then tends to configure itself into 'pro- or anti-' Bank positions. This might be called, tongue-in-cheek, a Strategy for the Sustainable Development of the World Bank.

The East Asian Miracle can be read as the latest expression of this strategy. East Asia and industrial policy came to centre stage in the late 1980s, as the US and European economies continued to limp and East Asian economies continued to soar. The new element in the situation, compared to, say, a report on Africa or the Bank's poverty work in the late 1980s, is that the number two shareholder was putting pressure on the Bank to endorse, or at least make some concession to, its non-orthodox views about development principles. The mere centrality of the issue in the development debate would not have been sufficient to prompt the Bank to make a special study, for the issue was at once too indirectly tied to lending and too likely to annoy the Japanese or to complicate the Bank's policy formula.[72] But when Japan agreed to pay for the study and to drop its opposition to the operational directive on financial sector reform the Bank could not say no.

These initiating circumstances made it important for the team leader to

[71] Peter Gibbon, 'The World Bank and the New Politics of Aid', *European Journal of Development Research*, vol. 5, no. 1, (1993) pp. 35–62.

[72] I worked in the Bank's Trade Policy division in 1987–88, at the time when a team from the division was formulating a paper setting out the Bank's trade policy and its empirical and conceptual underpinnings. As a member of the same small division, I repeatedly urged the team to examine East Asia's import-control regime, and especially to consider whether the regime contained design features that enabled Japan, Korea, and Taiwan—all three having highly protected economies for long periods—to escape some of the expected neoclassical costs. I indicated possible mechanisms (as in 'Managing Trade: Taiwan and South Korea as Challenges to Economics and Political Science', *Comparative Politics*, vol. 25, no. 2, (1993) pp. 147–67; and, 'How to Protect Exports from Protection: Taiwan's Duty Drawback Scheme', *The World Economy*, vol. 14, September 1991, pp. 299–310), and offered to provide relevant literature. But the team was unwilling even to consider the possibility that protection East Asian-style might have brought benefits as well as costs, and the trade policy paper refers to the import-control regimes in East Asia *only* in terms of their liberalization. See 'Strengthening Trade Policy Reform', World Bank, Washington DC, November 1989.

32

be someone known to be solidly in the mainstream of Bank thinking, not a doctrinaire free marketeer. John Page met this condition; his pedigree, as a student of Ian Little's and protégé of Anne Krueger's,[73] was conservative, but he had subsequently espoused more pragmatic views. Likely candidates from the East Asia vice-presidency were either free marketeers or too much under their hierarchical command. Even so, the universalistic and non-institutional ethos of neoclassical economics meant that no premium was given to selecting people for the core team who had expertise in East Asia—whether Bank staff or consultants. Any Bank economist is expected to be an expert on a country or region within a matter of months.

As we have seen, the East Asia vice-presidency was excluded. True, it got the country studies, but these were largely ignored by the core team. Yet the East Asia vice-presidency could not be prevented from being the major reviewer, because in the higher level review committees the East Asia vice-president met the Research vice-president on equal terms—and with much more personal influence in the Bank where he had spent his whole career. If the East Asia vice-president decided to do so, he could effectively prevent or at least delay the report in its path to the Board, and so hinder its publication. The cross-pressures among the Japanese sponsors, the core team, and the East Asian vice-presidency help to explain the report's inconsistencies.

Inconsistency as a Register for Change

The inconsistencies should not be seen simply as 'mistakes'. The authors may have left them in—to the extent that they were aware of them[74]—in an attempt to *widen* the grounds of debate without generating a backlash that would cause the report to be dismissed as incompetent or ideological, and the Bank to be accused of changing its mind. The pro-industrial policy statements, though at odds with the rest of the report, may function as attractor points by enabling those wishing to put new questions on the agenda to claim legitimacy from the *Miracle* study. This, it could be argued, is the most likely way that big organizations change their minds; sharp changes are rare.

The Japanese have influenced the Bank enough to provide attractor points beyond those in the *Miracle* study itself. The several studies of Japanese economic policy and civil service organization sponsored by the Bank at about the same time—and also paid for by the Japanese—provide a set of policy ideas that can legitimize further work in these domains, outside and inside the Bank. In particular, the Bank's impri-

---

[73] Ian Little was professor of economics at Oxford University, Anne Kreuger was World Bank vice-president for research, and both are well-known conservative economists. See for example Little, *Economic Development: Theory, Policy and International Relations*, New York 1982.

[74] My argument does not imply that these techniques were deliberately deployed in an attempt to maintain the Bank's central beliefs. One does not need to embrace postmodernism to agree that people's commitment to a particular paradigm has a large subjective element—is underdetermined by the evidence—and that they are largely unaware of how the commitment is protected, by themselves and others, from contrary evidence or interpretations.

matur can help legitimize the idea of 'Japan as model' for *Japan's* use in its own more dirigist Asian aid strategy, further strengthening the constituency for these ideas. It may also be argued that the Bank's softening of its stand against directed credit, as of 1995, owes something to the wider Japanese pressure on the Bank. Compared to the 1980s, the Bank is now less likely to insist that directed credit and interest rate subsidies should always be avoided. It is more likely to insist simply that the onus must be on the proposer to explain the special circumstances justifying directed credit in a given case.[75] The shift is small but not trivial, and gives the Bank more flexibility in responding to Japan's continued use of directed credit.

Although the Japanese government has ceased pressuring the Bank, it has not stopped promulgating its ideas in developing countries. Seeing 'the Japanese approach to industrial policy' as a new export product, it is building up an enormous capacity for teaching Asian bureaucrats, industrialists and scholars about the Japanese approach to industrial policy. One of the leading figures in this campaign recently declared, 'Free market theory has failed in many areas like Russia, Eastern Europe, and Sub-Saharan Africa because it is too short sighted and too market oriented. Not enough attention was paid to these countries' own economic and social structures... Japan started from a planned economy post war, to become gradually liberalized over the years. I would say we are now 80 per cent of the way to being a free market economy. In developing countries it should be more like 50 per cent. We are not saying that developing countries should imitate Japan. But they do need to study an alternative to neo-classical economic theory'. To supply them with such an alternative, in 1995 between 500 and 600 foreign government officials will attend courses in economic development run by the ministries of international trade and industry, finance, foreign affairs, and the Bank of Japan. Scores of Japanese officials will also leave Tokyo on secondment to governments in developing countries, or to swell the small ranks of Japanese officials in multilateral development agencies. Most of the countries targeted for receiving this attention are also lucrative markets for Japanese goods.[76]

The argument raises two wider points. The first is about the Bank's research function. The Bank's legitimacy depends upon the authority

---

[75] And it would point out that the question cannot be debated without making several distinctions: credit may be directed by region, by urban/rural, by small firm/large firm, by sector, by sub-sector; it may contain a larger or smaller element of subsidy; the amount of subsidy may be calculated in relation to the cost of lending or in relation to the price that the lender would otherwise charge; directed credit may comprise a larger or a smaller percentage of total credit, and so on.

[76] The quoted official is Mr Katsuhisa Yamada, director of Japan's Institute of Developing Economies. See William Dawkins, 'Pedlars of the Japanese Model to Developing World', *Financial Times*, 7 February 1995. The Japanese are also helping to keep the debate going in the OECD academic world. During 1994 OECF invited scholars in OECD countries to write short comments on the *Miracle* study. For the eight comments from UK-based respondents plus two Japanese commentaries on the *Miracle* see *Journal of Development Assistance* (Research Institute of Development Assistance, OECF), vol. 1, NO. 1, JULY 1995 (in English). OECF's OECD country offices have also arranged meetings with academics in their respective countries to discuss papers such as the Economic Planning Agency's 'Possibility of the Application of Japanese Experience from the Standpoint of the Developing Countries', November 1994.

of its views; like the Vatican, and for similar reasons, it cannot afford to admit fallibility. At the same time, many of the Bank's research publications, especially the high visibility ones like the *World Development Reports*, are really *advocacy* statements, steered by the bedrock perception that the Bank must act as a counterweight to all the gravitational pulls towards excessive government intervention—which justifies erring on the side of markets. Hence for good organizational and political reasons the Bank's research is biased towards the conclusion that 'there is no alternative' to government policies that stay within the bounds of 'strengthening the enabling environment for private sector development'. The Bank's endorsement of this tenet is important for its authoritative image in the eyes of the interlocking social groups who embrace the 'Washington consensus'. The research must also be largely quantitative, for numbers and econometric technique themselves confer authority. Research that meets these criteria thus helps to maximize staff commitment internally and authoritative reputation externally, and in turn colours the 'reality' against which those leaders of economic opinion check their expectations of the future. But its conclusions are not necessarily those that are most consistent with the evidence.

The second point concerns the Bank's autonomy. Our case study shows the Bank fending off a challenge to its way of seeing from its second largest shareholder. On the face of it, this looks like autonomy. It seems consistent with William Ascher's argument that 'the viability of a development objective or strategy to be implemented through the World Bank depends not only on the acquiescence of the obvious international actors—the nation states through their formal institutional representation and their various pressures—but also on its congruence with the professional role models of the relevant staff. If the staff perceives the strategy or objectives as a "decline in standards", as requiring them to become more "political" vis-à-vis the borrower governments . . . its viability is doubtful unless altered role models can be quickly inculcated, new incentives provided, or rapid staff turnover undertaken.'[77]

The problem is not that this argument is wrong, as far as it goes, but that it stops short of asking about the structure of power in which the Bank operates, and how that structure affects the Bank's response to new development approaches. The story of *The East Asian Miracle* shows the determining importance of essentially American values and interests in the functioning of the Bank.[78] But the influence is exerted not mainly from the American government to the senior management of the Bank—if we look just at this relationship we see considerable autonomy, though the President has always been American. The influence comes partly through the Bank's dependence on world financial markets, and the self-reinforcing congruence between the values of the owners and managers of financial capital and those of the US state. It also

[77] Ascher, 'New Development Approaches and the Adaptability of International Agencies', p. 436.
[78] American hegemony in the Bank is eclipsed or ceded in regions where other major countries have particular interests. France's ex-colonies in West Africa are a good case in point. There the Bank acts within narrow limits set by the Elysée's advisor on African Affairs, occultly coordinating with the Ministre de la Coopération and French military intelligence.

comes through the Bank's staffing and professional norms. Not only are Americans greatly over-represented in the professional and managerial ranks but, at least as important since the beginning of the 1980s, is a second channel of influence—the conquest of managerial positions by economists, and the recruitment of economists, including some from the developing countries, predominantly from North American and British universities (virtually none from Japanese universities). This channel of influence is obscured by talking of 'professionalism' as a source of the Bank's autonomy, without also talking about the *content* of that professionalism and from which member state's intellectual culture it comes.

By examining such factors we can see how the Bank forms part of the external infrastructural power of the US state, even though it by no means bows to every demand of the US government. Whereas the Japanese state uses its strong *domestic* infrastructural power directly to leverage its external reach—especially in Southeast Asia and China—the US state, with much weaker domestic infrastructural power, relies upon its dominance of international organizations like the World Bank and the IMF to keep those organizations pursuing goals that augment its own external reach. The Bank's stance as honest broker allows it to insist on the acceptance of those goals more openly than the US could itself. The story of *The East Asian Miracle* shows how this process worked itself out in one particular case.

[5]

'In the foothills'

Relations between the IMF and civil society

Jan Aart Scholte

Formally, and also largely in practice, multilateral institutions deal in the first place with states. However, in the post-Westphalian circumstance that has arisen in the contemporary globalising world, multilateral governance is not a question of the states-system alone. Since the 1970s, most of the main global regulatory agencies have experienced a major expansion of exchanges with actors in civil society. Global governance has thereby become at least a triangular affair, with complex relationships between national governments, multilateral institutions, and civic associations (see further Scholte 1997, 1999b).

This general shift from Westphalian 'international organisation' to post-sovereign 'global governance' is clearly seen in the recent history of the International Monetary Fund (hereafter IMF, or 'the Fund'). The IMF has since the 1970s experienced major growth in its competences, resources and authority. In the late twentieth century the Fund has not only been shaped by its member states (stronger governments in particular), but has also exerted considerable influence over them (weaker governments in particular).

Not surprisingly, given the far-reaching significance of IMF activities for much contemporary public policy, numerous civil society organisations across the world have over the past several decades developed keen interest in the Fund. Many of these non-state actors (including business associations, academic institutions, trade unions, non-governmental organisations (NGOs), religious groups, etc.) have by-passed national governments to seek direct contact with the IMF. Concerned citizens have wanted to understand and interrogate this new major player in governance. Interest groups have wanted to lobby and perhaps to extract advantage from this important locus of policy-making.

This chapter examines these burgeoning, yet so far little studied, relations between civil society and the IMF (see also Scholte 1998, 1999b). The first section below sets the context by elaborating on the expansion of the Fund in the globalising political economy of the late twentieth century. The second section surveys the range of contacts that have developed between the IMF and civil society. The third section reviews the aims that the Fund and the various civic associations have pursued *vis-à-vis* each other. The next two sections examine the strategies and tactics that the parties have employed in their interactions. The sixth section discusses the impacts that civil society has had on both the substantive policies and the operating procedures of the IMF. The seventh section highlights several major limitations to these relationships, in terms of biased access, general shallowness, and the frequent absence of a veritable dialogue. The eighth section lays out the main forces which have to date hindered a fuller development of exchanges between the Fund and civil society. A further section suggests several reforms which could enhance the contributions of IMF-civil society relations to more effective and democratic global economic governance.

The issues at hand here are important. Both the IMF and civic organisations are players of growing significance in world politics. Current dynamics of globalisation suggest that the involvement of civil society in global governance is for the time being irreversible and, indeed, likely further to expand. If conducted well, contacts between the Fund and civic groups can make substantial contributions to more effective and democratic regulation of macro-economic affairs. A healthy dialogue can increase information flows, stimulate policy debates, involve stakeholders in policy-making, advance civic education, and help to legitimate Fund activities. However, if handled badly, IMF-civil society relations can undermine policy efficacy and undercut democracy. For example, the exchanges could be highly exclusive and favour the privileged; or they could be poorly informed and disrupt policy processes; or they could be treated merely as public relations exercises. A key challenge for global governance in the twenty-first century is therefore to design and execute exchanges between multilateral institutions and civil society in ways that minimise their possible pitfalls and maximise their potential benefits.

To date, links between civil society and the IMF have remained underdeveloped. As an Executive Director of the Fund has acknowledged, 'When it comes to managing "participation", the IMF is only in the foothills; and some people want us back in the valleys' (interview with author). It is hoped that the present research may help IMF-civil society relations to reach higher elevations.

Growth of the IMF

The International Monetary Fund emerged from the Bretton Woods Conference in July 1944. During its first quarter-century of operations, the Fund was mainly concerned to establish and manage the international regime of fixed (but adjustable) exchange rates. Its interventions with member governments were relatively infrequent and brief; they were generally limited to countries of the North; and they were mainly restricted to monetary and trade policies.

The IMF lost much of its old role with the end of the dollar-centred fixed-rate system in 1971; however, the rapid globalisation of money and finance since the 1960s has prompted the Fund to reinvent itself with a much expanded agenda (Vries 1986; James 1996). For one thing, the IMF has since 1978 exercised so-called 'surveillance', scrutinising both the economic policies of individual member-states and the performance of the world economy as a whole. Second, the Fund has since the 1970s intervened more intensely with many client governments by designing for them not only traditional stabilisation measures for short-term corrections of the balance of payments, but also structural adjustment packages for medium- and long-term economic reconstruction. IMF-sponsored structural adjustment programmes began in the South during the 1970s and extended to the East in the 1990s with the transition in those countries from state socialism to a market-based economy. In the process the scope of Fund conditionality (i.e. the policies that a state must follow in order to use IMF resources) has widened to encompass liberalisation, privatisation, fiscal reform and more. Third, the 'second generation' IMF has undertaken major training and technical assistance activities, largely in order to provide poorly equipped states with staff and tools that can better handle the policy challenges of contemporary globalisation. Fourth, the Fund has pursued various initiatives to promote stability in global financial markets, including several major rescue operations.

To handle this enlarged agenda, the IMF has undergone substantial institutional growth. Its Executive Board now meets in at least three (long) sessions each week. Staff numbers have more than tripled, from 750 in 1966 to about 2,600 in 1998 (IMF 1966: 133; http://imf.org/external/np/ext/facts/glance.htm). Since the 1970s the Fund has developed its own 'diplomatic service', with resident representatives stationed in sixty-eight countries by 1998. From 1970 the IMF has had its own money form, the Special Drawing Right (SDR). Quota subscriptions to the Fund have grown from the equivalent of twenty-one billion SDRs in 1965 to 212 billion SDRs in 1999. Various other sources (gold stocks, the General Arrangements to Borrow, etc.) have given the IMF potential access to tens of billions of additional SDRs for lending purposes (IMF 1995a; GAO 1998).

Given this growth in competences and resources, the IMF has in the late twentieth century become a major site of economic governance. Its voice carries far in global markets, in national economic policies, and eventually in local and household budgets. In these circumstances it is hardly surprising that the Fund has since the 1970s attracted progressively more attention from civil society.

Range of contacts

The IMF has since its creation maintained at least sporadic contacts with certain parts of civil society (such as academic associations). However, the number and impact of its links with civic groups were on the whole negligible until the 1980s. The main growth in the frequency, range and sophistication of interchanges between civil society and the Fund has occurred during the 1990s.

All manner of actors in civil society have developed contacts with the Fund. For example, national bankers' associations in most IMF programme countries have held periodic meetings with Fund officials, as has the Institute of International Finance with its 1999 membership of over 300 financial services providers headquartered in fifty-six countries (http://www.iif.com). Many national industrial associations and chambers of commerce have likewise regularly exchanged views with IMF staff. A wide range of think tanks like the Institute for International Economics (IIE) and the Cato Institute in Washington and the Overseas Development Institute (ODI) in London have often contributed to discussions of IMF approaches to macro-economic policy. The labour movement

Relations between the IMF and civil society   259

has actively engaged the Fund through both national and transborder trade union coalitions. The International Confederation of Free Trade Unions (ICFTU) has figured especially importantly in this regard (ICFTU 1988: 50–1; ICFTU 1992: 43–8; ICFTU 1996: 66–8). A multitude of development NGOs in both the South and the North have lobbied the IMF at its headquarters and in the field. Prominent examples include the Washington-based Development GAP, the Brussels-based European Network on Debt and Development (EURODAD), the various Oxfam groups across the world, and the Swiss Coalition of Development Organisations. A few environmental NGOs like the United States branch of Friends of the Earth (FOE-US) have campaigned actively on the Fund since the late 1980s. Meanwhile other NGOs (e.g. concerned with human rights, the status of women, corruption and peace) have had sporadic interchanges with the global monetary institution. Finally, the IMF has maintained contacts with a number of Christian churches and orders as well as certain religious NGOs like the Washington-based Center of Concern.

These various parts of civil society have engaged the IMF at a number of different points in the institution. Especially since the early 1990s, the present Managing Director (MD), Michel Camdessus, has given considerable priority to cultivating links with business circles, trade unions and churches. Since the mid-1990s, the three Deputy Managing Directors have also increased their contacts with civic groups. The twenty-four Executive Directors (EDs), who represent national governments at IMF headquarters, have (with varying mixes of enthusiasm and reluctance) in the 1990s held increasing numbers of interviews with civil society representatives. Within the staff, the Fund has greatly expanded its External Relations Department (EXR), first established in 1981. A Public Affairs Division has existed in EXR since 1989, *inter alia* to handle the IMF's day-to-day relations with civil society groups. More exchanges with civic associations have also taken place in the 1990s through the operational departments of the Fund, especially Policy Development and Review (PDR) and the Fiscal Affairs Department (FAD). For the rest, contacts between IMF officials and civic circles have transpired in the field, through staff missions and resident representatives.

In sum, then, a complex web of relations has developed since the 1980s between civil society and the IMF. On the side of civil society, the exchanges have involved a host of business associations, academic institutes, trade unions, NGOs and religious organisations. On the side of the Fund, the exchanges have involved management, external relations officials, operational staff in Washington, and missions and resident representatives in the field.

Aims of engagement

As might be expected, given the variety of constituencies just described, civic organisations have pursued diverse objectives in their lobbying of the IMF. For example, business associations have primarily aimed to advance the commercial interests of their members, both specifically (through the promotion of particular policy measures) and generally (through the support of business-friendly macro-economic policy frameworks). Mainstream think tanks like the IIE and the Brookings Institution have engaged the Fund in the hope of improving its performance, usually within the existing broad lines of policy.

In contrast, various other voices in civil society have challenged the reigning policy frameworks at the IMF. For example, trade unions have sought to reverse the claimed negative effects of Fund-sponsored policies on employment levels and working conditions. A host of NGOs, religious organisations and reform-minded academic institutes have aimed to halt the purported adverse consequences of IMF-supported structural adjustment on the poor (Watkins 1995: chapter 3). Many of the same circles have urged the Fund to support major reductions in the external debt burdens of the South. A few environmentalist groups like FOE-US and the World Wide Fund for Nature have hoped to place issues of ecological sustainability at the heart of the IMF agenda (Reed 1996). Other critics in civil society have argued that Fund policies should be changed to remove their disproportionately greater costs to women (Woestman 1994). Several NGOs have moreover demanded that IMF conditionality be reformulated to promote human rights, reductions in military spending, and an end to corruption.

Along with these desired changes in substantive IMF policies, some civic groups have aimed to alter certain of the Fund's operating procedures. For example, a number of campaigners have argued for changes in the voting system at the IMF in order to reduce the dominant voice of a handful of governments. In addition, under the slogan of 'ownership', advocates of increased democracy in Fund operations have also urged greater participation by client governments and civil societies in the formulation and implementation of IMF-supported programmes. With reference to 'transparency', many advocates of change have demanded greater openness about policy-making processes at the IMF: e.g. what decisions have been taken; by whom; from among which options; and on the basis of what information. On the theme of 'accountability', various activists have pressed the Fund to establish comprehensive, systematic and transparent mechanisms of policy evaluation.

As for the IMF, it has sought increased contact with civil society in the 1990s mainly in the hope of building support for the macro-economic policies that the Fund sponsors. Both management and staff at the IMF have become convinced that overtures to business associations, labour unions, religious groups and NGOs can help to construct a popular base for worldwide economic restructuring on the neo-liberal lines which the Fund has favoured. Many an IMF official has in recent years declared that 'a broad-based social consensus is needed to sustain a Fund programme' or that 'we have to persuade the population that an adjustment package is legitimate' (interviews with the author).

In addition, the IMF has taken some of its initiatives *vis-à-vis* civil society with the aim of securing its resource position. In particular, the Fund has learned that a poor public image can complicate the approval of quota increases and other requested monies, especially by the United States Congress. In another episode, the IMF created its Visitors' Center in 1986 when the municipal government of

Washington, D.C. threatened otherwise to deny permission for an extension of the headquarters building. (It is a sign of changed times that the Fund needed no outside pressure a decade later to decide on a substantial expansion of the Visitors' Center.)

Strategies

In pursuing the aims noted above, civil society organisations have adopted one or a mixture of three broad strategies: conformism, reformism and radicalism. Those who have taken what might be called a 'conformist' approach to the IMF have broadly accepted the institution's existing premises, policy frameworks and operating procedures. A conformist strategy implies working through the Fund's own terms: that is, the promotion of liberal capitalism; the methodology of neoclassical economics and so on. In contrast, reformers and radicals have challenged the status quo at the IMF, though they are divided on how this challenge should be mounted. Whereas reformers believe that the existing Fund can be reconstructed so that it produces more effective and democratic policy, radicals see the organisation as incorrigible and pursue its contraction or outright abolition (Jordan 1996). Reformers usually welcome opportunities to meet, debate and work with the IMF, while radicals tend to regard any collaboration as a recipe for cooptation.

This threefold categorisation of strategies is of course a simplification; nevertheless, it remains an analytically useful characterisation of the range of approaches taken in civil society *vis-à-vis* the IMF. Broadly speaking, business associations have tended to fall towards the conformist end of the spectrum. Trade unions, NGOs and religious bodies have generally operated somewhere in the reformist and/or radical realms. Meanwhile research institutes have worked across all bands. Thus, for example, the Brookings Institution has taken a conformist line, the Washington-based Overseas Development Council (ODC) has taken a reformist approach, and the Heritage Foundation has taken a radical outlook.

As for the IMF, its overall strategy in relations with civil society has followed two main strands: one proactive and the other reactive. On the proactive side, the Fund has since the late 1980s pursued concerted public relations efforts to win friends and influence people. IMF officials have sought to retain their existing backers in civil society and, more importantly, to 'educate' and 'correct' their critics. Firmly convinced of the merits of Fund-sponsored policies, management and staff have presumed that once people 'understand' the IMF, everyone will support its activities.

On the reactive side, the Fund has sought to contain criticism in civil society, especially from radicals, in order that such opposition does not harm the IMF's work and reputation. In the late 1980s Camdessus declared that the Fund would no longer stay silent in response to attacks on its performance. Subsequently IMF officials have quickly and emphatically defended their organisation against critical academic studies, editorials, press reports, conference resolutions and so on.

262   *Jan Aart Scholte*

Tactics

Both civic groups and the IMF have in the 1990s become considerably more sophisticated in dealing with each other. In earlier years, civic activists tended to hold *ad hoc* street protests against the Fund, to submit petitions, to write letters to the Managing Director, and to publish journal articles. A few of these initiatives attained impressive proportions, such as the marches that accompanied the 1988 Annual Meetings in Berlin, the 'IMF riots' in Venezuela in February 1989 that left over 300 dead, and a 1989 petition to the Fund from Save the Rainforest that held nearly 28,000 signatures from five major member countries. However, on the whole these initiatives were not designed and executed in ways that would shift IMF policy. Before 1990 only a few business and academic organisations such as the Institute of International Finance (IIF), the Japan Center for International Finance (JCIF), the IIE and ODI held face-to-face meetings with Fund officials on detailed policy questions.

Some civic associations have continued to this day to sponsor demonstrations, letter-writing campaigns and the like in respect of the Fund, but other more precisely targeted and sustained activities have developed as well. For example, several civil society campaigns to influence the IMF have hired professional lobbyists, consultants and/or information officers. Certain organisations based outside the USA (e.g. the ICFTU and Oxfam International) have set up bureaux in Washington *inter alia* to monitor the Fund. Increasing numbers of deputations from business associations, trade unions, religious organisations and NGOs have called at IMF headquarters for interviews with EDs and officials from relevant functional and area departments. On other occasions, civic groups have invited management and staff of the Fund to their own events. For instance, the IIF, the JCIF and the ICFTU have frequently included participation from the IMF in their seminars on topics such as global finance and structural adjustment. The ED from Switzerland has accompanied staff from the Swiss Coalition of Development Organisations in joint fact-finding missions to Ghana in 1993 and Bangladesh in 1996.

Civic associations have also developed political sophistication with their use of indirect pressure on the Fund, for example, via national governments. The most advanced tactics of this kind have developed in the USA, where lobbies have since the late 1970s intervened with some effect variously to promote, oppose or attach conditions to congressional approval of increased monies for the IMF. Other civil society engagement of national legislatures on issues concerning the Fund has transpired during the 1990s in Britain, Ireland and programme countries like Haiti where a structural adjustment package requires the approval of the representative assembly. In Germany, the Netherlands, Switzerland and the USA, certain civic associations have discussed IMF policies with the national ministry of finance and central bank.

Civil society groups have also indirectly pursued influence on the IMF via other global governance agencies. In this vein the ICFTU has linked up with the International Labour Organisation to advocate a larger social dimension in Fund programmes. On similar lines EURODAD has engaged with the European Commission, in particular the Structural Adjustment Unit of Directorate General VIII. Meanwhile many activists have hoped that campaigns for change targeted at the World Bank might reverberate on the Fund.

Turning to non-official circles, a number of lobby groups have in the 1990s given increased attention to civic education about the IMF. To this end they have issued popular information packs, organised symposia, and produced several films concerning the Fund (e.g. Torfs 1996; Maryknoll n.d.). NGOs have since the mid-1990s maintained half a dozen listservs on the Internet with continually updated information about the IMF. Some organisations like Oxfam have cultivated links with the mainstream press in the hope of reaching the wider public via newspapers and the broadcast media.

Finally, civic associations have in the 1990s advanced their tactics *vis-à-vis* the IMF with improved communications among themselves. For example, NGOs have held a Forum alongside all IMF/World Bank Annual Meetings since 1986. NGOs and trade unions have (separately) also convened a number of regional gatherings where Fund-related issues have been discussed. Lower telephone charges, faxes, electronic mail and the World Wide Web have enabled activists with access to these technologies to develop closer day-to-day contacts with one another. With such means a substantial network has grown since 1994 around the theme of '50 Years Is Enough'. By 1998 this coalition to limit the powers of the Bretton Woods institutions encompassed over 200 US-based associations plus 180 partner organisations in sixty-five countries (http://www.50years.org).

As for the IMF, it has pursued its strategies of self-promotion and self-protection on the largest scale through publications. A Pamphlet Series was started already in 1965, and the biweekly *IMF Survey* was launched in 1972; however, the Fund did not issue any popular information booklets until 1988 (Driscoll 1988a, 1988b; Landell-Mills 1988). In the 1990s the External Relations Department has greatly expanded the IMF publications programme with books, reports, brochures and regularly updated fact sheets. The Public Affairs Division has accumulated a worldwide mailing list of some 700 addresses and distributes materials to these individuals and groups in three languages. EXR has also produced several films about the IMF and has made the organisation publicly accessible on the Internet since 1995 (http://www.imf.org/).

The Fund has also given increased attention in the 1990s to cultivating its image in and through the mass media. The institution has expanded its flow of press releases, news briefs and public information notices to scores per year. IMF officials have also regularly issued rejoinders on the letters pages to what they regard as inaccurate reporting of Fund activities and their consequences. Meanwhile the Managing Directors and Executive Directors of the IMF have in recent years granted newspaper, magazine and broadcast interviews on a scale unheard of in an earlier generation. Management has likewise encouraged IMF mission chiefs and resident representatives to cultivate links with the press in programme countries. In 1993 EXR initiated media training courses for Fund staff, which had by 1996 involved over 325 employees (IMF 1994: 186; IMF 1996: 193).

Many other IMF outreach activities have taken the form of face-to-face meetings. For instance, Camdessus and his three deputies have during the 1990s given dozens of speeches to civic associations and other audiences. The Managing Director and the First Deputy MD, Stanley Fischer, have on various occasions met privately with representatives of civil society both in Washington and on their frequent travels abroad. In 1996, delegations of Executive Directors met with business organisations, trade unions and other civic associations during tours of the Middle East and Eastern Europe. Meanwhile EXR has since 1990 organised a number of external relations missions abroad, where IMF staff have met with civic groups in selected countries including China, India, South Africa and Ukraine. More routinely, IMF mission chiefs and resident representatives have given briefings on Fund policies and procedures to a variety of civic associations in programme countries. Scores of civil society organisations have in the 1990s received invitations to attend the IMF/World Bank Annual Meetings, where the hosts have *inter alia* provided an NGO Room with full communications facilities.

The IMF has also pursued some tactics of indirect influence on civil society. In particular, the Fund has repeatedly argued – both in public declarations and in private urgings – that national governments should take the lead in forging popular support behind IMF-sponsored policies. On a few occasions (e.g. in Venezuela in 1996), Fund staff have worked closely with a government to 'sell' a structural adjustment programme to business groups, political parties, labour unions and church leaders. IMF officials have also engaged civil society through the United Nations, for instance, at UN-sponsored global conferences on environment and development in 1992, on social development in 1995, and on women also in 1995.

Impacts on IMF policy

To recapitulate the preceding sections, since the 1980s multifarious actors in civil society have engaged the IMF with a variety of aims, through diverse strategies, and with increasingly sophisticated campaign tactics. Concurrently, multiple parts of the Fund have developed relations with civil society, normally with fairly focused aims and strategies, and likewise employing increasingly sophisticated tactics. Yet what significance have relations between civil society and the IMF acquired in terms of policy impacts?

Needless to say, it is impossible to determine exactly the degree to which civic associations have affected IMF behaviour. The Fund's actions result from a complex interplay of circumstances of which inputs from civic groups are but one. Yet although the effects cannot be precisely measured, it is clear that civil society has over the last two decades had noteworthy influences both in reinforcing the primary lines of IMF policies and in shifting some of their secondary aspects.

Organisations pursuing conformist strategies towards the Fund have often played an important role in bolstering the IMF's existing policy frameworks. Bankers' associations, chambers of commerce and mainstream economic research institutes have rarely pushed the Fund to depart from its prevailing

Relations between the IMF and civil society   265

assumptions, modes of analysis and broad prescriptions. When these circles have exerted pressure, they have normally urged the Fund to make minor amendments or to perform better, that is, within established policy lines. To be sure, such criticisms have sometimes been sharply worded: e.g. on how the IMF might have miscalculated a target indicator; or how the Fund might have failed to anticipate a financial crisis. However, conformist groups have not attacked the primary Fund prescriptions, namely, for stabilisation, liberalisation, deregulation, privatisation, tax reform, a streamlined civil service, etc. On the contrary, mainstream business associations and think tanks have usually explicitly or implicitly endorsed these neo-liberal formulas. Contacts with conformist circles in civil society have thereby had an important effect of reinforcing the confidence of Fund officials in their established approaches to surveillance, conditionality, debt problems, and so on.

At the same time, civic associations pursuing changes at the IMF have made some impact in shifting both substantive policies and operating procedures in the institution (see further Scholte forthcoming). On the substantive side, inputs from trade unions, NGOs, development studies institutes and other critics have encouraged the Fund to reconsider its approach to conditionality in certain respects. Most prominently, IMF-sponsored programmes have since the mid-1990s given greater attention to the so-called 'social dimension' of structural adjustment. 'Safety nets' are now regularly incorporated into the package to protect, for example, health and education services (IMF 1995b; Chu and Gupta 1998). In addition, Fund research and policy have since the mid-1990s occasionally given attention to issues of environmental degradation, gender consequences of macro-economic policy, and corruption (Gandhi 1996; Stotsky 1996; Mauro 1997). On the question of external debt, persistent pressure from a variety of religious bodies and NGOs have helped to nurture a recognition in the Fund that these burdens form a hindrance to development in the South. Indeed, in 1996 the IMF together with the World Bank launched the Highly Indebted Poor Countries (HIPC) Initiative, a programme which has for the first time included modest relief on repayments to the two multilateral institutions (Boote and Thugge 1997).

With regard to operating procedures, inputs from civic associations have encouraged the IMF to adopt a number of steps in the 1990s toward greater transparency, accountability and participation. In respect of openness, the Fund has not only massively increased its production of public relations material (as noted earlier), but it has also since the mid-1990s released substantial numbers of policy documents and other details about its advice to governments. In addition, the IMF has answered calls for greater accountability in its operations with (hesitant) moves to develop a policy evaluation programme (Wood and Welch 1998). Finally, Fund management and staff have become more sensitive to a need for greater participation by client governments and civil societies in the formulation of IMF-supported policies.

In relation to the aims for change specified earlier, the shifts in policies and *modus operandi* just described constitute fairly modest alterations. Labour protection, poverty eradication, ecological sustainability, gender equity and

266   *Jan Aart Scholte*

human rights have not become central planks of IMF conditionality. The Fund has not come close to endorsing debt write-offs for the South. Some IMF operations continue to be cloaked in secrecy. Evaluation mechanisms for Fund policies remain underdeveloped. IMF officials are often still unclear how to move from the rhetoric of 'ownership' to the practice of participation.

On the other hand, none of these issues figured on the Fund agenda at all before the 1990s. Seen in this light, the IMF has undergone some reform in the broad directions that many civic activists have advocated. More generally, critics in civil society have stimulated searching debates in the 1990s about the desirable shape of global economic governance.

Limitations

As the preceding sections have indicated, contacts between the International Monetary Fund and civil society have become more numerous, more intricate and more influential than many observers of global economic governance appreciate. Nevertheless, the links remain in important respects underdeveloped. On three major counts, the relationships have manifested dangers for policy efficacy and democracy through the IMF.

The first key limitation concerns bias. The various parts of civil society have had unequal access to a dialogue with the Fund. In a rough ranking, academic institutions and business associations have tended to have easiest entry to the IMF. Trade unions have generally occupied second place. (Christian) religious groups, development NGOs and environmental NGOs have broadly come third, while many other groups including smallholder associations and women's organisations have had almost no contact with the IMF. Other biases in the relationships have favoured associations based in the North over groups located in the South and the East. In class terms, the great majority of contacts have involved university-educated, computer-literate, (relatively) high-earning English speakers. Owing to an urban-rural divide, organisations based in towns (especially national capitals) have usually had greater access to the Fund than groups in the countryside. Women have been severely under-represented both in the professional staff of the IMF and in the civic associations with which the Fund has had most contacts (i.e. business groups, economic research institutes and trade unions). Given these various biases, IMF-civil society relations have often poorly represented the various constituencies with a stake in the Fund's activities. The contacts have to this extent tended to reproduce or even enlarge structural inequalities and associated arbitrary privileges in the world political economy.

The second major shortcoming in IMF-civil society relations to date has been their overall shallowness. On both sides, most participants in these interchanges have remained inadequately informed about each other and have not given sufficient priority to developing their relationships. In spite of the many initiatives described earlier, links between civic associations and the Fund have on the whole been only weakly institutionalised and haphazardly sustained. The Executive Board has not yet formally articulated what purposes contacts with civil society should serve; nor has management carefully considered what institutional mechanisms would best advance the dialogue. In civil society, only a few associations like the IIF, the ICFTU, FOE-US and the Cato Institute have pursued sustained, focused, carefully researched campaigns to influence Fund policies. Many activists advocating change in the IMF have struggled *against* with only vague ideas about what they are struggling *for.* In these circumstances of overall superficiality on both sides, the Fund has missed many potentially valuable inputs from civic partners, while many initiatives from civil society toward the IMF have been ill-informed and misdirected.

The third core problem in IMF-civil society relations has concerned shortfalls in reciprocity. That is, the parties have tended to enter discussions with inadequate readiness to listen to, learn from, and be changed by the other side. A dialogue of the deaf has arisen especially when the general public relations strategy of the Fund has clashed with the reformist and radical strategies of many civic associations. On the whole, exchanges between these civic groups and the IMF have involved insufficient negotiation of differences. Civic organisers have complained that 'the IMF won't have a frank discussion about the problems of its policies', that 'you cannot critique in a dialogue with the Fund', and that 'if you're too insistent in expressing a different point of view, IMF people tell you to keep quiet' (interviews with the author). For their part, Fund officials have frequently objected that '[NGOs] spend the whole time telling us we're wrong', that 'it's hard to get a dialogue going with such people', and that 'some NGOs are just rabid' (interviews with the author). These difficulties have often prompted the IMF to focus its contacts with civil society more on conformist groups, to the relative neglect of challengers. Such a marginalisation of critics (whether deliberate or unconscious) could give the Fund an exaggerated sense of popular endorsement of its policies and might at some point generate a backlash against the institution.

Constraints on relations

The underdevelopment of relations just described has rarely resulted from ill will on the part of either IMF officials or civil society organisers. If blame is to be allocated, then it has lain principally with: (a) the limited resources that the parties have had to hand; and (b) certain deeper structures (e.g. related to institutional culture and the organisation of the world political economy) that the parties have inherited.

Neither civil society nor the Fund have had sufficient resources to realise the full potential of their relationships with each other. In terms of personnel, for example, the IMF staff has included no 'civil society experts' beyond a handful of public affairs officers in EXR. Other Fund officials have usually been overstretched with other responsibilities that are accorded a higher priority than dialogue with civic groups. Likewise, most civic organisations have lacked personnel with expertise regarding the IMF.

As for finances, the Fund has in the late 1990s allocated just 3.6 per cent of its fairly modest operating budget to cover all external relations activities (IMF 1997: 225). Meanwhile, apart from a few well-endowed think tanks and business lobbies, most civic groups have struggled on small budgets. NGO campaigns on the IMF have usually depended on small short-term grants from a handful of donors.

With regard to information, the IMF has accumulated but a meagre store of data concerning civic organisations. On the civil society side, although increased transparency at the Fund in the 1990s has improved matters, much crucial information regarding policy substance and process in the institution remains inaccessible to the public. As one experienced civic organiser from Africa has objected, 'How can we ever influence the IMF if we barely know it?' (interview with the author).

Both civic groups and the IMF have done little to compensate for their limited personnel, funds and information by coordinating their efforts. For example, the Fund has rarely drawn on the greater expertise and information regarding civic contacts which is available from the World Bank and various United Nations agencies. In civil society, although new technologies have helped to improve communications between associations in the 1990s, the various organisations have often failed to share intelligence and coordinate initiatives.

In addition to – and compounding – these resource shortfalls, several structural conditions of the world political economy have also hampered a fuller development of IMF-civil society relations in the late twentieth century. One of these barriers has related to the particular institutional characteristics of the Fund. As an organisation, the IMF has been highly monolithic and tightly run under a hierarchical, interventionist management. This institutional context has arguably discouraged Fund staff from developing more extensive and open discussions with civic groups.

Difficulties of access to the IMF for civil society have also resulted from the culture of secrecy that has traditionally enveloped all of monetary and financial regulation. To be sure, there are sound arguments for discretion in some Fund activities. For instance, devaluations, interest rate changes and the like clearly should not be publicised in advance. However, institutions of macro-economic policy-making like the IMF have tended to drape the cloak of secrecy over much more than sensitive matters. As noted earlier, the Fund has in the 1990s shifted its views on the balance between the need to know and the need for confidentiality in favour of the former. All the same, an embedded culture of secrecy does not dissolve quickly.

A third structural circumstance of the late twentieth century, namely, the power of neo-liberalism, has helped to produce both biased access and shortfalls in reciprocity in IMF-civil society relations. The neo-liberal paradigm has prescribed liberalisation, deregulation, privatisation and liberal democracy as a universal formula for the good society in the contemporary globalising world. Following the stagnation of post-colonial socialism in the South, the collapse of central planning in the East, and the retreat of corporatist welfarism in the North, neo-liberal ideology has reigned supreme across the world in the 1980s and 1990s. Alternative visions propounded in some civic circles – such as neo-mercantilism, Keynesianism, socialism, feminism and environmentalism – have in these times been readily marginalised. The structural power of neo-liberalism has enabled the IMF readily to reject unorthodox talk and to concentrate its contacts with civil society on sympathetic quarters like business associations and mainstream think tanks. Indeed, some campaigners for IMF reform have – deliberately or unconsciously – shifted their language in the direction of neo-liberalism in order to obtain a more serious hearing from the Fund.

Meanwhile embedded social hierarchies have played an important role in creating uneven access to the IMF for the different parts of civil society. In other words, the previously noted unequal entry has not been accidental. Social structures in the contemporary world political economy have systematically favoured the North over the South and the East, propertied and professional classes over poorer and less literate circles, urban centres over rural areas, and men over women. Such inequalities are easily (indeed, usually unconsciously and inadvertently) reproduced; they are but rarely (usually only with deliberate and persistent efforts) counteracted.

Another structural hierarchy – namely, that which has favoured the state over other social actors – has helped to keep most relations between the IMF and civil society shallow. True, as highlighted at the start of this chapter, states are far from the sole players in emergent post-Westphalian politics. Governments have lost sovereignty in its traditional sense of supreme, absolute, comprehensive and unilateral control over a territorial jurisdiction. On the other hand, states have become anything but powerless, and they have clung jealously to the *claim* that they always have the final say in governance. By the letter of international law, in the mindset of IMF staff, and also among many civic organisers, the Fund is seen to be responsible first and foremost to states and only secondarily, if at all, to civil society. Both the Fund and civic groups have usually limited their direct contacts to levels that national governments would tolerate.

Finally, IMF-civil society contacts have to date remained under-developed owing to insufficient attention on the part of civic organisations to their democratic credentials. Many of these groups – including some which have pressed hardest for a democratisation of the Fund – have not done enough to secure their own representativeness, consultation processes, transparency and accountability (see Bichsel 1996). These shortcomings have dented the credibility of many NGOs in particular and have allowed the IMF and states to take these associations less seriously than they might otherwise have done.

In sum, some very powerful social forces have hindered the development of a wider and deeper dialogue between civic groups and the Fund. Given the major resource limitations and inauspicious structural conditions reviewed above, it is not surprising that IMF-civil society relations have often had a partial, shallow and troubled character.

Towards the future

How might current shortcomings in relations between civil society and the IMF be overcome? They are by no means inevitable and incorrigible. After all, the contacts have over the past two decades already become more extensive and richer than any observer in 1980 might have imagined. True, major increases in resources and fundamental transformations in world structures would be required

270   *Jan Aart Scholte*

for exchanges between the Fund and civil society to realise their full potential to enhance efficacy and democracy in global economic governance. However, more modest and immediately feasible steps could substantially improve the situation in the short and medium term.

For one thing, both the IMF and civic associations could clarify their objectives in engaging with one another. On the side of the Fund, the Executive Board could formulate explicit general aims for the organisation's relations with civil society. Drawing on these guidelines, department heads could issue specific instructions to mission teams, resident representatives and other relevant staff. Many civil society groups could also establish more explicit, specific and practicable goals for their initiatives *vis-à-vis* the IMF.

The dialogue between the Fund and civic groups could also benefit from further development of institutional mechanisms. For example, the IMF's Articles of Agreement could be amended to 'legalise' the Fund's contacts with civic associations. More concretely, the IMF could at national level join with government, civil society actors and perhaps other global governance agencies like the World Bank to establish a consultative framework regarding Fund and other multilateral involvements in the country concerned. In addition, the IMF could include on its staff specifically designated 'civil society liaison officials' who would, with the consent of the governments concerned, be included in the Fund teams for designated countries. In civil society, meanwhile, many associations could alter their institutional procedures with a view to enhancing their democratic credentials.

Tight budgetary constraints for the time being preclude major increases in resources for IMF-civil society relations; however, it is to be hoped that, given the stakes involved, donors and managers might see fit to enlarge financial allocations at least somewhat. For civil society, such funds could be used in the first place to build capacity regarding the Fund, particularly in programme countries. Such capacity building would require a commitment of multiple years' funding rather than one-off short-term grants.

The Fund could use a modest expansion of allocations *inter alia* to hire the previously mentioned civil society liaison officials. In addition, monies could be used to give relevant IMF officials short training courses on cooperation with civil society. The Fund could furthermore use extra funds to increase its distribution of information to civic groups (particularly in the South and the East) which do not have access to the Internet. The IMF could also at limited expense expand and systematise a data base on civil society organisations. This task would probably be done most efficiently in collaboration with other multilateral institutions, for example through the Non-Governmental Liaison Service of the United Nations.

Finally, relations between civil society and the IMF could benefit from a number of shifts in attitude. For example, all parties could accord a higher priority to developing their mutual relations. IMF officials could go further in shifting their general approach from one of selling policies to one of discussing options. Civic organisers could do more to move beyond criticisms of the Fund to concrete suggestions for improvement. To encourage greater participation of marginalised circles, all parties in the IMF-civil society dialogue could make a habit of regularly asking 'who is missing'? Finally, both civic associations and the Fund could nurture greater sensitivity to questions of their accountability. In post-Westphalian times, non-state actors can no longer shift all responsibility for policy outcomes on to governments.

Conclusion

As seen from the preceding discussion, IMF contacts with civic associations illustrate the general contemporary trend whereby 'international organisation' of the Westphalian system has mutated into 'global governance' involving complex interlinkages of states, multilateral institutions and civil society. The Fund has since the 1970s grown into a major regulatory agency with some relative autonomy from its member governments. Over the same period, increasing numbers of civic groups have sought to learn about and influence the IMF, often by-passing states to establish direct links with the multilateral agency. Both civic organisations and the Fund have in their mutual relations pursued a variety of (progressively more sophisticated) aims, strategies and tactics.

Although a shift to a new multilateralism from below, identified in the introduction of this book, has not yet materialised, these interchanges have made some notable policy impacts at the IMF. On the one hand, inputs from business associations and mainstream think tanks have often reinforced the Fund's established policies. These conformist circles have underwritten and helped to fine tune orthodox approaches to stabilisation, neo-liberal prescriptions for structural adjustment, and conventional responses to external debt problems. On the other hand, inputs from trade unions, religious organisations, NGOs and reform-minded academic institutes have helped in the 1990s to induce marginal shifts in IMF conditionalities, first steps toward relief on multilateral debts for poor countries, and substantial moves toward greater transparency in Fund operations.

Yet relations between the IMF and civil society could, with further development, offer much more for effective and democratic global governance. The interchanges need to be more sustained and better informed. The dialogue needs to be more open, reflexive and creative. Access needs to be geared toward wider participation on equal terms. A number of immediately practicable steps are available to advance these ends, for example in terms of policy clarifications, institutional innovations, new resource allocations and attitudinal shifts. Such moves can help to ensure that emergent global governance through the IMF contributes to prosperity, equity, democracy, social cohesion and ecological sustainability.

Note

Research for this chapter has been supported through a grant under the Global Economic Institutions Programme of the Economic and Social Research Council in the United Kingdom (award no. L120251027). I am grateful to more than 130 persons in civil society, the IMF and other official circles who have shared with me their experiences of and reflections on relations between the Fund and civic groups. Interviews and correspondence were conducted on condition of non-attribution.

272   *Jan Aart Scholte*

References

Bichsel, A. (1996) 'NGOs as agents of public accountability and democratization in intergovernmental forums', in W. M. Lafferty and J. Meadowcroft (eds), *Democracy and the Environment: Problems and Prospects*, Cheltenham: Edward Elgar.

Boote, A. R. and K. Thugge (1997) *Debt Relief for Low-Income Countries: The HIPC Initiative*, Washington: International Monetary Fund, Pamphlet Series no. 51.

Chu, K.-Y. and S. Gupta (1998) *Social Safety Nets: Issues and Experience*, Washington, D.C.: International Monetary Fund.

Driscoll, D. D. (1988a) *What Is the International Monetary Fund?* Washington, D.C.: International Monetary Fund.

—— (1988b) *The IMF and the World Bank: How Do They Differ?* Washington, D.C.: International Monetary Fund.

Gandhi, V. P. (ed.) (1996) *Macroeconomics and the Environment*, Washington, D.C.: International Monetary Fund.

GAO (1998) *International Monetary Fund: Observations on Its Financial Condition*, Washington, D.C.: United States Government General Accounting Office.

http://www.50years.org

http://www.iif.com

http://www.imf.org

ICFTU (1988) *Report of the Fourteenth World Congress*, Brussels: ICFTU.

—— (1992) *Report on Activities/Financial Reports 1987–1990*, Brussels: ICFTU.

—— (1996) *Report on Activities/Financial Reports 1991–94*, Brussels: ICFTU.

IMF (1966) *Annual Report 1966*, Washington, D.C.: International Monetary Fund.

—— (1994) *Annual Report 1994*, Washington, D.C.: International Monetary Fund.

—— (1995a) *Financial Organization and Operations of the IMF*, Washington, D.C.: International Monetary Fund, Pamphlet Series No. 45, fourth edn.

—— (1995b) *Social Dimensions of the IMF's Policy Dialogue*, Washington, D.C.: International Monetary Fund, Pamphlet Series No. 47.

—— (1996) *Annual Report 1996*, Washington, D.C.: International Monetary Fund.

—— (1997) *Annual Report 1997*, Washington, D.C.: International Monetary Fund.

James, H. (1996) *International Monetary Cooperation since Bretton Woods*, New York: International Monetary Fund and Oxford University Press.

Jordan, L. (1996) 'The Bretton Woods challengers', in J. M. Griesgraber and B. G. Gunter (eds), *Development: New Paradigms and Principles for the Twenty-First Century*, London: Pluto.

Landell-Mills, J. (1988) *Helping the Poor: The IMF's New Facilities for Structural Adjustment*, Washington, D.C.: International Monetary Fund.

Maryknoll (n.d.) *Banking on Life and Debt*, film by Maryknoll World Productions.

Mauro, P. (1997) *Why Worry about Corruption?* Washington, D.C.: International Monetary Fund, Economic Issues Series No. 6.

Reed, D. (ed.) (1996) *Structural Adjustment, the Environment and Sustainable Development*, London: Earthscan.

Scholte, J. A. (1997) 'The globalization of world politics', in J. Baylis and S. Smith (eds), *The Globalization of World Politics: An Introduction to International Relations*, Oxford: Oxford University Press.

—— (1998) 'The IMF meets civil society', *Finance and Development* 35, 3: 42–5.

—— (1999a) 'Civil society and a democratisation of the International Monetary Fund', in P. Yeros , S. O. Vandersluis and and S. Owen (eds), *Poverty in World Politics: Whose*

Global Era? London: Macmillan.

—— (1999b) 'Globalisation and governance', in P. Hanafin and M. S. Williams (eds), *Identity, Rights and Constitutional Transformation*, Aldershot: Ashgate.

—— (forthcoming) 'Social movements and the International Monetary Fund', in R. O'Brien *et al.*, *Contesting Global Governance: The Global Economic Institutions – Social Movement Nexus*, Cambridge: Cambridge University Press.

Stotsky, J. G. (1996) *Gender Biases in Tax Systems*, Washington, D.C.: International Monetary Fund, Discussion Paper 96/99.

Torfs, M. (1996) *The IMF Handbook: Arming NGOs with Knowledge*, Brussels: Friends of the Earth Europe.

Vries, M. de (1986) *The IMF in a Changing World, 1945–85*, Washington, D.C.: International Monetary Fund.

Watkins, K. *et al.* (1995) *The Oxfam Poverty Report*, Oxford: Oxfam UK and Ireland.

Woestman, L. (1994) *Male Chauvinist SAPs: Structural Adjustment and Gender Policies*, Brussels: EURODAD/WIDE.

Wood, A. and C. Welch (1998) *Policing the Policemen: The Case for an Independent Evaluation Mechanism for the IMF*, London and Washington: Bretton Woods Project and Friends of the Earth-US.

Journal of Common Market Studies

Vol. 34, No. 3
September 1996

European Integration from the 1980s:
State-Centric *v.* Multi-level Governance*

GARY MARKS

Department of Political Science, University of North Carolina,
Chapel Hill, NC 27599-3265, USA

LIESBET HOOGHE

Department of Political Science, University of Toronto
Toronto, ONT M5S 3GS, Canada

KERMIT BLANK

Department of Political Science, University of North Carolina,
Chapel Hill, NC 27599-3265, USA

Abstract

This article takes initial steps in evaluating contending models of EU governance. We argue that the sovereignty of individual states is diluted in the
European arena by collective decision-making and by supranational institutions. In addition, European states are losing their grip on the mediation of
domestic interest representation in international relations. We make this
argument along two tracks. First, we analyse the conditions under which
central state executives may lose their grip on power. Next, we divide up the
policy process into stages and specify which institutional rules may induce
various actors to deepen EU policy-making.

* We would like to thank Simon Bulmer, Jim Caporaso, Stephen George, John Keeler, Peter Lange, Andrea
Lenschow, Christian Lequesne, Mark Pollack, Michael Shackleton, and Helen Wallace for their useful
criticisms, comments and suggestions. We are indebted to Ivan Llamazares and Leonard Ray for research
assistance.

342 GARY MARKS, LIESBET HOOGHE AND KERMIT BLANK

I. Introduction

Developments in the European Union (EU) over the last decade have revived debate about the consequences of European integration for the autonomy and authority of the state in Europe. The scope and depth of policy-making at the EU-level have dramatically increased. The EU has almost completed the internal market and has absorbed the institutional reforms of the Single European Act (1986) which established qualified majority voting in the Council of Ministers and increased the power of the European Parliament. The Maastricht Treaty (1993) further expanded EU competencies and the scope of qualified majority voting in the Council, and provided the European Parliament with a veto on certain types of legislation. The Maastricht Treaty is a landmark in European integration quite apart from its ambitious plan for a common currency and a European central bank by the end of this century.

Our aim in this article is to take stock of these developments. What do they mean for the political architecture of Europe? Do these developments consolidate nation-states or do they weaken them? If they weaken them, what kind of political order is emerging? These are large and complex questions, and we do not imagine that we can settle them once and for all. Our strategy is to pose two basic alternative conceptions – state-centric governance and multi-level governance – as distinctly as possible and then evaluate their validity by examining the European policy process.

The core presumption of state-centric governance is that European integration does not challenge the autonomy of nation-states (Mann, 1994; Milward, 1992; Moravcsik, 1991, 1993, 1994; Streeck, 1996). State-centrists contend that state sovereignty is preserved or even strengthened through EU membership. They argue that European integration is driven by bargains among Member State governments. No government has to integrate more than it wishes because bargains rest on the lowest common denominator of the participating Member States. In this model, supranational actors exist to aid Member States, to facilitate agreements by providing information that would not otherwise be so readily available. Policy outcomes reflect the interests and relative power of Member State executives. Supranational actors exercise little independent effect.

An alternative view is that European integration is a polity creating process in which authority and policy-making influence are shared across multiple levels of government – subnational, national, and supranational (Marks, 1992, 1993; Hooghe,1996). While national governments are formidable participants in EU policy-making, control has slipped away from them to supranational institutions. States have lost some of their former authoritative control over individuals in their respective territories. In short, the locus of political control has changed. Individual state sovereignty is diluted in the EU by collective decision-making among national governments and by the autonomous role of the European Parliament, the European Commission, and the European Court of Justice.

We make this argument in this article along two tracks. First we analyse the variety of conditions under which central state executives will voluntarily or involuntarily lose their grip on power. Second, we examine policy-making in the EU across its different stages against the background of contending state-centric and multi-level approaches to European governance.

II. Two Models of the European Union

The models which we outline below are drawn from a large and diverse body of work on the European Union, though they are elaborated in different ways by different authors. Our aim here is not to replicate the ideas of any particular writer, but to set out the basic elements that underlie contending views of the EU so that we may evaluate their validity.

The core ideas of the *state-centric model* are put forward by several writers, most of whom call themselves intergovernmentalists (Hoffmann, 1966, 1982; Taylor, 1991; Moravcsik, 1991, 1993; Garrett, 1992; Milward, 1992; Streeck, 1996; for an intellectual history see Caporaso and Keeler, 1993).[1] This model poses states (or, more precisely, national governments) as ultimate decision-

---

[1] While the roots of the state-centric model lie in (neo)realism (see, for an overview, Caporaso, 1995), there are a variety of state-centric approaches to European integration which take issue with certain neorealist assumptions and which attempt to encompass domestic politics as an influence on the formation of state preferences. The most interesting of these is 'liberal institutionalism' which, despite its nuanced view of interstate co-operation and state preference formation, is firmly in the state-centric mould.

Liberal institutionalism focuses on how international institutions foster gains from co-operation where they otherwise might not arise. International institutions diminish anarchy, but the state-centric perspective remains intact: states are unitary actors and state preferences are determined exogenously or by domestic politics (Caporaso, 1995). 'The basic claim ... is that the EC can be analysed as a successful intergovernmental regime designed to manage economic interdependence through negotiated policy co-ordination. ... An understanding of the preferences and power of its Member States is a logical starting point for analysis' (Moravcsik, 1993, p. 474).

This approach allows that European institutions are strong: 'Strong supranational institutions are often seen as the antithesis of intergovernmentalism. Wrongly so' (Moravcsik, 1993, p. 507). But they are at the service of Member States, not independent: 'The unique institutional structure of the EC is acceptable to national governments only insofar as it strengthens, rather than weakens, their control over domestic affairs, permitting them to attain goals otherwise unachievable' (Moravcsik, 1993, p. 507). Milward claims that ' ... the political machinery of the Community resembles the court of a minor eighteenth-century German state. There is a numerous and deferential attendance around the president of the Commission. A hierarchical bureaucracy attends to the myriad facets of relationships with the surrounding greater powers, for every decision has to be finely attuned to the wishes of the real powers to which the Community's continued existence is useful. The struggles to appoint to its offices are like those within the Imperial Diet' (Milward, 1992, p. 446).

European institutions are not essentially different from other international institutions. All serve a precise function: 'Like other international regimes, EC institutions increase the efficiency of bargaining by providing a set of passive, transaction-cost reducing rules' (Moravcsik, 1993, p. 518). Consequently, supranational actors cannot achieve political autonomy. In this respect, the EU looks strikingly similar to a consociational regime: 'Consociational theory sees the state apparatus as being an umpire rather than a promoter of any specific ideology. ... [P]ressures to enlarge the role of the Commission as umpire are increased rather than diminished as integration proceeds' (Taylor, 1991, pp.118-19).

The state-centric model claims that Member States have EU institutions firmly under control. 'The EC regime ... fixes interstate bargains until the major European powers choose to negotiate changes' (Moravcsik, 1993, p. 31). In effect, 'the most fundamental task facing a theoretical account of European integration is to explain these bargains' (Moravcsik, 1993, p. 473). To do so, one should refer back to the preferences of participating states: 'EC institutions appear to be explicable as the result of conscious calculations by Member States' (Moravcsik, 1993, p. 507). And when states choose to transfer sovereignty to supranational institutions, 'their principal national interest will be not only to define and limit that transfer of sovereignty very carefully but also meticulously to structure the central institutions so as to preserve a balance of power within the integrationist framework in favor of the nation-states themselves' (Milward and Sørensen, 1993, p. 19).

In the most general sense, European integration has served to rescue the nation-state. 'The European Community has been its buttress, an indispensable part of the nation-state's post-war construction. Without it, the nation-state could not have offered to its citizens the same measure of security and prosperity which it has provided and which has justified its survival' (Milward, 1992, p. 3). '[S]tates will make further surrenders of sovereignty if, but only if they have to in the attempt to survive' (Milward, 1992, p. 446). Stanley Hoffmann arrived at the same conclusion along somewhat different lines: 'in areas of key importance to the national interest, nations prefer the certainty, or the self-controlled uncertainty, of national self-reliance, to the uncontrolled uncertainty of the untested blender. ... The logic of diversity implies that, on a vital issue, losses are not compensated by gains on other (and especially not on other less vital) issues: nobody wants to be fooled .... The logic of integration deems the uncertainties of the supranational functional process creative; the logic of diversity sees them as destructive past a certain threshold: Russian roulette is fine only as long as the gun is filled with blanks' (Hoffmann, 1966, p. 882).

Despite these gloomy predictions, by the early 1990s, the annual regulatory output of the European Community was greater than that of most individual states and 75–80 per cent of national legislation was subject to prior consultation with the European Commission (Majone, 1994). How do state-centrists account for this expansion? Some argue that state competencies have merely shifted: 'The European nation-state has lost some economic functions to the EC and some defense functions altogether, while gaining functions in what had previously been more private and local spheres. Overall, the bars of the [national] cage may not have changed very much. Citizens still need to deploy most of their vigilance at the national level' (Mann, 1993, p. 130). For others, state sovereignty is still intact: ' ... policymaking in the Community has not in itself detracted from national sovereignty: what is changed is the wish of national legislatures and governments to do certain things rather than their legal or constitutional right or capacity to do them' (Taylor, 1991, p. 123). Still others worry less about the scope as long as Member States control the depth of European intrusion. And here voluntarism and the individual veto – 'fundamental decisions in the EC can be viewed as taking place in a non-coercive unanimity voting system' (Moravcsik, 1993, p. 498) – combine to make outcomes converge to the lowest common denominator. 'The need to compromise with the least forthcoming government imposes a binding constraint on the possibilities for greater co-operation, driving EC agreements toward the lowest common denominator. 'A lowest common denominator outcome does *not* mean that final agreements perfectly reflect the preferences of the least forthcoming government – since it is generally in its interest to compromise somewhat rather than veto an agreement – but only that the range of possible agreements is decisively constrained by its preferences' (Moravcsik, 1993, p. 501). However, many outcomes cannot be characterized as lowest common denominator (see our argument below), a point that some state-centrists are now conceding (Moravcsik, 1995, fn 3).

Community institutions that try to challenge Member States do not get very far: 'As for the common organs set up by the national governments, when they try to act as a European executive and parliament, they are both condemned to operate in the fog maintained around them by the governments and slapped down if they try to dispel the fog and reach the people themselves' (Hoffmann, 1966, p. 910).

One contribution of liberal institutionalism, and of Andrew Moravcsik's work in particular, lies in the attempt to specify the conditions under which 'international cooperation ... tends on balance to *strengthen* the domestic power of executives *vis-à-vis* opposition groups' (Moravcsik, 1994, p. 7, his emphasis). However, even though the billiard ball of the nation-state is cracked open to understand state preferences, state-centrists resort to unitary actor assumptions to analyse interstate bargaining: 'Groups articulate preferences; governments aggregate them' (Moravcsik, 1993, p. 483).

makers, devolving limited authority to supranational institutions to achieve specific policy goals. Decision-making in the EU is determined by bargaining among state executives. To the extent that supranational institutions arise, they serve the ultimate goals of state executives. The state-centric model does not maintain that policy-making is determined by state executives in every detail, only that the overall direction of policy-making is consistent with state control. States may be well served by creating a judiciary, for example, that allows them to enforce collective agreements, or a bureaucracy that implements those agreements. But such institutions are not autonomous supranational agents. Rather, they have limited powers to achieve state-oriented collective goods.

EU decisions, according to the state-centric model, reflect the lowest common denominator among state executive positions. Although Member State executives decide jointly, they are not compelled to swallow policies they find unacceptable because decision-making on important issues operates on the basis of unanimity. This allows states to maintain individual as well as collective control over outcomes. While some governments are not able to integrate as much as they would wish, none is forced into deeper collaboration than it really wants.

State decision-making in this model does not exist in a political vacuum. In this respect, the state-centric model takes issue with realist conceptions of international relations which focus on relations among unitary state actors. State executives are located in domestic political arenas, and their negotiating positions are influenced by domestic political interests. But – and this is an important assumption – those state arenas are discrete. That is to say, state decision-makers respond to political pressures that are *nested* within each state. So, the 15 state executives bargaining in the European arena are complemented by 15 separate state arenas that provide the sole channel for domestic political interests at the European level. The core claim of the state-centric model is that policy-making in the EU is determined primarily by state executives constrained by political interests nested within autonomous state arenas that connect subnational groups to European affairs.[2]

---

[2] States or state leaders are conceived as monopolizing the interface between the neatly separated arenas of European and domestic politics. European decision-making is seen as 'a process that takes place in two successive stages: governments first define a set of interests, then bargain among themselves in an effort to realize those interests' (Moravcsik, 1993, p. 481). State-centrists make short shrift of interest group representation in Brussels: 'Even when societal interests are transnational, the principal form of their political expression remains national' (Moravcsik, 1991, p. 26). European and national politics belong to two different worlds because there is no need for direct interplay: 'If parties have organized themselves only in a superficial way in the European Parliament, that is because no more has been needed ... it is within the nation that political parties have to fulfill their task of organizing a democratic consensus' (Milward, 1992, p. 446). Other state-centrists argue that domestic and EU arenas are nested rather than interconnected because it is in the interest of state executives to keep them that way: 'the EC does not diffuse the domestic influence of the

One can envision several alternative models to this one. The one we present here, which we describe as *multi-level governance*, is drawn from several sources (Marks, 1992, 1993; Sbragia, 1992, 1993; Schmitter, 1992a, b; Majone, 1994, 1995; Pierson, 1996; Leibfried and Pierson, 1995; see also Caporaso and Keeler, 1993 for an overview). Once again, our aim is not to reiterate any one scholar's perspective, but to elaborate essential elements of a model drawn from several strands of writing which makes the case that European integration has weakened the state.

The multi-level governance model does not reject the view that state executives and state arenas are important, or that these remain the *most* important pieces of the European puzzle. However, when one asserts that the state no longer monopolizes European level policy-making or the aggregation of domestic interests, a very different polity comes into focus. First, according to the multi-level governance model, decision-making competencies are shared by actors at different levels rather than monopolized by state executives. That is to say, supranational institutions – above all, the European Commission, the European Court, and the European Parliament – have independent influence in policy-making that cannot be derived from their role as agents of state executives. State executives may play an important role but, according to the multi-level governance model, one must also analyse the independent role of European level actors to explain European policy-making.

Second, collective decision-making among states involves a significant loss of control for individual state executives. Lowest common denominator outcomes are available only on a subset of EU decisions, mainly those concerning the scope of integration. Decisions concerning rules to be enforced across the EU (e.g. harmonizing regulation of product standards, labour conditions, etc.) have a zero-sum character, and necessarily involve gains or losses for individual states.

Third, political arenas are interconnected rather than nested. While national arenas remain important for the formation of state executive preferences, the multi-level model rejects the view that subnational actors are nested exclusively within them. Instead, subnational actors operate in both national and supranational arenas, creating transnational associations in the process. States do not monopolize links between domestic and European actors, but are one among a variety of actors contesting decisions that are made at a variety of levels. In this perspective, complex interrelationships in domestic politics do not stop at the nation-state, but extend to the European level. The separation between domestic

executive; it centralizes it. Rather than "domesticating" the international system, the EC "internationalizes" domestic politics. While cooperation may limit the *external* flexibility of executives, it simultaneously confers greater domestic influence ... In this sense, the EC strengthens the state' (Moravcsik, 1994, p. 3, his emphasis).

and international politics, which lies at the heart of the state-centric model, is rejected by the multi-level governance model. States are an integral and powerful part of the EU, but they no longer provide the sole interface between supranational and subnational arenas, and they share, rather than monopolize, control over many activities that take place in their respective territories.

III. Sources of Multi-Level Governance

Why would states allow competencies to be shifted out of their own hands to supranational or subnational institutions? Why would states allow their own sovereignty to be weakened? Why would states tolerate European integration if it threatened their own political control? These questions are commonly posed by state-centrists who wish to analyse the sources of European integration. One way to answer them is to argue that states receive something important in return. They give up a measure of external control, but they are thereby empowered *vis-à-vis* domestic interests (Moravcsik, 1994). Or the loss of control is superficial. According to Milward and Sørensen, when nation-states choose to transfer sovereignty to common institutions, 'their principal national interest will be not only to define and limit that transfer of sovereignty very carefully but also meticulously to structure the central institutions so as to preserve a balance of power within the integrationist framework in favor of the nation-states themselves' (Milward and Sørensen, 1993, p. 19).

There are doubtless other answers to these questions but, before we go any further, we need to take a second look at the questions themselves, for they fulfil the dictum that 'he who asks the question, supplies the answer'. They conflate two different meanings of the term 'state'. In the first place, the state is an institution, i.e. a particular constellation of formal (and informal) rules that specify the location, extent and basis of legitimate authority in a society. From this standpoint, which reflects the normal meaning of the word in political science, the state is a set of socially accepted norms or rules that structure authority irrespective of any particular set of rulers who happen to be in positions of authority.

In its second usage, the term 'state' refers to central state executives, national governments, or whole countries as political actors. This conception is derived from international relations, and it is a legacy of the realist understanding of international relations as a system determined by countries operating as discrete and autonomous actors. This usage is ubiquitous in commentary and theoretical analysis of the EU, as when one reads that the United Kingdom wants to weaken supranational institutions, that Germany acquiesced to monetary union, or that particular Member States support or oppose expanding the role of the European Parliament. This way of framing observation is not merely shorthand, for it is

348   GARY MARKS, LIESBET HOOGHE AND KERMIT BLANK

based on theoretically pregnant suppositions about how one should conceive the EU.

Our starting point in this article is to make a clear distinction between institutions and actors, i.e. between the state (and the EU) as sets of rules and the particular individuals, groups, and organizations which act within those institutions. This has the decided advantage of leading one away from reified accounts, common in the state-centric literature, of the goals, preferences, desires, and plans of states, towards an *actor-centred* approach in which one specifies particular actors as participants in decision-making.

When writers refer to the state as an actor, they usually have in mind one or more of the following: public administrators, parliamentarians, judges, the armed forces, subnational executives and, most importantly in the context of European Union decision-making, party leaders serving in national governments. From this perspective, the question is not, 'why do states give up sovereignty in the process of European integration?' but 'why do particular actors (party leaders in national governments) change institutional rules (e.g. shift competencies to the European Union)?'.

It makes little sense to conceive of whole states or national governments as the key actors in European decision-making. One cannot assume that those serving in national governments give priority to sustaining the state as an institution. This is an empirical matter. Institutions influence the goals of those who hold positions of power within them, but it is unlikely that political actors will define their own preferences solely in terms of what will benefit their institution. The degree to which an actor's preferences will reflect institutional goals depends, in general, on the extent to which an institution structures the totality of that individual's life, on how positively or negatively the institution is viewed, on the strength of contending institutional, personal and ideological loyalties, and on the length of time in which the individual expects to stay within that institution.

The key actors we are concerned with here are elected politicians in the central state executive. Their tenure of office is relatively brief. Unlike judges, army officers, civil servants – or Commission officials – they can expect to remain in their positions for a matter of years rather than decades. Many are committed to substantive policy goals that are not derived from the goal of strengthening state executive control. And, most importantly, sustaining their tenure in government requires electoral success. Whatever substantive goals a political leader has, their implementation depends on winning the next election, maintaining party (and, in some cases, coalition) cohesion, and fostering ties with strategic constituencies.

There are two sets of reasons why government leaders may wish to shift decision-making to the supranational level: the political benefits may outweigh the costs of losing political control or there may be intrinsic benefits having to do with shifting responsibility for unpopular decisions or insulating decision-making from domestic pressures.[3]

1. Costs v. *benefits of decisional reallocation.* Reallocating competencies to the supranational level may be an effective means of providing information and other resources to meet the transaction costs involved in formulating, negotiating, and implementing collective decisions (Majone, 1995, 1994; Williamson, 1985, 1993; Moe, 1987, 1990). Decisional reallocation may have significant costs for government leaders, but these costs may (a) be less politically salient than the benefits of more efficient delivery of collective policies; or (b) they may be lagged with respect to the benefits, and therefore of less weight for political leaders having a high discount rate. The relative importance of these conditions depends on the potential efficiency gains to be realized by centralizing decision-making in a particular policy area, the domestic electoral and party-political context facing government leaders, and their substantive policy goals.

From this perspective, sovereignty is merely one goal among others. To the extent that political leaders have a short time horizon (and thus a high discount rate), and the substantive policy stream of European integration is more salient for powerful domestic constituencies than its decisional implications, so state sovereignty may be sacrificed for efficient policy provision. It is worth stressing that we are not making the argument that supranational empowerment is a Pareto-optimal outcome for Europeans. It suffices that government leaders are able to reap a private gain by instituting a Pareto-suboptimal policy (for example agricultural subsidies) as a means, say, to reward a powerful constituency.

2. Intrinsic benefits of decisional reallocation. Government leaders may shift decision-making to the supranational level because they positively wish to do so. In the first place, they may prefer to avoid responsibility for certain policies. A recent highly publicized case where a government was clearly relieved to be impotent was the conflict in the UK in 1995 over the transportation of calves to the Continent in crates for eventual slaughter. In response to the (sometimes violent) demonstrations of animal rights' advocates in British ports, William Waldegrave, the Minister of Agriculture, explained that the British government could not be blamed because effective decision-making was made in Brussels. He advised opponents of the policy to demonstrate in Brussels rather than in the UK, which they promptly did.

Second, government leaders may shift decision-making to insulate it from political pressures. The autonomy of central banks is designed on this premise. The same logic can lead a government to cede competencies to the European Commission or to an independent agency within the EU. Recent examples

---

[3] Paul Pierson has developed an interesting set of arguments about 'gaps' in state executive control that parallel several points made in this section (1996).

include the decision on the part of national governments to give the Commission considerable authority over European mergers, and to envisage the creation of an independent European central bank with exclusive responsibility for monetary policy. By insulating policy-making in this way, government leaders seek to control policy after they have left office. To the extent that leaders face a trade-off between preserving state sovereignty and assuaging a particular constituency, shifting the electoral balance in their party's favour, or institutionalizing deep-seated preferences, they may sacrifice state sovereignty.

Historically, the creation of nation-states in Western Europe enabled rulers to mobilize and enhance their resource base. State-building was a means to more effective war making, more efficient national markets, a larger economic base, and more efficient means for ruling elites to extract taxes from it. But the fit between the institution of the state and the preferences of political elites is not written in stone. If we regard states as sets of commonly accepted rules that specify a particular authoritative order, then we need to ask how such rules may change over time and whether and how they will be defended. The point we make in this section is that states may be weakened by government elites if they seek to achieve their own policy goals and respond to competitive pressures generated within liberal democracies.

Limits on Individual State Executive Control

The most obvious constraint on the capacity of a national government to determine outcomes in the EU is the decision rule of qualified majority voting in the Council of Ministers for a range of issues from the internal market to trade, agriculture and the environment. In this respect the EU is clearly different from international regimes, such as the UN or WTO, in which majoritarian principles of decision-making are confined to symbolic issues.

State-centrists have sought to blunt the theoretical implications of collective decision-making in the Council of Ministers along two lines of argument.

The first is that while state executives may sacrifice some independence of control by participating in collective decision-making, they more than compensate for this by their increased ability to achieve the policy outcomes they want. Moravcsik has argued at length that collective decision-making actually enhances state executive control because state executives will only agree to participate insofar as 'policy coordination increases their control over domestic policy outcomes, permitting them to achieve goals that would not otherwise be possible' (1993, p. 485). By participating in the European Union, state executives are able to provide policies, such as a cleaner environment, higher levels of economic growth, etc. that could not be provided autonomously. But two entirely different conceptions of power are involved here, and it would be well to keep them separate.

STATE-CENTRIC *V.* MULTI-LEVEL GOVERNANCE   351

On the one hand, power or political control may be conceptualized as control over persons. *A* has power over *B* to the extent that she can get *B* to do something he would not otherwise do (Dahl, 1961). This is a zero-sum conception: if one actor gains power, another loses it. This conception of power underlies Max Weber's definition of state sovereignty as the monopoly of legitimate coercion within a given territory, and although this definition has been contested, most subsequent theorists of the state have continued to view sovereignty in terms of the extent to which states control the lives of those in their territories.

By contrast, power conceived as the ability to achieve desired outcomes involves not only power over persons, but power over nature in the broadest sense. From this standpoint one would evaluate the power of an institution as a function of its success in achieving substantive goals, rather than in terms of its relations with other actors. Logically, this would lead one to say that a successful national government in a federal European state has more control than a less successful national government in a confederal state.

The latter conception is not invalid, for concepts can be used in any way one wishes to use them. However, it confuses two phenomena that we have already sought to untangle: institutionally rooted relations of power among political actors, and the ability of political actors to achieve substantive policy goals. One of the causal dynamics that may lead government leaders to shift decision-making away from the institution in which they are located, as we have argued above, is precisely that they may achieve desired policy outcomes by so doing.

State-centrists have also claimed that majoritarianism in the Council of Ministers camouflages, but does not invalidate, state sovereignty. They argue that treaty revisions, new policy initiatives, and certain sensitive areas remain subject to unanimity and hence the national veto; that the Luxembourg Compromise gives state executives the power to veto any decision under majority rule that they deem contravenes their vital national interests; and that, ultimately, a state executive could pull out of the EU if it so wished.

The Luxembourg veto is available to national governments only under restricted conditions and even then, it is a relatively blunt weapon. As we detail below, the Luxembourg veto is restricted by the willingness of other state executives to tolerate its use in a particular case. In one famous case, an attempt to veto annual agricultural prices in 1982 by the UK government was actually rejected by the other Member State executives. The Luxembourg veto is a defensive rather than an offensive weapon in that it can only be used to reject a particular course of action, not select another. The German government barred a Council decision to reduce agricultural prices for cereals and colza in 1985, but it was unable to stop the Commission from achieving the required reductions by resorting to its emergency powers (Teasdale, 1993).

352   GARY MARKS, LIESBET HOOGHE AND KERMIT BLANK

From the standpoint of physical force, Member States retain ultimate sovereignty by virtue of their continuing monopoly of the means of legitimate coercion within their respective territories. If a national government broke its treaty commitments and pulled out of the EU, the EU itself has no armed forces with which to contest that decision. Here the contrast between the European Union and a federal system, such as the United States, seems perfectly clear. In the last analysis, states retain ultimate coercive control of their populations.

But monopoly of legitimate coercion tells us less and less about the realities of political, legal, and normative control in contemporary capitalist societies. A Weberian approach, focusing on the extent to which states are able to monopolize legitimate coercion, appears more useful for understanding the emergence and consolidation of states from the twelfth century than for understanding changes in state sovereignty in the latter half of the twentieth century. Although the EU does not possess armed forces, it requires no leap of imagination to argue that a national government is constrained by the economic and political sanctions – and consequent political-economic dislocation – that it would almost certainly face if it revoked its treaty commitments and pulled out of the European Union. Analyses of the ultimate sovereignty of Member States and the sanctions available to the EU under extreme circumstances have an air of unreality about them because, under present and foreseeable circumstances, they remain entirely hypothetical.

Limits on Collective State Executive Control

We have argued that government leaders may have positive grounds for shifting decision-making to supranational institutions and that they do not exert individual control over binding collective decisions in the Council of Ministers. Here we argue that there are reasons for believing that even collectively, national governments are constrained in their ability to control supranational institutions they have created at the European level.

1. The treaty process. In the first place, while state executive control of the big decisions, the treaties, is impressive, it is not complete. State executives play a decisive role in drafting the basic treaties and major legislation underlying the EU, such as the Single European Act and the Maastricht Treaty, but they are far less dominant in most areas of day-to-day policy-making.

Because state representatives are the only legally recognized signatories of the treaties undergirding the EU, they are actually empowered in the process of formulating treaties. If a domestic group wishes to influence a clause of a formal EU treaty it must adopt a state-centric strategy and focus pressure on its national government. Treaty making is the realm of negotiation among national leaders, the national veto, and side-payments to bring recalcitrant national governments on board.

In the pre-Maastricht era, the process of ratification was dominated by state executive leaders through party control of national legislatures. Not only did they determine the content of treaties, but they could be reasonably confident that those treaties would be accepted in their respective domestic arenas.[4] European integration was a technocratic process, involving co-ordination among state executives to achieve limited and contingent policy goals. The course of European integration was pragmatic, not politicized, and state representatives dominated decision-making to the virtual exclusion of other political actors. When this incremental pattern of state executive decision-making was interrupted, as it was by de Gaulle in the 1960s and Thatcher in the 1980s, it was to reassert state sovereignty as a constraint on European integration.

In the wake of the Maastricht Treaty, the process of treaty ratification has shifted beyond the control of state executives to the politicized realms of party-political competition, parliamentary debates and mass referendums. The Maastricht Treaty itself gives only subtle hints to the intensity of response it generated. It lacks any coherent institutional blueprint or constitutional ambition, but is an assembly of discrete and vague policy initiatives that, with the major exception of proposed monetary union, are an extension, rather than an overhaul, of the existing framework. One of the hallmarks of the Treaty, and a clue to the alienation felt by many Europeans, is that it is written in opaque Euro-legalese which is virtually unintelligible to the uninitiated. But whatever the reasons for its tumultuous reception, it has implanted the expectation that state executives must submit future treaties to thorough democratic scrutiny. State executive leaders still have considerable power to frame basic alternatives, but they no longer control the treaty process as a whole.

2. Constraints on the ability of state executive principals to control supranational agents. From a transaction analysis standpoint, it is not feasible for Member State executives to plan for all possible future ambiguities and sources of contention, so they create institutions, such as the European Commission and the European Court of Justice, that can adapt incomplete contracts to changing circumstances (Majone, 1995; Pierson, 1996). According to agency theory, a principal exerts control by selecting his agent, creating a structure of incentives to induce the required behaviour (Williamson, 1985). If a principal finds out at some later date that an agent is not acting in the desired way, he can always fire the agent or reform the incentives. Scholars who have applied principal–agent theory to American political institutions have found that the effectiveness of such incentives and disincentives is limited (Moe, 1990). In the EU the ability of principals, i.e. Member State executives, to control supranational agents is constrained by the multiplicity of principals, the mistrust that exists among them,

---

[4] The only exception was the European Defence Community which was voted down in the French Assemblée in 1954. After that débâcle, the European Political Community was quietly dropped as well.

impediments to coherent principal action, informational asymmetries between principals and agents and by the unintended consequences of institutional change. We discuss these briefly in turn.

Multiplicity of principals. It is one thing for a single principal to control an agent. It is quite different for several principals to control an agent. And it is yet another thing for several principals prone to competition and conflict to control an agent. Supranational institutions in the EU are not external to conflicts among Member State executives, but are intimately involved in them and are able to extend their role as a result. One of the consequences of the multiplicity of contending principals is that basic treaties of the EU tend to be ambiguous documents providing ample room for diverse interpretations on the part of both principals and agents. The treaties are hammered out in interstate negotiations in which each state executive wishes to win domestic acclaim for having made collective progress in solving a variety of policy problems, but where each has a veto on the content of the agreement. There is a powerful incentive to ambiguity on points of contention to allow each participating government to claim success in representing national interests.

The basic treaties of the EU have legitimated Commission initiatives in several policy areas, yet they are vague enough to give the Commission wide latitude in designing institutions. This was the case in the creation of structural policy which, in the wake of the Single European Act, was transformed by the Commission from a side-payment transferring resources from richer to poorer countries to an interventionist instrument of regional economic development (Hooghe, 1996).

The European Court does not act merely as an agent in adapting Member State agreements to new contingencies, but actively adjudicates disagreements among Member State executives, a role that places it in a position of authority not merely as the supreme judiciary in Europe, but one that is above all Member State actors, state executives included (Volcansek, 1992; Burley and Mattli, 1993; Lenaerts, 1992).

Constraints on change. Because the decision rule for major institutional change is unanimity, it is often remarked that this poses a high hurdle for integration. However, unanimity applies for *any* institutional change in the EU, whether it empowers supranational institutions or reins them in. Supranational actors need only dent the united front of state executives in order to block a proposed change. The logic of lowest common denominator under unanimity voting limits the ability of state executives to shorten their collective leash on supranational institutions, as well as embark on new integrationist measures. Once a suprana-tional institution has a power or powers beyond those necessary to serve as a mere agent of state executives, it needs only to gain support from one or more principals to sustain its position.[5]

Informational asymmetries. Agents may gain a potent source of influence if they develop access to information or skills that is not available to principals (Majone, 1995, 1994; Eichener, 1992). As a small and thinly staffed organization, the Commission has only a fraction of the financial and human resources available to national governments, but its position as interlocutor with national governments, subnational authorities and numerous interest groups gives it a unique informational base. The Commission's job in reducing transaction costs of policy co-ordination among Member State governments provides it with unparalleled access to information and, therefore, the means for independent influence *vis-à-vis* those governments.

Detailed regulation as a response to mutual mistrust. It is in the collective interest of Member State executives to enact certain common regulations, but each may be better off if others adhere to them while it defects. To contain defection, state executives have created a Court of Justice with unprecedented powers of adjudication among Member State actors, as described below. A further consequence of mutual mistrust is the highly detailed character of European regulation. While state executives are induced to ambiguity in the high politics of treaty making, they give the Commission latitude to formulate very precise regulations on specific policies. Instead of determining general provisions that are broadly applicable ('relational contracting'), state executives allow the Commission to propose legislation that approximates a 'complete contract', legislation that is designed to straightjacket principals and so reduce their scope for evasion (Majone, 1995). This allows the Commission to legitimate its role in technocratic terms, as the hub of numerous highly specialized policy networks of technical experts designing detailed regulations.

Unintended consequences of institutional change. A final limit on the capacity of state executives to control their supranational agents lies in their inability to forecast precisely the effects of their own collective actions. The complexity of policy-making across disparate territories and multiple actors, the changing patterns of mutual interaction among policy arenas, the sensitivity of EU decision-making to international and domestic exogenous shocks – these contribute to a fluid and inherently unpredictable environment which dilutes the

---

[5] As is apparently what has happened in the case of the EU's cohesion policy. The Commission managed to secure its considerable role in this policy area by gaining the support of some recipient governments, thwarting the attempts on the part of the governments of the UK, France, Germany and Spain to limit severely the Commission's power (Marks, 1996).

356   GARY MARKS, LIESBET HOOGHE AND KERMIT BLANK

extent to which Member State decisions at time T_0 can control supranational actors at T_1.

IV. Policy-Making in the European Union

The questions we are asking have to do with who decides what in European Union policy-making. If the state-centric model is valid, we would find a systematic pattern of state executive dominance. That entails three conditions. National governments, by virtue of the European Council and the Council of Ministers, should be able to impose their preferences collectively upon other European institutions, i.e. the European Commission, the European Parliament and the European Court of Justice. In other words, the latter three European institutions should be agents effectively controlled by state-dominated European institutions. Second, national governments should be able to maintain individual sovereignty *vis-à-vis* other national governments. And thirdly, national governments should be able to control the mobilization of subnational interests in the European arena. If, however, the multi-level governance model is valid, we should find, first, that the European Council and Council of Ministers share decisional authority with supranational institutions; second, that individual state executives cannot deliver the outcomes they wish through collective state executive decisions; and, finally, that subnational interests mobilize directly in the European arena or use the EU as a public space to pressure state executives into particular actions.

We divide the policy-making process into four sequential phases: policy initiation, decision-making, implementation and adjudication. We focus on informal practices in addition to formal rules, for it is vital to understand how institutions actually shape the behaviour of political actors in the European arena.

Policy Initiation: Commission as Agenda-setter with a Price – Listen, Make Sense, and Time Aptly

In political systems that involve many actors, complex procedures and multiple veto points, the power to set the agenda is extremely important. The European Commission alone has the formal power to initiate and draft legislation, which includes the right to amend or withdraw its proposal at any stage in the process, and it is the think-tank for new policies (Article 155, EC). From a multi-level governance perspective, the European Commission has significant autonomous influence over the agenda. According to the state-centric model, this formal power is largely decorative: in reality the European Commission draws up legislation primarily to meet the demands of state executives.

At first sight, the practice of policy initiation is consistent with a state-centric interpretation. Analysis of 500 recent directives and regulations by the French Conseil d'Etat found that only a minority of EU proposals were spontaneous initiatives of the Commission. Regulatory initiative at the European level is demand driven rather than the product of autonomous supranational action, but the demands come not only from government leaders. A significant number of initiatives originate in the European Parliament, the Economic and Social Committee, regional governments, and various private and public-interest groups (Majone, 1994).

Such data should be evaluated carefully. For one thing, regulatory initiative at national and European levels is increasingly intermeshed. In its report, the Conseil d'Etat estimated that the European Commission is consulted beforehand on 75–80 per cent of French national legislation. Jacques Delors' prediction that by the year 2000 about 80 per cent of national economic and social legislation would be of Community origin has a solid base in reality (Majone, 1994). Moreover, it is one thing to be the first to articulate an issue, and quite another to influence how that issue will be taken up, with whom, and under what set of rules. And in each of these respects the influence of the Commission extends beyond its formal role, partly because of its unique political and administrative resources, discussed below, and partly because the Council is stymied by intergovernmental competition.

An organization that may serve as a powerful principal with respect to the Commission is the European Council, the summit of the political leaders of the Member States (plus the President of the Commission) held every six months. The European Council has immense prestige and legitimacy and a quasi-legal status as the body which defines 'general political guidelines' (Title 1, Art. D, Treaty of the European Union). However, its control of the European agenda is limited because it meets rarely and has only a skeleton permanent staff. The European Council provides the Commission with general policy mandates rather than specific policy proposals, and such mandates have proved to be a flexible basis for the Commission to build legislative programmes.

More direct constraints on the Commission originate from the Council of Ministers and the European Parliament. Indeed, the power of initiative has increasingly become a shared competence, permanently subject to contestation, among the three institutions. The Council (Article 152, EC) and, since the Maastricht Treaty, the European Parliament (Article 138b, EC) can request the Commission to produce proposals, although they cannot draft proposals themselves (Nugent, 1994). Council Presidencies began to exploit this window in the legal texts from the mid-1980s, when state executives began to attach higher priority to the Council Presidency (Nugent, 1994). Several governments bring detailed proposals with them to Brussels when they take over the Council

Presidency. Another way for the Council to circumvent the Commission's formal monopoly of legislative proposal is to make soft law, i.e. by ratifying common opinions, resolutions, agreements, and recommendations (Nugent, 1994; Snyder, 1994).

The effect of this on the Commission's agenda-setting role is double edged. On the one hand, the Commission finds it politically difficult to ignore detailed Council initiatives or soft law, even though their legal status is vague (Snyder, 1994). On the other hand, state executives are intent on using the European arena to attain a variety of policy goals, and this gives the Commission allies for integrationist initiatives.

The European Parliament has made use of its newly gained competence in Article 138b. In return for the approval of the Santer Commission in January 1995, it extracted from the Commission President a pledge to renegotiate the code of conduct (dating from 1990) between the two institutions in an effort to gain greater influence on the Commission's pen, its right of initiative.

The European Council, the Council, and the European Parliament have each succeeded in circumscribing the Commission's formal monopoly of initiative more narrowly, though none can claim that it has reduced the position of the Commission to that of an agent. Agenda-setting is now a shared and contested competence among the four European institutions, rather than monopolized by one actor.

But the diffusion of control over the EU's agenda does not stop here. Interest groups have mobilized intensively in the European arena and, while their power is difficult to pinpoint, it is clear that the Commission takes their input seriously. The passage of the Single European Act precipitated a rapid growth of European legislation and a corresponding increase in interest group representation in Europe. An outpouring of case study research suggests that the number and variety of groups involved is as great, and perhaps greater, than in any national capital. National and regional organizations of every kind have mobilized in Brussels, and these are flanked by a large and growing number of European peak organizations and individual companies from across Europe. According to a Commission report, some 3,000 interest groups and lobbies, or about 10,000 people, were based in Brussels in 1992. Among these there are 500 'Euro-groups' which aggregate interests at the European level (McLaughlin and Greenwood, 1995). Most groups target their lobbying activity at the European Commission and the European Parliament, for these are perceived to be more accessible than the secretive Council (Mazey and Richardson, 1993).

Subnational authorities now mobilize intensively in Brussels. Apart from the Committee of the Regions, established by the Maastricht Treaty, individual subnational authorities have set up almost 100 regional offices in Brussels and a wide variety of interregional associations (Hooghe and Marks, 1996; Hooghe, 1995a; Marks *et al.,* 1996).

Agenda-setting is therefore increasingly a shared and contested competence, with European institutions competing for control, and interest groups and subnational actors vying to influence the process. This is not much different from the situation in some national polities, particularly those organized federally.

As a consequence, it is often difficult to apportion responsibility for particular initiatives. This is true for the most intensively studied initiative of all – the internal market programme – which was pressed forward by business interests, the Commission, and the European Parliament, as well as by state executives (Cameron, 1992; Moravcsik, 1991; Cowles, 1995; Majone, 1994; Dehousse, 1992; Garrett and Weingast, 1993). Because the Commission plays a subtle initiating role, its influence is not captured by analysis of which institution formally announces a new policy. For example, the White Paper on *Growth, Competitiveness and Employment* was publicly mandated by the European Council in June 1993, but it did so in response to detailed guidelines for economic renewal tabled by the Commission President.

The Commission has considerable leverage, but it is conditional, not absolute. It depends on its capacity to nurture and use diverse contacts, its ability to anticipate and mediate demands, its decisional efficiency, and the unique expertise it derives from its role as think-tank of the European Union.

The Commission is always on the look-out for information and political support. It has developed an extensive informal machinery of advisory committees and working groups for consultation and pre-negotiation, some of which are made up of Member State nominees, but others of interest group representatives and experts who give the Commission access to independent information and legitimacy. The Commission has virtually a free hand in creating new networks, and in this way it is able to reach out to new constituencies, including a variety of subnational groups.

An example of this strategy was the creation of an Advisory Council for Local and Regional Authorities in 1988 to advise the Commission on initiatives in cohesion policy. The Commission hoped to mobilize support from below for a 'partnership' approach to structural programming in which the Commission, national and subnational authorities would jointly design, finance, and implement economic development programmes. Jacques Delors and the Commission realized that they would need significant external support to overcome the reluctance of several Member State governments to give subnational governments greater influence over economic development policy. One of the Commission's longer-term goals was to institutionalize regional participation, and a step was taken in this direction with the establishment of a Committee of the Regions in 1993. While the Commission alone was not responsible for this outcome –

pressure by the German Länder and the Belgian regions on their respective governments was pivotal – the experience of the Advisory Council laid the groundwork (Hooghe, 1996).

The extent to which the Commission initiates policy (Article 155) depends also on its alacrity. A striking example of this is the European Energy Charter, a formal agreement between Russia and west European states guaranteeing Russian energy supply after the collapse of the Soviet Union (Matlary, 1993). An EU policy came into being because the Commission pre-empted an alternative intergovernmental approach preferred by the Dutch, German, and British governments. Acting on a vague mandate of the European Council in June 1990, the Commission negotiated a preliminary agreement with the Russian government in 1991. Member State executives, presented with a *fait accompli*, accepted the European Community as the appropriate forum for the Charter and gave the Commission a toe-hold in international energy policy (Matlary, 1993), a noteworthy incursion in a policy area which had been dominated by national governments.

The Commission's capacity to move quickly is a function of its internal cohesion. An example from industrial policy illustrates the limits of the Commission's agenda-setting power when it is internally divided. In Spring 1990, Europe's largest electronics firms pressured the Commission for a European strategy in the semi-conductors' sector as a means of securing EU financial support and market protection. The Commission was paralysed for months as a result of internal disagreements. When it eventually produced a policy recommendation for a European industrial policy in the beginning of 1991, most firms had shifted their strategy to other arenas. The French firms, Bull and Thomson, had obtained guarantees from the French government for financial support, while others like Siemens and Olivetti were exploring strategic alliances with American or Japanese firms (Ross, 1993, 1995).

As the think-tank of the European Union, the Commission has responsibility for investigating the feasibility of new EU policies, a role that requires the Commission to solicit expertise. In this capacity it produces annually 200–300 reports, White Papers, Green Papers, and other studies and communications (Ludlow, 1991). Some are highly technical studies about, say, the administration of milk surpluses. Others are influential policy programmes such as the 1985 White Paper on the Internal Market (Cameron, 1992; Sandholtz and Zysman, 1989), the 1990 reform proposals for Common Agricultural Policy which laid the basis for the European position in the GATT negotiations, or the 1993 White Paper on *Growth, Competitiveness and Employment* which argued for more labour market flexibility.

As a small and thinly staffed organization, the Commission has only a fraction of the resources available to central state executives, but its position as interlocutor with national governments, subnational authorities and a large variety of interest groups gives it unparalleled access to information. The Commission has superior in-house knowledge and expertise in agriculture, where one-quarter of its staff is concentrated. It has formidable expertise in external trade and competition, the two other areas where Commission competence is firmly established. In other areas, the Commission relies on Member State submissions, its extensive advisory system of public and private actors, and paid consultants (Nugent, 1995).

The European Commission is a critical actor in the policy initiation phase, whether one looks at formal rules or practice. If one surveys the evidence one cannot conclude that the Commission serves merely as an agent of state executives. The point is not that the Commission is the only decisive actor. We discern instead a system of multi-level governance involving competition and interdependence among the Commission, Council, and European Parliament, each of which commands impressive resources in the intricate game of policy initiation.

Decision-making: State Sovereignty in Retreat

According to the Treaties, the main legislative body in the EU is not the European Parliament, but the Council of Ministers, an assembly of Member State executives. Until the Single European Act, the Council was the sole legislative authority. The thrust of the state-centric argument is to give great weight to the legislative powers of state executives in the decision-making stage. At this stage, state executives may be said to be in complete control. They adjust policies to their collective preferences, define the limits of European collaboration, determine the role of the European Commission and the ECJ and, if need be, curtail their activities. If previous decisions have unintended consequences, these can be corrected by the Council.

There is some plausibility to this argument, but it is one-dimensional. In the first place, one must take into account the serious constraints under which individual governments have operated since the Single European Act. Second, one should recognize that even collectively, state executives exert conditional, not absolute, control. State executive dominance is eroded in the decision-making process by the legislative power of the European Parliament, the role of the European Commission in overcoming transaction problems, and the efforts of interest groups to influence outcomes in the European arena.

The most transparent blow to state sovereignty has come from the successive extension of qualified majority voting under the Single European Act and the Maastricht Treaty. Qualified majority voting is now the rule for most policy areas covered by the original Treaty of Rome, including agriculture, trade, competition policy, transport, and policy areas concerned with the realization of the internal market, though there are important exceptions which include the EU budget, taxation, capital flows, self-employed persons and professions, visa policy (qualified majority from 1 January 1996), free movement of persons, and rights of employed persons (Dinan, 1994; Nugent, 1994; Schmitter, 1992b). The decision-making rules are complex, but the bottom line is clear: over broad areas of EU competence individual state executives may be outvoted.

The practice of qualified majority voting is complicated by the Luxembourg Compromise and by a 'veto culture' which is said to have predominated in the Council of Ministers. Under the Luxembourg Compromise state executives can veto decisions subject to majority rule if they claim that their national vital interests are at stake. The Luxembourg Compromise features far more strongly in academic debates about the EU than in the practice of European politics. It was invoked less than a dozen times between 1966 and 1981, and it has been used even less frequently since that time.

The Luxembourg Compromise was accompanied by a 'veto culture' which inhibited majority voting if a state executive expressed serious objections. During the 1970s, this led to the virtual paralysis of the Community as literally hundreds of Commission proposals were blocked. But the effectiveness of the veto culture was its undoing. It eroded during the 1980s as a result of growing intolerance with deadlock on the part of the European Parliament and most national leaders (Teasdale, 1993). The turning point was the inability of the British government in 1982 to veto a decision on agricultural prices to extract a larger British budgetary rebate. A qualified majority vote was taken at the meeting of Council of Ministers despite British objections.

Thereafter, state executives became more reluctant to invoke the compromise or tolerate its use by others. The last successful use of the Luxembourg veto was in June 1985, when the German government blocked a Council decision to reduce agricultural prices for cereals and colza. Since the Single European Act, which made majority voting the norm in a large number of areas, there has been just one attempt to invoke the compromise, and this failed. The Greek government vetoed a Council proposal concerning adjusted green exchange rates in 1988 in order to extract a more favourable exchange rate for the green drachma, but found itself isolated in the Council and was forced to retract the veto. In 1992–93, the French government threatened to veto the agricultural package of the GATT agreement, but eventually settled for a financial compensation package to cover what amounted to a 'discreet climbdown' (Teasdale, 1993). As Nugent has observed, the Luxembourg Compromise 'is in the deepest of sleeps and is subject only to very occasional and partial awakenings' (1994).

In this context, second order rules about the adoption of alternative voting procedures are extremely important. Amendments to the Council's Rules of Procedure in July 1987 have made it much easier to initiate a qualified majority vote. While previously only the Council President could call a vote, it now suffices that one representative – and that could be the Commission – demands a ballot and is supported by a simple majority of the Council (Nugent, 1994).

One of the most remarkable developments in the 1980s has been the transformation of the notion of 'vital national interest'. State executives wishing to exercise a Luxembourg veto have become dependent on the acquiescence of *other* state executives. They can no longer independently determine whether their vital national interest is at stake. As the British (1982), German (1985), Greek (1988) and French (1992–93) cases suggest, the conditions are restrictive (Nugent, 1994; Wallace, 1994; Teasdale, 1993). The Luxembourg Compromise has come to operate effectively only for decisions which involve some combination of the following characteristics: the perception of an unambiguous link to vital national interests; the prospect of serious domestic political damage to the government concerned; a national government which can credibly threaten to damage the general working of the European Union. While it originally legitimized unconditional defence of state sovereignty (de Gaulle vetoed the budgetary reform of 1965 on the grounds that it was too supranational), the notion of vital national interest has evolved to justify only defence of substantive interests, not defence of national sovereignty itself.

Even if a Member State executive is able to invoke the Luxembourg Compromise, the veto remains a dull weapon. It cannot block alternative courses of action, as the German Federal government experienced in 1985 after it had stopped a Council regulation on lower prices for cereal and colza. The Commission simply invoked its emergency powers and achieved virtually the same reductions unilaterally (Teasdale, 1993). Moreover, a veto rarely settles an issue, unless the status quo is the preferred outcome for the vetoing government. But even in the two cases where the status quo was more desirable than the proposed change (the German and French cases), neither government was able to sustain the status quo. The German government was bypassed by the Commission; the French government was unable to block the GATT accord and, moreover, received only modest financial compensations in return for its acquiescence (Teasdale, 1993).

All in all, since the mid-1980s, the Luxembourg Compromise has been a weak instrument for the defence of state sovereignty. The British, German, Greek and French governments did not gain much by invoking or threatening to invoke it. Each came to accept that its options were severely constrained by European decisions. The Luxembourg Compromise is now mainly symbolic for domestic consumption. In each of the four cases the ensuing crisis enabled embattled governments to shift responsibility in the face of intense domestic pressure. Although national governments were not able to realize their substantive aims, they could at least claim they fought hard to achieve them.

364   GARY MARKS, LIESBET HOOGHE AND KERMIT BLANK

State executives have built a variety of specific safeguards into the Treaties. There are numerous derogations for particular states, especially on matters of taxation, state aids, monetary policy and energy policy. The Single European Act and the Maastricht Treaty preserve unanimity for the most sensitive or contested policy areas.

These qualifications soften the blow to national sovereignty. But a sensible discussion of the overall situation turns on the *extent* to which national sovereignty has been compromised, rather than on whether this has happened. Even under the doubtful premise that the Council is the sole decision-maker, it is now the case that state sovereignty has been pooled among a group of states in most EU policy areas (Wessels, 1992; Scharpf, 1994).

Collective state control exercised through the Council has diminished. That is first of all due to the growing role of the European Parliament in decision-making. The SEA and the Maastricht Treaty established co-operation and co-decision procedures which have transformed the legislative process from a simple Council-dominated process into an complex balancing act between Council, Parliament and Commission. Since the Maastricht Treaty, the two procedures apply to the bulk of EU legislation. The procedures are designed to encourage consensual decision-making between the three institutions. It is impossible for the Council to take legislative decisions without the support of at least one of the two other institutions unless it is unanimous. Moreover, the procedures enhance the agenda-setting power of the European Parliament (Tsebelis, 1994, 1995).

The co-operation procedure gives the Commission significant agenda-setting capacity (Tsebelis, 1994; Garrett and Weingast, 1993; Schmitter, 1992a; Weiler, 1991; compare with sceptical early prognoses: Bieber *et al.*, 1986). It may decide to take up or drop amendments from either the Council or Parliament, a power that makes it a broker – a consensus crafter – between the two institutions.

The intermeshing of institutions is particularly intricate under the co-decision procedure, under which the Parliament obtains an absolute veto, although it loses some agenda-setting power to the Council. If the Parliament or Council rejects the other's positions, a conciliation committee tries to hammer out a compromise. The committee consists of representatives from both institutions, with the Commission sitting in as broker. A compromise needs the approval of an absolute majority in the Parliament and a qualified majority in the Council. If there is no agreement, the initiative returns to the Council, which can then make a take-it-or-leave-it offer, which the Parliament can reject by absolute majority. So the Parliament has the final word.

Even though the outcome of the co-decision procedure is likely to be closer to the preferences of the Council than those of the Commission or Parliament (Tsebelis, 1995), it does not simply reflect Council preferences. Under both procedures the Council is locked in a complex relationship of co-operation and contestation with the two other institutions. This is multi-level governance in action, and is distinctly different from what would be expected in a state-centric system.

The erosion of collective state control goes further than this. It is difficult for state executives to resolve transaction costs in the egalitarian setting of the Council, particularly now, given that there are 15 such actors (Garrett and Weingast, 1993; Scharpf, 1988; Majone, 1994). The Council usually lacks information, expertise, and the co-ordination to act quickly and effectively, and this induces it to rely on the European Commission for leadership (Nugent, 1995).

The Commission, as a hierarchical organization, is usually able to present a more coherent position than the Council. Furthermore, Commission officials bring unusual skills to the negotiation table. As administrators, they have often been working on a particular policy issue for years; career mobility tends to be lower than for top echelons of most national administrations (Bellier, 1994). In addition, they have access to information and expertise from a variety of sources in the European Union. They tend to be exceptionally skilled political negotiators acclimatized to the diverse political styles of national representatives and the need to seek consensual solutions (Majone, 1993; Nugent, 1995; Bellier, 1994). Formal decision rules in the Council help the Commission to focus discussion or broker compromise. While Member State representatives preside at Council of Ministers' meetings and Council working groups, the Commission sits in to clarify, redraft, and finalize the proposal – in short, it holds the pen.

While recent theoretical literature has often stressed the intergovernmental character of the European Union, most of the empirical literature has emphasized the influence of the Commission. Cowles (1995), Bornschier and Fielder (1995), Sandholtz and Zysman (1989), and Cameron (1992) have demonstrated this leadership/broker role for the internal market programme; Sandholtz (1992), Peterson (1991) and Pollack (1995) for technology policy (Esprit, Race); Sandholtz (1993) for telecommunications; Cram (1993), Eichener (1992) and Majone (1994) for social policy; Ross (1993) for industrial policy; Matlary for energy policy (1993); Tömmel (1992), Marks (1996) and Hooghe (1996) for cohesion policy.

Cohesion policy offers an example of how the Commission may step beyond its role of umpire to become a negotiator. In establishing the framework for structural funds for 1994–99 in the summer of 1993, Commission officials negotiated bilaterally with officials from the relevant states. It was the Belgian presidency which acted as umpire. In such cases, the Commission becomes effectively a 13th (or, since 1995, a 16th) partner around the bargaining table (Hooghe, 1996). This can even be true for the most intergovernmental aspect of

366   GARY MARKS, LIESBET HOOGHE AND KERMIT BLANK

European Union politics: treaty bargaining, as an example from Maastricht illustrates. When the British government refused the watered down social provisions in the Maastricht Treaty, Jacques Delors put on the table his original, more radical, social policy programme of 1989 and proposed to attach it as a special protocol to the Treaty, leaving Britain out. Faced with the prospect that the whole negotiation might break down, the other 11 state executives hastily signed up to a more substantial document than they had originally anticipated (Pierson, 1996; Lange, 1993).

In sum, the Council is the senior actor in the decision-making stage, but the European Parliament and the Commission are indispensable partners. The Commission's power is predominantly soft in that it is exercised by subtle influence rather than sanction. Except for agriculture, external trade and competition policy, where it has substantial executive autonomy, it can gain little by confrontation. Its influence depends on its ability to craft consensus among institutions and among Member State executives. However, extensive reliance on qualified majority voting has enabled the Commission to be bolder, as it does not have to court all state executives at once.

The European Parliament's position is based more on formal rules. Its track record under co-operation and co-decision shows that it does not eschew confrontations with the Council. In return for its assent to enlargement and the GATT-agreement in 1994, it extracted from the Council a formal seat in the preparatory negotiations for the intergovernmental conference of 1996–97. In the meantime, it is intent on making the most of its power, even if it treads on the toes of its long-standing ally, the European Commission. During its hearings on the Santer Commission in January 1995, the European Parliament demanded that the Commission accept parliamentary amendments 'as a matter of course', and withdraw proposals that it rejects (reiterated by EP President Klaus Haensch in an interview for the *European*, 20–26.1.95). Commission officials have described these proposals as 'outrageous' on the grounds that the Commission 'would more or less lose its ability to operate' (*Financial Times*, 14–15.1.1995).

As a whole, EU decision-making can be characterized as one of multiple, intermeshing competencies, complementary policy functions, and variable lines of authority – features that are elements of multi-level governance.

Implementation: Opening the European arena – Breaking the State Mould

Multi-level governance is prominent in the implementation stage. Although the Commission has formal executive powers and national governments are in principle responsible for implementation, in practice these competencies are shared. On the one hand, national governments monitor the executive powers of the Commission closely, though they do so in conjunction with subnational governments and societal actors. On the other hand, the Commission has become involved in day-to-day implementation in a number of policy areas, and this brings it into close contact with subnational authorities and interest groups. As in the initiation and decision-making stage, mutual intrusion is contested.

The Commission's formal mandate gives it discretion to interpret legislation and issue administrative regulations bearing on specific cases. It issues 6–7,000 administrative regulations annually (Nugent, 1994; Ludlow, 1991). However, only a tiny proportion of the Commission's decisions are unilateral. Since the 1980s, with the institutionalization of comitology, the Council and the individual national governments have become intimately involved. Many regulations have their own committee attached to them. Balancing Commission autonomy and state involvement is an open-ended and conflictual process in the European Union, and this is also apparent in comitology. Rules of operation vary across policy areas and are a source of contention between the Commission, usually supported by the Parliament, and the Council (St.Clair Bradley, 1992). Some committees are only advisory; others can prevent the Commission from carrying out a certain action by qualified majority vote; and a third category must approve Commission actions by qualified majority. In each case the Commission presides.

At first sight, comitology seems to give state executives control over the Commission's actions in genuine principal–agent fashion. But the relationship between state actors and European institutions is more complex. Comitology is weakest in precisely those areas where the Commission has extensive executive powers, e.g. in competition policy, state aids, agriculture, commercial policy and the internal market. Here, the Commission has significant space for autonomous action (McGowan and Wilks, 1995; Nugent, 1994, 1995).

State-centrists may argue that state executives prefer to delegate these powers to achieve state-oriented collective goods, such as control over potential distortion of competition or a stronger bargaining position in international trade. But one result is that state executives have lost exclusive control in a range of policy areas. To mention just three examples among the many discussed in this chapter: they no longer control competition within their borders; they cannot aid national firms as they deem fit; they cannot autonomously conduct trade negotiations.

German regional policy had to be recast because it ran foul of the European Commission's competition authority. The Commission's insistence in the 1980s that regional aid to western Länder be curtailed has provoked several disputes among Länder and between Länder and the Federal government. By 1995, the traditional system of *Gemeinschaftsaufgabe* was on the brink of collapse (Anderson, 1996).

Although comitology involves state actors in the European Commission's activities, this intermeshing is not necessarily limited to *central* state actors. Because the issues on the table are often technical in nature, Member State governments tend to send those people who are directly responsible or who are best informed about the issue at home. These are regularly subnational officials, or representatives of interest groups or other non-governmental bodies. Subnational participation in comitology is prevalent for Member States organized along federal or semi-federal lines (see, on Germany, Goetz, 1994; on Belgium, Hooghe, 1995b). But, in recent years, subnational actors have been drawn into the European arena from more centralized Member States (see, for France, Lequesne, 1994).

To the extent that EU regulations affect policy areas where authority is shared among central and subnational levels of government, effective implementation requires contacts between multiple levels of government. Environmental policy is an example of this, for in several European countries competencies in this area are shared across different territorial levels. To speed up implementation of environmental law, the Commission began in 1990 to arrange so-called 'package' meetings to bring together central, regional and local government representatives of a Member State. Such meetings are voluntary, but in the first year of its operation seven countries made use of them. The Spanish central government, for example, was keen to use the Commission's presence to pressure its autonomous provinces into compliance with EU environmental law, but to do so it conceded them access to the European arena.

The majority of participants in comitology are not national civil servants, but interest group representatives (particularly from farming, union, and employer organizations) alongside technical experts, scientists and academics (Buitendijk and van Schendelen, 1995). These people are mostly selected, or at least approved of, by their national government. One can plausibly assume that national governments find it more difficult to persuade technical experts, interest group representatives, and private actors than their own officials to defend the national interest. In practice therefore, comitology, which was originally a mechanism for central state oversight over Commission activities, has had the intended consequence of deepening the participation of subnational authorities and private actors in the European arena.

A second development which has received little attention in the literature is the direct involvement of Commission officials in day-to-day policy implementation. The Commission was never expected to perform ground-level implementation, except in unusual circumstances (such as competition policy, fraud, etc.). Yet, in some areas this has changed. The most prominent example is cohesion policy, which now absorbs about one-third of the EU budget. The bulk of the money goes to multi-annual regional development programmes in the less developed regions of the EU. The 1989 reform prescribes the involvement of Commission, national, regional, local and social actors on a continuing basis in all stages of the policy process: selection of priorities, choice of programmes, allocation of funding, monitoring of operations, evaluation and adjustment of programmes. To this end, each recipient region or country is required to set up an elaborate system of monitoring committees, with a general committee on top, and a cascade of subcommittees focused on particular programmes. Commission officials can and do participate at each level of this tree-like structure. Partnership is implemented unevenly across the EU (Marks, 1996; Hooghe and Keating, 1994), but just about everywhere it institutionalizes some form of direct contact between the Commission and non-central government actors including, particularly, regional and local authorities, local action groups and local businesses. Such links break open the mould of the state, so that multi-level governance encompasses actors within as well as beyond existing states.

Adjudication: An Activist Court in a Supranational Legal Order

State-centrists have argued that a European legal order and effective European Court of Justice (ECJ) are essential to state co-operation (Garrett and Weingast, 1993; Garrett, 1995; Moravcsik, 1993). Unilateral defection is difficult to detect, and thus it is in the interest of states to delegate authority to a European Court to monitor compliance. The ECJ also mitigates incomplete contracting problems by applying general interstate bargains to future contingencies. In this vein, the ECJ may be conceptualized as an agent of constituent Member States. However, a number of scholars have argued convincingly that the ECJ has become more than an instrument of Member States (Burley and Mattli, 1993). The Court has been active in transforming the legal order in a supranational direction. But the Court could not have done this without a political ally at the European level: the European Commission. Nor could it have established the supremacy of European law without the collaboration of national courts, and this collaboration has altered the balance of power between national courts and national political authorities.

Through its activist stance, the ECJ has laid the legal foundation for an integrated European polity. By means of an impressive body of case law, the Court has established the Treaty of Rome as a document creating legal obligations directly binding on national governments and individual citizens alike. Moreover, these obligations have legal priority over laws made by the Member States. Directly binding legal authority and supremacy are attributes of sovereignty, and their application by the ECJ indicates that the EU is becoming a constitutional regime.

The Court was originally expected to act as an impartial monitor 'to ensure that in the interpretation and application of the treaties the law is observed' (Article 164 EEC, Article 136 Euratom, Article 31 ECSC) but, from the beginning, the Court viewed these interstate treaties as more than narrow agreements. The Court's expansive role is founded on the failure of the treaties to specify the competencies of major EU institutions (Weiler, 1991). Instead, the treaties set out 'tasks' or 'purposes' for European co-operation, such as the customs union (Treaty of Rome), the completion of the internal market (Single European Act) or economic and monetary union (Maastricht Treaty). The Court has constitutionalized European law and expanded European authority in other policy areas by stating that these were necessary to achieve these functional goals (Weiler, 1991).

Court rulings have been pivotal in shaping European integration. However, the ECJ depends on other actors to force issues on the European political agenda and condone its interpretations. Legislators (the European Council, Council of Ministers, Commission and Parliament) may always reverse the course set by the Court by changing the law or by altering the Treaties. In other words, the ECJ is no different from the Council, Commission or European Parliament in that it is locked in mutual dependence with other actors.

One outcome of this interlocking is the principle of 'mutual recognition', which became the core principle of the internal market programme in the landmark case of *Cassis de Dijon* (1979) in which the Court stated that a product lawfully produced in one Member State must be accepted in another. Some have argued that the ruling was based on the ECJ's reading of the interests of the most influential state executives, France and Germany (Garrett and Weingast, 1993), but detailed analysis of the evidence suggests that the Court made the decision autonomously, notwithstanding the opposition of the French and German governments (Dehousse, 1992; Alter and Meunier-Aitsahalia, 1994; Majone, 1995). It was the Commission that projected the principle of mutual recognition onto a wider agenda, the single market initiative, and it did this as early as July 1980 when it announced to the European Parliament and the Council that the *Cassis* case was the foundation for a new approach to market harmonization (Alter and Meunier-Aitsahalia, 1994).

National courts have proved willing to apply the doctrine of direct effect by invoking Article 177 of the Treaty of Rome which stipulates that national courts may seek 'authoritative guidance' from the ECJ in cases involving Community law. In such instances, the ECJ provides a preliminary ruling, specifying the proper application of Community law to the issue at hand. While this preliminary ruling does not formally decide the case, in practice the Court is rendering a judgment of the 'constitutionality' of a particular statute or administrative action in the light of its interpretation of Community law. The court that made the referral cannot be forced to acknowledge the interpretations by the ECJ, but if it does, other national courts usually accept these decisions as a precedent. Preliminary rulings expand ECJ influence, and judges at the lowest level gain a *de facto* power of judicial review, which had been reserved to the highest court in the state (Burley and Mattli, 1993). Article 177 gives lower national courts strong incentives to circumvent their own national judicial hierarchy. With their support, much of the business of interpreting Community law has been transferred from national high courts to the ECJ and lower courts.

ECJ decisions have become accepted as part of the legal order in the Member States, shifting expectations about decision-making authority from a purely national-based system to one that is more multi-level. The doctrines of direct effect and supremacy were constructed over the strong objections of several Member State executives. Yet, its influence lies not in its scope for unilateral action, but in the fact that its rulings and inclusive mode of operation create opportunities for other European institutions, particularly the Commission, for private interests, and national institutions (lower national courts), to influence the European agenda or enhance their power.

V. Conclusion

Multi-level governance does not confront the sovereignty of states directly. Instead of being explicitly challenged, states in the European Union are being melded gently into a multi-level polity by their leaders and the actions of numerous subnational and supranational actors. State-centric theorists are right when they argue that states are extremely powerful institutions that are capable of crushing direct threats to their existence. The institutional form of the state emerged because it proved a particularly effective means of systematically wielding violence, and it is difficult to imagine any generalized challenge along these lines. But this is not the only, nor even the most important, issue facing the state. One does not have to argue that states are on the verge of political extinction to believe that their control of those living in their territories has significantly weakened.

It is not necessary to look far beyond the state itself to find reasons that might explain how such an outcome is possible. When we disaggregate the state into the actors that shape its diverse institutions, it is clear that key decision-makers, above all those directing the state executive, may have goals that do not coincide with that of projecting state sovereignty into the future. As well as being a goal in itself, the state may sensibly be regarded as a means to a variety of ends that are structured by party competition and interest group politics in a liberal democratic setting. A state executive may wish to shift decision-making to the supranational level because the political benefits outweigh the cost of losing control. Or a state executive may have intrinsic grounds to shift control, for example to shed responsibility for unpopular decisions.

Even if state executives want to maintain sovereignty, they are often not able to do so. A state executive can easily be outvoted because most decisions in the

372   GARY MARKS, LIESBET HOOGHE AND KERMIT BLANK

Council are now taken under the decision rule of qualified majority, and moreover, even the national veto, the ultimate instrument of sovereignty, is constrained by the willingness of other state executives to tolerate its use. But the limits on state sovereignty are deeper. Even collectively, state executives do not determine the European agenda because they are unable to control the supranational institutions they have created at the European level. The growing diversity of issues on the Council's agenda, the sheer number of state executive principals and the mistrust that exists among them, and the increased specialization of policy-making have made the Council of Ministers reliant upon the Commission to set the agenda, forge compromises, and supervise compliance. The Commission and the Council are not on a par, but neither can their relationship be understood in principal–agent terms. Policy-making in the EU is characterized by mutual dependence, complementary functions and overlapping competencies.

The Council also shares decision-making competencies with the European Parliament, which has gained significant legislative power under the Single European Act and the Maastricht Treaty. Indeed, the Parliament might be conceived of as a principal in its own right in the European arena. The Council, Commission and Parliament interact within a legal order which has been transformed into a supranational one through the innovative jurisprudence of the European Court of Justice. The complex interplay among these contending institutions in a polity where political control is diffuse often leads to outcomes that are second choice for all participants.

The character of the Euro-polity at any particular point in time is the outcome of a tension between supranational and intergovernmental pressures. We have argued that, since the 1980s, it has crystallized into a multi-level polity. States no longer serve as the exclusive nexus between domestic politics and international relations.

Direct connections are being forged among political actors in diverse political arenas. Traditional and formerly exclusive channels of communication and influence are being sidestepped. With its dispersed competencies, contending but interlocked institutions, shifting agendas, multi-level governance opens multiple points of access for interests, while it privileges those interests with technical expertise that match the dominant style of EU policy-making. In this turbulent process of mobilization and counter-mobilization it is patently clear that states no longer serve as the exclusive nexus between domestic politics and international relations. Direct connections are being forged among political actors in diverse political arenas.

However, there is nothing inherent in the current system. Multi-level governance is unlikely to be a stable equilibrium. There is no widely legitimized constitutional framework. There is little consensus on the goals of integration.

As a result, the allocation of competencies between national and supranational actors is ambiguous and contested. It is worth noting that the European polity has made two U-turns in its short history. Overt supranationalist features of the original structure were overshadowed by the imposition of intergovernmental institutions in the 1960s and 1970s (Weiler, 1991). From the 1980s, a system of multi-level governance arose, in which national governmental control became diluted by the activities of supranational and subnational actors.

These developments have engendered strong negative reactions on the part of declining social groups represented in nationalist political movements. Ironically, much of the discontent with European integration has been directed towards state executives themselves and the pragmatic and elitist style in which they have bargained institutional change in the EU.

The EU-wide series of debates unleashed by the Treaty of Maastricht have forced the issue of sovereignty onto the agenda. Where governing parties themselves shy away from the issue, it is raised in stark terms by opposition parties, particularly those of the extreme right. Several Member State govern-. ments are, themselves, deeply riven on the issues of integration and sovereignty. States and state sovereignty have become objects of popular contention – the . outcome of which is as yet uncertain.

References

Alter, K. and Meunier-Aitsahalia, S. (1994) 'Judicial Politics in the European Community. European Integration and the Pathbreaking Cassis de Dijon Decision'. *Comparative Political Studies*, Vol. 26, pp. 535–61.

Anderson, J. (1996) 'Germany and the Structural Funds. Reunification Leads to Bifurcation'. In Hooghe, L. (ed.), *Cohesion Policy and European Integration. Building Multi-Level Governance* (Oxford: Oxford University Press.)

Bellier, I. (1994) 'Une culture de la Commission européenne? De la rencontre des cultures et du multilinguisme des fonctionnaires'. In Mény, Y., Muller, P. and Quermonne, J-L (eds), *Politiques Publiques en Europe* (Paris: L'Harmattan).

Bieber, R., Pantalis, J. and Schoo, J. (1986) 'Implications of the Single Act for the European Parliament'. *Common Market Law Review*, Vol. 23, pp. 767–92.

Bornschier, V. and Fielder, N. (1995) 'The Genesis of the Single European Act. Forces and Protagonists Behind the Relaunch of the European Community in the 1980s: The Single Market'. Unpublished paper.

Buitendijk, G.J. and van Schendelen, M.P.C.M. (1995) 'Brussels Advisory Committees: A Channel for Influence'. *European Law Review*, Vol. 20, pp. 37–56.

Bulmer, S. J. (1994) 'Institutions, Governance Regimes and the Single European Market: Analyzing the Governance of the European Union'. Presented at the Conference of Europeanists, Chicago, 31 March–2 April.

Burley, A-M. and Mattli, W. (1993) 'Europe before the Court: A Political Theory of Legal Integration'. *International Organization*, Vol. 47, pp. 41–76.

374   GARY MARKS, LIESBET HOOGHE AND KERMIT BLANK

Cameron, D. (1992) 'The 1992 Initiative: Causes and Consequences.' In Sbragia, A.M. (ed.), *Europolitics: Institutions and Policymaking in the 'New' European Community* (Washington, D.C.: Brookings Institution).

Caporaso, J.A. (1996) 'The European Union and Forms of State: Westphalian, Regulatory or Post-Modern?'. *Journal of Common Market Studies*, Vol. 34, No. 1, pp. 29–52.

Caporaso, J. A. and Keeler, J.T.S. (1993) 'The European Community and Regional Integration Theory.' Paper presented at the Third Biennial International Conference of the European Community Studies Association. Washington, D.C., 27–29 May.

Cowles, M. G. (1995) 'Setting the Agenda for a New Europe: The ERT and EC 1992.' *Journal of Common Market Studies*, Vol. 33, No. 4, pp. 501–26.

Cram, L. (1993) 'Calling the Tune without Paying the Piper? Social Policy Regulation: The Role of the Commission in European Community Social Policy'. *Policy and Politics*, Vol. 21, pp. 135–46.

Dahl, R.A. (1970) *Modern Political Analysis* (New York, Prentice-Hall).

Dehousse, R. (1992) 'Integration versus Regulation ? On the Dynamics of Regulation in the European Community'. *Journal of Common Market Studies*, Vol. 30, pp. 383–402.

Dinan, D. (1994) *Ever Closer Union? An Introduction to the EC* (Basingstoke: Macmillan).

Eichener, V. (1992) *'Social Dumping or Innovative Regulation? Processes and Outcomes of European Decision-Making in the Sector of Health and Safety at Work Harmonization'*. EUI Working Paper.

Garrett, G. (1992) 'International Cooperation and Institutional Choice: The EC's Internal Market'. *International Organization*, Vol. 46, pp. 533–60.

Garrett, G. (1995) 'The Politics of Legal Integration in the European Union'. *International Organization*, Vol. 49, pp. 17–81.

Garrett, G. and Weingast, B. (1993) 'Ideas, Interests, and Institutions: Construction of the EC's Internal Market'. In Goldstein, J. and Keohane, R. (eds), *Ideas and Foreign Policy* (Ithaca N.Y.: Cornell University Press).

Goetz, K. (1994) 'National Governance and European Integration: Intergovernmental Relations in Germany'. *Journal of Common Market Studies*, Vol. 33, pp. 91–116.

Hoffmann, S. (1966) 'Obstinate or Obsolete? The Fate of the Nation State and the Case of Western Europe'. *Daedalus*, Vol. 95, pp. 892–908.

Hoffmann, S. (1982) 'Reflections on the Nation-State in Western Europe Today'. *Journal of Common Market Studies*, Vol. 21, pp. 21–37.

Hooghe, L. (1995a) 'Subnational Mobilisation in the European Union'. *West European Politics*, Vol. 18, pp. 175–98.

Hooghe, L. (1995b) 'Belgian Federalism and the European Community'. In Keating, M. and Jones, B. (eds), *Regions in the European Union* (Oxford: Clarendon Press), pp. 135–66.

Hooghe, L. (1996) 'Building a Europe with the Regions. The Changing Role of the European Commission.' In Hooghe, L. (ed.), *Cohesion Policy and European Integration: Building Multi-Level Governance* (Oxford: Oxford University Press).

Hooghe, L. and Keating, M. (1994) 'The Politics of EU Regional Policy'. *Journal of European Public Policy,* Vol. 1, pp. 367–93.

Hooghe, L. and Marks, G. (1996) 'Territorial Restructuring in the European Union: Regional Pressures'. In Cassese, S. and Wright, V. (eds), *La restructuration de l'Etat dans les pays d'Europe occidentale.* (Paris: Editions La Découverte, Collection 'Recherches').

Lange, P. (1993) 'The Maastricht Social Protocol: Why Did They Do It?' *Politics and Society,* Vol. 21, pp. 5–36.

Leibfried, S. and Pierson, P. (ed.) (1995) *European Social Policy. Between Fragmentation and Integration* (Washington, D.C.: Brookings Institution).

Lenaerts, K. (1992) 'The Role of the Court of Justice in the European Community: Some Thoughts about the Interaction between Judges and Politicians'. University of Chicago Legal Forum.

Lequesne, C. (1994) 'L'administration central de la France et le système politique européen: mutations et adaptations depuis l'Acte unique'. In Mény, Y., Muller, P. and Quermonne, J-L. (eds), *Politiques publiques en Europe* (Paris: L'Harmattan).

Ludlow, P. (1991) 'The European Commission'. In Keohane, R.O. and Hoffmann, S. (eds) *The New European Community: Decisionmaking and Institutional Change* (Boulder, Col.: Westview Press).

McGowan, L. and Wilks, S. (1995) 'The First Supranational Policy in the European Union: Competition Policy'. *European Journal of Political Research,* Vol. 28, pp. 141–69.

McLaughlin, A. and Greenwood, J. (1995) 'The Management of Interest Representation in the European Union.' *Journal of Common Market Studies,* Vol. 33, No. 1, pp. 143–56.

Majone, G. (1993) 'Deregulation or Re-regulation? Policy-Making in the European Community since the Single Act'. Unpublished paper.

Majone, G. (1994) 'The European Community as a Regulatory State'. Unpublished paper.

Majone, G. (1995) 'The Development of Social Regulation in the European Community: Policy Externalities, Transaction Costs, Motivational Factors'. Unpublished paper.

Mann, M. (1993) 'Nation-states in Europe and Other Continents: Diversifying, Developing, Not Dying'. *Daedalus,* Vol. 13, pp. 115–40.

Marks, G. (1992) 'Structural Policy and 1992'. In Sbragia, A. (ed.), *Euro-Politics. Institutions and Policymaking in the 'New' European Community* (Washington D.C.: Brookings Institution).

Marks, G. (1993) 'Structural Policy After Maastricht'. In Cafruny, A. and Rosenthal, G. (eds), *The State of the European Community* (New York: Lynne Rienner).

Marks, G. (1996) 'Decision-making in Cohesion Policy. Describing and Explaining Variation'. In Hooghe, L. (ed.), *Cohesion Policy and European Integration: Building Multi-Level Governance* (Oxford: Oxford University Press).

Marks, G., Salk, J., Ray, L. and Nielsen, F. (1996) 'Conflict, Cracks and Conflicts: Regional Mobilization in the European Union'. *Comparative Political Studies,* Vol. 29.

376   GARY MARKS, LIESBET HOOGHE AND KERMIT BLANK

Matlary, J. H. (1993) 'Quis Custodiet Custodes? The European Commission's Policy-Making Role and the Problem of Democratic Legitimacy'. Paper presented at the Third Biennial International Conference of the European Community Studies Association. Washington D.C., 27–29 May.

Mazey, S. and Richardson, J. (1993) 'EC Policy-Making: An Emerging European Policy Style?'. In Liefferink, D. and Lowe, P. (eds), *European Integration and Environmental Policy* (Scarborough, Ontario: Belhaven Press).

Milward, A. (1992) *The European Rescue of the Nation-State* (Berkeley: University of California Press).

Milward, A. and Sørensen, V. (1993) 'Interdependence or Integration? A National Choice'. In Milward, A., Ranieri, R., Romero, F. and Sørensen, V. (eds), *The Frontier of National Sovereignty: History and Theory, 1945–1992* (New York: Routledge).

Moe, T. M. (1987) 'Interests, Institutions and Positive Theory: The Politics of the NLRB'. *Studies in American Political Development*, Vol. 2, pp. 236–99.

Moe, T. M. (1990) 'The Politics of Structural Choice: Toward a Theory of Public Bureaucracy'. In Williamson, O.E. (ed.), *Organization Theory from Chester Barnard to the Present* (Oxford: Oxford University Press).

Moravcsik, A. (1991) 'Negotiating the Single European Act: National Interests and Conventional Statecraft in the European Community'. *International Organization*, Vol. 45, pp. 651–88.

Moravcsik, A. (1993) 'Preferences and Power in the European Community: A Liberal Intergovernmental Approach'. *Journal of Common Market Studies*, Vol. 31, pp. 473–524.

Moravcsik, A. (1994) 'Why the European Community Strengthens the State: Domestic Politics and International Cooperation'. Presented at the Annual Meeting of the American Political Science Association, New York, 1–4 September.

Moravcsik, A. (1995) 'Liberal Intergovernmentalism and Integration: A Rejoinder'. *Journal of Common Market Studies*, Vol. 33, No. 4, pp. 611–28.

Nugent, N. (1994) *The Government and Politics of the European Community* (Basingstoke: Macmillan).

Nugent, N. (1995) 'The Leadership Role of the European Commission: Explanatory Factors'. Paper presented to the Research Conference of the University Association for Contemporary European Studies at the University of Birmingham, 18–19 September.

Peterson, J. (1991) 'Technology Policy in Europe: Explaining the Framework Programme and Eureka in Theory and Practice'. *Journal of Common Market Studies*, Vol. 29, No. 3, pp. 269–90.

Pierson, P. (1996) 'The Path to European Integration: An Historical Institutionalist Perspective'. *Comparative Political Studies*, Vol. 29, pp. 123–63.

Pollack, M. A. (1995) 'Creeping Competence: The Expanding Agenda of the European Community'. *Journal of Public Policy*, Vol. 14, pp. 95–146.

Ross, G. (1993) 'Sidling into Industrial Policy: Inside the European Commission'. *French Politics and Society,* Vol. 11, pp. 20–44.

Ross, G. (1995) *Jacques Delors and European Integration* (Oxford: Oxford University Press).

Sandholtz, W. (1992) 'ESPRIT and the Politics of International Collective Action'. *Journal of Common Market Studies,* Vol. 30, No. 1, pp. 1–21.

Sandholtz, W. (1993) 'Institutions and Collective Action: The New Telecommunications in Western Europe'. *World Politics,* Vol. 45, pp. 242–70.

Sandholtz, W. and Zysman, J. (1989) '1992: Recasting the European Bargain'. *World Politics,* Vol. 42, pp. 95–128.

Sbragia, A. (1992) 'Thinking About the European Future: The Uses of Comparison'. In Sbragia, A. (ed.), *Europolitics: Institutions and Policymaking in the 'New' European Community* (Washington D.C.: Brookings Institution).

Sbragia, A. (1993) 'The European Community: A Balancing Act'. *Publius,* Vol. 23, pp. 23–38.

Scharpf, F. (1988) 'The Joint Decision Trap: Lessons from German Federalism and European Integration'. *Public Administration,* Vol. 66, pp. 239–78.

Scharpf, F. (1994) 'Community and Autonomy Multilevel Policymaking in the European Union'. *Journal of European Public Policy,* Vol. 1, pp. 219–42.

Schmitter, P. C. (1992a) 'Interests, Powers and Functions: Emergent Properties and Unintended Consequences in the European Polity'. Center for Advanced Study in the Behavioral Sciences (typescript).

Schmitter, P. (1992b) 'The Emerging Europolity and its Impact upon Euro-Capitalism'. In Boyer, R. (ed.), *Contemporary Capitalism: The Embeddedness of Institutions*

Snyder, F. (1994) 'Soft Law and Institutional Practice in the European Community'. In Martin S. (ed.), *The Construction of Europe: Essays in Honour of Emile Noel* (Dordrecht: Kluwer).

St. Clair Bradley, K. (1992) 'Comitology and the Law Through a Glass, Darkly'. *Common Market Law Review,* Vol. 29, pp. 693–721.

Streeck, W. (1996) 'Neo-Voluntarism: A New European Social Policy Regime? In Marks, G., Scharpf, S., Schmitter, P.C. and Streeck W. (eds), *Governance in the Emerging Euro-Polity* (London: Sage).

Streeck, W. and Schmitter, P.C. (1991) 'From National Corporatism to Transnational Pluralism: Organized Interests in the Single European Market'. *Politics and Society,* Vol. 2, pp. 133–64.

Taylor, P. (1991) 'The European Community and the State: Assumptions, Theories and Propositions'. *Review of International Studies,* Vol. 17, pp. 109–25.

Teasdale, A. (1993) 'The Life and Death of the Luxembourg Compromise'. *Journal of Common Market Studies,* Vol. 31, No. 4, pp. 567–79.

Tömmel, I. (1992) 'System-Entwicklung und Politikgestaltung in der Europäischen Gemeinschaft am Beispiel der Regionalpolitik'. *Politische Vierteljahresschrift, Sonderheft* Vol. 23, pp. 185–208.

Tsebelis, G. (1994) 'The Power of the European Parliament as a Conditional Agenda Setter'. *American Political Science Review,* Vol. 88, pp. 128–42.

378   GARY MARKS, LIESBET HOOGHE AND KERMIT BLANK

Tsebelis, G. (1995) 'Will Maastricht Reduce the Democratic Deficit?' *APSA-Comparative Politics Newsletter,* Vol. 1, pp. 4–6.

Volcansek, M. L. (1992) 'The European Court of Justice: Supranational Policy-Making'. *West European Politics,* Vol. 15, pp. 109–21.

Wallace, W. (1994) *Regional Integration: The Westeuropean Experience* (Washington: Brookings Institution).

Weiler, J. H. H. (1991) 'The Transformation of Europe'. *Yale Law Review,* Vol. 100, pp. 2403-83.

Wessels, W. (1992) 'Staat und (westeuropäische) Integration. Die Fusionsthese'. *Politische Vierteljahresschrift, Sonderheft,* Vol. 23, pp. 36–60.

Williamson, O. E. (1985) *The Economic Institutions of Capitalism* (New York: Free Press).

Williamson, O. E. (1993) 'Transaction Cost Economics and Organization Theory'. *Industrial and Corporate Change,* Vol. 2, pp. 107–56.

[7]

Review of International Political Economy 2:4 Autumn 1995: 600–631

Regions, states and the European Union: modernist reaction or postmodern adaptation?

James Anderson and James Goodman

Department of Geography, The Open University

ABSTRACT

How is European integration best conceptualized? How and why are relations between regions, states and the European Union changing? This article combines theoretical and empirical analysis of recent developments, especially the partial 'unbundling' of state sovereignty and the growth of sub-state regionalism in response to intensified global competition. It explores the uses and limitations of 'postmodern' and 'new medieval' conceptualizations of territoriality; the possibility that globalization is producing a fundamental shift in the underlying time-space of territorial politics; and the increasing need to differentiate between the various roles of the state, as globalization impacts very unevenly on different policy areas. The European Union has been characterized as the world's 'first truly postmodern international political form' and the empirical analysis confirms significant 'unbundling' of territorial sovereignty. Sub-state regionalism is encouraged by some of the central institutions of the EU and by forces within the regions themselves responding to the Single European Market. However, more ambivalent and contradictory stances are taken by the member states, especially the United Kingdom and the Republic of Ireland which are among the most centralized and 'anti-regionalist'. Supra-state and sub-state developments continue to be crucially conditioned by the power of states; and analogies to the very different circumstances of medieval Europe have to be substantially qualified, not least because the differences are as revealing as the similarities. This perspective helps steer a path between underestimating and exaggerating contemporary changes.

KEYWORDS

European integration; globalization; territorial sovereignty; regionalism; 'new medievalism'; 'postmodernity'.

REGIONS, STATES AND THE EUROPEAN UNION

1 INTRODUCTION

Sub-state regional politics are becoming more important within the European Union. The 'nation states' are widely seen as being eroded 'from below' by regionalism and 'from above' by EU institutions and globalization – a pincer movement transforming traditional conceptions of territorial sovereignty and national identity. There are arguments that the Single European Market and global economic competition demand a more federalized and regionalized Europe; and hopes that a transformation of sovereignty in the EU and SEM will supersede sub-state national conflicts such as in Northern Ireland. There have even been suggestions that a new 'Europe of the Regions' is replacing the 'Europe of States'. Regionalism is seen by some as signalling the 'end of territorially based sovereignty' (Kaldor 1993) and providing an alternative to nationalism. There are however counter arguments that, far from signalling 'the end of the nation state', European integration is controlled by the member states and is a means by which they are preserving their own powers. In some respects states may simply be reacting to maintain the status quo; but perhaps in other respects they are adapting, even giving encouragement, to the emergence of new economic and political relationships at suprastate and substate levels.

These issues emerged as important concerns in research interviews about the implications of European integration for the national conflict in Ireland and for relations between Northern Ireland and the Republic of Ireland as neighbouring 'regions' in EU terms (Anderson, 1994; Anderson and Goodman, 1994). There were prior questions about the nature of European integration and how the roles of states and regions might be changing; and there were problems with how our interviewees conceptualized these issues, whether in 'realist', 'functionalist' or 'postnationalist' ways (Anderson and Goodman, 1993). In contrast, this article explores alternative 'new medieval' and 'postmodern' conceptualizations of territoriality and sovereignty in the EU, arguing that these provide a more fruitful perspective from which to examine 'Europeanization' and contemporary developments such as the growth of substate regionalism. This growth is encouraged by some of the central institutions of the EU, and by the impact of the Single Market – or more precisely by regional interests responding to the SEM and more generally to globalization. But both regionalism and 'Europeanization' are crucially conditioned by the continuing power of states, whether they resist these changes in 'modernist reaction' or encourage or adjust to them in 'postmodern adaptation'.

A contrast between 'postmodernity' and 'modernity' and comparisons with 'premodernity', along with the related historical analogy of a 'new medievalism', are useful in signalling the possibility that the

ARTICLES

contemporary globalization of our 'shrinking world' is producing a fundamental shift in the underlying time-space of territorial politics. Although used only with specific reference to issues of sovereignty and territoriality, the terms 'new medieval' and 'postmodern' highlight two related sets of problems, conceptual and empirical. Conceptual problems about how to characterize contemporary change are addressed in section 2, while section 3 focuses on empirical questions about the growth of regionalism and 'Europeanization', their implications for states, and the difficulties of steering a path between underestimating and exaggerating the changes.

As 'postmodernists' have emphasized, these changes 'exceed the representational capabilities of traditional international relations theory' (Der Derian, 1992: 7), and the ontological openness of 'postmodernity' allows room for interesting questions about developments in the international political economy. Here, however, use of the concept is restricted to the ontology of state sovereignty, excluding the postmodernists' epistemological relativism (see Callinicos, 1991). Furthermore, as we shall argue, there are reasons for qualifying even this restricted ontological usage. Similarly, the related analogy of 'new medievalism' opens up interesting questions about overlapping sovereignties and the increasing complexity of territorialities, and it underlines the need to supersede the simple binary oppositions of 'domestic/foreign' or 'inside/outside' which have stunted the study of 'international' integration (see Walker, 1993). But, again, it will also be necessary to qualify the analogy to the very different circumstances of medieval Europe, and not least because the differences are as revealing as the similarities. We reject the fashionable and generally reactionary use of 'new medievalism' to imply a return to a supposed 'dark age' of disorder and social chaos, but even a restricted application to issues of territoriality has its limitations. Indeed we shall argue that our world lacks the sort of 'universal order' which gave coherence to medieval Christendom. Contemporary political configurations are in some respects more complex, which does not necessarily imply 'disorder'. There is a continuity of old along with new political forms – for which the overall label of 'late' rather than 'post' modernity might be preferable.

A central aspect of this contemporary complexity is the increasing need to differentiate between the various roles of the state, as globalization impacts very unevenly on different policy areas. Among the most affected is economic development, the area where states have been assumed to have lost much of their former power, and also the area which provides much of the focus for the growth of regional and local politics, as regions and localities strive to attract investment capital. So in assessing changes in sovereignty or in state or regional forces, we need to note that what is true of one aspect of state power may not be

REGIONS, STATES AND THE EUROPEAN UNION

true of another. States may lose power in some policy areas but gain it in others. If so, generalizations about 'the end of territorial sovereignty' or the 'death of the nation-state', while containing a grain of truth, may be completely misleading. By the same token, we would need to distinguish in what sense and to what degree regions are becoming politically more important.

These developments have advanced furthest in the European Union – according to John Ruggie's (1993) revealing analysis, the world's 'first truly postmodern international political form' – and it is in this context that section 3 addresses the empirical questions about regions, states and international integration. It focuses on the changing relationships between regionalism, the EU, and the member states, with particular reference to the United Kingdom and the Republic of Ireland which are among the most centralized and 'anti-regionalist' of all the states in the EU. Regional development in the EU may be acquiring a dynamic that is increasingly autonomous from particular states but this hardly justifies predictions of a post-nationalist 'Europe of the Regions'. Territoriality may be changing but 'postmodernity' does not mean what some of the more over-enthusiastic 'post-modernists' think it means.

2 TERRITORIALITY AND 'POSTMODERNITY'

While currently dominant interpretations of European integration (2.1) can be characterized as 'modern', contemporary transformations of territoriality can be seen in terms of 'new medievalism' and a 'postmodernity' which involves a partial or selective 'unbundling' of sovereignty (2.2). But although the EU may be 'postmodern' in some senses, the emerging configurations of political space are a mixture of new and old forms which vary for different state roles and aspects of power (2.3).

2.1 Realism, functionalism and 'post-nationalism'

European integration is usually interpreted in one of three broad ways: 'realist', 'functionalist' or 'post-nationalist', and each raises problems. The 'realists' have seen integration in terms of inter-governmental relations between independent states which leave the traditional form of territorial sovereignty intact. As will be confirmed in section 3, this is clearly not the case in the EU. The main alternative approach has been to see the 'low politics' of economic or functional integration in civil society as the means of achieving the changes in the 'high politics' of state sovereignty and national identity which are a necessary part of transnational integration. However, this 'functionalist' approach has generally failed to appreciate that joint membership of the EU would lead to 'divergence' as well as 'convergence' between different states and regions; and it has systematically underestimated the need for proactive political, most typically state, intervention to achieve integration (e.g., in Ireland the lack of appropriate cross-border political institutions has been a major impediment to a 'purely' economic integration of North and South (Anderson, 1994)).

Some of the same problems arise with the 'post-nationalist' position, and not surprisingly as it developed out of functionalism under the influence of over-enthusiastic 'postmodernists'. It rightly points to the transformative potential of globalization and transnational economic and cultural 'networks' in a 'shrinking world'. It becomes very problematical, however, when it posits the 'postmodern' death of the nation-state in a federal 'Europe of the Regions', and when it suggests that 'cultural' or 'regional' identities can now be separated from 'political' or 'national' ones and that nationalism is becoming an anachronistic irrelevance. For instance, Richard Kearney, Ireland's leading 'postmodernist', has asked 'are we heading for a bureaucratic Euro-state which will homogenize culture and centralize power *or* for a democratic European federation of decentralized and equal regions?' (Kearney, 1988: 9). In our opinion the simple answer is *'neither'* and Kearney is asking the wrong questions. Genuinely 'equal regions' are an impossibility, at least under capitalism, and a 'federation' of regions is highly unlikely; but so too is 'centralized power' in a 'Euro-state', whether democratic or bureaucratic.

So 'post-nationalism', like realist and functionalist conceptualizations, has severe limitations. Ironically, the Euro-federalist vision involves a *mis*reading of postmodernity by self-styled 'postmodernists'. They seem to miss the real political import of 'postmodern' conditions. Partly this is because they exaggerate the transformations of sovereignty, territoriality and statehood resulting from globalization, but is also because they fail to recognize the genuinely new configurations of territoriality which are beginning to emerge.

2.2 The 'unbundling' of territoriality

The debate about whether the EU is regionalizing Europe or enhancing state power involves a false polarization: European integration both reflects state interests and at the same time increases regionalism – the two are basically opposite sides of the same coin (Anderson and Goodman, 1994). The EU is, however, widely interpreted as a 'transitional' political form between, on the one hand, inter-governmentalism and the modern system of independent states, and, on the other hand, a European 'superstate', a 'United States of Europe' or a federal state in which regions and regionalism replace nations and nationalism. Much of the debate around European integration is about which of the two will win out in the future. But maybe in some respects 'the future' has

REGIONS, STATES AND THE EUROPEAN UNION

already arrived, maybe 'this is it', neither a basic continuation of the modern system of states, nor a federal state in embryo, but something quite different from both, an 'intermediate' form which is distinct in its own right rather than merely 'transitional'?

This would be consistent with Hedley Bull's (1977) insightful hypothesis of a 'new medievalism' – 'a secular reincarnation of the system of overlapping or segmented authority that characterised medieval Christendom'. This could emerge, he reasoned, because of, among other things, a 'regional integration of states', as in the EU, and 'a disintegration of states' because of substate nationalist and regionalist pressures 'from below'. Crucially, according to Bull, the emergence of 'new medieval' territorialities would not require anything as clear cut or decisive as 'the death of the nation-state' or a 'Europe of Regions'. On the contrary, a return to 'overlapping or segmented authority' would be most likely where the pressures 'from above and below' achieve more partial and ambiguous changes, undermining but not relocating sovereignty as presently understood. The situations to look for include an intermediate stage 'where, while one could not speak of a European state, there was real doubt . . . as to whether sovereignty lay with national governments or with the organs of the "community"'; similarly, 'the disintegration of states would be theoretically important only if it were to remain transfixed in an intermediate state' in which substate nationalisms or regionalisms substantially undermined but did not succeed in replicating existing state sovereignty (Bull, 1977: 264–7). Bull ultimately rejected his own hypothesis, but developments since he wrote in the 1970s provide further support for it, though, as we shall conclude, it is necessary to relax his condition of global 'universality' being achieved.

Following up Bull's hypothesis, and also David Harvey's (1989) discussion of postmodernity as the greatest transformation in our experiences of time-space since the Renaissance, Ruggie (1993) focuses on territoriality to argue for a 'postmodern' EU which is neither a traditional intergovermental arrangement of sovereign states nor an emerging federal state. He reaches this conclusion looking only at state and suprastate institutions, but his argument is given added force by the growth of substate regionalism. Territorial sovereignty is the key to modern as distinct from medieval polities, and by extension the 'unbundling' of territoriality is the key to the contemporary spatial reorganization of politics. This is reflected for example in the increasing ambiguity about what is 'foreign' and what is 'domestic' in a world where:

> IBM is Japan's largest computer exporter, and Sony is the largest exporter of television sets from the United States . . . in which . . . a Japanese concern assembling typewriters in . . . Tennessee, brings an antidumping case before the US International Trade

ARTICLES

> Commission ... against ... an American firm that imports type-
> writers into the United States from its offshore facilities in
> Singapore and Indonesia.
>
> (Ruggie, 1993: 172)

It is not just that state borders are becoming more porous – in varying degrees they always have been. Previous historical transformations have been represented as 'the world turned upside down', but now the appropriate metaphor might be 'the world turned inside out'?

To appreciate the argument we need to sketch the medieval to modern transformation before dealing with contemporary change from 'modernity' to 'postmodernity'. The basic point is that we may be seeing the superimposition of new forms of territoriality reminiscent of medieval Europe where:

> people identified with communities and political units which were generally much smaller (and in some cases much larger) than the supposedly 'natural' nation or present-day states: their parish or diocese, manor, guild or city, whilst many were subjects of city-states, duchies or principalities. These small units were often part of a complex hierarchy of political or cultural entities, such as the Church of Rome, the Hanseatic League, or the dynastic Habsburg Empire.
>
> (Anderson, 1986: 115)

Political sovereignty was shared between a wide variety of secular and religious institutions and different levels of authority – feudal knights and barons, kings and princes, guilds and cities, bishops, abbots, the papacy – rather than being based on territory *per se* as in modern times. Furthermore, the different levels of overlapping sovereignty typically constituted *nested* hierarchies (e.g., parish, bishopric, arch-bishopric; manor, lordship, barony, duchy, kingdom), and people were members of higher level collectivities not directly but only by virtue of their membership of lower level bodies.

The rise of the modern state, and what distinguished it from medieval predecessors, centred on the removal or displacement of these complex nested hierarchies, and the development of state sovereignty as absolute and undivided authority within a precisely delimited territory. Later on territorial sovereignty was 'democratized' as something to be exercised by 'the nation'. Individuals deemed to belong to the nation belonged *directly* 'in their own right', rather than through membership of lower level bodies and the 'territorial' state became also the 'nation' state (Anderson, 1986: 124–8).

This transition from medieval to modern involved an historical process of increasing differentiations between 'domestic' and 'foreign', 'internal'

REGIONS, STATES AND THE EUROPEAN UNION

and 'external', 'belonging' and 'not belonging'. It was bound up with what Harvey (1989: 242–4) described as 'a radical reconstruction of views of space and time', initiated in the Renaissance and exemplified by (among other things) the invention of perspective from a single fixed viewpoint. This radically transformed perceptions and representations of space and it shaped western visual art up to the early twentieth century, when 'cubists' reintroduced multiple perspectives in paintings and again showed things from different sides and angles.

For Ruggie there were analagous and related transformations of political space. The invention of single-point perspective (reputedly by Brunelleschi in Florence about 1425) brought precision and perspective from a single point of view, the viewpoint of a single subjectivity. What was true in the visual arts became true of politics, as the principle of 'territorial contiguity' gained dominance over the principle of 'transterritorial' dynastic rule:

> Political space came to be defined *as it appeared from a single fixed viewpoint*. The concept of sovereignty, then, was merely the doctrinal counterpart of the application of single-point perspectival forms to the spatial organization of politics . . . territorially defined, territorially fixed, and mutually exclusive state formations [were] the distinctive feature of the modern system of rule . . . a peculiar and historically unique configuration of territorial space.
>
> (Ruggie, 1993: 144, 153, 163)

In a sense sovereignty over everything, secular and spiritual, was 'bundled' together in territorial 'sovereign' states. But from the beginning there had to be a partial 'unbundling' for international transactions, most notably inter-state diplomacy, to be possible. Regular communication between mutually exclusive territorial states required the establishment of permanent foreign embassies; accommodating them required making an exception to totally exclusive territoriality by inventing fictitious 'extraterritorial' spaces. Additional instances of 'unbundled' territoriality included 'various types of functional regimes, common markets, political communities, and the like' (Ruggie, 1993: 164–5). Now, with growing transnational interdependency and 'space-time compression' (Harvey, 1989), such instances are multiplying. The process of 'unbundling' is accelerating, and transnational networks, regulatory regimes and forms of authority, often defined primarily in functional rather than territorial terms, are becoming much more important (see McGrew, 1995). Qualitatively new or 'postmodern' territorialities could be the result.

Harvey's (1989) political economy approach is for the most part silent on how the modern state and states system might be affected by 'space-time compression' and conditions of postmodernity, while the

ARTICLES

orthodoxies of international relations theory are misleading in either completely exaggerating or ignoring their effects:

> The orthodox liberal position that these developments somehow imply the growing irrelevance of states is ... fundamentally misplaced [but] the standard realist ground for rejecting the transformational potential of these developments is equally misplaced ... [t]here is an extraordinarily impoverished mind-set ... that is able to visualize long-term challenges to the system of states only in terms of entities that are institutionally substitutable for the state. Since global markets and transnational corporate structures (not to mention communications satellites) are not in the business of replacing states, they are assumed to entail no potential for fundamental international change.
>
> (Ruggie, 1993: 141, 143)

In fact, as Susan Strange (1994) suggests, states may be losing some of their autonomy, not because power has 'gone upwards' to other political institutions such as the EU, but because it has 'gone sideways' to economic institutions and global market forces, and in some respects has 'gone nowhere' or just 'evaporates' as economics outruns politics and political control is simply lost.

Ruggie interprets such changes in terms of our changing experience of space-time, as analysed by Harvey and others, and specifically in terms of a switch back from singular to multiple perspectives. Just as early twentieth-century 'cubists' reintroduced multiple perspectives into western art, again showing things from different sides and angles, so postmodernity in political space may mean that the 'single-point perspective' and 'singular sovereignty' of independent statehood is (sometimes) displaced by multiple and overlapping sovereignties. State sovereignty and territoriality may be experiencing a related transformation with the result that there is no longer one fixed viewpoint or perspective from which to see territorial sovereignty or unambiguously differentiate between 'foreign' and 'domestic'.

2.3 The EU and 'postmodern' politics

According to Ruggie (1993: 140, 171–2), it is in the EU that 'the process of unbundling territoriality has gone further than anywhere else'; the EU 'may constitute the first "multiperspectival polity" to emerge since the advent of the modern era'. Relations between the (presently) twelve member states can no longer realistically be seen as simply involving twelve separate, single viewpoints: the twelve do sometimes act as a collectivity which has its own singularity; the central institutions which were set up by the states, particularly the European Commission and

REGIONS, STATES AND THE EUROPEAN UNION

Parliament, are now also to some extent actors in their own right; and in defining their own interests each of the twelve states increasingly takes into account or internalize at least some of the interests of the other eleven and the views expressed in the central institutions. This configuration is 'multiperspectival' or 'postmodern' in being distinctly different from (and not necessarily transitional to) a European 'super-state' which, as Bull (1977) noted, would simply relocate or replicate the typically modern form of territorial sovereignty at a different geographical scale, a 'United States of Europe' replicating the USA.

However, rather than 'celebrating' the EU as 'postmodern', we need to analyse the limitations of its 'postmodernity' and qualify some of Ruggie's conclusions. Although a new form of polity, the EU is still territorial, and in many respects 'singular sovereignty' remains dominant, whether exercised by the member states or by the EU as a political collective. For example, 'Fortress Europe', particularly as seen from the external viewpoint of an intending immigrant, can display exactly the same unfriendly 'singularity' as a conventional territorial state. Furthermore, one consequence of state borders within the EU becoming more porous, and of individual states not trusting other member states to properly police their external EU borders, is that there are increasing social controls and surveillance deep inside state jurisdictions (e.g. in relation to immigrants), where previously frontier checks were the main mechanism of control (see Bunyan, 1993). Another example of such a shift was seen when, with the establishment of the Single Market, customs officials were redeployed away from frontier posts to work on checking firms' financial returns. Perhaps it is not too fanciful to see these shifts in terms of *reversing* the medieval to modern movement whereby authority in the 'territorial state' came to depend on the defence and 'impenetrability' of territorial borders.

Other important qualifications to the 'postmodernity' of the EU, highlighting continuity as well as change, relate to the partiality or selective nature of territorial 'unbundling' which varies greatly between different state roles and aspects of power. Indeed the concept of 'unbundling' (as distinct perhaps from 'unravelling') should be taken to imply selectivity, in contrast to an undiscriminating 'bundling' of everything together in traditional territorial sovereignty. Largely in response to heightened international competition, the member states have 'pooled' some of their authority and resources at the European level, and some powers, particularly with respect to economic policy, have been ceded to the central Commission. But in other policy areas, such as 'security' or 'defence', there has been much less 'pooling' or 'ceding', and the EU's involvement in the area of 'welfare' is mostly limited to equalizing the conditions of capitalist competition within the neo-liberal Single Market. As already noted, the uneven impacts of globalization are making it increasingly necessary to distinguish between the different roles of the state, and to some extent the distinctions are between the spheres of production and of reproduction. Cox has argued that states are being 'internationalized' by globalization:

> The state becomes a transmission belt from the global to the national economy, where heretofore it had acted as a bulwark defending domestic welfare from external disturbances. . . . Power within the state becomes concentrated in those agencies in closest touch with the global economy – the offices of presidents and prime ministers, treasuries, central banks. The agencies that are more closely identified with domestic clients . . . become subordinated.
>
> (Cox, 1992: 30–1)

This should not be taken to mean that states are 'in decline' or becoming unimportant, as distinct from experiencing qualitative change. With greater insecurity in the 'new world disorder' even a weakened 'bulwark' might be seen as better than none. Furthermore, the idea that globalization is concentrating power in a few 'internationalized' parts of the central state needs to be balanced by the growing importance of regional or local politics precisely because of globalization; and here it is important to appreciate that the 'local state' is part of the state rather than a separate rival.

While we might agree with Ruggie that the EU is the first 'postmodern multiperspectival polity', this applies only to some state roles but not to others, and in neither case is it necessarily cause for 'celebration'. Where the EU is 'postmodern', as in some economic policy areas, we might want to criticize its 'multiperspectival' politics. Its 'democratic deficit' is at least partly due to the diffuseness and lack of 'singularity' in its decision-making structures, particularly the relative powerlessness of its central Parliament. Conversely, and indeed sometimes as a necessary corollary to 'postmodernity', the member states are in some respects traditionally 'modern', and we have seen that that can also be true of the EU itself as a territorial entity.

A more detailed empirical analysis of regionalism and European integration will confirm that the partiality of territorial 'unbundling' is producing a complex political amalgam of new and old forms (section 3), and that we need to make further qualifications to 'medieval' and 'premodern' analogies (section 4).

3 REGIONALISM IN THE EU

The main motive and context for European integration has been increasing global competition (3.1), and this largely explains the encouragement of substate regionalism by some of the central institutions of the

REGIONS, STATES AND THE EUROPEAN UNION

EU and by forces within the regions themselves (3.2). Relationships between regionalism and the member states have been much more ambivalent or contradictory, perhaps especially in the case of the United Kingdom and the Republic of Ireland (3.3).

3.1 Globalization and the EU

Since the ending of the post-war boom, the EU has developed largely as a response to intensified economic competition in global markets, and as both a consequence and a cause of changes in the economic role of states. Particularly since the mid-1970s, 'national' capital in western Europe and elsewhere has increasingly internationalized. There has been an historic shift variously described as a movement from 'state-centred Fordism' to 'globalized post-Fordism', or from 'state capitalism' – the integration of national capital and the nation-state – to the transnational integration of capitals across different states and a loosening of their ties with a particular state and territory.

This is the main reason for assuming a significant transformation in the role of states. Their responses, however, have been highly variable, disjointed and sometimes contradictory. States have adapted to internationalized economic forces, privatizing and deregulating, acting in combination and creating supranational institutions, and to varying degrees allowing autonomous regional adaptations at substate level. But they have also reacted to globalizing forces by seeking to retain their own powers of social control and social reproduction, increasing their control in some areas to compensate for a loss of control in others. They have formed 'macro' regional international combinations, such as the EU and the North American Free Trade Area, in order to engage in a 'neo-mercantilist' competition between larger economic blocs rather than between single states; and in some cases they have also increased their appeals to exclusivist forms of nationalism.

The internationalization of financial and productive capital in the world economy has rendered the traditional levers of 'national' economic policy less effective. The new globalized regimes of accumulation have led to a 'trans-state' capitalism (Gill and Law 1989) which still needs the state but is not orientated to it. However, partly because of the emergence of multiple levels of political authority in the realm of economic policy, there has been a strengthening of other state roles. The result is a hybrid configuration with sovereignty reduced in some respects and strengthened in others.

By the early 1990s one third of all private capital was owned by multinational corporations and their sales accounted for 25 per cent of global GDP (United Nations, 1993). With privatization and deregulation, companies have been acting less as 'national champions' and more as

ARTICLES

transnational or global operators. This is particularly true of the EU which is highly integrated into international flows of trade, finance and investment. In 1992 international trade was generally equivalent to between a quarter and a half of the GDP of member states (e.g. 26 per cent of GDP in the case of Germany, and 56 per cent of GDP for the Irish Republic), whereas in Japan it amounted to only 9.4 per cent of GDP and in the USA only 7.4 per cent.[1] In the 1980s EU states received over 80 per cent of all foreign direct investment (FDI) going to developed countries; and both their inflows and outflows of FDI grew exponentially (e.g. from about £4 billion to £20 billion in the case of the UK) (Das, 1993; Agnew, 1994).

There is a high degree of economic integration between the different EU countries. For example, 49 per cent the FDI involving the UK consists of flows either to or from other EU member states. Similarly, 60 per cent of EU exports in 1990 were destined for other EU economies (the figure having risen from 53 per cent in 1980). This contrasts for instance with Japan which is dependent on the Asia-Pacific region for only 36 per cent of its export earnings[2] (Hine, 1993). Unable to prevent the evasion of exchange controls on trans-state capital movements because of the large Eurodollar market, states had to deregulate their capital markets in the 1980s (Frieden, 1991). One outcome is that in Europe there has been a greater 'decay of that older relationship between national capitalism and national solidarity'; this helps explain both the widespread acceptance of the neo-liberal argument that states have 'lost control' of macroeconomic policy, and why instead member states have increasingly put their faith in greater 'action at the community level'.[3]

Here there is a significant ideological dimension to ideas about economic globalization, for they have helped in the propagation and legitimation of neo-liberal or 'New Right' deregulation by the EU and by the states themselves. Neo-liberal ideology about all-powerful 'global markets' has provided excuses for the inadequacies of state policies, allowing governments to opportunistically feign 'powerlessness' in the face of global forces. But while the rhetoric downplays the continuing importance of states and state intervention, its ideological character is revealed by the fact that neo-liberal governments have departed completely from their own scripts on key issues (e.g. economic recovery in the 1980s depended on government intervention, especially the USA's soaring federal budget deficit and sharply increased arms expenditure; and the 'Black Monday' stock market crash of October 1987 was prevented from becoming a 1930s style slump only by massive state funding of the banking system as monetarists became Keynesians overnight).

However, while states are far from 'powerless', those in the EU have increasingly acted collectively, and in generally neo-liberal ways, in the

REGIONS, STATES AND THE EUROPEAN UNION

face of heightened competition from North American and East Asian economies. As Helmut Kohl put it: 'Europe can hold its own in world-wide competition with Japan and North America only if it acts as one'.[4] In the belief that there were 'no national solutions to economic issues', a consensus developed on the need for exchange rate stability, balanced fiscal and monetary policies, labour market flexibility, more market integration, and the need for EU-wide action to achieve these objectives.[5] This generated a programme of accelerated neo-liberal integration in the late 1980s.[6] Along with deregulation in national economies, there was a partial re-regulation at the EU level, and an international or 'neo-' mercantilism developed to foster 'European champions' (Cornett and Caporaso, 1993: 228). The result has been a further concentration of transnational capital and economic power within the EU. Indeed in 1992 the Directorate-General for Competition Policy expressed concern at the concentration of production and control in larger and larger EU conglomerates (CEC, 1992: 428).

In response to these developments, the 'Maastricht Treaty' sought to harmonise macroeconomic policies and establish a common EU currency. Guidelines were set for levels of government debt, inflation rates, and central bank policies, in addition to the guidelines for trade, competition and regional policies already established through the Single European Act. Reducing unemployment came to be defined as a 'European' issue by member states and the European Commission, further recognition that 'it is no longer possible for nation states to be the motors of recovery'.[7]

Integration has forced states into a process of shared policy making which requires them to accept the consequences of so-called 'framework' decisions, agreeing to 'constrain their autonomy in order to facilitate collective action' (Puchala, 1993: 88). There has been a progressive dilution of veto powers in the Council of Ministers, and the exercise of sovereignty by member states has been substantially changed as whole swathes of economic policy are dominated by 'common' EU policies for external trade, currency control, agriculture, regional development and other matters.[8] Global competitive pressures to pursue common external policies have strengthened EU institutions, giving them a neo-mercantilist international legal 'personality' (House of Lords, 1985). The year of the SEM completion, 1992, saw the birth of 'a tougher, more outward looking' Commission, most notably with respect to its key role in the GATT negotiations over trading relations with North America and East Asia, and in the granting – or rather limiting – of East European access to EU markets.[9]

In summary, EU institutions have acquired significant powers, primarily over economic matters; they express common interests and exercise power in the name of the Union, constituting a dimension of

ARTICLES

political authority additional to that of the member states themselves. They have helped create a 'multiperspectival' political space which can no longer be reduced simply to the sum of (currently) twelve 'singular' sovereignties. With the increased political authority, if not 'formal' sovereignty, of functionally-defined economic regulatory regimes at the EU level, it seems that what Ruggie called the principle of 'territorial contiguity' is becoming less dominant and that 'transterritorial authority' is regaining some of its pre-modern importance. But of course there remain fundamental tensions between the tendencies towards federalism and the continuation of an essentially economic bloc dominated by inter-governmentalism; and, as already argued, there is unlikely to be a clear-cut resolution in either direction. For instance, when it assessed the impact of the 'Maastricht Treaty' on state sovereignty, the German constitutional court defined the EU as a '*Staatenverbund*' – not a federal European state, nor a confederation, nor simply a concert of states, but an 'association' of states that has no competence to determine its own sphere of competence.[10] The EU is essentially a new 'hybrid'. As we have seen (2.3, above), its 'democratic deficit' is at least partly due to the lack of 'singularity' in its decision-making structures, and public debate on this issue is likely to intensify with the review of EU institutional structures expected in 1996.

3.2 The EU and substate regions

Globalization and the 'macro' regionalism of the states combining in the EU are encouraging 'micro' or substate regionalism (Cox, 1992: 34); uneven development between substate regions is 'sapping the old state structures from within' (Nairn, 1977); and these processes are being furthered both by central institutions of the EU and by forces within the regions.

With economic power increasingly located in international capital markets and in multinational corporations as well as in EU institutions, 'national' economies are becoming less central to economic prosperity at substate levels. The mechanisms of 'national' economic management have been weakened, and direct 'local–global' contacts are increasing as localities compete to attract investment. Devising and implementing economic development (or survival) strategies at substate levels has become much more important. The 'national' economies have become much more 'regionalized' since the 1970s, as highlighted by successive Commission Reports on regional development (CEC, 1979, 1984, 1987 and 1990). By 1987, before the establishment of the Single Market, inter-regional disparities were already becoming more important than inter-state disparities. Whilst the latter had remained relatively constant, inter-regional inequalities were shown to have been widening at

REGIONS, STATES AND THE EUROPEAN UNION

an alarming rate (CEC, 1987: 63). The difference between the twenty-five regions with the highest unemployment rate and those with the lowest unemployment rate within the 11 EC states (excluding Greece) had widened from 5.7 percentage points in 1976 to 14.6 in 1985.[11] There was concern not only that this would impede European integration, but also that the very process of integration would itself exacerbate the problem, particularly when weak regions were subjected to stronger competition in the Single Market.

Concerns about the possible negative effects of integration on regional development had been raised as early as 1970. Then the 'Werner Report' on economic and monetary union argued that an EC-wide regional policy was a necessary component of any move to accelerated integration (CEC, 1970). In 1990, two years before the official 'completion' of the Single Market and during negotiations over closer monetary and political union, the fourth regional report showed that unemployment disparities had remained relatively constant since 1985 despite increased expenditure on EU regional funds (CEC, 1990: Tables A and C). Since 1988 this still limited regional compensation has been more concentrated in the regions most 'in need' – regions with declining industries, agricultural regions, declining urban regions, frontier regions, peripheral regions, and regions generally 'lagging behind' (CEC, 1987). In 1987 the Commission had speculated that integration was undermining the attempts at maintaining cohesion, but in its 1990 report on disparities, the Commission sought some consolation for the weaker regions in the notion of 'specific regional competitive advantages' within the SEM. Drawing on the more optimistic versions of the 'post-Fordist' future, it asserted that with 'flexible specialization' reducing the importance of 'scale economies', the less advantaged regions could become better off by producing specialized products for 'niche' markets (CEC, 1990: section 9.3, 80–1).

This perspective was central to the Commission's 1991 discussion document on regional policy, *Europe 2000*. It argued that 'new location factors' were opening up economic opportunities for peripheral regions, that 'flexible production systems' were making firms more mobile and that their location decisions were increasingly influenced by qualitative 'lifestyle' factors (CEC, 1991). Drawing on the experience of 'Silicon Glen' in Scotland, Rennes in France, the Pais Vasco in Spain, and South Wales, and noting the potential of information technology and telecommunications for altering 'comparative advantage', *Europe 2000* argued that increased mobility could help the 'periphery' and 'promote a more balanced distribution of economic activity' (CEC, 1991: 199).

However, this upbeat conclusion underplays the continuing, and indeed sharpening, difficulties faced by peripheral economies in times of economic depression when 'core' and 'periphery' generally diverge.

ARTICLES

Since the mid-1970s there have been widening disparities in levels of unemployment and income between the three main subdivisions of the EU: the 'vital axis' from northern Italy and central Germany through parts of Belgium and France to south-east England; the 'orbit of underdevelopment' in southern Italy, southern Spain and Greece; and the 'Atlantic arc' from Portugal to Ireland and northern and western parts of the UK (Dunford and Perrons, 1995).

Redistributive measures to counter the negative effects of integration have understandably been criticized as very limited: EU regional funds, for instance, amount to a mere 0.24 per cent of EU GDP, and they compare unfavourably with the expected efficiency gains of the Single Market which will largely accrue to 'core' regions (Perrons, 1992: 187). There are also demands for qualitatively different and more 'interventionist' measures, such as the redirection of capital flows at the EU level. This has become more urgent as economic integration has accelerated, stimulating intra-industry rather than inter-regional trade (Begg, 1989). The policy of developing 'European champions' to compete in global markets has directly undermined development prospects in the less developed regions (Amin *et al.*, 1992: 320). Efforts to achieve 'nominal cohesion' in terms of equalizing tax rates, exchange rates and inflation, as embodied in the deflationary 'convergence criteria' of the Maastricht Treaty, may well further damage the weaker economies, worsen inter-regional inequalities and undermine the process of achieving 'real convergence' between the regions (Williams *et al.*, 1991). Furthermore, competition between regions to attract investment tends to hold down local income levels and work against economic cohesion.[12] These problems were reflected in the necessity to set the 'ERM bands' at 15 per cent in 1993 and in the failure to meet the nominal 'convergence criteria' almost as soon as they had been agreed.

The economic prospects of the EU as a whole may hinge on its ability to reduce social and regional inequalities and maintain acceptable levels of effective demand across all regions (Dunford and Perrons, 1995). Concern about the widening of social divisions between and within regions and cities led to calls for neo-Keynesian reflation and 'supply-side Keynesianism' at the EU level. EU institutions such as the European Parliament have argued that the need for 'real' social cohesion and the 'well-being of all citizens' – rather than neo-liberal deregulation – should guide EU policy (European Parliament, 1991b).

This has been reflected in EU urban policies, in attempts to revise the Maastricht 'convergence criteria', in the 'European Recovery Programme' of limited reflation, and in the Delors' 'white paper' on reducing unemployment. Interventionism has moved up the political agenda as the possibility of fiscal reflation at the EU level has been combined with a range of supply-side policies targeted on the less-advantaged regional

REGIONS, STATES AND THE EUROPEAN UNION

economies on the periphery of the SEM. Contrary to neo-liberal ideology, globalization does not mean that states have 'lost control' of macroeconomic policy, but it may mean that it is now more difficult to operate demand-side policies and achieve non-inflationary growth. Thus it is argued that there is a need for Keynesian policies to be complemented by supply-side measures delivered primarily by non-market institutions: economic growth depends on 'comparative institutional advantage', and going beyond traditional Keynesianism requires 'fine-targeted' labour market and industrial policies (Matzner and Streeck, 1991: 7–8). Whereas Keynesian demand management is typically state-wide, 'fine-targeted' supply-side policies and 'institutional' or 'socio-' economics imply a more selective regional or local focus. 'Fine-targeting' is best carried out by local or regional authorities and is a further argument for strengthening regional institutions and policies, rather than simply relying on state-wide or EU-wide measures.

In any event, the Commission has attempted to counter socio-spatial problems by encouraging development strategies in the regions. The Commission has come to assume a crucial role in the calculation of relative regional deprivation, and its ranking of regions for the distribution of aid has increased the political significance of regions and regionalism. Its regional strategy has tended both to undermine existing state authority and legitimize regional movements. Regional interests have worked in alliance with EU institutions to challenge the development priorities of member states; and there has been a proliferation of disputes over 'national' and regional priorities and over the use of EU regional funds for state expenditure programmes (the 'subsidiarity' and 'additionality' debates). In some cases – most notably in Portugal, Greece and the Irish Republic – this has led to the creation (or re-creation) of political or administrative structures in the regions (Leonardi *et al.*, 1992).[13]

Building on these alliances of 'bureaucratic elitism' with 'emotional populism' (Kolinsky, 1978), the Commission proposed in the 'Maastricht' negotiations that the EU should set up a 'Committee of the Regions' to act as the 'upper house' of the European Parliament. The idea of a powerful and accountable tier of representation at the EU level was later 'watered down' by state representatives in the European Council, and the Committee as set up in 1994 has only a consultative role. Nonetheless, it is expected that its powers will be progressively enhanced, particularly after the 1996 review of EU institutions, as the Committee comes to provide a platform for the large and growing number of influential elected representatives from powerful regional governments in states such as Germany and Spain.[14]

The legitimacy of regionalism has also been enhanced by the European Parliament and its Regional Policy Committee. The two 'Regions of the Community' conferences which the Parliament sponsored jointly with

ARTICLES

regional associations in 1984 and in 1991 played a key role in driving forward the Commission's agenda. The 1984 conference led directly to the creation of the Association of European Regions (in 1985 – it now has 171 members) and the Consultative Council of Local and Regional Authorities (established in 1988). The 1991 conference ensured that the 'Committee for the Regions' was not written out of the 'Maastricht Treaty' by the European Council when it met to approve the Treaty in December 1991 (European Parliament, 1991a).

Partly because of encouragement from EU institutions, but also on their own initiative and in response to the 'threats and opportunities' of the SEM, substate regional interests have been demanding more powers and resources. Across the EU they are attempting to gear their regions to the needs of international capital, 'plugging into' transnational markets and networks and seeking to develop regionally-focused systems of innovation. Weaker regions have seen this as a way of reversing regional deprivation, or achieving what some observers have called 'regional inversion' (Suarez-Villa and Roura, 1993). In many cases the regional authorities have played a key, neo-corporatist role in stimulating economic development, linking 'Eurocrats', multinational companies, the local bourgeoisie and the local trade union movement (Harvie, 1990). In this context the lack or weakness of regional political structures is increasingly seen as having a debilitating effect on regional economic performance (European Dialogue, 1993; Leonardi *et al.*, 1992: 265).

This applies particularly in the relatively 'over-centralized' UK and the Irish Republic. Fearing further political marginalization and economic 'peripheralization' in the Single Market, many regionalist groupings such as the Campaign for a Scottish, for a Welsh and, in England, for a Northern Assembly, have argued that regional autonomy is urgently required (European Dialogue, 1993; Scott and Millar, 1992). In England and in the UK's 'national' regions, neo-corporatist 'partnerships' have been established at local and regional levels to maximize opportunities in the SEM (for instance the 'North-West Regional Association' and the 'West Midlands Regional Forum'). These typically bring together local politicians, commercial and industrial interests, trade unions and educational establishments, and they have made inputs into plans for the 1995–9 tranche of regional funds (Birch and Holliday, 1993; Rose, 1992).[15] In London the need to jointly lobby for European regional development funds brought together the Conservative-controlled London Boroughs Association and the Labour-controlled Association of London Authorities.[16]

In Northern Ireland a coalition including business organizations and local authorities established the 'Northern Ireland Centre in Europe'; and business interests are campaigning for North–South economic integration in an all-Ireland regional economy (Anderson, 1994). In the Irish

REGIONS, STATES AND THE EUROPEAN UNION

Republic there are some substate groupings, such as the 'Campaign for the West', which are demanding greater recognition of regional needs and calling for the formation of regional representative bodies to devise and implement economic development programmes. Mirroring developments in Northern Ireland, a consensus is growing within the Southern business community about the need for an 'all Ireland' economy and for North–South institutions to achieve it.

Increased demands for more regional autonomy are paralleled by an upsurge of trans-state inter-regional cooperation, manifested in a multiplicity of regional groupings and associations reaching across the EU's member states. The SEM offers new transnational opportunities for relatively advantaged regions, but it also threatens effective exclusion for regions and groups which are already disadvantaged. The resulting insecurities (see Massey, 1993), and the failure to achieve 'real' inter-regional cohesion in constructing the deregulated Market, have actually sharpened divisions between regions. However this too has encouraged inter-regional alliances spanning different EU states; and while many are 'at best . . . embyonic: at worst . . . the wishful thinking of . . . vested interests' (Cochrane, 1993), there can be little doubt that some of the alliances reflect substantial economic and political tendencies.

Unsurprisingly, it is the more prosperous regions which have taken the lead in forging new inter-regional development axes. Catalonia, Lombardy, Baden-Wurttemburg and Rhône-Alpes – the so-called 'four motors' of the EU – have carved out a place for themselves in the new European economy, forming 'another association of the "haves" ' similar to the OECD or the G-7 group of industrialized states at the global level (Cooke 1993).[17] Set up in September 1988, this association was explicitly designed to help these strong regions take a 'pathbreaking role' in the new Europe. Baden-Wurttemburg, for instance, saw the alliance as part of a strategy of 'working with the various stronger regions of Europe',[18] while Catalonia saw it as a means of pursuing its own interests rather than making common cause with poorer regions of Spain (Gallagher, 1990). Other 'core' regions are organizing along sectoral lines in 'regions of traditional industry' or 'motor industry cities and regions', or they are seeking to develop common interests with geographically contiguous regions.[19]

Regional associations are only rarely aimed at linking the interests of 'core' and 'peripheral' regions, and for the most part peripheral regions are forced to bargain for individual membership of the 'core' associations. Wales for instance has established links with the 'four motors' (Mitchell, 1991). This, and divergences between rich and poor regions, has encouraged the less prosperous to more clearly define their common interests at the EU level, through the Conference of Peripheral Maritime Zones, for example, or by linking with a neighbouring peripheral region as in the case of the North and South of Ireland.[20]

ARTICLES

The recent growth of regional interests seeking to devise and implement economic strategies for their areas has thus been a direct consequence of globalization and, more specifically, of integration in the EU and the SEM. The related building of inter-regional linkages, formal associations of regional bodies, and collective institutional expressions of regional interests at the EU level, are all contributing to a multiple layering of power and to the process of selectively 'unbundling' territoriality.

3.3 Substate regionalism and the member states

Despite significant 'unbundling' of their sovereignty, however, the member states continue to have crucial conditioning effects on regionalism. In the first instance regionalism is only possible within limits set by the states. As economic powers have been ceded to the Commission, states have strengthened their political control by 'institutionalizing intergovernmentalism', through exercising limited veto powers in the Council of Ministers (since 1966), meeting to agree common positions in 'European Political Cooperation' (since 1969), setting the pace for integration at meetings of the heads of state in the 'European Council' (since 1974), and acting through the 'Committee of Permanent Representatives' (since the 1970s) in order to acquire a 'consultative' role in the different stages of policy making and implementation (Taylor, 1983; Weiler, 1990).

Through increased integration the states have 'strengthened their own capacity for territorial management' (Keating and Jones, 1991: 324). They have attained more say in wider global arenas and greater leverage over economic forces than they would otherwise have. Consequently EU institutional structures provide a 'framework for attempting the resolution of existing national difficulties rather than an opportunity for transcending them' (Taylor, 1983). It is the states that determine what is and what is not deemed to constitute a 'region' of the EU. The Union's division into 174 regional and 829 subregional units simply reflects the institutional divisions set up and currently used by the member states. The Commission has pointed to the negative consequences of relying on the very heterogeneous regional subdivisions which result; and it admits that 'the values of statistical indicators are not independent of the regional framework selected' (CEC, 1990: Annex O; CEC, 1987: 11).

Some states have decentralized administration to regional authorities or established constitutional guarantees of regional autonomy (Vandamme, 1981). Their objectives have included the democratization of state structures, and the containment of regionalist and nationalist movements, absorbing centripetal pressures and preventing

REGIONS, STATES AND THE EUROPEAN UNION

geographical fragmentation. Just as Germany's *Lander* were established as a means of countering centralism and rekindling democracy after the Second World War, so in Italy, Spain, Portugal and Greece during the 1970s and early 1980s the process of setting up elected regional authorities has reflected a general concern to revive democratic participation. The Spanish, Italian, and Portuguese constitutions have granted substantial autonomy to island regions and 'historic nations' which, like the *Lander* in Germany, act as regional governments. Holland and Denmark have provincial assemblies with some powers, and since 1981 France has established regionally elected councils. Although some of the plans for decentralizing power to regional authorities have yet to be implemented (particularly in Portugal and Greece), and some of the regional bodies have only limited powers (for instance in France), elected regional bodies have established themselves as a permanent feature of political life in four of the five largest EU states and in several of the smaller ones (Keating, 1988; Leonardi *et al.*, 1992; Council of Europe, 1988).

The UK and the Irish Republic are the two most notable exceptions.[21] Fearing the 'break-up' of the UK into its constituent 'national' regions, British nationalists have had difficulty in viewing the EU as anything other than a threat to British sovereignty (Anderson, 1989), while in the Irish Republic parliamentary politicians often refuse to see 'over-centralization' as a political issue.[22] However even in the UK there have been changes. For example, regional planning groups were re-created by the neo-liberal Thatcher government in 1988, nine years after it had abolished them. In 1991 provision was made in the Planning and Compensation Act for local authorities to combine together to draw up regional plans; in 1992 the Department of the Environment began encouraging the formation of regional planning fora in each of the 'Standard Regions';[23] and in 1993 regional aid programmes were decentralized to inter-departmental committees based in new 'Standard Region' offices.[24] But while these measures may have helped contain regionalist and nationalist pressures, they have signally failed to assuage demands for the creation of regionally elected political bodies.

The state response to regional pressures in the Irish Republic has also been minimalist. In order to oversee the distribution of EU funds, the government was forced by the Commission to re-establish regional advisory bodies in 1988, one year after it had dissolved them as part of a budget cut.[25] Complaints about the lack of regional consultation on the 1989–94 expenditure programme also led to Commission intervention; and in 1993 care was taken to ensure a substantial regional input. But, contrary to the recommendations of the 1987 European Parliament Report on regional issues in Ireland, and the Irish government's own inquiry into local government in 1990, regional bodies remain largely

ARTICLES

administrative and are not directly elected (European Parliament, 1987; DSO, 1990).

In principle, both the British and Irish governments are committed to North–South cooperation in Ireland, but in practice both have generally given priority to immediate internal matters.[26] For example, in 1990 Irish government restrictions on cross-border shopping trips to Northern Ireland were maintained by the then Minister of Finance, Albert Reynolds, with the suspicion that he was more interested in maintaining his party's vote in border constituencies than in furthering Ireland's integration.[27] Until recently the need to improve North–South, Dublin–Belfast transport links has been routinely sidelined by Dublin governments, and it was only in 1992, after sustained pressure from Irish business interests North and South, that funds from the 1993–9 funding programme were committed to improving these links.[28] Likewise, the Irish government's exchange rate policy in the aftermath of the UK's departure from the ERM reflected an aspiration to membership of a German-led 'fast track' to monetary union, intermingled with hopes of the South gaining greater economic independence from UK: this also implied greater detachment from Northern Ireland in contradiction to the professed goal of North–South economic integration.[29]

However, the subsequent devaluation of the punt in the ERM confirmed the Republic's position on the 'outer periphery' of the SEM, and it underscored the need to maximize Ireland's indigenous North–South economic potential.[30] Irish government policy has recently become more orientated to the needs of indigenous industry and of particular regional or subregional economies (DSO, 1992). But its practical responses, like those of the UK, have generally been piecemeal and inadequate. While Southern political leaders remain formally committed to the ideal of an all-Ireland state, in practical terms they prioritize the interests of their own highly centralized state over the interests of an all-Ireland economy and of their own subregions. As the former Taoiseach Garret Fitzgerald recently pointed out, 'the priority for the Dublin government is to achieve security and stability', and its policies are orientated to the Republic of Ireland electorate rather than to interests defined in terms of Ireland as a whole.[31]

In summary, it seems that the ruling political establishments in all EU states have struck compromises both with other EU elites and with substate regional interests. In the UK and the Republic state responses to regionalism have been particularly minimalist and tend to be phrased only in terms of administrative devolution. In France there is a strategy of 'defensive regionalization' with the state allowing some political autonomy to elected regional authorities but only within a firmly uniform and centralist all-France political structure (Holohan, 1993).[32] Other approaches include non-uniform limited regional autonomy as in

REGIONS, STATES AND THE EUROPEAN UNION

Spain and Italy, or federal structures as in Germany and Belgium. But due to continuing changes in the global economy, the compromises are often unstable. States have responded to the process of globalization by attempting to maximize security and stablility, but the institutions they construct are constantly in the process of being undermined. Failure at one level rebounds onto others, so for example the failure of states to meet the economic needs of regional interests has encouraged the emergence of regional movements. Permanent interaction and often conflict over economic policy between the different layers of authority has become a constant theme of EU politics. The result, within an increasingly regionalized EU framework, is that while the state has remained a *central player* it is no longer the *central place* in capital accumulation.

4 CONCLUSIONS

The empirical analysis of the EU, the member states and the regions confirms that there is now significant 'unbundling' of territorial sovereignty. Globalization and integration in the EU have altered the role of states and regions; and the evidence of increasing substate regionalism provides additional support for Ruggie's (1993) conclusion, based on suprastate developments, that the EU is a 'postmodern' political form. The evidence, however, also points to the partiality of the 'unbundling' process and hence to the elements of continuity in new political arrangements, and especially to the continuing importance of states within them. Such partial 'unbundling', particularly in the sphere of economic production, has been both a cause and, in part, a consequence of growing substate regionalism.

The partiality is directly related to an increasing differentiation of state roles as globalization impacts very unevenly on different policy areas. It is therefore increasingly important to distinguish between the various aspects of state involvement in society – between, for example, the sphere of production on the one hand and the spheres of reproduction and social control on the other. There has been much less 'unbundling' with respect to the latter, with, for instance, the EU having a relatively limited role in social welfare, and the regions a limited role in social control. Thus while state power may be transferred or seep away in some spheres, it may be augmented in others. Blanket generalizations about 'the end of territorial sovereignty' or the 'death of the nation-state' are therefore completely misleading.

State elites do have less control over globalized economic forces as power has seeped away to global markets, and as some state controls have been transferred to suprastate collectivities as in the case of the EU. But contrary to neo-liberal ideology, states continue to play crucial roles in servicing economic development and in providing conditions

ARTICLES

favourable to capital accumulation. The need for 'fine-targeted supply side Keynesianism' is one important reason why regional and local branches of the state have taken on an increased importance.

With these changes the ground has been shifting underneath established conceptions of sovereignty, and 'new medieval' and 'postmodern' conceptualizations provide fruitful alternatives. They highlight multiple levels and overlaps of authority; and they usefully signal a shift in the underlying time-space of politics while helping to avoid exaggerating the changes. However, even restricted usage of the concepts, specifically referring to the ontology of territoriality, has limitations. In particular, analogies to the very different circumstances of medieval or 'pre-modern' Europe have serious inadequacies which are themselves revealing, for the differences indicate or arise from the greater complexity of the contemporary world. This is not to say it is more 'disordered', though two differences are the relative absence of the unifying 'universalism' and of the nested hierarchies which were important ordering principles of medieval Christendom.

Modern democracies are more complex partly because sovereignty now belongs to 'the people' or 'the nation', at least in theory if not always in practice. It is now 'our sovereignty' which is being 'unbundled'. Thus democracy as presently constituted tends to be undermined by the 'unbundling' of territoriality; and this, not surprisingly, generates popular resistance and democratic opposition, as seen for example in the difficulties which several EU states experienced when holding referenda to gain popular ratification of closer European union. One democratic response to territorial 'unbundling' is simply to react against it, by, for example, voting against transfers of power to EU institutions. Another, quite different, response is to accept it but work towards reducing the EU's 'democratic deficit' by strengthening its central institutions and particularly the European Parliament. This of course implies ongoing tensions between democratic accountability via states or directly through EU institutions, with federalization continuing to be 'arrested' in some 'intermediate stage' which would be consistent with Bull's 'new medievalism'. It implies a need for new transnational forms of democracy and accountability as well as (not instead of) the need make states more democratic, but here the 'medieval model' is unhelpful to say the least.

At the same time our more complex world lacks the sort of 'universalism' which stemmed from the basically theocratic and unifying political system of medieval Christendom. Bull stressed that to qualify as a 'new medievalism', the new political order would have to be 'universal', 'all over the globe'. But state forms and political and cultural allegiances are extremely uneven across the world, and this global diversity would seem to rule out a secular reincarnation of the 'universality'

REGIONS, STATES AND THE EUROPEAN UNION

which cemented the relatively self-contained 'world' of medieval Europe. Indeed, the contemporary European continent, never mind the world as a whole, could be said to lack a modern equivalent of the unifying 'world view' or 'moral order' which combined all aspects of life – economic, social, cultural, ideological – over most of medieval Europe. There may now be 'one world' in terms of a highly interdependent global system of capitalist production and exchange, but in many respects it is still composed of 'separate worlds' in ideological and political terms. The world has been integrated in a capitalist global economy, but this has not been matched by anything approaching the cultural homogeneity of medieval Europe. As well as making for greater complexity, this integration of 'separate worlds', some dominant, others subordinate, may also make for more social and political instability. The European Union may be the world's 'first truly postmodern international political form' but there is little evidence of this particular arrangement being replicated in the other major economic blocs.

The third important difference from the medieval era is the relative absence of ordered hierarchies. As we saw, sovereignty in medieval Europe was typically divided between different institutions and levels which constituted nested hierarchies, and people were members of higher collectivities not directly but by virtue of their membership of lower level bodies. Now, in contrast, the typical hierarchies are *not nested*: hierarchies may still exist, but not in a medieval 'chain of command' sense; and people are often *directly* members of international networks, not via national bodies. Likewise, small local groups increasingly deal directly with transnational institutions, not via larger intermediaries, and regional groups and institutions deal directly with their counterparts in other states without the respective states necessarily having any involvement. Indeed the growth of direct 'local–global' interrelationships which bypass central state institutions is an esential aspect of the contemporary territorial 'unbundling'.

The 'escape' from nested hierarchies, together with the lack of universalism and the presence of formal democracy, implies a greater complexity than in medievalism. 'Postmodern' territoriality may have some limited similarities to 'premodern' counterparts but history does not simply repeat itself. States, once born, are continuing to exist rather than being tidily removed to clear the ground for new polities. Their powers and roles may be changing, but they continue to co-exist and interact with a plethora of other, different kinds of political communities, institutions, organizations, associations and networks. Globalization is overlaying the mosaic of states with other forms of political community, non-state polities and non-political market relations which are shaped by different forms of authority, 'territorial', 'non-territorial' and 'functional'.

ARTICLES

Thus while the EU is in some respects 'postmodern', contemporary reality is a mixture of new and old forms. For some purposes, territoriality and 'territorial contiguity' are becoming less dominant as modes of social organization and control, and 'non-territorial' authority is regaining some of the importance it had in medieval times. But for other purposes the modern nation-state with its sovereignty defined by (often the same old) territorial boundaries seems as firmly rooted as ever. This duality helps to explain the persistence of nationalism, the continuing attachment to statehood, and the fact that globalization can 'call forth' nationalist revivals (Calhoun, 1994) at the same time as it 'internationalizes'. Given such continuities, 'late' rather than 'post' modernity is probably a better overall label for the contemporary political world.

The state has not been superseded 'from above', or replaced 'from below'; rather, it has adapted to the changing reality of global power and the shifting demands of substate forces. Political restructuring cannot be reduced to the simple arithmetic of a 'zero-sum game' in which losses at one level of institutional politics automatically mean gains at another. As in the 'new medieval' analogy, the pressures on nation-states 'from above and below' may well result in partial and ambiguous changes which lead to doubts about where authority really lies. The various contending pressures are likely to produce ongoing conflict between 'old' and 'new' political forms, between a reactive longing for traditional 'modernist' polities and a more adaptive acceptance or encouragement of 'postmodern' arrangements. If the EU is widely seen as an economic success, more adaptive responses are likely to predominate. If, however, it is seen as failing to deliver prosperity – failing even in its 'chosen' economic sphere where 'postmodern adaptation' is most advanced – there could well be more 'modernist reaction' with more reliance on nation-states and nationalisms.

NOTES

An earlier version of this article was presented at the Annual Conference of the Sociological Association of Ireland, Derry, 13–15 May 1994. Our thanks to those who gave us comments and criticisms, especially Douglas Hamilton, Paschal Preston, Liam O'Dowd, Graham Thompson, and the three anonymous referees for *RIPE*.

1 *Financial Times*, 19 January 1993.
2 *Financial Times*, 19 January 1993.
3 *Guardian*, 11 December 1993. See also European Parliament (1983) *The Recovery of the European Economy* (the 'Albert–Ball' Report).
4 *Financial Times* 4 January 1993.
5 *Financial Times* 19 October 1992.

REGIONS, STATES AND THE EUROPEAN UNION

6 *Financial Times* 18 March 1993.

7 See 'And one for all' by Ken Coates MEP, *New Statesman and Society*, 6 November 1992.

8 The pressure to define common EU interests, rather than particular 'national' interests, is somewhat enhanced by the restricted powers of 'co-decision' that have been granted to the European Parliament, and by the advisory roles that have been accorded to the Economic and Social Committee and the Committee of the Regions.

9 As a former Polish Defence Minister has argued, EU policy could hardly be less friendly considering the haggling over East European imports which amounted to no more than 1 per cent of the EU's total imports (*Independent*, 26 January 1993; *Financial Times* 2 May 1993).

10 The Court's 85-page judgment established a Bundsestag Europe monitoring committee (*Financial Times* 21 March 1993 and 11 November 1993; *Independent*, 22 November 1993 and 30 October 1993; *Guardian*, 13 October 1993).

11 For the nine member states of 1970 the gap widened from 4.3 percentage points to 11.4. Unemployment rates are based on ILO figures (CEC, 1987: 63 and 134, Table 3.2.3–2).

12 *Financial Times*, 17 December 1992; 'Europe of the Regions', *Centre for Local Economic Strategies*, Bulletin 17, June 1991)

13 Earlier the Council of Europe organized conferences for a range of European regions – including frontier regions (1972), peripheral maritime regions (1975), Alpine regions (1978) and island regions (1981) (Council of Europe, 1988).

14 Charles Grey, Chair of the Local Government International Bureau, confirmed this at a conference on 'The Nation-State, Supranationalism and Democratic Control: Economic Policy and the European Union', London European Research Centre, University of North London, April 1994.

15 *Financial Times*, 18 June 1993; and *Financial Times*, West Midlands Special Survey, 14 July 1993.

16 Association of Local Authorities and London Boroughs Association Press Release, 15 March 1994.

17 *Guardian*, 25 April 1992. See also 'The four motors are driving off', *Fortnight*, 296, June 1991.

18 As the Economics Minister of Baden-Wurttemberg, H. Shauffler, put it in the AER journal *Regions of Europe*, 2 November 1990, 126, Strasbourg.

19 *The European*, 17 January 1992. For instance Nord-Pas de Calais, Kent and the three Belgium regions, Wallonia, Flanders and Brussels, established a 'Euroregion' partnership in 1987 – see Thompson, R. (1992) 'European policy and funding', *The Planner*, TCPSS Proceedings 27/11/92; also Cochrane (1993).

20 The Commission has attempted to develop linkages between less powerful regions under Article 10 of the ERDF regulations (for instance, funding joint economic ventures involving Donegal, North Jutland, South West Flanders and Galway).

21 UK centralization increased with the abolition of metropolitan authorities in 1986, with the transfer of administrative powers from local government to centrally-appointed quangos or to Whitehall, and with the dissolution in 1993 of some relatively powerful authorities at the regional and county level, just as the Commission has grown to recognize them as 'key points of contact' – see *The New Europe: Implications for UK Local Government*, Association of County Councils, February 1992.

ARTICLES

In the Irish Republic local administration is largely conducted through county councils whose chief executives are appointed by central government. Here too centralization has increased in recent years: in 1988 the national Roads Authority took over responsibility for major roads, and the Agriculture and Food Development Authority took responsibility for agriculture; in 1992 responsibility for environmental protection was handed over to an appointed central agency – see Sinnott, R. (1992) 'Regional elites, regional powerlessness and the European Regional Programme in Ireland' (in Leonardi (ed.) 1992: 71–109).

22 In 1990 the Taoiseach, Charles Haughey, argued that the EC-wide tendency to devolve power to subnational regions would have little impact on Ireland (*Irish Times*, 12 May 1990).

23 Department of the Environment, *The Functions of Local Authorities in England*, HMSO (1992).

24 *Financial Times*, 5 November 1993.

25 *Irish Times*, 13 October 1987.

26 *Irish Times*, 5 June 1993.

27 *Financial Times*, 20 June 1990; *Irish Times*, 13 June 1990; *Belfast Telegraph*, 8 June 1993.

28 Public finances and EU structural funds had been used to improve Dublin–Cork, Dublin–Wexford, Dublin–Galway and Dublin suburban transport links, rather than Dublin–Belfast links (*Irish Times*, 5 June 1990, *Irish News*, 20 March 1992).

29 *Irish Times*, 3 and 12 February 1993 and 2 August 1993, and *Financial Times*, 1 February 1993.

30 *Sunday Tribune*, 7 February 1993; see also Munck, 1993.

31 *Irish Times*, 25 September 1993.

32 This was illustrated by the refusal to recognize the existence of a distinctive Corsican people; in the Statutes of the Corsican regional government, the French state permits the expression of substate identity only in so far as it is integrated into the French political system and conforms to its definition of the French 'nation' (Holohan, 1993).

REFERENCES

Agnew, J. (1994) 'The territorial trap: the geographical assumptions of International Relations theory', *Review of International Political Economy*, 1(1): 53–80.

Amin, A., Charles, D. and Howells, J. (1992) 'Corporate restructuring and cohesion in the new Europe', *Regional Studies* 26(4): 319–31.

Anderson, J. (1986) 'Nationalism and geography', in J. Anderson (ed.) *The Rise of the Modern State*, pp. 115–42, Brighton: Harvester Press.

—— (1994) 'Problems of inter-state economic integration: Northern Ireland and the Irish Republic in the Single European Market', *Political Geography* 13(1): 53–73.

Anderson, J. and Goodman, J. (1993) 'European integration and the national conflict in Ireland', in R. King (ed.) *Ireland, Europe and the Single Market: Geographical Perspectives*, Geography Society of Ireland Special Publications, No.8: 16–30, Dublin: GSI.

—— (1994) 'European and Irish integration: contradictions of regionalism and nationalism', *European Urban and Regional Studies*, 1(1): 49–62.

REGIONS, STATES AND THE EUROPEAN UNION

Anderson, J.J. (1989) 'Sceptical reflections on a Europe of regions: Britain, Germany and the ERDF', *Journal of Public Policy* 10: 417–47.

Begg, I. (1989) 'European integration and regional policy', *Oxford Review of Economic Policy* 5(2): 90–104.

Birch, M. and Holliday, I. (1993) 'Institutional emergence: the case of the North-West of England', *Regional Politics and Policy* 3(2): 29–51.

Bull, H. (1977) *The Anarchical Society*, London: Macmillan.

Bunyan, T. (1993) *Statewatching in the New Europe*, London: Statewatch.

Calhoun, C. (1994) 'Nationalism and civil society: democracy, diversity and self-determination', *International Sociology* 8(4): 387–411.

Callinicos, A. (1991) *Against Postmodernism*, Polity Press: Cambridge.

Cochrane, A. (1993) 'Beyond the nation state? – building the Euro-region', in N. Bullmann (ed.) *Die Politik der Dritten Ebene Regionen im Prozess der EG – Integ*, Berlin: Nomos.

CEC (Commission of the European Communities) (1970) *Report to the Council and the Commission on the realisation by stages of Economic and Monetary Union in the Community*, CEC: Brussels.

—— (1979, 1984, 1987, 1990) *The Regions of the Enlarged Community: Periodic reports on the social and economic situation and development of the regions of the Community*, Luxemburg: Office for the Official Publications of the EC.

—— (1991) *Europe 2000: The Outlook for the Development of the Community's Territory*, COM 91, 452, Luxemburg: Office for the Official Publications of the EC.

—— (1992) *Twenty-First Report on Competition Policy*, Directorate-General for Competition Policy, Luxemburg: Office for the Official Publications of the EC.

Cooke, P. (1993) 'Globalisation of economic organisation and the emergence of regional interstate partnerships', in C. Williams (ed.) *The Political Geography of the New World Order*, pp. 46–59, London: Belhaven Press.

Cornett, L. and Caporaso, J. (1993) ' "And still it moves!" State interests and social forces in the European Community', in J. Rosenau and E. Czempiel (eds) *Governance without Government: Order and Change in World Politics*, pp. 219–49, Cambridge: Cambridge University Press.

Council of Europe (1988) *The Allocation of Powers to the Local and Regional Levels of Government in the Member States of the Council of Europe*, Strasbourg.

Cox, R.W. (1992) 'Global perestroika', in R. Miliband and L. Panitch (eds) *Socialist Register*, pp. 26–44, London: Merlin Press.

Das, D. (1993) 'Contemporary trends in the international capital markets', in D. Das (ed.) *International Finance*, pp. 3–27, London: Routledge.

Der Derian, J. (1992) *Antidiplomacy: Spies, Terror, Speed and War*, Oxford: Blackwell.

Dublin Stationery Office (1990) *Local Government and Reform*, Report of the Advisory Expert Committee (the 'Barrington Report'), Dublin.

—— (1992) *Ireland in Europe, A Shared Challenge: Economic Cooperation on the Island of Ireland in an Integrated Europe*, Dublin.

Dunford, M. and Perrons, D. (1995) 'Regional inequality, regimes of accumulation and economic development in contemporary Europe', in *Transactions of Institute of British Geographers* (forthcoming).

European Dialogue (1993) *Power to the People? Economic Self Determination and the Regions*, Conference Report, Roberts A. (ed.) London: European Dialogue/Freidrich Ebert Foundation.

ARTICLES

European Parliament (1987) *Report on Behalf of the Committee on Regional Policy and Regional Planning – The Regional Problems of Ireland* ('Hume Report'), A2 – 109/87, July, Luxembourg: EP.

—— (1991a) 'The regions of the Community and social and economic cohesion on the eve of the completion of the internal Market, *Report and Minutes of the Second EP/Regions of the Community Conference, Strasbourg 27–29 November 1991*, Luxembourg: EP.

—— (1991b) *Opinion of the Committee on Economic and Monetary Matters and Industrial Policy on the Fourth Periodic Report*, Ribiero Rapporteur, EN/PR/ 111473 PE, October, Luxembourg: EP.

Gallagher, T. (1990) 'Autonomy in Spain', in B. Crick (ed.), *National Identities*, Political Quarterly Special Edition, London: Blackwell.

Gill, S. and Law, D. (1989) 'Global hegemony and the structural power of capital', *International Studies Quarterly* 33: 475–99.

Harvey, D. (1989) *The Condition of Postmodernity*, Oxford: Basil Blackwell.

Hine, R. (1993) 'Regionalism and integration of the world economy', *Journal of Common Market Studies* 30(2): 115–23.

Holohan, W.D. (1993) 'French forms of regionalisation: a specific response to European integration and claims for regional autonomy', paper to conference on Peripheral Regions and European Integration, ESRC Research Seminar, Queens University, Belfast, 23–24 April 1993.

House of Lords (1985) *The External Competence of the European Communities*, European Communities Sub Committee, 1984–5, 16th Report, July 1985, London: HMSO.

Kaldor, M. (1993) 'Civil society and democratic renewal', in A. Roberts (ed.) *Power to the People? Economic Self Determination and the Regions*, Conference Report, European Dialogue/Freidrich Ebert Foundation: London.

Kearney, R. (1988) 'Introduction: thinking otherwise', in R. Kearney (ed.) *Across the Frontiers*, pp. 7–29, Dublin: Wolfhound Press.

Keating, M. (1988) *State and Regional Nationalism: Territorial Politics and the European State*, London: Harvester.

Keating, M. and Jones, B. (1991) 'Scotland, Wales – Peripheral assertion and European integration', *Parliamentary Affairs* 44(3) July: 311–24.

Kolinsky, M. (1978) *Divided Loyalties*, Manchester: Manchester University Press

Leonardi, R. (ed.) (1992) 'The regions and the European Community: the regional response to the Single Market in the underdeveloped areas', *Regional Politics and Policy – An International Journal*, Special Issue, 2 (1).

McGrew, A. (1995) 'World order and political space', in J. Anderson, C. Brook and A. Cochrane (eds) *A Global World? Reordering Political Space*, Oxford: Oxford University Press.

Massey, D. (1993) 'Power-geometry and a progressive sense of place', in Bird *et al* (eds), *Mapping the Futures*, pp. 59–70, London: Routledge.

Matzner, E. and Streeck, W. (eds) (1991) *Beyond Keynesianism: The Socio-economics of Production and Full Employment*, Brighton: Edward Elgar.

Munck, R. (1993) *The Irish Economy: Results and Prospects*, London: Pluto Press.

Nairn, T. (1977) *The Break-up of Britain: Crisis and Neo-nationalism*, London: New Left Books.

O'Dowd, L. and Corrigan, J. (1992) 'National sovereignty and cross-border cooperation: Ireland in a comparative context', paper to Sociological Association of Ireland Annual Conference, Cork, 8–10 May 1992.

Perrons, D. (1992) 'The regions and the Single Market', in M. Dunford *et al* (eds) *Cities and Regions in the New Europe*, pp. 170–195, Belhaven: London.

REGIONS, STATES AND THE EUROPEAN UNION

Puchala, D. (1993) 'Western Europe', in R. Jackson and A. James (eds) *States in a Changing World*, pp. 69–93, Oxford: Clarendon Press.

Rose, E. (1992) 'A Europe of regions – the West Midlands of England: planning for metropolitan change in Brimingham', *Landscape and Urban Planning*, 22: 229–42.

Ruggie, J. (1993) 'Territoriality and beyond: problematizing modernity in international relations', *International Organisation* 47(1) 139–74.

Scott, A. and Millar, D. (1992) 'Subsidiarity and the Scottish dimension – a discussion paper', presented to Europe of the Regions Conference, Edinburgh, November 1992.

Strange, S. (1994) 'The power gap: the member states and the world economy', paper to conference on 'The Nation-State, Supranationalism and Democratic Control: Economic policy and the European Union', London European Research Centre, University of North London, 14 April 1994.

Suarez-Villa, L. and Roura, J. (1993) 'Regional economic integration and the evolution of disparities', *Papers in Regional Science* 72(4) 369–87.

Taylor, P. (1983) *The Limits of European Integration*, London: Croom Helm.

United Nations (1993) *World Investment Report: Transnational Organizations and Integrated Production*, New York: UN.

Vandamme, J. (1981) 'Regionalism in Europe', in D. Demeron (ed.) *Regionalism and Supranationalism*, London: Political Studies Association.

Walker, R.B.J. (1993) *Inside/Outside: International Relations as Political Theory*, Cambridge: Cambridge University Press.

Williams, K. (1991) 'What kind of regional policy?' *Local Economy*, 5(4) February: 330–46.

Competition & Change, 1995 Vol. 1, pp. 31–50
Reprints available directly from the publisher
Photocopying permitted by license only

The State and the Global City: Notes Towards a Conception of Place-Centered Governance

Saskia Sassen

Professor of Urban Planning, Columbia University, New York, NY 10027, USA

Re-examines the proposition of a declining signficance of the state in the global economy. Argues that this proposition has been fed by an over-emphasis on the hypermobility of capital and a conceptual background that posits a mutually exclusive relation between the national and the global. Shows that a) the state itself has been transformed by its participation in the design and implementation of global economic systems; and b) even the most global and hypermobile industries, such as finance and the advanced corporate services, are ultimately embedded in a global grid of linkages and sites with great concentrations of material facilities and work processes, many of them strategic to the operation of hypermobile capital. Because of its strategic character and the density of resources and linkages it concentrates, this global grid could be a space for focused regulatory activity by an inter-state system that has itself become more internationalized. But it would require considerable innovation in the frameworks for and objects of regulation.

Globalization has transformed the meaning of, and the sites for, the governance of economies. One of the key properties of the current phase in the long history of the world economy is the ascendance of information technologies, the associated increase in the mobility and liquidity of capital, and the resulting decline in the regulatory capacities of national states over key sectors of their economies. This is well illustrated by the case of the leading information industries, finance and the advanced corporate services, the focus of this essay. These tend to have a space economy that is transnational and is partly embedded in electronic spaces that override conventional jurisdictions and boundaries. Yet, this is also a space economy which reveals the need for strategic sites with vast concentrations of resources and infrastructure, sites that are situated in national territories and are far less mobile than much of the general commentary on the global economy suggests. This signals possibilities for governance and a role for national states not typically foreseen in propositions about the declining significance of the state in the global economy.

Here I want to examine the underside of globalization in order to show that the dominant line of theorization with its emphasis on the hypermobility and liquidity of capital is a partial account; further, it is partial in a way that carries significant implications for questions of state and non-state centered regulatory capacities and, more generally, questions of governance and accountability in a global economy. The organizing focus in this brief essay is the space economy of information industries at a time when the development of telematics maximizes the potential for geographic dispersal and mobility. I will seek to show how the space economy for major new transnational economic processes diverges in significant ways from the duality of global/national presupposed in much analysis of the global economy. The substantive rationality for this inquiry is to add to our understanding of questions of governance and accountability in the global economy.

Two propositions organize my analysis (see Sassen 1991; 1994; forthcoming, for more extensive accounts). One is that to a large extent the global economy materializes in concrete processes situated in specific places, and that this holds for the most advanced information industries as well. We need to distinguish between the capacity for global transmission/communication and the material conditions that make this possible.

The second proposition is that the spatial dispersal of economic activity made possible by telematics contributes to an expansion of central functions if this dispersal is to take place under the continuing concentration in control, ownership and profit appropriation that characterizes the current economic system. More conceptually, we can ask whether an economic system with strong tendencies towards such concentration can have a space economy that lacks points of physical agglomeration.

From these two propositions I have derived a series of analytic pathways into questions of place and production and thereby into the place-boundedness of key processes of economic globalization. Recovering this place-boundedness also illuminates certain aspects about the role of the state in today's global information economy which are easily lost in discussions of the hypermobility of information outputs.

But precisely because they are deeply embedded in telematics, advanced information industries also shed light on questions of control in the global economy that not only go beyond the state but also beyond the notions of non-state centered systems of coordination prevalent in the literature on governance. They are questions of control that have to do with the orders of magnitude that can be achieved in the financial markets thanks to the speed in transactions made possible by the new technologies. Among the best examples are the foreign currency markets: they operate largely in electronic space and have achieved volumes that have left the central banks incapable of exercising the influence on exchange rates they are expected to have. Here are questions of control that arise out of the properties of the new information technologies, notably the immense speed-up of transactions, rather than out of the extension of the economy beyond the state.

Regulatory Capacities and Space Economies: Preliminary Notes

Current forms of economic transnationalism have a number of characteristics that matter for an examination of questions of governance. Two are particularly important (see Sassen, forthcoming for a more extensive discussion). One of these is that many key components of economic globalization today do not strengthen the inter-state system, in contrast to the situation during the three decades after WWII. A second one is that the state remains as the ultimate guarantor of the "rights" of global capital, i.e. the protection of contracts and property rights.

There follows a brief discussion of each of these in order to set a context for the ensuing examination of global cities and the emergent transnational urban system as potentially significant sites for the implementation of mechanisms for governance and accountability in the global economy.

1. Globalization and the Inter-State System

During the Pax Americana, economic internationalization had the effect of strengthening the inter-state system. Leading economic sectors, especially manufacturing and raw materials extraction, were subject to international trade regimes that contributed to build the inter-state system. Individual states adjusted national economic policies to further this type of international economic system, doubtless often pressured by the hegemonic power of the US. (Even though already then certain sectors did not fit comfortably under this largely trade dominated inter-state regime: out of their escape emerged the euro-markets and off-shore tax havens of the 1960s).

The breakdown of the Bretton Woods system produced an international governance void rapidly filled by multinationals and global financial markets. This has fed the notion of the shrinking role of the state and the debate about non-state centered systems of governance (Jessop 1990; Rosenau 1992; Young 1989; Kooiman and van Vliet 1993; Leftwich 1994). According to some (see Panitch 1996; Mittelman 1996; Drache and Gertler 1991) the neoliberalism of the 1980s has redefined the role of states in national economies and in the inter-state system. Further, the structure of the state itself in developed countries has undergone a shift away from those agencies most closely tied to domestic social forces, as was the case in the U.S. during the Pax Americana, and towards those closest to the transnational process of consensus formation.

A focus on international finance and corporate services brings to the fore the extent to which the forms of economic globalization evident in the last two decades have not necessarily had the effect of strengthening the inter-state system. Furthermore, the ascendance of international finance has produced regulatory voids that lie beyond not only states but also the inter-state system. Existing systems of governance and accountability for transnational economic activities and entities leave much ungoverned when it comes to these industries. In this regard, an analysis of these industries can help bring to the fore the differences between the role of the state in earlier forms of internationalization and the current globalization of economic activity evident in some (but by no means all) economic sectors.

One way of illustrating this weakened articulation of the growth dynamic of finance and corporate services to the state and inter-state system is by examining what we could think of as the new valorization dynamic embedded in the ascendance of these industries–that is, a new set of criteria for valuing or pricing various economic activities and outcomes. (For more detail see Sassen 1994: chapters 4 and 6.) We are seeing the formation of an economic complex with properties clearly distinguishing it from other economic complexes in that the articulation of its valorization dynamic with the public economic functions of the state is quite weak compared with Fordist manufacturing, for example.

2. Guaranteeing the Global Rights of Capital

Even though transnationalism and deregulation have reduced the role of the state in the governance of economic processes, the state remains as the ultimate guarantor of the rights of capital whether national or foreign. Firms operating transnationally want to ensure the functions traditionally excercised by the state in the national realm of the economy, notably guaranteeing property rights and contracts. The state here can be conceived of as representing a technical administrative capacity which cannot be replicated at this time by any other institutional arrangement (Sassen, forthcoming); furthermore, this is a capacity backed by military power.

But this guarantee of the rights of capital is embedded in a certain type of state, a certain conception of the rights of capital, and a certain type of international legal regime: It is largely the state of the most developed and most powerful countries in the world, western notions of contract and property rights, and a new legal regime aimed at furthering economic globalization.[1]

Deregulation has been widely recognized as a crucial mechanism to facilitate the globalization of various markets and industries because it reduces the role of the state. But deregulation can also be seen as negotiating on the one hand the fact of globalization, and, on the other, the ongoing need for guarantees of contracts and property rights for which the state remains as the guarantor of last instance (Panitch, 1996; Sassen, forthcoming; see also Negri 1995). The deregulation of key operations and markets in the financial industry can be seen as a negotiation between nation-based legal regimes and the formation of a consensus among a growing number of states about furthering the world economy (Mittelman, 1996; Trubek *et al.*, 1993). In other words, it is not simply a matter of a space economy extending beyond a national realm. It also has to do with the formation and legitimation of transnational legal regimes that are operative in national territories. National legal fields are becoming more internationalized in some of the major developed economies and transnational legal regimes become more important and begin to penetrate national fields hitherto closed (e.g., Trubek *et al.*, 1993; Aman, 1995).[2] The state continues to play a crucial role in the production of legality around new forms of economic activity.[3]

Transnational economic processes inevitably interact with systems for the governance of national economies. There are few industries where deregulation and transnationalization have been as important to growth as in international finance and advanced corporate services. What deregulation in finance makes clear is that it has had the effect of partly de-nationalizing national territory: e.g. the International Banking Facilities in the U.S. can be seen as such an instance. Yet another, more familiar

---

[1] For instance, France which ranks among the top providers of information services and industrial engineering services in Europe and has a strong, though not outstanding, position in financial and insurance services has found itself at an increasing disadvantage in legal and accounting services. French law firms are at a particular disadvantage because anglo-saxon law dominates in international transactions. Foreign firms with offices in Paris dominate the servicing of the legal needs of firms operating internationally, for both French and foreign firms operating out of France (Carrez 1991).

[2] The hegemony of neo-liberal concepts of economic relations with its strong emphasis on markets, deregulation, free international trade has influenced policy in the 1980s in USA and UK and now increasingly also in continental Europe. This has contributed to the formation of transnational legal regimes that are centered in Western economic concepts. Through the IMF and IBRD as well as GATT this vision has spread to the developing world. An issue that is emerging as significant in view of the spread of western legal concepts is the critical examination of the philosophical premises about authorship and property that define the legal arena in the West (e.g. Coombe 1993.)

[3] Many of these changes, of course, required explicit government action. Pastor's study [*Congress and the Politics of U.S. Foreign Economic Policy, 1929–1976*] on the U.S. about the arduous legislative road to open up the country to foreign investment is a good case in point.

instance, can be found in various forms through which manufacturing production has been internationalized: e.g. export processing zones which fall under special regimes that reduce the obligations of firms to the state, notably regarding taxes and labor legislation (see, e.g. Bonacich *et al.*, 1994; Gereffi 1996; Morales 1994; Mittelman 1996). Insofar as global processes materialize in concrete places, they continue to operate under sovereign regulatory umbrellas, but they do so under new emergent transnational regimes and, often, under conditions of a de-nationalizing of national territory.

It is through the formation of such transnational regimes and the de-nationalizing of national territory that the state guarantees a far broader range of rights of national and foreign capital. These rights are often in addition to those guaranteed through strictly national regimes. In this regard, deregulation and other policies furthering economic globalization cannot simply be considered as an instance of a declining significance of the state. Deregulation is a vehicle through which a growing number of states are furthering economic globalization and guaranteeing the rights of global capital, an essential ingredient of the former. Deregulation and kindred policies constitute the elements of a new legal regime dependent on consensus among states to further globalization.

3. Elements for New Policy Frameworks

A focus on the space economy of information industries elaborates and specifies the meaning of deregulation insofar as important components of these industries are embedded in particular sites within national territories and others are located in electronic spaces that escape all conventional jurisdictions or borders.

To help situate my particular question here in the broader governance debate let me refer to one of the working argumentations that organize the larger project on which this brief essay is based: A focus on leading information industries in a strategic subnational unit such as the global city illuminates two conditions that are at opposite ends of the governance challenge posed by globalization and are not captured in the more conventional duality of national-global. These two contrasting conditions are place-boundedness and the virtualization of economic space.

Regarding the first, a focus on leading information industries in global cities introduces into the discussion of governance the possibility of capacities for regulation derived from the concentration of significant resources, including fixed capital, in strategic places, resources that are essential for participation in the global economy. The considerable place-boundedness of many of these resources contrasts with the hypermobility of information outputs. The regulatory capacity of the state stands in a different relation to hypermobile outputs than to the infrastructure of facilities, from fiber optic cable served office buildings to specialized workforces, present in global cities.

At the other extreme, the fact that many of these industries operate partly in electronic spaces raises questions of control that derive from key properties of the new information technologies, notably the orders of magnitude in trading volumes made possible by speed and the fact that electronic space is not bound by conventional jurisdictions. Here it is no longer just a question of the capacity of the state to govern these processes, but also of the capacity to do so on the part of the private sector, that is, of the major actors involved in setting up and operating in these electronic markets. Elementary and well known illustrations of this issue of control are stock market crashes attributed to electronic program trading, and globally implemented decisions to invest or disinvest in a currency, or an emerging market which resemble a sort of worldwide stampede, all facilitated by the fact of global integration and instantaneous execution worldwide. Mexico's recent crisis and its aftermath are an illustration of this; so is the fall of the U.K. bank Barings.

The specific issues raised by these two variables, i.e. place-boundedness and speed/virtualization, are quite distinct from those typically raised in the context of the national-global duality. A focus on this duality leads to rather straightforward propositions about the declining significance of the state *vis à vis* global economic actors. This is partly a result of the overarching tendency in economic analyses of globalization and information industries to emphasize certain aspects: industry outputs rather than the production process involved, the capacity for instantaneous transmission around the world rather than the infrastructure necessary for this capacity, the inability of the state to regulate those outputs and that capacity insofar as they extend beyond the nation-state. And all of this is by itself quite correct; but it is a partial account of the implications of globalization for governance.

A focus on key properties of the new information technologies, such as speed, and their implications for questions of governance illuminates the extent to which we may be confronting a whole new configuration, one that cannot be addressed along the lines dominating much of the thinking about governance in a global economy. It is not just a question of coordination and order in a space economy that transcends a single state, but a qualitatively new variable: technologies that produce outcomes which the existing institutional apparatus both private and governmental cannot handle because they are processes embedded in a speed that has made current mechanisms for management and control obsolete. It is impossible to address this subject here in depth (see Sassen, forthcoming for a more detailed analysis).

A focus on place, and particularly the type of place I call global cities, on the other hand, brings to the fore the fact that many of the resources necessary for global economic activities are not hypermobile and could, in principle be brought under effective regulation. But this would be a type of regulation focused not on the outputs of information industries – which are indeed hypermobile and circulate in electronic spaces – but on the infrastructure. Essential to this proposition is an understanding of the extent to which key components of the leading information industries are place-bound and conversely, the extent to which key components of what we call the global economy actually materialize in places.

A refocusing of regulation onto infrastructures and production complexes in the context of globalization contributes to an analysis of the regulatory capacities of states that diverges in significant ways from understandings centered on hypermobile outputs and global telecommunications. One crucial piece of such an analysis is a detailed examination of the importance of place and place-boundedness in global economic processes. This is the subject in the remainder of this paper.

Place and Production Complex in the Global Economy

The analysis of the space economy developed here is centered in the notion that we cannot take the existence of a global economic system as given, but rather need to examine the particular ways in which the conditions for economic globalization are produced. This entails examining not only communication capacities and the power of multinationals, but also the underside of the global economy.

The capabilities for global operation, coordination and control contained in the new information technologies and in the power of the multinationals need to be produced. By focusing on the production of these capabilities we add a neglected dimension to the familiar issue of the power of large corporations and the new technologies. The emphasis shifts to the *practice* of global control: the work of producing and reproducing the organization and management of a global production system and a global marketplace for finance, both under conditions of economic concentration.

I see the producer services, and most especially finance and advanced corporate services, as industries producing the organizational commodities necessary for the implementation and management of global economic systems (Sassen 1991: chapters 2–5).[4] Over the last few years we have seen the growth of a rich literature on the producer services, including major information industries such as international finance and advanced corporate services (e.g., Daniels 1985; Delaunay and Gadrey 1987; Noyelle and Dutka 1988; Daniels and Moulaert 1991). With a few exceptions (e.g., Castells 1989; Sassen 1991; Knox and Taylor 1995; Drennan 1992; Mitchelson and Wheeler 1994; Corbridge *et al.* forthcoming) the literature on producer services has not necessarily been concerned with the operation of the global economy as such, nor has it been seen as part of the literature on globalization.[5]

Introducing the research on producer services into our analysis of the global economy helps us explore how the categories of place and production process are involved in economic globalization. These are two categories that are easily overlooked in analyses of the hypermobility of capital and the power of multinationals. Developing categories such as place and production process does not negate the centrality of hypermobility and power. It adds other dimensions and in so doing intersects with the regulatory role of the state in a distinct way and one that diverges from much international political economy.

---

[4] Producer services are intermediate outputs, that is, services bought by firms. They cover financial, legal, and general management matters, innovation, development, design, administration, personnel, production technology, maintenance, transport, communications, wholesale distribution, advertising, cleaning services for firms, security, and storage. Central components of the producer services category are a range of industries with mixed business and consumer markets. They are insurance, banking, financial services, real estate, legal services, accounting, and professional associations.

[5] There is, however, a rapidly growing literature on the impact of globalization on cities which in various ways incorporates examinations of producer services, including, besides the ones already listed above, Friedmann 1986; Fainstein *et al.* 1993, Hitz *et al.* 1995, von Petz *et al.* 1992, Machimura 1992, Frost and Spence 1992, Rodriguez and Feagin 1991, Knox and Taylor 1995, Levine 1993, *Le Debat*, 1994.

One of the central concerns in my work has been to look at cities as production sites for the leading service industries of our time, and hence to recover the infrastructure of activities, firms and jobs, that is necessary to run the advanced corporate economy, including its global components. Specialized services are usually understood in terms of specialized outputs rather than the production process involved. A focus on the production process in these service industries allows us a) to capture some of their locational characteristics and b) to examine the proposition that there is a new dynamic for agglomeration in the advanced corporate services because they function as a production complex, a complex which serves corporate headquarters yet has distinct locational and production characteristics. It is this producer services complex, more so than headquarters of firms generally, that benefits and often needs a city location. We see this dynamic for agglomeration operating at different levels of the urban hierarchy, from the global to the regional. Some cities concentrate the infrastructure and the servicing that produce a capability for global control and servicing.

In brief, with the potential for global control capability, certain cities are becoming nodal points in a vast communications and market system. Advances in electronics and telecommunication have transformed geographically distant cities into centers for global communication and long-distance management. But centralized control and management over a geographically dispersed array of plants, offices, and service outlets does not come about inevitably as part of a "world system." It requires the development of a vast range of highly specialized services and of top level management and control functions.

The next three sections develop these subjects in greater detail.

1. Globalization and Service Intensity

The globalization of economic activity has raised the scale and the complexity of transactions, thereby feeding the demand for top-level multinational headquarter functions and for advanced corporate services. This demand for specialized services is further fed by a second major process, the growing service intensity in the organization of all industries (Sassen 1991: chapter 5; 1994: chapter 4). This has contributed to a massive growth in the demand for services by firms in all industries, from mining and manufacturing to finance and consumer services. To this we should add the growing demand by firms for non-specialized services, notably industrial services.

Two of the key variables that make these processes relevant to cities and to the argument in this paper are: a) the rapid growth in the last fifteen years in the share of services bought by firms rather than produced in-house; and b) the existence of agglomeration economies in the production of specialized services. If firms continued to produce most of their services in-house as used to be the case, particularly with the large vertically integrated firms, cities might have been less significant production sites for services. Service activities would have moved out of cities as part of the moves by the larger firms of which they were but one component; there could conceivably have been far more geographic dispersal of specialized service jobs than there is now, though these jobs would of course have been included in the industrial classification of the larger firms, which were not necessarily service firms.

I discuss these two variables next.

a) The growing demand for corporate services

The increase in the share of bought services can be seen in the figures on growth in producer services jobs, in the numbers of producer services firms, and, perhaps most sharply, in the figures from the national input-output tables for the U.S. Figures on employment and numbers of firms in producer services have by now become familiar and have been published widely. That cannot be said for the figures from the national input-output tables; I analysed these figures for several years and several industries within major sectors and found a clear trend of growth in the value of bought service inputs for the industries examined (Sassen, forthcoming).[6]

The sharp rise in the use of producer services has been fed by a variety of processes.[7] Among these are the territorial dispersal, whether at the regional, national or global level, of multi-establishment firms. Firms operating many plants, offices and service outlets must coordinate planning, internal administration and distribution, marketing and other central headquarters activities. Formally, the development of the modern corporation and its massive participation in world markets and foreign countries has made planning, internal administration, product development and research increasingly important and complex. Diversification of product lines, mergers, and transnationalization of economic activities all require highly specialized services.

For all firms, whether they operate globally or regionally, the rise of litigation, the growing importance of insurance, advertising, and outside financing have all contributed to a growing need for specialized services. Further, as large corporations move into the production and sale of final consumer services, a wide range of activities, previously performed by free-standing, independent consumer service firms, are shifted to the central headquarters of the new corporate owners. Regional, national or global chains of motels, food outlets, flower shops, require vast centralized administrative and servicing structures. The complexity of these will in turn generate a demand for specialized corporate services bought from specialized firms, something far less likely in the small independently owned consumer service firm. A parallel pattern of expansion of central high-level planning and control operations takes place in governments, brought about partly by the technical developments that make this possible and partly by the growing complexity of regulatory and administrative tasks.

A brief examination of the territorial dispersal entailed by transnational operations of large enterprises can serve to illustrate some of the points raised here. For instance the numbers of workers employed abroad by the largest one hundred non-financial

---

[6] Using input-output tables from 1972 to 1987 we examined the use of service-based commodities in 11 four digit SIC industries (ranging from wholesale trade to mining). The service-based industries examined as the intermediate commodity input, down to the four digit SIC code, included among others, Finance and Insurance, and Business Services. For the sake of simplicity, the following figures cover the 1972 to 1982 period only because after this date the comparison becomes too complicated to describe in a footnote. Of all the industry combinations studied, the level of service inputs from the Finance industry was most prominent, tripling from 1972 to 1982, in Banking, Wholesale Trade, and Insurance. The use of Business Services increased sharpest in the following industry groups: Motor Vehicles and Equipment, Insurance Carriers, Wholesale Trade, and Banking. The use of business services in Banking more than tripled from 1972 to 1982. (See Sassen and Orlow for a full description; also in Sassen forthcoming).

[7] For a discussion of the literature and the broader trends lying behind the possibility of the formation of a free-standing producer services sector, (Sassen 1991: Chapter 5).

transnational corporations worldwide are rather large. (For detailed figures on this and the following items, see UNCTC, 1992, 1993; Sassen 1994: chapter 4). Thus about half of Exxon's and IBM's and about a third of Ford Motors' and GM's total workforce is employed outside the US. We know furthermore that large transnationals have very high numbers of affiliates. Thus in 1990 German firms had over 19,000 affiliates in foreign countries, up from 14,000 in 1984; and the U.S. had almost 19,000. Finally, we know that the top transnationals have very high shares of foreign operations: the top ten largest transnational corporations in the world had 61% of their sales abroad. The average for the 100 largest corporations was almost 50%.

What these figures show is a vast operation dispersed over a multiplicity of locations. This generates a large demand for producer services, from international accounting to advertising. Operations as vast as these feed the expansion of central management, coordination, control and servicing functions. Some of these functions are performed in headquarters, some are bought or contracted for therewith feeding the growth of the producer services complex.

b) The formation of a new production complex
As for the second variable, agglomeration economies, the issue here is why has there not been more dispersal of specialized service firms, particularly since these are among the most advanced and intensive users of telematics and hence could, supposedly locate anywhere. In order to understand why such a large share of these firms is concentrated in cities, and often in dense spatial concentrations reminiscent of industrial districts, we need to focus on the actual production process in these services.

The evidence on the locational patterns of the leading information industries shows sharp economic concentration in major cities. For instance, New York City accounts for 35% of earnings in producer services, compared to little over 3% of the national population, and between a fourth and a fifth of all producer services exports in the U.S., which total about US$ 40 billion annually (Drennan 1991). London accounts for about 40% of producer services exports in the U.K., and Paris accounts for 40% of all producer services employment in France and over 80% of the advanced corporate services (Cordier 1992; Le Debat 1994). There are many other such examples.

According to standard conceptions about information industries, the rapid growth and disproportionate concentration of producer services in major cities should not have happened. Because many of these services are thoroughly embedded in the most advanced information technologies, producer services could be expected to have locational options that bypass the high costs and congestion typical of major cities. It is my argument that in order to understand their sharp concentration in large cities we need to focus on the actual production process in these industries.

The production process in these services benefits from proximity to other specialized services. This is especially the case in the leading and most innovative sectors of these industries. Complexity and innovation often require multiple highly specialized inputs from several industries. The production of a financial instrument, for example, requires inputs from accounting, advertising, legal expertise, economic consulting, public relations, designers, and printers. The particular characteristics of production of these services, especially those involved in complex and innovative operations, explain their pronounced concentration in major cities. The commonly heard explanation that high level professionals require face-to-face interactions, needs to be refined in several ways. Producer services, unlike other types of services, are not necessarily dependent on spatial proximity to the consumers, i.e. firms, served. Rather, economies occur in such specialized firms when they locate close to others that produce key inputs or whose proximity makes possible joint production of certain service offerings. The top-of-the-line accounting firm can service its clients at a distance, but the nature of its service depends on proximity to other specialists, from lawyers to programmers. Moreover, it is well known that many of the new high-income professionals tend to be attracted to the amenities and lifestyles that large urban centers can offer. Frequently, what is thought of as face-to-face communication is actually a production process that requires multiple simultaneous inputs and feedbacks. At the current stage of technical development, immediate and simultaneous access to the pertinent experts is still the most effective way, especially when dealing with a highly complex product. The concentration of the most advanced telecommunications and computer network facilities in major cities is a key factor in what I refer to as the production process of these industries.[8]

Further, time replaces weight in these sectors as a force for agglomeration. In the past, the pressure of the weight of inputs from iron ore to unprocessed agricultural products, was a major constraint pushing toward agglomeration in sites where the heaviest inputs were located. Today, the acceleration of economic transactions and the premium put on time, have created new forces for agglomeration. This is increasingly not the case in routine operations. But where time is of the essence, as it is today in many of the leading sectors of these industries, the benefits of agglomeration are still extremely high – to the point where it is not simply a cost advantage, but an indispensable arrangement. This is further underlined by the centrality of the market in many of the most speculative and innovative branches of finance. Speculation and innovation in the context of deregulation and globalization have profoundly altered market operation in the industry, promoting far greater instability. Under these conditions, agglomeration carries additional advantages insofar as the market becomes a key site for new opportunities for profit and speed is of the essence. (Sassen 1991: chapters 2–4; Mitchelson and Wheeler 1994; but see also Lyons and Salmon 1995).

---

[8] The telecommunications infrastructure also contributes to concentration of leading sectors in major cities. Long-distance communications systems increasingly use fiber optic wires. These have several advantages over traditional copper wire: large carrying capacity, high speed, more security, and higher signal strength. Fiber systems tend to connect major communications hubs because they are not easily spliced and hence not desirable for connecting multiple lateral sites. Fiber systems tend to be installed along existing rights of way, whether rail, water or highways (Moss 1991). The growing use of fiber optic systems thus tends to strengthen the major existing telecommunication concentrations and therefore the existing hierarchies.

This combination of constraints suggests that the agglomeration of producer services in major cities actually constitutes a production complex. This producer services complex is intimately connected to the world of corporate headquarters; they are often thought of as forming a joint headquarters-corporate services complex. But in my reading, we need to distinguish the two.[9] Although it is true that headquarters still tend to be disproportionately concentrated in cities, over the last two decades many have moved out. Headquarters can indeed locate outside cities, but they need a producer services complex somewhere in order to buy or contract for the needed specialized services and financing. Further, headquarters of firms with very high overseas activity or in highly innovative and complex lines of business tend to locate in major cities. In brief, firms in more routinized lines of activity, with predominantly regional or national markets, appear to be increasingly free to move or install their headquarters outside cities. Firms in highly competitive and innovative lines of activity and/or with a strong world market orientation appear to benefit from being located at the center of major international business centers, no matter how high the costs.

Both types of firms, however, need a corporate services complex to be located somewhere.[10] Where this complex is located is probably increasingly unimportant from the perspective of many, though not all, headquarters. From the perspective of producer services firms, such a specialized complex is most likely to be in a city rather than, for example, a suburban office park. The latter will be the site for producer services firms

---

[9] It is common in the general literature and in some more scholarly accounts to use headquarters concentration as an indication of whether a city is an international business center. The loss of headquarters is then interpreted as a decline in a city's status. The use of headquarters concentration as an index is actually a problematic measure given the way in which corporations are classified.

Which headquarters concentrate in major international financial and business centers depends on a number of variables. First, how we measure or simply count headquarters makes a difference. Frequently, the key measure is size of firm in terms of employment and overall revenue. In this case, some of the largest firms in the world are still manufacturing firms and many of these have their main headquarters in proximity to their major factory complex, which is unlikely to be in a large city due to space constraints. Such firms are likely, however to have secondary headquarters for highly specialized functions in major cities. Further, many manufacturing firms are oriented to the national market and do not need to be located in an international business center. Thus, the much publicized departure of major headquarters from New York City in the 1960s and 1970s involved these types of firms. If we look at the Fortune 500 largest firms in the U.S. (cf. "*Fortune Magazine 500 list*") many have left New York City and other large cities. If instead of size we use share of total firm revenue coming from international sales, a large number of firms that are not part of Fortune 500 list come into play. For instance, in the case of NYC the results change dramatically: 40% of U.S. firms with half their revenue from international sales have their headquarters in New York City.

Secondly, the nature of the urban system in a country is a factor. Sharp urban primacy will tend to entail a disproportionate concentration of headquarters no matter what measure one uses. Thirdly, different economic histories and business traditions may combine to produce different results. Further, headquarters concentration may be linked with a specific economic phase. For instance, unlike New York's loss of top Fortune 500 headquarters, Tokyo has been gaining headquarters. Osaka and Nagoya, the two other major economic centers in Japan are losing headquarters to Tokyo. This is in good part linked to the increasing internationalization of the Japanese economy and the corresponding increase in central command and servicing functions in major international business centers. In the case of Japan, extensive government regulation over the economy is an added factor contributing to headquarter location in Tokyo insofar as all international activities have to go through various government approvals.

[10] For example, Wheeler (1986) examined the spatial linkages between major U.S. corporations and financial institutions and found that corporations do not necessarily use the firms available in their location but rather tend to work with firms located higher up in the metropolitan hierarchy, a trend that is particularly strong for large corporations. Schwartz (1992) found that large firms located in the New York metropolitan area continued to use Manhattan firms for most of their service needs.

but not for a services complex. And only such a complex is capable of handling the most advanced and complicated corporate demands.

Elsewhere (Sassen 1994: chapter 5), a somewhat detailed empirical examination of several cities served to explore different aspects of this trend towards spatial concentration.[11] Here there is space only for a few observations. The case of Miami, for instance, allows us to see, almost in laboratory-like fashion, how a new international corporate sector can become implanted in a site. It allows us to understand something about the dynamic of globalization in the current period and how it is embedded in place. Miami has emerged as a significant regional site for global city functions though it lacks a long history as an international banking and business center as is the case for such global cities as New York or London.

The case of Toronto, a city whose financial district was built up only in recent years, allows us to see to what extent the pressure towards spatial concentration of financial firms is embedded in an economic dynamic rather than simply being the consequence of having inherited a built infrastructure from the past, as one could think was the case in older centers such as London or New York.[12] But the case also shows that it is

---

[11] A very different category through which some of these issues can be examined is that of "centrality." The spatial correlates of centrality today can assume a multiplicity of forms, ranging from the traditional central business district as well as a metropolitan grid of economic nodes intensely connected via telematics. Examing the evidence for a number of major cities I found a clear trend towards centrality, but with a far broader range of spatial correlates than the traditional CBD. Telematics and the growth of a global economy, both inextricably linked, have contributed to a new geography of centrality (and marginality). Simplifying an analysis made elsewhere (Sassen 1994), I identify four forms assumed by centrality today. First, while there is no longer a simple straightforward relation between centrality and such geographic entites as the downtown, or the central business district as was the case in the past, the CBD remains a key form of centrality. But the CBD in major international business centers is one profoundly reconfigured by technological and economic change. Second, the center can extend into a metropolitan area in the form of a grid of nodes of intense business activity. This regional grid of nodes represents, in my analysis, a reconstitution of the concept of region. Far from neutralizing geography the regional grid is likely to be embedded in conventional forms of communications infrastructure, notably rapid rail and highways connecting to airports. Ironically perhaps, conventional infrastructure is likely to maximize the economic benefits derived from telematics. I think this is an important issue that has been lost somewhat in discussions about the neutralization of geography through telematics. Third, we are seeing the formation of a transterritorial "center" constituted via telematics and intense economic transactions. The most powerful of these new geographies of centrality at the inter-urban level binds the major international financial and business centers: New York, London, Tokyo, Paris, Frankfurt, Zurich, Amsterdam, Los Angeles, Sydney, Hong Kong, among others. But this geography now also includes cities such as Sao Paulo and Bombay. The intensity of transactions among these cities, particularly through the financial markets, trade in services, and investment has increased sharply, and so have the orders of magnitude involved. Fourth, new forms of centrality are being constituted in electronically generated spaces (Sassen, forthcoming). The city is a strategic site in the first three of these forms of centrality.

[12] In his study of the financial district in Manhattan, Longcore found that the use of advanced information and telecommunication technologies has a strong impact on the spatial organization of the district because of the added spatial requirements of "intelligent" buildings. (See also Moss 1991). A ring of new office buildings meeting these requirements was built over the last decade immediately around the old Wall street core, where the narrow streets and lots made this difficult; furthermore, renovating old buildings in the Wall Street core is extremely expensive and often not possible. The occupants of the new buildings in the district were mostly corporate headquarters and the financial services industry. These firms tend to be extremely intensive users of telematics and availability of the most advanced forms typically is a major factor in their real estate and locational decisions. They need complete redundancy of telecommunications systems, high carrying capacity, often their own private branch exchange, etc. With this often goes a need for large spaces. For instance, the technical installation backing a firm's trading floor is likely to require additional space the size of the trading floor itself.

particularly certain industries which are subject to the pressure towards spatial concentration, notably finance and its sister industries (Gad 1991; Todd 1995).

The case of Sydney illuminates the interaction of a vast, continental economic scale and pressures towards spatial concentration. Rather than strengthening the multipolarity of the Australian urban system, the developments of the 1980s – increased internationalization of the Australian economy, sharp increases in foreign investment, a strong shift towards finance, real estate and producer services – contributed to a greater concentration of major economic activities and actors in Sydney. This included a loss of share of such activities and actors by Melbourne, long the center of commercial activity and wealth in Australia (Daly and Stimson 1992).

Finally, the case of the leading financial centers in the world today is of continued interest since one might have expected that the growing number of financial centers now integrated into the global markets would have reduced the extent of concentration of financial activity in the top centers.[13] One would further expect this given the immense increases in the global volume of transactions. Yet the levels of concentration remain unchanged in the face of massive transformations in the financial industry and in the technological infrastructure this industry depends on.[14]

For example, international bank lending grew from US$1.89 trillion in 1980 to US$6.24 trillion in 1991 – a fivefold increase in a mere ten years. New York, London and Tokyo accounted for 42% of all such international lending in 1980 and for 41% in 1991 according to data from the Bank of International Settlements, the leading institution worldwide in charge of overseeing banking activity. There were compositional changes: Japan's share rose from 6.2% to 15.1% and the UK's fell from 26.2% to 16.3%; the U.S. share remained constant. All increased in absolute terms. Beyond these three, Switzerland, France, Germany, and Luxembourg bring the total share of the top centers to 64% in 1991, which is just about the same share these countries had in 1980. One city, Chicago dominates the world's trading in futures, accounting for 60% of worldwide contracts in options and futures in 1991.

This concentration in the top centers is partly a function of the concentration of the most advanced technical financial capabilities in these centers. And it is partly a function of various macro-economic conjunctures, notably the perceived high risk of new markets in combination with the ease with which money can be shifted back and forth, as is illustrated by the current flight from the so-called emergent markets after the December 1994 Mexican devaluation of the peso and the ensuing financial crisis for foreign investors.

---

[13] Furthermore, this unchanged level of concentration has happened at a time when financial services are more mobile than ever before: globalization, deregulation (an essential ingredient for globalization), and *securitization* have been the key to this mobility – in the context of massive advances in telecommunications and electronic networks. One result is growing competition among centers for hypermobile financial activity. In my view there has been an overemphasis on competition in general and in specialized accounts on this subject. As I have argued elsewhere (Sassen 1991: chapter 7), there is also a functional division of labor among various major financial centers. In that sense we can think of a transnational system with multiple locations. (See also Abu-Lughod 1995).

[14] Much of the discussion around the formation of a single European market and financial system has raised the possibility, and even the need if it is to be competitive, of centralizing financial functions and capital in a limited number of cities rather than maintaining the current structure in which each country has a financial center.

2. The Global Grid of Strategic Sites

The global integration of financial markets depends on and contributes to the implementation of a variety of linkages among the financial centers involved.[15] Prime examples of such linkages are the multinational networks of affiliates and subsidiaries typical of major firms in manufacturing and specialized services. Corporate service firms have developed vast multinational networks containing special geographic and institutional linkages that make it possible for client firms – transnational firms and banks – to use a growing array of service offerings from the same supplier (Marshall *et al.* 1986; Noyelle and Dutka 1988; Daniels and Moulaert 1991; Fainstein 1994: chapter 2; Leyshon *et al.* 1987).[16] There is also a growing number of less directly economic linkages, notable among which are a variety of initiatives launched by urban governments which amount to a type of foreign policy by and for cities. For example, New York State has opened business offices in several major cities overseas.

Whether these linkages have engendered transnational urban systems is less clear. It is partly a question of theory and conceptualization. So much of social science is profoundly rooted in the nation-state as the ultimate unit for analysis, that conceptualizing processes and systems as transnational is bound to engender much controversy. Even much of the literature on world or global cities does not necessarily posit the existence of a transnational urban system: in its narrowest form it posits that global cities perform central place functions at a transnational level. But that leaves open the question as to the nature of the articulation among global cities. If one posits that they merely compete with each other for global business, then they do not constitute a transnational system; in this case, studying several global cities becomes an instance of traditional comparative analyses.

If one posits that besides competing they are also the sites for transnational processes with multiple locations, then one can begin to posit the possbility of a systemic dynamic binding these cities. Elsewhere (1991: chapters 1 and 7) I have argued that in addition to the central place functions performed by these cities at the global level, as posited by Hall (1966), Friedmann and Wolff (1982) and Sassen (1982), these cities relate to one another in distinct systemic ways. For instance, the interaction among New York, London and Tokyo, particularly in terms of finance and investment, consists partly of

---

[15] There is a rapidly growing and highly specialized research literature focused on different types of economic linkages that bind cities across national borders (Castells 1989; Noyelle and Dutka 1988; Daniels and Moulaert 1991; Leyshon, Daniels and Thrift 1987; Sassen 1991).

[16] There is good evidence that the development of multinational corporate service firms was associated with the needs of transnational firms. The multinational advertising firm can offer global advertising to a specific segment of potential customers worldwide. Further, global integration of affiliates and markets requires making use of advanced information and telecommunications technology which can come to account for a significant share of costs – not just operational costs but also, and perhaps most important, research and development costs for new products or advances on existing products. The need for scale economies on all these fronts contributes to explain the recent increase in mergers and acquisitions, which has consolidated the position of a few very large firms in many of these industries, and further strengthned crossborder linkages among the key locations which concentrate the needed telecommunications facilities. They have emerged as firms that can control a significant share of national and international markets. The rapid increase in direct foreign investment in services is strongly linked with the growing tendency among leading service firms to operate transnationally. Subcontracting by larger firms and the multiplicity of specialized markets has meant that small independent firms can also thrive in major business centers. (Sassen 1991; Noyelle and Dutka 1988; Leyshon, Daniels and Thrift 1987).

a series of processes that can be thought of as the chain of production in finance. Thus in the mid 1980s Tokyo was the main exporter of the raw material we call money while New York was the leading processing center in the world. It was in New York that many of the new financial instruments were invented, and where money either in its raw form or in the form of debt was transformed into instruments that aimed at maximizing the returns on that money. London, on the other hand, was a major entrepot which had the network to centralize and concentrate small amounts of capital available in a large number of smaller financial markets around the world, partly a function of its older network for the administration of the British empire. This is just one example suggesting that these cities do not simply compete with each other for the same business. There is, it seems to me, an economic system that rests on the three distinct types of locations these cities represent.[17] In my view, there is no such thing as a single global city, unlike what was the case with earlier imperial capitals – a single world city at the top of a system. The global city is a function of the global grid of transactions, one site for processes which are global because they have multiple locations in multiple countries. (See also Abu-Lughod 1995; Smith and Timberlake 1995).

If finance and the advanced corporate services are in fact embedded in such trasnational systems then this might be a rather significant factor in examinations of the possibilities for regulation. The pursuit of profits in these industries is not only dependent on deregulation and globalization but also on a complex and dense grid of linkages and sites. The hypermobility of these industries and the associated difficulties for regulation are only part of the picture, albeit the most intensely studied and debated one; the global grid of linkages and sites within which this hypermobility is embedded and through which it flows is potentially another part of the picture, and one that will require more research to elucidate.

Conclusion: Regulating the Global Grid of Places

Including cities in the analysis of economic globalization and the ascendance of information industries adds three important dimensions to the study of economic globalization. First, it decomposes the nation state into a variety of components that may be significant in understanding international economic activity and regulatory capacities. Second, it displaces the focus from the power of large corporations over governments and economies to the range of activities and organizational arrangements

---

[17] The possibility of such a transnational urban system raises a question as to the articulation of such cities in their national urban systems. It is quite possible that the strengthening of cross-national ties among the leading financial and business centers is likely to be accompanied by a weakening of the linkages between each of these cities and their hinterlands and national urban systems (Sassen 1991). Cities such as Detroit, Liverpool, Manchester, Marseille, the cities of the Ruhr, and now increasingly Nagoya and Osaka, have been affected by the territorial decentralization of many of their key manufacturing industries at the domestic and international level. This process of decentralization has contributed to the growth of service industries that produce the specialized inputs to run spatially dispersed production processes and global markets for inputs and outputs. These specialized inputs – international legal and accounting services, management consulting, financial services – are heavily concentrated in business and financial centers rather than in manufacturing cities.

necessary for the implementation and maintenance of a global network of factories, service operations and markets; these are all processes only partly encompassed by the activities of transnational corporations and banks. Third, it contributes to a focus on place and on the strategic concentrations of infrastructure and production complexes necessary for global economic activity. Processes of economic globalization are thereby reconstituted as concrete production complexes situated in specific places containing a multiplicity of activities. Focusing on cities allows us to specify a global geography of strategic places as well as the microgeographies and politics unfolding within these places.

The transformation in the composition of the world economy, especially the rise of finance and advanced services as leading industries, is contributing to a new international economic order, one dominated by financial centers, global markets, and transnational firms.[17] Correspondingly we may see a growing significance of other political categories both sub- and supra-national. Cities that function as international business and financial centers are sites for direct transactions with world markets.

These cities and the globally oriented markets and firms they contain mediate in the relation of the world economy to nation-states and in the relations among nation-states. Transnational economic processes inevitably interact with systems for the governance of national economies. Further, the material conditions necessary for many global economic processes – from telematics infrastructure to the producer services production complex – need to be incorporated in examinations of questions of governance and accountability in the global economy. They signal the possibility of novel forms of regulation and conditions for accountability.

In sum, an analysis focused on place and production has the effect of decoding globalization; the latter is conceptually reconstituted in terms of a transnational geography of centrality consisting of multiple linkages and strategic concentrations of material infrastructure. Globalization can then be seen as embedded and dependent on these linkages and material infrastructure. To a considerable extent, global processes are this grid of sites and linkages.

The existence of such a transnational grid of places and linkages that constitute the infrastructure for the globalization of finance and other specialized services points to regulatory possibilities. Precisely because of its strategic character and because of the density of resources and linkages it concentrates, this new geography of centrality could in turn be a space for concentrated regulatory activity. But the type of regulatory frameworks and operations it would entail need to be discovered and invented, as does the meaning of accountability and democratization of the new global information economy.

References

Abu-Lughod, Janet Lippman (1995) "Comparing Chicago, New York and Los Angeles: testing some world cities hypotheses" In Paul L. Knox and Peter J. Taylor (eds) World Cities in a World-System. Cambridge, UK: Cambridge University Press. pp. 171–191.

Aman, Jr. Alfred C. (1995) "A Global Perspective on Current Regulatory Reform: Rejection, Relocation, or Reinvention?" *Indiana Journal of Global Legal Studies.* Vol 2, pp. 429–464

Bonacich, Edna, Lucie Cheng, Norma Chinchilla, Nora Hamilton and Paul Ong (eds) (1994) *Global Production: The Apparel Industry in the Pacific Rim.* Philadelphia: Temple University Press.

Coombe, Rosemary J. "The Properties of Culture and the Politics of Possessing Identity: Native Claims in the Cultural Appropriation Controversy." *The Canadian Journal of Law and Jurisprudence,* Vol. VI, No. 2, July 1993, pp. 249–85.

Corbridge, S., Martin, R. and Thrift, N. (eds) *Money, Power and Space.* (Forthcoming).

Cordier, Jean (1992) "Paris, place financiere et bancaire." In M. Berger and C. Rhein (eds), *L'Ile de France et la recherche urbaine.* STRATES-CNRS Univ. Paris 1, et Plan Urbain-DATAR.

Daly, M.T. and Stimson, R. (1992) "Sydney: Australia's Gateway and Financial Capital" Chap. 18. In E. Blakely and T.J. Stimpson (eds) *New Cities of the Pacific Rim* Institute for Urban & Regional Development, University of California, Berkeley.

Daniels, Peter W. (1985) *Service Industries: A Geographical Appraisal.* London and New York: Methuen.

Daniels, Peter W. and Moulaert, Frank (eds) (1991) *The Changing Geography of Advanced Producer Services.* London and New York: Belhaven Press.

Delauney, Jean Claude and Jean Gadrey (1987) *Les Enjeux de la Societe de Service.* Paris: Presses de la Fondation des Sciences Politiques.

Drache, D. and Gertler, M. (eds) (1991) *The New Era of Global Competition: State Policy and Market Power.* Montreal: McGill-Queen's University Press.

Drennan, Mathew P. (1992) "Gateway Cities: The Metropolitan Sources of US Producer Service Exports." *Urban Studies,* 29(2), 217–235.

Fainstein, Susan (1994) *The City Builders: Property, Politics, and Planning in London and New York.* Cambridge, Mass.: Blackwell.

Fainstein, S., Gordon, I. and Harloe, M. (1993) *Divided Cities: Economic Restructuring and Social Change in London and New York.* New York: Blackwell.

Friedmann, John (1986) "The World City Hypothesis." *Development and Change,* 17, 69–84.

Frost, Martin and Nigel Spence (1992) "Global City Characteristics and Central London's Employment." *Urban Studies,* 30(3), 547–558.

Gad, Gunter (1991) "Toronto's Financial District." *Canadian Urban Landscapes-1,* 203–207.

Gereffi, Gary (1996) "The Elusive Last Lap in the Quest for Developed Country Status." In Mittelman, James H. (ed) *International Political Economy Yearbook, Vol 9,* Lynne Rienner Publishers.

Hitz, Hansruedi, *et. al.* (eds) (1995) *Financial Metropoles in Restructuring: Zurich and Frankfurt En Route to Postfordism.* Zurich: Rootpunkt.

Jessop, Robert (1990) *State Theory: Putting Capitalist States in Their Place.* University Park: Pennsylvania State University Press.

Knox, Paul and Peter J. Taylor (eds) (1995) *World Cities in a World-System.* Cambridge: Cambridge University Press.

Kooiman, Jan and Martin van Vliet (1993) "Governance and Public Management." In K.A. Eliassen and J. Kooiman (eds) Managing Public Organizations: Lessons from Contemporary European Experience. London: Sage, pp. 58–72.

Leftwich, A. (1994) "Governance, the State, and the Politics of Development" *Development and Change*, 24(4), 363–386.

Levine, Marc. (1993) *Montreal*. Philadelphia: Temple University Press.

Longcore, T.R. "Information Technology and World City Restructuring: The Case of New York City's Financial District." (Unpublished thesis, Department of Geography, University of Delaware). 1993.

Lyons, Donald and Scott Salmon (1995) "World cities, multinational corporations and urban hierarchy: the case of the United States." In Knox and Taylor (eds) op.cit. pp. 98–114.

Machimura, Takashi (1992) "The Urban Restructuring Process in the 1980s: Transforming Tokyo into a World City," *International Journal of Urban and Regional Research*, 16–1, 114–128.

Markusen, A. and Gwiasda, V. "Multipolarity and the Layering of Functions in the World Cities: New York City's Struggle to Stay on Top." *International Journal of Urban and Regional Research*.

Marshall, J.N. *et al. Uneven Development in the Service Economy: Understanding the Location and Role of Producer Services*. Report of the Producer Services Working Party, Institute of British Geographers and the ESRC, August 1986.

Mitchelson, Ronald L. and James O. Wheeler (1994) "The Flow of Information in a Global Economy: The Role of the American Urban System in 1990." *Annals of the Association of American Geographers*, 84(1), 87–107.

Mittelman, James (ed) *International Political Economy Yearbook* , Vol. 9, 1996.

Morales, Rebecca (1994) *Flexible Production: Restructuring of the International Automobile Industry*. Cambridge, UK: Polity press.

Moss, Mitchell (1991) "New Fibers of Urban Economic Development. *Portfolio: A Quarterly Review of Trade and Transportation*, 4(1), 11–18.

Negri, Toni (1995) "A quoi sert encore l'Etat." *Pouvoirs Pouvoir*, Vol. 25–26 of *Futur Anterieur*, pp. 135–152. (Paris: L'Harmattan).

Noyelle, T. and Dutka, A.B. (1988) *International Trade in Business Services: Accounting, Advertising, Law and Management Consulting*. Cambridge, MA: Ballinger Publishing.

von Petz, Ursula, und Klaus M. Schmals (eds) (1992) *Metropole, Weltstadt, Global City: Neue Formen der Urbanisierung*. Dortmund: Dortmunder Beitrage zur Raumplanung, Vol. 60, Universitat Dortmund.

Panitch, Leo (1996) "Rethinking the Role of the State in an Era of Globalization." In Mittelman (ed) op.cit.

Rodriguez, Nestor P. and Feagin, J.R. (1986) "Urban Specialization in the World System." *Urban Affairs Quarterly*, 22(2), 187–220.

Rosenau, J.N. (1992) "Governance, order, and change in world politics," In Rosenau and E.O. Czempiel (eds) Governance without Government: Order and Change in World Politics. Cambridge: Cambridge University Press, pp. 1–29.

Sassen, Saskia (Forthcoming) *On Governing the Global Economy*. The Leonard Hastings Memorial Schoff Lectures delivered at Columbia University, to be published by Columbia University Press.

— (2000) *Cities in a World Economy*. Thousand Oaks, California: Pine Forge/Sage Press. New Edition

50   S. Sassen

— (2000)*The Global City: New York, London, Tokyo*. Princeton University Press. New Edition
—- (1982) "Recomposition and Peripheralization at the Core." In *Immigration and Changes in the New International Division of Labor*. San Francisco: Synthesis Publications, pp. 88–100.
Sassen, Saskia and Bradley J. Orlow (1995) "The Growing Service Intensity in Economic Organization: Evidence from the Input-Output Tables." (Department of Urban Planning, Columbia University, New York City).
Smith, David A. and Michael Timberlake (1995) "Cities in global matrices: toward mapping the world system's city system." In Knox and Taylor (eds) op.cit., pp. 79–97.
Schwartz, Alex (1992) "The geography of corporate services: a case study of the New York urban region." *Urban Geography*, 13(1), 1–24.
Stimson, Robert J. "Process of Globalisation and Economic Restructuring and the Emergence of a New Space Economy of Cities and Regions in Australia." Presented at the Fourth International Workshop on Technological Change and Urban Form: Productive and Sustainable Cities, Berkeley, California, USA. April 14–16, 1993.
Todd, Graham (1995) "'Going Global' in the semi-periphery: world cities as political projects. The case of Toronto." In Knox and Taylor (eds) op.cit. 192–214.
Trubek, David M., Yves Dezalay, Ruth Buchanan, John R. Davis. "Global Restructuring and the Law: the Internationalization of Legal Fields and Creation of Transnational Arenas." Working Paper Series on the Political Economy of Legal Change. N. 1. Madison, Wisconsin: Global Studies Research Program, University of Wisconsin.
United Nations Conference on Trade and Development, Programme on Transnational Corporations (1993) *World Investment Report 1993: Transnational Corporations and Integrated International Production*. New York: United Nations.
United Nations (1992) *World Investment Report 1992: Transnational Corporations as Engines of Growth*. New York.
Wheeler, James O. (1986) "Corporate Spatial Links with Financial Institutions: The Role of the Metropolitan Hierarchy." *Annals of the Association of American Geographers*, 76(2), 262–274.
Young, O.R. (1989) *International Cooperation: Building Regimes for Natural Resources and the Environment*. Ithaca: Cornell University Press.

[9]

Global Capitalism and Liberal Myths: Dispute Settlement in Private International Trade Relations

A. Claire Cutler

The range of possible responses to the problems posed by 'the globalisation of liberalism' is vast and of considerable complexity. However, a crucial characteristic of these problems is the presupposition that two separate, though related, spheres of activity exist: one is private and concerns the economic, the other is public and concerns the political. The globalisation of liberalism is then framed by the attempt to sort out the character of the relationship between these two spheres. It is posited, for example, that forces of global capitalism are related to the homogenisation of political structures in the form of liberal states. The problem then is 'how as a result of international pressures, states are compelled more and more to conform to each other in their internal arrangements'.[1] This approach defines the international system 'as primarily one constituted by economic activity, and the spread of capitalism on a world wide scale'.[2] The genesis of international society is historically and sociologically related to 'how capitalism as a socio-economic system spreads, the role that values and norms, including the concept of sovereignty, play within it, and the changing balance of coercion and consent involved in the reproduction of that society'.[3] Therefore, this focus raises significant concerns regarding the definition and measurement of expanding capitalism, and the definitions of liberal states and the liberal international order.

This article, in contrast, considers the more fundamental distinction between the political and economic spheres. The boundary between public and private authority structures and property rights has shifted over time, in response to changing historical, social, political, and economic forces. The concept of 'historic blocs' or 'configurations of social forces upon which state power ultimately rests' is useful for capturing this complex set of forces that constitutes state/society relations under different historical conditions.[4] The article focuses on the derivation of the public/private distinction in the context of international

---

1. Fred Halliday, 'International Society as Homogeneity: Burke, Marx, Fukuyama', *Millennium: Journal of International Studies* (Vol. 21, No. 3, 1992), p. 1. 435.
2. *Ibid.*, p. 442.
3. *Ibid.*, p. 443.
4. Robert W. Cox, *Production, Power, and World Order: Social Forces in the Making of History* (New York, NY: Columbia University Press, 1987), p. 105.

© Millennium: Journal of International Studies, 1995. ISSN 0305-8298. Vol. 24, No. 3, pp. 377-397

Millennium

trade relations. More specifically, the concern is with the differentiation between private and public international trade law. A review of the historical evolution of private dispute settlement in international trade illustrates how, during different historic blocs, economic and political elites have manipulated the boundary between the two spheres as a means of regulating commerce and, at times, of insulating international commercial transactions from national and democratic controls. This account offers a stark contrast to conventional historical narratives, which focus on the continuity of international trade regulation and often use transaction cost analysis as a key explanatory tool.[5]

The story of the constitution of the sphere of private trade relations is important because it is a significant chapter in the story of the constitution of the capitalist global political economy. The private international trade regime facilitates the mobility and expansion of capital. Private institutions and actors articulate and enforce norms that provide the foundation for contractual exchange, by establishing property rights and standards of liability that minimise barriers to commercial exchange and capital mobility. Moreover, the norms governing private commercial exchange are so foundational that they are both constitutive of the state/society relations of modern capitalism, and are attributes of the capitalist order.[6]

Liberal mythology plays a central role in the construction of these spheres. This article identifies four liberal myths that are critical to the constitution of the private sphere and that serve to differentiate it from the public sphere. These myths concern the natural, neutral, consensual, and efficient nature of private commercial exchange relations. The article argues that these liberal myths form the foundation for the separation of economic and political processes, giving rise to the association of economics with the private sphere and politics with the public sphere, and rationalising their differential treatment. Economics becomes the domain of private activity, and is thus removed from politics and practices of democratic accountability. The analysis suggests that, although global capitalism and liberal mythology may be effecting a homogenisation of political structures, these structures, while capitalist, are only mythically liberal. In other words, forces of global capitalism are contributing to an erosion of societal and democratic controls and facilitating the denationalisation of capital. Understanding these developments is important to the theory and practice of

---

5. Harold Berman and Colin Kaufman, 'The Law of International Commercial Transactions (*Lex Mercatoria*)', *Harvard International Law Journal* (Vol. 19, No. 1, 1978), pp. 221-22 and 272-73, and Leon E. Trakman, *The Law Merchant: The Evolution of Commercial Law* (Littleton, CO: Fred B. Rothman and Co., 1983), pp. 9, 13, 23, and 39.

6. The view that the private sphere is constitutive of the capitalist order is clearly evident in the treatment of legal norms or 'juridical and political relations' as primary and not simply as part of the superstructure of capitalism. For the view that juridical forms are 'constituent of productive relations themselves' and 'attributes' of 'particular productive systems', see Ellen Meiksins Wood, 'The Separation of the Economic and Political in Capitalism', *New Left Review* (Vol. 127, 1981), pp. 78-79.

international relations, because they signal the danger posed by globalising forces and hegemonic practices that threaten the demise of liberal democracy.

The article traces the evolution of the public/private distinction over three phases in the development of dispute settlement practices under private international trade law. It illustrates how the boundary between public and private authority in the settlement of commercial disputes has shifted over time, in response to the changing interests of economic and political elites and the development of liberal mythology. The next two sections develop the conceptual foundation for the analysis of the public/private spheres, while the subsequent section introduces the private international trade law regime and places the arbitration norm at the centre of dispute settlement processes. This is followed by a brief history of the arbitration norm which illustrates how the norm evolved in the context of shifting boundaries between public and private authority. The last section addresses the implications of these four liberal myths for the theory and practice of international relations.

Four Liberal Myths

Four myths form the foundation for the distinction between the public and private spheres. They originate in liberal political economy and posit the natural, neutral, consensual, and efficient nature of private exchange relations.

The first myth is that the private ordering of economic relations is consistent with natural or normal economic processes. In this vein, international trade law distinguishes between normal and deviant trade relations. Private international trade law deals with normal and natural activity, while public international law deals with deviant, unnatural behaviour. As Kennedy notes:

> [i]n normal situations, governments adopt a passive *laissez-faire* attitude. The regime of 'private international law' sustains trade rules about property and contract, mechanisms to stabilize jurisdictional conflicts while liberating private actors to choose forums, and *ad hoc* mechanisms of dispute resolution. The dominant players are private traders, and to a far greater extent than in even the most *laissez-faire* national system, they legislate the rules that govern their trade through contract. And when governments do participate, they operate 'commercially'—as private actors.[7]

In contrast, public international trade law deals with unnatural activities like dumping, cartels, subsidies, price supports, and the like. The regime in the public sphere is thus regarded as 'supplemental' to the private, in that it deals with the reduction or punishment of interventionist abnormalities.

---

7. David Kennedy, 'Turning to Market Democracy: A Tale of Two Architectures', *Harvard International Law Journal* (Vol. 32, No. 2, 1991), p. 380.

Millennium

The second myth posits the neutral and apolitical nature of the private sphere. Liberalism represents the world as a series of dichotomies: the public/private constitutes one central division of authority, and the domestic/international another.[8] Under liberalism, private relations are associated with the domain of neutral economic processes, while public relations are related to the realm of politics. As a political theory, liberalism 'purports to be neutral, advancing only the goals of liberty and procedural justice.... Liberal ideology provides the mode of governance, based on liberty, and a dispute resolution process, based on the rule of law'.[9] As a legal theory, liberal-inspired contract law embodies and reproduces the separation of the spheres, associating the private sphere with neutral and objective processes of resource allocation and the public sphere with contentious and political processes of resource distribution.[10] Liberalism deems the private sphere to operate according to neutral principles. It does not question the 'rightness or propriety of dividing international life into spheres of sovereign authority', but 'presenting itself as a neutral and objective system, liberal legality provides no awareness of its hidden substantive commitments'.[11] Contract law is endowed with objective foundations and has the 'appearance of being self-contained, apolitical, and inexorable' as it regulates transactions amongst market participants who are presumed to be of equal bargaining power.[12] Its role is to facilitate exchange, ensuring procedural fairness, but it does not inquire into the substantive fairness of a transaction. Thus, the law functions as a 'mechanism of exclusion', reproducing 'the relationship it posited between law and society', in the attempt 'to project a stable relationship between spheres it creates to divide'.[13]

The identification of certain types of activity as 'private', and thus apolitical, removes that activity from public scrutiny and review. This process of transforming public and political activity into private and apolitical activity is a central 'structural separation' of capitalism, and may be 'the most effective defense mechanism available to capital'.[14] It also contributes to the third liberal myth concerning the consensual and noncoercive nature of private exchange

8. For an interesting account of the possible relationship between these two dichotomies, see Justin Rosenberg, *The Empire of Civil Society: A Critique of the Realist Theory of International Relations* (London and New York, NY: Verso, 1994).

9. Nigel Purvis, 'Critical Legal Studies in Public International Law', *Harvard International Law Journal* (Vol. 32, No. 1, 1991), pp. 100-101. See also Will Kymlicka, 'Liberal Neutrality', in James Sterba (ed.), *Justice: Alternative Political Perspectives*, Second Edition (Belmont, CA: Wadsworth Publishing Company, 1992), pp. 252-72.

10. Generally, see Morton J. Horowitz, 'Law and Economics: Science or Politics?', *Hofstra Law Review* (Vol. 8, 1979-80), pp. 905-12.

11. Purvis, *op. cit.*, in note 9, p. 102.

12. Morton J. Horowitz, 'The Rise of Legal Formalism', *American Journal of Legal History* (Vol. 19, 1975), p. 252. Horowitz notes that most of the basic dichotomies in legal thought, including that between law and politics and between distributional and allocational goals, 'arose to establish the objective nature of the market and to neutralize and hence diffuse the political and redistributional potential of law'. *Ibid.*, p. 254.

13. David Kennedy, 'A New Stream of International Law Scholarship', *Wisconsin International Law Journal* (Vol. 7, No. 1, 1988), p. 8.

14. Wood, *op. cit.*, in note 6, p. 67.

relations. Mark Rupert cogently illustrates how the coercive aspects of the exchange relationship are obscured by what appear to be impersonal market forces and natural economic laws. 'To the extent that capitalism is supported by an explicitly coercive power, that power is situated in the putatively communal sphere occupied by the state, and appears as law and order enforced in the public interest'; the private sphere is 'insulated from explicitly communal and political concerns, the "private" powers of capital are ensconced in the sanctuary of civil society....'[15]

The fourth liberal myth posits the inherent efficiency of the private regulation of commercial relations. This myth also draws upon the other myths, since, for liberals, it is not difficult to derive the value of efficiency from allegedly natural, neutral, and consensual processes. Indeed, the proponents of enhanced private regulation of international commerce invoke precisely these attributes to support liberal-inspired functional and transaction cost analysis of private regulation.[16] Private regulation is thus said to produce greater efficiencies by reducing the costs of doing business and by achieving greater economies.

While liberalism provides a rationale for the distinction between the two spheres, it provides no sense of the history and the function of their separation. It is simply unhistoric to posit the distinction as a natural division, for it has not always figured as part of the natural world. Moreover, it is reductionist to attribute the complex public/private and state/society relationships to functional efficiency arguments. Transaction cost and efficiency arguments do not capture the complex character of the historic blocs that give rise to different permutations of the private/public distinction. They conflate the modern and medieval periods, and therefore miss crucial shifts in the boundary between public and private authority. In addition, they fail to grasp the essentially coercive and political nature of private commercial exchange relations. The next section considers very generally how a more careful historicisation of the private/public distinction could be developed. This provides the framework for a more detailed enquiry into the history of private international trade law.

Historicising the Public/Private Distinction

Michael Walzer associates the public/private distinction with the liberal practice of the 'art of separation', wherein 'political community is separated from the sphere of economic competition and free enterprise'.[17] In the private sphere of free economic exchange, there are no restrictions on prices or the quality of

---

15. Mark Rupert, *Producing Hegemony: The Politics of Mass Production and American Global Power* (Cambridge: Cambridge University Press, 1995), pp. 22-24.
16. Bernado M. Cremades and Steven L. Plehn, 'The New Lex Mercatoria and the Harmonization of the Laws of International Commercial Transactions', *Boston University International Law Journal* (Vol. 2, No. 3, 1984), pp. 317-18, 326-33, and 347, and Trakman, *op. cit.*, in note 5, pp. 97-102.
17. Michael Walzer, 'Liberalism and the Art of Separation', *Political Theory* (Vol. 12, No. 3, 1984), pp. 315-30.

goods bought and sold: *caveat emptor* prevails. However, while Walzer justifies the liberal art of separation on the grounds that it is a 'necessary adaptation to the complexities of modern life', he recognises that critics on the left are suspicious of the practice, regarding it as an ideological rather than a practical enterprise' and 'an elaborate exercise in hypocrisy'.[18] Moreover, the separation obscures significant temporal and geographical differences in the ordering of public/private relations.

The early work of Jürgen Habermas is particularly useful in addressing these concerns and in understanding the historical evolution and the nature of the public/private distinction.[19] Importantly, Habermas shows how the development of capitalism was central to the association of politics with the public sphere and economics with the private sphere. Habermas' illustration of how the spheres historically acquired different meanings is also significant.[20]

While the public/private categories were of Greek origin, they were transmitted to medieval Europe through Roman civilisation and law. However, the categories known to ancient Greek and Roman civilisations did not hold the same meanings that they hold today. In ancient Greece, the public sphere included the *polis*—the Greek city-state composed of free citizens—and public life took place in the *agora*, or market place. In contrast, private life, which included the production of wealth, took place in the home, or *oikos*. The public sphere came to be associated with freedom, while the private was the realm of obscurity and necessity. The Romans inherited the Hellenic view, but reproduced the categories in terms of property rights: *res publicas* referred to public property, and *res privatus* referred to private property. The Roman distinctions were in use in the Middle Ages, but Habermas notes that these were not yet the categories of an 'emancipated society'.[21] It took the liberation of the peasants and the breakdown

---

18. *Ibid.*, pp. 317 and 319.
19. Jürgen Habermas, *The Structural Transformation of the Public Sphere: An Inquiry into a Category of Bourgeois Society*, trans. T. Burger (Cambridge, MA: The MIT Press, 1994).
20. *Ibid.*, pp. 14-26. Habermas provides an account of the origin, transformation, and degeneration of the bourgeois public sphere in the context of the development of capitalism in Germany, France, and Britain. He has been criticised for providing an idealised account that misrepresents history, neglects the gendered and exclusionary nature of the public sphere, and is thus suspect as an emancipatory theory. See the various selections in Craig Calhoun (ed.), *Habermas and the Public Sphere* (Cambridge, MA, and London: The MIT Press, 1992), and R.B.J. Walker, 'Social Movements/World Politics', *Millennium* (Vol. 23, No. 3, 1994), pp. 679-84. Arguably, there are other interpretations of the development of the state and the derivation of the public/private distinction. See Anthony Giddens, *A Contemporary Critique of Historical Materialism, Volume 1: Power, Property and the State* (London: Macmillan, 1981), and *Volume 2: The Nation-State and Violence* (Oxford: Polity Press, 1985); or Ellen Wood, *The Pristine Culture of Capitalism* (London: Verso, 1991). However, Habermas' account of the distinction between the private and public spheres and the changing nature of the distinction in the context of evolving capitalist practice and concepts of private law is useful at an abstract level, to provide a general framework for conceptualising the private/public distinction.
21. Habermas, *op. cit.*, in note 19, p. 76.

Global Capitalism and Liberal Myths

of feudal patterns of ownership to furnish the foundation for property rights conceived in terms of the opposing spheres of public and private.

Habermas illustrates how the development of the public/private distinction was inextricably bound up with the evolution of capitalism and the emergence of a bourgeois social order. This order began to take shape in financial and trade exchanges during and after the thirteenth century in northern Italy. Later, it spread to other parts of Europe. The early history of the private sphere was constituted by the activities of merchants engaged in long-distance trade, which gave rise to the growth of private merchant corporations and joint stock companies. Here too we find the beginning of the tension between the private and the public spheres. The former came to be regarded as a domain of unregulated economic exchange. The latter came to be associated with regulation imposed by what was to become the mercantilist state. However, the private sphere had to be freed from mercantilist regulation before it could be private in a 'positive' sense, as opposed to a negative sense of simply not being public. With the expansion and liberation of the market 'the commodity owners gained private autonomy; the positive meaning of "private" emerged precisely in reference to the concept of free power of control over property that functioned in a capitalist fashion'.[22]

Moreover, and of critical importance to this discussion, Habermas illustrates this development by reference to the foundations of private commercial law. These foundations emphasised the natural and consensual nature of economic exchange relations. The conception of a commercial contract founded upon the free will of the parties was 'modelled on the exchange transaction of freely competing owners of commodities'.[23] Private law reduced relationships between private people to private contracts, assuming that the laws of the free market were of a model or natural character. Legal rights ceased to be determined by estate and birth. Instead, they were determined by 'fundamental parity among owners of commodities in the market'.[24] The adage 'from status to contract' encapsulates the evolution from feudal to capitalist conceptions of property rights.[25] Private law 'secured the private sphere in the strict sense, a sense in which private people pursued their affairs with one another free from impositions by estate and state, at least in tendency'.[26]

As mercantilism gradually disappeared, the private sphere came to be regulated by private law and the nation-state.[27] The law was, in theory at least, supposed to operate amongst equals and in a neutral fashion, protecting commercial

---

22. *Ibid.,* p. 74.
23. *Ibid.,* p. 75.
24. *Ibid.*
25. *Ibid.,* p. 77.
26. *Ibid.,* p. 75.
27. For mercantilism generally, see Eli Heckscher, *Mercantilism* (New York, NY: Macmillan, 1955), and for an historical sociological account of the development of the private sphere, see Giddens, *Power, Property and the State, op. cit.,* in note 20, pp. 182-202.

Millennium

freedoms and markets. State intervention was frowned upon as interfering with the 'natural' operation of the market, which, for merchant law, translated into the ability to predict transaction costs in accordance with rational and calculable expectations.

The discussion of the problems associated with the public/private distinction will be taken up again after consideration of the private international trade law regime. For now, Habermas' account of the emergence of the public/private distinction in post-medieval Europe provides a useful general framework for constructing a new history of international trade law. Within this framework, different historical blocs have created the two spheres and manipulated the boundary between them.

Private International Trade: A Return to 'Medieval Internationalism'?

It is commonly asserted that international commerce is witnessing a revival of 'medieval internationalism' in the growing adoption of international arbitration as the chosen method for resolving international commercial disputes.[28] Today, private international trade disputes are resolved predominantly through international arbitration, as opposed to adjudication in national courts of law. Indeed, arbitration has replaced adjudication as the norm for resolving international commercial disputes.[29] Hundreds of institutions engage in commercial arbitration throughout the world: the International Chamber of Commerce Court of Arbitration (ICC), the American Arbitration Association, and the London Court of Arbitration are among the most significant.[30] The recourse to private arbitration is encouraged by states who are participating in creating uniform and mandatory rules that provide for the recognition and enforcement of foreign arbitral awards. States are adopting legislation that curtails the power of national courts to intervene in private arbitrations and that limits the ability of judicial authorities to set aside arbitration awards.[31]

The use of private means to resolve disputes between commercial actors evokes images of medieval merchants who, travelling from market to market, 'carried their law, as it were, in the same consignment as their goods, and both law and goods remained in the places they traded and became part of the general

---

28. See Clive M. Schmitthoff, 'International Business Law: A New Law Merchant', *Current Law and Social Problems* (Vol. 2, 1961), pp. 131-32, 144-46, and 152.

29. See Gerald Aksen, 'The Need to Utilize International Arbitration', *Vanderbilt Journal of Transnational Law* (Vol. 17, No. 1, 1984), pp. 11-17; Thomas E. Carbonneau, 'Arbitral Adjudication: A Comparative Assessment of its Remedial and Substantive Status in Transnational Commerce', *Texas International Law Journal* (Vol. 19, No. 1, 1984), pp. 33-114; and Richard J. Graving, 'The International Commercial Arbitration Institutions: How Good a Job are They Doing?', *American University Journal of International Law and Policy* (Vol. 4, No. 2, 1989), pp. 319-76.

30. For a comprehensive list of arbitration institutions, see 'List of Arbitral Institutions', *Yearbook of Commercial Arbitration* (Vol. 13, 1988), pp. 713-37.

31. The United Nations Convention on the Recognition and Enforcement of Foreign Arbitral Awards, 10 June 1958, UN Doc. A/Conf. 9/22, curtails the power of national courts to intervene in private arbitrations.

Global Capitalism and Liberal Myths

stock of the country'.[32] Medieval commercial disputes were settled by merchant juries who sat in courts of 'pie powder' (*piepoudres*).[33] The law applied was called the law merchant, *lex mercatoria*, and was renowned for the speed, justice, and efficiency with which disputes were settled. The law merchant evolved as a distinct and autonomous body of law regulating the activities of merchants who were granted significant immunities from local laws and regulations.[34] It was considered to be the *jus commune* or common law of the medieval period.[35] It achieved such universality in the European trading world that it even came to be regarded as the *jus gentium*, or the law of nations 'known to merchants throughout Christendom'.[36]

Similarities in dispute settlement in the medieval and modern periods are so striking that they suggest a renaissance of medieval practices. Indeed, trade experts agree that the law merchant courts operated more like modern arbitration tribunals than like courts of law.[37] Symmetry in the norms applied and an emphasis on informal, speedy, and just settlements characterise arbitral proceedings in both periods. Trade experts maintain that, in the absence of protections that stabilise expectations by rendering transaction costs predictable and property rights secure, actors will not engage in commercial transactions.[38] Therefore, these experts invoke classical and neo-classical liberal economic principles to explain both the emergence of the medieval law merchant and its symmetry with modern practices.[39] Moreover, in order to promote private regulation, they reproduce liberal myths about the private sphere's natural, neutral, consensual, and efficient character.[40] The superiority of the system of private regulation and arbitration is thus represented as a natural result of the reasonableness and efficiency of allowing merchants maximum scope for managing their own affairs. The right of freedom of contract becomes the legal

---

32. Wyndham Bewes, *The Romance of the Law Merchant* (London: Sweet and Maxwell, 1923), p. vi.
33. The courts of pie powder were named thus because, according to lore, justice was administered 'as speedily as the dust could fall or be removed from the feet of the litigants'. C. Gross (ed.), *Select Cases Concerning the Law Merchant, Volume I* (London: Bernard Quaritch, 1892), p. xiv.
34. See A.T. Carter, 'The Early History of the Law Merchant in England', *The Law Quarterly Review* (Vol. 17, No. 67, 1901), pp. 232-51.
35. See René David, 'The International Unification of Private Law', in *International Encyclopaedia of Comparative Law: The Legal Systems of the World, Their Comparison and Unification, Volume II* (The Hague: Mohr, Tublingen Martinus Nijhoff, 1972), Chapter 5.
36. Frederick Pollock and Frederick W. Maitland, *History of English Law, Volume I* (Cambridge: Cambridge University Press, 1898), p. 467.
37. See Schmitthoff, *op. cit.*, in note 28, p. 134, and Cremades and Plehn, *op. cit.*, in note 16, pp. 332 and 335.
38. See D.M. Day, *The Law of International Trade* (London: Butterworths, 1981), pp. 1-10, and Berman and Kaufman, *op. cit.*, in note 5, pp. 221-23.
39. See Trakman, *op. cit.*, in note 5, pp. 1-6; Cremades and Plehn, *op. cit.*, in note 16, pp. 319 and 347; Carbonneau, *op. cit.*, in note 29, pp. 58-59; and Berman and Kaufman, *op. cit.*, in note 5, pp. 224-25 and 272-77.
40. See Trakman, *op. cit.*, in note 5, pp. 99-105; Cremades and Plehn, *op. cit.*, in note 16, pp. 326-27; and Graving, *op. cit.*, in note 29, p. 324.

Millennium

equivalent of the liberal principles of freedom of trade, commerce, and markets.[41]

While some legal theorists explicitly engage in transaction cost analysis to explain the origin and continuing influence of law merchant practices,[42] it is students of 'new institutional theory' who develop this approach most fully.[43] The emergence of an institution like the law merchant is explained as a response to the transaction and information costs and insecurity experienced by merchants engaging in trade over wide geographical regions.[44] It is argued that the merchant courts provided an efficacious system for settling merchant disputes and for enforcing transactions.[45] Self-regulation by merchants · included the imposition of the sanctions of market exclusion, bankruptcy, and loss of reputation, and provided the foundation for a system of private adjudication suited to the needs of commercial actors. By centralising enforcement in merchant courts, the system provided invaluable information about the credit-worthiness of those with whom a merchant traded, and functioned as a valuable reputation system which enforced honesty. According to this logic, the system of private enforcement made commercial exchange over time and space possible, by lowering the costs of exchange and providing merchants with some security that their agreements would be honoured. However, a review of the history of

41. The influence of liberal economic thought on commercial law is profound. For a brilliant discussion of the liberal foundations of modern contract law, see Patrick S. Atiyah, *The Rise and Fall of Freedom of Contract* (Oxford: Clarendon Press, 1979). Certainly, among Anglo-American scholars the tendency is to assume *a priori* the validity of liberal economic accounts of the efficiency value of the private international trade regime. The presumption is that the reduction of legal uncertainty will generate greater trade. See Elizabeth Hayes Patterson, 'United Nations Convention on Contracts for the International Sale of Goods: Unification and the Tension between Compromise and Domination', *Stanford Journal of International Law* (Vol. 22, 1986), p. 266, n. 7. Economic theories of law, like that developed by Richard A. Posner, explicitly develop transaction cost analysis, although it is related to domestic and not international law. Posner's ideas on the evolution of primitive legal orders do, however, provide interesting suggestions for conceptualising international law. See his 'A Theory of Primitive Society, With Special Reference to Law', *Journal of Law and Economics* (Vol. 23, No. 1, 1980), pp. 1-54, and 'The Ethical and Political Basis of the Efficiency Norm in Common Law Adjudication', *Hofstra Law Review* (Vol. 8, 1980), pp. 487-514.
42. See Bruce Benson, 'The Spontaneous Evolution of Commercial Law', *Southern Economic Journal* (Vol. 55, No. 3, 1988/89), pp. 644-61.
43. A pioneering work in this regard is Paul R. Milgrom, Douglas C. North, and Barry R. Weingast, 'The Role of Institutions in the Revival of Trade: The Law Merchant, Private Judges, and the Champagne Fairs', *Economics and Politics* (Vol. 2, No. 1, 1990), pp. 1-23. See also North and Robert P. Thomas, *The Rise of the Western World: A New Economic History* (Cambridge: Cambridge University Press, 1973); North, *Structure and Change in Economic History* (New York, NY: Norton, 1981); North, *Institutions, Institutional Change and Economic Performance* (Cambridge: Cambridge University Press, 1990); and Hendrick Spruyt, 'Institutional Selection in International Relations: State Anarchy as Order', *International Organization* (Vol. 48, No. 4, 1994), pp. 527-57.
44. Milgrom, North, and Weingast, *op. cit.*, in note 43, pp. 19-21.
45. *Ibid.*, pp. 4-6.

Global Capitalism and Liberal Myths

dispute settlement under the law merchant reveals that there are problems in applying liberal transaction cost analysis to the medieval political economy, and then drawing a direct link from this to modern practices. This revelation supports charges that new institutionalism has a 'need for history', and that it effectively reduces the political landscape to efficiency arguments.[46] The supposed symmetry of the medieval and modern law merchant begins to break down when one considers the absence of a clear conceptual distinction between the public and the private spheres in the medieval period, and then the subsequently shifting boundary between public and private authority structures.

Dispute Settlement under the Law Merchant (*Lex Mercatoria*)

Legal historians and trade experts identify three phases in the evolution of the law merchant.[47] They divide the evolution of the regime into a first phase of medieval internationalism in the eleventh to sixteenth centuries, a second phase of nationalisation and localisation in the seventeenth to nineteenth centuries, and a third phase of modern internationalism in the twentieth century. This is presented as evidence of a continuous, albeit rather uneven, existence of merchant law and practice.[48] However, when we concentrate on the separation of the private and public spheres, it becomes clear that the history of international trade law is, in fact, marked by sharp discontinuities and changes.

During the first phase, dispute settlement through private arbitration was the norm. Conceptually, however, the public/private distinction was not yet developed, and, in practice, public authorities exercised local controls with limited impact on international commerce. The arbitration norm weakened in the second phase, as states sought to regulate international commerce and national adjudication became the norm. This period witnessed a clear articulation of the conceptual distinction between the public and private spheres. In practice, the public sphere expanded and the private sphere contracted as state elites increased intervention into international commercial relations. Private arbitration has emerged strongly in the third phase, although now it is conducted with the full support of the state. The boundary between the public and private spheres is shifting, as matters previously regarded as public are today being delegated to private actors. Tensions between political and commercial elites over the extent to which international commercial relations should be subject to state regulation, and conflicts over the nature of that regulation, are reflected in the shifting location of the boundary and the changing content of each sphere. Each of the three phases will be considered briefly below.

---

46. Spruyt, *op. cit.*, in note 43, pp. 532-33.
47. Berman and Kaufman, *op. cit.*, in note 5, pp. 224-29, and Schmitthoff, *op. cit.*, in note 28, pp. 131-42.
48. Berman and Kaufman, *op. cit.*, in note 5, pp. 272-73.

Millennium

Phase I: The Medieval Law Merchant

Medieval law merchant practices exhibited widespread acceptance of private arbitration in the settlement of disputes.[49] The courts of pie powder originated in this phase, and sat in fairs, markets, and seaport towns. The right to hold a fair court, for example, formed part of the grant of the right to hold a fair, which was issued by the king or local lord. The grant established the jurisdiction of the fair court and provided for its general administration. The law applied was the law merchant and judgements were rendered by juries of merchants. Fair courts throughout England and the continent applied the law merchant, enforcing transactions which were unenforceable in the local common and civil law courts. The common and civil law courts did not have jurisdiction over contracts entered into or torts committed abroad, and did not recognise or enforce the instruments commonly utilised by merchants. The various financial, insurance, transport, and maritime instruments (*e.g.*, bills of exchange, letters of credit, partnership agreements, general average agreements, charterparties, sea loans, and bare promises) used by merchants could only be enforced under the law merchant and in merchant courts. The merchant courts thus operated independently and at the suit of merchants, evidencing considerable merchant autonomy. They emphasised procedural and evidentiary informality, which contributed further to their unique character.

Merchant autonomy in dispute resolution derived both from the inability of the 'inchoate nation-state system' to regulate the 'geographically dynamic' activities of the medieval merchant, and from a hands-off approach to foreign merchants who were regarded as providing valuable revenues and supplies of foreign goods.[50] Local political, religious, and guild authorities lacked the capacity to regulate international transactions, while the local courts and legal systems did not recognise law merchant transactions, and therefore were powerless to regulate or enforce them.

What is particularly significant about the medieval phase is that merchant autonomy in dispute settlement contrasted rather sharply with the intensity with which local commercial exchanges were regulated to protect consumers. Local traders were subject to strict consumer protections, in the form of the requirements of just prices and liability for defects in the quality of goods.[51] Local markets were strictly controlled for supply or price manipulation by forestalling (purchasing before market), regrating (purchases by middlemen), and

---

49. Generally, see William C. Jones, 'An Inquiry into the History of the Adjudication of Mercantile Disputes in Great Britain and the United States', *University of Chicago Law Review* (Vol. 25, No. 3, 1958), pp. 445-64.

50. Cremades and Plehn, *op. cit.*, in note 16, p. 318. See also Henri Pirenne, *Economic and Social History of Medieval Europe* (London: Kegan Paul, 1937), and Shepard Clough and Charles Cole, *Economic History of Europe*, Revised Edition (Boston, MA: D.C. Heath and Company, 1946).

51. See Cornelius F. Murphy, 'Medieval Theory and Products Liability', *Boston College Industrial and Commercial Law Review* (Vol. 3, No. 1, 1961-2), pp. 29-37.

Global Capitalism and Liberal Myths

engrossing (cornering the market). Sales were limited to the open market (*market ouvert*) and churchmen enforced the prohibition against usury, albeit rather selectively.[52] Foreign merchants were often exempted from local price, quality, and interest restrictions. In return, merchants engaged in international transactions provided a valuable source of foreign exchange and revenue from the payment of customs duties and taxes. This suggests that, in addition to simply being unable to regulate international transactions in any significant way, the local authorities were unwilling to do so. Thus, while '[t]he ability of the merchant class to both generate and enforce its own norms of behaviour allowed it to achieve a large degree of independence from these local sovereigns',[53] one must also consider the reluctance of the local authorities to interfere.

The absence of a clear distinction between the public and private spheres reflects medieval political arrangements. The distinguishing feature of medieval Europe was the decentralisation of political authority, 'overlapping feudal jurisdictions, plural allegiances, and asymmetrical suzerainties'.[54] Ecclesiastical authorities and local political leaders exercised control over local transactions; however, their ability to discipline international commercial transactions was very limited. The 'picture of an authoritarian control is everywhere in evidence; yet the lines of the agencies of supervision are far from clean-cut. The activities of a people passing out of feudalism do not lend themselves to our distinction between public and private'.[55]

Phase II: Nationalising the Law Merchant

During the second phase in the development of the regime the public/private distinction emerged. With the development of a system of territorial-based sovereign states, and with the movement from feudalism to capitalism, the public/private distinction came to be firmly established. State-building projects involved the nationalisation and control of foreign commercial activities (which were increasing in volume). The consolidation of states signalled a change in both the ability and the willingness of political authorities to regulate international commercial transactions. The result was a contraction of the private sphere, as merchant autonomy and private dispute settlement declined. Effective enforcement came to be associated with the state. Indeed, dispute settlement and enforcement became functions of the public sphere, as the geographic expansion of commercial relations rendered the self-enforcement system of merchants less successful and more costly. The collection of information regarding the credit-

---

52. Clough and Cole, *op. cit.*, in note 50, p. 55.
53. Cremades and Plehn, *op. cit.*, in note 16, p. 319.
54. J.L. Holzgrefe, 'The Origins of Modern International Relations Theory', *Review of International Studies* (Vol. 15, No. 1, 1989), p. 11. See also John Gerard Ruggie, 'Continuity and Transformation in the World Polity: Toward a Neorealist Synthesis', *World Politics* (Vol. 35, No. 2, 1983), pp. 261-85.
55. Walton H. Hamilton, 'The Ancient Maxim Caveat Emptor', *Yale Law Journal* (Vol. 40, No. 8, 1931), p. 1141.

worthiness and honesty of merchants became more expensive. The sanctions of market exclusion and loss of reputation became difficult to enforce as markets proliferated in number, as commerce extended to far away places, and as the practice of simultaneous exchange in markets was replaced by non-simultaneous exchanges over time and space. The imposition of the sanction of bankruptcy and the enforcement of agreements became the prerogatives of states and thus came to be contingent upon national intervention, as states adopted laws and procedures governing the enforcement and execution of commercial agreements.

During this period, the expansion of trade through colonisation, the development of mercantilist doctrine, and the advent of capitalism brought new insights into the role of commerce in determining national power.[56] Political authorities developed a new understanding of the importance of regulating international commerce for achieving national welfare goals and political autonomy. This understanding, coupled with the development of the institutional and legal machinery capable of disciplining international transactions, rendered states more willing and more able to regulate international trade.

Thus, the balance between public and private authority shifted in favour of the former, as state authority replaced the overlapping authority structures of the medieval period. Moreover, states exercised stronger and more comprehensive control than did the local religious and political authorities of the earlier phase. Notable, however, is the profound change in the nature of public regulation. Medieval paternalistic and religious restraints were replaced by a permissive and facultative approach inspired by liberal political economy, which appeared later in the period. Liberalism sanctioned capitalist business techniques and provided a normative and a theoretical rationale for free market principles. It provided a foundation for assumptions concerning the natural, neutral, consensual, and efficient nature of private regulation. The widespread acceptance and legitimacy of prices established under freedom of contract or by the market, the weakening influence of strict liability standards for defective goods, and the growing legitimacy of interest charges show the increased importance of free market principles and the value of facilitating exchange. While establishing the terms of a contract became a private activity, its enforcement became a public, judicial activity.

The trend towards increasing reliance upon national judicial enforcement was bolstered by the incorporation of the jurisdiction of merchant courts into national judicial systems. States differed in the extent to which national courts assumed jurisdiction over commercial matters. England and the United States adopted unitary systems, wherein the national courts assumed jurisdiction for most commercial matters. In France, special commercial courts and commercial jurisdictions were retained, while the jurisdiction of the merchant courts was assumed by a special commercial division of the national court in Germany.

---

56. For a discussion of these developments, see Cox, *op. cit.*, in note 4, pp. 111-50.

Global Capitalism and Liberal Myths

Despite considerable judicial hostility towards the recognition and enforcement of arbitral awards, reliance on private arbitration still persisted in many states.[57]

Thus, in the second phase, national adjudication and enforcement became the norm, as conflict over the placement of the boundary between public and private authority was resolved in favour of the former. However, as a norm, national regulation was only moderately strong, given the continuing recourse to private arbitration in some jurisdictions.

Phase III: The Modern Law Merchant

The twentieth century is said to be witnessing a revival of the 'medieval internationalism' of the first phase.[58] A decline in the universality of the law merchant, caused by the proliferation of national differences in phase II, has generated a movement for the unification of international commercial law. The unification movement is being advanced by an historic bloc committed to facilitating the expansion of capitalism. The bloc is comprised of an elite group of merchants, trade lawyers, trade associations, and government officials working in combination with intergovernmental efforts to unify commercial law and practice.[59] The unification of commercial law facilitates exchange and the mobility of capital by reducing legal barriers to exchange and thereby reducing the costs of contracting. It is also effecting a relocation of the border between the private and public domains. Curiously, state elites are participating in narrowing the powers of the public sphere and broadening those of the private sphere.

The unification movement seeks to recreate the tradition of *jus commune*, which disappeared as international commercial law was assimilated by national legal systems. It has made such progress in restoring the universality of international commercial norms that some suggest that there is now a basis for a global common law and a universal commercial code.[60] The movement is assisting in the consolidation of capitalism by placing renewed emphasis on the primacy of liberal, capitalist values, which function to free international transactions from state regulation. Proponents of the new law merchant, predominantly representatives of Western industrialised states, stress the self-regulating abilities and capacities of merchants.[61] In asserting either explicitly

---

57. See Jones, *op. cit.*, in note 49, pp. 461-63. See also Carbonneau, *op. cit.*, in note 29, pp. 40-57, for a review of English, American, and French arbitration practices.
58. See Schmitthoff, *op. cit.*, in note 28, pp. 139-40.
59. For the significance of arbitration institutions and a transnational mercantile community to the unification of commercial law, see Graving, *op. cit.*, in note 29, pp. 321-22, and Berman and Kaufman, *op. cit.*, in note 5, p. 222. These institutions and the transnational mercantile community are constituent elements of the neoliberal historical bloc analysed by Stephen Gill elsewhere in this issue.
60. Francis A. Gabor, 'Emerging Unification of Conflicts of Laws Rules Applicable to the International Sale of Goods: UNCITRAL and the New Hague Conference on Private International Law', *Northwestern Journal of International Law and Business* (Vol. 7, No. 4, 1986), p. 726.
61. See Carbonneau, *op. cit.*, in note 29, pp. 100-101, and Trakman, *op. cit.*, in note 5, pp. 97-105.

Millennium

or implicitly that the purpose of commercial regulation is to facilitate international economic exchange, they claim that the best way to achieve efficiency and certainty is to give maximum play to the principles of merchant autonomy, freedom of contract, and private arbitration. Although recognising that states have legitimate interests in regulating international commercial activities, they emphasise that such regulation should be permissive, suppletive, and facultative.[62] While national public policy concerns establish mandatory limits to freedom of contract, such limits should be sensitive to the international dimension of transactions[63] and the furtherance of international comity. Mandatory public policy rules should be recognised as 'exceptions from' the basic principle of freedom of contract. Freedom of contract is 'a delegation by the state to individuals of the power to enter into binding contracts' according to self-determined terms: arbitration is regarded as a logical and necessary corollary of this power.[64]

Part of the rationale for freeing international commercial transactions from national controls is that, as 'private' transactions between contracting parties, international commercial transactions are essentially apolitical and value-neutral in their more general application. However, while liberal neutrality is accepted by most practitioners and academics in the industrialised world,[65] this view is not universal. The primacy accorded to merchant autonomy and private arbitration is challenged by those who posit that private trade relations are not value-neutral, but are inherently 'political'.[66] Asserting the belief that legal rules operate very much in a distributional manner, determining who has access to which markets, goods, and services and on what terms, they posit the overwhelming importance of justice and equitable considerations. They seek to limit the laissez-faire approach, and argue that commercial law should exercise a distributive function by promoting fairness and equality in exchange, and by protecting weaker parties. Critics argue that unrestricted reliance upon merchant autonomy and freedom of contract are unacceptable foundations for the unification of commercial law.

Many vital questions are at stake, ranging from the reconciliation of common and continental law to the protection of the weaker party and the

---

62. *Ibid.*

63. Kazuaki Sono, 'Restoration of the Rule of Reason in Contract Formation: Has There Been Civil and Common Law Disparity?', *Cornell International Law Journal* (Vol. 21, No. 3, 1988), p. 485.

64. Cremades and Plehn, *op. cit.,* in note 16, p. 328.

65. See Schmitthoff, *op. cit.,* in note 28, pp. 140-41, 144, and 152-53, and Clive M. Schmitthoff, 'Nature and Evolution of the Transnational Law of Commercial Transactions', in Norbert Horn and Clive M. Schmitthoff (eds.), *The Transnational Law of International Commercial Transactions* (Deventer: Kluwer, 1982), pp. 20-21. Graving, *op. cit.,* in note 29, p. 324, identifies neutrality as the central advantage of arbitration.

66. For the East-West and North-South differences in unifying sales law, see Alejandro M. Garro, 'Reconciliation of Legal Traditions in the UN Convention on Contracts for the International Sale of Goods', *The International Lawyer* (Vol. 23, No. 2, 1989), pp. 443-83.

Global Capitalism and Liberal Myths

satisfactory regulation of transactions between parties from different social
and economic systems or from developed and underdeveloped countries, and
it would be irrational madness to leave the legal responses to these problems
to an uncontrolled laissez-faire in a world in perpetual strife. It is a fact that
the economic and political matters involved in international trade
transactions considerably exceed the narrow margins of private interests
which are often—and mistakenly—understood to be the only concerns in the
private law regulation of international commercial issues.[67]

It is argued that merchant autonomy 'tends to annihilate freedom of contract' and
does not guarantee a fair result for weaker parties, like the developing
countries.[68] Such countries have very limited resources to effect the terms of
exchange with multinational enterprises. This is particularly true when
contracting occurs under standard form agreements or contracts of adhesion,
which are presented on a 'take it or leave it' basis. There have been attempts to
revive notions of equity as the foundation for the determination of prices and for
the rules governing liability for defective goods, but these attempts have largely
failed.[69] Attempts to modify the contract rules governing the sale, transport,
financing, and insurance of goods have also been largely unsuccessful in
equalising contractual relations between merchants in developed and developing
countries.[70]

These attempts are made even more difficult by the re-emergence of arbitration
as the preferred method for settling commercial disputes. Freeing international
commercial transactions 'from stringent requirements of the domestic law of the
forum or foreign law' is regarded as a major role of arbitration and reflects
important shifts in public policy.[71] Undoubtedly, the growing trend among states
to accept limits on the abilities of national courts to intervene in commercial
arbitrations reflects significant pragmatic considerations. The inability of national
judicial systems to deal with both the growth in commercial transactions and the
expansion in commercial litigation has been significant in reordering domestic
attitudes towards arbitration.[72] Domestic courts are simply unable to respond
adequately and cost-effectively to the increased volume of commercial cases and
to the increasing complexity of commercial transactions. In addition, most states
recognise the economic benefits that flow from reducing the transaction costs of
enforcement, and from encouraging stability in the enforcement of property
rights. However, it is the consolidation of an historic bloc premised upon liberal

---

67. Horacio A. Grigera Naon, 'The UN Convention on Contracts for the International
Sale of Goods', in Horn and Schmitthoff (eds.), *op. cit.*, in note 65, p. 91.
68. Gyula Eörsi, 'Contracts of Adhesion and the Protection of the Weaker Party in
International Trade Relations', in UNIDROIT, *New Directions in International Trade
Law, Volume I* (New York, NY: Oceana Publications, 1977), p. 157.
69. See Patterson, *op. cit.*, in note 41.
70. See Garro, *op. cit.*, in note 66.
71. Mark Buchanan, 'Public Policy and International Commercial Arbitration', *American
Business Law Journal* (Vol. 26, No. 3, 1988), p. 513.
72. See Carbonneau, *op. cit.*, in note 29.

mythology concerning the natural, 'apolitical', consensual, and efficient nature of private economic regulation that enables arbitration to insulate global capital from national regulation. Economic and political elites draw on liberal mythology concerning the superiority of private regulation to establish national and international private regulatory structures, which effectively delegate enforcement powers to the private sphere. The development of an international institutional context for arbitration, centered around the work of the United Nations Commission on International Trade Law and the many private arbitration institutions, is critical to the strength of the arbitration norm.[73] Liberal mythology has the sanction of states and is reproduced by cooperative governments and corporate elites in their rhetoric and in the law. Merchant autonomy in the medieval period operated largely due to the absence of the state. Today, merchant autonomy exists with the endorsement and support of state elites. Furthermore, states participate in the construction of the myths by according private actors wide scope in both structuring and enforcing their international commercial agreements. Liberal mythology forms the foundation for the public/private distinction and has important implications for the theory and practice of international relations.

'Apolitical' Politics

Clive M. Schmitthoff, a leading scholar of international commercial law, attributes the success of the law merchant in regulating international commercial transactions to the 'apolitical' nature of private trade relations.[74] Law merchant norms, he argues, have attained near universality in application because, irrespective of their level of development and political, economic, or social characteristics, all states have buyers and sellers, investors, lenders, and borrowers engaged in private exchanges.[75] As long as these private actors conduct their transactions within the terms of national law and public policy, it is assumed that no matters of a 'political' nature will arise. The designation of commercial transactions as essentially 'private' removes them from the sphere of the political, which is significant for international relations. When coupled with the belief that the private ordering of exchange relations is natural, the designation obscures significant differentiation in state/society relations over time and space. The public and private spheres have changed as historic blocs vested them with different contents. Moreover, among Western states, the 'image of direct and exceptional public intervention to preserve normal private commerce has become increasingly anachronistic as new forms of property ownership, corporate finance and control, public-private partnerships...and secondary markets have emptied the central categories of private property and public policy

---

73. See Graving, *op. cit.*, in note 29, p. 325.
74. Schmitthoff, 'Nature and Evolution of the Transnational Law of Commercial Transactions', *op. cit.*, in note 65, pp. 20-21.
75. *Ibid.*

of much of their iconic meaning'.[76] While the public/private distinction is of declining force in Western states, it continues to operate in states with newly acquired market structures. Rather than effecting greater homogenisation of state/society relations throughout the world, the proliferation of market democracy is arguably producing greater heterogeneity.

Furthermore, the private sphere has never operated in the neutral and consensual manner posited by liberalism. The legal presumption of the equal bargaining power of contracting parties is plainly incredible for transactions involving parties from states with asymmetric economic, technical, and legal capabilities. This is precisely the sort of argument directed at the modern law merchant by states with little bargaining power, which face obstacles to market entry.[77] Attempts to modify the laws better to accommodate development and equity concerns have been largely unsuccessful. Some changes in the rules of a marginal nature have been made, but the basic principles inspired by liberal political economy remain the core of the regime. By removing economic activity from the sphere of public scrutiny and accountability, the regime insulates commercial exchange from challenge. The public/private distinction creates what Hoffmann refers to as a 'zone of irresponsibility', wherein the public aspects of private activities are unregulated and unaccountable.[78] State and corporate elites are able to shield their activities from democratic influence, thus enhancing the further consolidation of capitalism.

The posited efficiency of the private sphere reinforces belief in the superiority of private regulation. However, this provides an unhistoric and reductionist account of state/society relations. As rationalist theories premised upon an atomistic ontology and an empirical epistemology, functional theories and transaction cost analysis produce unhistoric conceptions of the state.[79] Janice Thomson shows how state control of the economy was not meant to be 'functional to society', but evolved in the historical context of state-building and different approaches to the state's 'war-making capability'.[80] The unhistoric nature of these approaches collapses the distinction between state and society and obscures potential antagonism between political elites and society. Moreover, efficiency explanations do not capture the shifting balance between public and private authority. They do not explain why political elites found it useful to regulate dispute settlement in the second phase of the regime, but not in the third phase. Furthermore, such analysis is incapable of accounting for the influence of

---

76. Kennedy, *op. cit.*, in note 7, p. 381.
77. See Patterson, *op. cit.*, in note 41, and Garro, *op. cit.*, in note 66.
78. Stanley Hoffmann, 'The Crisis of Liberalism', *Foreign Policy* (Vol. 98, 1995), p. 175.
79. For a good discussion of this problem in the context of criticisms of neorealism, see Rupert, *op. cit.*, in note 15, Chapter 1.
80. Janice Thomson, 'State Sovereignty in International Relations: Bridging the Gap Between Theory and Empirical Research', *International Studies Quarterly* (Vol. 39, No. 2, 1995), p. 221.

national power and state interests, because all that is of heuristic and analytical value is reduced to efficiency concerns.[81]

The implications of these deficiencies are of particular importance to international relations theory. Conceptually, the notions of private agency and authority in international relations are hard to reconcile with the dominant statist discourse. The significance of private power to the international political economy suggests that some profound transformations are at work and requires more scholarly attention. In addition, the tendency of liberal mythology to conflate the medieval and modern periods, and to reduce politics and history to economic activity, suggests significant analytical limitations to liberal analysis. However, there is another, perhaps more compelling reason for probing the private and public spheres. Normatively, the public/private distinction has a particularly invidious effect. It provides the foundation for legal practices that generate and perpetuate inequalities, while advancing the mythology of their value-neutrality and efficiency. This creates a universe of thought and practice that is resistant to criticism and change.

The institutions of capitalism created, and now perpetuate, a distinction that serves to buttress and reproduce a self-sustaining view of the world. Significant developments suggest that the world has moved beyond modernity into a condition of post-modernity, characterised by globalised capitalism and definitions of political identity that challenge the dominant statist logic. Challenges to the capitalist order posed by simultaneously fragmenting and globalising influences are being met by the attempt of core states to 'bind the core' and further to consolidate capitalism.[82] The law merchant responds by reproducing the myth of the superiority and 'apolitical' nature of private regulation, thereby assisting in insulating the core from challenge. It contributes to the 'disembedding of liberalism', as capital is further denationalised and insulated more securely from government intervention and democratic controls.[83]

---

81. Stephen Krasner identifies analytical and heuristic weaknesses in market failure approaches to international regimes in their inability to investigate relative capabilities and the questionable relevance of power concerns to the solution of market failures. See his 'Global Communications and National Power: Life on the Pareto Frontier', in David A. Baldwin (ed.), *Neorealism and Neoliberalism: The Contemporary Debate* (New York, NY: Columbia University Press, 1993), p. 243. For what continues to be a good discussion of many deficiencies of functional analysis, see Stephan Haggard and Beth Simmons, 'Theories of International Regimes', *International Organization* (Vol. 41, No. 3, 1987), pp. 491-517.

82. For discussions of the range of globalising forces that are integrating the world, but are simultaneously disintegrating previously embedded institutions and practices, see Fredric Jameson, *Postmodernism, or The Cultural Logic of Late Capitalism* (Durham, NC: Duke University Press, 1991), and Stephen Gill, 'Gramsci and Global Politics: Towards a Post-Hegemonic Research Agenda', in Gill (ed.), *Gramsci, Historical Materialism and International Relations* (Cambridge: Cambridge University Press, 1993), pp. 1-18.

83. For the idea of 'disembedded liberalism', see John Gerard Ruggie, 'Trade, Protectionism and the Future of Welfare Capitalism', *Journal of International Affairs* (Vol. 48, No. 1, 1994), pp. 1-11, as well as his contribution to this issue.

Global Capitalism and Liberal Myths

As a discipline, International Relations is not very good at seeing fundamental discontinuity. More specifically, theorists often overlook 'the question of whether the modern system of states may be yielding in some instances to postmodern forms of configuring political space'.[84] It is hoped that this article contributes to the recognition that '[r]epresentations of space are not "merely" epistemic; functions of how one "just happens to think". They are related to the dominant political and material conditions of different eras'.[85] The public/private distinction separates space into political and economic domains. Liberalism then vests the separation with natural, practical, and ideological value. In so doing, the hegemony of capital is rendered more palatable and, ultimately, more secure as the core is insulated from challenge. For those uncomfortable with this picture, it is important to look behind the mythology and to reveal the processes by which hegemony reproduces itself, because, as Robert Cox suggests, '[h]egemony is like a pillow: it absorbs blows and sooner or later the would-be assailant will find it comfortable to rest upon'.[86]

A. Claire Cutler is Assistant Professor in the Political Science Department, University of Victoria, Victoria, British Columbia, Canada, V8W 3P5

84. John Gerard Ruggie, 'Territoriality and Beyond: Problematizing Modernity in International Relations', *International Organization* (Vol. 47, No. 1, 1993), pp. 143-44.
85. John Agnew, 'Timeless Space and State-Centrism: The Geographical Assumptions of International Relations Theory', in Stephen J. Rosow, Naeem Inayatullah, and Mark Rupert (eds.), *The Global Economy as Political Space* (London and Boulder, CO: Lynne Reinner Publishers, 1994), p. 102.
86. Robert W. Cox, 'Gramsci, Hegemony and International Relations: An Essay in Method', *Millennium* (Vol. 12, No. 2, 1983), p. 173.

[10]

Review of International Political Economy 1:1 Spring 1994

Passing judgement: credit rating processes as regulatory mechanisms of governance in the emerging world order

Timothy J. Sinclair

Center for International and Strategic Studies, York University, Toronto

ABSTRACT

This article argues that certain knowledge-producing institutions located in the American financial industry – debt security or bond rating agencies – are significant forces in the creation and extension of the new, open global political economy and therefore deserve the attention of international political economists as mechanisms of 'governance without government'. Rating agencies are hypothesized to possess leverage, based on their unique gate-keeping role with regard to investment funds sought by corporations and governments. The article examines trends in capital markets, the processes leading to bond rating judgements, assesses the form and extent of the agencies' governance powers, and contemplates the implications of these judgements for further extension of the global political economy and the form of the emerging world order.

Commercial credit is the creation of modern times and belongs in its highest perspective only to the most enlightened and best governed nations. Credit is the vital arm of the system of modern commerce. It has done more – a thousand times more – to enrich nations than all the mines of the world.[1]

INTRODUCTION

This article is about the rise of non-state forms of international authority, and the transformative effects these are having on economic relationships and political processes in the emerging post-Cold War world. Until the erosion of Soviet dominance over eastern Europe in the fall of 1989, and the subsequent collapse of the Soviet Union itself, international political relations were conditioned by an overriding concern with the maintenance of an effective security framework in which possible threats could be contained.[2] With the end of the Cold War, and the obsolescence of many of the relationships undergirding this phenomenon, the atten-

ARTICLES

tion of much of the scholarly international relations community has shifted from these concerns. While this very visible drama has been playing itself out on the nightly television news another has been unfolding behind closed doors. Starting in the early 1960s, offshore capital markets – places where funds are raised by selling debt obligations and equity outside the constraints of government regulation – have rapidly become global in character, stimulated initially by a desire on the part of American financiers to get around the restrictive US banking laws created during the Depression.[3] During the 1970s, and into the first half of the 1980s, the freedom of these non-national money markets was matched by a slackening of regulation within domestic finance industries, led by the United States. Other governments, including those of Britain, Japan and Canada were obliged to follow this path or suffer declines in their own finance sectors, as funds were relocated to more open markets.[4] Accordingly, during the 1980s, 'many of the boundaries between national financial markets dissolved and a truly global capital market began to emerge'.[5]

What questions does the decline of Cold War tensions and the development of a global capital market raise? Among these are: What will be the new organizing principles of the emerging world order? Where will authority be derived in the post-Cold War era of global capital mobility? What new conceptual tools will scholars need to understand these phenomena? This article evaluates these questions through an analysis of debt security rating processes. Debt security rating is portrayed in this article as a significant mechanism of authority in its own right, and as an exemplar of the form of authority that is organizing the emerging world order. Accordingly, the generalizations developed here will have applicability beyond the capital markets. Leading off the article is an evaluation of trends in the division of authority between global civil society and national states.[6] Rosenau's notion of 'governance without government' is then introduced as a way of understanding the new found influence of non-state institutions.[7] Subsequently, the article evaluates specific developments within international finance that have influenced which institutions and processes have gained authority and which have diminished in power. These developments point to the significance of the rating agencies. Some basic background material is then provided on the agencies, followed by a discussion of debt security rating processes. What information goes into a rating and how this material is analysed are examined here. A more theoretical section follows in which the governance 'powers' of the rating institutions are elaborated. This discussion is followed by an appraisal of the implications of rating agency governance for investment, policy and national determination. Finally, the article returns to the broader theme of the future character of the emerging world order in light of the mechanism identified.

PASSING JUDGEMENT: CREDIT RATING PROCESSES

GOVERNANCE

The development of the *global political economy* (GPE) has irreparably changed the authority structures that developed with the rise of the Western state system subsequent to Westphalia.[8] 'At the core of the new order', suggests Rosenau, is '. . . a relocation of authority that [has] transformed the capacities of governments'.[9] The 'state-centric system' of the Westphalian order is now being replaced by a 'multicentric system', bifurcated between state and non-state actors.[10] Because of the transnational character of many economic, political and climatic developments, 'national governments are decreasingly competent to address and resolve major issues confronting their societies'.[11] This does not mean that the sovereignty of states has ended, but rather, that the 'exclusivity and scope of their competence' has altered significantly, 'narrowing the range within which their authority and legitimacy are operative'.[12] These developments may also be interpreted as expressive of a political strategy. Gill has labelled this strategy the 'new constitutionalism', which seeks to 'place restraints on the democratic control of public and private economic organization and institutions', premised on neo-liberal assumptions about the efficiency of market forces. He suggests that some states, such as the US, are likely to be less accountable to international market forces than others, based on their divergent positions within the GPE, and thus that 'some states are more sovereign than others in the emerging world order'.[13]

Both Rosenau's and Gill's respective conceptions of the emerging world order problematize the mainstream assumptions about interstate relations and the nature of authority itself. The orthodox, neo-realist understanding of authority in international relations has been one that focuses on the legally binding actions of governments.[14] Ferguson and Mansbach propose that authority be understood instead as a process in which 'law is only one possible source of legitimacy that enhances the capacity of political actors to govern effectively . . .'[15] This implies that authority is socially constructed and based on some measure of voluntary compliance, as was the *auctoritas* of the Roman Senate. *Auctoritas* had the character of 'more than a counsel and less than a command; rather a counsel with which one could not properly avoid compliance'.[16] Based on such a notion of authority, 'a wide range of governmental and non-governmental entities may, in fact, govern effectively and thus be an "authority" or "polity" within their particular domain(s)'.[17]

Following in the conceptual footsteps of Foucault, Rosenau has developed a useful way of thinking about these shifts in the location of authority in the emerging world order. He argues that the crucial category to think about is governance: the 'system of rule'.[18] It only exists when it is accepted by the majority, whereas governments can function (up to a point) despite opposition. Governance may exist without government where there are 'regulatory mechanisms in a sphere of activity which function effectively even though they are not endowed with formal authority'.[19] Similarly, one can conceive of government without governance. However, essential to identifying a regulatory mechanism is observing 'intentionality'.[20] Governance only exists in self-conscious arrangements, and must be distinguished from arrangements which derive from the 'aggregation of individual decisions'.[21] For example, a market is an aggregation of individual decisions and does not express governance in this sense, whereas market rules or institutions that intervene in markets represent self-conscious arrangements and thus regulatory mechanisms of governance.[22] The following section discusses the context in which the regulatory mechanisms of governance examined in this article have developed.

THE CHANGING FORM OF GLOBAL CAPITAL MARKETS

The argument is that the nature of wholesale financing has changed significantly over the last decade or so, and that this has affected the nature of the authority exercised in the capital markets by regulatory mechanisms. According to Sassen, since the 1980s, the 'marketplace has assumed new strategic and routine economic functions'.[23] Financing has increasingly become *disintermediated*, which has created information problems for those wishing to lend money and for those wishing to borrow. This process has led to the disempowerment of traditional intermediating institutions, notably banks, and the empowerment of others, such as debt security rating agencies.

Two ways of organizing the allocation of investment funds have been in competition with each other since the rise of the GPE. The primary way in which funds have been loaned and borrowed has been through banks. Banks act as financial intermediaries in that they bring together the suppliers of funds and the users of funds. They borrow money, in the form of deposits, and lend at their own risk to borrowers. Those who deposit money in banks and those who borrow from them do not establish a contractual relationship with each other, but only with the bank.[24] Banks cover the costs of intermediation and make a return on their investment by charging the users or borrowers of funds more than they pay to the suppliers or lenders of funds. This structure is threatened by the trend toward disintermediation. In this process, flows of funds between borrowers and lenders avoid the direct use of financial intermediaries, for instance, in cases in which companies withdraw their funds from banks and lend them directly to each other, or when corporations issue commercial paper that may merely be underwritten by a bank or investment bank.[25] Globally, bank lending decreased from 37 per cent

PASSING JUDGEMENT: CREDIT RATING PROCESSES

of total capital movements in the 1977–81 period to 14 per cent in 1982–6. Portfolio, as opposed to direct forms of investment grew during the same period from 36 per cent in 1972–6, to 65 per cent of total investment in 1982-6. Most of this was funded through securities offerings.[26] Commercial banks increasingly take on the characteristics of investment or merchant banks, organizing issues, underwriting them, buying and selling debt in the secondary market, but not carrying these obligations on their own balance sheets.[27]

Why has this trend toward disintermediation developed? Part of this story clearly has to do with the locus of control evident in securities issues versus either equity or bank debt.[28] Banks typically want covenants that limit the application of funds by the borrower so that their interest stream is covered first. They might also place limits on the leveraging of the corporation that prevent it from raising its debt load, hindering management's plans for new plant and equipment. Moreover, '[b]ank lending is inherently more expensive than securitisation' because of the high overhead costs generated by the credit monitoring function of intermediation.[29] The high interest rates and elevated loan defaults of the 1980s made these differentials very significant. In the case of equity finance, stock holders may expect some involvement in the major decisions of the corporation, as is their right as owners of the enterprise.

What are the implications of this trend? Has the authority that used to reside in banks dissipated, or has it taken a new form? Disintermediation creates an information problem for suppliers and users of funds.[30] In an intermediated environment a lender can depend on the prudential behaviour of the bank, which is regulated and required to maintain a certain liquidity under the Basle standards. There is relatively low risk to the supplier of funds where intermediation is the norm. However, in a securitized funds environment in which no institution stands between the supplier of funds and the user, the supplier must make a judgement about the likelihood of repayment by the user. Given the high transaction costs of gathering this information for individual funds suppliers it is not surprising that institutions have developed to provide judgements on the creditworthiness of security issuers.[31] Because there is no merchant relationship between providers of these judgements and the users of this knowledge with regard to the funds themselves, this is not the same form of relationship that banks have had with their customers. The providers of the judgement risk only their credibility, not their balance sheet when they conduct this business. This interest is in making an accurate rating, not in determining which are reliable credits for the purpose of furthering their own balance sheet. However, in a disintermediated GPE, in which the creation and sale of knowledge seems to be displacing more traditional financial relationships from centre stage, these institutions of

137

capital market judgement may have become regulatory mechanisms of governance. It is to these mechanisms – the debt security rating agencies – that this article now turns.

DEBT SECURITY RATING

Debt security rating agencies had their beginnings in the early part of this century as a result of failed railroads, Florida land schemes and other property deals in the far West of the United States.[32] Two major agencies dominate the market in ratings, listing around US$3 trillion each.[33] A host of smaller agencies compete for market niches. The two major agencies are Moody's Investors Service (Moody's) and Standard & Poor's Ratings Group (S&P). Both are headquartered in New York. Moody's is owned by Dun and Bradstreet, the information concern, while S&P is a subsidiary of McGraw-Hill, the publishing company. S&P is split into two major groups, one that deals with debt rating, and the other with equity analysis. A demarcation line separates the two parts of the corporation. Moody's concern themselves exclusively with debt, although parts of their parent corporation conduct equity research.[34] Both agencies have branches in London, Paris, Frankfurt, Tokyo and Sydney. Two American agencies dominate the second tier. These are Fitch Investors Service and Duff & Phelps. Fitch is mainly in the business of municipal and corporate rating, while Chicago-based Duff & Phelps exclusively rates industrial corporations. Neither has any presence outside the USA, although Fitch did have a European presence at one time. IBCA, a London-based agency that has its roots in rating banks, has in recent years expanded its business into the corporate area. It now has offices in New York, Paris, Madrid and Tokyo. It recently merged with Euronotation of France, in what may be the first step toward the creation of a 'true European rating agency'.[35] In addition, there are a host of domestically focused agencies in a number of countries, including Japan, France, Canada, Israel, Brazil, Mexico, South Africa, and most recently, the Czech Republic.[36] Rumours constantly circulate in the financial press about the creation of a German rating agency.[37]

What do bond raters actually do? Bond raters make judgements on the 'future ability and willingness of an issuer to make timely payments of principal and interest on a security over the life of the instrument'. [38] The more likely 'the borrower will repay both the principal and interest, in accordance with the time schedule in the borrowing agreement, the higher will be the rating assigned to the debt security'.[39] Ratings are made on corporations, financial institutions, municipalities, and sovereign governments in terms of long-term obligations such as bonds or short-term obligations such as commercial paper. The processes that lead to a rating will be discussed below. The product the bond raters produce is a

PASSING JUDGEMENT: CREDIT RATING PROCESSES

letter symbol reflecting a relative ranking on a scale from most to least creditworthy. The agencies are adamant that a debt rating is 'not a recommendation to purchase, sell, or hold a security, inasmuch as it does not comment as to market price or suitability for a particular investor', because investors' risk/return trade-offs vary.[40] What bond raters do must be distinguished from equity analysis, where a buy/sell recommendation is fundamental. It has become a convention in the industry to distinguish between investment and speculative grade credits as a result of US state laws enacted during the interwar period which limited the investment opportunities of pension funds to those above a certain benchmark.[41] S&P provide four categories of investment grade, from AAA to BBB and seven of speculative grade, from BB to D (for default). Moody's rank from Aaa to Baa3, and Ba1 to C respectively.[42] Both agencies have other scales for short-term debt obligations such as commercial paper. Bond raters maintain surveillance over the issues they rate and will warn investors when they consider that developments may lead to a revision to an existing rating in either an upward or downward direction. The following section of this article investigates the elements of the rating process.

RATING METHODOLOGY

Most securities issuers approach the rating agencies themselves to initiate the rating determination, although the bond raters do on occasion approach the issuer when they become aware that a major issue is about to be offered for sale. Recently, Securities and Exchange Commission (SEC) Rule 415 has allowed issuers to file in advance in order to sell a given value of securities in the US when market conditions are agreeable. This has meant that corporations have been able to bring a new issue to market at very short notice. As a consequence, 'it has become common practice for issuers' managements to meet with S&P analysts on a regular, reasonably frequent basis, regardless of whether a new issue is imminent'.[43] Three types of information flow into the rating process. The first type of information is the publicly available kind. This includes quantitative information such as audited financial statements and qualitative information such as media reports on the state of the industry, municipality or country. The second type is the information disclosed by the issuer themselves. This includes up-to-date financial information on the operating position of the entity. But it also includes qualitative information on accounting policy, management experience and skill, competitive position and corporate strategy. The third type of information is provided by competitors of disgruntled former employees of the issuer, amongst others. The bond raters claim this sort of information is uncommon and is treated sceptically, but they exhibit no qualms about asking

ARTICLES

questions of the issuer based on these anonymous tips.[44] These information flows are always supplemented with extensive meetings between issuer and rater. The actual rating is made by vote in a rating committee, sometimes disparagingly referred to as the 'Star Chamber', on the recommendation of the analytical team.[45] The composition of the rating committees and the internal deliberations within the rating agencies on any particular issue are kept strictly confidential. The judgement that is made by the committee weighs the quantitative and qualitative factors in each case because 'there is no formula for combining these scores to arrive at a rating conclusion'. Accordingly, 'such judgements are highly subjective. Yet that is at the heart of every rating.'[46] The rating is generally subject to appeal by the issuer. But there is no regulatory requirement for this: rating opinions are defendable as free speech within the terms of the First Amendment to the Constitution of the United States.[47]

Rating methodology varies by the nature of the credit. In the case of industrial debt, it is important to understand that ratings do not reflect merely the accounting or financial position of the enterprise. While that is considered fundamental to the likelihood of successful repayment of obligations, understanding financial risk is not sufficient. Financial considerations such as debt/equity ratios of various kinds are considered alongside business risk factors that influence the probability of a sufficient stream of funds flowing into the business to meet obligations.[48] In the case of municipalities, the bond raters make judgements about the future prospects for the tax base and the professionalism of local government, amongst other variables.[49] This led to controversy when Moody's downgraded the City of Detroit in November 1992. City officials considered that they had met the stringent quantitative criteria for greater confidence, which had to do with the City budget, while Moody's based its negative view of the City on 'extraordinarily weak credit fundamentals' in Detroit itself, such as depopulation (the City is expected to shrink to 400,000 by 2012, from around one million people in 1992, which is already down 44 per cent on 1950), maximal tax rates and unemployment at twice the US average. Moreover, the vast majority of the City residents are poor. Raymon L. Flynn, the Mayor of Boston and past president of the United States Conference of Mayors, is critical of the inclusion of factors such as these by the bond raters because he believes these are the sort of issues that should be judged by the electorate and do not impact directly on creditworthiness.[50] In the case of sovereign credits, a judgement has to be made by the agencies not just about the capacity to repay but also the willingness to repay. This is an important consideration because 'the enforceability of a legal claim against a sovereign government by a foreign investor is limited at best'.[51]

Creditworthiness is a dynamic condition and the quality of the rating output immediately starts to deteriorate as new events occur which

PASSING JUDGEMENT: CREDIT RATING PROCESSES

impact on the liquidity and solvency of the debtor. Accordingly, the agencies place a great deal of emphasis on monitoring the condition of issuers on a continuous basis. This allows them to react to events more readily and give appropriate signals to the market about the condition of an issuer. This is important, because one of the major criticisms of the agencies has been the backward or historical focus of much of their credit analysis.[52] Attention to surveillance presumably improves the quality of analysis, based on a much deeper institutional knowledge of their credits by rating analysts, and consequently heightened awareness of likely risks. The willingness of firms to subject themselves to this monitoring has been heightened by the aforementioned SEC Rule 415, as taking advantage of 'shelf registration' in the market requires up-to-date ratings.[53] The surveillance relationship can readily be characterized in terms of an instituted system of rule, in which information is gathered as a prelude to possible discipline, should that information reveal a break in the understanding – or rating – that underpinned the relationship.[54] That discipline may take the form of a rating review and rating change, or a listing on Moody's 'Watchlist' and S&P's 'Credit Watch' lists which signal positive and negative rating implications of events or trends. Importantly, S&P place emphasis on the fact that credibility is gained when the 'record demonstrates' that an issuer's actions are consistent with its plans. This credibility may carry an issuer over a rough patch, because, 'Once earned, credibility can support the continuity of a particular credit rating' despite, say, short-term liquidity problems.[55] The next section of this article evaluates the extent to which the rating agencies can be considered mechanisms of governance.

RATING AGENCIES AS REGULATORY MECHANISMS OF GOVERNANCE

> The Masters of the Universe were a set of lurid, rapacious plastic dolls. . . . They were unusually vulgar, even for plastic toys. Yet one fine day, in a fit of euphoria, after [Sherman McCoy] had picked up the telephone and taken an order for zero-coupon bonds that had brought him a $50,000 commission, *just like that*, this very phrase had bubbled up into his brain. On Wall Street he and a few others – how many? – three hundred, four hundred, five hundred? – had become precisely that. . . Masters of the Universe. There was . . . no limit whatsoever![56]

Three developments have contributed to the growth of the regulatory authority of debt security rating during the era of the GPE. These are the structural power of disintermediated debt finance, the knowledge structure that has developed around economic and financial analysis in the GPE, and the coordinative position of rating agencies with regard to

ARTICLES

economic and financial behaviour. The first development has been discussed above. Disintermediation has led to the growth of the structural power of securitized finance, in which structural power is understood as the capacity to condition the context in which events occur, as opposed to the behavioural power over the course of events themselves, by shaping the conceptual frameworks that market actors use to understand situations and the subsequent range of choices they consider to be within the acceptable range.[57] The same process has reduced the structural power of banks and public authorities. An article in *The Wall Street Journal* just prior to the 1992 US presidential election ruminated on this power. The report posed the question of whether the debt security market 'may now hold unprecedented power – perhaps even veto power – over US economic policy'.[58] US federal debt, it reported, stood at around $3 trillion, with interest costs of approximately $200 billion per year. If President Clinton was thought likely to pursue a strategy perceived to be inflationary (and therefore reduces the yield on fixed income securities such as US Treasury bonds) the reaction, according to the *Journal*, is likely to be 'swift and painful' in the electronically-linked secondary market. This would in turn raise the price or interest rate the Treasury would have to offer to clear the market in new US Treasury bonds. Because 'many other long-term rates, such as mortgage rates are keyed to the Treasury debt, rising long-term rates can stagger the economy'. This power has led the players in the debt security market to be labelled 'bond vigilantes', because when inflation threatens their earnings 'they act as vigilantes to restore law and order to the market and the economy'. According to the *Journal*, Clinton's plans at the time of the election seemed to imply a $20 billion net increase in federal spending in the 1994 fiscal year. If bond buyers were to react with even modest anxiety to this prospect and send long-term rates up by, possibly, one percentage point, the US deficit would increase by $20 billion, effectively doubling to $40 billion the net cost of President Clinton's new policies. But this is an unlikely scenario, concluded the *Journal* reporters at the time because, according to Edward Yardeni of C.J. Lawrence Inc., the bond vigilantes are 'forcing Clinton to recognize that they will be *voting* every day the bond market is open', and if Clinton ignores them, he will find out very quickly who is in the 'driver's seat'. Makers of public policy, like corporate executives who want access to cheap finance, must acknowledge the structural power of disintermediated finance and incorporate debt security markets into their policy agendas and market plans at the earliest stages, and not as an afterthought. This precognition must in turn expand the authority of rating agencies as these institutions are a primary vehicle through which the actions of issuers are examined and judged.

The second factor which contributes to the regulatory capacity of rating agencies is their provision of knowledge to the increasingly de-

PASSING JUDGEMENT: CREDIT RATING PROCESSES

centralized financial markets. Strange has argued that knowledge structures exist which have the effect of valuing or devaluing different forms of knowledge.[59] She considers that a knowledge structure 'determines what knowledge is discovered, how it is stored, and who communicates it by what means to whom and on what terms'.[60] This structure, created by the dominant social forces and their major concerns, comprises a certain pattern of incentives and constraints on the development of forms of knowledge. The structural empowerment of the capital markets has been matched by a new valuation of certain forms of knowledge. The creation of the Euromarkets and the deregulation of capital movements characteristic of the past 20 years have greatly increased the mobility of money within the global economy.[61] Walter B. Wriston, the former Chair of Citicorp, has concluded from these developments that an 'information standard' now exists in which the mobility of investment funds is maximized through the rapid information transfers possible with contemporary communications technology.[62] This standard acts as a constraint on forces that would seek to create, for example, more narrowly regulated environments for investment, as the owners and managers of those funds will seek to circumvent possible controls on the freedom to maximize. However, raw information is not the most important consideration. What is crucial is the valuation placed on analytic frameworks having to do with economic and financial advice. This valuation has grown because of the increased uncertainty resulting from the greater volatility of international financial transfers. Corporations and governments want to reduce or at least specify the amount of risk they are assuming.[63] However, the increasing demand for this form of information and the consequent growth in its authoritativeness belies the processes of judgement which are central to it. These processes are based on certain assumptions tied to dominant interests in society, as Strange's conception of a knowledge structure implies. What is characteristic of this framework is the domination of narrow assumptions about market efficiency, in which undistorted price signals are the objective and state intervention is generally considered meddlesome.[64] Typically, 'transition costs' (such as unemployment) are not factored into the advice but assumed to be outweighed by the new environment created. However, this is merely an 'article of faith' of this framework, as Granovetter has pointed out.[65]

Foucault argued that 'particular technical devices' or 'intellectual technology' such as writing, listing, and numbering render a realm knowable and therefore potentially controllable. These procedures of inscription of 'objects' such as the economy, the corporation and so on are 'rendered in a particular conceptual form', which have implications for governance.[66] Rather than a series of ideas which exist in a political vacuum, knowledge is, in fact, as Smith has argued, a form of social organization with

ARTICLES

dominating and subordinating dimensions.[67] Her argument is that knowledge, once produced, loses its connection with those who have created it. It becomes 'externalized' and debates, findings and opinions come to stand alone and acquire 'facticity'.[68] Illustrating this phenomenon, Leo C. O'Neill observed that [sic] 'what makes our ratings such a strong factor in the market is that they take into account all the factors that surround a debt obligation and *reduce it to a letter symbol which is easily understood'*.[69] This process, which limits the conceptual universe of social actors involved, can be seen in the salience that ratings have acquired, for example, in the corporate planning process in the US.[70] Ratings are also ubiquitous in advertising. Both the Union Bank of Switzerland and Credit Suisse used ratings in print advertisements during 1992, most notably in *The Economist*. One of these advertisements, for Union Bank, began with the line, 'There are three standards for measuring banks: Moody's, S&P's and our clients.' Ratings have also been used in television commercials, most recently for Canada Trust.[71]

The final factor which has contributed to the regulatory capacity of rating agencies is the fact that they are institutions in what is an increasingly deinstitutionalized context, where traditional forms of authority and organization are less and less evident. Banks are no longer the sources of authority they once were, and governments have increasingly become (sic) 'nightwatchmen' over their capital markets rather than allocators or managers of capital investment. This leaves few institutions left with oversight and knowledge of the market, other than market participants. This must increase the structural power of debt rating agencies. That rating agency judgements are increasingly the subject of media analyses probably reflects the understanding that the 'bean counters' have become important sources of coordination within an increasingly decentralized system. A 'steering mechanism' seems to have developed,[72] albeit imperfectly, to contain some of the contradictions generated by the liberalization of markets and provide a 'degree of orderliness' to corporate behaviour.[73] According to Mintz and Schwartz, this 'orderliness' has two aspects. The first aspect relates to situations where the agencies 'directly intervene in the affairs of a corporation' and in 'certain circumstances . . . dictate corporate policy'.[74] The other dimension captures the broader sense of rating agency power as mechanisms of regulatory governance, through the exercise of structural power. In this dimension, the agencies can be seen to in part create a 'set of de facto rules' which 'responsible corporate citizens' must honour or 'risk financial disfavour'.[75] According to Mintz and Schwartz, this has created a situation of hegemonic control in which corporate activity is conditioned by the desire to appeal to the preferences of the rating agencies so as to gain access to cheap capital, or conversely, not to lose such competitively advantageous access.[76] It seems that the 'internationalized policy pro-

PASSING JUDGEMENT: CREDIT RATING PROCESSES

cess', which provides some measure of coordination within the GPE, occurs not just at the level of relations between states, but within transnational capital itself. Two considerations are important with regard to these transnational regulatory institutions. The first of these is the inadequacy of the existing interstate framework for macroeconomic coordination. Group of Seven or European Union structures have not proven themselves adequate to meet these challenges, as the global exchange crisis in the fall of 1992 has indicated. Yet the process of articulating and reinforcing the knowledge structure of economic and financial analysis through non-state institutions seems to have produced considerable change at the microeconomic policy level, as exemplified by some Latin American countries. The second consideration is that these forms of governance are, of course, private in nature, not subject to the usual forms of public accountability. Governance of the type identified here may reflect and in turn help to constitute a world order in which the demands of investment maximization are increasingly unchallenged. The following section explores the implications of rating agencies considered as regulatory mechanisms of governance.

IMPLICATIONS OF AGENCY GOVERNANCE

What you consumed over your lifetime was in part borrowed, and even today it still is . . . but at the end of the day if people don't believe it, then someone will pull the plug . . . the only difference between an African Third World state and a Canada or New Zealand is that they actually hit the end of their credit limit very quickly; we're given much more rope to hang ourselves with . . . but when your credit rating is on the line, that focuses the mind.[77]

Growth in the structural power of debt security rating can be assessed in three broad categories. The first set of implications is for investment, the second is for policy choice and the third is for national determination. What are the implications for investment? The investigation of rating agency governance for investment is broken down into three sets of questions. First, the question of cost of capital. Do ratings make a difference to the cost of debt? Second, there is the important issue of the perception of the role of ratings. What tells us that people in the market think that ratings are crucial? Finally, there is the question of the perception of rating agencies as powerful. Are bond raters acknowledged as quasi-public authorities? Is it a widespread view that bond raters are part of the context of the market, although there may be criticism of them at the margins?

The primary influence on the new issue and secondary corporate bond markets as a whole are shifts in interest rates.[78] These determine the price that issuers as a collective must offer to attract funds into their market and

ARTICLES

away from other investment opportunities such as banks, the stock market and real estate. Beyond these general influences there are the particular circumstances of the debt instrument itself. For example, whether the bond is backed by a sinking fund, in which the issuing company sets aside revenue for the purpose of debt repayment.[79] Other things being equal, the primary factor that distinguishes between different bonds is the creditworthiness of the borrower. However, as Foster observes: 'There is a dispute in the literature over whether debt-security ratings convey new information to capital market participants (that is, beyond that already in the public domain from other sources).'[80] It may be the case that the market has made its own assessment of the creditworthiness of the issuer. Quantitative analysis has not progressed sufficiently to attribute causation. This controversy is even more pronounced with regard to the impact of downgrades on yield spreads in the secondary market, as one rater observed.[81]

Despite the confusion in the quantitative literature, ratings are certainly perceived to have a major influence on the cost of capital by market participants.[82] It is these perceptions, rather than an inherent reality, that ultimately shapes the impact that ratings have on economic and financial policy. If issuers believe that ratings and the gradations between them are very important this will shape their commercial behaviour. If bond holders believe ratings to be important information this will influence their decisions to buy and sell debt. There are two levels on which market actors and others perceive ratings to be important. The first of these has to do with what Gill and Law have called the behavioural form of power.[83] At this level the actions of rating agencies are perceived to have a direct effect upon market perception and thus upon the views of debt issuers and their behaviour. As Mintz and Schwartz comment, at this level the agencies reveal their capacity to 'directly intervene in the affairs of a corporation'.[84] The clearest instance of this form of leverage is the impact of rating downgrades on the US auto industry. The history of rating actions goes back to the early 1970s, in the case of the Chrysler corporation. However, the most prominent recent example of the perceived behavioural leverage of rating agencies is General Motors (GM).

At the end of 1991, GM announced it had made a 'disastrous $4.5 billion loss' on operations.[85] Subsequently, the corporation declared that it would close 21 plants and cut 74,000 jobs.[86] According to Cox, this 'was intended, by appearing as a token of the corporation's intention to increase competitiveness, to deter a down-grading of its bond rating which would have increased the corporation's cost of borrowing'.[87] The perceived threat of a downgrade was reinforced by *The Wall Street Journal*, which noted that the threat of a rating reduction had 'hung heavily' over Robert C. Stempel, GM's chairman at the time, and had 'pushed' him to speed up the announcement of restructuring plans.[88] However, Stempel's

PASSING JUDGEMENT: CREDIT RATING PROCESSES

strategy did not work and the huge corporation was downgraded by Moody's in January 1992, and by Standard & Poor's in March of that year.[89] In justifying their action Moody's officials said that they considered the auto maker's restructuring plans were unlikely to solve its competitive problems.[90] Pressure on GM from the agencies did not end with these downgradings. According to Judith H. Dobrzynski of *Business Week*, 'the prospect of sinking credit ratings that would deny it access to equity and commercial paper, eventually prompted independent directors' to pressure GM's 'old guard', as personified by Chairman Stempel, the 'deliberative engineer', to quit in late October 1992.[91] Subsequently, further warnings of possible downgrades in the form of rating reviews came from the agencies, including the possibility of the relegation of GM debt to junk bond status.[92] Although the agencies subsequently acknowledged some improvement in operating performance at GM, what seems to have tipped the agencies into the further downgrades of late November 1992 and February 1993 were unfunded pension costs and escalating medical benefit liabilities which threatened to substantially degrade GM's balance sheet.[93] As S&P commented,

> Servicing its massive benefits obligations will be a substantial drain on the company's financial resources – and a significant competitive disadvantage – for the foreseeable future. . . . GM's unfunded pension liability increased to $14.0 billion at year-end 1992, from $8.4 billion one year earlier . . . the company has reported a retiree medical liability of $24 billion . . . reflecting not only assumption revisions, but the failure to negotiate with the United Auto Workers an agreement to cap future benefits. Adjusting for these liabilities effectively eliminates GM's consolidated net worth, in contrast to GM's reported equity of $6.2 billion at year-end 1992.[94]

Fearing this sort of judgement, which has hampered General Motors Acceptance Corporation (GM's finance company subsidiary) by raising the cost of commercial paper sales, GM has been forced to raise bank lines of credit instead, 'completing the largest bank credit package ever', with the attendant costs of intermediation, as discussed elsewhere in this article.[95] GM has also been raising relatively high-cost equity capital in response to the impact of reduced credit ratings on the cost of debt finance.[96]

The second type of leverage the agencies possess is structural power. Because it has to do with frameworks of thought, structural power is much harder to detail empirically and disentangle from other influences on the way managers think and act. However, it is also probably the more significant aspect of the relationship between rating agencies and the capital markets. A flavour of this structural power can be picked up from trade journals such as *Institutional Investor* and *Euromoney*, which act as

ARTICLES

mouthpieces for industry concerns about rating proficiency. These help to spread the understanding amongst pension fund managers – the lenders of funds – and corporate CFOs (chief finance officers) and their public sector equivalents – the borrowers of funds – that rating agencies expect more than just getting the numbers right from credits, that credits are expected to show foresight in management and business acumen, as well as financial prudence.[97] A measure of the structural power of the rating agencies can be gained from Glen Yago's observation that 'In some of my discussions in Washington [relating to the junk bond phenomenon], I found Congressional leaders who mistakenly thought that rating and credit analysis of bonds was done by government agencies and federally mandated.'[98] Another indication of the structural power of rating agencies is that US corporations often write ratings targets into their corporate plans for the coming financial year.[99] As Emmer commented, those corporations that failed to follow this path learnt in 1991, during a time of stringent bank credit rationing, the costs of not adopting this standard. Indeed, interviews in London confirmed the fact that recessionary conditions have heightened the structural leverage of rating agencies, as alternative sources of credit, such as bank loans, dry up and as difficult operating conditions induce a desire to play a more cautious commercial game.[100] These factors place a greater emphasis on taking the views of rating agencies into account prior to rating determinations.

If rating agencies have behavioural and structural leverage over corporations it becomes a question of whether rating agencies are a new form of financial intermediation? Has the old type of intermediation by banks simply given way to a new intermediary in the form of a rating agency? The answer to this question seems to be no. Rating agencies do not have the same relationship to borrowers and lenders as banks do. They neither lend nor borrow like banks, and thus have entirely different legal obligations. Nor do they place their balance sheets directly on the line when they issue a rating. While their credibility is at stake (and the importance of this cannot be understated) this does not establish the same incentives on behaviour as entering into a financial transaction. There is no pecuniary advantage to the rating agency from any particular rating determination, whereas this is the case with financial transactions between banks and their customers. Thus, the nature of the contract in either case places different incentives on banks and rating agencies which lead to different roles in the market and distinguishable effects on capital allocation. Bond raters simply want to issue a rating which reflects the probability of repayment at the contracted rate of interest at the right time. Banks want to minimize their cost of borrowing and maximize their real return from lending, within the context of competing suppliers of capital. The different incentives on bond raters and suppliers of capital is reflected in the common criticism of bond raters made within the

PASSING JUDGEMENT: CREDIT RATING PROCESSES

financial markets, that they look at creditworthiness in historical terms, once removed from what is happening in the market.[101]

A further implication for investment could be that the international growth of ratings through the creation of agencies modelled on American lines and through the establishment of foreign subsidiaries by the American agencies will export US models of financial orthodoxy. An element of this orthodoxy would appear to be a characteristically short-term investment horizon. This tendency reveals itself in the concern of pension fund managers with the quarterly performance of their assets and their readiness to dump a security in the secondary market when it is not performing at an acceptable yield.[102] As Ronald D. Peyton, of Callan Associates, a pension fund consulting firm, commented to *Business Week*, 'I doubt there's an investment manager in America whose contract doesn't have a 30-day cancellation clause.'[103] These time horizons, which raise the risks and therefore the cost of capital in the US, seem to exist because of the relatively distant relationship between suppliers and users of capital.[104] A major element of this antagonism is the lack of information investors have on the businesses they invest in. Only the 'outward manifestations' given in quarterly earnings data are considered funda-mental in investment decision making.[105] The high cost of capital has business investment and management consequences which inhibit long-term planning for competitiveness, as seems to have been the case in differences between Japan and the United States.[106] Debt security rating agencies contribute to the divorce between suppliers and users of capital to the extent that their analysis merely reflects orthodox US theories of finance, and perhaps to the extent that they seek a uniform comparative system of rating world wide. Moreover, ratings themselves, as expressions of a 'neutral' judgement about a corporation, can often take on a life of their own and 'crowd out' analysis by the investor. This may be especially the case with large institutional investors such as pension funds.[107] Ratings may also have the effect of making some corporations overly prudent in their business activities. Ratings may become objectives in themselves, enshrined in corporate plans even where this raises the cost of capital for the concern in question and lowers long-term profitability.[108] This mark of esteem seems to have been of special concern to the Swiss banks who, as discussed, use their AAA ratings in advertising. It would be ironic if the international growth ratings based on US methodology and assumptions led to this sort of outcome overseas, just as US business leaders are calling for a greater role for the equity investor in corporate governance, so as to create the sort of 'patient capital' that has existed in countries with a more 'relational investing' system.[109]

The second set of implications of debt security rating governance have to do with policy choice in the liberal democracies. Governments have

ARTICLES

increasingly financed their deficits with foreign debt during the 1980s. They 'now have to care about their international credit ratings' because they have to borrow in foreign currencies or have obligations to foreign investors.[110] In 1991, for example, non-resident investors held C$149.2 billion of Government of Canada and provincial bonds, an 84 per cent increase from the C$81.3 billion they held in 1985.[111] Governments are now much more effectively accountable to the 'bond vigilantes' and 'Masters of the Universe' and their agents than previously. Local policy decisions will be judged from the perspective of these external interests, within the context of assumptions about a liberal trade order and the free movement of capital within the GPE. Their debt exposures mean that governments are constrained to respond to this perspective. As Cox notes, among the very first acts of the new provincial government of Ontario in 1990 was for the recently installed Premier to visit New York to discuss credit issues with the rating agencies and other debt market players.[112] Even where the actual magnitude of a downgrade is minor, as was the case when Standard & Poor's reduced the rating on the Government of Canada's C$9 billion debt denominated in foreign currency, the impact on the credibility of the issuer can be immense. As *The Globe and Mail* (Toronto) commented at the time,

> While the downgrade is expected to increase the federal government's borrowing costs only marginally in the near future, [private] investment officials said the action sent alarms throughout international markets that Canada's financial health is eroding. 'It's a warning bell that the country's finances are deteriorating. This will only add to investor worries about Canada,' a New York investment executive said.[113]

For the developing countries, ratings provide perhaps the supreme seal of approval in their struggle to obtain development funds at a less than exorbitant cost, and with less risk than the recycled petrodollars they obtained from banks on floating interest rate contracts during the 1970s. Accordingly, in a recent *Euromoney* supplement on Mexico, there is a lengthy discussion of the probability of that country acquiring an investment grade rating from Moody's and S&P.[114]

Finally, there is the question of national determination and response to the growth of the US agencies' extra-US activities. Ten years ago Moody's and S&P had no analysts outside the USA. In 1993, they each had around 100 employees altogether in Europe, Japan and Australia. S&P opened a new branch in Toronto during the spring of 1993. Questions arise then, especially in times of tension and transformation in European–American and Japanese–American relations, about the aspirations of the major United States rating agencies. Will countries find that the regulation of their financial systems, ways of reporting financial information, industry

PASSING JUDGEMENT: CREDIT RATING PROCESSES

practices and financial cultures change in accord with an American agenda? Who is likely to resist the spread of the American agencies? Is the internationalization of rating simply another step toward greater global financial integration, or do the American agencies represent a more parochial interest in financial organization? There is growing resentment toward the US agencies in Europe which seems to have crystallized around the 1991 downgrading of Credit Suisse, the early 1992 downgrading of Swiss Bank Corporation and the longer-term problem that foreign agencies have had in getting SEC recognition in the USA as Nationally Recognized Statistical Rating Organizations (NRSROs).[115] NRSRO status is important because under many state laws US pension funds may not purchase bonds that have not been given an investment grade rating by an NRSRO, but only agencies rating US issues have been given this status by the SEC.[116] These are all US agencies with the exception of IBCA, which has established a branch in New York, seemingly in order to qualify. Regulation is much less significant in Europe, although this is a developing situation. These tensions have led to private discussions in London, Paris and Frankfurt about the establishment of a possible Europe-wide agency to compete with the major US-based agencies.[117] In addition to this concern, which reflects the cross-national significance of the SEC, Europeans complain that 'being based in the US, the two global agencies simply don't understand non-US businesses'.[118]

CONCLUSIONS

The argument of this article is that debt security rating agencies are exemplars of the new location and form of authority that is shaping international relations in the emerging world order. There are three aspects to this authority. The first has to do with the division of authority between state and non-state institutions, the second concerns the distribution of power among non-state institutions, and finally, the third has to do with conflict between rising and declining sectors of finance. The rise of the GPE and the decline of exogenous threats has changed the balance of authority between institutions of government and institutions of global civil society. Global civil society has become relatively empowered while state institutions have become less significant in the way things get done. Although both elected authority and what might be called 'manifest authority' are bound together in many ways in terms of the reproduction of political order, the argument here is that the shift in authority, as exemplified by debt security rating, has changed the character of that order in significant ways.

The second aspect of authority in the emerging world order to consider is its sectoral character. Although a shift from 'high' to 'low' politics, and

ARTICLES

from state to non-state institutions within the GPE has been identified, a relocation of authority within the GPE itself is observed. This transformation has involved the erosion of the control formerly exercised by some of the great industrial concerns, and a corresponding increase in the leverage available to financial forces and those industries in which information is the raw material and knowledge the product. The downgrading of General Motors by the rating agencies reflects this shift. Accordingly, finance may, to use Robert Cox's words, have increasingly 'become decoupled from production to become an independent power, an autocrat over the real economy'.[119]

The final aspect of the relocation of authority to consider are the transformations within the financial realm itself. International political economy has expended a great deal of its initial research effort on studying the activities of the major international banks and their regulation. This made a lot of sense when the LDC debt crisis threatened to overwhelm the international credit system. However, that risk did not materialize and banks have subsequently become the preserve of the most marginal users of funds in the United States, and increasingly elsewhere. In global capital markets, banks have been exposed to much greater competition by their governments and have come under pressure to play the markets like any other investor. The increased cost of this activity has been passed along to funds users, raising the cost of capital to them, reducing their demand and spurring the drive to securitization. With the growth of alternative mechanisms for gathering information about credits and producing saleable knowledge about them, the rationale for banking intermediation of credit allocation is threatened. Banks will – in the medium term at least – continue to be major pools of funds because of their retail activities. But they will become less like lenders and more like portfolio managers, and consequently less like sources of authority in the market and more like just another part of the market itself.[120] The creation of knowledge and the passing of judgement, based on a strategic position in the production of financial, economic and policy information, will increasingly fall to debt security rating agencies.

What will be the effect of all this upon the emerging world order? Two probable scenarios come to mind. On one hand, the regulatory mechanisms of governance identified in this article could engender a much more thoroughgoing hegemony than has been seen before. During the Cold War, the coherence of transnational relations was maintained by exogenous threats from the Soviet Union. The regulatory mechanism identified, and perhaps others like it, have the character of endogenous forces, at least as far as the advanced industrial societies are concerned. This will probably mute opposition, or as seems to be the case in Europe, channel that opposition into rating competition. For the developing countries, it seems that they are now playing a game with a very different

PASSING JUDGEMENT: CREDIT RATING PROCESSES

referee. Rating agencies, as mechanisms of governance without government do not invoke quite the same nationalist hostility that interstate regulation seems to, especially for elites in these countries, infused with a neo-liberal business ethos. The medium-term effect could be to further the strategy of new constitutionalism by removing many areas of domestic policy debate from the political arena, and to undermine radical intellectual elites as a new form of intellectual orthodoxy – economic and financial analysis – becomes the dominant framework in which policy issues are cast. On the other hand, this form of governance may be fragile. An order characterized by governance based in global civil society could conceivably be less dynamic than one with an active political executive. This could reduce the adaptive capacity of the global system, just as threats from transboundary problems like global warming become much more of a concern. It will certainly be the case that this order will be less inclusive than in the past. This may mean that the trend to urban decay typified by the City of Detroit may accelerate and spread to other areas of the world as they too come to be judged by this regulatory mechanism.

NOTES

Versions of this research have been presented at the annual meetings of the British International Studies Association, University College Swansea, 14–16 December 1992, the International Studies Association, Acapulco, 23–27 March 1993, and the Canadian Political Science Association, Carleton University, Ottawa, 6–8 June 1993. Among those who have helped to clarify the arguments and text are Stephen Gill, Robert W. Cox, David Leyton-Brown, Susan Strange, Eric Helleiner, Robert J. O'Brien, Randall Germain, Kendall Stiles, Tony Porter, Mark Neufeld, Barry Gills, Ronen Palan, Mark Amen, R.B.J. Walker, James N. Rosenan, Lewis W. Pauly, Chris Robinson and Andrew McDonald. For interview access and documentation, acknowledgements are due to Leo C. O'Neill, Glenn S. Goldberg, Edward Z. Emmer, Joanne W. Rose and Mark Goebel of Standard & Poor's Ratings Group, Dana B. Collins at Moody's Investors Service, Claire G. Cohen of Fitch Investors Service, and Brian I. Neysmith of Canadian Bond Rating Service. Responsibility for the arguments and any errors of fact remain mine.

1 This quotation, from a speech by Daniel Webster in the United States Senate, 18 March 1834, appears on a plaque above the main entrance to Moody's Investors Service, New York City.
2 John J. Mearsheimer, 'Back to the Future: instability in Europe after the Cold War', *International Security* 15, no. 1 (summer 1990), pp. 5–56.
3 Susan Strange, *States and Markets: An Introduction to International Political Economy* (New York: Basil Blackwell, 1988), p. 104.
4 Ibid., p. 108.
5 'Fear of finance: a survey of the world economy', *The Economist*, 19 September 1992, p. 5.
6 By global civil society, I include the ideas, non-state institutions and social forces that have developed in concert with the global political economy. I am not referring here to a participatory conception of society as a counterhegemonic force, say, that developed in eastern Europe at the time of the

ARTICLES

1989 revolutions. Instead, I use civil society as an analytical category in the ideal-typical sense, as discussed by John Keane. See his 'Introduction' in John Keane (ed.) *Civil Society and the State: New European Perspectives* (London: Verso, 1988). I thank Barry Gills and Ronen Palan for pointing out the potential confusion in my previous use of this term.

7 I am grateful to Susan Strange for pointing out the salience of non-governmental authorities such as these in private correspondence with the author, 14 January 1992.

8 Two major processes are evident in the development of the GPE. The first of these, the internationalization or globalization of capital, is the growth in the mobility and fungibility of investment in both its direct and portfolio forms. The second process has to do with changes in the policy outputs of governments, which, taken together, give rise to the transnationalization of state authority. On the global political economy, see Stephen Gill, *American Hegemony and the Trilateral Commission* (Cambridge: Cambridge University Press, 1990), p. 243, and Stephen Gill and David Law, *The Global Political Economy: Perspectives, Problems, and Policies* (Baltimore, MD: The Johns Hopkins University Press, 1988), pp. xvii–xxiii.

9 James N. Rosenau, 'The relocation of authority in a shrinking world'. *Comparative Politics* 24, no. 3, April 1992, p. 256.

10 Ibid.

11 Ibid.

12 Ibid. On this theme see also David N. Gibbs, 'Taking the state back out: business power and the fallacies of statism', paper presented to the annual meeting of the American Political Science Association, Chicago, September 1992.

13 Stephen Gill, 'Gramsci and global politics: towards a post-hegemonic research agenda' in Stephen Gill (ed.) *Gramsci, Historical Materialism and International Relations* (Cambridge: Cambridge University Press, 1993), pp. 10–11.

14 Yale H. Ferguson and Richard W. Mansbach, 'Between celebration and despair: constructive suggestions for future international theory', *International Studies Quarterly* 35, no. 4, December 1991, p. 376.

15 Ibid.

16 Theodor Mommsen, cited by Leonard Krieger, 'Authority' in Philip P. Wiener (ed.) *Dictionary of the History of Ideas: Studies in Selected Pivotal Ideas*, vol. I (New York: Charles Scribner's Sons, 1973), p. 143.

17 Ferguson and Mansbach, op. cit. note 14, p. 376.

18 James N. Rosenau, 'Governance, order, and change in world politics' in James N. Rosenau and Ernst-Otto Czempiel (eds) *Governance without Government: Order and Change in World Politics* (Cambridge: Cambridge University Press, 1992), p. 4. On Foucault, see Peter Miller and Nikolas Rose, 'Governing the economy', *Economy and Society* 19, no. 1, February 1990, pp. 1–31.

19 Rosenau, op. cit. note 18, p. 5.

20 Ibid.

21 Ibid.

22 Ibid., p. 6.

23 Saskia Sassen, *The Global City: New York, London, Tokyo* (Princeton, NJ: Princeton University Press, 1991), p. 6.

24 Graham Bannock and William Manser, *International Dictionary of Finance* (London: Hutchinson/*The Economist*, 1989), p. 86.

25 On disintermediation, see Bannock and Manser, ibid. p. 66. Also see David Stimpson (ed.) *Global Credit Analysis* (London/New York: IFR

PASSING JUDGEMENT: CREDIT RATING PROCESSES

Publishing/Moody's Investors Service, 1991), pp. 4–11. Commercial paper is an unsecured, short-term debt obligation, which matures within one year of issue. On commercial paper, see John Downes and Jordan Elliot Goodman, *Dictionary of Finance and Investment Terms*, 3rd edn (New York: Barron's, 1991), p. 76.

26 These figures are taken from the *Balance of Payments Yearbook* (Washington: International Monetary Fund, various years) as cited in Randall Germain, 'From money to finance: the international organization of credit', paper presented to the 1992 annual meeting of the Canadian Political Science Association, Prince Edward Island, June 1992, p. 14. Further evidence of the disintermediation trend can be found in Stimpson, op. cit. note 25, pp. 4–11.

27 Bannock and Manser, op. cit. note 24, p. 34.

28 Germain, op. cit. note 26, p. 14.

29 'Time to leave: a survey of world banking'. *The Economist*, 2 May 1992, p. 9.

30 On the impact of communications technology on this information problem in the securities markets, see Richard O'Brien, *Global Financial Integration: The End of Geography* (London: The Royal Institute of International Affairs/Pinter Publishers, 1992), p. 10.

31 I am grateful to Chris Robinson for pointing out the transaction cost argument to me. Further elaboration of this approach can be found in Oliver E. Williamson, *The Economic Institutions of Capitalism: Firms, Markets, Relational Contracting* (New York: Free Press, 1985).

32 Interview with Leo C. O'Neill, President, Standard & Poor's Ratings Group, New York City, 18 August 1992.

33 Interview with Edward Z. Emmer, Executive Managing Director, Corporate Finance, Standard & Poor's Ratings Group, New York City, 17 August 1992.

34 Interview with Joanne W. Rose, Vice President and General Counsel, Standard & Poor's Ratings Group, New York City, 16 February 1993.

35 Rupert Bruce, 'Debt-rating agencies fill the gap'. *The International Herald Tribune*, 14–15 November 1992, p. 11.

36 Susan Greenberg, 'New rating agency causes a stir', *The Guardian*, 13 February 1993.

37 Richard Waters, 'Rating agencies complete merger', *The Financial Times*, 21 October 1992.

38 *Moody's Investors Service: Consistency, Reliability, Integrity* (New York: Moody's Investors Service, ND), p. 3.

39 George Foster, *Financial Statement Analysis*, 2nd edn (Englewood Cliffs, NJ: Prentice-Hall, 1986), p. 498.

40 Standard & Poor's Ratings Group, *Ratings Handbook*, vol. 1, no. 5, August 1992, p. 183.

41 Interview with Leo C. O'Neill.

42 For a complete breakdown of these scales for S&P, see the S&P *Ratings Handbook*, August 1992, pp. 183–7. For Moody's scales, see Stimpson, op. cit. note 25, pp. 71–86.

43 Standard & Poor's Ratings Group, *S&P's Corporate Finance Criteria* (New York: Standard & Poor's Corporation, 1992), p. 9.

44 Interview with Brian I. Neysmith, President, Canadian Bond Rating Service, Montreal, 16 June 1992.

45 Vivian Lewis, 'Too big for their boots?', *The Banker*, October 1990, p. 12.

46 *S&P's Corporate Finance Criteria*, op. cit. note 43, p. 15.

47 Interview with Joanne W. Rose.

48 With regard to ratio analysis, S&P have developed and published sectoral criteria for debt leverage positions that influence their judgement of any

ARTICLES

particular issuer's balance sheet. See *S&P's Corporate Finance Criteria*, op. cit. note 43, p. 9.

49 The search for the relative weighting of these factors in determining ratings has fostered an extensive literature of its own. Although this work emphasizes the significance of administrative and political variables, these have proven stubbornly resistant to the application of quantitative analytical tools. See, for example, George S. Cluff and Paul G. Farnham, 'A problem of discrete choice: Moody's Municipal Bond Ratings', *Journal of Economics and Business*, vol. 37, December 1985, pp. 277–302.

50 Barbara Presley Noble, 'A downgraded Detroit cries foul', *The New York Times*, Tuesday 3 November 1992, p. C1.

51 Standard & Poor's Ratings Group, *Standard & Poor's Ratings Guide* (New York: McGraw-Hill, 1979), p. 231.

52 On this concern, see Margaret A. Elliott, 'Rating the debt raters', *Institutional Investor* 22, no. 14, December 1988, pp. 109–12 and Fran Hawthorne, 'Rating the raters', *Institutional Investor* 24, no. 9, July 1990, pp. 121–7. See also 'OK, so what is quality?', *Euromoney* supplement, September 1991, pp. 36–44 (especially p. 40).

53 *S&P's Corporate Finance Criteria*, op. cit. note 43, p. 9.

54 For a discussion of surveillance in these terms, see Christopher Dandeker, *Surveillance, Power and Modernity: Bureaucracy and Discipline from 1700 to the Present Day* (New York: St Martin's Press, 1990), pp. 39–40. See also Anthony Giddens, *The Nation-State and Violence* (Berkeley and Los Angeles, CA: University of California Press, 1987).

55 Standard & Poor's Ratings Group, *S&P's Structured Finance Criteria* (New York: Standard & Poor's Corporation, 1988), pp. 16–17.

56 Tom Wolfe, *The Bonfire of the Vanities* (New York: Bantam, 1988), p. 12.

57 On behavioural and structural power see Hugh Ward, 'Structural power – a contradiction in terms?', *Political Studies* 35, no. 4, December 1987, pp. 593–610; Strange, op. cit. note 3, pp. 24–9; Gill and Law, op. cit. note 8, pp. 71–5; Stephen Gill and David Law, 'Global hegemony and the structural power of capital', *International Studies Quarterly* 33, no. 4, December 1989, pp. 475–99.

58 Douglas R. Sease and Constance Mitchell, 'The vigilantes: world's bond buyers gain huge influence over US fiscal plans', *The Wall Street Journal*, 6 November 1992, p. A1. Italics applied for emphasis. For a subsequent treatment of this issue once Clinton was inaugurated, see Thomas T. Vogel, Jr and Terrence Donnelly, 'Treasury bond prices surge on strong buying at 30-year sale and Clinton deficit remarks', *The Wall Street Journal*, 12 February 1993, p. C16.

59 Strange, op. cit. note 3, pp. 115–34.

60 Ibid., p. 117.

61 Ibid., pp. 102–4.

62 Jeffry A. Frieden, *Banking on the World: The Politics of American International Finance* (New York: Harper & Row, 1987), p. 114. See also Walter B. Wriston, *The Twilight of Sovereignty: How the Information Revolution is Transforming Our World* (New York: Charles Scribner's Sons, 1992), pp. 55–73.

63 It may also be the case that this form of knowledge has gained new salience because of the development of what Castells has termed the 'informational mode of development', in which, as in foreign exchange or stock speculation, 'knowledge intervenes upon knowledge itself in order to generate higher productivity'. Manuel Castells, *The Informational City: Information Technology, Economic Restructuring, and the Urban–Regional Process* (Oxford: Basil Blackwell, 1989), p. 10.

PASSING JUDGEMENT: CREDIT RATING PROCESSES

64 Stephen Gill, 'The emerging world order and European change', in Ralph Miliband and Leo Panitch (eds) *New World Order? Socialist Register 1992* (London: Merlin, 1992), p. 177.

65 Mark Granovetter, 'Economic action and social structure: the problem of embeddedness', in Mark Granovetter and Richard Swedberg (eds) *The Sociology of Economic Life* (Boulder, CO: Westview, 1992), p. 73.

66 Miller and Rose, op. cit. note 18, pp. 6–7. On this theme, see also William H. Melody, 'The information society: implications for economic institutions and market theory', *Journal of Economic Issues* 19, no. 2, June 1985, pp. 523–39.

67 Dorothy E. Smith, *The Conceptual Practices of Power: A Feminist Sociology of Knowledge* (Toronto: University of Toronto Press, 1990), p. 61.

68 Ibid., p. 66.

69 Interview with Leo C. O'Neill. Italics have been applied for emphasis.

70 Interview with Edward Z. Emmer.

71 'Independent bond rating agencies judge Canada Trust as safe as the major banks', broadcast on Canadian Broadcasting Corporation, station CBLT Toronto, January–March 1992.

72 Gill, op. cit. note 8, p. 214.

73 Beth Mintz and Michael Schwartz, 'Sources of intercorporate unity', in Michael Schwartz (ed.) *The Structure of Power in America: The Corporate Elite as a Ruling Class* (New York: Holmes & Meier, 1987), p. 22.

74 Ibid., p. 30.

75 Ibid., p. 22.

76 Ibid., p. 30.

77 Comments by Simon Upton, New Zealand Associate Minister of Finance, *W5 with Eric Malling*, CTV television network, Toronto, 28 February 1993.

78 Staff of the New York Institute of Finance, *How the Bond Market Works* (New York: New York Institute of Finance, 1988), p. 10.

79 Ibid., pp. 175–6.

80 Foster, op. cit. note 39, pp. 515–16.

81 Interview with Brian I. Neysmith.

82 It was precisely this constraint, and the high interest rates charged by banks, that led to the issuance of high-yield or junk bonds starting in the late 1970s, based on arguments made by Michael Milken, formerly of Drexel Burnham Lambert. As a result of research he had conducted at business school, Milken argued that non-investment grade credits were a lot less likely to default than rating agencies had maintained, and that they were therefore deserving of better ratings, or at least better access to non-bank finance at discounted prices. On Milken and his arguments for high-yield financing, see Glen Yago, *Junk Bonds: How High Yield Securities Restructured Corporate America* (New York: Oxford University Press, 1991), pp. 14–27, and Alvin Toffler, *Power Shift: Knowledge, Wealth, and Violence at the Edge of the 21st Century* (New York: Bantam, 1990), pp. 43–57. I thank Stephen Gill for pointing this out to me.

83 Gill and Law, op. cit. note 57, p. 480.

84 Mintz and Schwartz, op. cit. note 73, p. 30.

85 Kathleen Kerwin, James B. Treece and Zachary Schiller, 'GM is meaner, but hardly leaner', *Business Week*, 19 October 1992, p. 30.

86 Joseph B. White and Bradley A. Stertz, 'GM's debt is downgraded by Moody's', *The Wall Street Journal*, 8 January 1992, p. A2.

87 Robert W. Cox, 'Global perestroika', in Ralph Miliband and Leo Panitch (eds) *New World Order? Socialist Register 1992* (London: Merlin, 1992), p. 29.

88 White and Stertz, op. cit. note 86.

ARTICLES

89 Joseph B. White, 'General Motors debt ratings are cut by S&P', *The Wall Street Journal*, 16 March 1992, p. A2.

90 White and Stertz, op. cit. note 86.

91 Judith H. Dobrzynski, 'A GM postmortem: lessons for corporate America', *Business Week*, 9 November 1992, p. 87; Kathleen Kerwin, James B. Treece and Zachary Schiller, 'Crisis at GM: turmoil at the top reflects the depth of its troubles', *Business Week*, 9 November 1992, p. 84.

92 Joseph B. White, 'S&P issues new warning on GM stock', *The Wall Street Journal*, 12 November 1992, p. A3.

93 Ibid., and Joseph B. White and Neal Templin, 'GM to disclose more details on pension gap', *The Wall Street Journal*, 16 November 1992, p. A3. Joseph B. White, 'GM's ratings on debt, paper cut by Moody's', *The Wall Street Journal*, 25 November 1992, p. A3. Kathleen Kerwin, 'GM isn't running on fumes – yet', *Business Week*, 30 November 1992, pp. 35–6. Joseph B. White, 'GM ratings are downgraded by S&P, but stock jumps on car sales data', *The Wall Street Journal*, 4 February 1993, p. A4.

94 'General Motors Corp. and related entities', *Standard & Poor's Creditweek*, 22 February 1993, p. 44 and 46.

95 'GM secures $20.6 billion in credit lines with banks', *The Wall Street Journal*, 20 May 1993, p. A3.

96 Kerwin, op. cit. note 93, and White, op. cit. note 92.

97 See, for example, Ida Picker, 'The ratings game', *Institutional Investor* 25, no. 9, August 1991, pp. 73–7, and 'OK, so what is quality?', *Euromoney* supplement, September 1991, pp. 36–44.

98 Yago, op. cit. note 82, p. 5.

99 Interview with Edward Z. Emmer.

100 Interviews that contributed to this view were, amongst others, those with Jock Paton, Director, Standard & Poor's Ratings Group, London, 9 December 1992, and Jan B. Konstanty, Managing Director, Moody's Investors Service, London, 11 December 1992.

101 Hawthorne, op. cit. note 52.

102 'Opening our eyes to market myopia', *Business Week* special issue, 'Reinventing America: meeting the new challenges of a global economy', 1992, p. 134.

103 Ibid., p. 138.

104 See Peter Hall, *Governing the Economy: The Politics of State Intervention in Britain and France* (Oxford: Polity, 1986) for an analysis of relations between suppliers and users of capital.

105 Michael T. Jacobs, *Short-Term America: The Causes and Cures of Our Business Myopia* (Boston, MA: Harvard Business School Press, 1991), p. 9.

106 Ibid., p. 12.

107 Ibid., p. 17.

108 Interview with Edward Z. Emmer.

109 'Opening Our Eyes', op. cit. note 102, pp. 134 and 138.

110 Cox, op. cit. note 87, p. 29.

111 Jacquie McNish, 'S&P cuts Canada's rating on foreign currency debt', *The Globe and Mail* (Toronto), 15 October 1992, p. B1. See also 'Canada keeps triple-A debt rating', *The Globe and Mail* (Toronto), 29 January 1993, p. B9.

112 Cox, op. cit. note 87, p. 29.

113 McNish, op. cit. note 111.

114 'Flavour of the month'. *Euromoney* supplement, 'Mexico: no turning back', January 1992, pp. 24–33.

115 'Swiss cheesed off with rating agency', *The Globe and Mail* (Toronto), 5 November 1991, p. B9.

PASSING JUDGEMENT: CREDIT RATING PROCESSES

116 Interviews with Leo C. O'Neill and Joanne W. Rose. The two Canadian agencies (Canadian Bond Rating Service and Dominion Bond Rating Service) were in the process of reapplying for NRSRO status during the summer of 1993.

117 Waters, op. cit. note 37.

118 Richard Waters, 'The awesome power of a triple-A', *The Financial Times*, 14 May 1992.

119 Cox, op. cit. note 87, p. 29. See also Peter Drucker, 'The changed world economy', *Foreign Affairs* 64, no. 4, spring 1986, p. 783.

120 'Time to Leave', op. cit. note 29, p. 11.

[11]

Global Governance 3 (1997),83–102

From Place to Planet:
Local Knowledge and
Global Environmental Governance

⊕

Ronnie D. Lipschutz

Even though there is desperate need for worldwide change, limited by the knowledge my place makes possible, I hesitate to legislate the law of other places. . . . To act in the world and make it better you have to be someone, be somewhere, tied to institutions, related to people. And be limited by that body, place, and time. You have to have a place, a home.
—*Wade Sikorski, 1993*[1]

One of the central issues facing human civilization at the end of the twentieth century is governance: Who rules? Whose rules? What rules? What kind of rules? At what level? In what form? Who decides? On what basis? Many of the problems that give rise to questions such as these are transnational and transboundary in nature, with the result that the notion of global "management" has acquired increasing currency in many circles. This is especially true given that economic globalization seems to point toward a single integrated world economy, in which the sovereign state appears to be losing much of its authority and control over domestic and foreign affairs. Contrary to the expectations of neofunctionists and others, however, global economic integration is not generating a parallel process in the political realm. Rather, what we see is political fragmentation and the emergence of a multilevel and very diffuse system of governance, within which "local" management, knowledge, and rule are of growing importance to coordination within domestic and international political "hierarchies" as well as among regions and countries. The issue of environmental protection and restoration, in which these contrary trends are evident, illustrates this proposition. In this essay,[2] I examine the relationship between local knowledge and global environmental governance, and the role of what I call "global civil society" in fostering such governance. I propose that, to a growing degree, it is in functional areas such as these that we must look to see the emerging outlines of twenty-first-century global politics.

Knowledge is defined here as a system of conceptual relationships—both scientific and social—that explains cause and effect and offers the possibility of human intervention and manipulation in order to influence or direct the outcomes of certain processes. *Local knowledge* encompasses such knowledge as well as the specific and sui generis social and cultural elements of bounded social units. *Civil society* includes those political, cultural, and social organizations of modern societies that are autonomous of the state but part of the mutually constitutive relationship between state and society. *Global civil society* extends this concept into the transnational realm, where it constitutes something along the lines of a "regime" composed of local, national, and global nongovernmental organizations (NGOs). Finally, *governance* is, in Ernst-Otto Czempiel's words, the "capacity to get things done without the legal competence to command that they be done."[3] In this sense, it is a form of authority rather than jurisdiction.

I begin with a discussion of the much-noted phenomenon of economic integration accompanied by political fragmentation, and its political and social implications. Although, at first glance, this might not seem relevant to the question of environmental governance, it is central. If there is a causal, or even dialectical, relation between the two processes, global governance becomes a quite different proposition from "global management." I propose that such governance is as likely to rest with management functions centered in civil society, both local and global, as it is with states and governments.

Next, I consider what global civil society can and cannot do where environmental protection and restoration are concerned. It cannot—in the near term, at least—change the big structures or systems that drive much of the destruction and degradation of nature of which we are increasingly aware. At the same time, however, agency and action are not impossible, and alternatives are not foreclosed. I then consider a central question implied by this analysis: Where must people act, and under what conditions, in order to begin a process of changing practices on a larger scale? Here I consider the ways in which the menu of possibilities in any given place is constrained by those big structures but not fully determined by them. To paraphrase others: Women and men can make history, so long as they are aware of the conditions established by those who have come before.

Finally, I conclude with a discussion of governance and the problem of, as one author has put it, "coordination without hierarchy." I argue that we must look to the growing number of alliances, coalitions, networks, and projects that link together more local environmental protection and management efforts and work with a wide range of transnational and international organizations. This emerging system of global governance is functionalist rather than comprehensive: it does not presage a world government with black helicopters, but it does add up to more than an "international community."

W(h)ither the Global Polity:
Growing Together or Coming Apart?

Back in 1990—in what now seems like ancient times—the Public Broad-casting System televised a miniseries titled *After the Warming*. With James Burke as writer/commentator/guide, the program provided graphic illus-trations of an imagined future in 2050, looking back on a chaotic past dis-rupted by global warming. The impacts were, of course, widespread and horrific: how else to illustrate the premise of the show? But the proffered solution was somewhat hubristic: a "Planetary Management Authority" (PMA) run, "of course" (as Burke put it), by Japan. The PMA—housed in a futuristic building that even today looks garish and anachronistic—would consist of a formidable system of computers and sensing devices that, utilizing a complex climatic model, could assess the impacts on global climate of human activities all over the planet. As necessary, the PMA would issue appropriate directives to mitigate or ameliorate the cli-matic consequences: a global panopticon, in other words (but within a prison in which the inmates would be free to run riot); not a World State but a World Manager, with complete authority and power.

Such a centralized management system is quite improbable. It flies in the face not only of logic but also of a contemporary global politics that is characterized as much by fragmentation within existing polities as global economic integration among them. But why are economic integra-tion and political fragmentation linked, and what is the relevance of this process to the arguments advanced in this essay? The relationship between the two suggests that the global management problem will be even more difficult than has been so far imagined, inasmuch as the number of sovereign or semisovereign entities participating in world politics—and subject to transboundary effects—could well increase over the coming decades from the fewer than two hundred we now have to many more. That is not the only complication: Many of these entities may not even ex-ercise effective political control over their own juridical territories, which is now the case in various "failed" states—states subject to ethnic wars and other types of conflict—around the world. Environmental protection, and the governance it entails, might well require political arrangements differ-ent from the international cooperation among states we now take for granted, a point to which I will return.

Global economic integration is a condition whose origins are to be found in the nineteenth century, with the Industrial Revolution, the rise of English liberalism, and the institutionalization of free trade as propagated by the Manchester School. With fits, starts, and retreats, such integration has spread into virtually all corners of the world, creating myriad webs of material linkages and changing even the lives of those who, at first glance, seem quite remote from the global economy. The fact that such integration has become so widespread does not, of course, mean that all places in the world share in the resulting benefits, as growing domestic and global gaps between rich and poor indicate. But the global economy requires such disparities if it is to operate most efficiently. Indeed, it is uneven development that makes capitalism so dynamic, and it is the constant search for new combinations of factors of comparative advantage that drives innovation; the fact that there are multiple economic "systems" present in any one location simply adds to the dynamism of that process. Today's comparative advantage may, consequently, be tomorrow's competitive drag.

The political implications of such a process have not been given much serious thought. Contrary to the arguments of much of neoclassical trade theory and political advocates of free trade, comparative advantage no longer appears to be a feature of states as a whole—it has never really been, although the loosening of state control over national economies has made this more visible in recent years—but of region and locale, where the combination of material, technological, and intellectual factors is, perhaps only momentarily, fortuitous. The specific comparative advantages of a place such as Silicon Valley—in many ways, a historical accident as much as the result of deliberate policy—may in the future have only limited spillover in terms of a country as a whole. These conditions, moreover, seem not to be easily reproduced in the short term. The competition among places to attract investment and jobs thus becomes more of a zero-sum than a positive-sum game, and this point is not lost, for example, on U.S. states and cities that have established foreign trade offices in various global cities and regularly send trade missions abroad as well.

Capital has its choice of locations in which to invest and can pick and choose among them. Cities, communities, places—and to a certain degree, labor—are much more constrained, and have a limited menu of factors of production that can be flaunted to attract capital. An article in the *San Francisco Examiner,* describing the activities of a consulting firm providing city and regional marketing programs for economic development, compared economic development programs to those "of an international arms dealer—selling weapons to one ruler and then making a pitch to the neighboring potentate based on the new threat. Part of the pitch for these [economic development] programs is that a region needs its own program to survive against the rival programs of other areas."[4] Such competition may become the cause of considerable political antagonism, against both the neighbors who win and the authorities who have contributed to these conditions of competitive struggle in the first place.

How such antagonisms play themselves out is contextual and contingent, of course, and often depends on preexisting social and political "fault lines" that fracture under the pressures of real, potential, or imagined competition. In some places, these fault lines were intended to be administrative but were drawn up in ethnic or national terms; in other places, the fault lines are linguistic, religious, clan based, "tribal," or even vaguely cultural. It goes almost without saying that those places in which people have fallen to killing each other have nothing to offer global capital—they have quite literally fallen "out of history"—whereas those places able to break away from the political grip of larger polities, as Slovenia escaped the competitive drag of Serbia, could find themselves well placed to participate in the global economy. Inevitably, this process of political fracturing and fragmentation will lead to a much more complex and "neofederalized" global system, which our modern concepts of international system, nation-state, and power will hardly begin to describe.

Some have suggested that we confront a "new medievalism"; others have proposed as organizing principles "heteronomy" or "heterarchy."[5] In discussing the first of these three concepts, Ole Wæver argues that "for some four centuries, political space was organized through the principle of territorially defined units with exclusive rights inside, and a special kind of relations on the outside: International relations, foreign policy, without any superior authority. There is no longer one level that is clearly *the* most important to refer to but, rather, a set of overlapping authorities."[6] What is important here is the concept of *authority*—in the sense of the ability to get things done because of one's legitimacy as opposed to one's ability to apply force or coercion—rather than "law" or "power." As John Ruggie points out, in a political system—even a relatively unsocialized one—*who* has "the right to act as a power" (or an authority) is at least as important as the *capability* of actors to force others to do their bidding.[7]

In the emerging heteronomy, authority will be increasingly fragmented among many centers of political action, often on the basis of specific issues rather than territories. In a way, this will generate a form of functionalism (really, functional differentiation) rather than federalism, inasmuch as different authorities will deal with specific problems—some spatial, others not—toxic wastes moving through a neighborhood here, protection of a marsh there. And because these problems are embedded within a global economic system, such functionalism will inevitably reach beyond localities into and through that global system.

This is not the same as the functionalism of the 1960s. Whereas older theories of functionalism envisioned political *integration* as the outcome of international functional coordination, it appears that contemporary functionalism may lead to something quite different, a consequence of the marriage of local knowledge and governance at multiple levels. In the present instance, functionalism can be understood as a consequence of rapid *innovation*, of the generation of new scientific-technical and social knowledge(s) required to address different types of contemporary issues and problems.[8] Inasmuch as there is too much scientific and social knowledge for any one actor, individual or collective, to assimilate, it becomes necessary to establish knowledge-based alliances and coalitions whose logic is only partly based on space or, for that matter, hierarchy. "Local" knowledge is spatially situated while "organizational" knowledge—how to put knowledge together and use it—is spaceless; combined, the two become instrumental to technical and social innovation.[9] Several examples follow.

In the environmental arena, such arrangements are represented by, for example, the Climate Action Network, a global alliance of regional coalitions made up of national and local environmental organizations and individuals. These actors are engaged in a continuous and reciprocal exchange of knowledge and practice, some of it universal, some of it contingent and contextual. Members and organizations participate in local educational activities, regional and national lobbying, and international negotiations, such as those dealing with the UN Framework Convention on Climate Change. Two other examples are the Global Rivers Environmental Education Network (GREEN), which has projects in 136 countries, and the River Watch Network (RWN), based in Vermont. GREEN "seeks to improve the quality of watershed and rivers, and thereby the lives of people. GREEN uses watersheds as a unifying theme to link people within and between watersheds. . . . Each watershed project is unique, and how it develops depends upon the goals and situation of the local community. . . . As they share cultural perspectives, students, teachers, citizens and professionals from diverse parts of the world are linked by a common bond of interest in and concern for water quality issues."

RWN is more focused on the linkages between technological and scientific competence and political action, without much reference to larger goals. As RWN's materials put it, "We can help you clean up your river."

> River pollution . . . is generated by all of us and its solution requires active citizen participation. Federal, state and local governments are frequently unable to tackle these water quality problems because their resources for river monitoring are severely limited. . . . Gathering and interpreting scientifically credible water quality data underlies every River Watch effort. . . . RWN will never just send you a kit with a page of instructions for water sampling. . . . Each River Watch program is individually designed to meet the particular needs of its community and the conditions of its river. . . . RWN staff are river experts *and* community organizers.[10]

Both networks are only part of a growing worldwide effort to protect and restore river and stream watersheds.[11]

Acquisition of such knowledge and practices also leads to new forms and venues of authority, in that only those with access to such capabilities can act successfully. In some sense, the management function finds itself at that level of social organization where the appropriate combination of local and global knowledges come together. This level is more likely to be local—in the lab, the research group, the neighborhood, the watershed—than global. Or, as Richard Gordon puts it, "Regions and networks . . . constitute interdependent poles within the new spatial mosaic of global innovation. Globalization in this context involves not the leavening impact of universal processes but, on the contrary, the calculated synthesis of cultural diversity in the form of differentiated regional innovation logics and capabilities. . . . The effectiveness of local resources and the ability to achieve genuine forms of cooperation with global networks must be developed from within the region itself."[12] Such functionalist regionalization points back toward the political fragmentation discussed above: lines must be drawn somewhere, whether by reference to nature, power, authority, or knowledge. From a constructivist perspective, such lines may be as "fictional" as those that currently separate one county from another. Still, they are unlikely to be wholly disconnected from the material world, inasmuch as they will have to map onto already existing patterns and structures of social and economic activity.

The Agency-Structure Question Redux: History Counts

Where in this emergent structure is there a space for agency, for organized political action? At its core, the agent-structure debate is more than just an obscure discussion among academics; it is really about the possibilities of political action in a world where, as John Agnew, a geographer, puts it: "[People] are *located* according to the demands of a spatially extensive division of labour, the global system of material production and distribution, and variable patterns of political authority and control."[13] In citing Agnew, however, I do not mean to argue that people's lives are determined by these patterns—only that their choices must be made within the constraints imposed by them (and the histories of the places where they are located). Large-scale opportunities to engineer genuine ideational and material change are rare, however, and the "stickiness" of structures and the institutions that accompany these patterns can defy all efforts to change them.[14]

What and where then are the possibilities for action if they are not to be found at the macrolevel? To discover these, we must look to the history of social, economic, and political entities—history does count. Any social situation in which people, either individually or collectively, find themselves is a product of history, as Marx pointed out; to this, we might add, it is both the history of people and the history of places, *made by people*. To understand how one has arrived at a particular time and place one has to know first what has come before and second how our "conventional" histories of the past may have been misleading or misinformed (intentionally or not). In the language of economics, the present is a product of path dependency; in the language of cultural studies, it is a consequence of how we have acted on what was thought to have happened. This history, in turn, says something about the menu of choices for the future available at any given time.

While such statements might seem self-evident, and perhaps even simplistic, they are neither: most of our routine behaviors are the result of habit, of repetition, of unquestioned circumstances, of *institutions and associated practices*.[15] This is the context within which we make ordinary choices; indeed, it is the realm of the microeconomists' rational actor. But as the discussion above suggests, there are constraints on choices: choices must be imagined to be realized and, although many might be possible in theory, not all that might be imagined are necessarily feasible in political terms.[16] As John Thompson has put it, "As constellations of social relations and reservoirs of natural resources, specific institutions form a relatively stable framework for action and interaction; they do not determine action but *generate* it in the sense of establishing, loosely and tentatively, the parameters of permissible conduct."[17] Sometimes, however, social constraints make what is a necessary choice very difficult, if not almost impossible. It is at this point that human agency becomes important, as the individual actor struggles to move away from habit-driven actions that simply reproduce the status quo.

The patterns—or "historical structures"—described by Agnew (and others, such as Robert Cox and Stephen Gill) do put people in their place, but this does not mean that they are then left without choices.[18] As John Walton argues,

> The constitution of local society . . . is far more than an imposition or small-scale reflection of the national state. On the contrary, it is the evolving product of multiple influences—the people, the economy, natural resources, intermediate levels of state authority, local accommodation to some broader designs, determined resistance to others and, perhaps above all, collective action founded on cultural meaning. Action takes place within social structures that forcibly shape experience, yet people live in local societies where particular customs, exigencies, and choices mediate structural constraints. On the ground people construct their lives in consciously meaningful ways that cannot be read from state-centered directives any more than they can be deduced from modes of economic production.[19]

Beyond this, there are historical junctures at which the "menu of choices" expands, so to speak, offering alternative paths that might not be available at other times. Agency is thus a matter of being aware of alternatives and helping to foster conditions under which meaningful choices can be made.

Such agency should be distinguished from one form more common to contemporary or modernizing societies: consumer preference, choice, or autonomy—sometimes called "GREEN consumerism" when it involves choosing "environmentally friendly" products—which is not agency at all. Rather, it is a response to particular profit-seeking strategies pursued by capital. It is not my intention to dismiss environmentally driven consumer behavior as irrelevant—it does have real impacts—but rather to point out that it is subject to very real constraints imposed by others. And, although environmental protection mediated via markets can improve various types of environmental quality, these do not (and cannot) alter fundamental institutional structures and practices.

Making Choices, Taking Action

If individualistic choice and action are not sufficient to effect changes in the habit-driven behaviors characteristic of people in particular social and political contexts, what is? Norman Long points out that "effective agency . . . requires organizing capacities; it is not simply the result of possessing certain persuasive powers or forms of charisma . . . . *Agency (and power) depend crucially upon the emergence of a network of actors who become partially, though hardly ever completely, enrolled in the "project" of some other person or persons* . . . . It becomes essential, therefore, for social actors to win the struggles that take place over the attribution of specific social meanings to particular events, actions and ideas."[20]

These struggles over the "attribution of specific social meanings" are not about science or data or cost-benefit ratios or any of the things that are quantifiable; they are about ontologies and epistemologies of place, life, and history, within which the methods and findings of science and economics are tools, or means to an end. Again, not all social meanings are available—the repertoire is limited by history, political economy, and culture—but successful agency is possible when a context can be explained in terms of one or more of the meanings in the repertoire. What is central, therefore, to effective social action is the ability to recognize the relationship between choices and meanings; indeed, such an ability is central to politics, inasmuch as the articulation of the relationship is essential for successfully "enrolling" people in a "project."

It now begins to become apparent how and why, at the international level, management projects are so difficult to effect. While power and wealth are important, they do not include all sources of social authority, especially those that may play central roles, akin to Gramscian hegemony, in the domestic politics of culturally different societies. Consider the question of climate change, which is ordinarily described in terms of impacts that are difficult to quantify with great precision, especially in regional or local terms (e.g., a 2–3°C *average* rise in global temperature as a result of a doubling of CO_2 levels in the atmosphere). Implicit in these numbers is the notion that everyone will be affected to his or her detriment. Consequently, echoing Dr. Pangloss, the present—the status quo ante of the future—is the "best of all possible worlds." The intended result of such an assumption is, as Deborah Stone points out, the creation of a "natural community"[21]—inhabitants of the Blue Planet, whether animal, vegetable, or mineral—with a shared interest. In this case, that interest in preventing or minimizing global environmental change requires the construction of a shared, albeit artificial, history and culture around the process, which allows a group of actors to negotiate a "text" on which they can all agree. The text, in turn, will tell a story with a specific social meaning.

Thus, for example, in the preamble to the Framework Convention on Climate Change, signatories "acknowledge that the global nature of climate change calls for the widest possible cooperation by all countries and their participation in an effective and appropriate international response, in accordance with their common but differentiated responsibilities and respective capabilities and their social and economic conditions."[22] As posed in the document, this is a story about a problem and the conditions the signatories deem necessary to resolve it. What is not told here—or, for that matter, anywhere in the convention itself—are the actual *social meanings* that the parties and their societies bring to the negotiations. These meanings can be read in the controversies that litter the growing literature and debates on the potential political, economic, and social impacts of climate change. Conversely, the collective social meaning embedded in the convention by the delegates may have little or no meaning to the members of the societies that must ultimately implement the terms of the document. It is unlikely, therefore, that these individuals will "enroll" in this project in the absence of such an accepted meaning. In other words, to be implemented successfully, the Framework Convention on Climate Change must have many different social meanings, each of which is context dependent, but each of which may be "essentially contested" by other parties to the convention. The result is that a textual resolution mostly depends on how a particular story is told and on whose social meaning is more compelling and able to garner more votes.

In the midst of struggles over meaning, then, history counts not only in terms of explaining how one has arrived at a particular place but also how convincing is the story to be told. This, in turn, has much to do with being able to make choices under constrained conditions, inasmuch as the ways in which a story is told will generate different projects and programs. The politics of meanings, as described here, explain why crises offer the greatest opportunities for agency and social change. It is during these times that conditions become "underdetermined," that people are ready and willing to seek and follow new solutions to their immediate dilemma, and that political entrepreneurs are most able to mobilize followers around specific projects.[23]

While we tend to focus on large-scale crises—statewide or international—these might not be the most important ones in terms of social and political change. Crises occur at all different levels and spatial scales. The death throes of a formerly stable community may hardly be noticed by those outside of it; indeed, a community's complete disappearance may hardly cause a ripple in the larger society. To those who are members of that community, however, the ripple is a tidal wave. But, to carry the metaphor a bit further, such a wave washes away old mental constraints as well as old modes of production: what might have seemed anathema before is now a matter of necessity. Structures still matter, but less so than they might have mattered at another time; choices about the future are now possible. Crises of one sort or another, at these scales, are not that uncommon; they are "deviations" from the structures of everyday life. More to the point, they offer the possibility of changing institutions and putting in place new governance arrangements.

To make this point entirely clear, consider the case of the Mattole River watershed in northern California, on the "Lost Coast," and the threat to the indigenous salmon run in that river. Several different stories can be told about this problem. One has to do with the erosive effects of logging and ranching along the river's watershed and the resulting obstructions to salmon seeking their spawning grounds.[24] A second blames depletion of the local fishery on sport and commercial fishers, who are engaged in what appears to be a Hardinesque "tragedy of the commons." A third suggests that the decline of the salmon is a result of a number of complex, interacting factors and that responsibility cannot be placed on any one activity or group of actors; it must, instead, be explained through an examination of the history of Agnew's "spatially extensive division of labour, the global system of material production and distribution, and variable patterns of political authority and control,"[25] and the cultural, social, and political roles of each actor within the region. Each of these stories suggests different projects, with different outcomes; but the third, which is most inclusive, is also the most open-ended, inasmuch as it establishes no single blame and points to the need for a shared effort to save a resource that is of critical meaning to the valley's residents.

Another example can be found in the campaign to "save the Amazon rain forest." Here we find, on the one side, indigenous groups, rubber tappers, and, in some instances, *garimpieros* (small-scale Brazilian gold miners, who hold no legal title to the places they mine), regional research organizations, social movements in Brazilian cities, international environmental organizations based in the United States and Europe, industrialized country governments, and international organizations. Arrayed somewhat in opposition to this coalition are the Brazilian government and military, organizations of ranchers and landowners, Brazilian state governments, other industrialized country governments and, in all likelihood, national and international corporate actors.[26]

What is this campaign ultimately about? It involves negotiating over the terms of the story that will prove most compelling as a "project," and whether this story is a local, regional, national, or global one. At each level, the meaning enrolls different actors and points to different political outcomes. Of course, such stories are never finalized; as Marianne Schmink and Charles Wood put it,

> Ideological positions (and repositioning) such as these are not mere reflections of material interests. Nor are they static features of people's consciousness. To the contrary, . . . ideologies . . . [are] part of the arsenal of weapons the contestants actively forge and mobilize in the contest over boundaries and the content of accepted discourse. In the process, they alter the definitions of themselves and their understanding of the world around them. Social action therefore has a *constitutive* property. [Through this] . . . the preferences, interests, and ideas that define individuals—and that become the basis for collective action—are formed or constituted in the process of actions that engage participants in a dispute. From this perspective, people act not merely to meet preexisting ends but also to constitute themselves as persons and groups with particular and desired attributes. Because the interests that characterize different social groups are as much formed as they are revealed in the contests in which people are engaged, they are mutable and subject to continual redefinition.[27]

Environmental change and degradation often take the form of microlevel crises in which conditions become underdetermined. When the trees or fish give out, when the air or water become unbearably polluted, when toxic wastes bubble up in backyards, the people living in a place, a community, are faced with the disruption of their accustomed way of life. To them, such a situation is a crisis; they *must* respond. The first—and sometimes the only—impulse is to attack those powerholders or institutions deemed responsible for the crisis; the second impulse is often to organize politically to seek redress or rectification; the third is to make sure the crisis does not happen again.

Love Canal—whether it was a health hazard or not[28]—is notable not because it was a toxic waste dump with local impacts but because it became the locus of political agency in the face of big and mostly immovable institutions and structures. Moreover, the lessons learned from Love Canal were transmitted, through a variety of means, to other individuals and communities facing similar circumstances. One local crisis crystallized a whole realm of innovative social and political action, a newly emergent element of global civil society.[29] This pattern, which has been, and is being, repeated in a myriad of places around the world, around a broad range of environmental issues and problems, is becoming a globalized arrangement in the process. On this point—albeit in reference to events on a larger scale—John Ruggie has argued that "periods of fundamental political transition—of transformation—are characterized by a generalized loss of predictability and control among social actors. The reestablishment of an effective system of rule once again fixes parametric conditions."[30]

This, then, is the basis for the possibilities open to agency: the ability to place historically in a given context, making strategic decisions about how that history is to be told, and understanding how the confluence of structures provides openings for different futures. Of course, no choices are final, although they can and do foreclose other choices, both in the present and in the future. But, final or not, such choices are best made at the most localized level at which they make practical and political sense, especially if we acknowledge that decisions made at the supralocal level cannot be very sensitive to local conditions and might, in fact, engender local resistance that undermines such decisions. It is also clear from this argument that, somehow, localized agency becomes a necessary, albeit not a sufficient, element of environmental governance. The key question, which I address in the following section, is whether it is possible to nurture a governance system that privileges local choice and at the same time takes into account global complexities, connections, *and* justice.

Who Rules? Whose Rules? From Global Environmental Management to Global Environmental Governance

Much can be learned about the relationship between locally based civil society, knowledge, and global governance by examining the histories of environmental projects at the local and regional levels. For example, in his study of the century-long struggle against Los Angeles by the residents of the Owens Valley in eastern California, John Walton discusses how local groups engaged in resistance to the state and were successful only when they were able to draw on the expanding authority of the federal state, and the legitimation of various environmental strategies, as a means of putting pressure on the city to alter its patterns of water removal from the valley.[31] In a broader sense, this coalition took advantage of local knowledge, as well as a nationally redefined ideology of ecology legitimated by the U.S. federal government, to recast social meanings for political purposes. Whereas Los Angeles tapped the Owens Valley water sources for industrial and urban growth, both the local residents and Washington, D.C., sought to conserve water and restore the landscape by framing the conflict in terms of an increasingly accepted story of environmental protection and restoration. This is not to suggest that self-interest was absent from the scenario but to point out that collective action required collective meanings.

Beyond this, the insight provided by Walton's story is that our conventional concepts of the state and governance are, at present, too limited. The state—even a federal one—is not restricted to discrete levels of government; it is more than that. As Theda Skoçpol points out: "On the one hand, states may be viewed as organizations through which official collectivities may pursue collective goals, realizing them more or less effectively given available state resources in relation to social settings. On the other hand, states may be viewed more macroscopically as configurations of organizations and action that influence the meanings and methods of politics for all groups and classes in society."[32]

Skoçpol perhaps offers a conception of the state that is too broad in encompassing society, but her point is, in my view, an important one. The state is more than just its constitution, agencies, rules, and roles; it is embedded as well in a system of governance. As James Rosenau argues, "Governance . . . is a more encompassing phenomenon than government. It embraces governmental institutions, but it also subsumes informal, nongovernmental mechanisms whereby those persons and organizations within its purview move ahead, satisfy their needs, and fulfill their wants. . . . Governance is thus a system of rule that is as dependent on intersubjective meanings as on formally sanctioned constitutions . . . of regulatory mechanisms in a sphere of activity which function effectively even though they are not endowed with formal authority."[33] From this view, state and civil society are mutually constitutive, and where the state engages in *government*, civil society often plays a role in *governance*. What is striking, especially in terms of relationships between environmental organizations and institutionalized mechanisms of government, is the growth of institutions of governance at and across *all* levels of analysis.

What this implies is that, even though we recognize that there is no world government as such, there is an emerging system of *global governance*. Subsumed within this system of governance are both institutionalized regulatory arrangements—some of which we call "regimes"—and less formalized norms, rules, and procedures that pattern behavior without the presence of written constitutions or material power. This system is not the state, as we commonly understand the term, but it is state-like, in Skoçpol's second sense. Indeed, we can see emerging patterns of behavior in global politics very much like those described by Walton in the case of the Owens Valley: alliances between coalitions in global civil society and the international governance arrangements associated with the UN system.[34] In the Amazon case, too, each of the actors has, in one way or another, acquired a certain amount of "governance authority" within a poorly specified political, economic, and/or social realm. Each of the actors, at one time or another, finds it useful to ally with others, at other levels, to put pressure on yet other actors, at still other levels. The result might look more like a battlefield than a negotiation—and, indeed, violence is an all-too-real component of this particular campaign—but, while there is no definitive ruler, the process is not entirely without rules or structure.

To push this argument further, let us return for a moment to what scholars of international environmental policy and politics regard as the sine qua non of their research: the fact, as it is often put, that environmental degradation respects no borders. This feature automatically thrusts many environmental problems into the international realm, where, we are reminded, there is no government and no way to regulate the activities of sovereign states. From this follows the need for international cooperation to internalize transboundary effects, a need that leads logically to the creation of international environmental regimes. Such regimes, it is often noted, are the creation of states, and scholars continue to argue about the conditions necessary for their establishment and maintenance. Whether they undermine the sovereignty of states or are, in themselves, a form of state building is as yet unclear; what is less recognized or acknowledged is that some regimes are merely the "tip of the iceberg" of necessary action, so to speak, or they will be if they reach fruition.

Much of the implementation and regulation inherent in regimes such as the emerging one addressing climate change and other transboundary problems must, as I have suggested, take place at the regional and local levels, in the places where people live, not where their laws are made. If this climate regime is successful—whatever "success" means in such a context—it will, for all practical purposes, function as a global institution of governance with elements at the local, regional, provincial, national, and international levels. It will, in effect, transfer some of the jurisdictional responsibilities of the state both upward and downward, enhancing political authority at the global as well as local level.

But the politics of this and similar regimes will make domestic politics simple by comparison. Rather than two- or even three-level games,[35] what we see, and will see more of, are "*n*-level games," in which intermediate levels are squeezed or strong-armed by those above and below.[36] This is commonly discussed in terms of coalitional strategies between grassroots social movement organizations and international institutions, but, in fact, these coalitions are much more complex, often link multiple levels as well as multilevel actors, and may also shift and change as a situation demands. What should we call such a process? Clearly, it is governance, but not government (although it does contain elements of government); at the same time, it does not mark the end or disintegration of the state as an institutionalized form of politics (although it might, of course, mark the end of *particular* states).

Perhaps these arrangements are best understood as a dialectical relationship between two mutually constitutive structures: states and global civil society. This can be seen more clearly by considering the relationship of domestic civil societies to the state in which they are located. In many states, civil society and state are mutually constitutive. Each is necessary for the functioning of the other, and each serves to legitimate the other. At times, moreover, civil society fulfills a regulatory function in place of the state, as is the case with, for example, the medical and legal professional associations found within the United States and other countries.[37] These associations not only provide credentials to practitioners, through certification of practitioners' knowledge, but they also provide a set of rules and norms to which a practitioner must adhere, at the risk of losing her or his license to practice.

While these rules and norms have a moral quality to them—as, for example, in the Hippocratic Oath—there is clearly the element of self-interest about them, too. And this is true of most, if not all, of the associations of civil society. Not everyone observes *all* of the norms and rules to which they have subscribed *all* of the time, but the adherence rate is generally pretty good. More to the point, the members of these associations internalize these rules and norms and follow them, whether the element of self-interest is evident or not.[38] Rules, in other words, take the place of explicit rule; governance replaces government; informal networks of coordination replace formal structures of command. Governance is effected.

One Earth, Many Worlds

How, then, are we to proceed? I would argue that, rather than via global hierarchy or markets, nature will most likely be protected via governance through social relations of the type discussed above, in which shared norms, cooperation, trust, and mutual obligation play central roles. Such governance seems increasingly characteristic of the emerging global political economy characterized by economic integration and political fragmentation. The fundamental units of governance are, in this system, defined by both function and social meanings, anchored to particular places but linked globally through networks of knowledge-based relations. Coordination occurs not only because each unit plays a functional role where it is located, but also because the functional units share goals with other functional units. Relations such as these develop when the costs of acquiring information through "normal" channels becomes too great; both bear a remarkable resemblance to transactions and economies centered on kinship relations, in which "trust" and "membership" replace formal hierarchies and markets. The phenomenon of networking also resembles the form of organization described above, a form that is characteristic of relations within global civil society. It is a form that lends itself to cooperation without centralization, without "global management."

Such a system need not necessarily be a second-best one, either. There is reason to think that a governance system composed of collective actors at multiple levels with overlapping authority, linked together through various kinds of networks, might be as functionally efficient as a highly centralized one.[39] Such a decentralized system of governance has a number of advantages over a real or imagined hierarchical counterpart. As Donald

Chisholm points out, "Formal systems often create a gap between the formal authority to make decisions and the capacity to make them, owing to a failure to recognize the necessity for a great deal of technical information for effective coordination. Ad hoc coordinating committees staffed by personnel with the requisite professional skills appear far more effective than permanent central coordinating committees run by professional coordinators."[40] Chisholm goes on to argue that formal systems work so long as appropriate information, necessary to the function and achievement of their goals, is available. The problem is that "strict reliance on formal channels compounds the problem [of trying to prevent public awareness of bureaucratic failure]: reliable information will not be supplied, and the failure will not be uncovered until it is too late to compensate for it. Informal channels, by their typically clandestine nature and foundation on *reciprocity and mutual trust,* provide appropriate means for surmounting problems associated with formal channels of communication."[41]

Compare this observation with Richard Gordon's discussion of the organizational logic of innovation: "While strategic alliances involve agreements between autonomous firms, and are oriented towards strengthening the competitive position of the network and its members, inter-firm relations *within* the alliance itself tend to push beyond traditional market relations. Permanently contingent relationships mediated by strict organizational independence and market transactions—the arms-length exchange structure of traditional short-term linkages—are replaced by long-term relations intended to endure and which are mediated by highly personalized and detailed interaction . . . . *Cooperative trust, shared norms and mutual advocacy overcome antagonistic independence and isolation.*"[42]

In policy terms, this is not a very satisfying or parsimonious framework. It does not provide an entry for either easy explanation or manipulation. It relies on the possibly heroic assumption that people can and will help create social choice mechanisms, in their collective self-interest, that may also help protect nature. But it offers more than global management of a passive or resistant population. It suggests that people, acting locally, can have real and significant global impacts. Such social and political change will not occur quickly, nor will it come easily, and it will never encompass the entire world. But, at the very least, by illuminating and examining change where it is under way, we can offer to others a model of action based on local knowledge that might, over the longer term, make a meaningful difference. ⊕

Notes

Ronnie D. Lipschutz is associate professor of politics and director of the Stevenson Program on Global Security at the University of California, Santa Cruz. His research is concerned with the social and political impacts of globalization on the nation-state.

1. Wade Sikorski, "Building Wilderness," in Jane Bennett and William Chaloupka, eds., *In the Nature of Things: Language, Politics, and the Environment* (Minneapolis: University of Minnesota Press, 1993), p. 28.

2. This essay is based on Ronnie D. Lipschutz, with Judith Mayer, *Global Civil Society and Global Environmental Governance: The Politics of Nature from Place to Planet* (Albany: State University of New York Press, 1996). An earlier version was presented on a panel, Knowledge Dynamics of Global Governance, at the annual meeting of the International Studies Association, Chicago, 22–25 February 1995, and will appear in revised form in Martin Hewson and Timothy Sinclair, eds., *Approaches to Global Governance Theory* (forthcoming). Financial and other support for this research was provided by the University of California Systemwide Institute on Global Conflict and Cooperation at UC–San Diego, the Center for German and European Studies at UC-Berkeley, the Social Science Division and Academic Senate at UC–Santa Cruz, and the Monterey Institute of International Studies in Monterey, California.

3. Ernst-Otto Czempiel, "Governance and Democratization," in James N. Rosenau and Ernst-Otto Czempiel, eds., *Governance Without Government: Order and Change in World Politics* (Cambridge: Cambridge University Press, 1992), p. 250.

4. Louis Trager, "All's Fair in Selling Growth to Cities," *San Francisco Examiner*, 22 January 1995, p. C-1.

5. The best-known discussion of the "new medievalism" is to be found in Hedley Bull, *The Anarchical Society: A Study of Order in World Politics* (New York: Columbia University Press, 1977), pp. 254–255, 264–276, 285–286, 291–294. The notion of "heteronomy" is found, among other places, in John G. Ruggie, "Continuity and Transformation in the World Polity: Toward a Neorealist Synthesis," *World Politics* 35, no. 2 (January 1983):274, note 30. The term *heterarchy* comes from Christopher A. Bartlett and Sumantra Ghoshal, "Managing Innovation in the Transnational Corporation," in Yves Doz and Gunnar Hedlund, eds., *Managing the Global Firm* (London: Routledge, 1990), pp. 215—255; quoted in Richard Gordon, "Globalization, New Production Systems and the Spatial Division of Labor," in Wolfgang Litek and Tony Charles, eds., *The Division of Labor: Emerging Forms of World Organization in International Perspective* (Berlin: Walter de Gruyter, 1995), p. 181.

6. Ole Wæver, "Securitization and Desecuritization," in Ronnie D. Lipschutz, ed., *On Security* (New York: Columbia University Press, 1995), pp. 46–86, note 59.

7. John G. Ruggie, "International Structure and International Transformation: Space, Time, and Method," in Ernst-Otto Czempiel and James N. Rosenau, eds., *Global Changes and Theoretical Challenges* (Lexington, Mass.: Lexington Books, 1989), p. 28.

8. The following paragraphs are based on Gordon, "Globalization, New Production Systems and the Spatial Division of Labor."

9. Judith Mayer has pointed out that even organizational knowledge is, to a large degree, also contextual, inasmuch as successful organization aimed at solving a localized functional problem must be based on a solid understanding of local social relations. Personal communication, 26 January 1995.

10. Both of these quotes can be found in Lipschutz, *Global Civil Society and Global Environmental Governance*, p. 158 (emphasis in original).

11. A more detailed discussion can be found in Roger A. Coate, Chadwick F. Alger, and Ronnie D. Lipschutz, "The United Nations and Civil Society: Creative Partnerships for Sustainable Development," *Alternatives* 21, no. 1 (January-March 1996):93–122.

12. Gordon, "Globalization, New Production Systems and the Spatial Division of Labor," pp. 196, 199.

13. John Agnew, "Representing Space—Space, Scale and Culture in Social Science," in James Duncan and David Ley, eds., *Place/Culture/Representation* (London: Routledge, 1993), p. 262.

14. James N. Rosenau, "Before Cooperation: Hegemons, Regimes, and Habit-Driven Actors in World Politics," *International Organization* 40, no. 4 (autumn 1986): 849–894.

15. Rosenau, "Before Cooperation." See also the discussion of institutions in Ronnie D. Lipschutz and Judith Mayer, "Not Seeing the Forest for the Trees: Property Rights, Constitutive Rules, and the Renegotiation of Resource Management Regimes," in Ronnie D. Lipschutz and Ken Conca, eds., *The State and Social Power in Global Environmental Politics* (New York: Columbia University Press, 1993), pp. 246–273, which is based, in part, on Oran Young, *Resource Regimes—Natural Resources and Social Institutions* (Berkeley: University of California Press, 1982).

16. Norman Long, "From Paradigm Lost to Paradigm Regained? The Case for an Actor-Oriented Sociology of Development," in Norman Long and Ann Long, eds., *Battlefields of Knowledge: The Interlocking of Theory and Practice in Social Research and Development* (London: Routledge, 1992), pp. 24–25.

17. John Thompson, *Studies in the Theory of Ideology* (Berkeley: University of California Press, 1984), p. 135 (emphasis in original).

18. Robert Cox, *Production, Power and World Order* (New York: Columbia University Press, 1987); Stephen Gill, ed., *Gramsci, Historical Materialism and International Relations* (Cambridge: Cambridge University Press, 1993).

19. John Walton, *Western Times and Water Wars: State, Culture, and Rebellion in California* (Berkeley: University of California Press, 1992), p. 287.

20. Long, "From Paradigm Lost to Paradigm Regained?" pp. 23–24 (emphasis added).

21. Deborah A. Stone, *Policy Paradox and Political Reason* (Glenview, Ill.: Scott, Foresman, 1988), p. 135.

22. International Negotiating Committee for a Framework Convention on Climate Change, *United Nations Framework Convention on Climate Change* (Geneva: UNEP/WMO Information Unit on Climate Change, n.d.), p. 2.

23. Ronnie D. Lipschutz and Beverly Crawford, "Economic Globalization and the 'New' Ethnic Strife: What Is to Be Done?" Policy Paper no. 25 (San Diego: Institute on Global Conflict and Cooperation, UC–San Diego, May 1996), pp. 7–8.

24. See, for example, William K. Stevens, "Dwindling Salmon Spur West to Save Rivers," *New York Times,* 15 November 1994 (national edition), p. B7; Glen Martin, "Salmon Lose Struggle for Shasta River," *San Francisco Chronicle,* 22 August 1994, p. A1.

25. Agnew, "Representing Space," p. 262.

26. Susanna B. Hecht and Alexander Cockburn, *The Fate of the Forest: Developers, Destroyers and Defenders of the Amazon* (New York: HarperPerennial, 1990); Marianne Schmink and Charles H. Wood, *Contested Frontiers in Amazonia* (New York: Columbia University Press, 1992); João Pacheco de Oliveira Filho, "Frontier Security and the New Indigenism: Nature and Origins of the Calha Norte

Project," in David Goodman and Anthony Hall, eds., *The Future of Amazonia: Destruction or Sustainable Development?* (New York: St. Martin's Press, 1988), pp. 155–178; David Cleary, "After the Frontier: Problems with Political Economy in the Modern Brazilian Amazon," *Journal of Latin American Studies* 25, no. 2 (May 1993): 331–350; Susanna B. Hecht, "The Logic of Livestock and Deforestation in Amazonia," *BioScience* 43, no. 10 (November 1993): 687–696.

27. Schmink and Wood, *Contested Frontiers in Amazonia,* pp. 17–18. Or, as Charles Lipson says in a somewhat different context, the outcomes of social negotiations "do not have fixed meanings or decontextualized significance. Rather, they are continually reproduced and redefined in the dispute process as the actors use or resist existing standards." Lipson, *Standing Guard: Protecting Foreign Capital in the Nineteenth and Twentieth Centuries* (Berkeley: University of California Press, 1985), p. 32.

28. See Charles T. Rubin, *The Green Crusade: Rethinking the Roots of Environmentalism* (New York: Free Press, 1994), p. 219; see also the discussion in Sherry Cable and Charles Cable, *Environmental Problems, Grassroots Solution: The Politics of Grassroots Environmental Conflict* (New York: St. Martin's Press, 1994), pp. 75–84.

29. Andrew Szasz, *Ecopopulism* (Minneapolis: University of Minnesota Press, 1994).

30. Ruggie, "International Structure and International Transformation," p. 28.

31. Walton, *Western Times and Water Wars.*

32. Theda Skoçpol, "Bringing the State Back In: Strategies of Analysis in Current Research," in Peter B. Evans, Dietrich Reuschemeyer, and Theda Skoçpol, eds., *Bringing the State Back In* (Cambridge: Cambridge University Press, 1985), p. 20.

33. James N. Rosenau, "Governance, Order, and Change in World Politics," in Rosenau and Czempiel, eds., *Governance Without Government,* pp. 4–5.

34. A good illustration of this process can be found in Franke Wilmer, *The Indigenous Voice in World Politics* (Newbury Park, Calif.: Sage, 1993).

35. The notion of two-level games was originally developed by Robert D. Putnam, "Diplomacy and Domestic Politics: The Logic of Two Level Games," *International Organization* 42, no. 3 (summer 1988): 427–460; see also Peter B. Evans, Harold K. Jacobson and Robert D. Putnam, eds., *Double-Edged Diplomacy: International Bargaining and Domestic Politics* (Berkeley: University of California Press, 1993).

36. See Janie Leatherman, Ron Pagnucco, and Jackie Smith, "International Institutions and Transnational Social Movement Organizations: Transforming Sovereignty, Anarchy, and Global Governance," Kroc Institute for International Peace Studies, Notre Dame University, August 1994, Working Paper 5: WP: 3.

37. Personal communication from Robert Meister.

38. Fred Hirsch, *Social Limits to Growth* (Cambridge: Harvard University Press, 1976), pp. 120–121, 137–140, 146.

39. Much of the following discussion is based on Donald Chisholm, *Coordination Without Hierarchy: Informal Structures in Multiorganizational Systems* (Berkeley: University of California Press, 1989).

40. Ibid., p. 11.

41. Ibid., p. 32 (added emphasis).

42. Gordon, "Globalization, New Production Systems and The Spatial Division of Labor," pp. 183–184 (first emphasis in original; second emphasis added).

[12]

The Real New World Order

Anne-Marie Slaughter

THE STATE STRIKES BACK

MANY THOUGHT that the new world order proclaimed by George Bush was the promise of 1945 fulfilled, a world in which international institutions, led by the United Nations, guaranteed international peace and security with the active support of the world's major powers. That world order is a chimera. Even as a liberal internationalist ideal, it is infeasible at best and dangerous at worst. It requires a centralized rule-making authority, a hierarchy of institutions, and universal membership. Equally to the point, efforts to create such an order have failed. The United Nations cannot function effectively independent of the major powers that compose it, nor will those nations cede their power and sovereignty to an international institution. Efforts to expand supranational authority, whether by the U.N. secretary-general's office, the European Commission, or the World Trade Organization (WTO), have consistently produced a backlash among member states.

The leading alternative to liberal internationalism is "the new medievalism," a back-to-the-future model of the 21st century. Where liberal internationalists see a need for international rules and institutions to solve states' problems, the new medievalists proclaim the end of the nation-state. Less hyperbolically, in her article, "Power Shift," in the January/February 1997 *Foreign Affairs*, Jessica T. Mathews describes a shift away from the state—up, down, and sideways—to supra-state, sub-state, and, above all, nonstate actors. These new players have multiple allegiances and global reach.

ANNE-MARIE SLAUGHTER is the J. Sinclair Armstrong Professor of International, Foreign, and Comparative Law at Harvard Law School.

Anne-Marie Slaughter

Mathews attributes this power shift to a change in the structure of organizations: from hierarchies to networks, from centralized compulsion to voluntary association. The engine of this transformation is the information technology revolution, a radically expanded communications capacity that empowers individuals and groups while diminishing traditional authority. The result is not world government, but global governance. If government denotes the formal exercise of power by established institutions, governance denotes cooperative problem-solving by a changing and often uncertain cast. The result is a world order in which global governance networks link Microsoft, the Roman Catholic Church, and Amnesty International to the European Union, the United Nations, and Catalonia.

The new medievalists miss two central points. First, private power is still no substitute for state power. Consumer boycotts of transnational corporations destroying rain forests or exploiting child labor may have an impact on the margin, but most environmentalists or labor activists would prefer national legislation mandating control of foreign subsidiaries. Second, the power shift is not a zero-sum game. A gain in power by nonstate actors does not necessarily translate into a loss of power for the state. On the contrary, many of these nongovernmental organizations (NGOS) network with their foreign counterparts to apply additional pressure on the traditional levers of domestic politics.

A new world order is emerging, with less fanfare but more substance than either the liberal internationalist or new medievalist visions. The state is not disappearing, it is disaggregating into its separate, functionally distinct parts. These parts—courts, regulatory agencies, executives, and even legislatures—are networking with their counterparts abroad, creating a dense web of relations that constitutes a new, transgovernmental order. Today's international problems—terrorism, organized crime, environmental degradation, money laundering, bank failure, and securities fraud—created and sustain these relations. Government institutions have formed networks of their own, ranging from the Basle Committee of Central Bankers to informal ties between law enforcement agencies to legal networks that make foreign judicial decisions more and more familiar. While political scientists Robert Keohane and Joseph Nye first observed its emergence in the 1970s, today

The Real New World Order

transgovernmentalism is rapidly becoming the most widespread and effective mode of international governance.

Compared to the lofty ideals of liberal internationalism and the exuberant possibilities of the new medievalism, transgovernmentalism seems mundane. Meetings between securities regulators, antitrust or environmental officials, judges, or legislators lack the drama of high politics. But for the internationalists of the 1990s—bankers, lawyers, businesspeople, public-interest activists, and criminals—transnational government networks are a reality. Wall Street looks to the Basle Committee rather than the World Bank. Human rights lawyers are more likely to develop transnational litigation strategies for domestic courts than to petition the U.N. Committee on Human Rights.

> The state is not disappearing, it is disaggregating.

Moreover, transgovernmentalism has many virtues. It is a key element of a bipartisan foreign policy, simultaneously assuaging conservative fears of a loss of sovereignty to international institutions and liberal fears of a loss of regulatory power in a globalized economy. While presidential candidate Pat Buchanan and Senator Jesse Helms (R-N.C.) demonize the U.N. and the WTO as supranational bureaucracies that seek to dictate to national governments, Senators Ted Kennedy (D-Mass.) and Paul Wellstone (D-Mich.) inveigh against international capital mobility as the catalyst of a global "race to the bottom" in regulatory standards. Networks of bureaucrats responding to international crises and planning to prevent future problems are more flexible than international institutions and expand the regulatory reach of all participating nations. This combination of flexibility and effectiveness offers something for both sides of the aisle.

Transgovernmentalism also offers promising new mechanisms for the Clinton administration's "enlargement" policy, aiming to expand the community of liberal democracies. Contrary to Samuel Huntington's gloomy predictions in *The Clash of Civilizations and the New World Order* (1996), existing government networks span civilizations, drawing in courts from Argentina to Zimbabwe and financial regulators from Japan to Saudi Arabia. The dominant institutions in these networks remain concentrated in North America and Western Europe, but their

Anne-Marie Slaughter

impact can be felt in every corner of the globe. Moreover, disaggregating the state makes it possible to assess the quality of specific judicial, administrative, and legislative institutions, whether or not the governments are liberal democracies. Regular interaction with foreign colleagues offers new channels for spreading democratic accountability, governmental integrity, and the rule of law.

An offspring of an increasingly borderless world, transgovernmentalism is a world order ideal in its own right, one that is more effective and potentially more accountable than either of the current alternatives. Liberal internationalism poses the prospect of a supranational bureaucracy answerable to no one. The new medievalist vision appeals equally to states' rights enthusiasts and supranationalists, but could easily reflect the worst of both worlds. Transgovernmentalism, by contrast, leaves the control of government institutions in the hands of national citizens, who must hold their governments as accountable for their transnational activities as for their domestic duties.

JUDICIAL FOREIGN POLICY

JUDGES ARE building a global community of law. They share values and interests based on their belief in the law as distinct but not divorced from politics and their view of themselves as professionals who must be insulated from direct political influence. At its best, this global community reminds each participant that his or her professional performance is being monitored and supported by a larger audience.

National and international judges are networking, becoming increasingly aware of one another and of their stake in a common enterprise. The most informal level of transnational judicial contact is knowledge of foreign and international judicial decisions and a corresponding willingness to cite them. The Israeli Supreme Court and the German and Canadian constitutional courts have long researched U.S. Supreme Court precedents in reaching their own conclusions on questions like freedom of speech, privacy rights, and due process. Fledgling constitutional courts in Central and Eastern Europe and in Russia are eagerly following suit. In 1995, the South African Supreme Court, finding the death penalty unconstitutional under the national constitution, referred to decisions from national and supranational courts around the world,

The Real New World Order

including ones in Hungary, India, Tanzania, Canada, and Germany and the European Court of Human Rights. The U.S. Supreme Court has typically been more of a giver than a receiver in this exchange, but Justice Sandra Day O'Connor recently chided American lawyers and judges for their insularity in ignoring foreign law and predicted that she and her fellow justices would find themselves "looking more frequently to the decisions of other constitutional courts."

> National and international judges are networking, creating new global relationships.

Why should a court in Israel or South Africa cite a decision by the U. S. Supreme Court in reaching its own conclusion? Decisions rendered by outside courts can have no authoritative value. They carry weight only because of their intrinsic logical power or because the court invoking them seeks to gain legitimacy by linking itself to a larger community of courts considering similar issues. National courts have become increasingly aware that they and their foreign counterparts are often engaged in a common effort to delimit the boundaries of individual rights in the face of an apparently overriding public interest. Thus, the British House of Lords recently rebuked the U.S. Supreme Court for its decision to uphold the kidnapping of a Mexican doctor by U.S. officials determined to bring him to trial in the United States.

Judges also cooperate in resolving transnational or international disputes. In cases involving citizens of two different states, courts have long been willing to acknowledge each other's potential interest and to defer to one another when such deference is not too costly. U.S. courts now recognize that they may become involved in a sustained dialogue with a foreign court. For instance, Judge Guido Calabresi of the Second Circuit recently allowed a French litigant to invoke U.S. discovery provisions without exhausting discovery options in France, reasoning that it was up to the French courts to identify and protest any infringements of French sovereignty. U.S. courts would then respond to such protests.

Judicial communication is not always harmonious, as in a recent squabble between a U.S. judge and a Hong Kong judge over an insider trading case. The U.S. judge refused to decline jurisdiction in favor of the Hong Kong court on grounds that "in Hong Kong they practically give you a medal for doing this sort of thing [insider trading]." In

CORBIS - BETTMANN

Let's keep talking: judicial networking is born

response, the Hong Kong judge stiffly defended the adequacy of Hong Kong law and asserted his willingness to apply it. He also chided his American counterpart, pointing out that any conflict "should be approached in the spirit of judicial comity rather than judicial competitiveness." Such conflict is to be expected among diplomats, but what is striking here is the two courts' view of themselves as quasi-autonomous foreign policy actors doing battle against international securities fraud.

The most advanced form of judicial cooperation is a partnership between national courts and a supranational tribunal. In the European Union (EU), the European Court of Justice works with national courts when questions of European law overlap national law. National courts refer cases up to the European Court, which issues an opinion and sends the case back to national courts; the supranational recommendation guides the national court's decision. This cooperation marshals the power of domestic courts behind the judgment of a supranational tribunal. While the Treaty of Rome provides for

The Real New World Order

this reference procedure, it is the courts that have transformed it into a judicial partnership.

Finally, judges are talking face to face. The judges of the supreme courts of Western Europe began meeting every three years in 1978. Since then they have become more aware of one another's decisions, particularly with regard to each other's willingness to accept the decisions handed down by the European Court of Justice. Meetings between U.S. Supreme Court justices and their counterparts on the European Court have been sponsored by private groups, as have meetings of U.S. judges with judges from the supreme courts of Central and Eastern Europe and Russia.

The most formal initiative aimed at bringing judges together is the recently inaugurated Organization of the Supreme Courts of the Americas. Twenty-five supreme court justices or their designees met in Washington in October 1995 and drafted the ocsa charter, dedicating the organization to "promot[ing] and strengthen[ing] judicial independence and the rule of law among the members, as well as the proper constitutional treatment of the judiciary as a fundamental branch of the state." The charter calls for triennial meetings and envisages a permanent secretariat. It required ratification by 15 supreme courts, achieved in spring 1996. An initiative by judges, for judges, it is not a stretch to say that ocsa is the product of judicial foreign policy.

Champions of a global rule of law have most frequently envisioned one rule for all, a unified legal system topped by a world court. The global community of law emerging from judicial networks will more likely encompass many rules of law, each established in a specific state or region. No high court would hand down definitive global rules. National courts would interact with one another and with supranational tribunals in ways that would accommodate differences but acknowledge and reinforce common values.

THE REGULATORY WEB

THE DENSEST area of transgovernmental activity is among national regulators. Bureaucrats charged with the administration of antitrust policy, securities regulation, environmental policy, criminal law enforcement, banking and insurance supervision—in short, all the

Anne-Marie Slaughter

agents of the modern regulatory state—regularly collaborate with their foreign counterparts.

National regulators track their quarry through cooperation. While frequently ad hoc, such cooperation is increasingly cemented by bilateral and multilateral agreements. The most formal of these are mutual legal assistance treaties, whereby two states lay out a protocol governing cooperation between their law enforcement agencies and courts. However, the preferred instrument of cooperation is the memorandum of understanding, in which two or more regulatory agencies set forth and initial terms for an ongoing relationship. Such memorandums are not treaties; they do not engage the executive or the legislature in negotiations, deliberation, or signature. Rather, they are good-faith agreements, affirming ties between regulatory agencies based on their like-minded commitment to getting results.

National regulators track their quarry through cooperation.

"Positive comity," a concept developed by the U.S. Department of Justice, epitomizes the changing nature of transgovernmental relations. Comity of nations, an archaic and notoriously vague term beloved by diplomats and international lawyers, has traditionally signified the deference one nation grants another in recognition of their mutual sovereignty. For instance, a state will recognize another state's laws or judicial judgments based on comity. Positive comity requires more active cooperation. As worked out by the Antitrust Division of the U.S. Department of Justice and the EU's European Commission, the regulatory authorities of both states alert one another to violations within their jurisdiction, with the understanding that the responsible authority will take action. Positive comity is a principle of enduring cooperation between government agencies.

In 1988 the central bankers of the world's major financial powers adopted capital adequacy requirements for all banks under their supervision—a significant reform of the international banking system. It was not the World Bank, the International Monetary Fund, or even the Group of Seven that took this step. Rather, the forum was the Basle Committee on Banking Supervision, an organization composed of 12 central bank governors. The Basle Committee was created by a simple agreement among the governors themselves. Its members meet

The Real New World Order

four times a year and follow their own rules. Decisions are made by consensus and are not formally binding; however, members do implement these decisions within their own systems. The Basle Committee's authority is often cited as an argument for taking domestic action.

National securities commissioners and insurance regulators have followed the Basle Committee's example. Incorporated by a private bill of the Quebec National Assembly, the International Organization of Securities Commissioners has no formal charter or founding treaty. Its primary purpose is to solve problems affecting international securities markets by creating a consensus for enactment of national legislation. Its members have also entered into information-sharing agreements on their own initiative. The International Association of Insurance Supervisors follows a similar model, as does the newly created Tripartite Group, an international coalition of banking, insurance, and securities regulators the Basle Committee created to improve the supervision of financial conglomerates.

Pat Buchanan would have had a field day with the Tripartite Group, denouncing it as a prime example of bureaucrats taking power out of the hands of American voters. In fact, unlike the international bogeymen of demagogic fantasy, transnational regulatory organizations do not aspire to exercise power in the international system independent of their members. Indeed, their main purpose is to help regulators apprehend those who would harm the interests of American voters. Transgovernmental networks often promulgate their own rules, but the purpose of those rules is to enhance the enforcement of national law.

Traditional international law requires states to implement the international obligations they incur through their own law. Thus, if states agree to a 12-mile territorial sea, they must change their domestic legislation concerning the interdiction of vessels in territorial waters accordingly. But this legislation is unlikely to overlap with domestic law, as national legislatures do not usually seek to regulate global commons issues and interstate relations.

Transgovernmental regulation, by contrast, produces rules concerning issues that each nation already regulates within its borders: crime, securities fraud, pollution, tax evasion. The advances in technology and transportation that have fueled globalization have made it more

Anne-Marie Slaughter

difficult to enforce national law. Regulators benefit from coordinating their enforcement efforts with those of their foreign counterparts and from ensuring that other nations adopt similar approaches.

The result is the nationalization of international law. Regulatory agreements between states are pledges of good faith that are self-enforcing, in the sense that each nation will be better able to enforce its national law by implementing the agreement if other nations do likewise. Laws are binding or coercive only at the national level. Uniformity of result and diversity of means go hand in hand, and the makers and enforcers of rules are national leaders who are accountable to the people.

BIPARTISAN GLOBALIZATION

SECRETARY OF STATE Madeleine Albright seeks to revive the bipartisan foreign policy consensus of the late 1940s. Deputy Secretary of State Strobe Talbott argues that promoting democracy worldwide satisfies the American need for idealpolitik as well as realpolitik. President Clinton, in his second inaugural address, called for a "new government for a new century," abroad as well as at home. But bipartisanship is threatened by divergent responses to globalization, democratization is a tricky business, and Vice President Al Gore's efforts to "reinvent government" have focused on domestic rather than international institutions. Transgovernmentalism can address all these problems.

Globalization implies the erosion of national boundaries. Consequently, regulators' power to implement national regulations within those boundaries declines both because people can easily flee their jurisdiction and because the flows of capital, pollution, pathogens, and weapons are too great and sudden for any one regulator to control. The liberal internationalist response to these assaults on state regulatory power is to build a larger international apparatus. Globalization thus leads to internationalization, or the transfer of regulatory authority from the national level to an international institution. The best example is not the WTO itself, but rather the stream of proposals to expand the WTO's jurisdiction to global competition policy, intellectual property regulation, and

The Real New World Order

other trade-related issues. Liberals are likely to support expanding the power of international institutions to guard against the global dismantling of the regulatory state.

Here's the rub. Conservatives are more likely to favor the expansion of globalized markets without the internationalization that goes with it, since internationalization, from their perspective, equals a loss of sovereignty. According to Buchanan, the U.S. foreign policy establishment "want[s] to move America into a New World Order where the World Court decides quarrels between nations; the wto writes the rules for trade and settles all disputes; the imf and World Bank order wealth transfers from continent to continent and country to country; the Law of the Sea Treaty tells us what we may and may not do on the high seas and ocean floor, and the United Nations decides where U.S. military forces may and may not intervene." The rhetoric is deliberately inflammatory, but echoes resound across the Republican spectrum.

Transgovernmental initiatives are a compromise that could command bipartisan support. Regulatory loopholes caused by global forces require a coordinated response beyond the reach of any one country. But this coordination need not come from building more international institutions. It can be achieved through transgovernmental cooperation, involving the same officials who make and implement policy at the national level. The transgovernmental alternative is fast, flexible, and effective.

A leading example of transgovernmentalism in action that demonstrates its bipartisan appeal is a State Department initiative christened the New Transatlantic Agenda. Launched in 1991 under the Bush administration and reinvigorated by Secretary of State Warren Christopher in 1995, the initiative structures the relationship between the United States and the eu, fostering cooperation in areas ranging from opening markets to fighting terrorism, drug trafficking, and infectious disease. It is an umbrella for ongoing projects between U.S. officials and their European counterparts. It reaches ordinary citizens, embracing efforts like the Transatlantic Business Dialogue and engaging individuals through people-to-people exchanges and expanded communication through the Internet.

Anne-Marie Slaughter

DEMOCRATIZATION, STEP BY STEP

TRANSGOVERNMENTAL NETWORKS are concentrated among liberal democracies but are not limited to them. Some nondemocratic states have institutions capable of cooperating with their foreign counterparts, such as committed and effective regulatory agencies or relatively independent judiciaries. Transgovernmental ties can strengthen institutions in ways that will help them resist political domination, corruption, and incompetence and build democratic institutions in their countries, step by step. The Organization of Supreme Courts of the Americas, for instance, actively seeks to strengthen norms of judicial independence among its members, many of whom must fend off powerful political forces.

Individuals and groups in nondemocratic countries may also "borrow" government institutions of democratic states to achieve a measure of justice they cannot obtain in their own countries. The court or regulatory agency of one state may be able to perform judicial or regulatory functions for the people of another. Victims of human rights violations, for example, in countries such as Argentina, Ethiopia, Haiti, and the Philippines have sued for redress in the courts of the United States. U.S. courts accepted these cases, often over the objections of the executive branch, using a broad interpretation of a moribund statute dating back to 1789. Under this interpretation, aliens may sue in U.S. courts to seek damages from foreign government officials accused of torture, even if the torture allegedly took place in the foreign country. More generally, a nongovernmental organization seeking to prevent human rights violations can often circumvent their own government's corrupt legislature and politicized court by publicizing the plight of victims abroad and mobilizing a foreign court, legislature, or executive to take action.

Responding to calls for a coherent U.S. foreign policy and seeking to strengthen the community of democratic nations, President Clinton substituted the concept of "enlargement" for the Cold War principle of "containment." Expanding transgovernmental outreach to include institutions from nondemocratic states would help expand the circle of democracies one institution at a time.

The Real New World Order

A NEW WORLD ORDER IDEAL

TRANSGOVERNMENTALISM OFFERS its own world order ideal, less dramatic but more compelling than either liberal internationalism or the new medievalism. It harnesses the state's power to find and implement solutions to global problems. International institutions have a lackluster record on such problem-solving; indeed, NGOs exist largely to compensate for their inadequacies. Doing away with the state, however, is hardly the answer. The new medievalist mantra of global governance is "governance without government." But governance without government is governance without power, and government without power rarely works. Many pressing international and domestic problems result from states' insufficient power to establish order, build infrastructure, and provide minimum social services. Private actors may take up some slack, but there is no substitute for the state.

Transgovernmental networks allow governments to benefit from the flexibility and decentralization of nonstate actors. Jessica T. Mathews argues that "businesses, citizens' organizations, ethnic groups, and crime cartels have all readily adopted the network model," while governments "are quintessential hierarchies, wedded to an organizational form incompatible with all that the new technologies make possible." Not so. Disaggregating the state into its functional components makes it possible to create networks of institutions engaged in a common enterprise even as they represent distinct national interests. Moreover, they can work with their subnational and supranational counterparts, creating a genuinely new world order in which networked institutions perform the functions of a world government—legislation, administration, and adjudication—without the form.

These globe-spanning networks will strengthen the state as the primary player in the international system. The state's defining attribute has traditionally been sovereignty, conceived as absolute power in domestic affairs and autonomy in relations with other states. But as Abram and Antonia Chayes observe in *The New Sovereignty* (1995), sovereignty is actually "status—the vindication of the state's existence in the international system." More importantly, they demonstrate that in contemporary international relations, sovereignty has been redefined to mean "membership . . . in the regimes that make

Anne-Marie Slaughter

up the substance of international life." Disaggregating the state permits the disaggregation of sovereignty as well, ensuring that specific state institutions derive strength and status from participation in a transgovernmental order.

Transgovernmental networks will increasingly provide an important anchor for international organizations and nonstate actors alike. U.N. officials have already learned a lesson about the limits of supranational authority; mandated cuts in the international bureaucracy will further tip the balance of power toward national regulators. The next generation of international institutions is also likely to look more like the Basle Committee, or, more formally, the Organization of Economic Cooperation and Development, dedicated to providing a forum for transnational problem-solving and the harmonization of national law. The disaggregation of the state creates opportunities for domestic institutions,

> Globe-spanning networks will strengthen the state in the international system.

particularly courts, to make common cause with their supranational counterparts against their fellow branches of government. Nonstate actors will lobby and litigate wherever they think they will have the most effect. Many already realize that corporate self-regulation and states' promises to comply with vague international agreements are no substitute for national law.

The spread of transgovernmental networks will depend more on political and professional convergence than on civilizational boundaries. Trust and awareness of a common enterprise are more vulnerable to differing political ideologies and corruption than to cultural differences. Government networks transcend the traditional divide between high and low politics. National militaries, for instance, network as extensively as central bankers with their counterparts in friendly states. Judicial and regulatory networks can help achieve gradual political convergence, but are unlikely to be of much help in the face of a serious economic or military threat. If the coming conflict with China is indeed coming, transgovernmentalism will not stop it.

The strength of transgovernmental networks and of transgovern-mentalism as a world order ideal will ultimately depend on their accountability to the world's peoples. To many, the prospect of

The Real New World Order

transnational government by judges and bureaucrats looks more like technocracy than democracy. Critics contend that government institutions engaged in policy coordination with their foreign counterparts will be barely visible, much less accountable, to voters still largely tied to national territory.

Citizens of liberal democracies will not accept any form of international regulation they cannot control. But checking unelected officials is a familiar problem in domestic politics. As national legislators become increasingly aware of transgovernmental networks, they will expand their oversight capacities and develop networks of their own. Transnational NGO networks will develop a similar monitoring capacity. It will be harder to monitor themselves.

Transgovernmentalism offers answers to the most important challenges facing advanced industrial countries: loss of regulatory power with economic globalization, perceptions of a "democratic deficit" as international institutions step in to fill the regulatory gap, and the difficulties of engaging nondemocratic states. Moreover, it provides a powerful alternative to a liberal internationalism that has reached its limits and to a new medievalism that, like the old Marxism, sees the state slowly fading away. The new medievalists are right to emphasize the dawn of a new era, in which information technology will transform the globe. But government networks are government for the information age. They offer the world a blueprint for the international architecture of the 21st century.✪

Part II
New Actors, Norms and Issues

[13]

Bringing the Firm Back In: Multinationals in International Political Economy

Lorraine Eden

> The state is based on the concepts of territoriality, loyalty, and exclusivity, and it possesses a monopoly of the legitimate use of force...[T]he market is based on the concepts of functional integration, contractual relationships, and expanding interdependence of buyers and sellers...The tension between these two fundamentally different ways of ordering human relationships has profoundly shaped the course of modern history and constitutes the crucial problem in the study of political economy.[1]

INTRODUCTION

International political economy (IPE) is a focus of inquiry that seeks to explain international politico-economic relations and how they affect the global systems of production, exchange and distribution.[2] IPE sees the nation-state as the key actor in the global system, the organiser of the international political order. The state is treated as the alternative to the market which is seen as the organiser of economic relations. As the above quote shows, much of the IPE literature has concentrated on this conflict between 'states and markets'; indeed, Susan Strange has written a book with this very title.[3]

The concept of states versus markets is, however, flawed because the market is a structure, not an actor, and hence a poor counterpoint to the state. The appropriate counterpoint is the multinational enterprise (MNE), the key nonstate actor dominating both domestic and international markets. The largest 600 MNEs now generate worldwide sales of over one billion dollars each and together produce one-quarter of world gross domestic product.[4] The crucial problem in the study of political economy as we move into the twenty-first century is the tension between states and multinationals, not states and markets. It is time to bring the firm, *i.e.*, the multinational enterprise, back into IPE.

Multinationals are studied in the IPE literature; however, their presence is often implicit rather than explicit, or segregated from other questions.[5] Some IPE perspectives devote more attention to multinationals than others (*e.g.*, dependency versus regime theories). Indeed, the terms used by various authors to identify this international organisational structure (*e.g.*, multinational enterprise (MNE), multinational corporation (MNC) and transnational corporation (TNC)) often reveal the perceptions of multinationals within different paradigms or disciplines.[6]

© Millennium Journal of International Studies, 1991.ISSN 0305-8298. Vol. 20, No. 2 pp. 197-224

Millennium

However identified, all IPE perspectives need to take account of the 'new style MNEs' of the 1990s in thinking about global issues and problems. These new style firms, or global corporations, operate with worldwide strategies, investments and sales, making them the chief vehicle for increasing interdependence among national economies.[7] IPE must come to terms with the globalisation of markets through multinational enterprises.

The purpose of this paper is to further the process of 'bringing the firm back into IPE'. The paper first reviews the treatment of multinationals in various strands of the literature, arguing that IPE traditionally focuses on five faces or images of the MNE: the product life cycle, sovereignty at bay, the law of uneven development, the obsolescing bargain, and the changing international division of labour. A review of these faces is followed by a summary of current thinking in the international business studies (IBS) literature on global multinationals, focusing on the Ownership-Location-Internalisation (OLI) paradigm, the international value chain, and strategic management of MNEs.[8] The last section of the paper deals with implications of multinationals for the concept of states versus markets, and for the five faces multinationals traditionally assumed in IPE. The paper concludes that a clearer focus on the MNE as an institutional actor with goals, strategies and structures is necessary for a better understanding of state-MNE relations in the 1990s.

FACES OF THE MULTINATIONAL ENTERPRISE IN IPE

Each of the major perspectives in IPE – liberalism, nationalism and Marxism – has a different view of the MNE.[9] The liberal perspective views multinationals as an integrating force in the world economy. Because MNEs transfer resources between countries according to comparative advantage, they are a force for progress, increasing wealth and lessening income inequalities between developed and developing countries. MNEs are seen by liberals as generally beneficial in their role as promoters of a more integrated world order, offsetting the mercantilist tendencies of nation-states. The nationalist and neomercantilist perspectives perceive MNEs as potential threats to the power of the state. Because MNEs respond to global profit motives, conflict between state goals and MNE goals is inevitable. MNEs need to be regulated, both by national governments and internationally, according to the nationalist perspective, to ensure that state autonomy and sovereignty are maintained. The important question is how to manage multinationals to ensure that they enhance domestic industrial capacity, national sovereignty and state security. Lastly, the Marxist critiques, particularly the Latin American dependency writings, view MNEs as oligopolistic transnational capitalists that systemically exploit and promote underdevelopment in the periphery and semiperiphery. MNEs act at the behest of their home states, enhancing imperialism and permanently creating global income inequalities. Radical theorists argue that MNEs make alliances with transnational elites such as domestic capitalists in the semiperiphery, but that such development is stunted because it remains dependent on relations with the core.

While IPE perspectives have different underlying views of the MNE, five faces or images are covered in all the paradigms and in the major IPE texts.[10] Three of these faces (the product life cycle, sovereignty at bay and the obsolescing bargain) were developed by Raymond Vernon;[11] the other two images (the law of uneven development and the international division of labour) by Stephen Hymer.[12] The first three faces of the MNE as outlined above fall within mainstream perspectives in IPE (liberal, nationalist); the latter faces within the radical IPE approach (Marxist). The first three faces take the world order as it exists and try to make the state-MNE relationship work more smoothly; they are thus exercises in problem-solving theory. The next two faces take an historical approach, appraising the changing role of MNEs and the need to change the existing world order, and are therefore exercises in critical theory.[13] Two of the faces (*i.e.*, sovereignty at bay and the obsolescing bargain) explicitly focus on the conflict between multinationals and states, and therefore are more attentive to the MNE as an actor within markets than most of the IPE literature. A brief summary of the five faces of MNEs in IPE follows.

The Product Life Cycle Model

Products have a life cycle where they move from being new to mature to obsolete. New products need frequent product and process changes in their pre-paradigm stage. As a result the production process is unstandardised, labour intensive and high cost, and needs to take place close to consumers. As product design matures, production becomes more capital intensive. Eventually significant economies of scale are achieved through mass production of standardised products.

The product cycle model as developed by Vernon explains the rise of MNEs from particular home countries in terms of the life cycle of the manufactured goods these firms produce. New products, developed first in the US, were exported to Europe once product designs had stabilised.[14] As the technology matured and foreign demand increased, US firms established branch plants to supply foreign demand and the profits from overseas production were used to generate new products. Vernon later revised the model to argue that foreign direct investment (FDI) was caused by the desire of oligopolistic MNEs to erect barriers to entry in foreign markets in order to maintain their market share.[15] In the later version, MNEs respond to local demands based on incomes and factor scarcities (*e.g.*, energy in Japan). Once the oligopoly becomes mature, the members use economies of scale in production, marketing and research and development as entry barriers to new firms. The oligopolists match each other move for move, generating a bunching of FDI. Eventually the oligopoly becomes senescent, the barriers fail to deter entry and cost competitiveness becomes key to survival. In this phase, MNEs shift production to the lowest cost locations and export products back to the home countries.

The product cycle model has lost its significance with the end of the technological gap and the narrowing of per capita income differentials within the Triad (*i.e.*, the US, Japan and the European Community). However, the model is still used to point out the essential market seeking character of FDI, the importance of technology in MNE activities, the flow of (albeit mature) technology from the parent firm to its subsidiaries, the rents that MNEs earn on overseas sales and production, and the substitutability between FDI and trade.

Millennium

Sovereignty at Bay

The phrase 'sovereignty at bay' has become a metaphor for the eventual decline of the nation-state in relation to MNEs that are above state control.[16] However, this was not the message of the book. As Vernon wryly notes, 'practically every reader remembers the title of the book; but scarcely anyone will accurately recall its context...the label (but not the contents) became generic'.[17] The original argument was that MNEs were used by home governments to extend their jurisdictional reach beyond their territorial limits; the US in particular practised this extraterritoriality.[18] Host governments also attempted to restrain and direct foreign subsidiaries located within their borders. The conflict between the social goals of states and the profit goals of MNEs generated significant tensions that were exacerbated by the shrinkage in international space, the narrowing gap in consumer tastes and the higher levels of international trade and capital flows. Vernon argued that nation-states would have to take action to constrain MNEs, facing the inherent conflicts in their 'double personality'. This would involve sorting out the problems of overlapping jurisdictions, double taxation, and their innate global reach.

In a later assessment of the sovereignty at bay theory, Vernon concludes that the three assumptions underlying the theory remain accurate: (1) host states want the benefits FDI can bring; (2) the policies of foreign subsidiaries reflect the overall strategic interests of the MNE; and (3) MNEs can serve as a conduit through which one state attempts to affect other states. While the 1971 book failed to predict the vast wave of nationalisations in the 1970s by Least Developing Country (LDC) governments, the problem of multiple jurisdiction still remains, and in fact has worsened since the 'number of players and intensity of the game' has risen.[19]

The question of whether states or MNEs are 'at bay' remains unsettled. Vernon and Spar argue that, although the 1980s were a relatively peaceful period of MNE-state relations, the problem of overlapping jurisdictions and states' capacities to monitor and control MNEs still exist.[20] As long as the United States insists on its right to regulate affiliates of US multinationals, Vernon and Spar foresee continued tensions. Moran, on the other hand, concludes from the case studies in his book that multinationals are at bay, not states.[21] State demands on the firms within their borders are escalating, paralysing MNEs caught between competing jurisdictions.

The Obsolescing Bargain

Kobrin calls the obsolescing bargain model the 'currently accepted paradigm of Host Country-MNC relations in international political economy'.[22] The model was developed by Vernon and has spawned an enormous literature.[23] These publications are among the best studies of MNEs in international political economy since they usually contain extensive analyses of particular industries, MNE global investment strategies, and the constraints these pose for state development policies.

The bargaining-power model explains the development of host country-MNE relations over time as a function of the goals, resources and constraints of each party. The model assumes that: (1) each party possesses assets valuable to the other; (2) each party has the ability to withhold these assets, thus giving it potential bargaining power with regard to the other; (3) each party is constrained in its exercise of this power; (4) the party with the larger actual bargaining power gains a larger share of the benefits; and (5) the game is positive sum so that both parties can win absolutely, although only one can win in relative terms.

The key argument of the model is that MNE-host state relations are dynamic and evolve over time. Prior to the entry of the MNE, the host government is assumed to be in a weak bargaining position. Given the uncertainty of investing in a new country, and the number of options open to the MNE, the state must offer concessions in order to attract entry. However, once the investment has been made, bargaining power shifts towards the host state. Over time, the uncertainty dissipates; the MNE commits more and more immobile resources that can be used as hostages; and the host country becomes less dependent on the MNE for capital, technology and access to markets as the FDI resource package diffuses throughout the economy. Thus the host state is likely to insist on renegotiating the bargain to capture more of the benefits. The MNE must either keep the host country dependent on it for new technology, products or access to export markets, give in to state demands, or exit. The obsolescing bargain model has been applied to many extractive (mining, petroleum) and manufacturing (autos, computers) industries. Kobrin concludes that manufacturing is not subject to the structurally based obsolescence of depletable resource industries.[24] Where the foreign subsidiary is part of a globalised industry or where technology is rapidly changing, the bargain may not obsolesce, and so the model may be inappropriate. Moran, however, notes that competition among MNEs for host country markets can strengthen the position of LDC governments, and concludes more optimistically that LDC states can use FDI to improve their developmental prospects over time.[25]

The Law of Uneven Development

The first of the critical (in Cox's sense) faces of the MNE is developed by Hymer who posits two laws of monopoly capitalism.[26] The first, the law of increasing firm size, documents the growth in size and complexity as the organisational structures of firms changed from local workshops to MNEs. He argued that MNEs create a spatial division of labour across the globe that corresponds to the vertical division of labour within the MNE. The corporate hierarchy becomes divided geographically into three divisions: top management in the largest core cities, white collar co-ordination in smaller core cities, and blue collar production distributed globally. As a result, the core becomes progressively more developed and the periphery less developed. This provides the second law, the law of uneven development. The oligopolistic behaviour of MNEs and their large size further exacerbates uneven development through tax avoidance, erosion of state power, and footloose production sites.

Hymer's uneven development argument is part of a broader dependency perspective that sees multinationals as the agent of external process that produce underdevelopment in the periphery.[27] One recent extension of Hymer's international class hierarchy is made by Cox who argues that as production and

Millennium

exchange became more internationalised in the 1970s, social forces mobilised and a transnational historic bloc emerged.[28] The members of this bloc – MNEs, multinational banks and internationalist institutions – are linked by transnational forces and have a shared ideology. Whereas Hymer focuses on a three level pyramid of production, Cox sees world classes being formed with the highest world class being a managerial class made up of labour and capitalists who work in the transnational historic bloc.

The Changing International Division of Labour

The division of labour has been a subject of inquiry since Adam Smith first discussed the advantages of specialisation in a pin factory.[29] Throughout the twentieth century the primary method of production has been Fordism.[30] The Fordist production process is based on the increasing division of tasks, the separation of skilled from unskilled labour, the mechanisation of skilled tasks, Taylorist methods of control, the assembly line and just-in-case inventories. Fordism is a capital intensive system, designed to achieve economies of scale through mass production of standardised products.

Hymer was the first to integrate the concept of the MNE with the concept of Fordist production to develop a theory of the international division of labour (IDL).[31] The IDL had four components, according to Hymer: firm expansion (the law of increasing firm size), hierarchy (the creation of a world hierarchy of classes), class conflict (conflict between the international managerial class and domestic classes), and the internationalisation of production (the movement of capital abroad through foreign direct investment). Throughout the 1860-1970 period, MNEs went abroad to gain access to raw materials in the periphery, exporting these materials for processing in the core. This old international division of labour was perceived by both Marxist and *dependency* scholars to be exploitative of the South.

In the 1970s, however, the type of FDI exported to the periphery states began to change. US multinationals, following the logic of the product cycle, began to search for cheaper labour sites and to move the production of mature technology products to developing countries. This new IDL, or NIDL, characterised the spread of FDI to the periphery from the early 1970s to the present. Asian and Latin American developing countries encouraged the inflow of this new type of foreign investment by setting up export processing zones with cheap, docile labour forces, tax incentives and minimal regulations. Most recently, the NIDL appears to be changing again (the new NIDL!) as MNEs adopt knowledge intensive methods of production, reducing the labour and materials content of production processes and outputs. This shift, referred to as post-Fordism, systemofacture or lean production, is reflected in the adoption by MNEs of new information technology products and Japanese flexible production processes.

In summary, the IPE literature views MNEs as oligopolistic firms that control and organise production facilities in two or more countries. The firms are usually in manufacturing or resource industries, have parents headquartered in the US or Western Europe, and expand abroad through wholly owned foreign affiliates. MNE relationships with their home countries are usually assumed to be amicable,

Bringing the Firm Back In: Multinationals in IPE

whereas host country relationships are more adversarial. Developing countries are used by multinationals as sources of raw material and/or cheap labour inputs. FDI provides a package of capital, technology and management skills to host countries; however, FDI also brings a loss of sovereignty and the ability of home states to influence host development. In this writer's opinion, the political economy model that best captured host country-multinational relationships is the obsolescing bargain model. The analyst's view of the future of MNE-state relations depends on the IPE perspective that is adopted: there may be a sovereignty at bay world where MNEs dominate states, a mercantilist version where states dominate, or a dependency version where the periphery remains permanently dependent on the transnational capital from core states.

Let us now turn to the current thinking about global MNEs in the international business studies (IBS) literature and see how this literature differs from the five faces of the MNE in international political economy.

MULTINATIONALS IN INTERNATIONAL BUSINESS STUDIES

Within international business studies (IBS), research on multinationals falls into three time periods: the 1950s to mid-1970s, the mid-1970s to mid-1980s and the mid-1980s onwards.[32] The focus of inquiry has shifted from a macro approach to FDI, to an examination of the firm as an institution, to a focus on the value adding activities of MNEs. Regardless of the focus, the perspectives all fall broadly within what IPE scholars would define as liberalism. All are exercises in problem solving and little attempt is made to examine MNEs from a critical perspective. While the work of neomarxists such as Hymer are known to IBS scholars, only contributions in a liberal context are carried over to IBS.[33] There are crossovers between IPE and IBS. Vernon's contributions are well known; the product cycle, sovereignty at bay and the obsolescing bargain are discussed in the IBS textbooks. Similarly, the obsolescing bargain is considered by IBS scholars, as well as by IPE scholars, to characterise host country-MNE relations. Most IPE scholars are aware of John Dunning's work on multinationals, and his explanation for the growth of MNEs, the OLI (ownership, location and internalisation) paradigm, is covered in several IPE texts.[34] The existence of research centres on MNEs, *e.g.*, Vernon and his colleagues at Harvard and Dunning and his colleagues at the University of Reading, has facilitated interchange between scholars from different disciplines. The UN Centre on Transnational Corporations (UNCTC) has also encouraged this. Kindleberger's work on FDI and Chandler's work on the business history of MNEs are known to both groups. [35]

However, in spite of these crossovers it is clear that the IBS focus on multinationals differs from that of the IPE scholars, with IPE scholars generally taking the more critical view. In addition, the IPE literature, with the exception of recent work on the international division of labour, lags behind IBS research on global multinationals. The outline of current IBS research given below has not crossed over into mainstream IPE thinking on multinationals. The complexity of international value-adding activities of MNEs in the 1990s and its implications for states and markets remain to be explored.

Millennium

Explaining MNEs: The OLI Paradigm

International business studies has taken three approaches to the study of the MNE. Initially the IBS literature took a macro approach, examining issues such as the substitutability of FDI and international trade, the effects of FDI on host countries, the composition and location of FDI, and the US as the largest home country.[36] While various definitions of the MNE existed, the simplest was that MNEs were enterprises that owned and managed production establishments in more than one country. In the mid-1970s the focus shifted from looking at the act of FDI to examining the institution making the investments abroad.[37] The MNE is now seen as an institutional structure that co-ordinates activities across borders. While there are many individual theories about the MNE, the generally accepted paradigm containing the various theories for understanding the existence, patterns and growth of the MNE is the eclectic or OLI paradigm developed by John Dunning.[38]

The OLI paradigm argues that MNEs form and grow because they possess three sets of advantages relative to other firms. These advantages of ownership, locational and internalisation are sometimes referred to as the OLI tripod. All three sets of advantages must be taken into account simultaneously in order to explain the existence of multinationals and the reasons for their growth and success in certain sectors or countries. These advantages can also be used to analyze MNE decisions about locating, expanding or divesting abroad.[39]

Since the mid-1980s there has been another shift, this time to thinking about the international value adding or production activities of the MNE rather than the firm's institutional structure. This shift in focus to international production by MNEs has several motives. First, the work done by Michael Porter and other IBS scholars in the United States on strategic management of MNEs, along with new concepts such as the value chain (more on this below), have infiltrated the OLI model. Second, there has been an enormous increase, since the early 1980s, both in crossborder alliances between firms in the same industry within the Triad economies and in alternative contractual arrangements such as subcontracting in the LDCs. The focus on the firm as a single entity has therefore been broadened to examine clusters of firms and nonequity investment relationships.[40] Third, the increasing use by states of aggressive industrial policies in high-technology sectors designed to increase national competitiveness has focused attention on the role states can play in engineering long run competitive advantage.[41] Fourth, the technological revolution that has been occurring as information technology and biotechnology transform production and distribution methods has generated more attention to crossborder technology, service and data flows.[42] Fifth, the move of Japanese firms from exporting to setting-up production plants in the United States and Europe has drawn attention to process technology changes (*e.g.*, just-in-time, flexible automation) that are affecting the value adding strategies of MNEs.[43] Sixth, the rapid rise of MNEs in services such as banking, business services and retailing has shifted attention away from manufacturing and natural resource multinationals and toward explaining international production of services. All of these factors have influenced the definition of an MNE in the international business studies literature. Dunning's new definition for a global MNE is:

Bringing the Firm Back In: Multinationals in IPE

an orchestrator of production and transactions within a cluster, or network, of cross border internal and external relationships, which may or may not involve equity investment, but which are intended to serve its global interest.[44]

These new style MNEs have ownership, locational and internalisation advantages which explain their growth and success in international markets.

1. Ownership Advantages

MNEs have ownership advantages on which they can earn rents in foreign locations and which allow MNEs to overcome the cost disadvantage of producing in foreign markets. These advantages are usually intangible, based either on knowledge or oligopoly, and can be transferred relatively costlessly within the MNE. Knowledge advantages include product and process innovations, marketing and management skills, patents, brand names, *etc.*; whereas oligopolistic advantages include economies of scale and scope, and privileged access to various resources. Ownership advantages arise from one of three sources: (1) the firm's size and access to markets, resources and/or intangibles; (2) the firm's ability to co-ordinate complementary activities (*e.g.*, manufacturing and distribution); and (3) the 'global scanning' ability, which allows MNEs to exploit differences between countries. These core competencies provide potential access to a wide variety of markets, contribute significantly to customer satisfaction, and are difficult to imitate.[45] However, they are not fixed for the firm; ownership advantages require identification and continuous investment to prevent their dissipation and/or obsolescence. The advantages can be lost if firms do not understand and invest sufficiently and effectively in their areas of competency. Some of the most recent work on MNEs is now turning to this problem, focusing on issues such as: (1) the core competencies of various MNEs in the same industrial sector and why they vary across countries[46]; (2) the underlying structures which states can provide to help generate successful firms[47]; (3) how technological advantages can be generated, appropriated and sustained over time[48]; (4) the role of entrepreneurial culture as an advantage[49]; and (5) whether firm-specific advantages are necessary to explain the existence of MNEs.[50]

2. Internalisation Advantages

Internalisation advantages arise from exploiting the differences among exogenous imperfections faced by MNEs in external markets. Exogenous imperfections are of two types. The first group are inherent to certain types of markets, arising, for example, from the public good aspect of knowledge, from uncertainty and from the existence of transactions costs in all external markets. Through using markets internal to the firm, the MNE can reduce uncertainty and transactions costs and generate knowledge more efficiently. The second type are state-generated imperfections (such as tariffs, foreign exchange controls and subsidies). State policies in the internalisation literature are considered as inefficient policies to be arbitraged by MNEs, implying that internalisation is a welfare improving activity. MNEs with global horizons are thus seen as efficient actors, offsetting the

Millennium

inefficient activities of states with their national horizons (a very different perspective from IPE scholars!). Internalisation theory therefore predicts that hierarchy (the vertically or horizontally integrated firm) is a better method of organising transactions than the market (trade between unrelated firms) whenever markets are imperfect. By replacing an external or missing external market with an internal, hierarchical control structure, the impact of market failures can be reduced.

Internalisation advantages can also be generated by exploiting oligopolistic rivalry among competing MNEs, when the firms themselves create or worsen market defects.[51] Oligopolistic imperfections include exertion of monopoly power, cross-subsidisation of markets and opportunistic exploitation of suppliers or buyers. IPE scholars have tended to emphasise endogenous imperfections created by MNEs as international oligopolists, starting with Hymer's laws of uneven development and increasing firm size. Most internalisation theorists, however, have de-emphasised this aspect, focusing on MNEs as efficient internalisers of market imperfections.[52] Some IBS scholars do take exception, arguing that internalisation is not just a passive response to market failure but also one of the rules of the game for firms trying to avoid risks by creating barriers to entry for competitors.[53]

Internalisation helps prevent the dissipation of, and increase the rents from, the core competencies of the MNE. The early internalisation literature of the late 1970s and early 1980s assumed that it would be more profitable for MNEs to earn rents on their ownership advantages and service foreign markets through wholly owned subsidiaries than by exporting or licensing to foreign markets. More recent work has extended the OLI model to other arrangements such as joint ventures and subcontracting, and has shown that FDI is not always the most effective choice for the MNE.[54] Firms face a wide range of options in contractual arrangement for transacting goods, services and factors across borders. The range extends from the polar case of markets – buying or selling to unrelated firms at arm's length in external markets (this is considered low control, but has a high risk of dissipation of ownership advantages) – to the polar case of hierarchies – all transactions take place between wholly owned affiliates in an internal market where the firms are related and not at arm's length; (this is a high control, low risk option).[55] There are a variety of contractual arrangement options in between, offering varying amounts of control and risk to the MNE. Internalisation theory predicts that MNEs compare the costs and benefits of alternative modes and select the most profitable.[56]

Contractual relationships within the MNE have varied historically. Until the mid-1970s most MNEs preferred the wholly-owned subsidiary; more recently MNEs have increasingly moved to nonequity contractual arrangements. State strategies for import substituting industrialisation in the 1950s and 1960s encouraged MNEs to choose the wholly-owned subsidiary as a vehicle for entry into developing countries. However, the rise in host regulations and wave of nationalisations in the 1970s encouraged MNEs to switch to nonequity investments. Low interest rates and easy bank loans also facilitated this move. Nonconventional MNEs and new MNEs without ready access to financial capital also often chose what we can call the foreign minority investment (FMI) route in preference to FDI. The situation changed in the early 1980s as real interest rates

Bringing the Firm Back In: Multinationals in IPE

rose and bank lending to LDCs dried up. Given the shortage of FDI inflows into developing countries, many have been forced to liberalise their investment policies to attract capital. Structural adjustment policies endorsed by the World Bank and the International Monetary Fund are also encouraging this policy change. While developing countries are now more willing to allow inflows of FDI, multinationals have come to realise that foreign minority investments have their own advantages. MNEs can earn rents on their ownership advantages without owning or financing investments in developing countries by concentrating on supplying technology, marketing and management skills while the host country partner puts up the equity capital and does the actual production. Thus more of the risk but also more of the potential gains are shifted to the host country. Oman notes that small or latecomer MNEs (*e.g.* from the four Asian tigers) use minority investment more than the FDI route, and that even the largest multinationals will use this strategy in protected or isolated markets.[57]

3. Locational Advantages

The third advantage possessed by MNEs is their access to factors of production in foreign countries, *i.e.*, locational or country-specific advantages. Ownership advantages must be used in combination with immobile factors in foreign countries to induce foreign production. These country specific advantages determine which countries are hosts to MNE foreign production. Locational advantages can be broken into three categories: economic, social and political factors, all of which can be expected to change over time. Country risk analysis is used by MNEs and multinational banks to estimate the advantages of different locations. Economic advantages are based on a country's factor endowments of labour, capital, technology, management skills and natural resources. In addition, market size and transportation and communications can make a host location more or less economically attractive. Noneconomic or social advantages include the psychic distance between countries in terms of language, culture, ethnicity, and business customs. Political advantages include general host government attitudes towards foreign MNEs and specific policies that affect FDI and production such as trade barriers and investment regulations. Foreign production is expected to move to countries that are geographically close and have similar incomes and tastes to the home country, and have good factor endowments and low factor costs.[58]

Dunning has recently argued that IBS scholars need to pay more attention to the role of locational advantages as underlying factors affecting the core competencies of the MNE.[59] In fact, the impact of political factors on all three elements of the OLI tripod has been underestimated. The lack of coverage of MNEs in the IPE literature is matched by the lack of coverage of the state in international business.[60] Some work has been started in this area. Ostry focuses specifically on the political economy of policy making in the United States, the European Community and Japan, looking at the role MNEs have played in the Uruguay Round of the GATT and in the development of national policies for high-technology industries.[61] Rugman and Verbeke examine the interactions between government trade policies and MNEs using a series of two-by-two matrices to characterise firm strategies.[62]

The OLI paradigm traditionally has focused on the why, how and where questions: Why do firms go abroad? How do they choose modes of entry? Where do they go? The management of these firms once abroad received less attention. In this regard, the American strategic management literature, based on the concept of the value chain, is an essential prerequisite to understanding the new style MNEs of the 1990s.

Strategic Management and the International Value Chain

The theory of strategic management was developed initially in the United States.[63] Strategic management theorists model firms engaging in a range of activities called the value chain. The value chain consists of primary activities (functions involved in the physical creation of the product such as extraction, processing, assembly, distribution, sales and service) and support activities (functions that provide the infrastructure necessary to support the primary activities such as research and development, finance, marketing). Each firm must decide the shape and length of its value chain, *i.e.*, the number of products it produces, the number of value adding activities in which it engages, and the number of geographical areas in which these activities take place. These decisions depend on the firm's overall management strategy. The choice of overall strategy for the MNE affects its choice of structure and location.

The international value chain concept recognises that MNEs have additional strategies that are not available to domestic firms. MNEs can locate stages of the value chain in different countries, or have several plants at the same stage of the value chain in different locations. MNEs can adopt differing positions depending on the country location and the position of the affiliate within the MNE. According to Porter global strategies for MNEs fall into one of four categories: global cost leadership or differentiation (selling a wide range of products globally); global segmentation (selling a narrow range of products worldwide or, alternatively, a wide range in a subset of countries); protected markets (seeking shelter from foreign competition markets are protected by host governments); and national responsiveness (developing products that meet local needs in particular countries).[64] MNEs can adopt a wider range of strategies than can domestic firms by taking advantage of economic, political, geographic, social and cultural differences among countries.[65]

The combination of the OLI paradigm and the value chain thus provides a simple explanation for the existence of vertically and horizontally integrated MNEs. A horizontally integrated MNE produces the same product or product line (*i.e.*, at the same stage of the value chain) in two or more plants located in different countries. A basic motivation for horizontal integration is the additional rents in the foreign location that can be earned on the MNE's firm- specific assets. Usually horizontal integration occurs at the final assembly and sales stages for market-driven manufacturing MNEs as states demand nationally responsive MNEs or MNEs seek shelter behind protectionist barriers erected by states. A vertically integrated MNE, on the other hand, controls and co-ordinates two or more different value adding activities such as resource processing and manufacturing. The basic motivation for vertical integration is the avoidance of exogenous transactions and governmental costs associated with external markets. Uncertainty and incomplete futures markets combine to raise barriers to contract making between unrelated firms, particularly in natural resource industries and industries where quality control is essential.[66] Government barriers can be avoided through such techniques as transfer pricing of intrafirm trade and financial flows, and leading and lagging of payments.[67]

1. Managerial Structures of Global Multinationals

The managerial structure of a firm describes its executive lines of authority and responsibility, lines of communication, information flows and how they are channelled and processed.[68] There are many kinds of international managerial structures available to MNEs.[69] In the 1970s most American multinationals followed nationally responsive or shelter strategies based on supplying products to segmented national markets. MNEs decentralised day-to-day operations to national subsidiaries, but used centralised service staffs for headquarters functions such as financial planning and policymaking.[70] Hymer's vision of the three level pyramid of decision making within the MNE was an accurate characterisation of the command and control structure of most MNEs.

Information technology is changing this, however.[71] Telecommunications networks can be used to link MNE affiliates worldwide, providing centralised corporate data bases for use by both headquarters and affiliates. This improves centralised control by the parent firm and creates new information channels within the organisation. The parent firm can monitor foreign operations more effectively with fewer middle managers to analyse and relay information. In addition, information technology is homogenising tastes through increasing the mobility of consumers and information. International brand recognition (*e.g.*, Sony, Gucci) is increasing. The advantages of moving to a global cost leadership or differentiation strategy are encouraging the integration of local and international planning. The more integrated the structure, the less the local autonomy of the affiliate and the greater the centralisation and co-ordination functions of the parent. MNEs are moving to organisational structures that more effectively promote global planning objectives. As a result, the tension between the national objectives of states, both home and host governments and the global goals of MNEs is more likely to increase in the 1990s.

2. Locational Choices of Global Multinationals

In the general OLI framework outlined above, the ownership advantages of the multinational enterprise give it advantages over domestic firms in going abroad. The internalisation advantages imply that the MNE can best profit from its advantages through a hierarchy of vertical and horizontal intrafirm equity and nonequity linkages. However, neither of these two factors determines where the MNE invests. Location, like structure, tends to follow strategy, *i.e.*, the particular location selected by the MNE depends on the strategic role that the affiliate is to play within the multinational. MNEs go abroad for many reasons: gaining access to low-cost foreign inputs such as natural resources and labour, being close to foreign markets, earning rents on ownership advantages, and pre-empting competition by

Millennium

rival firms. The list can be reduced to three general categories that influence plant location: securing natural resources, reducing costs, and gaining access to foreign markets. Locational decisions determine initial FDI and subsequent trade patterns; both horizontal and vertical FDI have resulted in substantial growth in intrafirm trade flows in the post-war period.[71] Locational advantages are the key to determining which countries become host countries for the MNE, and depend on whether the purpose of the investment is resource seeking, cost reduction, or market access. In setting up a foreign plant, global MNEs can choose among several different types of locational structures. Given the basic purpose behind the investment, some structures are more likely than others. Since states often want to influence the nature of the foreign investments offered by an MNE, it is clearly crucial for states to know what the underlying purpose of the investment is. Strategies designed to encourage more local production of R&D may be useless if the foreign factory has been set up simply to take advantage of low labour costs. The various locational structures available to the MNE fall into three categories corresponding to the three strategies, resource seeking, cost reducing and market access. These are outlined below and illustrated in Figure 1:[72]

Resource seeking strategic investments:
Extractors secure natural resources essential to the production process. The key factor driving location is the need to be close to raw materials. *Processors* turn raw materials into fabricated materials through refineries, smelters and fabricators. If the weight-to-value ratio is high, economies of scale at the two stages similar, and foreign tariffs on processed imports low, extracting and processing may occur in the same plant.

Cost reducing strategic investments:
Offshores use cheap local inputs such as low wage labour to produce components or assemble inputs which are then re-exported to the MNE for further assembly. Many investments in export processing zones are of this type. As wage rates rise, footloose offshores move from country to country searching for lower cost sites. *Source factories* provide access to low-cost inputs, but also carry responsibility for developing and producing specific components for the MNE. Sources are globally rationalised plants where the factory produces subcomponents for final assembly and sale elsewhere. These factories are tightly integrated into MNE networks since output is sold within the MNE.[73]

Market access strategic investments:
Importers facilitate MNE sales in a host country by providing marketing, sales, service and warehousing facilities. Most Japanese early investments in Europe and North America were importer factories. *Local servers* are also designed to service local markets, but they normally assemble subcomponents for domestic sale (*e.g.*, bottling plants, drug packaging). Where state regulations require MNEs to maintain a local presence, local servers are normally chosen as the choice of location. *Focused factories* are globally rationalised firms that produce one or two product lines in mass production runs for final sale in local and foreign markets, exchanging these product lines for those produced of other focused factories

within the MNE family. They are relatively autonomous and nationally responsive units with some process technology facility.

Miniature replicas are plants that assemble and sell a full range of products, similar to the parent in the local market, generally due to a shelter strategy adopted by the MNE in response to host country trade barriers. Miniature replicas are likely to be costly, inefficient plants in domestic markets are small. *Lead factories* are equal partners with the parent firm in developing new technology and products for global markets. Lead factories are placed in strategic locations within the Triad and are insiders in each of their major locations. *Outposts* are R&D intensive investments set up by MNEs from one of the Triad countries in the other Triad markets to source knowledge worldwide and to act as a window on technology developments. MNEs are now moving abroad to improve access to technology and share research and development costs with strategic partners such as universities, governments and rival firms. Programmes such as ESPRIT in Europe are encouraging the formation of outposts.

Figure 1 illustrates both the concept of the MNE's value chain and the range of strategic locational choices available to the firm. Each investment is placed in the appropriate part of the MNE's value chain depending on whether the general motivation for foreign production is resource seeking, cost reduction or market access. The higher the vertical placement, the greater the amount of technological innovation expected from the factory.

In summary, each MNE, depending on the length of its value chain and the nature of the industries in which it competes, consists of a set of foreign affiliates, strategically located according to their underlying resource, cost or market function. These affiliates are part of the firm's direct value chain if they are owned and controlled by the parent firm. They become part of the MNE's indirect value chain if the foreign factories are linked to the MNE through contractual arrangements or strategic alliances.

The choice of location strategy is partly dependent on the age of the affiliate.[74] Firms may first go abroad by setting up extractors, offshores or importers. As the plant matures, a growth in functions is likely. Extractors may take on processing functions, offshores become sources, and importers become focused factories. Locational factors can influence this upgrading. Cascading tariff structures in Triad countries deter offshore processing and assembly. In mature industries such as automobiles, global MNEs follow integrative strategies that are cost driven, using source factories to divide production among affiliates and subcontractors, assembling the final products locally to meet domestic content requirements. Government-controlled industries such as telecommunications and aircraft, on the other hand, tend to adopt more nationally responsive strategies, *e.g.*, miniature replicas and focused factories.[75]

The revolution in information technology (IT) is also affecting the locational choices of MNEs. Natural resources and unskilled labour are being eliminated as sources of competitive advantage, while highly skilled workers are in increased demand. Given the global mobility of capital, MNEs are moving to set up factories in Triad cities to gain access to new technology. With the short product life cycles that the IT revolution has partly generated, access to the latest technology becomes more important. Just as in the 1970s, the MNEs set up offshore factories to take

Millennium

FIGURE 1: LOCATIONAL STRATEGIES OF MULTINATIONALS

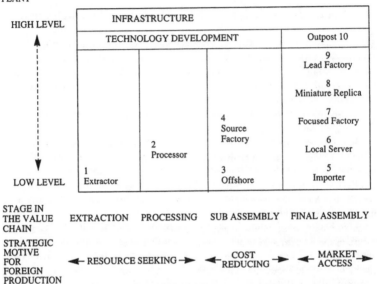

LEVEL OF
TECHNOLOGICAL
ACTIVITIES
PERFORMED
BY THE FOREIGN
PLANT

advantage of cheap labour through source factories, in the 1990s MNEs are setting up outposts and lead plants to take advantage of cheaper and newer sources of knowledge.[76] In the 1990s, knowledge-intensive production requires worldwide access to knowledge and this is replacing the search for cheap labour as the driving force behind MNE's foreign location strategies.

In summary, the field of international business studies is a rapidly growing area, where the focus of inquiry has shifted from explaining the act of FDI, to analysing the firm making the investments, to examining the international value adding activities of MNEs. The key ideas behind IBS are the OLI paradigm, the value chain and strategic management as tools explaining the organisational and locational structures of the new style MNEs of the 1990s. While there have been some crossovers between IBS and IPE scholars, particularly the work of Raymond Vernon, the concepts of the OLI tripod and the international value chain and their implications for states and markets have been little discussed by IPE scholars. In this last section, we turn to bringing the firm back into IPE.

BRINGING THE FIRM BACK IN: MULTINATIONALS IN IPE

As outlined above, IBS scholars have tried to understand and explain the new style MNEs of the 1990s. They are giant firms, linked by equity and nonequity

Bringing the Firm Back In: Multinationals in IPE

relations in clusters, engaged in two-way flows of products, investments and technology within the Triadic economies. What implications does the IBS literature have for the faces of the MNE portrayed in the IPE literature? First, we examine some implications for the concept of states versus markets, and then for the five faces of MNEs in the IPE literature.

Bringing the Firm Back In: MNEs, Markets and Globalisation

IPE scholars argue that increasing interdependence or globalisation in the 1980s has exacerbated the tension between states and markets as neomercantilistic states jockey for competitive advantages in a shrinking world. However, if one examines the concept of globalisation more closely, the dominance of multinationals in this process becomes clear.

The globalisation of markets has been well documented.[77] It is a multifaceted phenomenon with at least three components. The first, convergence, refers to the trend within the Triad countries for the underlying production, financial and technology structures to approach a common average standard. For example, the technology gap between the United States and Europe and Japan has substantially lessened. Per capita income differentials have narrowed considerably. Although some would argue that the United States is still the global hegemon, it clearly acts in a multipolar world. Consumer tastes within the Triad countries have become more homogeneous, leading to the development of global markets and global products. OECD tariff rate differentials, both among countries and among product classifications, have narrowed, as have corporate tax differentials, further encouraging the globalisation of markets.

The second measure of globalisation, synchronisation, refers to the increasing macroeconomic tendency for the Triad economies to move in tandem, experiencing similar business cycle patterns. This has partly been hastened by the G7 states agreeing after the Plaza Accord to synchronise their economies more closely through monetary, fiscal and exchange rate policies. Increasingly, states are also using similar microeconomic and structural policies, *e.g.*, liberalisation, deregulation, privatisation, to encourage development and growth. The third component, interpenetration, has received the most attention. It refers to the growing importance of trade, investment and technology flows, both inwards and outwards, within each domestic economy. Trade and investment flows have grown faster than world GDP consistently since the 1950s, and this trend has accelerated since the mid-1980s. Two-way or intra-industry flows dominate intra-OECD patterns.[78]

A closer look at these three measures of globalisation, however, makes clear the importance of multinationals as the engineers or agents of this increasing interdependence. Statistics document the overwhelming importance of MNEs in today's markets.[79] While only a portion of MNEs are truly global, the 500 largest account for about 80 per cent of all foreign production and have sales turnovers of at least $US 100 billion.[80] Investment, trade and technology flows within the Triad economies are increasingly dominated by MNEs with global strategies. Eighty per cent of MNE activities are now within Triad countries, mostly two-way flows in similar industries.[81]

Millennium

MNEs now dominate all the underlying structures of the global economy: production, finance, technology, security, energy and trade. Let us now turn to the five faces of MNEs in IPE and attempt to show how these faces need to be modified for the new style MNEs of the 1990s.

Bringing the Firm Back In: Faces of the MNE in IPE

1. The Product Life Cycle

The problems with the product cycle model of FDI are well known, with Vernon himself arguing that it has become obsolete.[82] The first version of the model suffers from several problems. In the first place, its single focus on the market seeking motive for FDI and inattention to the choices of foreign factories available to the MNE is too limited. The model assumes that firms set up abroad once foreign demand is high enough to justify the additional costs of producing in a foreign location. However, as argued above, global MNEs have at least three motives for going abroad: resource seeking, cost reduction and market access. Second, the model assumes that MNEs produce technologically sophisticated goods initially developed in their home markets. MNEs are viewed as the creators of technology, transferring it outwards to foreign affiliates. However, with the elimination of the technological gap, the homogenisation of tastes and the ease of international communications among the Triad economies, global MNEs now have lead plants and outposts in the major Triad markets in order to take advantage of domestic technology. Thus the parent firm is importing products and technology from its foreign affiliate abroad in a reversal of the model's prediction. In addition, the product cycle model cannot explain where or when particular products are developed in the Triad, or why there are mutual cross investments by MNEs in each other's markets.[83] The focus on manufactured goods rather than services is also problematic. The increasing volume of trade and FDI in services such as banking and engineering services does not fit the model well.

Vernon's second product cycle model, where the firms are strategic rivals engaged in battles over global market share does, however, describe today's oligopolistic global MNEs. It is surprising that the second version of the model still receives less attention than the first. Interpreted in a Triad-non-Triad framework where product cycles are short and research and development costs high, only the largest firms can afford to be technological leaders. Thus strategic alliances are increasingly being used in the Triad among global MNEs to exchange complementary technologies.[84] These alliances strengthen the position of global MNEs versus other firms, and the position of Triad countries versus other nations. Note that the creation of knowledge through strategic alliances is not itself the problem; problems arise because global MNEs operate in oligopolistic world markets where ownership advantages can be exploited to earn oligopolistic rents. However, the second product cycle model argues that the oligopoly itself becomes mature and obsolescent. With the information technology revolution, even mature products are undergoing rejuvenation. It is hard to argue that markets are maturing, and with the wide range of products which global MNEs produce and sell, generalisations about obsolescence are hard to justify. Thus the utility of the product cycle model in explaining today's global MNEs is somewhat limited.

Bringing the Firm Back In: Multinationals in IPE

2. Sovereignty at Bay

This is the twentieth anniversary of Vernon's sovereignty at bay thesis. Vernon and Spar argue that the model, interpreted as conflicts between states and MNEs, remains an accurate portrayal of MNE-state relations.[85] Extra-territoriality is still a problem as long as home countries such as the US maintain their rights to enforce domestic regulations on overseas affiliates of domestic MNEs. Two trends may check this somewhat. First, the trend to substitute foreign minority investments for FDI means that 'quasi-affiliates' may not be subject to the same home regulations. With the limits of the firm becoming less discernible (*e.g.*, are cross licenses, subcontracts and joint ventures part of the MNE?), it becomes more difficult for home and host states to enforce regulations such as transfer pricing and taxation rules. Second, the inflow of foreign investments is turning the United States into a host country. Its domestic policies for MNEs (antitrust, tax, national treatment, patent laws) were set up when the United States was a home country. With cross-cutting investments, US goals can be expected to change, albeit slowly, as foreign subsidiaries press for more favourable treatment in the United States.[86]

Vernon's three assumptions should also be modified to accommodate the global firms of the 1990s. First, states want economic, social and political benefits from the MNEs in their midst. With Triad countries being both home and host states simultaneously, pressures will be put on both domestic and foreign MNEs. Second, MNEs are caught between internal pressures for a globally integrative strategy and external pressures for a nationally responsive strategy. Different MNEs, depending on their structures and locational choices, will choose different mixes of integration and national responsiveness. Third, minority investments allow a more nationally responsive strategy while reducing the risks and costs involved in foreign production. Fourth, states are increasingly using domestic firms to further national competitiveness and strategic goals. Thus states, while now less attentive to the ownership of a particular plant, are demanding more contribution to national competitiveness.

An obvious extension, given the escalating demands for competitiveness by home states, is to apply the obsolescing bargain model in the home country-MNE situation. It is clear that Triad states are demanding more from the MNEs within their midst.[87] The usual assumption is that home states and MNEs have common interests. However, given the crosshauling of investments and the intra-industry nature of trade and investment flows, it becomes difficult to identify global MNEs in terms of their ownership. Nationality may be becoming a technical or legal term without real meaning. When firms are allied to each other through webs of co-operative arrangements, it becomes difficult for them to identify which firms are rivals, and where their national allegiance lies. MNEs are likely to respond in different ways to pressures depending on the rapidity of change they face and the homogeneity of firms in the industry.[88] Their willingness to co-operate with home country policies should vary depending on their value chains, their locational and organisational structures and the equity and nonequity arrangements to which they are tied.

While both MNEs and Triad states appear to have more options, both groups

Millennium

face increasing pressures: MNEs from other global rivals, states from domestic interest groups. Domestic regulation of MNEs has little effect unless accompanied by information exchanges among states. International regulations of MNEs remain toothless and nonbinding. One possible regulatory regime might emerge from the Uruguay Round. If the General Agreement on Tariffs and Trade (GATT) is extended to cover more investment issues (intellectual property rights, trade related investment measures), there may emerge codes of conduct which like-minded states can sign, effectively creating an international club within which MNEs are regulated.[89] It is unlikely that developing countries would be willing to join such a club; however, with substantial two way flows of investments, Triad states may find it to their mutual benefit to regulate MNE actions regionally. The inclusion of FDI measures within the Canada-US free trade agreement is one signal of this possible trend in state-MNE relations.

3. The Obsolescing Bargain

The theory of global MNEs adds further complications to the obsolescing bargain model. On the one hand, host states are faced with a shortage of savings, both domestic and international, with which to finance investments. Thus the need for inflows from MNEs has never been higher and host country bargaining power probably never been less, particularly for the least developed countries in sub-Saharan Africa. In addition, with more MNEs following global strategies focused on knowledge intensive production, the country-specific advantages of many developing countries are not high enough to attract global MNEs. The declining resource and labour intensity of production and the need to locate upstream suppliers close to final production are causing some MNEs to shift production from the South to the North.[90] Lastly, with well defined locational strategies, MNEs locate foreign plants in order to achieve particular purposes. The ability of host states to demand these affiliates move up the value chain and add more value locally becomes difficult. Host states need to understand the overall strategy of global MNEs and how their affiliates fit into this strategy. While the host state and domestic interest groups may see foreign firms as levers of change and adopt strategies that target particular MNE policies, affiliates vary in their will and capacity to respond.[91]

On the other hand, as MNEs delink foreign production from ownership, more firms that are willing to unbundle the FDI package – for a price. As Oman notes, while host countries may call such inflows foreign investments, in many cases the foreign firm is really engaged in exporting (*e.g.*, turnkey plants).[92] When the MNE is a seller of access to its core competencies, the divergence of interests between the MNE and the host state is more profound since the two are effectively locked in a bilateral monopoly. As an investor however, the MNE has a shared interest with the host state in maximising the overall profit on the project, even though they differ over the relative gains. Thus host LDCs now may face more options in terms of foreign inflows but minority investments may not be as attractive in the long run.

Bringing the Firm Back In: Multinationals in IPE

4. The Law of Uneven Development

Hymer's concern with the inequity of the FDI process, its tendency to concentrate wealth and highly paid jobs in the North, remains a present concern of IPE scholars. The focus of international business studies on the MNE as an efficient international unit, arbitraging markets and state-generated imperfections is not one for which critical IPE theorists have much sympathy. Although it should be stated that movement is occurring in both directions. IBS scholars are becoming more concerned about the oligopolistic tendencies of global MNEs; while IPE scholars are faced with the graduation of some Asian countries to income levels above certain members of the Triad, demonstrating that periphery states can engineer their own movement up the development ladder using foreign investment.[93]

The new-style MNEs of the 1990s, however, may play out the law of uneven development by widening the income gap between the richest and poorest countries. With FDI almost occurring totally within Triadic economies and strategic alliances among Triad MNEs producing most technology, the technology gap between the North and the poorest countries of the South (*e.g.*, sub-Saharan Africa) is likely to widen. While lead plants may be located in more than one country (decentralising Hymer's top management jobs), they will only be found within the Triad. As the newly industrializing economies graduate to more capital and knowledge intensive production plants, the poorest LDCs may well be left with only resource seeking and cost reducing foreign investments. Without a more open trading order that encourages LDC exports of labour intensive manufactured products to the North and attracts MNE investments, uneven development – a wealthy core, fast growing semiperiphery and stagnant periphery – may well continue.

5. The Changing International Division of Labour

It is on this face that IPE and IBS scholars are closest; but, while both have focused on technological change, the two groups have had quite different concerns. IPE scholars, worried about the impact on developing countries, have generally taken a critical view of the worldwide sourcing strategies of MNEs and also fear the movement of production from the South to the North under post-Fordism. Most IBS scholars, on the other hand, have been interested in the impact of technological change on cost-savings and competitiveness for the Triad economies. Both groups agree, however, that the tendency to uneven development may be exacerbated by information technology.

Changes in product and process technology are encouraging the introduction of flexible manufacturing systems in manufacturing plants. Low-cost labour is no longer the focus of MNE worldwide sourcing. Sourcing new products and processes from other Triad partners is now key for the new-style MNEs. Offshores are therefore likely to be more footloose in the 1990s, moving back to the OECD countries. As some authors have argued, the newly industrializing economies may have difficulty retaining their share of MNE value added unless they increase their locational advantages.[94]

217

Millennium

Nevertheless the impact of post-Fordism on service sector MNEs has been little studied by either group; nor has there been much examination of the effects on the various MNE locational strategies.[95] If MNEs secure natural resources through nonequity investments and are less attentive to labour costs, there are still a number of factors that will determine the choice of location. Further research on the impact of choices on LDCs is needed.

In conclusion, the new five faces of the MNE outlined above differ from the general ones presented in the IPE literature. The international business studies literature calls for more attention to the specificities of global MNEs: their goals, strategies, structures and locational patterns. The key characteristics of the new-style MNEs are their clusters of equity and nonequity relationships, the increasing importance of access to foreign knowledge rather than resources or labour inputs, and their complicated patterns of international value chains. From the brief outline presented here, we conclude that more work on upgrading the five faces is necessary; IPE scholars need to 'move up the value chain' in their analyses of the multinational within IPE.

CONCLUSIONS

The purpose of this paper was to examine the ways in which multinationals are treated within international political economy and to document the need to 'bring the firm back in'. The paper reviewed the faces which multinationals assume in the IPE literature, contrasted these with the research on MNEs within international business studies, and made a first attempt to integrate the new developments in the business literature into IPE theory.

Just as Evans, *et. al.*, assert that 'critique and prescription have tended to overshadow and constrain analysis' of the state within international relations, so too has the IPE literature boxed the MNE into the undifferentiated concept of the market.[96] Critique and prescription within IPE have constrained analysis of the MNE. Whereas IPE takes a general approach that focuses on foreign direct investment as a process, the IBS literature has opened the box in order to understand the MNE as an institution and as an actor that engages in international productive activities. As markets have become increasingly globalised and dominated by large firms, a clearer focus on the MNE as an institutional actor with goals, strategies and structures is needed in the study of international political economy. MNEs are an increasingly dominant actor in both domestic and international markets and in international politics. Without a better understanding of this actor's goals, structures and institutional processes, our comprehension of the sources and uses of power in international political economy remains imprecise. More careful analyses of the causes and consequences of MNE responses to state actions can lead to a better understanding of the efficacy of state policies, and of state-MNE relations. Nuanced and sophisticated studies of the MNE are needed, both in terms of the underlying structures – production, finance, technology, security, trade, energy – of the global economy, and of the web of bargains that drive world efficiency, equity, development and growth. The crucial problem for the study of IPE as we

Bringing the Firm Back In: Multinationals in IPE

move into the twenty-first century is the tension between states and multinationals, the two key actors in the global economy, not between states and markets. It is time to bring the firm – the MNE – back into international political economy.

Lorraine Eden is Associate Professor at the
Norman Paterson School of International Affairs,
Carleton University, Ottawa, Ontario, Canada K1S 5B6.

REFERENCES

An earlier version of this paper was presented at the annual meeting of the International Studies Association in Vancouver, March 19-24, 1991. Research assistance was provided by Jeremy Byatt and Susan Olsen. I would also like to thank Derek Baas, Michael Dolan, Richard Higgott, Barbara Jenkins, Christopher Maule, Maureen Molot, Angela Nembavlakis, Tony Porter, Yimin Qi, Susan Strange, Raymond Vernon, the students in my MNEs course, the outside referees and the editors of *Millennium* for helpful comments. I assume responsibility for any remaining errors and for the views expressed in this paper.

1   Robert Gilpin, *The Political Economy of International Relations* (Princeton, NJ: Princeton University Press, 1987), pp. 10-11.

2.   Susan Strange, *States and Markets: An Introduction to IPE* (London: Pinter, 1988), p. 18; Roger Tooze 'Perspectives and Theory: A Consumer's Guide', in Susan Strange (ed.), *Paths to International Political Economy* (London: Allen and Unwin, 1984), p.12.

3.   Strange, *op. cit.,* in note 2. Strange has more recently argued that IPE must be looked at from the viewpoint of the MNE because multinationals exercise power and the aim of IPE is to look for sources and effects of power. See Susan Strange, 'An Eclectic Approach', in Craig Murphy and Roger Tooze (eds.), *The New International Political Economy* (Boulder, CO: Lynne Rienner 1991), pp. 40-49.

4.   United Nations Center for Transnational Corporations (UNCTC), *Transnational Corporations in World Development* (New York: United Nations, 1988), Chapter 1.

5.   For example, the following books cover multinationals in one chapter (Spero devotes two), but pay little attention to MNEs outside these pages: Robert Gill and David Law, *The Global Political Economy: Perspectives, Problems and Policies* (Baltimore, MD: Johns Hopkins University Press, 1988); Gilpin, op. cit., in note 1; Robert Isaak, *International Political Economy: Managing World Economic Change* (Englewood Cliffs, NJ: Prentice Hall, 1991); and Joan Spero, *The Politics of International Economic Relations* 4th ed. (New York: St. Martins Press, 1990). R. D. McKinley and R. Little, *Global Problems and World Order* (Madison, WI: University of Wisconsin Press, 1986) and Strange, *op. cit.* note 2. Each explicitly discuss MNEs or foreign direct investment over about 20 pages. I take these books as representative of current IPE texts.

6.   For example, political scientists have historically used the term MNC. Economists tend to use MNE, arguing that all multinationals are enterprises but not all are incorporated. There may also be a regional bias, with American scholars using MNC and British scholars using MNE. UNCTAD and the UNCTC use the term TNC on the grounds that MNE or MNC implies multinational ownership whereas most multinationals are owned by residents of one country, according to Horst Heininger, 'Transnational corporations and the Struggle for the Establishment of a New World Order', in Alice Teichova, Maurice Levy-Leboyer, and Helga Nussbaum (eds.), *Multinational Enterprise in Historical Perspective* (Cambridge: Cambridge University Press, 1986). The term MNF has been dropped since a multinational may consist of several firms. D.K. Fieldhouse, 'The Multinational: A Critique of a Concept', in Alice Teichova, *et. al., op. cit.* documents the history of the term multinational corporation since its first use in 1960, arguing that the concept has been taken up and misused by a variety of interest groups.

7.   The term new style MNEs is used by John Dunning, *Explaining International Production* (Boston, MA: Unwin Hyman, 1988), Chapter 13; Sylvia Ostry, *Governments and Corporations in a Shrinking World: Trade and Innovation Policies in the United States, Europe, and Japan* (New York: Council on Foreign Relations, 1990) refers to them as global corporations.

8.   In both cases page length must make our examination somewhat cursory; interested readers are directed to the bibliographies and summaries cited here and in these readings for more extensive treatments.

Millennium

9.   See Jeffery Frieden and David Lake (eds.), *International Political Economy* (New York: St. Martin's Press, 1987); Gill and Law, *op. cit.*, in note 5, Chapters 3-7, 11; Robert Gilpin, 'Three Models of the Future', in C.F. Bergsten and L.B. Krause (eds.), *World Politics and International Economics* (Washington, D.C.: The Brookings Institution, 1975), Chapter 6; Gilpin, *op. cit.*, in note 1, Chapters 2 and 6; Heininger, *op. cit.*, in note 6; Isaak, *op. cit.*, in note 5, Chapter 6; David Leyton-Brown, 'The Roles of the Multinational Enterprise in International Relations' in David Haglund and Michael Hawes (eds.), *World Politics, Interdependence and Dependence* (Toronto: Harcourt, Brace, Javanovich, 1990); McKinley and Little, op. cit., in note 5, pp. 97-98, 130-36 and 154; Theodore Moran (ed.), *Multinational Corporations; The Political Economy of Foreign Direct Investment,* (Lexington, MA.: Lexington Books, 1985), Chapters 1, 7, 13; Spero, *op. cit.*, in note 5, Chapters 4, 8; and Strange, *op. cit.*, in note 2, pp. 74-87.

10.   Robert T. Kurdle, 'The Several Faces of the Multinational Corporation: Political Reaction and Policy Response', in W. Ladd Holsti and F. LaMond Tullis (eds.), *An International Political Economy* (Boulder, CO.: Westview Press, 1985) argues that host countries see the multinational enterprise as having three faces: extension (as an extension of the home country), rival (as a rival to the host country), and resource (as a resource transfer package to the host country). All three of these faces fall within one of the five faces of MNEs of IPE: the obsolescing bargain model. In addition, the extension and rival faces are captured in the sovereignty at bay argument.

11.   See all of the following by Raymond Vernon: 'International Investment and International Trade in the Product Cycle', *Quarterly Journal of Economics* (Vol. 80, No. 2, May 1966); Sovereignty at Bay (Harmondsworth: Penguin Books, 1971); *Storm Over the Multinationals* (Cambridge, MA: Harvard University Press, 1977); 'The Product Cycle Hypothesis in the New International Environment', *Oxford Bulletin of Economics and Statistics* (Vol. 41, No. 4, Nov. 1979); 'Sovereignty at Bay: Ten Years Later', *International Organization* (Summer 1981), reprinted in Moran, *op. cit.*, in note 9.

12.   See Steven Hymer 'The Multinational Corporation and the Law of Uneven Development', in Jagdish Bhagwati (ed.), *Economics and World Order* (New York: McMillan, 1971), and 'The International Division of Labour' in R.B. Cohen, N. Felton, J. van Liere and M. Nkosi, (eds.), *The Multinational Corporation: A Radical Approach, Papers by Stephen Herbert Hymer* (Cambridge: Cambridge University Press, 1979).

13.   On the differences between problem solving and critical theory see Robert Cox, 'Social Forces: States and World Order', *Millennium Journal of International Studies* (Vol. 10, No. 2, 1981), pp. 126-55.

14.   Vernon, *op. cit.*, in note 11, 1966.

15.   Vernon, *op. cit.*, in note 11, 1971: pp. 65-112, 1977: 89-101, and 1979.16.Gilpin, *op. cit.*, in note 9.

17.   Raymond Vernon, *op. cit.*, in note 9, 1981, p. 247.

18.   Vernon, *op. cit.*, in note 11, pp. 231-47.

19.   Vernon, *op. cit.*, in note 17, 1981.

20.   Raymond Vernon and Debra Spar, *Beyond Globalism: Remaking American Foreign Economic Policy* (New York: Macmillan, 1990), pp.109-39.

21.   Moran, *op. cit.*, in note 9, p. 274.

22.   Steven J. Kobrin, 'Testing the Bargaining Hypothesis in the Manufacturing Sector in Developing Countries', *International Organization* (Vol. 41, 1987), p. 610.

23.   Vernon, *op. cit.*, in note 11, 1971: pp. 46-59, and 1977: pp. 151-73. See Chapter 1, the citations in its footnotes and the case studies in Moran, op. cit., in note 9 for a review of the literature to the mid-1980s. See also Barbara Samuels, Managing Risk in Developing Countries (Princeton, NJ: Princeton University Press, 1990) Chapter 1 and the bibliography for an update.

24.   Kobrin, *op. cit.*, in note 22, pp. 634-37.

25.   Moran, *op.cit.*, in note 9, pp. 264-69.

26.   Hymer, *op. cit.*, in note 12, 1971. See also Hymer, op. cit., in note 12, 1979, and Hugo Radice (ed.), *International Firms and Modern Imperialism* (London: Penguin, 1975).

27.   The arguments are not developed in detail here. See, for example, Samir Amin, *Unequal Development* (Hassocks: Harvester, 1976); Rhys Jenkins, TNCs and Uneven Development: *The Internationalization of Capital and the Third World* (London: Methuen, 1987), and Richard Newfarmer (ed.), *Profits, Progress and Poverty* (Notre Dame: University of Notre Dame Press, 1985).

28.   Cox, *op.cit.*, in note 13; see also Robert Cox, *Production, Power and World Order: Social Forces in the Making of History* (New York: Columbia University Press, 1987).

29.   See James Caporaso (ed.), *A Changing International Division of Labour* (Boulder, CO: Lynne Reiner Publishers), Chapter 1, for a theoretical overview of the literature on the international division of labour. Mark Casson, *Multinationals and World Trade: Vertical Integration and the Division of Labour in World Industries* (London: Allen and Unwin, 1986), Chapter 2, relates this literature to the economic theory of the vertically integrated MNE.

Bringing the Firm Back In: Multinationals in IPE

30.   See Folker Froebel, Jurgen Heinrichs and Otto Kreye, 'The World Market for Labour and the World Market for Industrial Sites', *Journal of Economic Issues* (Vol. 12, No. 4, 1978), pp. 843-858; Kurt Hoffman and Raphael Kaplinsky, *Driving Force: The Global Restructuring of Technology, Labour and Investment in the Automobile and Components Industries* (Boulder, CO: Westview Press, 1988).

31.   Hymer, *op. cit.*, in note 12, 1979.

32.   John Dunning, 'The Globalization of Firms and the Competitiveness of Countries', in John Dunning, Bruce Kogut and Magnus Blomstrom (eds.), *Globalization of Firms and Competitiveness of Nations* (Crafoord Lectures, Lund: Lund University Institute of Economic Research, 1990).

33.   For example, Hymer's early work on the oligopolistic advantages of MNEs that allow them to cover the costs of foreignness in going abroad is a key component of the OLI paradigm outlined below. However, his later neomarxist writings are not discussed. Dependencia views are almost totally ignored.

34.   For example, Gill and Law, *op. cit.*, in note 5, and Strange, *op. cit.*, in note 4.

35.   Charles Kindleberger, *American Business Abroad: Six Lectures on Direct Investment* (New Haven, CT: Yale University Press, 1969). See Alfred Chandler: 'Technological and Organizational Underpinnings of Modern Industrial Multinational Enterprise: The Dynamics of Competitive Advantage', in Alice Teichova *et al.*, *op. cit.*, in note 6, and *Scale and Scope: The Dynamics of Industrial Capitalism* (Harvard: Belknap Press of Harvard University, 1990). The early work on the MNE as an actor was developed in Stephen Hymer's 1960 Doctoral dissertation, written under Charles Kindleberger. See Hymer, The International Operations of National Firms: A Study of Direct Investment (Ph.D. Thesis, MIT; published by MIT Press under the same title in 1976). Their works on oligopolistic motives for FDI are now known in IBS as the Hymer-Kindleberger approach.

36.   Kindleberger, *op. cit.*, in note 35, 1969; Charles Kindleberger, ed. *The International Corporation* (Cambridge, Mass.: MIT Press, 1970); Richard Caves, *Multinational Enterprise and Economic Analysis* (Cambridge, U.K.: Cambridge University Press, 1982).

37.   Good summaries of the various theories can be found in John Cantwell, 'A Survey of Theories of International Production' (Mimeo: University of Reading Department of Economics, 1990), and Dunning, *op. cit.*, in note 7, Chapters 1,2 and 12, For a short summary see John Dunning, 'The Theory of International Production', in Khosrow Fatemi (ed.), *International Trade: Existing Problems and Prospective Solutions* (New York: Taylor and Francis, 1989).

38.   There are many references but several of the best known are gathered together in Dunning, *op. cit.*, in note 7. See also Dunning, *op. cit.*, in note 37 for a concise summary of the development of the OLI model; John Dunning, 'The Study of International Business: A Plea for a More Inter-disciplinary Approach', *Journal of International Business Studies* (Fall, 1989), pp. 411-36 for current directions in IBS; Dunning, op.cit, in note 325 on globalisation, MNEs and competitiveness; Casson, op. cit., in note 29; Mark Casson, *The Firm and the Market: Studies in Multinational Enterprise and the Scope of the Firm* (Oxford: Basil Blackwell and Cambridge, Mass: MIT Press, 1987); and Cantwell, *op. cit.*, in note 37.

39.   Cantwell, *op. cit.*, in note 37, argues that the eclectic paradigm can be analyzed at the macro (economy), meso (industry) or micro (firm) level. Dunning, *op. cit*, in note 37, pp. 68-69 shows how these advantages can vary at each level. For an application of this model to the pharmaceutical industry see Lorraine Eden, 'Pharmaceuticals in Canada: An Analysis of the Compulsory Licensing Debate', in Alan Rugman (ed.), *International Business in Canada: Strategies for Management* (Toronto: Prentice Hall, 1989).

40.   Farok Contractor and Peter Lorange, *Cooperative Strategies in International Business* (Lexington, Mass:Lexington Books, 1988) and Charles Oman, *New Forms of Investment in Developing Countries: Mining, Petrochemicals, Automobiles, Textiles, Food* (Paris: Development Centre of the OECD, 1990) document the growing nonequity linkages among MNEs. Charles Kindleberger, 'The "New" Multinationalization of Business', *ASEAN Economic Bulletin* (November 1988), pp. 113-24, argues, however, that many of these so-called 'new forms of international business' are not new (*e.g.*, joint ventures) and may not be efficiency based.

41.   On international competitiveness strategies see Michael Porter: *The Competitive Advantage of Nations* (New York: The Free Press, 1990a), and 'The Competitive Advantage of Nations', *Harvard Business Review* (March-April, 1990b), pp. 73-93; Ostry, *op. cit.*, in note 7; Alan Rugman and Alain Verbeke, *Global Corporate Strategy and Trade Policy* (London and New York: Routledge, 1990).

42.   See Lorraine Eden, 'Multinational Responses to Trade and Technology Changes: Implications for Canada', in Don McFetridge (ed.), *Foreign Investment, Technology and Growth* (Ottawa: Investment Canada, 1991); UNCTC, *op. cit.*, in note 4; and Rob van Tulder and Gerd Junne, *European Multinationals in Core Technologies* (New York: John Wiley, 1988) on information technology and its potential impacts on MNE organisational and locational structures.

Millennium

43.   Eden, *op. cit.*, in note 42; UNCTC, *op. cit.*, in note 4; Van Tulder and Junne, *op. cit.*, in note 56.

44.   Dunning, *op. cit.*, in note 7, p. 327.

45.   C.K. Prahalad and Gary Hamel, 'The Core Competence of the Corporation', *Harvard Business Review* (May-June 1990), pp. 78-91.

46.   See Ian Giddy and Stephen Young, 'Conventional Theory and Unconventional Multinationals: Do New Forms of Multinational Enterprise Require New Theories?' in Alan Rugman (ed.) *New Theories of the Multinational Enterprise* (London: Croom Helm, 1982), pp. 55-78, on the ownership advantages of 'nonconventional' MNEs. They argue that multinationals from LDCs and small countries tend to rely more heavily on nonequity joint ventures, do not have innovation based advantages, and tend to be imitators, fast followers or niche players. See also Oman, *op. cit.*, in note 40.

47.   The key work initiating this study is Porter, *op. cit.*, in note 55, 1990a. A much shorter and more readable summary can be found in Porter, *op. cit.*, in note 41, 1990b. Porter argues that home states can generate sustainable competitive advantages in domestic firms by encouraging the development of a domestic competitiveness diamond. This diamond has four points: (1) factor conditions, (2) related and supporting industries, (3) demand conditions, and (4) firm strategy and industry structure.

48.   At a micro level, David Teece, 'Profiting from Technological Innovation', in David Teece (ed.) *The Competitive Challenge: Strategies for Industrial Innovation and Renewal* (Cambridge, Mass.: Ballinger Publishing, 1987), pp. 185-219, is most useful in identifying the roles of the initial innovator, the fast followers and the owners of specialised and co-specialised assets. At a macro level, John Cantwell, *Technological Innovation and Multinational Corporations* (Oxford: Basil Blackwell, 1989), and Cantwell, *op. cit.*, in note 37, develop a model of the MNE and technological competence.

49.   Mark Casson, *Enterprise and Competitiveness: A Systems View of International Business* (Oxford: Clarendon Press, 1990) examines the economic and cultural determinants of firm performance, arguing that culture-specific transactions costs explain most performance differences. He examines the roles of the entrepreneur as a risk taker, problem solver and global scanner. Determinants of entrepreneurial culture are discussed, applied in case studies of the United States and Japan, and then extended to examine joint ventures and the impacts of MNEs on LDCs.

50.   This last issue has caused some considerable internal debate among the British IBS scholars. See the summary in Cantwell, *op. cit.*, in note 37.

51.   Dunning, *op. cit.*, in note 32, p. 60, calls these internalisation advantages arising from structural market failure.

52.   Cantwell, *op. cit.*, in note 37, p.13; Alan Rugman, Don Lecraw and Lawrence Booth, *International Business: Firm and Environment* (Toronto: McGraw Hill, 1985), pp. 104-108.

53.   Francois Chesnais, 'Multinational Enterprises and the International Diffusion of Technology', in Giovanni Dosi *et al.*(eds.), *Technical Change and Economic Theory* (London and New York: Pinter Publishers, 1988).

54.   Contractor and Lorange, *op. cit.*, in note 40, 1988.

55.   Markets versus hierarchies theory, referred to as the new institutional economics, was recently linked to IPE in Beth Yarbrough and Robert Yarbrough, 'International Institutions and the New Economics of Organization', *International Organization* (Vol. 44, No. 2, Spring 1990), pp. 235-59. For an application of the theory of governance to international regimes see Lorraine Eden and Fen Hampson, 'Clubs are Trumps: Towards a Taxonomy of International Regimes', *CITIPS Working Paper 90-02* (Ottawa: Carleton University, 1990). It is interesting that the IPE literature sets up its polar cases as states versus markets, whereas the IBS literature uses markets versus hierarchies. In both sets of literature markets are the alternative to the primary unit of analysis.

56.   Erin Anderson and Hubert Gatignon, 'Modes of Foreign Entry: A Transactions Cost Analysis', *Journal of International Business Studies* (Vol. 17, No.3, 1986), pp. 1-26.

57.   Oman, *op. cit.*, in note 40.

58.   Freidrich Schneider and Bruno Frey, 'Economic and Political Determinants of Foreign Direct Investment', *World Development* (Vol. 13, No.2, 1985), pp. 161-75. Dunning, *op. cit.*, in note 7, divides locational advantages into environmental, systemic and policy factors. While the interpretations are somewhat similar, the triad of economic, social and political factors is easier to differentiate.

59.   Dunning, *op. cit.*, in note 32.

60.   Dunning, *op. cit.*, in note 7 contains approximately 40 pages on the state and state policies. Just as the major IPE textbooks pay insufficient attention to the MNE, so do the major MNE textbooks provide too little study of the state. One recent exception is a new book on government-business relations by Jack Behrman and Robert Grosse, *International Business and Government: Issues and Institutions* (Columbia, South Carolina: University of South Carolina Press, 1990).

61.   Ostry, *op. cit.*, in note 7.

62.   Rugman and Verbeke, *op. cit.*, in note 41.

Bringing the Firm Back In: Multinationals in IPE

63.   See by Michael Porter, *Competitive Strategy* (New York: The Free Press, 1980), *Competitive Advantage* (New York: The Free Press, 1985); Porter (ed). *Competition in Global Industries* (Cambridge, Mass.: Harvard Business School Press, 1986); and Porter, 'Changing Patterns of International Competition' in David Teece (ed.), *The Competitive Challenge: Strategies for Industrial Innovation and Renewal* (Cambridge, Mass: Ballinger Publishing Co., 1987). See also Yves Doz, *Strategic Management in Multinational Enterprises* (Oxford: Pergamon Press, 1986); Christopher Bartlett and Sumantra Ghoshal, *Managing Across Borders* (Boston: Harvard Business School Press, 1989).

64.   Porter, *op. cit.*, in note 63, 1986, pp. 46-49.

65.   Doz, *op. cit.*, in note 63; Anant Negandhi and Arun Savara (eds.), *International Strategic Management* (Lexington, Mass: Lexington Books, 1989).

66.   Mark Casson, 'Transactions Costs and the Theory of the Multinational Enterprise', in Alan Rugman (ed.), *New Theories of the Multinational Enterprise* (London and Canberra: Croom Helm, 1982); Porter, op. cit., in note 63, 1986; Nigel Grimwade, *International Trade: New Patterns of Trade, Production and Investment* (London and New York: Routledge, 1989).

67.   Lorraine Eden, 'The Microeconomics of Transfer Pricing', in Alan Rugman and Lorraine Eden (eds.), *Multinationals and Transfer Pricing Management* (London and New York: Croom Helm and St. Martins Press, 1985).

68.   Stefan H. Robock and Kenneth Simmonds, *International Business and Multinational Enterprises* (Homewood and Boston: Irwin, 1989), p. 253.

69.   Business International, *Organizing for International Competitiveness: How Successful Corporations Structure Their World Wide Operations* (New York: Business International, 1988) identifies seven generic types: (1) the international division where one unit within the MNE is responsible for all international operations; (2) worldwide regional where the MNE's affiliates are divided into regional divisions; (3) national subsidiaries where each host country constitutes a division; (4) worldwide product divisions where the MNE is organized into several domestic businesses each of which is responsible for its own worldwide operations; (5) worldwide functional divisions based on major functions, *e.g.*, administration, manufacturing, research and development; (6) matrix structures that focus on two characteristics (product, function, region), providing a dual chain of command; and (7) mixed where the MNE combines two or more of the above structures. Business International concludes that the mixed and matrix structures, due to their synergistic properties, are likely to dominate MNE organisational structures in the 1990s. See also OECD, *Recent Trends in International Direct Investment* (Geneva: OECD, 1987).

70.   Peter F. Drucker, 'The Coming of the New Organization', *Harvard Business Review* (Jan.-Feb. 1988), pp. 45-63.

71.   Grimwade, *op. cit.*, in note 66, pp. 143-215.

72.   For more discussion of these locational strategies in the context of technology and trade policy changes facing US multinationals with Canadian affiliates, see Eden, *op. cit.*, in note 42. This paper adds an additional locational strategy (the world product mandate) which is not considered here due to its specific Canadian context.

73.   Gary Gereffi, in 'International Subcontracting and Global Capitalism: Reshaping the Pacific Rim', presented at the PEWS conference on Pacific-Asia and the Future of the World System, University of Hawaii at Manoa, March 28-30, 1991, refers to offshores as 'export processors' and source factories as 'component suppliers', pp. 5-8.

74.   Kasra Ferdows, 'Mapping International Factory Networks', in Kasra Ferdows (ed.), *Managing International Manufacturing* (Amsterdam: North Holland, 1989).

75.   Doz, *op. cit.*, in note 63.

76.   Lynne K. Mytelka, 'Knowledge-Intensive Production and the Changing Internationalizatio n Strategies of Multinational Firms', in James Caporaso (ed.), *A Changing International Division of Labour* (Boulder, CO: Lynne Reinner).

77.   Doz, *op. cit.*, in note 63, Ch.6; Investment Canada, 'The Business Implications of Globalization', *Investment Canada Working Paper Series*, No. 1990-V.(Ottawa: Government of Canada, 1990); UNCTC, *op. cit.*, in note 4, Part I.

78.   Asim Erdlick (ed.), *Multinationals as Mutual Invaders: Intra-industry Direct Foreign Investment* (New York: St. Martins Press, 1985), Grimwade, *op. cit.*, in note 66, Ch.1; Investment Canada, *op. cit.*, in note 77; OECD, Structure and Organization of Multinationals (Geneva: OECD, 1987); UNCTC, *op. cit.*, in note 4.

79.   Investment Canada, 'International Investment: Canadian Developments in a Global Context', *Investment Canada Working Paper 1990-VI* (Updated) (Ottawa: Investment Canada, 1991), OECD, *op. cit.*, in note 78; UNCTC, *op. cit.*, note 4.

80.   Dunning, *op. cit.*, in note 7, p. 328.

81.   Dunning, *op. cit.*, in note 32, pp. 24-25; Grimwade, op. cit., in note 66.

Millennium

82.   Vernon, *op. cit.*, in note 11, 1977 and 1979.

83.   The link to Porter's (*op. cit.*, in note 41, 1990a,b) diamond of competitive advantage may provide a clue; *i.e.* sophisticated consumers and strong competitive rival firms in the home country can generate an explosion of new products. Thus, as Porter argues individual countries may have a comparative advantage in particular industries such as Northern Italy in textiles. See also Erdlick, *op. cit.*, in note 78.

84.   Mytelka, *op. cit.*, in note 76.

85.   Vernon and Spar, *op. cit.*, in note 20.

86.   Helen Milner, *Resisting Protectionism: Global Industries and the Politics of International Trade* (Princeton, NJ: Princeton University Press, 1988); Helen Milner and David Yoffie, 'Between Free Trade and Protectionism: Strategic Trade and a Theory of Corporate Trade Demands', *International Organization* (Vol. 43, No. 2, Spring 1989), pp. 239-72. One obvious example of this change is the Exon- Florio amendment which requires the Committee on Foreign Investment in the United States (CFIUS) to review large inward FDI projects for their national security effects. The CFIUS has been around for some time, but that its functions have been and are likely to be increased, partly to monitor Japanese takeovers of US firms. Another interesting question arises as to whether Japanese and European states will attempt to apply extraterritoriality to affiliates in the United States.

87.   Benjamin Cohen, 'The Political Economy of International Trade', *International Organization* (Vol. 44, No. 2, Spring 1990), pp. 261-81; Ostry, op. cit., in note 7; David Richardson, 'The Political Economy of Strategic Trade Policy', *International Organization* (Vol. 44, No.1, Winter, 1990), p. 107-35.

88.   Milner and Yoffie, *op. cit.*, in note 108.

89.   Eden and Hampson, *op. cit.*, in note 70.

90.   Gerd Junne, 'Automation in the North: Consequences for Developing Countries Exports', in Caporaso (ed.), *op. cit.*, in note 29.

91.   Samuels, *op. cit.*, in note 28. Some optimism may be provided by Ferdows, *op. cit.*, in note 74 who argues that as subsidiaries mature they tend to adopt more technologically sophisticated functions within the MNE; *e.g.*, offshores moving up to source factories. This is already happening in the Mexican maquiladoras where the old plants (offshores) tend to be simple, female dominated and labour intensive operations (*e.g.*, in textiles) while the new plants (source factories) are more technology and capital intensive and operate with a higher proportion of male workers (*e.g.*, in autos and advanced electronics assembly). See Gary Gereffi, Mexico's Maquiladoras Industries: What Is their Contribution to National Development and Transnational Integration in North America?', presented at the conference Facing North/Facing South: A Multidisciplinary Conference on Canadian-US-Mexican Relations, University of Calgary, May 2-4, 1991.

92.   Oman, *op. cit.*, in note 40.

93.   Magnus Blomstrom, *Transnational Corporations and Manufacturing Exports from Developing Countries* (New York: United Nations, 1990); UNCTC, op. cit., in note 4. Joel Migdal's recent book *Strong Societies and Weak States: State-Society Relations and State Capacities in the Third World* (Princeton: Princeton University Press, 1988), however, documents the difficulties governments in the Third World face in mobilising their resources for development purposes.

94.   Junne, *op. cit.*, in note 90; James Womack, Daniel Jones and Daniel Roos, *The Machine that Changed the World* (New York: Rawson Associates, 1990. Locational advantages can be increased through technological upgrading and/or trade linkages. For example, Womack *et. al.*, see small sized auto plants moving to Mexico in response to a North American Free Trade Agreement. See also Eden, *op. cit.*, in note 42.

95.   Lavalin, a Canadian engineering MNE, in the mid-1980s shifted its drafting work from Canada to India where unit labour costs were lower. With the introduction of CAD-CAM in Canada, the MNE recently shifted the drafting work back to Canada. This example demonstrates the importance of technological infrastructure for both manufacturing and services in developing countries.

96.   Peter Evans, Dietrich Rueschemeyer and Theda Skocpol, 'On the Road to a More Adequate Understanding of the State', in Evans *et al.*(eds.), *Bringing the State Back In* (Cambridge: Cambridge University Press, 1985), p. 363.

[14]

An Overview of Relations with National Governments

JOHN H. DUNNING

The relationship between TNCs and national governments has always been an un-
easy—if not a downright hostile—one.
History is replete with examples of the mistrust and tensions between the two parties.
Sometimes—particularly at the turn of the
present century and in the 1970s[1]—this has
exploded into direct confrontation and has
led to the expropriation or nationalisation of
foreign-owned assets. But, for the most
part, the divergence of interests has been
confined to the kinds of economic activity
and behaviour governments expect of
TNCs (and their subsidiaries) and the
sharing out of the economic rents arising
from those activities.

In particular, questions about the appropriateness of the technology transferred by
TNCs, their monopoly power, their labour
practices, their effects on the environment,
and their ability to evade taxes by manipu-
lative transfer pricing, were hotly debated
in the 1970s and documented in a plethora
of reports published by the then United Nations Centre on Transnational Corporations
(UNCTC)—now part of UNCTAD.

Developing countries—particularly those
in Latin America—were also concerned lest
too much inbound foreign investment
would lead to increased economic *dependencia* between recipient and investing
countries, and an unacceptable erosion of
the former countries' sovereignty. Smaller
developed countries felt they lacked the
clout to safeguard their economic interests;
hence their support, in the 1970s, for the

John Dunning, Graduate School of Management, Rutgers University, 180 University Avenue,
Newark, NJ 07102, USA.

1356-3467/98/020280-05 © 1998 Carfax Publishing Ltd

Debate

efforts of such multilateral institutions as UNCTAD, the UN Institute for Training and Research (UNITAR) and the United Nations Commission on Transnational Corporations,[2] to promote more harmonised policies towards TNCs (e.g. on matters related to restrictive practices, technology transfer, entry and local performance requirements); and to formulate a code of conduct for TNCs. And, indeed, throughout the following decade, much of the attention of the Commission, and of regional institutions such as the OECD, was directed to designing and implementing behavioural codes both for corporations and for national governments, so that each could at least be better informed about the other's goals and expectations.

Although the code prepared by the UNCTC for the Commission never came to fruition, the discussions and interchange of views between the representatives of TNCs and national governments provided a valuable learning experience for each. Unquestionably, over the years, national authorities became better informed about the costs and benefits of foreign direct investment (FDI); as, indeed, did the TNCs of the development objectives of the host governments, and of their ability to formulate and implement the development strategies which would best advance these ends.

In the meantime, political and economic events in the global economy, coupled with a new generation of technological advances, were hatching a new scenario for government–TNC relationships. As a result, since the mid 1980s, the general complexion of the interface between national governments and TNCs has shifted from being predominantly adversarial and confrontational to being non-adversarial and cooperative. Admittedly, conflicts of interest, particularly on the sharing of the benefits of inbound FDI, still remain; but, for the most part, the debate about the pros and cons of economic dependence, or interdependence, is now conducted in the context of the globalisation of economic activity, rather than

that of the strategies and behaviour of TNCs *per se*.

Overwhelmingly, the thrust of the last two decades has been to welcome inward investment and to take a more positive and relaxed stance on outward FDI. According to UNCTAD (various dates), over the decade 1986–95, more than 80 countries liberalised their policies towards inbound TNC activity. Between 1991 and 1995 alone, of more than 500 changes introduced in the foreign investment regimes of 50 or more countries, no fewer than 98 per cent were in the direction of liberalisation or investment promotion.[3] Indeed, in 1997, UNCTAD followed up a report published in 1996 on *Incentives and Foreign Direct Investment* with another entitled *Survey of Best Practices in Investment Promotion*.[4] Both documents were directed towards identifying and designing an appropriate package of fiscal and other incentives, a favourable investment climate, a coherent regime of investment promotion agencies, and the policies and practices which governments and agencies might best follow to attract new FDI and facilitate the operations of established investors. This is a far cry from the polemic of, and the policies prescribed by, the UNCTC in the 1970s, when the main item on the agenda was how to maximise the benefits of inward investment, and to ensure that TNCs and their subsidiaries conformed to the existing economic policies and development strategies of host governments.[5]

A close scrutiny of the annual *World Investment Reports* published by UNCTAD in the 1990s reveals that, although many of the issues of concern to both developed and developing countries about inbound FDI remain unchanged, they are now being aired within the context of these countries being increasingly integrated into the world economy—at a regional as well as a global level. Furthermore, action taken to ameliorate any adverse affects of TNCs, and to promote the prudential supervision of their activities, is increasingly being directed towards securing supranational mechanisms powerful enough to achieve their

John H. Dunning

objectives, while avoiding counterproductive actions on the part of national governments, either to encourage or to control inbound FDI.[6]

There are two principal reasons for the more constructive and less adversarial interface between governments and TNCs which has evolved since the mid 1970s. The first is the deceleration of economic growth in many parts of the world economy, China constituting the major exception. This, together with the innovation and implementation of new labour-saving technologies, and the increasing mobility of intangible assets—especially information and organisational skills—across national boundaries, has added to the pressure on countries to attract foreign investment from wherever they can get it.

The second factor has been the opening up of new territories in the world—especially in Asia—which has meant that the locational options for multinational investment have widened. This has occurred at a time when technological advances and competitive pressures have impelled firms to be more vigorous in seeking out the most cost-efficient locations for their value-added activities.

These two factors have led to a reprioritisation of the objectives of governments and a change in their attitudes towards TNC activity. From a focus on political sovereignty and constrained economic interdependence in the 1960s and 1970s, the contemporary need of nation-states is for their indigenous resources to be productively used and allocated in such a way that conforms to the needs of a global village, characterised by an easy movement of intangible assets across geographic space. In the 1990s nations have begun to realise that, to achieve many of their economic and social goals, they have to offer at least as attractive opportunities for production and market access to the main wealth creators as do their (main) foreign competitors.

As part and parcel of this reorientation of objectives, governments have initiated several strategic policies which are, directly or indirectly, affecting their relationships with TNCs. The first, as we have already described, has been the deregulation and liberalisation of many national markets and of policies towards FDI. Second, the promotion of freer trading and investment regimes in each of the three main industrial regions of the world, viz. North America, Western Europe and East Asia, has not only changed the locational parameters facing TNCs. It is also compelling national administrations to examine more carefully the pulling power of their own resources and capabilities—including the legal and institutional infrastructure for wealth-creating activities—to mobile investors. The dramatic increase in intra-firm trade in the European Union over the past 30 years is just one example of the impact of regional integration on the location of TNC activities.

Third, and perhaps of greatest long-term importance, is the reappraisal of strategic macro-organisational (or micro-management) policies by governments. In situations in which trade and FDI are determined by the distribution of natural factor endowments, the value-added activities of firms in different countries are essentially complementary to, rather than substitutable for, each other. Governments then do not need to behave strategically in their trade or FDI policies. At the other extreme, governments may engage in structurally distorting import substitution or domestic economic policies aimed at protecting or advancing the development of indigenous industry.

It is, indeed, becoming widely recognised, e.g. by the World Bank in its 1997 *World Development Report*,[7] that markets, firms (including TNCs) and governments are best regarded as partners in advancing economic development and national competitiveness, and that the objectives of the two parties are becoming more mutually consistent. This, in turn, suggests that governments are now having to pay more attention to increasing or restructuring the domestic value-adding activities of TNCs, or their affiliates, rather than simply seek-

282

ing to gain the maximum share of the economic rent generated by these activities. They have also realised—often by hard and bitter experience—that the adoption of structurally distorting economic policies or confrontational stances towards TNCs is often counterproductive; and that the end result of such policies and stances is that the level and structure of domestic production is sub-optimal. By adopting market-friendly policies which promote the efficient development of both foreign and domestically owned assets, governments are increasingly acting as partners with, rather than protagonists against, TNCs in their wealth-creating responsibilities.

We have acknowledged that this change in TNC–government economic relations is shown in various ways—not least of which is the liberalisation of policies towards FDI. However, the extent and form of the restructuring of government policies and the *raison d'etre* behind it differs markedly among countries. At the one extreme, countries such as Japan, Korea and Singapore have adopted holistic and integrated strategies towards promoting the long-term competitiveness of their indigenous resources and capabilities; and have done so in the light of both the perceived strategies of their foreign competitors and the likely response of their own and foreign firms to them. By contrast, the macro-organisational policies of most Western governments—notably the USA and UK in the 1980s—have been fragmented and uncoordinated, and only recently have they begun to take more explicit account of the impact of inward or outward investment on their national capabilities, and the possible reactions of other governments to their own policies.[8] There is some evidence that the globalisation of the world economy, coupled with the recognition that the key to industrial competitiveness rests in the continual upgrading of created assets, many of which are mobile across national boundaries, is making for more long-sighted educational, technology and industrial policies by Western governments.

However, much remains to be done to educate policy makers on the implications of the global economy, especially the increasing role of international business activities for domestic economic governance.[9]

In conclusion, a word of caution is necessary. As yet, it is not possible to assert whether the new and constructive alliance between TNCs and national governments is here to stay, or whether it is specific to the current phase of a transient world economy. Certainly, it would be incorrect to infer that all is 'sweetness and light' between the two parties. Areas of substantial difference on issues to do with transfer pricing, environmental protection, allocation of export markets, human resource management and business practices—not to mention those which are culturally or ideologically sensitive—still remain. In a book to be published later this year, Professor Raymond Vernon—perhaps the world's leading scholar on the political economy of TNC activity—warns of troubled times ahead, particularly in cases where, for one reason or another, the TNCs are finding it difficult to keep pace with the demands of the global marketplace, and/or where governments cannot cope with these same demands.[10]

In this respect, the current experiences of several Asian governments and their own TNCs provide a salutary reminder that economic interdependence is a two-edged sword and that the real test of the staying powers of any partnership between TNCs and national governments is not when businesses and economies are booming, but when they are facing hard times. It is then, according to Vernon, that the pressure from aggrieved constituents is most likely to break out, with adverse affects both on national interests and those of TNCs. Widening the Asian troubles to those of the global economy at large, it would seem our future concern about the TNC–government relationship should focus less on these two factors, and more on the world economic scenario in which they operate. The more regional and multina-

Leslie Sklair

tional institutions, such as the World Bank, World Trade Organization (WTO), the UN and the G7 group of political leaders, can help the world economy steer a predictable path to sustained and balanced growth, and promote social cohesion among the key wealth-creating constituents, the less likely are the tensions and destructive policies of the 1970s to recur—and the more likely will the TNC–government partnership take root and flourish.

Notes

1. Most noticeably as exemplified in the gunboat diplomacy of the USA in protection of its foreign investments in Central America in the early 1900s; the exploitation of mineral resources by *Union Minière* in the Congo before the First World War; and the unacceptable intervention by ITT in the political affairs of Chile in the 1970s.
2. To which the UNCTC provided the research, information and policy advisory back-up services.
3. The exact number of countries introducing such changes varied from year to year.
4. UNCTAD, *Incentives and Foreign Direct Investment* (UNCTAD, 1996) and *Survey of Best Practices in Investment Promotion* (UNCTAD, 1997).
5. Such policies and strategies—whatever they were—were assumed to be inviolate and not open to question.
6. In the former case, for example, by engaging in local tournaments on investment incentives; and in the latter, by market-distorting local performance requirements.
7. See, for example, the World Bank, *World Development Report: The State in a Changing World* (Oxford University Press, 1997).
8. See, for example, the various publications on UK industrial competitiveness put out by the Department of Trade and Industry (DTI) in the 1990s (e.g. DTI, *Competitiveness: Forging Ahead* (HMSO, 1995) and *Competitiveness: Creating the Enterprise Centre of Europe* (HMSO, 1996)) and the increasingly important informative and data-collection role played by the Invest in Britain Bureau and some of the regional investment agencies.
9. Some suggestions are offered by several authors. See, for example, J. H. Dunning (Ed.), *Governments, Globalization and International Business* (Oxford University Press, 1997).
10. Raymond Vernon, *In the Hurricane's Eye: The Troubled Prospects of Multinational Enterprises* (Harvard University Press, forthcoming).

TNCs as Political Actors

LESLIE SKLAIR

Few researchers on TNCs would deny that they engage in political activities of various types. In this short note I shall address two questions: (i) what forms do these activities take and are they effective? And (ii) do they enhance or undermine democracy?

My argument is that, while TNCs have always been political actors, the demands of the global economy require them to be political in a more systematic sense than previously. For this purpose, I argue, we can identify a transnational capitalist class, led by the TNCs, and composed of four main interlocking groups: TNC executives and their local affiliates; globalising bureaucrats; globalising politicians and professionals; and consumerist elites (merchants and media). While each of these groups performs distinct functions, personnel are often interchangeable between them. Key individuals can belong to more than one fraction at the same time, and the transition from membership of one to another group is more or less routinised in many societies.

Leslie Sklair, Department of Sociology, London School of Economics, Houghton Street, London WC2A 2AE, UK.

1356-3467/98/020284-04 © 1998 Carfax Publishing Ltd

Debate

Historically, the relationship between the economic power and the political power of TNCs has been highly controversial. While the involvement of ITT in the bloody coup against President Allende's government in Chile in 1973 appears to be the exception rather than the rule in the second half of the twentieth century, there is a growing body of research to suggest that major corporations are currently using more subtle methods to achieve political objectives that will serve their economic interests. Two telling examples are the Codex Alimentarius Commission (Codex) and the corporate lobby inside the European Union (EU).

Codex was established in 1963 to increase world trade in food through mandatory international standards, the implication being that these international standards are liable to be lower than the strictest national standards imposed on food TNCs. While Codex is an intergovernmental body run by the Food and Agriculture Organization (FAO) and the World Health Organization (WHO), detailed research by Avery, Drake & Lang reveals substantial and in some cases decisive involvement by TNCs and their allies.[1] Their study of the 2578 people who attended the 1989–91 session of Codex documents participation by 105 countries and 140 food and agrochemical companies; there were 660 industry representatives compared with 26 from public interest groups (Nestlé alone had 38, more than most countries). At the two meetings on food additives and contaminants, 41 per cent of those present were from TNCs and industry federations; and at the meetings on pesticide residue levels, 127 (33 per cent) were from TNCs, compared with 80 from all the developing countries. While consumer groups and professionals independent of the TNCs are campaigning for reforms to the Codex process, the signs are that WTO procedures and the proposed Multilateral Agreement on Investment (MAI) currently being negotiated at the OECD will increase rather than diminish the power of food and agrochemical TNCs to cut corners.

Corporate Europe Observatory, a research centre in Amsterdam, argues that the European Roundtable of Industrialists (ERT), comprised of the leaders of 45 key European TNCs, has completely shifted the emphasis of policy making in the European Union in its own interests.[2] ERT performs an agenda-setting role in Europe for global free trade and international competitiveness. ERT was founded in 1983 by a group of visionary captains of industry, notably Agnelli of Fiat, Dekker of Philips and Gyllenhammer of Volvo. Corporations prominent in ERT today include BP, Daimler–Benz, Fiat, Shell and Siemens. The European Centre for Infrastructure Studies (ECIS), an offshoot of ERT, is also said to have been instrumental in persuading the European Commission to establish the Trans-European Networks (TENs), 150 infrastructure projects which threaten over 60 nature sites, without consulting the European Parliament. ECIS, founded by Umberti Agnelli of Fiat in 1994, includes regional and national governments, municipalities, EU institutions, research institutes, banks and corporations. In a familiar pattern for globalising elites, former Commission Vice-President Henning Christopherson joined the Board of ECIS when he left the Commission. So it is not too far-fetched to argue that ECIS has been influential in shaping EU transport policy.

One central consequence of the political efficacy of TNCs is the failure of government to shift the balance from private cars and lorries to public transport and rail freight, despite almost universal rhetoric on the need to do this. Two European examples will suffice. German milk is freighted to Greece to be made into feta cheese and then sent back to Germany for sale; in the 1960s, most European countries had their own Unilever soap factories, now there is one huge factory in England to supply all of Europe. In the past, TNCs strove to bring production close to consumption; but now, because production and distribution technology allows the supply chain to be stretched and information

Leslie Sklair

technology keeps the system together, this is no longer necessary. German milk companies and Unilever thus contribute to the enormous increase in long-distance transport of goods through Europe because lean production and 'just-in-time' (key concepts for economic globalisation) make production much more 'efficient' for the producers and, in a sense, for consumers too, if the real prices of the products actually fall, but more 'inefficient' for road users and those who lose jobs.[3]

The European Union and the US government, along with the TNCs, have established a Transatlantic Business Dialogue (TABD) to pursue globalisation-friendly policies. According to its US business coordinator, 'TABD is a private-sector force designed to respond to the new reality of trade; namely that companies are functioning globally and their involvement in the making of international trade policy is a natural outgrowth of such globalisation'.[4] This is, of course, one small organisation among thousands of others, but its leading personnel includes a European Commissioner (Sir Leon Brittain); senior executives from major European and US corporations; high officials from the US Treasury and State Department; and the former GATT Secretary-General, Peter Sutherland.

I have spent so much of my limited space on this obscure report from the Corporate Europe Observatory about these obscure lobby groups because it so perfectly illustrates my thesis that the TNCs do work, quite deliberately and often rather covertly, as political actors and often have direct access to those at the highest levels of formal political and administrative power with considerable success.[5] Such research could, I am sure, be replicated for most countries, perhaps most cities, in the world. Everywhere we find corporate executives, globalising bureaucrats, politicians and professionals and consumer elites (merchants, marketers, advertisers) telling us in public and doing their best to ensure in private that the globalising agenda of contemporary capitalism driven

by the TNCs and their allies is inevitable and, eventually, in the best interests of us all. They would see Codex, ERT and the Transatlantic Business Dialogue as doing a fine job in paving the way to universal prosperity.[6]

The question is: does this present a problem for democracy? In one sense, it does not. TNCs are legal bodies with every right to act legally in defence of their interests. They are owned by millions of individual shareholders whose main interest is in seeing the value of their investment increase, though effective control is usually vested in small groups of owner-executives and institutional shareholders.

The other side of the matter is that all major trade and investment treaties are profoundly undemocratic in structure and process. In 1994, just before the US Congress was due to vote on the Uruguay Round of GATT, legislation that would establish the more all-encompassing WTO, the Washington-based organisation, Public Citizen, offered to donate US$10 000 to the charity of choice of any member of Congress who had read the 500-page agreement and who could answer 10 questions about it. Only one member, a 'free-trader', eventually accepted the challenge, and as a result he changed his vote from for to against the agreement (after having voted for NAFTA which, presumably, he had not read). Congress approved GATT in December 1994, the inference being that most US legislators voted for an agreement that would fundamentally change the global economy without knowing what was in it in any detail.[7] Neither do legislators in the member countries of the European Union appear, on the whole, to be better informed than those in the USA on such matters. So, apart from the big issues about whether to join or accede to treaties, which are occasionally put to the vote in a referendum, our elected representatives appear to nod through on a regular basis critically important legislation that affects our daily lives in many different ways. As the evidence from Codex, the EU and environmental legislation in general sug-

Debate

gests, the interests of the TNCs may be better represented precisely because the TNCs have the resources and the commercial motivation to see that their interests *are* fully represented. Even such a relatively well-endowed organisation as Greenpeace Germany has only one Brussels-based lobbyist. To quote again from the Corporate Europe Observatory report, 'in comparison with the swarms of industry lobbyists to be found in Brussels corridors, environmentalists are an endangered species'.[8]

The political activities of the TNCs and their allies, therefore, raise serious doubts about how well our democracies are working with respect to everyday economic issues, such as global trade and investment, the environment and the health and safety of workers and citizens in general. The attempts by bodies like the ILO and the now-dismantled UN Centre on Transnational Corporations to develop universal codes of conduct to encourage the best practices of TNCs and to outlaw their much-documented bad practices all over the world have come to very little, and any new MAI promises to give more freedoms to the TNCs without imposing many compensating responsibilities. All this is done in the name of globalisation, free trade and international competitiveness and the hope that, somehow, it will eventually make poor people better off.

Notes

1. N. Avery, M. Drake & T. Lang, *Cracking the Codex* (National Food Alliance, 1993). This is summarised in Tim Lang & Colin Hines, *The New Protectionism* (Earthscan, 1993), pp. 100–3.
2. See Corporate Europe Observatory, *Europe, Inc.: Dangerous Liaisons between EU Institutions and Industry*, Amsterdam, May 1997.
3. Unilever's 'product life cycle' analysis is one of the most progressive environmental policies of any TNC ('Environmental Report', Unilever, 1996), but it appears to have little impact on the globalising dynamic implicit in corporate strategy.
4. Cited in *Europe, Inc.*, p. 28. Research on such bodies is only beginning, and in the interests of democratic accountability it is important that such phenomena be exposed to public scrutiny.
5. Other examples that could be cited from the early 1990s are the binational coalition of US and Mexican corporate interests that swung the legislatures in favour of the North American Free Trade Agreement (NAFTA) and the Business Council for Sustainable Development that shut out critical discussion of corporate impact on the environment at the Earth Summit in Rio and subsequently in the UN Commission on Sustainable Development. Rough equivalents of the ERT are the Business Roundtable in the USA and Keidanren in Japan, dominated by major TNCs. The activities of the TNCs active on the Advisory Committee for Trade Policy and Negotiations of the WTO are also relevant here.
6. For a theoretical discussion that attempts to provide a Gramscian basis for the argument that global capitalism needs to be politically active to sustain its project and creates elite social movements based on the TNCs, see my 'Social Movements for Global Capitalism: The Transnational Capitalist Class in Action', *Review of International Political Economy*, Vol. 4, No. 3 (1997), pp. 514–38.
7. Ralph Nader & Lori Wallach, 'GATT, NAFTA, and the subversion of the democratic process', in: Jerry Mander & Edward Goldsmith (Eds), *The Case against the Global Economy and for a Turn toward the Local* (Sierra Club Books, 1996), ch. 8. The 43 chapters in this book, an early manifesto for the anti-TNC International Forum on Globalisation, provide many good examples of the political actions of TNCs and the growing opposition to them.
8. *Europe, Inc.*, p. 57. For the (sometimes) violent corporate onslaught on the environmental movement, see Andrew Rowell, *Green Backlash: Global Subversion of the Environment Movement* (Routledge, 1996).

New Political Economy, Vol. 3, No. 2, 1998

Do They Really Rule The World?

ANDREW WALTER

A recent book by David Korten entitled *When Corporations Rule the World* captures the essence of much contemporary concern that global, mobile firms are increasingly able to impose their preferences upon relatively immobile governments, workers and citizens.[1] Much contemporary 'globalisation theory' sweeping through the halls of academia also suggests that states (and citizens) have largely lost the power to tax, manage the domestic business cycle and enact various kinds of regulatory constraints upon capital. In this short contribution, I argue that such broad claims are exaggerated, and I try to explain an anomaly. The anomaly is that 'global firms' often fail in their demands that important host states adopt inward investment rules or regimes allowing their full operational flexibility; yet they have apparently unleashed policy competition between sub-state or sub-regional authorities eager to attract or retain investments. As the first claim will attract more abuse than the second, more space is devoted to it.

Structural power arguments and policy arbitrage

The core of the globalisation argument is that increasing capital mobility raises the bargaining power of firms *vis-à-vis* immobile states, citizens and factors (primarily labour). In this 'structural' version, by a process of regulatory arbitrage states are pushed into spontaneous or unilateral liberalisation, which coincides with the interest of capital agents. For example, Jan Art Scholte argues that '[global] firms can ...

with relative ease relocate production facilities and sales outlets to other jurisdictions if they find a particular state's regulations overly burdensome. Usually this threat alone is sufficient to make a state amenable to, *inter alia*, privatization and liberalization.'[2] A direct implication of this argument is that domestic rules relating to the treatment of FDI will increasingly reflect the interests and preferences of mobile firms rather than those of host states. On the face of it, there is much supporting evidence. Indeed, the overwhelming trend in the developing countries has been in the direction of the liberalisation of rules relating to inward foreign direct investment.

But this trend masks important anomalies. While the broad trend in developing countries in recent decades was towards the liberalisation of *entry and exit* of foreign investors into a number of sectors, many also shifted towards heavy usage of what some have referred to as 'creeping', rather than outright, expropriation. Perhaps most importantly, various performance requirements have been aimed at enhancing the contribution of FDI to the host economy, thereby constraining the operational flexibility of TNCs.[3] In recent years, many countries have been more willing to liberalise entry and exit regulations (including the right to financial transfers) than such operational restraints. The most important host developing countries, in particular, remain heavy users of such instruments in spite of their growing share of global FDI flows since the 1980s. They often also retain non-transparent screening procedures for entry, widespread use of limits

Andrew Walter, Department of International Relations, London School of Economics, Houghton Street, London WC2A 2AE, UK.

1356-3467/98/020288-05 © 1998 Carfax Publishing Ltd

on foreign ownership and outright prohibitions in designated 'strategic' sectors.[4]

This is inconvenient for the structural power argument. The bulk of FDI in the 1990s to the developing world has flowed to a handful of countries, in the following order of importance: China, Mexico, Malaysia, Argentina, Brazil, Indonesia, Hungary, Thailand, Poland, Colombia, Nigeria and Taiwan. The paradigm case is China, which maintained an extremely illiberal FDI regime while it rocketed to first place in terms of FDI inflows. If the policy arbitrage effect to which Scholte refers was powerful, these countries should have *more* rather than less liberal FDI regimes than countries receiving little FDI. But, if anything, there is an inverse relationship between the liberality of a developing country's FDI regime and its importance as a location for FDI. There are important exceptions: NAFTA has bound Mexico to what the US Trade Representative's office calls a 'state of the art investment regime' and Argentina is one of the only major developing countries to sign a bilateral investment treaty (BIT) with the USA. The US 'model BIT' prohibits the use of such restrictive policy instruments (along with various other things). For East Asian countries, however, their desire to retain such policy instruments for development purposes has meant that the USA has so far been unable to negotiate BITs with any of these countries, and not for want of trying.[5]

Collective action problems: the structural weakness of capital

The reason for this empirical anomaly in the broad trend towards liberalisation is obvious. The sheer attractiveness of East Asia as a location for international business means that these countries are in a much stronger bargaining position than sub-Saharan Africa. After considerable liberalisation of entry restrictions, the likes of Malaysia, Indonesia, China and Thailand have been able to retain often onerous operating restrictions upon TNCs because

there is more capital (and there are more TNCs) in the world economy than Asian tiger economies. If one automobile company dislikes the terms of a deal offered by the Chinese authorities, a competitor will take its place. Although China (and much more restrictive India) may be an exception because of the size of its domestic market, the heavy use of restrictive measures by the ASEAN countries has not prevented them from receiving a growing share of FDI flows either. Mobile international firms suffer from a basic collective action problem: as a group they cannot avoid investing in China, Malaysia or Indonesia because they have nowhere else to go. *Ceteris paribus*, firms prefer countries with liberal investment rules, but all things are never close to equal.

The collective action problem also applies to the financial markets. As with the debt crisis of the early 1980s, the recent financial crisis in Asia has necessitated IMF policy conditionality precisely because capital markets are so bad at imposing 'market conditionality'. Although some argue that the IMF simply does the bidding of global capital, it strains credibility to suggest that the markets consciously forced a regional currency crisis, with the massive losses this entailed, in order to push these countries into the loving arms of the IMF. The last thing markets expected was the bursting of the East Asian bubble. Similarly, while the latest IMF packages have entailed substantial easing of FDI restrictions, particularly in the financial sector, only the most paranoid conspiracy theorist could believe that this was part of a concerted TNC strategy. Hence, before the crisis, FDI inflows often strengthened rather than weakened the ability of states to resist the liberalisation preferences of TNCs. Once the crisis abates, and capital begins flowing back to the rapidly growing emerging market countries of Asia and Latin America, their ability to resist liberalisation pressures will grow again. Even the IMF may find that promises made in the heat of the crisis may not be carried out.

Andrew Walter

Structural weakness and political lobbying

In the face of their structural weakness, TNCs have resorted to old-fashioned political lobbying, particularly of their parent (home) governments. In a brave new world in which mobile capital could simply compete away restrictive state policies it did not like, there would be no need for such corporate lobbying and diplomacy. In the USA, the result of vocal corporate demands for diplomatic pressure on the major host developing countries to liberalise their FDI policies has been a multi-track US strategy of bilateral, regional and multilateral initiatives. However, the results of such activities have so far been disappointing for US (and other) TNCs. In East Asia, the bilateral strategy has failed: the list of countries with which the USA has successfully negotiated BITs is striking for its relative unimportance for US business. Efforts to obtain anything more than a weak non-binding investment agreement within APEC have come to nothing. The target countries have had little incentive to change this stance while FDI has been flooding in, and the US business sector has not favoured a tough policy of unilateral sanctions to ensure compliance because of the fear that this would jeopardise the market access they already enjoy.

The various multilateral initiatives that the USA has largely initiated have also been disappointing for business (with the exception of the recent telecoms and financial services agreements within the WTO). The results of the Trade Related Investment Measures (TRIMs) agreement in the Uruguay Round in particular were especially disappointing, leading to pressure for a separate initiative in a more conducive forum, which resulted in the opening of talks on the Multilateral Agreement on Investment in 1995. While the OECD was chosen because it was dominated by major capital exporting countries, the ultimate objective of US business and government was to place additional pressure on recalcitrant developing countries by

extending MAI (as a 'stand-alone' agreement) to 'like-minded' developing countries.

It is unlikely that MAI will answer the prayers of TNCs in this respect, in spite of a widespread view among opponents that it will provide unprecedented entry and operating flexibility for TNCs ('NAFTA on steroids', as North American NGOs refer to MAI). MAI opponents have been misled by the US-inspired negotiating approach, which first sets out general (liberal) rules and then turns to negotiating exceptions and reservations in the small print and the annexes. Even in the not-so-small print, OECD governments (including the US) fully intend to retain the right to regulate key aspects of TNC activity within their domestic jurisdictions, refusing key business demands such as the full inclusion of taxation in MAI. The USA has notably rejected the arguments of its own business community and everyone else that it should accept constraints upon the use of 'extra-territorial' measures for foreign policy purposes, as in the controversial Helms–Burton and Iran–Libya Sanctions acts. Other OECD governments have insisted on various exceptions to basic principles in areas such as privatisation, while Canada has demanded a blanket reservation for 'cultural' industries. In addition, US business lobbies dramatically underestimated the potential for the domestic politicisation of the MAI, and the mobilisation of labour and NGO groups has probably made the business insistence on no binding labour and environmental standards clauses in MAI untenable.

These factors have meant that an agreement was not reached by the original April 1998 deadline, and if the initiative does not collapse entirely, negotiations over the liberalisation or 'rollback' of country exceptions and reservations will be deferred. Moreover, even if a strong MAI were eventually to emerge, pressure on major host developing countries outside the OECD to accede will be limited (not only because they reject the labour and environmental clauses demanded by Northern

NGOs). First, developing country oppo- sition will probably continue to keep MAI out of the WTO for the time being, where linkage politics might be possible. Second, despite recent concessions on investment entry provisions by East Asian countries undergoing IMF-led structural adjustment programmes, it is implausible to think that the IMF could force these countries to accept much more general MAI provi- sions. Third, the OECD strategy of isolat- ing the recalcitrant developing countries is unlikely to put pressure on the major host states in East Asia as long as these coun- tries continue to attract a large share of global FDI flows to developing countries. This strategy in the end depends upon the structural market power of capital to force policy convergence upon non-MAI mem- bers and, as we have seen, this effect is weak.

Sub-state FDI competition

Does all this suggest there is nothing to the claims of globalisation theory? Not en- tirely. There does seem to be considerable pressure on governments to liberalise entry to international firms, in part thanks to the debt crisis of the 1980s and the associated demise of heavy import-substitution devel- opment models. In addition, at the margin, there may well be structural pressure on governments to make improvements in the operating conditions of mobile firms, such as to reduce levels of corporate taxation. Yet much work needs to be done to inves- tigate the extent of such effects; there are too many claims of the *post hoc, propter hoc* variety in the existing literature.

In fact, most of the existing evidence for policy arbitrage is at the sub-national or sub-regional integration agreement (RIA) levels rather than at the international level, and for good reason. Familiar anecdotes about Hoover moving production from France to Scotland to exploit lower labour costs and greater 'flexibility', or Mercedes Benz announcing a shortlist of 62 sites for a new US factory and unleashing an in- glorious 30-state bidding war, suggest that mobility does matter. This is because, at lower levels of political jurisdiction, the collective action dilemma passes from in- ternational firms to sub-federal states, re- gions or local authorities.

To oversimplify, consider the following simple two-stage model of a Japanese au- tomobile or electronics producer consider- ing building the kind of foreign factory that has received large incentive packages from US states or European sub-regions in recent years. In stage I of its location decision, the firm decides that a combi- nation of protectionist threat and commer- cial logic means that it has no choice but to locate inside the USA or the EU. In stage I, the mobile firm (and its competi- tors) has little bargaining power *vis-à-vis* the USA or the EU; all the cards are in the hands of the state/region. In stage II of the location decision, the firm finds that the number of site possibilities is very large. In fact, the possible number of sites will be many multiples of the available number of firms (in highly oligopolised industries) offering high-wage jobs in a technology- intensive industry. In stage II, the firm (and its competitors) can play off various sub-federal jurisdictions in the final loca- tion choice. Thus the federal government need offer no incentives for a firm to enter the US market, while Alabama and its various competitors feel they have no choice but to engage in an escalating in- centives war. This resolves some of the conflicting evidence about the relative im- portance of incentive packages in firms' location decisions.[6]

Important issues follow from this which require further research. First, if countries with large internal markets do not suffer a loss of bargaining power (and need not compete either on rules or in terms of incentives) *vis-à-vis* domestic market- orientated FDI, will they do so when the FDI is export-orientated? Much may depend on the location's access to key export mar- kets: Mexico's pulling power as a location for US-orientated exporters increased dra- matically as a result of NAFTA. This leads to a second issue: RIAs mean that nation-

Andrew Walter

states risk becoming 'sub-federal' competitors *vis-à-vis* highly mobile firms who simply need access to the broader regional market. If a semiconductor manufacturer is relatively indifferent between Ireland and Scotland as a production site from which it can access the whole European Economic Area (EEA) market, Ireland's special tax rate of 10 per cent for manufacturing FDI might be a considerable incentive. This helps explain the EU's recent concern about destructive 'tax competition'. However, in principle, regions (or the USA) can overcome such dilemmas through the harmonisation of policies and standards at agreed levels. (The EU has relatively successfully constrained the escalation of bidding wars in the past decade or so compared to the USA, in part because of the constraints imposed by EU competition law and regional policy, in part because of the lesser decentralisation of taxing power in most EU countries.)

Finally, there are two further qualifications to the extreme globalisation predictions. First, it is not clear that, if mobile firms are sensitive to policy rules at sub-federal levels within integrated regions, this will necessarily always lead to a 'race to the bottom'. Despite fears that mobile capital will arbitrage away high environmental standards in some countries, often we find US states or European regions advertising high environmental standards as part of their attractiveness as a location (similar 'race to the top' possi-

bilities arise with public infrastructure and human capital). Second, it is important to remember that much FDI is considerably less 'footloose' than the oft-repeated anecdotes imply. In particular, FDI in services, which constitutes the bulk of global FDI flows, often needs to locate near its customer base, though this might not apply to wholesale banking services.

Notes

1. David Korten, *When Corporations Rule the World* (Kumarian Press/Berrett-Koehler, 1995).
2. Jan Art Scholte, 'Global Capitalism and the State', *International Affairs*, Vol. 73, No. 3 (1997), p. 443.
3. For a general overview of this trend, see Charles Lipson, *Standing Guard: Protecting Foreign Capital in the Nineteenth and Twentieth Centuries* (University of California Press, 1985); and Charles Oman, *New Forms of International Investing in Developing Countries* (OECD, 1989).
4. For annual compilations on a country-by-country basis of the various policy instruments by which countries continue to regulate the operations of TNCs, see the investment sections of US Department of State, *Country Commercial Guides*, and US Trade Representative, *National Trade Estimates*.
5. A number of European countries have agreed BITs with East Asian countries but, unlike the USA, European countries have agreed exceptions to key principles such as national treatment (non-discrimination) and prohibitions against performance requirements in the interest of obtaining agreement.
6. I am grateful to Charles Oman of the OECD for clarifying this point.

[15]

National structures and multinational corporate behavior: enduring differences in the age of globalization

Louis W. Pauly and Simon Reich

Liberal and critical theorists alike claim that the world political economy is becoming globalized. If they are right, leading corporations should gradually be losing their national characters and converging in their fundamental strategies and operations. Multinational corporations (MNCs) should be the harbingers of deep global integration. In fact, recent evidence shows little blurring or convergence at the cores of firms based in Germany, Japan, or the United States.

In contrast to expectations now common both inside and outside academia regarding the imminent emergence of a truly global economy, this article shows that MNCs continue to diverge fairly systematically in their internal governance and long-term financing structures, in their approaches to research and development (R&D) as well as in the location of core R&D facilities, and in their overseas investment and intrafirm trading strategies. Durable national institutions and distinctive ideological traditions still seem to shape and channel crucial corporate decisions. Across the leading states of the three regions now commonly referred to

Much of the empirical material presented here originated in two reports commissioned by the Office of Technology Assessment: U.S. Congress 1993 and 1994. The authors were members of the original project team. William Keller led the team, and Paul Doremus was principally responsible for the research and development chapters and much of the statistical compilation upon which we rely in this article. Further empirical analysis related to the theme of this article can be found in the original reports as well as in the book, tentatively entitled *Multinationals and the Limits of Globalization*, which the four of us are now completing. For support that facilitated this article, Simon Reich thanks the Sloan Foundation and the International Affairs Fellowship Program of the Council on Foreign Relations. Louis Pauly is grateful for a sabbatical leave grant from the University of Toronto and a research grant from the Social Sciences and Humanities Research Council of Canada. Yoshiko Koda, Viktoria Murphy, and Arik Preis provided excellent research assistance. We are also indebted to many business executives, government officials, and scholars who commented, often critically, on various versions of the original Office of Technology Assessment reports as well as on the earlier drafts of this article, which were presented at the 1995 annual meetings of the International Studies Association and the American Political Science Association and at various university workshops. Special efforts were made by Alfred Chandler, Jonathan Crystal, Benjamin J. Cohen, Michael Donnelly, Kenneth Freeman, Lawrence Friedman, Robert Gilpin, William Greider, Peter Katzenstein, Stephen Krasner, Theodore Lowi, Michael Mastanduno, Helen Milner, John Odell, Alan Rugman, Richard Samuels, Harley Shaiken, Ulrike Schaede, Susan Strange, Raymond Vernon, and four anonymous reviewers, none of whom is responsible for the final result.

International Organization 51, 1, Winter 1997, pp. 1–30

as the "Triad," the foundations of corporate markets are not converging. Markets in this sense are not replacing political leadership and the necessity for negotiated adjustments among states.

Analytical context

The MNC—as empirical reality or as metaphor for the technological, financial, and managerial sinews of convergence in the contemporary world economy—is central to a number of contemporary research programs in the fields of international relations and international political economy. One strand of that research involves specifying the forces fundamentally driving corporate behavior and reshaping the relationship between that behavior and government policy.

Relying on the assumption that, at base, the logic of globally integrating markets ultimately drives corporate behavior, two important bodies of theory on the political implications of MNCs are now evolving. Although much more highly nuanced than their forebears in the 1960s and 1970s, recent studies within the liberal tradition suggest that increasingly mobile capital and the necessary responsiveness of firms to cross-national technological and financial incentives are beginning to constrain even leading industrial states and their societies in broadly comparable ways.[1] In complementary fashion, recent work in a more critical tradition explores the socioeconomic phenomenon of "globalization" and generally supports the idea that a noose, woven in substantial part by the intensifying operations of MNCs, is tightening around the neck of traditional forms of national political organization.[2] Only a small leap of imagination, a leap constantly made these days in scholarly circles, is necessary to draw central themes of these research programs together in the following terms.

Important industrial sectors currently are in ferment. Multinational firms at the center of those sectors are defining their interests ever more clearly in a global context. As they pursue those interests, they themselves become more alike through their interaction in increasingly integrated markets. Across a widening range of industries, transnational or global forces are reshaping basic corporate structures.[3] This is placing similar pressures on distinctive national institutions and policies. Consequent adaptations in those institutions and policies may not necessarily be "liberal" in the classic sense of the term; they may, to the contrary, rationalize cartels and other antiliberal agglomerations of power. Nevertheless, deep structural convergence at the level of the firm is profoundly changing the political economy of the world. In light of the history of economic nationalism, liberals imply, this transformation is probably not a bad thing, but its associated costs should be better understood. In light of the history of capitalism, their critical interlocutors respond,

---

1. Milner and Keohane 1996, chap. 1. Compatible arguments are made in Milner 1988; Rogowski 1989; Frieden 1991; Goodman and Pauly 1993; and Andrews 1994.
2. See Group of Lisbon 1995, 68–77; Carnoy, Castells, and Cohen 1993, 4–5; Castells 1991; Barnet and Cavanagh 1994; and Gill 1995.
3. Cerny 1995, 621.

this transformation may indeed be a bad thing for a substantial portion of the world's population, but it is, in any case, inevitable.

This article cuts into the middle of this stylized synthesis and explores the counterintuitive proposition that leading MNCs are *not* converging toward common patterns of behavior at their cores. In positive and more specific terms that lend themselves to comparative empirical testing, the proposition may be restated as follows: the institutional and ideological legacies of distinctive national histories continue significantly to shape the core operations of multinational firms based in Germany, Japan, and the United States. If basic insights behind current liberal and critical research programs are plausible, empirically oriented analysts should be able to cast serious doubt on such a proposition by finding fairly unambiguous evidence of basic structural and strategic convergence inside multinational firms themselves.

Using a different terminology in his magisterial *Scale and Scope,* Alfred Chandler sketched the rise before the 1940s of three fundamentally different kinds of industrial enterprise in Britain, Germany, and the United States.[4] In his conclusion, he asked whether such national patterns endure. Our research was motivated by the desire to contribute to an answer and to raise new theoretical and policy questions concerning its implications. We acknowledge at the outset that tracing the causal arrow— between the legacies of distinctive national histories, the core structures of firms, important firm strategies, and specific governmental policies responding to or seeking to affect corporate behavior—is not a simple matter. The empirical analysis of this article concentrates on the first three items and on the linkages among them.[5] This analysis convinces us that those linkages remain very strong.

A related but theoretically distinct body of thought has a long pedigree in the realist literature on MNCs. Some twenty years ago, to cite the most prominent and influential example, Robert Gilpin related the global spread of American firms after 1945 to the security interests and international political dominance of the United States.[6] *U.S. Power and the Multinational Corporation* represented a response to research that came to the fore in American academic circles from the 1960s onward, some of which left the impression of an impending split between corporations and the states that originally chartered them.[7] In the aftermath of oil, currency, and debt crises in later years, analysis of state–firm relations became more refined as states apparently returned to center stage.[8]

In Europe, meanwhile, a substantial body of research developed both on diverse host country reactions to multinational corporate expansion as well as on distinctions between American and British MNCs and their emerging Continental counterparts.[9]

4. Chandler 1990. Also see Chandler 1962, 1964, and 1977.

5. For an analysis of broad national structural variations that, unlike the present analysis, focuses on national and corporate competitiveness, see Porter 1990.

6. Gilpin 1975. Also see Hymer 1976 (based on a Ph.D. dissertation from 1960).

7. See Ball 1967; Cooper 1968; Morse 1970; Vernon 1971; Keohane and Nye 1972; and Wilkins 1974.

8. See Vernon 1977; Keohane and Nye 1977; Bergsten, Horst, and Moran 1978; Kudrle 1985; Robinson 1983; Ostry 1990; Dunning 1992a and 1992b; and Moran 1993.

9. See Dunning 1958; Servan-Schreiber 1967; Reddaway 1968; Turner 1970; Franko 1976; Stopford and Turner 1985; Hertner and Jones 1986; and van Tulder and Junne 1988.

Influenced by such work, research also commenced on the evolution of MNCs in Japan as well as in parts of the developing world.[10] In the 1990s, the revival of the European Community's single-market program stimulated new research in Europe. Although they noted behavioral discrepancies between European firms, these studies began to speculate about the emergence of new regional (as opposed to national or "Anglo-Saxon") corporate identities.[11] At the same time, U.S. scholars were again debating the question of whether the era of the global corporation, prematurely heralded in the 1960s, had finally arrived.[12]

The world had indeed changed a great deal since Gilpin's 1975 book first appeared.[13] Systemic power had become more diffuse, and national economies had become much more open. At the same time, intrafirm trade was accelerating and cross-border direct and portfolio investments were mushrooming. In certain industrial sectors, such as pharmaceuticals, semiconductors, and telecommunications, cross-border mergers and acquisitions, strategic alliances, and trumpeted international redeployments of corporate resources suggested a qualitative change in the nature of multinational corporate behavior. Careful comparative business studies suggested that receding national divergences might still be important in industries characterized by "regulated competition."[14] In many industrial sectors, however, the global corporation seemed a caricature no more.[15]

Argument

This article takes a different position. Certainly firms must continuously adapt to dynamic markets in order to survive, and certainly that adaptation must now take place in a world where short-term capital is highly mobile and where certain technologies are changing quite rapidly. But we argue that the underlying nationality of the firm remains the vitally important determinant of the nature of its adaptation. That nationality is not necessarily given by the location of corporate headquarters or the addresses of principal shareholders, although it usually still is. More fundamentally, it is given by historical experience and the institutional and ideological legacies of that experience, both of which constitute the essential structures of states. Because of them, we hypothesize, there remain systematic and important national differences in the operations of MNCs—in their internal governance and long-term financing, in their R&D activities, and in their intertwined investment and trading strategies.

We chose these operations for analysis because they provide a window on the very core of the MNC. They shed light on how MNCs are ultimately controlled and on the nature of their basic funding; where they locate and how they maintain the critical

10. See Tsurumi 1983; Campbell and Burton 1994; Wells 1983; and Lall et al. 1983.

11. See Franko 1991; and Jones and Schröter 1993.

12. Associated debate came prominently into public view, for example, in Reich 1990 and Tyson 1991.

13. For his own later reflections, see Gilpin 1987, chap. 6; and 1994.

14. Yoffie 1993.

15. The rising prominence of firms as political actors is highlighted by Stopford and Strange 1991; and Eden and Potter 1993.

mass of their R&D operations; and how they manage the linkage between trade and investment as their international expansions proceed.

Obviously, this is an ambitious agenda, especially within the confines of a short article. We nevertheless consider it important to take this initial step, especially in the context of the larger debates currently under way in the field of international political economy. With regard to the ultimate political implications of multinational firms, empirical research has tended to focus on the more obvious aspects of their behavior: where they place production facilities, how they market their products, and how they use and deepen short-term financial markets. Although the technical barriers to cross-disciplinary and broadly comparative analysis are daunting, scholars of politics must probe more deeply.

In the end, our analysis supports the view that national structures remain decisive. For scholars interested in the broader implications of corporate behavior, they do not just "matter." In analytical terms, they retain their priority with respect to other factors currently reshaping the world of the modern corporation.[16] The evidence we marshal below to test this argument strongly suggests that the domestic structures within which a firm initially develops leave a permanent imprint on its strategic behavior.[17]

To assess the extent to which we are really dealing with lagging indicators or something more fundamental, we adopt a theoretical stance more subtle than orthodox realism. Stephen Krasner recently captured some of this subtlety. When states are understood as institutional structures or polities, Krasner suggested, then the basic institutional structures of MNCs may be influenced or even determined by the characteristics of states. "In this perspective, institutional structures, not actors, are the units of analysis."[18]

Our approach has much in common with this understanding, but we go two steps further. First, the institutions worth emphasizing in such a conceptualization should be seen as embodying durable ideologies that link states and firms in distinctive ways. Second, those institutions and ideologies may be viewed as dynamic, but they change much more slowly than the firm-level operations rooted within them. Although corporate activity is not simply a product of internal organizational logic, the dominant causal arrow in such an analysis runs from slowly changing national structures through corporate structures and strategies to the actual behavior of firms in the marketplace.[19]

---

16. Our argument and evidence are not incompatible with a constructivist theoretical agenda, but they do challenge scholars probing the connection between global economic transformation and political identity to make clearer distinctions among states. See Ruggie 1993.

17. Adapting a term from electromagnetics, economists label such a process of marking "hysteresis," by which they typically imply a lagging effect after a causal force has been removed. See Krugman 1986; and Grossman and Richardson 1985. Business analysts refer in the same way and with the same implication to "corporate inertia" and "path dependence." Yoffie 1993, 17. Our argument and evidence raise strong doubts about the inevitable erosion of the effects of history.

18. Krasner 1996. Also see Sally 1994.

19. Philip Wellons's study of international banking provides an example of the plausible outcome of such causal reasoning. In one of the most "global" of industries, Wellons shows how banks from different home states do not behave alike in the face of similar opportunities and challenges. See Wellons 1987. Also see Wellons 1986; Biersteker 1987; Murtha and Lenway 1994; and Kapstein 1994.

6 International Organization

In essence, we modify what the theoretical literature of international political economy labels the domestic structures approach. The ideological dimension was not usually stressed in early theoretical work along these lines. We are not referring here, however, to what the older literature on MNCs called "economic nationalism," a concept that is too general to be of much analytical use. Adapting Emanuel Adler's terms, we see ideologies as providing broad orienting frameworks or belief systems that, when combined with national institutions, define "collective understandings" of roles, beliefs, expectations, and purposes. Richard Samuels, whose use of the term "technonationalism" we adapt below in the Japanese case, provides an exemplary model of how ideology and institutions can be mutually constitutive and mutually reinforcing.[20] Although such an approach can accommodate the fact that the core strategies and structures of corporations can and do change, it sees such developments as constrained by permissive changes in underlying institutional and ideological structures. The novelty of our analysis is to link such institutional and ideological structures not to governmental policy outcomes but to the most fundamental behavior of MNCs in a broadly comparative context. Where much related literature examines the influence of domestic structures on public-sector actors and policies, we probe their influence on the largest private-sector actors, actors that theorists of the internationalization/globalization phenomenon now commonly depict as increasingly autonomous.

Our empirical analysis deliberately focuses on leading MNCs from leading states. Firms from small home markets, often viewed as harbingers of a truly global economy, have long had to demonstrate high levels of external adaptability. There is nothing new in Swiss companies compensating for a small home market by expanding externally. Among the ranks of the world's largest public firms, however, the number of prominent firms from small home markets remains quite small. In terms of market valuation in 1995, Germany, Japan, and the United States accounted for seventy-five of the world's top one hundred firms. Britain accounted for eleven, but no other country accounted for more than five.[21] Moreover, although some of our evidence draws on the larger industrial base of the European Union, we view the German base as distinctive enough and regionally dominant enough to be the central analog to the American and Japanese cases. Of Europe's top one hundred firms, twenty-seven are German. They account for the largest share of European industrial production and sales, and, across key technology-intensive sectors, German firms hold a much larger—and rising—share of world production than firms based in any other European country.[22]

---

20. See, respectively, Katzenstein 1977; Adler 1987, 17; and Samuels 1994, 33–78. Other work in this tradition includes Krasner 1978; Zysman 1983; Gourevitch 1986; Hall 1986; Samuels 1987; Katzenstein 1984; Krauss and Reich 1992; Steinmo, Thelen, and Longstreth 1992; Hart 1992; Garrett and Lange 1995; Katzenstein 1996; and Markovits and Reich forthcoming.

21. *Wall Street Journal*, 2 October 1995, p. R32.

22. See Commission of the European Communities 1993, 27; and OECD 1994. Grieco 1990 employs a similar logic.

TABLE 1. *National differences that condition corporate structures and strategies*

	United States	Germany	Japan
Political institutions	Liberal democracy; divided government; highly organized interest groups	Social democracy; weak bureaucracy; corporatist organizational legacy	Developmental democracy; strong bureaucracy; "reciprocal consent" between state and firms
Economic institutions	Decentralized, open markets; unconcentrated, fluid capital markets; antitrust tradition	Organized markets; tiers of firms; bank-centered capital markets; universal banks; certain cartelized markets	Guided, bifurcated, difficult-to-penetrate markets; bank-centered capital markets; tight business networks/cartels in declining industries
Dominant economic ideology	Free enterprise liberalism	Social partnership	Technonationalism

In Table 1 we summarize the kinds of domestic structures in the United States, Germany, and Japan that we first suspected might exert a significant shaping influence on corporate behavior. Each of the structures is clearly an ideal type and can be unpacked. Indeed, a great deal of comparative research and contentious debate is devoted to just such a task.[23] As it reminds us, hard and fast demarcation lines are difficult to draw in the real world. Nevertheless, a critical mass of that research now associates these labels with recognizably different and relatively enduring patterns of economic and political organization. It also provides a basis for the central inference guiding our own more limited study. The weight of the evidence presented below strongly suggests that the putative relationship between such domestic structures and core aspects of multinational corporate behavior is not spurious.

It would obviously be simpleminded, however, to argue that one explanation captures the essential reality for all firms all of the time. The chemical industry, for example, is clearly subject to high transportation costs and particular hazards, which cannot help but influence some aspects of the behavior of all chemical companies regardless of nationality. Nevertheless, in basic corporate structures and strategies across a range of industrial sectors, striking differences of an aggregate nature remain. Market-led explanations, whether emphasizing the determinative force of product maturities, sectoral idiosyncrasies, or broad technological changes, are ultimately unsatisfying. The enduring institutional and ideological foundations within which leading firms remain most deeply embedded offer more plausible explanations.

23. See, for example, Berger and Dore 1996.

8 International Organization

Empirical evidence

To examine our central proposition we collected and analyzed a wide range of empirical evidence, including aggregate and sectoral statistical data, case studies, relevant secondary literature, and information culled from an series of confidential interviews undertaken between 1992 and 1994 with senior executives from MNCs in Europe, Japan, and the United States. The following is a summary of our findings.

Corporate governance and financing

U.S. corporate managers are highly constrained by dynamic and deep capital markets; their Japanese counterparts are effectively bound by complex but reliable networks of domestic relationships; and the managers of German MNCs retain a relatively high degree of operational independence. The circumstances of individual firms vary, but across the board such differences reflect the fact that corporations continue to govern themselves quite differently across the three home countries.[24] Those differences persist and are reflected in the varying priorities German, Japanese, and American MNCs assign to the maximization of shareholder value, to the autonomy of their managers, and to the stabilization of employer–employee relations.

The term "corporate governance" refers broadly to the rules and norms that guide the internal relationships among various "stakeholders" in a business enterprise, including owners, directors, managers, creditors, suppliers, employees, and customers. For comparative purposes, our emphasis here is on the central relationships between the managers of a corporation and the owners of voting shares. Those relationships are intermediated by boards of directors and focused on respective rights and obligations that are either specified in law or legitimated by long-standing custom and practice.[25] They are the products of unique national histories. Since MNCs span a number of legal jurisdictions, their governance often seems more complicated than it is for local firms. The core internal structures of almost all MNCs are nevertheless still clearly associated with prevailing norms in the jurisdiction within which their head offices are located. It is here that we observe the most direct influence of deeper institutions and ideologies.

Patterns of shareholding provide a starting point for understanding key differences. In the early 1990s, nearly 90 percent of the voting shares of publicly listed corporations in the United States were held by individual households, pension funds, and mutual funds. In Japan, that number was closer to 30 percent and in Germany closer to 15 percent. Conversely, banks held less than 1 percent of publicly listed shares in the United States but nearly 10 percent in Germany and 25 percent in Japan.

---

24. For accessible overviews of the issue, see Fukao 1995; and U.S. General Accounting Office 1993.
25. Inspired by Williamson 1988, much of the current and relevant analytical literature refers to the owners as "principals" and the managers as "agents."

At the same time, nonfinancial firms held a negligible number of such shares in the United States but 25 percent in Japan and nearly 40 percent in Germany.[26]

The dispersion and mobility of shareholders in the United States help to fixate the managers of American corporations on short-term financial performance, a fixation that may ultimately bolster competitive strengths by forcing rapid adjustments.[27] Over the long run, however, such imperatives can complicate life for firms that face direct competition in their home markets from rivals capable of longer-term planning because of their higher degree of insulation from capital market pressures. A few U.S. MNCs sometimes demonstrate similar capabilities but always within clear limits. The Ford Motor Company and Motorola—both of which have long-term shareholders with significant stakes derived from their original founders—are two examples of such American companies. German and Japanese MNCs, however, continue to demonstrate a general capacity in this regard. As Jay Lorsch and Elizabeth McIver put it, "In contrast to the United States' primary focus on shareholder value, these other countries' corporations are seen as durable national assets that serve a broad base of constituents. Quality products, market share, and employment are just as legitimate as goals as return on shareholder investment. While some US top managers and directors prefer this perspective themselves, they are swimming against the dominant national tide."[28]

More subtle differences in the character of relationships between banks and corporations also persist. In the United States, banks provide MNCs mainly with secondary financing, cash management, selective advisory work, and various other finance-related services. The historical trend, moreover, has been for corporations to reduce their reliance on commercial bank financing and to fund their long-term investments from retained earnings or directly from the capital markets.

Conversely, in Germany and Japan and across leading industrial sectors, banks perform a steering function. This function has evolved considerably as national industrial development has proceeded but nevertheless remains important. Before the financial bubble of the 1980s finally burst, commentators on Japan frequently argued that the centrality of banks was breaking down and that the long-term financing operations of Japanese MNCs were converging toward the American norm. Despite considerable weakness in bank balance sheets, such a proposition looks less plausible today. In Germany, it looks even less plausible.

In the United States, the ratio of bank loans to corporate financial liabilities, a rough measure of the relative importance of banks in the financing of corporations, fell into the 25–35 percent range from the early 1980s through the early 1990s. In both Germany and Japan, the comparable ratio stayed consistently in the 60–70 percent range. The numbers for bank deposits as a proportion of corporate financial

26. Data are from Deutsche Bundesbank, Tokyo Stock Exchange, ProShare, and Federal Reserve Board, cited in Kester 1993.
27. Roe 1994.
28. Lorsch and McIver 1992. Also see Lorsch and McIver 1989.

10   International Organization

assets show similar levels of divergence.[29] But such broad comparisons can oversimplify differences in deeper corporate structures.

Throughout the postwar period and in various high-technology sectors, most notably in electronics and transportation systems, Japanese MNCs became famous for pursuing aggressive strategies keyed to market share, not return on investment. Even recently, for example, the U.S. market share of Japanese auto manufacturers barely budged from 1993 (22.8 percent) through 1995 (22.4 percent), despite remarkable shifts in the relative value of the yen.[30] Probing the factors that continue to sustain this capacity has itself become something of a growth industry. Numerous studies have highlighted the linkage between such strategies and corporate governance and financing structures back home. Those structures appear to facilitate the sharing of information and the management of business and financial risks across allied firms in a manner that varies considerably from the American norm. Michael Porter encapsulated the distinction by labeling the Japanese system "patient capital," although it is unclear whether corporate owners or consumers constitute the more patient party. The distinction, however, is more complicated than the label implies.[31]

In Japanese MNCs, institutional cross-shareholding caps a complex system of corporate control. Large volumes of minority equity claims commonly are spread among lenders, customers, suppliers, and affiliates, and even small holdings can signify an important relationship. Despite some recent flux associated with an enormously wrenching economic restructuring, our research unearthed no evidence that such arrangements are now changing in a fundamental way. Indeed, in the course of an extensive series of interviews with senior corporate executives in Japan, we were repeatedly told that the reverse is true. A number of our interlocutors suggested, for example, that much of the widely reported turbulence experienced in the Japanese corporate equity market in the early 1990s reflected the exceptional efforts of some shareholders, mainly troubled financial institutions, to increase dividend flows at a time when the routine capital gains of the past could no longer be assured.[32] Certainly, as Table 2 shows, within the largest Japanese corporate networks changes in cross-shareholding arrangements over the past decade have been marginal.

Many of the executives we interviewed believed that successfully charting their way through the difficult 1990s depended on maintaining the essential structure of their equity bases and, more important, of the relationships thereby signified. Moreover, the prospect of punishment for breaches in network solidarity clearly exists. Bankers as well as their corporate clients explained to us repeatedly that all members of industrial groups understood that any firm contemplating appreciable sales of shares in related banks or companies would elicit immediate retaliation. The

29. IMF 1992, 3.

30. *New York Times,* 2 February 1996, C6.

31. Porter et al. 1992. See also Orru, Hamilton, and Suzuki 1989; Prowse 1992; Kester 1992; Pauly 1994; Johnson, Tyson, and Zysman 1989; Gerlach 1992; Aoki and Patrick 1994; Tilton 1996; and Uriu 1996.

32. Confidential interviews, Japan, 20 September–2 October 1993. Also see Lichtenberg and Pushner 1992.

TABLE 2. *Average cross-shareholdings within major Japanese corporate networks, in percentages*[a]

	Mitsui	Mitsubishi	Sumitomo	Fuyo	Sanwa	DKB
1980	17.62	29.26	26.74	16.26	16.78	14.12
1985	17.87	25.18	25.01	15.79	16.84	13.33
1988	17.09	26.87	24.42	15.29	16.38	12.24
1991	16.58	26.37	24.67	15.62	16.67	12.16
1992	16.58	26.33	24.65	15.62	16.72	12.19
1993	16.77	26.11	24.45	14.90	16.41	11.92

[a]Average of the ratios of stocks in one member company owned by other companies within the group. These are the largest of the networks of affiliated companies characteristic of the Japanese industrial economy. Commonly referred to as *keiretsu,* they are more accurately called *kigyō shūdan,* or enterprise groups. These six groups cross a diversity of markets, and each has a trading company and/or major commercial bank at its center. The banks are now Sakura Bank (after the merger of Mitsui Bank and Taiyo Kobe Bank), Mitsubishi Bank of Tokyo, Sumitomo Bank, Fuji Bank, Sanwa Bank, and Dai Ichi Kangyo Bank.
   Source. Kigyō Keiretsu Sōran 1987, 1990, 1993, and 1994. Tokyo: Toyo Keizai Shinposha.

consequent sense of responsibility for collectively managing difficult processes of restructuring within tight traditional constraints is palpable.[33]

Within Japan's leading industrial groups, furthermore, and especially during periods of crisis, managers continue to be constrained effectively and directly by their bankers and by the firms to which they supply key components. Affiliates are crucial, and arm's-length relationships still are not the norm. Hopelessly weak affiliates tend to be quickly and quietly liquidated or merged. Even apparently informal supplier ties can be decisive in such instances.

Obvious parallels exist in the case of Germany, although observers have often overemphasized the coordinating role of banks in the German industrial system. Especially in elite German MNCs, however, and most evidently during crises, the lead bank remains critically important. Although economists continue to debate the implications of this phenomenon and to underline the declining role of banks in small and medium-sized German firms, the evidence supporting its endurance in the largest and most outwardly oriented German firms remains convincing.[34]

The supervisory boards of German MNCs reinforce the functions of banks both directly and indirectly.[35] Bankers hold nearly 10 percent of the seats on the supervisory boards of the one hundred largest industrial corporations in Germany. By contrast, insurance companies hold approximately 2 percent of the seats; trade

33. Also see Lincoln, Gerlach, and Takahashi 1992.
34. See Edwards and Fischer 1994; and Baums 1994.
35. See Wever and Allen 1993; Ziegler, Bender, and Biehler 1985; and Coleman 1994.

unions, 12 percent; employees, 36 percent; other industries, 25 percent; individual investors, 10 percent; and governmental agencies, 5 percent.[36] In the largest German corporations, however, the lead bank also provides the board chairman. Since three banks dominate the corporate financing market, this means that many supervisory boards are interlocked. Underpinning such linkages are cross-shareholding arrangements, albeit to a lesser extent than in Japan. The bankers' role is further enhanced by peculiarities of Germany's proxy voting system, which in the case of MNCs often leaves banks effectively in control of over 50 percent of voting shares.

Our interviews provided no support for the increasingly common view that the power of banks in corporate Germany is broken. Similarly, despite talk about bold American moves toward German-style universal banking, long-standing sensitivities concerning financial concentration, a now-institutionalized decentralization and "vesting" of particularistic interests in the financial sector, and attendant difficulties in designing new risk-management techniques militate against deep-seated change in the U.S. system. For different reasons, we noted a similar reticence inside Japanese MNCs on the subject of fundamental change in patterns of corporate financing.

Prominent analysts commonly herald the dawn of a "Darwinian" global contest among competing corporate systems. As Franklin Edwards and Robert Eisenbeis put it, "Legal and institutional impediments that fail this test will cease to exist."[37] In such a context, it is ironic that we did not find evidence for, or credible expectations of, substantive convergence in core structures of corporate governance and basic financing across Germany, Japan, and the United States.

Research and development

The world's leading MNCs remain firmly rooted in distinctive national systems of innovation. Science and high technology–oriented American MNCs are somewhat more willing than others to invest in overseas R&D facilities, but on an annual basis such spending still represents less than 15 percent of their total R&D budgets. With an emphasis on the commercialization of production in technology-intensive sectors, Japanese firms conduct remarkably little R&D abroad, even in the United States where they have a very large production and sales presence. Mainly in certain sectors and in line with their own process-oriented traditions, German MNCs have made significant R&D commitments in the United States but limited investments elsewhere outside of Germany. Across the board, the vast majority of corporate R&D spending abroad is employed in efforts to customize products for local markets or to gather knowledge for transfer back home.

R&D sows the seeds for corporate futures. How much, how consistently, and where such activity takes place are therefore all vital questions, both for individual corporations and for the economies within which they operate. To move beyond the simplified portrait painted by aggregate statistics, our analysis differentiated between

---

36. Based on data from the Federal Association of German Banks in Schneider Lenné 1994, 303.
37. Edwards and Eisenbeis 1992.

basic activities and product customization facilities. Our findings indicate that convergence of a sort is taking place—but not the kind liberal analysts might anticipate. Leading firms from Germany, Japan, and the United States behave comparably in that they tend to maintain their basic R&D operations at home. Those operations comprise important building blocks for national systems of innovation that, though not completely autonomous or unchanging, do remain remarkably distinctive.[38] Significant variances are also reflected in overall corporate spending patterns, in the nature of R&D facilities abroad, and in the willingness to transfer key technologies outside the home base.

Differences in corporate R&D strategies have existed across the leading industrial states for many years. Japanese business spending on R&D as a percentage of gross domestic product (GDP), for example, rose rapidly throughout the 1980s and eclipsed that of the United States in 1989 before peaking in 1990 at 2.2 percent. Comparable U.S. spending fell consistently after peaking in 1985 at 2.1 percent, increased temporarily in 1991, and then resumed its pattern of decline. German firms, for their part, reduced their R&D spending precipitously in the late 1980s and early 1990s. At 1.7 percent of GDP in 1993, their spending was well below the levels registered by their Japanese and U.S. competitors.[39]

Beneath such statistics, other national patterns remained distinctive. In contrast to their U.S. counterparts, for example, Japanese chief executive officers typically note that when their firms are under duress, real cuts in R&D spending (as opposed to trimming back growth rates) are a last resort.[40] They view only the avoidance of cuts in permanent employment as more important than maintaining R&D budgets. This is reflected in relevant data. Before their widely noted troubles at the start of the 1990s, Japanese firms had increased their R&D spending by an average of 8 percent per year for an entire decade. Comparable figures for British, French, German, and U.S. firms were 1.6, 4.6, 3.9, and 3.9 percent, respectively.[41]

Sustained national differences are also reflected in patterns of corporate R&D spending abroad. Even though an absolute increase in R&D spending by foreign MNCs in the United States occurred during the last decade, an increase that appeared to be partly related to acquisitions in such R&D-intensive sectors as chemicals, U.S. firms remained more likely than their competitors to conduct R&D abroad. Even in their case, however, the scale of expansion from a low base was modest. In 1982, R&D spending by majority-owned foreign affiliates of U.S. manufacturers accounted for 8.7 percent of total corporate R&D budgets. One decade later, that amount increased only to 12.7 percent, despite a 43.2 percent expansion in total corporate R&D budgets. In addition, the manufacturing R&D intensity—that is, R&D spending as a percentage of total sales—is much higher for American MNCs in their home-based operations than it is in their foreign subsidiaries. In the early 1990s,

38. See Nelson 1993; Lundvall 1992; and Mowery 1994.
39. OECD (DSTI) 1994–95.
40. Confidential interviews with senior executives of Japanese MNCs, 20 September–2 October 1993, Japan.
41. U.S. Congress 1994, 62.

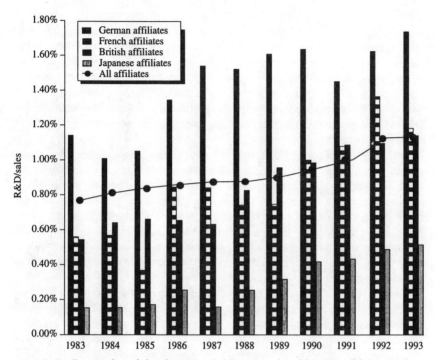

FIGURE 1. *Research and development (R&D) intensity of foreign affiliates in the United States, 1983–93*

Source. U.S. Department of Commerce, Bureau of Economic Analysis, *Foreign Direct Investment in the United States* (Washington, D.C.: Department of Commerce, annual surveys).

U.S. manufacturers reported an average R&D intensity of 2.1 percent at home, while their foreign subsidiaries registered 0.8 percent.[42]

Figure 1 graphs the ratio of R&D spending to sales for foreign firms in the United States. As the figure shows, R&D intensity has not changed dramatically over the past decade, and national patterns are consistent. German affiliates in particular were much more likely to conduct R&D in the United States than were their Japanese counterparts. In part, foreign R&D intensity in the United States correlates with the sectoral location of incoming foreign direct investment. German firms, and European firms more generally, have tended to invest proportionately more in manufacturing facilities in such sectors as pharmaceuticals. Japanese firms, as discussed below, have focused on wholesaling operations.

All things considered, the behavior of Japanese firms in the United States differs strikingly from their European counterparts. Figure 2 graphs the R&D intensity of

42. U.S. Congress 1994, 7.

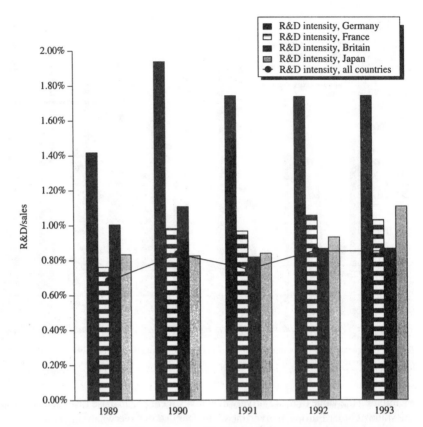

FIGURE 2. *Research and development (R&D) intensity of U.S. affiliates in foreign markets, 1989–93*

Sources. U.S. Department of Commerce, Bureau of Economic Analysis, *U.S. Direct Investment Abroad* (Washington, D.C.: Department of Commerce, annual surveys); and U.S. Department of Commerce, ·Bureau of Economic Analysis, *Survey of Current Business,* August 1987–August 1995.

U.S. affiliates in foreign markets. Looking at the two figures, German firms in the United States most closely replicate the R&D patterns of U.S.-based firms in Germany. In this regard, the data suggest a notable reciprocal interaction between U.S. and German MNCs. Conversely, the lower R&D intensity of Japanese MNCs in the United States and its incommensurability with the behavior of U.S. MNCs in Japan suggest a notable lack of reciprocal interaction.

In general, Japanese firms are the most reluctant to shift R&D activities abroad. While they formed by the early 1990s the largest national group of foreign investors in the United States (based on historical cost values), their U.S. operations had by far the lowest R&D intensities. Although historical cost analysis skews the comparison

16   International Organization

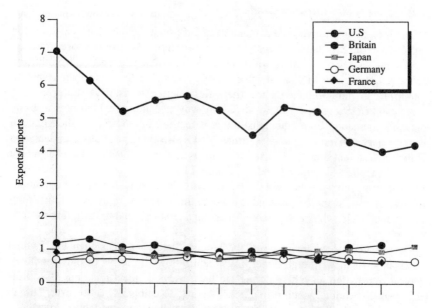

FIGURE 3. *Ratio of technology exports to imports for selected countries, 1982–93*

Source. Organization for Economic Cooperation and Development, *Main Science and Technology Indicators,* Economic Analysis and Statistics Division Database, no. 1 (1994) and no. 1 (1995).

by inflating the value of the relatively new investment of Japanese firms and deflating the value of older European investment, the fact that the overwhelming proportion of all inward flows of foreign direct investment into the United States occurred after 1980 tends to limit this effect. The outcome, in any event, is also reflected in aggregate data for R&D spending by manufacturing firms in the United States, which show Canadian affiliates in 1992 accounting for 19 percent, German affiliates for 16 percent (a comparable level to Swiss and British affiliates), and Japanese affiliates for 10 percent, despite their much larger market presence.[43]

Finally, MNCs based outside the United States also demonstrate a distinct tendency to limit the export of their core technological competencies. In the United States, conversely, technology exports are five times the level of technology imports. As Figure 3 shows, Germany, Japan, and other industrial economies have long maintained a ratio of less than 1 to 1. MNCs provide the channel for much of the flow of technology abroad, mainly from parents to affiliates. In comparative terms, the aggregate data suggest that U.S. MNCs are much more active in this regard than their counterparts in other countries.

43. Calculated based on data in U.S. Department of Commerce 1994, table H-4.

Investment and intrafirm trade

The foreign direct investment strategies of U.S. MNCs are broadly based on and reflective of the expectation of competitive inward flows. Moreover, those strategies incorporate a relatively high willingness to outsource key parts of production processes. American MNCs, in other words, rely much less than their rivals on intrafirm and intra-affiliate trading (hereafter referred to as IFT) strategies. The investment strategies of Japanese MNCs, by way of contrast, exhibit both a strong outward orientation from a home base that is secure from external challenge and a heavy reliance on intrafirm trade. German MNCs also exhibit an outward orientation in their investment strategies. That orientation is more selective than that of Japanese MNCs and reflects a narrower industrial base. Like Japanese corporations, however, German firms rely quite heavily on IFT. In short, the external investment operations of German and Japanese firms tend to enhance the prospects for overall exports from their home bases, while comparable American operations tend to substitute for U.S. exports.

Despite occasional fluctuations, the United States has long been the favored destination for new foreign direct investment inflows. In terms of outward flows, Japanese firms led all others during the latter years of the 1980s, but U.S. firms regained the leading position in 1991.[44] Aggregate comparison, however, fails to capture the markedly diverse corporate strategies that underpinned those flows.

Foreign investments undertaken by U.S. firms tend to be "trade-displacing." Their Japanese and, to a lesser but increasing extent, their German analogs tend to be "trade-creating."[45] In short, new overseas plants built by Japanese and increasingly by German MNCs tend to create conduits for increasing trade flows, specifically imports from their own home bases and affiliated networks.[46] For this reason, analysts have convincingly argued that such investment should be understood as "strategic."[47]

The hypothesis that Japanese and, to a lesser extent, German firms employ such a strategic approach is highly contentious, but aggregate statistical evidence continues to render it plausible. Across all of its manufacturing industries, for example, intrafirm exports as a percentage of total Japanese exports remained at about 40 percent from the late 1980s through the early 1990s.[48] The issue can be examined more rigorously, however, by comparing the direct investment behavior of foreign affiliates in the United States with that of U.S.-based multinationals abroad. The reliability of direct comparisons of IFT on a national basis is, however, severely limited by the lack of comparability of national databases and the complete absence of other statistical data sources.

---

44. Data from OECD 1994.

45. The question of whether high-technology intrafirm trade will decrease as firms become more deeply embedded in advanced host economies is contentious. See Vernon 1966, 190–207; Dunning 1977; Wells 1972; Helleiner 1981; and U.S. Congress 1994, 144–48.

46. See Kojima 1978; and Gilpin 1989.

47. Encarnation 1992. Also see Lincoln 1990; and Encarnation and Mason 1990.

48. See MITI 1989, tables 1-19 to 1-24; and MITI 1991, tables 1-22 to 1-27.

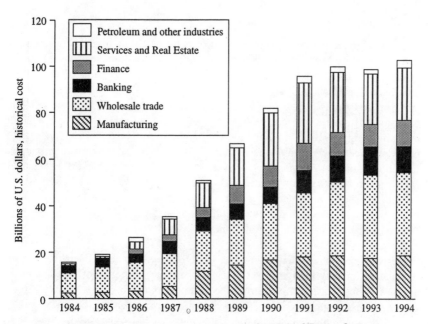

FIGURE 4. *Japan's direct investment position in the United States, by sector, 1984–94*

Source. U.S. Department of Commerce, Bureau of Economic Analysis, *Survey of Current Business,* August 1987–August 1995.

We can avoid this difficulty by focusing on meaningful bilateral comparisons within the same data set, such as the behavior of foreign affiliates in the United States compared with that of U.S.-based MNCs abroad. In 1992, Japanese firms as a group became for the first time the largest foreign investors in the United States. As Figure 4 shows, in a largely unrestricted environment the biggest proportion of this investment went into wholesaling facilities and distribution outlets. This stands in sharp contrast to the investment position of American MNCs in Japan, which is shown in Figure 5. U.S. MNC investment was heavily weighted toward manufacturing facilities.

Moreover, as a percentage of total foreign direct investment in the United States, Japanese investment in wholesaling operations in the United States rose from 41 percent of total incoming foreign direct investment in 1985 to 50 percent in 1993.[49] Many have argued that this emphasis on wholesaling operations reflects the relative youth of Japanese investments in the U.S. market by the standards of European firms and that over time it will fall to European levels; but the disparity is enormous. As a percentage of total foreign direct investment in the United States, the wholesaling operations of German firms fell from 15 percent in 1985 to 10.5 percent in 1993,

49. U.S. Congress 1994, 118.

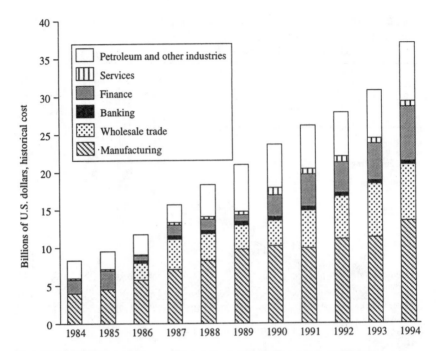

FIGURE 5. *U.S. direct investment position in Japan, by sector, 1987–94*

Source. U.S. Department of Commerce, Bureau of Economic Analysis, *Survey of Current Business,*
August 1987–August 1996.

while comparable figures for British firms were 13.9 and 9.9 percent, and for French
firms 1.5 and 2.7 percent, respectively.

The intrafirm trading operations of Japanese firms in the United States also
continued to grow during the 1990s in relative terms. By the end of the 1980s, for
example, IFT imports in the U.S. automobile sector accounted for an estimated
40–50 percent of all imports. Between 1988 and 1990, the value of intrafirm imports
by Japanese auto affiliates in the United States tripled to $4 billion. This represented
an increase from 75 to 95 percent of total intrafirm imports in this sector.[50] Japanese
auto executives expected this level to drop as their suppliers moved their own
operations to the United States, although this drop was likely to be due to the
replacement of direct IFT imports with indirect imports through traditional affiliated
networks.[51] In 1993, affiliated companies accounted for 43 percent of all suppliers to
Japanese auto transplants in the United States.[52]

50. OECD 1993, 20.
51. Confidential interviews with senior executives of Japanese MNCs, 20 September–2 October 1993,
Japan.
52. U.S. Congress 1994, 147.

TABLE 3. *Foreign content of intermediate goods purchased by foreign affiliates in the United States, by sector and country, 1990 and 1991*

	All countries		France		Germany		Japan		Great Britain	
	1990	1991	1990	1991	1990	1991	1990	1991	1990	1991
All industries	19.4	19.6	12.1	10.7	21.6	19.9	30.2	31.7	9.6	9.2
All manufacturing	16.7	17.3	17.3	16.2	21.4	20.9	28.4	28.0	9.4	10.0
Chemicals and allied products	12.1	13.2	9.6	9.5	18.4	18.5	5.1	7.2	11.6	13.2
Primary and fabricated metals	14.0	14.1	7.3	6.9	20.0	21.4	6.6	5.9	7.2	7.3
Nonelectrical machinery	31.0	30.4	NA[a]	20.3	25.9	25.5	48.5	45.3	12.9	9.5
Electric and electronic equipment	30.7	28.6	NA	37.5	43.7	39.2	41.4	38.1	11.3	14.3
Motor vehicles and equipment	40.4	45.1	NA	NA	NA	NA	49.3	52.8	NA	NA
Wholesale trade	32.3	33.9	11.6	12.1	39.9	39.6	34.6	38.3	15.3	12.2

[a]NA = data unavailable (suppressed to avoid disclosure of individual companies' data).
Source. Adapted from U.S. Department of Commerce, Bureau of Economic Analysis, *Survey of Current Business,* October 1993, 64, table 10.

Is such a pattern confined to the automobile industry? Alternatively, is it a product of anomalies in statistical databases? Examining variations in the foreign content of intermediate goods purchased by foreign affiliates in the United States across differing sectors addresses such questions and, as Table 3 shows, indicates that indeed a pattern does exist. In this respect, not only Japanese but also German affiliates differ markedly from other major investors in the United States.[53]

While the Japanese behavior generates considerable, if not always publicly expressed, antipathy among American corporate executives, the German behavior does not. The reason seems to be that the bilateral U.S.–German relationship is widely perceived to be more or less balanced in key industries.

Together with starkly divergent patterns of reliance on IFT by Japanese and German firms, such data suggest the importance not of investment maturity or governmental policies on the receiving end, but of purposive corporate strategies. As for the quite exceptional nature of the Japanese data, the overall emphasis of Japanese affiliates in the United States on IFT and wholesaling may help to explain

53. Confidential interviews with senior executives and government officials in Germany and the United States, 1–12 November 1993 and February–April 1994, respectively.

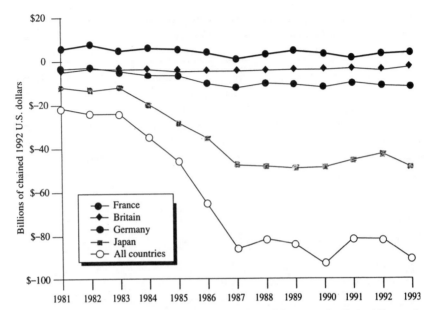

FIGURE 6. *Merchandise trade balance of foreign affiliates in the United States, by nationality of ownership, 1981–93*

Sources. U.S. Department of Commerce, Bureau of Economic Analysis, *Foreign Direct Investment in the United States,* table G-7/H-7 (Washington, D.C.: Department of Commerce, annual surveys); and U.S. Department of Commerce, Bureau of Economic Analysis, *Survey of Current Business,* October 1993.

the fact that they are alone among foreign investors in Europe and the United States in their strong preference for establishing new firms rather than acquiring existing ones.[54]

Some observers expected Japanese affiliates in the United States to begin reexporting from their new manufacturing facilities as they matured, but experience has confounded that expectation. The percentage of exports from Japanese affiliates as a proportion of their total sales actually fell—from over 12 percent in the early 1980s to approximately 6 percent in 1988 before rising marginally from that level in the early 1990s. Over the same period, IFT as a percentage of the value of all Japanese exports to the United States across all industries rose from 20 percent to over 50 percent.[55] Again, as Figure 6 displays, this pattern contrasts markedly with the collective behavior of MNCs from other major industrial countries in the United States, with the partial exception of those from Germany.

54. Yamawaki 1994, table 3-3, 97.
55. MITI 1989, tables 1-19 to 1-24; MITI 1991, table 1-11 and 1-22 to 1-27; and MITI 1993, table 2-16.

More broadly, since much of the aggregate flow of world imports and exports now occurs through intrafirm and affiliated networks, IFT constitutes a much higher proportion of bilateral flows between the United States and Japan than between the United States and Europe. Between 1983 and 1992, IFT accounted for an average of 70 percent of all U.S.-Japanese merchandise trade each year, compared with 43 percent of U.S.–European trade. Furthermore, over that same period and regardless of the direction of flow, Japanese MNCs accounted for fully 93 percent of IFT between Japan and the United States. In the end, the evidence suggests that IFT accounts for an overwhelming percentage of all U.S. imports from Japan and that Japanese firms control almost all of it. In contrast, and notwithstanding the fact that German firms tend to behave more like Japanese firms when it comes to intrafirm and affiliated trade, U.S.–European IFT is much more balanced in the aggregate.[56]

Counterpressures are widely reported to be building on both Japanese and German firms that will reduce their ability to use overseas operations as conduits for exports from their own facilities or from long-standing networks of suppliers in their home bases. Fluctuating currencies and domestic labor costs frequently are mentioned in this regard. Although anecdotes abound, we found little hard evidence of fundamental shifts in the overseas investment and trading strategies of American, German, and Japanese MNCs.

Conclusion

This article examined evidence on the question of structural and strategic convergence at the cores of leading MNCs across the Triad. In contrast to liberal or critical theories, which lead to credible expectations that the fundamental structures and strategies of multinational firms are converging in meaningful ways, we sketched remarkably enduring divergence across Germany, Japan, and the United States in patterns of internal governance and long-term financing. We also identified a tendency for MNCs based in those countries to maintain an overwhelming share of their R&D spending at home, and we noted stark national differences in willingness to export new technology from the home base. Finally, we found divergence along national lines in the strategic linkages firms construct between their overseas investments and their intrafirm and intra-affiliate trading activities: Japanese and, to a lesser extent, German firms lie on one end of the spectrum and American (and British) firms on the other. Table 4 briefly summarizes the most important patterns in the evidence.

Set out in this schematic fashion, none of these patterns will come as a surprise to students of comparative business history. But their endurance into the 1990s does raise important questions for students of international political economy in light of contemporary debates on the causes and consequences of deepening cross-national economic integration. Our analysis supports the view that recognizable and patterned

---

56. U.S. Congress 1994, 136–37.

TABLE 4. *Multinational corporate structures and strategies*

	United States	Germany	Japan
Direct investment	Extensive inward and outward	Selective/outward orientation	Extensive outward; limited competition from inward
Intrafirm trade	Moderate	Higher	Very high
Research and development	Fluctuating; diversified; innovation oriented	Narrow base/process, diffusion orientation	High, steady growth; high-technology and process orientation
Corporate governance	Short-term shareholding; managers highly constrained by capital markets; risk-seeking, financial-centered strategies	Managerial autonomy except during crises; no takeover risk; conservative, long-term strategies	Stable shareholders; network-constrained managers; takeover risk only within network/aggressive market share–centered strategies
Corporate financing	Diversified, global funding; highly price sensitive	Concentrated, regional funding; limited price sensitivity	Concentrated, national funding; low price sensitivity

differences persist in the behavior of leading MNCs. The precise nature of those differences in turn suggests that we not rule out as an explanation what is popularly termed corporate "nationality." Even when other possible influences on corporate behavior (for example, governmental policy on incoming foreign direct investment) provide identical background conditions, striking differences appear—most commonly along national lines.[57] In sum, the correlation between these patterns of corporate behavior and the domestic structures outlined earlier in this article is not likely to be spurious.[58]

Recall our orienting proposition on the link between basic domestic structures in the home base and core aspects of firm behavior. The evidence surveyed suggests a logical chain that begins deep in the idiosyncratic national histories that lie behind durable domestic institutions and ideologies and extends directly to structures of corporate governance and long-term corporate financing. Those structures in turn appear plausibly linked to continuing diversity in the corporate foundations of national innovation systems and in the varying linkages between foreign direct investment and IFT strategies.

Of course, the evidence only supports the claim of a causal link; it does not prove it. The evidence, however, comes from an examination of the three leading home states of contemporary MNCs and of a range of key industrial sectors. Additionally, we have examined core aspects of firm behavior in a comparative light. We conclude

57. For analysis of how domestic institutions influence and channel firm demands in the face of incoming foreign direct investment, see Crystal 1995.

58. Keller et al. forthcoming.

that a modified domestic structures approach provides a better fit for the patterns identified in the data than do alternative approaches, which draw their understanding of multinational corporate behavior from the relevant liberal, critical, or realist literatures sketched above. Neither liberal nor critical alternatives lead one to expect the persistent divergence found at the firm level. A straightforward realist alternative would miss important variations in the degree of that divergence and, with its traditional emphasis on central policymaking authorities, could easily lead to a misunderstanding of what that divergence means.

Consider several counterarguments. On the basis of the evidence, the contention that the particular mores evident in Japanese corporate technology development programs are becoming disconnected from the stabilizing influence of cross-held corporate equity bases and broader networks of managerial accountability in Japan seems implausible. Equally implausible is the argument that the investment behavior of German firms is becoming unhinged from the security provided by dominant banks back home. Finally, we consider it unlikely that the slightly more global behavior exhibited by U.S. firms in both their R&D and investment strategies is not related to deliberate efforts to compensate for the peculiarities of their highly dynamic and periodically unstable financial foundations.

In sum, we surmise that the behavior we have surveyed divides into three distinctive syndromes. Moreover, because the general lines of demarcation may credibly be labeled "national," the proposition that those syndromes are durably nested in broader domestic institutional and ideological structures cannot easily be dismissed. Such a conceptualization, we believe, is more precise and more useful in focusing further research than the much more amorphous concept of culture, which has been cited in recent work on the putative emergence of three increasingly integrated regional blocs.[59] At a time when many observers emphasize the importance of cross-border strategic alliances, regional business networks, and stock offerings on foreign exchanges—all suggestive of a blurring of corporate nationalities—our findings underline, for example, the durability of German financial control systems, the historical drive behind Japanese technology development through tight corporate networks, and the very different time horizons that lie behind American, German, and Japanese corporate planning. The gulf between nationally diverse domestic structures may narrow in the future, but we cannot count on leading MNCs to drive such a process.

Pending further research, our own answer to Chandler's question—whether differences like those sketched in *Scale and Scope* endure—must be in the affirmative. We have found little evidence to support the opposite view, namely, that such core patterns are inevitably eroding as a fully integrated global system of industrial enterprise and innovation emerges.

The implications of our analysis are diverse, but four deserve to be highlighted here. First, since multinational firms are key actors in the development and diffusion of new technologies, their national rootedness appears to remain a vital determinant

59. For example, see Rugman 1993.

of where future innovation takes place.[60] In this regard, the main danger for political and economic theorists is not underestimating the impact of technological change but extrapolating the future on the basis of atypical industrial sectors or anodyne exceptions drawn from the experiences of a few large firms from small states, where the size of home markets and the limitations of local resources have long required externally oriented strategies.

Second, the globalization template upon which much current theoretical and policy debate rests remains quite weak. German, Japanese, and U.S. corporations insert themselves into the home markets of their rivals, albeit with varying degrees of success. They then appear to adapt themselves at the margins but not much at the core. To the extent that fundamental differences in corporate structure and strategy create sanctuary markets or other difficult-to-surmount advantages, pressures will likely build from within corporations themselves for countervailing governmental responses. In Germany and Japan, for example, we consistently heard corporate decision makers heap derision on the idea that key technologies could ever be left to develop in markets organized around straightforward "laissez-faire" principles. Our evidence suggests further that the increasingly common idea, that mobile corporations are "arbitraging" diverse national structures and forcing deep structural convergence across diverse societies, is chimerical. Convergence may be apparent at the level of popular culture and perhaps not coincidentally in the sales reports and marketing campaigns of MNCs; but below the surface, where the roots of leading MNCs remain lodged, our research suggests durable sources of resistance. It also suggests the need for deeper analysis of the foundations of such apparently global markets as the oft-cited capital markets that link the interests of multinational intermediaries and their corporate clients.[61]

Third, and following on this latter point, our analysis is relevant to the growing debate over whether markets or, more precisely, huge sprawling commercial hierarchies are replacing states as allocators of public values. Our evidence does not speak directly to this debate, but it does imply that for leading societies any such shift is primarily an internal matter. To put the matter bluntly, power, as distinct from legitimate authority, may indeed be shifting within those societies, but it is not obviously shifting away from them and into the boardrooms of supranational business enterprises. Some of those societies may be structurally better equipped than others to deal with the consequences of internal power shifts. But none need to accept the now-conventional corporate line that such shifts are inevitable global phenomena. If certain domestic structures in leading societies are evolving in such a way as to render constraining corporate power more difficult, they should be adjusted internally. The situation would seem quite different, however, for societies not in possession of a large, diversified, and rooted industrial base. From their point of view, power may indeed be shifting in the direction of a few leading states and increasingly concentrated commercial hierarchies embedded in those states. Such

60. See David 1985; Krugman 1991; and Schwartz 1994.
61. See Cohen 1996; and Pauly forthcoming.

perceptions may help explain the apparently increasing efforts of many smaller states to negotiate adjustments and seek redress through multilateral institutions.

Finally, our reading of analytical literatures relevant to the contemporary study of multinational corporate behavior, together with our own initial empirical examination, leads us to conclude that further comparative elaboration and testing of a domestic structures approach to international theory at the level of the firm is worthwhile. At the center of important analytical and policy debates related to the themes of this article is the seminal work of American and British scholars, studying American and British firms, writing for American and British audiences, and exporting conclusions packaged as deductive theories to the rest of the world. The actual experiences of firms based in Germany and Japan, not to mention other industrialized and industrializing countries, are worthy of much deeper study as we try to understand the causes and consequences of multinational corporate behavior.

References

Adler, Emanuel. 1987. *The power of ideology.* Berkeley: University of California Press.

Andrews, David. 1994. Capital mobility and state autonomy. *International Studies Quarterly* 38:193–218.

Aoki, Masahiko, and Hugh Patrick, eds. 1994. *The Japanese main bank system.* New York: Oxford University Press.

Ball, George. 1967. Cosmocorp: The importance of being stateless. *Columbia Journal of World Business* 2(November–December): 25–30.

Barnet, Richard J., and John Cavanagh. 1994. *Global dreams: Imperial corporations and the new world order.* New York: Simon and Schuster.

Baums, Theodor. 1994. The German banking system and its impact on corporate finance and governance. In *The Japanese main bank system,* edited by Masahiko Aoki and Hugh Patrick. New York: Oxford University Press.

Berger, Suzanne, and Ronald Dore, eds. 1996. *National diversity and global capitalism.* Ithaca, N.Y.: Cornell University Press.

Bergsten, C. Fred, Thomas Horst, and Theodore Moran. 1978. *American multinationals and American interests.* Washington, D.C.: Brookings Institution.

Biersteker, Thomas J. 1987. *Multinationals, the state, and control of the Nigerian economy.* Princeton, N.J.: Princeton University Press.

Campbell, Nigel, and Fred Burton, eds. 1994. *Japanese multinationals.* London: Routledge.

Carnoy, Martin, Manuel Castells, and Steven Cohen. 1993. *The new global economy in the informational age.* University Park: Pennsylvania State University Press.

Castells, Manuel. 1991. *The informational city.* Cambridge, Mass.: Basil Blackwell.

Cerny, Philip G. 1995. Globalization and the changing logic of collective action. *International Organization* 49:595–625.

Chandler, Alfred D., Jr. 1962. *Strategy and structure.* Cambridge, Mass.: MIT Press.

———. 1964. *Giant enterprise.* New York: Harcourt Brace and World.

———. 1977. *The visible hand.* Cambridge, Mass.: Harvard University Press.

———. 1990. *Scale and scope.* Cambridge, Mass.: Belknap Press.

Cohen, Benjamin J. 1996. Phoenix risen: The resurrection of global finance. *World Politics* 48:268–96.

Coleman, William D. 1994. Banking, interest intermediation, and political power. *European Journal of Political Research* 26:31–58.

Commission of the European Communities. 1993. *Panorama of EC industry.* Luxembourg: Office of Official Publications of the European Communities.

Cooper, Richard. 1968. *The economics of interdependence.* New York: McGraw Hill.

Crystal, Jonathan. 1995. After protectionism: Political conflict over incoming foreign direct investment. Paper presented at the 91st annual meeting of the American Political Science Association, 31 August–3 September, Chicago.

David, Paul. 1985. Clio and the economics of QWERTY. *American Economic Review* 75:332–37.

Dunning, John H. 1958. *American investment in British manufacturing.* London: Allen and Unwin.

———. 1977. Trade, location of economic activity, and MNEs. In *The international allocation of economic activity,* edited by Bertil Ohlin, Per-Ove Hesselborn, and Per Magnus Wijkman. London: Macmillan.

———. 1992a. *Multinational enterprises and the global economy.* Reading, Mass.: Addison-Wesley.

———. 1992b. The global economy, domestic governance, strategies and transnational corporations. *Transnational Corporations* 1(3): 7–45.

Eden, Lorraine, and Evan Potter, eds. 1993. *Multinationals in the global political economy.* New York: St. Martin's.

Edwards, Franklin R., and Robert A. Eisenbeis. 1992. Financial institutions and corporate time horizons: An international perspective. Unpublished background paper for Porter 1992.

Edwards, Jeremy, and Klaus Fischer. 1994. *Banks, finance, and investment in Germany.* Cambridge: Cambridge University Press.

Encarnation, Dennis. 1992. *Rivals beyond trade.* Ithaca, N.Y.: Cornell University Press.

Encarnation, Dennis, and Mark Mason. 1990. Neither MITI nor America: The political economy of capital liberalization in Japan. *International Organization* 44:25–54.

Franko, Lawrence G. 1976. *The European multinational.* London: Harper and Row.

———. 1991. Global corporate competition. *Business Horizons,* November–December, 14–22.

Frieden, Jeffry. 1991. Invested interests: The politics of national economic policies in a world of global finance. *International Organization* 45:425–51.

Fukao, Mitsuhiro. 1995. *Financial integration, corporate governance, and the performance of multinational companies.* Washington, D.C.: Brookings Institution.

Garrett, Geoffrey, and Peter Lange. 1995. Internationalization, institutions, and political change. *International Organization* 49:627–55.

Gerlach, Michael. 1992. *Alliance capitalism.* Berkeley: University of California Press.

Gill, Stephen. 1995. Globalisation, market civilisation and disciplinary neo-liberalism. *Millennium* 24:399–423.

Gilpin, Robert. 1975. *U.S. power and the multinational corporation.* New York: Basic Books.

———. 1987. *The political economy of international relations.* Princeton, N.J.: Princeton University Press.

———. 1989. Where does Japan fit in? *Millennium* 18:329–42.

———. 1994. No one loves a political realist. Princeton University. Unpublished.

Goodman, John B., and Louis W. Pauly. 1993. The obsolescence of capital controls? Economic management in an age of global markets. *World Politics* 46:50–82.

Gourevitch, Peter. 1986. *Politics in hard times.* Ithaca, N.Y.: Cornell University Press.

Grieco, Joseph S. 1990. *Cooperation among nations.* Ithaca, N.Y.: Cornell University Press.

Grossman, G. M., and J. D. Richardson. 1985. *Strategic trade policy.* Papers in International Finance 15, International Finance Section, Department of Economics, Princeton University, Princeton, N.J.

Group of Lisbon. 1995. *Limits to competition.* Cambridge, Mass.: MIT Press.

Hall, Peter. 1986. *Governing the economy.* Oxford: Oxford University Press.

Hart, Jeffrey A. 1992. *Rival capitalists.* Ithaca, N.Y.: Cornell University Press.

Helleiner, Gerald K. 1981. *Intra-firm trade and the developing countries.* New York: St. Martin's.

Hertner, Peter, and Geoffrey Jones, eds. 1986. *Multinationals: Theory and history.* Aldershot, England: Edward Elgar.

Hymer, Stephen. 1976. *The international operations of national firms.* Cambridge, Mass.: MIT Press.

International Monetary Fund (IMF). 1992. *International capital markets: Developments, prospects, and policy issues.* Washington, D.C.: IMF.

Johnson, Chalmers, Laura D'Andrea Tyson, and John Zysman, eds. 1989. *Politics and productivity*. New York: Ballinger.

Jones, Geoffrey, and Harm G. Schröter, eds. 1993. *The rise of multinationals in continental Europe*. Aldershot, England: Edward Elgar.

Kapstein, Ethan. 1994. *Governing the global economy*. Cambridge, Mass.: Harvard University Press.

Katzenstein, Peter J., ed. 1977. *Between power and plenty*. Madison: University of Wisconsin Press.

————. 1984. *Small states in world markets*. Ithaca, N.Y.: Cornell University Press.

————. 1996. *The culture of national security*. Ithaca, N.Y.: Cornell University Press.

Keller, William W., Louis W. Pauly, Simon Reich, and Paul N. Doremus. Forthcoming. *Multinationals and the limits of globalization*. Princeton, N.J.: Princeton University Press.

Keohane, Robert O., and Joseph Nye, eds. 1972. *Transnational relations and world politics*. Cambridge, Mass.: Harvard University Press.

Keohane, Robert, and Joseph Nye. 1977. *Power and interdependence*. Boston: Little, Brown.

Kester, Carl. 1992. Industrial groups as systems of corporate governance. *Oxford Review of Economic Policy* 8(3): 24–44.

Kojima, Kiyoshi. 1978. *Direct foreign investment: A Japanese model of multinational business operations*. London: Croom Helm.

Krasner, Stephen. 1978. *Defending the national interest*. Princeton, N.J.: Princeton University Press.

————. 1996. Power politics, institutions, and transnational relations. In *Bringing transnational relations back in*, edited by Thomas Risse-Kappen. Cambridge: Cambridge University Press.

Krauss, Ellis S., and Simon Reich. 1992. Ideologies, interests, and the American executive: Toward a theory of foreign competition and manufacturing trade policy. *International Organization* 46:857–97.

Krugman, Paul, ed. 1986. *Strategic trade policy and the new international economics*. Cambridge, Mass.: MIT Press.

Krugman, Paul. 1991. *Geography and trade*. Cambridge, Mass.: MIT Press.

Kudrle, Robert T. 1985. The several faces of the multinational corporation. In *An international political economy*, edited by W. Ladd Hollist and F. Lamond Tullis. Boulder, Colo.: Westview.

Lall, Sanjaya, et al. 1983. *The new multinationals: The spread of third world enterprises*. New York: John Wiley and Sons.

Lichtenberg, Frank, and George Pushner. 1992. Ownership structure and corporate performance in Japan. NBER working paper no. 4092, National Bureau of Economic Research, Cambridge, Mass.

Lincoln, Edward. 1990. *Japan's unequal trade*. Washington, D.C.: Brookings Institution.

Lincoln, James, Michael Gerlach, and Peggy Takahashi. 1992. *Keiretsu* networks in the Japanese economy. *American Sociological Review* 57:561–85.

Lorsch, Jay, and Elizabeth McIver. 1989. *Pawns or potentates: The reality of America's corporate boards*. Boston: Harvard Business School Press.

————. 1992. Corporate governance and investment time horizons. Council on Competitiveness, Washington, D.C. Unpublished.

Lundvall, Bengt-Åke. 1992. *National systems of innovation*. New York: St. Martin's.

Markovits, Andrei S., and Simon Reich. Forthcoming. *The German predicament: Memory and power in the new Europe*. Ithaca, N.Y.: Cornell University Press.

Mason, Mark, and Dennis Encarnation, eds. 1994. *Does ownership matter? Japanese multinationals in Europe*. Oxford: Clarendon.

Milner, Helen. 1988. *Resisting protectionism*. Princeton, N.J.: Princeton University Press.

Milner, Helen, and Robert Keohane, eds. 1996. *Internationalization and domestic politics*. Cambridge: Cambridge University Press.

Ministry of International Trade and Industry (MITI). Industrial Policy Bureau, International Business Affairs Division. Various years. *Kaigai Toshi Tokei Soran* (Statistics of overseas investment). Tokyo: MITI.

Moran, Theodore, ed. 1993. *Governments and transnational corporations*. London: Routledge.

Morse, Edward. 1970. The transformation of foreign policies. *World Politics* 22:371–92.

Mowery, David C. 1994. *Science and technology policy in interdependent economies*. Boston: Kluwer.

Murtha, Thomas P., and Stefanie Ann Lenway. 1994. Country capabilities and the strategic state. *Strategic Management Journal* 15:113–29.

Nelson, Richard, ed. 1993. *National innovation systems: A comparative analysis.* New York: Oxford University Press.

Organization for Economic Cooperation and Development (OECD). 1994. *Review of foreign direct investment.* Paris: OECD.

———. Directorate for Science, Technology, and Industry (DSTI). 1993. *Globalisation of industrial activities: Sector case study of globalization in the automobile industry.* Paris: OECD.

———. DSTI. 1994–95. *Main science and technology indicators.* Paris: OECD.

Orru, Marco, Gary G. Hamilton, and Mariko Suzuki. 1989. *Patterns of inter-firm control in Japanese business.* Papers in East Asian Business and Development, no. 7. Davis: Institute of Governmental Affairs, University of California.

Ostry, Sylvia. 1990. *Governments and corporations in a shrinking world.* New York: Council on Foreign Relations Press.

Pauly, Louis W. 1994. National financial structures, capital mobility, and international economic rules. *Policy Sciences* 27:343–63.

———. Forthcoming. *Who elected the bankers? Surveillance and control in the world economy.* Ithaca, N.Y.: Cornell University Press.

Porter, Michael. 1990. *The competitive advantage of nations.* New York: Free Press.

Porter, Michael, et al. 1992. *Capital choices: A report to the Council on Competitiveness.* Washington, D.C.: Council on Competitiveness.

Prowse, Stephen D. 1992. The structure of corporate ownership in Japan. *Journal of Finance* 47:1121–40.

Reddaway, W. B., et al. 1968. *U.K. investment overseas.* Vols. 1 and 2. Cambridge: Cambridge University Press.

Reich, Robert B. 1990. Who is us? *Harvard Business Review* 68(January–February): 53–64.

Robinson, John. 1983. *Multinationals and political control.* New York: St. Martin's.

Roe, Mark J. 1994. *Strong managers, weak owners: The political roots of American corporate finance.* Princeton, N.J.: Princeton University Press.

Rogowski, Ronald. 1989. *Commerce and coalitions.* Princeton, N.J.: Princeton University Press.

Ruggie, John Gerard. 1993. Territoriality and beyond: Problematizing modernity in international relations. *International Organization* 47:139–74.

Rugman, Alan. 1993. Drawing the border for a multinational enterprise and a nation-state. In *Multinationals in the global political economy,* edited by Lorraine Eden and Evan Potter. New York: St. Martin's.

Sally, Razeen. 1994. Multinational enterprises, political economy and institutional theory. *Review of International Political Economy* 1(spring): 161–92.

Samuels, Richard. 1987. *The business of the Japanese state.* Ithaca, N.Y.: Cornell University Press.

———. 1994. *"Rich nation, strong army": National security and the technological transformation of Japan.* Ithaca, N.Y.: Cornell University Press.

Schneider Lenné, Ellen. 1994. The role of German capital markets. In *Capital markets and global governance,* edited by Nicholas Dimsdale and Martha Prevezer. Oxford: Clarendon.

Schwartz, Herman. 1994. *States versus markets.* New York: St. Martin's.

Servan-Schreiber, J. J. 1967. *Le défi Americain* (The American challenge). Paris: Denoël.

Steinmo, Sven, Kathleen Thelen, and Frank Longstreth. 1992. *Structuring politics.* Cambridge: Cambridge University Press.

Stopford, John, and Susan Strange. 1991. *Rival states, rival firms.* Cambridge: Cambridge University Press.

Stopford John, and Louis Turner. 1985. *Britain and the multinationals.* New York: John Wiley and Sons.

Tilton, Mark. 1996. *Restrained trade: Cartels in Japan's basic materials industries.* Ithaca, N.Y.: Cornell University Press.

Tsurumi, Yoshi. 1983. *Multinational management: Business strategy and government policy.* Cambridge, Mass.: Ballinger.

Turner, Louis. 1970. *Invisible empires: Multinational companies and the modern world.* London: Hamish Hamilton.

Tyson, Laura D'Andrea. 1991. They are not us. *American Prospect* (winter): 37–49.

Uriu, Robert M. 1996. *Troubled industries: Confronting economic change in Japan.* Ithaca, N.Y.: Cornell University Press.

U.S. Congress. Office of Technology Assessment. 1993. *Multinationals and the national interest: Playing by different rules.* Document no. OTA-ITE-569. Washington, D.C.: Government Printing Office.

———. 1994. *Multinationals and the U.S. technology base.* Document no. OTA-ITE-612. Washington, D.C.: Government Printing Office.

U.S. Department of Commerce. Bureau of Economic Analysis (BEA). 1994. *Foreign direct investment in the United States.* Washington, D.C.: Department of Commerce.

U.S. General Accounting Office. 1993. *Competitiveness issues: The business environment in the United States, Japan, and Germany.* Document no. GAO/GGD-93-124, August.

van Tulder, Rob, and Gerd Junne. 1988. *European multinationals in core technologies.* New York: Wiley.

Vernon, Raymond. 1966. International investment and international trade in the product cycle. *Quarterly Journal of Economics* 80:190–207.

———. 1971. *Sovereignty at bay.* New York: Basic Books.

———. 1977. *Storm over the multinationals.* Cambridge, Mass.: Harvard University Press.

Wellons, Philip. 1986. International debt: The behavior of banks in a politicized environment. In *The politics of international debt,* edited by Miles Kahler. Ithaca, N.Y.: Cornell University Press.

———. 1987. *Passing the buck: Banks, governments and third world debt.* Boston: Harvard Business School Press.

Wells, Louis T., ed. 1972. *The product life cycle and international trade.* Cambridge, Mass.: Harvard University Press.

———. 1983. *Third world multinationals.* Cambridge, Mass.: MIT Press.

Wever, Kirsten, and Christopher S. Allen. 1993. The financial system and corporate governance in Germany. *Journal of Public Policy* 13:183–202.

Wilkins, Mira. 1974. *The maturing of multinational enterprise: American business abroad from 1914 to 1970.* Cambridge, Mass.: Harvard University Press.

Williamson, Oliver. 1988. Corporate finance and corporate governance. *Journal of Finance* 43:567–91.

Yamawaki, Hideki. 1994. Entry patterns of Japanese multinationals in U.S. and European manufacturing. In *Does ownership matter? Japanese multinationals in Europe,* edited by Mark Mason and Dennis Encarnation. Oxford: Clarendon.

Yoffie, David, ed. 1993. *Beyond free trade: Firms, governments, and global competition.* Boston: Harvard Business School Press.

Ziegler, Rolf, Donald Bender, and Herman Biehler. 1985. Industry and banking in the German corporate network. In *Networks of corporate power,* edited by Fruns N. Stokman, Rolf Ziegler, and John Scott. Cambridge: Polity.

Zysman, John. 1983. *Governments, markets, and growth.* Ithaca, N.Y.: Cornell University Press.

[16]

Power Shift

Jessica T. Mathews

THE RISE OF GLOBAL CIVIL SOCIETY

THE END of the Cold War has brought no mere adjustment among states but a novel redistribution of power among states, markets, and civil society. National governments are not simply losing autonomy in a globalizing economy. They are sharing powers—including political, social, and security roles at the core of sovereignty—with businesses, with international organizations, and with a multitude of citizens groups, known as nongovernmental organizations (NGOs). The steady concentration of power in the hands of states that began in 1648 with the Peace of Westphalia is over, at least for a while.[1]

The absolutes of the Westphalian system—territorially fixed states where everything of value lies within some state's borders; a single, secular authority governing each territory and representing it outside its borders; and no authority above states—are all dissolving. Increasingly, resources and threats that matter, including money, information, pollution, and popular culture, circulate and shape lives and economies with little regard for political boundaries. International standards of conduct are gradually beginning to override claims of national or regional singularity. Even the most powerful states find the marketplace and international public opinion compelling them more often to follow a particular course.

The state's central task of assuring security is the least affected, but still not exempt. War will not disappear, but with the shrinkage of U.S. and Russian nuclear arsenals, the transformation of the

---

JESSICA T. MATHEWS is a Senior Fellow at the Council on Foreign Relations.

Power Shift

Nuclear Nonproliferation Treaty into a permanent covenant in 1995, agreement on the long-sought Comprehensive Test Ban treaty in 1996, and the likely entry into force of the Chemical Weapons Convention in 1997, the security threat to states from other states is on a downward course. Nontraditional threats, however, are rising—terrorism, organized crime, drug trafficking, ethnic conflict, and the combination of rapid population growth, environmental decline, and poverty that breeds economic stagnation, political instability, and, sometimes, state collapse. The nearly 100 armed conflicts since the end of the Cold War have virtually all been intrastate affairs. Many began with governments acting against their own citizens, through extreme corruption, violence, incompetence, or complete breakdown, as in Somalia.

These trends have fed a growing sense that individuals' security may not in fact reliably derive from their nation's security. A competing notion of "human security" is creeping around the edges of official thinking, suggesting that security be viewed as emerging from the conditions of daily life—food, shelter, employment, health, public safety—rather than flowing downward from a country's foreign relations and military strength.

The most powerful engine of change in the relative decline of states and the rise of nonstate actors is the computer and telecommunications revolution, whose deep political and social consequences have been almost completely ignored. Widely accessible and affordable technology has broken governments' monopoly on the collection and management of large amounts of information and deprived governments of the deference they enjoyed because of it. In every sphere of activity, instantaneous access to information and the ability to put it to use multiplies the number of players who matter and reduces the number who command great authority. The effect on the loudest voice—which has been government's—has been the greatest.

By drastically reducing the importance of proximity, the new technologies change people's perceptions of community. Fax machines,

---

[1] The author would like to acknowledge the contributions of the authors of ten case studies for the Council on Foreign Relations study group, "Sovereignty, Nonstate Actors, and a New World Politics," on which this article is based.

Jessica T. Mathews

satellite hookups, and the Internet connect people across borders with exponentially growing ease while separating them from natural and historical associations within nations. In this sense a powerful globalizing force, they can also have the opposite effect, amplifying political and social fragmentation by enabling more and more identities and interests scattered around the globe to coalesce and thrive.

These technologies have the potential to divide society along new lines, separating ordinary people from elites with the wealth and education to command technology's power. Those elites are not only the rich but also citizens groups with transnational interests and identities that frequently have more in common with counterparts in other countries, whether industrialized or developing, than with countrymen.

Above all, the information technologies disrupt hierarchies, spreading power among more people and groups. In drastically lowering the costs of communication, consultation, and coordination, they favor decentralized networks over other modes of organization. In a network, individuals or groups link for joint action without building a physical or formal institutional presence. Networks have no person at the top and no center. Instead, they have multiple nodes where collections of individuals or groups interact for different purposes. Businesses, citizens organizations, ethnic groups, and crime cartels have all readily adopted the network model. Governments, on the other hand, are quintessential hierarchies, wedded to an organizational form incompatible with all that the new technologies make possible.

Today's powerful nonstate actors are not without precedent. The British East India Company ran a subcontinent, and a few influential NGOs go back more than a century. But these are exceptions. Both in numbers and in impact, nonstate actors have never before approached their current strength. And a still larger role likely lies ahead.

DIAL LOCALLY, ACT GLOBALLY

No one knows how many NGOs there are or how fast the tally is growing. Published figures are badly misleading. One widely cited estimate claims there are 35,000 NGOs in the developing countries;

Power Shift

another points to 12,000 irrigation cooperatives in South Asia alone. In fact, it is impossible to measure a swiftly growing universe that includes neighborhood, professional, service, and advocacy groups, both secular and church-based, promoting every conceivable cause and funded by donations, fees, foundations, governments, international oganizations, or the sale of products and services. The true number is certainly in the millions, from the tiniest village association to influential but modestly funded international groups like Amnesty International to larger global activist organizations like Greenpeace and giant service providers like CARE, which has an annual budget of nearly $400 million.

> NGOs are able to push around even the largest governments.

Except in China, Japan, the Middle East, and a few other places where culture or authoritarian governments severely limit civil society, NGOs' role and influence have exploded in the last half-decade. Their financial resources and— often more important—their expertise, approximate and sometimes exceed those of smaller governments and of international organizations. "We have less money and fewer resources than Amnesty International, and we are the arm of the U.N. for human rights," noted Ibrahima Fall, head of the U.N. Centre for Human Rights, in 1993. "This is clearly ridiculous." Today NGOs deliver more official development assistance than the entire U.N. system (excluding the World Bank and the International Monetary Fund). In many countries they are delivering the services—in urban and rural community development, education, and health care—that faltering governments can no longer manage.

The range of these groups' work is almost as broad as their interests. They breed new ideas; advocate, protest, and mobilize public support; do legal, scientific, technical, and policy analysis; provide services; shape, implement, monitor, and enforce national and international commitments; and change institutions and norms.

Increasingly, NGOs are able to push around even the largest governments. When the United States and Mexico set out to reach a trade agreement, the two governments planned on the usual narrowly defined negotiations behind closed doors. But NGOs had a

Jessica T. Mathews

very different vision. Groups from Canada, the United States, and Mexico wanted to see provisions in the North American Free Trade Agreement on health and safety, transboundary pollution, consumer protection, immigration, labor mobility, child labor, sustainable agriculture, social charters, and debt relief. Coalitions of NGOs formed in each country and across both borders. The opposition they generated in early 1991 endangered congressional approval of the crucial "fast track" negotiating authority for the U.S. government. After months of resistance, the Bush administration capitulated, opening the agreement to environmental and labor concerns. Although progress in other trade venues will be slow, the tightly closed world of trade negotiations has been changed forever.

Technology is fundamental to NGOs' new clout. The nonprofit Association for Progressive Communications provides 50,000 NGOs in 133 countries access to the tens of millions of Internet users for the price of a local call. The dramatically lower costs of international communication have altered NGOs' goals and changed international outcomes. Within hours of the first gunshots of the Chiapas rebellion in southern Mexico in January 1994, for example, the Internet swarmed with messages from human rights activists. The worldwide media attention they and their groups focused on Chiapas, along with the influx of rights activists to the area, sharply limited the Mexican government's response. What in other times would have been a bloody insurgency turned out to be a largely nonviolent conflict. "The shots lasted ten days," José Angel Gurría, Mexico's foreign minister, later remarked, "and ever since, the war has been . . . a war on the Internet."

NGOs' easy reach behind other states' borders forces governments to consider domestic public opinion in countries with which they are dealing, even on matters that governments have traditionally handled strictly between themselves. At the same time, cross-border NGO networks offer citizens groups unprecedented channels of influence. Women's and human rights groups in many developing countries have linked up with more experienced, better funded, and more powerful groups in Europe and the United States. The latter work the global media and lobby their own governments to pressure leaders in developing countries, creating a circle of influence that is accelerating change in many parts of the world.

Power Shift

OUT OF THE HALLWAY, AROUND THE TABLE

IN INTERNATIONAL organizations, as with governments at home, NGOs were once largely relegated to the hallways. Even when they were able to shape governments' agendas, as the Helsinki Watch human rights groups did in the Conference on Security and Cooperation in Europe in the 1980s, their influence was largely determined by how receptive their own government's delegation happened to be. Their only option was to work through governments.

All that changed with the negotiation of the global climate treaty, culminating at the Earth Summit in Rio de Janeiro in 1992. With the broader independent base of public support that environmental groups command, NGOs set the original goal of negotiating an agreement to control greenhouse gases long before governments were ready to do so, proposed most of its structure and content, and lobbied and mobilized public pressure to force through a pact that virtually no one else thought possible when the talks began.

More members of NGOs served on government delegations than ever before, and they penetrated deeply into official decision-making. They were allowed to attend the small working group meetings where the real decisions in international negotiations are made. The tiny nation of Vanuatu turned its delegation over to an NGO with expertise in international law (a group based in London and funded by an American foundation), thereby making itself and the other sea-level island states major players in the fight to control global warming. *ECO*, an NGO-published daily newspaper, was negotiators' best source of information on the progress of the official talks and became the forum where governments tested ideas for breaking deadlocks.

Whether from developing or developed countries, NGOs were tightly organized in a global and half a dozen regional Climate Action Networks, which were able to bridge North-South differences among governments that many had expected would prevent an agreement. United in their passionate pursuit of a treaty, NGOs would fight out contentious issues among themselves, then take an agreed position to their respective delegations. When they could not agree, NGOs served as invaluable back channels, letting both sides know where the other's problems lay or where a compromise might be found.

Jessica T. Mathews

As a result, delegates completed the framework of a global climate accord in the blink of a diplomat's eye—16 months—over the opposition of the three energy superpowers, the United States, Russia, and Saudi Arabia. The treaty entered into force in record time just two years later. Although only a framework accord whose binding requirements are still to be negotiated, the treaty could force sweeping changes in energy use, with potentially enormous implications for every economy.

The influence of NGOs at the climate talks has not yet been matched in any other arena, and indeed has provoked a backlash among some governments. A handful of authoritarian regimes, most notably China, led the charge, but many others share their unease about the role NGOs are assuming. Nevertheless, NGOs have worked their way into the heart of international negotiations and into the day-to-day operations of international organizations, bringing new priorities, demands for procedures that give a voice to groups outside government, and new standards of accountability.

ONE WORLD BUSINESS

THE MULTINATIONAL corporations of the 1960s were virtually all American, and prided themselves on their insularity. Foreigners might run subsidiaries, but they were never partners. A foreign posting was a setback for a rising executive.

Today, a global marketplace is developing for retail sales as well as manufacturing. Law, advertising, business consulting, and financial and other services are also marketed internationally. Firms of all nationalities attempt to look and act like locals wherever they operate. Foreign language skills and lengthy experience abroad are an asset, and increasingly a requirement, for top management. Sometimes corporate headquarters are not even in a company's home country.

Amid shifting alliances and joint ventures, made possible by computers and advanced communications, nationalities blur. Offshore banking encourages widespread evasion of national taxes. Whereas the fear in the 1970s was that multinationals would become an arm of government, the concern now is that they are disconnecting from their home countries' national interests, moving jobs, evading taxes, and eroding economic sovereignty in the process.

Power Shift

The even more rapid globalization of financial markets has left governments far behind. Where governments once set foreign exchange rates, private currency traders, accountable only to their bottom line, now trade $1.3 trillion a day, 100 times the volume of world trade. The amount exceeds the total foreign exchange reserves of all governments, and is more than even an alliance of strong states can buck.

Despite the enormous attention given to governments' conflicts over trade rules, private capital flows have been growing twice as fast as trade for years. International portfolio transactions by U.S. investors, 9 percent of U.S. GDP in 1980, had grown to 135 percent of GDP by 1993. Growth in Germany, Britain, and elsewhere has been even more rapid. Direct investment has surged as well. All in all, the global financial market will grow to a staggering $83 trillion by 2000, a 1994 McKinsey

> Nowadays governments have only the appearance of free choice when they set out to make rules.

& Co. study estimated, triple the aggregate GDP of the affluent nations of the Organization for Economic Cooperation and Development.

Again, technology has been a driving force, shifting financial clout from states to the market with its offer of unprecedented speed in transactions—states cannot match market reaction times measured in seconds—and its dissemination of financial information to a broad range of players. States could choose whether they would belong to rule-based economic systems like the gold standard, but, as former Citicorp chairman Walter Wriston has pointed out, they cannot withdraw from the technology-based marketplace, unless they seek autarky and poverty.

More and more frequently today, governments have only the appearance of free choice when they set economic rules. Markets are setting de facto rules enforced by their own power. States can flout them, but the penalties are severe—loss of vital foreign capital, foreign technology, and domestic jobs. Even the most powerful economy must pay heed. The U.S. government could choose to rescue the Mexican peso in 1994, for example, but it had to do so on terms designed to satisfy the bond markets, not the countries doing the rescuing.

The forces shaping the legitimate global economy are also nourishing globally integrated crime—which U.N. officials peg at a staggering $750 billion a year, $400 billion to $500 billion of that in

Jessica T. Mathews

narcotics, according to U.S. Drug Enforcement Agency estimates. Huge increases in the volume of goods and people crossing borders and competitive pressures to speed the flow of trade by easing inspections and reducing paperwork make it easier to hide contraband. Deregulation and privatization of government-owned businesses, modern communications, rapidly shifting commercial alliances, and the emergence of global financial systems have all helped transform local drug operations into global enterprises. The largely unregulated multi-trillion-dollar pool of money in supranational cyberspace, accessible by computer 24 hours a day, eases the drug trade's toughest problem: transforming huge sums of hot cash into investments in legitimate business.

Globalized crime is a security threat that neither police nor the military—the state's traditional responses—can meet. Controlling it will require states to pool their efforts and to establish unprecedented cooperation with the private sector, thereby compromising two cherished sovereign roles. If states fail, if criminal groups can continue to take advantage of porous borders and transnational financial spaces while governments are limited to acting within their own territory, crime will have the winning edge.

BORN-AGAIN INSTITUTIONS

UNTIL RECENTLY, international organizations were institutions of, by, and for nation-states. Now they are building constituencies of their own and, through NGOs, establishing direct connections to the peoples of the world. The shift is infusing them with new life and influence, but it is also creating tensions.

States feel they need more capable international organizations to deal with a lengthening list of transnational challenges, but at the same time fear competitors. Thus they vote for new forms of international intervention while reasserting sovereignty's first principle: no interference in the domestic affairs of states. They hand international organizations sweeping new responsibilities and then rein them in with circumscribed mandates or inadequate funding. With states ambivalent about intervention, a host of new problems demanding attention, and NGOs bursting with energy, ideas, and calls for a larger role, international organizations are lurching toward an unpredictable, but certainly different, future.

Power Shift

International organizations are still coming to terms with unprecedented growth in the volume of international problem-solving. Between 1972 and 1992 the number of environmental treaties rocketed from a few dozen to more than 900. While collaboration in other fields is not growing at quite that rate, treaties, regimes, and intergovernmental institutions dealing with human rights, trade, narcotics, corruption, crime, refugees, antiterrorism measures, arms control, and democracy are multiplying. "Soft law" in the form of guidelines, recommended practices, nonbinding resolutions, and the like is also rapidly expanding.

> No longer of, by, and for the nation-state, international institutions lurch toward change.

Behind each new agreement are scientists and lawyers who worked on it, diplomats who negotiated it, and NGOs that back it, most of them committed for the long haul. The new constituency also includes a burgeoning, influential class of international civil servants responsible for implementing, monitoring, and enforcing this enormous new body of law.

At the same time, governments, while ambivalent about the international community mixing in states' domestic affairs, have driven some gaping holes in the wall that has separated the two. In the triumphant months after the Berlin Wall came down, international accords, particularly ones agreed on by what is now the Organization for Security and Cooperation in Europe and by the Organization of American States (OAS), drew explicit links between democracy, human rights, and international security, establishing new legal bases for international interventions. In 1991 the U.N. General Assembly declared itself in favor of humanitarian intervention without the request or consent of the state involved. A year later the Security Council took the unprecedented step of authorizing the use of force "on behalf of civilian populations" in Somalia. Suddenly an interest in citizens began to compete with, and occasionally override, the formerly unquestioned primacy of state interests.

Since 1990 the Security Council has declared a formal threat to international peace and security 61 times, after having done so only six times in the preceding 45 years. It is not that security has been abruptly and terribly threatened; rather, the change reflects the broadened scope of what the international community now feels it should poke

Jessica T. Mathews

its nose into. As with Haiti in 1992, many of the so-called Chapter VII resolutions authorizing forceful intervention concerned domestic situations that involved awful human suffering or offended international norms but posed little if any danger to international peace.

Almost as intrusive as a Chapter VII intervention, though always invited, election monitoring has also become a growth industry. The United Nations monitored no election in a member state during the Cold War, only in colonies. But beginning in 1990 it responded to a deluge of requests from governments that felt compelled to prove their legitimacy by the new standards. In Latin America, where countries most jealously guard their sovereignty, the OAS monitored 11 national elections in four years.

And monitoring is no longer the passive observation it was in earlier decades. Carried out by a close-knit mix of international organizations and NGOs, it involves a large foreign presence dispensing advice and recommending standards for voter registration, campaign law, campaign practices, and the training of clerks and judiciaries. Observers even carry out parallel vote counts that can block fraud but at the same time second-guess the integrity of national counts.

International financial institutions, too, have inserted themselves more into states' domestic affairs. During the 1980s the World Bank attached conditions to loans concerning recipient governments' policies on poverty, the environment, and even, occasionally, military spending, a once sacrosanct domain of national prerogative. In 1991 a statement of bank policy holding that "efficient and accountable public sector management" is crucial to economic growth provided the rationale for subjecting to international oversight everything from official corruption to government competence.

Beyond involving them in an array of domestic economic and social decisions, the new policies force the World Bank, the International Monetary Fund, and other international financial institutions to forge alliances with business, NGOs, and civil society if they are to achieve broad changes in target countries. In the process, they have opened themselves to the same demands they are making of their clients: broader public participation and greater openness in decision-making. As a result, yet another set of doors behind which only officials sat has been thrown open to the private sector and to civil society.

Power Shift

LEAPS OF IMAGINATION

AFTER THREE and a half centuries, it requires a mental leap to think of world politics in any terms other than occasionally cooperating but generally competing states, each defined by its territory and representing all the people therein. Nor is it easy to imagine political entities that could compete with the emotional attachment of a shared landscape, national history, language, flag, and currency.

Yet history proves that there are alternatives other than tribal anarchy. Empires, both tightly and loosely ruled, achieved success and won allegiance. In the Middle Ages, emperors, kings, dukes, knights, popes, archbishops, guilds, and cities exercised overlapping secular power over the same territory in a system that looks much more like a modern, three-dimensional network than the clean-lined, hierarchical state order that replaced it. The question now is whether there are new geographic or functional entities that might grow up alongside the state, taking over some of its powers and emotional resonance.

The kernels of several such entities already exist. The European Union is the most obvious example. Neither a union of states nor an international organization, the EU leaves experts groping for inadequate descriptions like "post-sovereign system" or "unprecedented hybrid." It respects members' borders for some purposes, particularly in foreign and defense policy, but ignores them for others. The union's judiciary can override national law, and its Council of Ministers can overrule certain domestic executive decisions. In its thousands of councils, committees, and working groups, national ministers increasingly find themselves working with their counterparts from other countries to oppose colleagues in their own government; agriculture ministers, for example, ally against finance ministers. In this sense the union penetrates and to some extent weakens the internal bonds of its member states. Whether Frenchmen, Danes, and Greeks will ever think of themselves first as Europeans remains to be seen, but the EU has already come much further than most Americans realize.

Meanwhile, units below the national level are taking on formal international roles. Nearly all 50 American states have trade offices abroad, up from four in 1970, and all have official standing in the World Trade

Jessica T. Mathews

Organization (WTO). German *Länder* and British local governments have offices at EU headquarters in Brussels. France's Rhône-Alpes region, centered in Lyon, maintains what it calls "embassies" abroad on behalf of a regional economy that includes Geneva, Switzerland, and Turin, Italy.

Emerging political identities not linked to territory pose a more direct challenge to the geographically fixed state system. The WTO is struggling to find a method of handling environmental disputes in the global commons, outside all states' boundaries, that the General Agreement on Tariffs and Trade, drafted 50 years ago, simply never envisioned. Proposals have been floated for a Parliamentary Assembly in the United Nations, parallel to the General Assembly, to represent the people rather than the states of the world. Ideas are under discussion that would give ethnic nations political and legal status, so that the Kurds, for example, could be legally represented as a people in addition to being Turkish, Iranian, or Iraqi citizens.

> The shift from national to another allegiance will be a cultural and political earthquake.

Further in the future is a proposed Global Environmental Authority with independent regulatory powers. This is not as far-fetched as it sounds. The burden of participating in several hundred international environmental bodies is heavy for the richest governments and is becoming prohibitive for others. As the number of international agreements mounts, the pressure to streamline the system—in environmental protection as in other areas—will grow.

The realm of most rapid change is hybrid authorities that include state and nonstate bodies such as the International Telecommunications Union, the International Union for the Conservation of Nature, and hundreds more. In many of these, businesses or NGOs take on formerly public roles. The Geneva-based International Standards Organization, essentially a business NGO, sets widely observed standards on everything from products to internal corporate procedures. The International Securities Markets Association, another private regulator, oversees international trade in private securities markets—the world's second-largest capital market after domestic government bond markets. In another crossover, markets become government enforcers when they adopt treaty standards as the basis for market judgments. States and NGOs are collaborating

Power Shift

ad hoc in large-scale humanitarian relief operations that involve both
military and civilian forces. Other NGOs have taken on standing operational roles for international organizations in refugee work and development assistance. Almost unnoticed, hybrids like these, in which states
are often the junior partners, are becoming a new international norm.

FOR BETTER OR WORSE?

A WORLD that is more adaptable and in which power is more diffused
could mean more peace, justice, and capacity to manage the burgeoning
list of humankind's interconnected problems. At a time of accelerating
change, NGOs are quicker than governments to respond to new
demands and opportunities. Internationally, in both the poorest and
richest countries, NGOs, when adequately funded, can outperform
government in the delivery of many public services. Their growth,
along with that of the other elements of civil society, can strengthen the
fabric of the many still-fragile democracies. And they are better than
governments at dealing with problems that grow slowly and affect
society through their cumulative effect on individuals—the "soft"
threats of environmental degradation, denial of human rights, population
growth, poverty, and lack of development that may already be causing
more deaths in conflict than are traditional acts of aggression.

As the computer and telecommunications revolution continues,
NGOs will become more capable of large-scale activity across national
borders. Their loyalties and orientation, like those of international civil
servants and citizens of non-national entities like the EU, are better
matched than those of governments to problems that demand transnational solutions. International NGOs and cross-border networks of local
groups have bridged North-South differences that in earlier years paralyzed cooperation among countries.

On the economic front, expanding private markets can avoid
economically destructive but politically seductive policies, such
as excessive borrowing or overly burdensome taxation, to which
governments succumb. Unhindered by ideology, private capital flows
to where it is best treated and thus can do the most good.

International organizations, given a longer rein by governments
and connected to the grassroots by deepening ties with NGOs, could,

Jessica T. Mathews

with adequate funding, take on larger roles in global housekeeping (transportation, communications, environment, health), security (controlling weapons of mass destruction, preventive diplomacy, peacekeeping), human rights, and emergency relief. As various international panels have suggested, the funds could come from fees on international activities, such as currency transactions and air travel, independent of state appropriations. Finally, that new force on the global scene, international public opinion, informed by worldwide media coverage and mobilized by NGOs, can be extraordinarily potent in getting things done, and done quickly.

There are at least as many reasons, however, to believe that the continuing diffusion of power away from nation-states will mean more conflict and less problem-solving both within states and among them.

For all their strengths, NGOs are special interests, albeit not motivated by personal profit. The best of them, the ablest and most passionate, often suffer most from tunnel vision, judging every public act by how it affects their particular interest. Generally, they have limited capacity for large-scale endeavors, and as they grow, the need to sustain growing budgets can compromise the independence of mind and approach that is their greatest asset.

A society in which the piling up of special interests replaces a single strong voice for the common good is unlikely to fare well. Single-issue voters, as Americans know all too well, polarize and freeze public debate. In the longer run, a stronger civil society could also be more fragmented, producing a weakened sense of common identity and purpose and less willingness to invest in public goods, whether health and education or roads and ports. More and more groups promoting worthy but narrow causes could ultimately threaten democratic government.

Internationally, excessive pluralism could have similar consequences. Two hundred nation-states is a barely manageable number. Add hundreds of influential nonstate forces—businesses, NGOs, international organizations, ethnic and religious groups—and the international system may represent more voices but be unable to advance any of them.

Moreover, there are roles that only the state—at least among today's polities—can perform. States are the only nonvoluntary political unit, the one that can impose order and is invested with the power to tax. Severely weakened states will encourage conflict, as they have in Africa,

Power Shift

Central America, and elsewhere. Moreover, it may be that only the nation-state can meet crucial social needs that markets do not value. Providing a modicum of job security, avoiding higher unemployment, preserving a livable environment and a stable climate, and protecting consumer health and safety are but a few of the tasks that could be left dangling in a world of expanding markets and retreating states.

More international decision-making will also exacerbate the so-called democratic deficit, as decisions that elected representatives once made shift to unelected international bodies; this is already a sore point for EU members. It also arises when legislatures are forced to make a single take-it-or-leave-it judgment on huge international agreements, like the several-thousand-page Uruguay Round trade accord. With citizens already feeling that their national governments do not hear individual voices, the trend could well provoke deeper and more dangerous alienation, which in turn could trigger new ethnic and even religious separatism. The end result could be a proliferation of states too weak for either individual economic success or effective international cooperation.

Finally, fearsome dislocations are bound to accompany the weakening of the central institution of modern society. The prophets of an internetted world in which national identities gradually fade, proclaim its revolutionary nature and yet believe the changes will be wholly benign. They won't be. The shift from national to some other political allegiance, if it comes, will be an emotional, cultural, and political earthquake.

DISSOLVING AND EVOLVING

MIGHT THE decline in state power prove transitory? Present disenchantment with national governments could dissipate as quickly as it arose. Continuing globalization may well spark a vigorous reassertion of economic or cultural nationalism. By helping solve problems governments cannot handle, business, NGOs, and international organizations may actually be strengthening the nation-state system.

These are all possibilities, but the clash between the fixed geography of states and the nonterritorial nature of today's problems and solutions, which is only likely to escalate, strongly suggests that the relative power of states will continue to decline. Nation-states may simply no

Jessica T. Mathews

longer be the natural problem-solving unit. Local government addresses citizens' growing desire for a role in decision-making, while transnational, regional, and even global entities better fit the dimensions of trends in economics, resources, and security.

The evolution of information and communications technology, which has only just begun, will probably heavily favor nonstate entities, including those not yet envisaged, over states. The new technologies encourage noninstitutional, shifting networks over the fixed bureaucratic hierarchies that are the hallmark of the single-voiced sovereign state. They dissolve issues' and institutions' ties to a fixed place. And by greatly empowering individuals, they weaken the relative attachment to community, of which the preeminent one in modern society is the nation-state.

If current trends continue, the international system 50 years hence will be profoundly different. During the transition, the Westphalian system and an evolving one will exist side by side. States will set the rules by which all other actors operate, but outside forces will increasingly make decisions for them. In using business, NGOs, and international organizations to address problems they cannot or do not want to take on, states will, more often than not, inadvertently weaken themselves further. Thus governments' unwillingness to adequately fund international organizations helped NGOs move from a peripheral to a central role in shaping multilateral agreements, since the NGOs provided expertise the international organizations lacked. At least for a time, the transition is likely to weaken rather than bolster the world's capacity to solve its problems. If states, with the overwhelming share of power, wealth, and capacity, can do less, less will get done.

Whether the rise of nonstate actors ultimately turns out to be good news or bad will depend on whether humanity can launch itself on a course of rapid social innovation, as it did after World War II. Needed adaptations include a business sector that can shoulder a broader policy role, NGOs that are less parochial and better able to operate on a large scale, international institutions that can efficiently serve the dual masters of states and citizenry, and, above all, new institutions and political entities that match the transnational scope of today's challenges while meeting citizens' demands for accountable democratic governance.◆

Third World Quarterly, Vol 16, No 3, 1995

NGO participation in the international policy process

LEON GORDENKER & THOMAS G WEISS

When viewed from the central vantage point of the United Nations (UN), each of the case studies above produces significant evidence that nongovernmental organisations (NGOs) have joined states as participants in organised international relations. At the same time, the principal participants in making policies and executing programmes in the international institutions in the UN realm remain government representatives. In each of the case studies, a complex set of equations emerges in which the variables are NGOs, intergovernmental organisations (IGOs) and governments.

Simple reference to these three categories of participants has a superficial and misleading quality. Day-to-day work is accomplished by people who, it can be assumed, have a variety of instructions or none at all from their governments or organisations. Relationships between NGOs and the United Nations vary from distant and indirect in the case of grassroots organisations to virtual equality in some human rights activities. In some instances, as in Partners in Action (PARinAC), mentioned by Cyril Ritchie in his essay on coalitions of organisations, the participation of NGOs as executing agencies is eagerly sought by an IGO, in this case the UN High Commission for Refugees (UNHCR), acting on behalf of governments. In other cases, as in the creation of environmental policies, as illustrated by Ken Conca, NGO participation has barely begun. Similarly, in the case of AIDS, described by Christer Jönsson and Peter Söderholm, NGOs participated in framing the epidemic as an international issue but had little direct role at the global level in managing programmes.

At the same time, in quantitative terms without reference to the character and aims of NGOs associated with the UN complex, the sheer numbers have mounted steadily and will likely stay at a high level. Moreover, the fact of mounting numbers has led—as suggested in the essay on coalitions, and in the case of Central America examined by Peter Sollis—to the creation of specialized meta-organisations. Yet the precise purposes of such coalitions, their membership and their relationships with IGOs and governments vary widely.

Reflections on theoretical approaches

Such descriptive conclusions only strengthen the scepticism expressed at the outset of this volume on the usefulness of conventional theoretical approaches to NGOs. The case studies describe nongovernmental organisations that challenge governments and their intergovernmental creations, even as these NGOs work parallel with governments and other NGOs that, in some respects, operate almost seamlessly with governments. Moreover, the attitude and actions of governments

0143-6597/95/030543-13 © 1995 Third World Quarterly

with respect to NGOs are hardly amenable to conventional strategic, zero-sum-based analyses that emphasise the power of competing states. It would make little sense, for instance, to attribute the activities of NGOs in Central America to the presumably overwhelming power of the United States. Nor would it explain much about human rights organisations to insist that their role is ultimately explained in the same manner.

Yet in varying magnitudes, states dispose of the most effective and far-reaching administrative apparatuses on earth. Both IGOs and NGOs, which for the sake of argument are assumed to be independent, usually need at least acquiescence from the state apparatus to operate effectively and reach goals. Governments engage IGOs to organise some of their cooperative common ventures, contributing funds as well as administrative capacities. Usually governments can ultimately open the way to, or suppress, NGO and IGO activities. Consequently, much activity attempts to convince governmental representatives at home and in IGO settings to take seriously, defer to, or follow NGO propositions.

In fact, all the case studies touch on a range of relationships between governments and NGOs. These are sometimes hierarchical, where governments exercise control over NGOs. As for IGOs, the fundamental effect on nongovernmental organisations has to do with access, which has become progressively broader and deeper. IGOs can also employ control by denial of, for instance, information or sometimes finances. Thus, many collaborative and cooperative relationships that mute conflicts between NGOs, governments and IGOs emerge from the case studies.

These findings support the proposition that a social approach and in particular interorganisation theory offers a promising way to understand the NGO phenomenon better. Further work would develop deeper information on how NGOs are constructed and how they operate. Interorganisation theory emphasises the quality of contact among NGOs through their personnel and among distinct policy and activity sectors; it does not assume a monolithic character of governments and IGOs. It makes identification of leaders and their organisational roles easier. In discussing NGO activity on AIDS, Jönsson and Söderholm explicitly use this approach to disclose the complexity and dynamism of relationships between NGOs and global IGO activity.

However, much remains to be done to approach a comprehensive theory of NGOs, either along social lines or from some other direction. The case studies here provide information and insights in that direction but, as anticipated, fall short of full explanation or observation of this tangled web of transnational relationships.

Dimensions

However remote, any general, testable theoretical approaches to NGOs may be, the case studies have developed much information that fills out the scheme of organisational dimensions set out in the introductory essay. At the same time, the studies show that much is still obscure and that some glaring gaps remain. The following pages point out some of the main findings.

NGO PARTICIPATION IN THE INTERNATIONAL POLICY PROCESS

Organisational dimensions

Nongovernmental organisations clearly operate in every geographic range from the community to the transnational. In discussing scaling up and scaling down, Peter Uvin calls attention to the impulses among NGOs to bridge several ranges. To a considerable degree, this bridging is related to the governmental contacts that NGOs seek and employ. Some NGOs, as Sollis's article on Central America suggests, have a regional range and connect with those at national and subnational levels. Conca points out, however, that few environmental organisations relevant to UN activities are truly transnational.

Data on the support base of NGOs is not highly developed in the case studies. Whether and how differences in organisational membership influence policy activities remains unclear. Democratic government of NGOs is an issue referred to in several case studies, but its effect is far from defined. In her essay on the women's movement, Martha Chen calls attention to the increasing number of women who attend the international conferences on women, although individual voluntary attendance and organisational representation are not quantified separately.

On the related subject of finances, Andrew Natsios identifies in his essay on humanitarian work a wide variation among NGOs, some of which refuse governmental funds, while others, including the new breed of 'super' NGOs, may be almost totally financed from public funds from governments and intergovernmental organisations. In the USA, legal rules provide that a nongovernmental organisation must raise 20% of its finances from private sources to be eligible for public funding. Nevertheless, some have grown to mega-proportions for this universe. Some NGO coalitions, as Ritchie describes in his essay on coordination, depend on IGOs for financing. Brief notice in several essays to philanthropic foundations implies the presence of endowment income, but few NGOs other than those mentioned appear to draw much from this source. Many of the essays mention contracting with governments and IGOs in the UN cluster as sources of finances for a set of nongovernmental organisations that deliver specific services.

Legal relationships affect NGOs in many ways. IGO regulations, dealt with by Antonio Donini in his essay on the UN bureaucracy, and by Ritchie, clearly affect access by NGOs. This relationship is especially highlighted in the case study by Conca on environmental organisations. Moreover, nongovernmental organisations can be inhibited or encouraged in their work at the community and national levels by the nature of local laws, as is noted by Sollis in his essay on state–UN–NGO relationships in Central America. The character of legal relationships between NGOs and other organisations clearly can be a focus of activity, as for example in the case of the environment, the status of women, and in the economic development field.

Several of the essays agree that the professionalism of personnel serving NGOs, especially those that have close relationships with the headquarters activities of IGOs, has risen markedly. This is also supported by the attention given by IGO personnel to NGOs in dealing with AIDS and with women's issues. Donini's examples of 'revolving door' personnel—people who move between intergovernmental and nongovernmental staffs—argue that professional standards in some NGOs and IGOs are equivalent.

Other findings related to personnel remain fragmentary. Although the use of research personnel in NGOs with technical, scientific or legal interests would seem indispensable, it remains hard to estimate either quantity or quality. Felice Gaer's essay on human rights, and the treatment of environmental organisations by Conca, give evidence of the payoff from high quality advance preparation for participation by NGOs in UN system meetings. The creation of intermediary organisations in Central America and in scaling up operations examined by Sollis and Uvin would appear to aim directly at employment of skilled personnel, either of a research or operational character.

Precisely how volunteers fit into NGOs in touch with the UN system remains rather obscure, even in the essays that speak of grassroots organisations and movements that go beyond defined NGO boundaries. By definition, grassroots organisations depend on voluntary participation. Such participation may extend to more upscale NGOs, at least in terms of boards of trustees. Membership organisations presumably have devices for representation of members, suggesting voluntary participation. Voluntary participation, moreover, has a close relationship with processes within NGOs. This is supposedly a precondition for accreditation to the Economic and Social Council of the UN (ECOSOC). Any generalisation about these issues, however, would depend on examination of NGO internal operations, and is beyond the scope of these essays.

Financing has a fundamental importance in the development of the mega-NGOs referred to by Natsios that operate in humanitarian emergencies. Much of this comes directly from governments and some comes via IGOs. Similar financing sources are evident in the Central American NGO picture developed by Sollis. In the AIDS field analysed by Jönsson and Söderholm, governments are the overwhelming source of funding for IGO programmes, but NGOs appear to operate to some extent on other financial bases. The women's movement, described by Chen, seems to be largely privately financed. How or whether endowments, except in the case of philanthropic foundations, figure in NGO financing is also not clear. As for income derived as compensation, with the spread of contracting for NGO services, this can be taken as an important channel for the specific transfer of financial resources.

Governance dimensions

Most NGOs probably exist to influence, to set direction for, or to maintain functions of governance or to operate where government authority does not. Consequently governance dimensions would be a strong presence in any inquiry about them. This is, in fact, the case in all of the studies. Donini points out that NGOs have even developed some roles in regard to the former diplomatic preserve of maintaining international peace and security.

In any case, NGOs are a strong presence at every contact point for transnational governance. Their presence differs, however, in specific areas. International conferences, as is shown in the cases of AIDS, the environment, human rights, women and humanitarian assistance, offer an entrance to deeper contacts between NGOs and the UN organisations. Some NGOs, equipped with expert knowledge and professional leadership, participate with special zeal and effect in the preparatory phases of such conferences. To some degree, NGO efforts at every stage shape the outcomes.

The global conferences both affect the agendas of intergovernmental agencies and are convened by them. The NGO presence and activity around the conferences convened by the United Nations and associated agencies is reconfirmed by the case studies. Donini calls attention to the changing environment for such association, while Ritchie makes it clear that many coalitions form and continue for the specific purpose of clamping NGOs and IGOs into a relationship with a set agenda.

Although the case studies focus on the UN agencies, national governments are never allowed to drift far from view. Gaer shows how the UN human rights organs provide a way for NGOs to embellish a critical and often adversarial relationship with national governments. Sollis discloses how NGOs working with IGOs have a virtually integral role in national governments in some instances in Central America, where a regional concept is also important. NGOs also seek contact, or cannot avoid it, with subnational governmental units, a point that is clear from both Natsios's and Uvin's discussions. In failed states, moreover, as Natsios's essay makes clear, NGOs take on some normal governmental programmes but not without misgivings about the propriety and result of such lack of normal contact with local authority. The frequent mention of grassroots organisation points to a community-level relationship for some NGOs.

Informal transnational relationships between NGO personnel and that of governments and IGOs is implicitly or explicitly demonstrated in all the case studies. It is especially emphasised in the case of the women's movement and AIDS. Since the governance dimensions are intended to highlight the variety of relationships between NGOs and authority, a variety of activities engaging the latter were set out. These include norm and policy setting, policy execution, contracting and inter-level mediation. In none of these are NGOs missing, although the depth and temporal extent of the contact vary greatly. For instance, Gaer and Chen show the constant and growing presence of NGOs in setting norms related to human and women's rights, while Conca's discussion of environmental agencies demonstrates a special density of contact during the norm-setting global conferences. Sollis reveals the involvement of NGOs in execution of policy. NGOs serving as contractors are engaged in the humanitarian activities discussed by Natsios. Ritchie's comments on coalitions and Uvin's analysis of scaling up and scaling down both have to do with NGOs related to interlevel mediation.

Strategic dimensions

Strategic dimensions supplement the data about governance dimensions by emphasising what is sought and what techniques are employed by NGOs in their relationships with various authorities engaged in governance processes.

As for goals, many and probably most of the NGOs in the case studies either concentrate on a single issue or a set of issues grouped around a particular topic. Gaer, for example, takes up some transnational human rights organisations that deal with no other subjects. At the same time, Gaer mentions representatives at the Vienna human rights conference with wider, multisectoral or broad social goals. In international cooperation on AIDS, Jönsson and Söderholm observe that some participating NGOs concentrate on persons with AIDS, while others aim at the position of homosexuals in society generally. In humanitarian emergencies, Natsios points to NGOs that aim narrowly at humanitarian relief or refugee issues in the short term, while others emphasise the continuum from relief to economic development that involves multisectoral approaches. Some of these organisations are church-related, and they define their aims in that light.

Both on women's issues, dealt with by Chen, and on arrangements for economic development, taken up by Uvin, some NGOs define their goals in terms of social ideology. For some feminists, wholesale changes in society are the goal, while some of the NGOs sponsoring grassroots development groups seek substantial changes in dominant economic structures.

Organisations that oppose the United Nations or the treatment of global issues by means of intergovernmental cooperation are unlikely to be visible in case studies focused on topics on the UN agenda. Yet it may be assumed that such organisations exist or that some NGO experience would lead to deep disillusion and therefore general opposition. These would be covered in a revolutionary/ rejectionist dimension. Some hints of such NGO aims occur in Uvin's essay, and by implication in Sollis's queries about the future of NGO programmes in Central America. Jönsson and Söderholm note that some AIDS activist NGOs find it difficult to cope with the UN milieu; they may well come to oppose both international programmes and policy making.

The case studies provide examples of every type of tactical mode in NGO strategy with regard to the United Nations and other authority. Probably a fair estimate would be that around UN headquarters and those of associated agencies advocacy/lobbying are the primary modes. Human rights activities analysed by Gaer provide a clear and familiar example. The coalitions described by Ritchie adopt a similar tactical mode, which also characterises NGO tactics at the global conferences on women and on the environment analysed by Chen and Conca.

The more passive monitoring mode is less visible than the positive tactic of advocacy/lobbying. It means following in an expert or at least informed manner the developments related to topics of particular interest to an NGO. All NGOs that concentrate on intergovernmental contacts and international conferences sponsored by the United Nations and associated agencies use the monitoring mode. Although the essays here provide little direct data on monitoring, it can be taken for granted in combination with the activities reported. In fact, Gaer's discussion of human rights indicates that intergovernmental organisations rely on the monitoring capacities of such independent NGOs as Amnesty International and Human Rights Watch. It is clearly also implied with regard to women's NGOs and coalitions described by Chen and Ritchie. On other governance lines, the frequency of monitoring is less certain, but the Sollis and Uvin essays give attention to intermediary organisations that could monitor UN activities on behalf of NGOs, but are unequipped to do so.

Mass propaganda and its specialised form, mass demonstrations, do not figure prominently in many of the case studies. Public reporting of human rights violations by NGOs may reach a wide audience and could be part of a mass propaganda programme, as hinted by Gaer, while reporting by environmental organisations, according to Conca, has a similar character. Women's organisations, too, have used such devices as the international tribunal reported by Chen. In these cases, mass communications media constitute an intervening organisational factor. This is not treated in the essays and in general poses difficult problems of description and analysis, which could be the nucleus of further specialised research.

A few single-issue NGOs concentrating on AIDS have used mass demonstrations to attempt to affect international conferences. The large presence of NGOs at the UN Conference on Environment and Development and at the women's conference could be viewed as mild mass demonstrations. In fact, showy mass demonstrations may only rarely be possible in international meetings; they could be easier to mount for local and national authorities, although this too is more a hypothesis than a finding.

Output dimensions

If strategic dimensions help disclose NGO relationships with authority, the output dimensions point in the direction of receivers of ultimate products, beneficiaries or end users. These dimensions tend markedly to reinforce each other and to overlap. One of the output dimensions, political feedback among governmental units, refers to the sometimes circuitous routes whereby the results of monitoring efforts and advocacy/lobbying are put before NGO membership and used in attempts to affect the policies of local or national authorities. This feedback process connects the decision-making in the UN system with that of national and local governments.

Because of its circuitousness, the process is difficult to trace, but the belief in its existence is manifest in the activities of NGOs in the human rights, women's movement and AIDS fields. Sollis provides data on how regional intermediary organisations in Central America affect governmental decisions in the region. Similar incidents are reported by Donini and Natsios.

Information, developed by NGOs of every persuasion, is stock in trade for them in looking towards ultimate consumers. It is a basic tool of political feedback in, for instance, the promotion of human rights as described by Gaer. A specialised use of information is in providing expert advice, noted in Chen's essay on women's movements, and is a standby of development NGOs at country sites. Other NGOs offer expert advice on the formation of grassroots organisations.

The case studies illustrate many instances of attempts to mobilise opinion by encouraging leadership. This is a significant function of intermediary organisations and an outcome sought by NGO participation in international conferences. The NGO activity in Central America, referred to by Sollis, in part had this aim. It is also a possible spin-off from the humanitarian activities analysed by Natsios, and is closely related to coalition-formation among NGOs described by Ritchie.

Nongovernmental organisations furnish material goods in humanitarian relief situations and in development activities, as illustrated in the studies by Natsios,

Sollis and Uvin. As mentioned earlier, this output is the mainstay of most NGO budgets. In humanitarian relief, large-scale distribution of material goods may occur, while in economic development the amounts are likely to be limited by the scale of projects, particularly by NGOs that tend to work in communities and on a small scale. NGOs also furnish material goods to each other in small amounts in the course of encouragement of networks and education of specific publics. Although the case studies do not take up this activity specifically, it is known that much trading of published materials among NGOs takes place, especially during intermediary functions and large gatherings. This was certainly the case with the women's movement and with human rights NGOs during the major gatherings documented by Chen and Gaer.

All NGOs implicitly encourage the creation of networks. This is quite explicit in the formation of the coalitions described by Ritchie and others. It was a by-product of the formal organising in Central America described by Sollis. Participation in global conferences, described by Conca and Chen, has this same effect. The human rights NGOs are old hands at trading information, a defining function of networks. Similar network-building was a prominent feature of NGO participation in transnational AIDS cooperation analysed by Jönsson and Söderholm.

Networking may link to education of specific publics. In this activity, NGOs seek to put before selected persons, such as senior officials of a bureaucracy, or business leaders in a country or a community, basic information about the subjects with which they are concerned. The implicit goal is to raise the level knowledge so that informed discourse can follow. Gaer and Chen demonstrate how well human rights NGOs and those involved with women's rights use this technique. Some NGOs are known deliberately to seek to inform academic audiences, although little evidence emerges from the case studies. With the education of members of a specific public, the possibility of further informal contact is heightened.

Negative potentials

The case studies as a whole suggest a vast range of energetic activities by nongovernmental organisations in many sectors of human life, whether dominated by the state apparatus or left to civil society. NGOs keep in touch with each activity by attenuated lines of communication and informal networks, some of which extend into governments and intergovernmental agencies. In international cooperation around the UN system, the case studies distinguish a large variety of dynamic practices and relationships. None of the case studies suggests anything approaching a static situation, although the direction of change can hardly be confidently discerned. Nor would it be accurate to think of this vast and highly pluralistic set of relationships as a substitute for the state.

Although the growth of NGOs may indicate vibrant participation in a civil society, it also suggests a potential difficulty. A modicum of state power remains necessary to support the essential order underpinning a society and to avoid civil war. The phenomenon of failed states suggests that 'inadequate stateness' may partly explain collapse. Moreover, nongovernmental organisations may compete for scarce resources. Without fungible resources, those going to NGOs from the United Nations Development Program's (UNDP) country allocations, for example, are unavailable for governments. Pluralism may have unintended costs if NGOs exacerbate the problem of inadequate central government capacity.

Yet, both international and local NGOs have become an unavoidable reality in the efforts by a rudimentary international community to respond to global problems. Because NGOs are increasingly important in world politics, theoretical and practical understandings of their activities are essential in comprehending the problems and prospects of the UN system. If the case studies open a window on this understanding, a great deal more needs to be done to approach a satisfactory and satisfying level of knowledge.

Both IGOs and NGOs thus have an intimate connection to the more general problem of global governance. The culture and character of nongovernmental organisations inclines them to act, rather than to contemplate and reflect. That adds yet more poignancy to exploring the relationships between IGOs, governments and NGOs in the context of global governance.

Ambiguities and dilemmas of NGO and UN interactions

In addition to the lessons and the consensus observations that resulted from the analyses in the preceding case studies, their discussion in Toronto, and our own research, several ambiguities also emerge, and present dilemmas facing policy makers. As such, they also constitute the skeleton of a future research agenda for scholars and policy analysts.

- The naïve and exaggerated notion that the outcome of NGO efforts is universally worthwhile is, in fact, contradicted by experience and analysis. There is no shortage of achievements, for example ranging from framing the agenda for human rights, women and the environment to delivery of technical assistance and humanitarian relief. At the same time, some activities that originally seemed justified by an implementing nongovernmental organisation have backfired in the longer run. Prominent examples can be drawn from the humanitarian arena, where the well-intentioned facilitation of the movement of refugees contributed to 'ethnic cleansing' and to the erosion of international norms. The development arena, too, is laden with examples of projects that were designed to introduce new technologies and production schemes, but that helped to destroy local capacities and the fabric of social structures. In short, any responsible NGO must try to anticipate negative externalities.
- Following this ambiguity is another one related to the mixture of conflict, competition, cooperation and cooptation as nongovernmental organisations determine how close their links should be with states or organisations of the UN system. These four 'Cs' could be viewed as a spectrum along which there are rather unclear boundaries; probably most would aim at the middle two categories on competition and cooperation. Even the extremes of conflict and cooptation can bring benefits, as several NGOs have demonstrated by using confrontational or rejectionist strategies (within the AIDS and environmental movements, for instance), or by becoming well integrated into UN program-

ming exercises for humanitarian emergencies. Moreover, as the examinations of cooperation in Central America or the coalition-building efforts within InterAction or the International Council of Voluntary Agencies (ICVA) suggest, there are few zero-sum outcomes. Policy makers and analysts are left with trying to determine the advantages and disadvantages of any partnership, at least for the present, on a case-by-case basis.

- The outcome that particular NGOs seek determines whether NGOs are better served by trying to define an issue narrowly (for example women and the environment) at the grassroots level and to concentrate efforts on well-circumscribed targets within logical organisational targets (for example the forthcoming Women's Conference in Beijing or the UN Environmental Programme) or, alternatively, whether it is better to 'mainstream' such issues into wider global concerns. To continue with these examples, it may be that both the causes of women's rights and sustainable development are better served by focusing educational efforts and advocacy upon more general issues of investment and development within the World Bank. The potential payoff from a change in policy by a major mainstream actor may dwarf more spectacular rhetorical gains in more narrowly focused institutional settings with ambitious agendas. Once again, generalising about the desired nature of a response depends on better data and analyses than we possess now. In fact, it may be that progress requires simultaneous efforts at both levels.
- The growth in NGO activity has had an impact at both ends of the spectrum of organisational size. On the one hand, a handful of 'super' nongovernmental organisations is emerging. In the humanitarian arena this means that eight to ten large conglomerates of international NGOs account for what may be 80% of the financial value of assistance in complex emergencies. Some of these are also involved in other operational areas with the UN system; but the same generalisations about human rights, the environment and women do not apply because there are no 'super' NGOs in these areas. With diminishing real public resources for development assistance, of which very little (perhaps 4% to 5%) has been devoted to education and advocacy, there are few 'super' agencies. At the other end of the spectrum—the community and local levels—the erosion and sometimes failure of state authority has permitted the emergence of an ever-increasing number of NGOs. Moreover, small and even minuscule international NGOs are also increasingly involved in the entire range of activities undertaken by the UN system. An evaluation of the advantages and disadvantages of the growth at both ends of the spectrum depends upon the issue area and may even depend upon the observer's evaluation of the necessity for enhancing the state capacity to provide at least a modicum of services. Although there is no nostalgia for the national security state of the past, clearly there is a downside to inadequate stateness.
- NGOs exist at the community, local, national, regional and international levels. These levels are obvious ones for analysis, but too little is known about links among them and about the direct and indirect feedback among the various levels. For example, powerful and influential international NGOs working on the AIDS pandemic can avoid the regulatory power of local and national authorities by linking directly with grassroots nongovernmental organisations.

NGO PARTICIPATION IN THE INTERNATIONAL POLICY PROCESS

Rather than direct confrontation, community-based and local NGOs working on human rights or the environment may decide to embarrass their state authorities indirectly through an international conference or a communication from an intergovernmental governing body. The relative merits of various tactics depend upon evaluations, yet to be accomplished, detailing and comparing the results of previous efforts.

- The nature of representation within nongovernmental organisations as well as within their coalitions, and by NGOs within international gatherings, is a source of some perplexity if not ambiguity for analysts. NGOs themselves are not necessarily democratic, which raises the question of who represents what to whom. Elections are hardly frequent occurrences within NGOs, which do not function the way representative governments do. And the elites of large NGOs at the summit or even at lower levels of expenditures may hardly be different from those of IGOs or the governments that they supposedly confront. NGO leaders may push their own personal agendas rather than those of constituents. Nevertheless, the introduction of nongovernmental concerns into international dialogue is healthy. Perhaps the best that can be hoped for may be a kind of crude balance at the local, national and international levels in which a mixture of governmental, intergovernmental and nongovernmental voices more closely reflects reality than a state-dominated framework with only a smattering of intergovernmental input.

On a related issue, the previous essays suggest that the demand by local and international NGOs for the right to be represented in international forums has not been matched with an adequate effort to define concomitant responsibilities to accompany such rights. Within certain NGO families, efforts to formulate codes of conduct that move in the direction of defining minimal obligations have been made. Numerous dilemmas are associated with the various forms of representation. Few unambiguous guidelines orient managers and decision-makers who seek to improve democratisation of the nongovernmental sector.

- The terms 'cooperation', 'collaboration', and 'coordination' are sprinkled liberally throughout international discourse and in the preceding essays. These concepts suggest a dilemma: cooperation and collaboration may be good, but on whose terms? Everyone favours coordination, but no one wishes to be coordinated. Joint ventures among NGOs and between them and members of the UN system involve unexpected as well as expected costs—human, temporal, financial, and lost autonomy—as well as benefits. Some experts argue that greater cooperation, coherence and centralisation are essential, especially during acute humanitarian emergencies. Others argue that the positive impact emanating from the diversity of NGOs and from competition among themselves and between this sector and the UN system outweighs purported benefits from pooling efforts. In any case, the different values and operating styles between NGOs and intergovernmental organisations, along with the NGOs' ferocious insistence on maintaining independence, probably preclude any far-reaching harmonisation of efforts.
- Independent statistical data from the Organization of Economic Cooperation and Development (OECD) and other institutions and the case studies here

indicate that NGOs are receiving greater resources from both private and public sources. Both governments and UN organisations increasingly rely on NGOs to deliver services. Nongovernmental organisations collectively now disperse more official development assistance (ODA) than does the entire UN system (excluding the Washington-based financial institutions). Moreover, in many countries they are powerful sources of employment and foreign exchange. This development is strikingly evident in complex emergencies where state authority is extremely weak and sometimes nonexistent. This trend calls for deeper analysis on the basis of more complete data. At a time of diminishing and fungible resources, financing local and international NGOs is sometimes simply subtracted from that originally intended for governments. Moreover, some NGOs employ dramatic images to elicit contributions from individuals and from bilateral donors and intergovernmental secretariats. This public relations technique often works against the more nuanced messages intended to educate donor constituencies about the root causes of conflict and poverty.

- The quality and characteristics of particular UN institutions can help or hinder the development of an effective partnership between local and international NGOs. Virtually nothing is known about the sociology and anthropology of the cultures within the UN family, except that they are clearly not monolithic. UNHCR and UNICEF not only contract for services from NGOs but also endeavour to involve them more intimately in project formulation and policy consultations. This may reflect the fact that these institutions have a relatively high number of staff members who themselves have previously worked in NGOs or are at least sympathetic to many of their values and programmatic emphases. This is very different from the relationships between the World Bank and nongovernmental organisations. Part of the explanation may, no doubt, lie in the possibility that the staff and managers in Washington know less about the strengths of both local and international NGOs. Moreover, the dimensions of the World Bank's projects and the incentives to its managers for large-scale implementation would seem to impede closer working relations with NGOs. Yet such comments are merely speculative, since too few resources have been devoted to analysing the composition and behaviour of international secretariats.

- Beginning with the establishment of the United Nations, and especially since the General Assembly adopted Resolution 1296 in 1968, officials from governmental, intergovernmental, and nongovernmental organisations have invested a seemingly disproportionate amount of energy in determining which NGOs qualify for official consultative status. Our own observations and virtually all of the case studies suggest that formal relationships may not be the most essential element in determining the efficacy, power and overall impact of NGO efforts, even efforts to influence opinion and help set international standards. In fact, the superficial characterisation of informality as marginal or weak does not appear to apply to the efforts to foster women's rights or appropriate policy reactions to the threat of AIDS. Moreover, other types of informal relationships, such as those that characterise efforts by knowledgeable technicians and are often labelled epistemic communities within the environmental and other arenas, may be every bit as influential as NGOs that enjoy consultative status.

Some concluding thoughts

Three overall conclusions, which may not be surprising but which are hardly trivial, may be set out with some confidence. First and most evident, far too little useful statistical information or even basic descriptive information exists about the phenomenon of NGOs that are active in the milieu surrounding the United Nations system. This makes theory-building and policy recommendations a hazardous, if not totally nonfeasible, undertaking. We have no convincing or well-tested models. This reflects the difficulties of groping in a rapidly evolving, uncertain global society.

Second, the age of innocence is over for NGOs as they relate to the UN system. There is a need to understand better and to contextualise fully any programmatic activity before taking action. The staff and constituencies of NGOs have generally believed that human and financial resources devoted to policy analysis and evaluation were irrelevant and even wasteful. They have preferred action to reflection. However, visceral reactions are no longer an adequate basis on which to base projects and programmes. The wrong kind of assistance to displaced persons, for instance, can worsen their situation and respect for international norms, and perhaps even prolong conflicts. Inappropriate development—involving the continued treatment of women as second-class citizens or the destruction of non-sustainable resources—may not necessarily be better than none at all. Fundraising of a sensational nature, even if effective, can undermine longer-run efforts to improve public knowledge about issues of direct consequence. Disarmament efforts occasionally may work against the type of security required to conduct normal activities. All of this is by way of saying that more reflection and less action is sometimes in order, and that NGO resources can and should legitimately be spent on analysis.

Third, we return to the point of departure and the final part of this volume's title, 'global governance'. Several prominent intellectuals, as well as august commissions, have struggled with this notion. We, however, posited the straightforward idea that it consists of more ordered and more reliable responses to problems that go beyond the individual and even collective capacities of states. The agreed and proverbial bottom line for all definitions of global governance, however, consists of enhanced transparency, accountability and participation. Under the right conditions, the growth in the number of local and international NGOs and in their roles and responsibilities at all levels, along with their increasing relevance to the operational and normative activities of the UN system, provides more opportunities to satisfy the requirements for improved transparency, accountability and participation.

[18]

Alternatives 23 (1998), 149–173

Social Movements and the Problem of Globalization

Cecelia Lynch*

There is a developing understanding among some "progressive" contemporary social movement groups that economic globalization poses the primary obstacle to the fulfillment of their goals. This understanding is well placed and overdue. Yet any effective response to globalization is predicated upon the ability of social movements to articulate a meaningful normative, or discursive, challenge. The particular form of contemporary social movements' inherited internationalist focus, along with both activists' and theorists' past rejection of issues and politics deemed too class-based, has resulted in what we might call the discursive demobilization of movements on questions of economic praxis. This article thus seeks to open dialogue about the ability of what currently constitutes the normative challenge to globalization on the part of contemporary movements to reverse this discursive demobilization.

"Globalization," a phenomenon that succeeds the concepts of "modernization" and "interdependence," now constitutes the touchstone of any discussion of the contemporary world political economy. At the same time, there is heightened interest in the role of social movements in processes of change in world politics, and consequently in what is termed by some "transnational" or "global" civil society.[1] As Stephen Gill points out, economic globalization affects society, on the group, national, and transnational levels: "[T]here are connections between the processes of economic globalization, and the way the outlook, expectations, and social choices of individuals and groups are being reshaped and reconfigured."[2]

Although globalization is much discussed, disparaged, or touted, depending on the audience, disagreement remains concerning whether it is highly or marginally significant, new or old, and a phenomenon of

*Dept. of Political Science, Northwestern University, Scott Hall, 601 University Place, Evanston, Ill., 60208-1006

lasting or ephemeral import. Consensus exists, however, on the definitional core of globalization. This consensus is perhaps best expressed by a prominent US journalist, who has defined globalization as "that loose combination of free-trade agreements, the Internet and the integration of financial markets that is erasing borders and uniting the world into a single, lucrative, but brutally competitive, marketplace."[3] Globalization promotes "an agenda of economic liberalization" in trade, investment, and finance. Many believe, for better or worse, that globalization also results in making states increasingly powerless to control their own economies; others charge that states adopt a rhetoric of powerlessness to divest themselves of broader social responsibilities.[4] In many ways, of course, the concept of globalization is not a new one.[5] The brutal competition for markets and profits has long divided international society into "winners" and "losers," or, in the current lexicon of some social movement activists, a system of "global apartheid."[6] Yet it is arguable that the work of contemporary social movements is currently being affected by global market processes in new ways, and that this fact opens up the potential for movement groups to make decisions regarding their stance vis-à-vis globalization that are capable of having a significant normative impact.

In thinking about the relationship between social movements and processes of globalization, one can make a type of causal claim that "the capitalist social movement," which, as Warren Magnussen reminds us, is involved, has generated a widespread reaction to the economic well-being that it promises but fails to deliver.[7] This causal claim is often heard regarding, for example, the genesis of right-wing party movements in Europe and militia movements in the United States, and the renaissance of nationalist movements everywhere. One can also claim that, regardless of the forces that generate particular social movements, globalization affects their goals, strategies, and meaning for international politics. Indeed, the control over decisionmaking wielded by market and financial power across the globe arguably constitutes the major challenge for the realization of the goals of contemporary social movements of all kinds—whether "progressive," right-wing, militarist, or xenophobic. I emphasize the second type of claim in this article: that contemporary globalization has significant implications for the work and meaning of the environmental, peace, and "rights-based" transnational movements; that is, the "universalistic" or "value-oriented" movements much analyzed since the late 1970s.[8] Focusing on the effects of globalization on these types of social movements limits the analysis largely to contemporary Western-based movements, but it also has unique features that in turn beg questions regarding the relationship between theories of social movements and civil society, and praxis.

Thus I first want to describe what social movements are in fact doing to address the "problem of globalization" (insofar as they perceive it to be a problem).[9] Next, I wish to assess the problem as well as potential of a normative challenge to globalization. In order to do this, I compare the constellation of contemporary movements against globalization with that of movement activism on the issue of "peace" and militarism at earlier points in the century. Finally, I wish to make several observations regarding the relationship between theorizing about social movements and civil society, and the practices of social movements themselves in world politics. In other words, analyzing the "problem of globalization" for social movements begs questions of what, in the end, social movements are capable of, how we might theorize about it, and the relationship between the construction of theoretical claims itself and the actions and discourses of social movements. I do not pretend to answer the question of whether the challenge of social movements to globalization can be successful, but do hope to highlight some of the major issues that social movements must confront in the process of making such a challenge, and that theorists must confront in the process of analyzing it.

The Problem of Globalization for Social Movements

The peace, environmental, and human-rights movements have each come up against processes of globalization in their efforts to achieve their goals. Peace movements (in the West) have been relatively quiescent since 1987, when the intermediate-range nuclear (INF) treaty, soon to be followed by START II, was signed by the United States and the Soviet Union. During the past two years or so, peace issues have received occasional bursts of renewed attention, first in 1995 when the Non-Proliferation Treaty (NPT) came up for renewal at the United Nations, and second when a Comprehensive Test Ban (CTB) was finally negotiated by that same body.

Debate on both of these treaties has focused on controls on existing stocks of nuclear weapons, especially given the highly charged issue of who—nuclear or nonnuclear power, First World or Third World, East or West, North or South—should bear the brunt of the effects of such restraints on sovereignty. The NPT, for example, has several essential components: controls on the spread of weapons-grade fissile material and weapons themselves, commitments on the part of nuclear-weapons powers to disarm, and "progress on measures designed to halt the arms race and to advance the cause of nuclear and general disarmament."[10] Yet the last component was barely given a hearing during the debate on the treaty's renewal. One major reason for this was that, given the political tension between the treaty's first two goals and the fact that many Third World states were willing, in the post–Cold War era, to make their agreement to sign an indefinite treaty contingent upon considerable concessions by nuclear-weapons powers, the desire to secure renewal trumped considerations of insuring compliance with all of the treaty's provisions. But the fact that renewal hinged on this issue also begs the question of how easy it is to ignore or drop challenges to market prerogatives, even when these markets concern highly sophisticated weapons and weapons of mass destruction.

Any challenge to "market" logic of meeting weapons demand with supplies has been made more difficult by the Clinton administration's change in policy regarding arms sales. The new administration policy, which essentially commodifies weapons, eliminates many of the separate rules by which arms were sold and transferred during the Cold War. This policy, by making explicit a new norm to commodify and hence deregulate arms in the post–Cold War era, has eroded further, and more seriously, the possibility of challenging the arms trade.[11]

Today, the major issue regarding constraints on weapons markets concerns the recent treaty to ban antipersonnel land mines. The debate surrounding this question is illustrative of the problem of the arms trade for peace movements: land mines are receiving considerable attention because their use has devastated the countryside in increasing numbers of states (Vietnam, Cambodia, Laos, Mozambique, Somalia, Bosnia—to name a selection) and because they are maiming increasing numbers of civilians, including children. The manifestations of land mines are thus visible (and a potential danger) to any foreign correspondent or CNN reporter. But land mines form only a small part of the arms equation for peace movements. The normative adherence to market forces—i.e., the belief that such forces should not or cannot be effectively challenged—means that social movements concerned with peace must parcel out the issue of the arms trade, addressing it bit by bit rather than head on.

The relationship between forces of globalization and human-rights movements is also problematic. Contemporary globalization has encouraged the creation of bonded labor markets throughout much of the world. But much of the focus of transnational human-rights movements has been on political and civil rights, torture, and genocide. With the decline of the International Labour Organization

as an effective voice and the decimation of labor unions in most industrialized societies, strengthened norms of labor rights have fallen
by the wayside. Moreover, UN rights conferences and conventions,
including the convention on the Rights of the Child promoted by
humanitarian NGOs and the series of international women's conferences promoted by women's groups, can both contribute to and dis-
tract attention from the ways in which globalization threatens basic
labor rights internationally. Where challenges to indentured servi-
tude, slave labor (especially in prostitution) and child labor (especially in the carpet and toy industries) do exist, they illuminate particular injustices while forgoing the opportunity to challenge the
"right" of firms to base investment decisions on the relative cost and
malleability of labor markets.[12]

The environmental movement's relationship and reaction to
processes of globalization is both similar and different to those of
the peace and human-rights movements. The environmental movement, since its experience in preparing for the Rio conference
(UNCED, the UN Conference on the Environment and Development), has moved toward direct conflict with market logic of extraction and production. On the international level, processes of globalization were called into question at Rio. The very notion of
"sustainable development," a major outcome of social movement participation in the conference, posed a challenge to market forces, in
that it put forth a norm of "fettered development," or development
constrained by attention to local needs and measures of environmental protection.[13] Overt international recognition of a sustainable
development norm represented the hope for significant expansion
of successful local efforts in many parts of the world to brake the
growing market control of environmental resources. Yet subsequently, environmental groups have been severely disappointed by
the implementation of Agenda 21, pointing out that most of the
funds provided to encourage environmentally sound economic policies have been funneled to multinational conglomerates that have
profited from them at the expense of local communities.

Perhaps more seriously, the push for "free" trade and low-wage
labor markets has directly affected the unity and work of the environmental movement, especially in North America. The debate over
the North American Free Trade Agreement (NAFTA) split the movement, resulting in bitter feelings and continued debate. At issue
was whether the so-called "side agreements" negotiated as part of
NAFTA could provide sufficient environmental and health safeguards to labor in all three countries and to communities, especially
along the US-Mexican border where the experience of *maquilladoras*

demonstrated the social and health costs of environmental degradation. Again, the implications of globalization for the environmental
movement concern in part whether or not the movement acquiesces
in parceling its goals. The NAFTA negotiations, including the
process of bargaining between well-funded North American environmental groups such as the Natural Resources Defense Council
(NRDC) and the US and Mexican governments, succeeded in creating a rift between movement groups on the question of whether or
not claims regarding the health of the environment and the impact
of environmental degradation on the health of workers could be
separated.[14]

It is possible, of course, that the logic of capital accumulation
and unequal distribution always formed the primary obstacle to the
realization of movements' goals (of demilitarization, the preservation of ecosystems, and respect for rights regardless of gender, race,
religion, income, or social position), but that it is only with the end
of the Cold War that the negative effects of this logic have been able
to take center stage.[15] Where social movements have recognized the
relationship between market practices and the fulfillment or lack
thereof of their own objectives, this recognition has been partial at
best. Yet suggestions that the market, capitalism, corporate power,
structural adjustment policies of international financial institutions,
and various other forms and nomenclatures of globalization hinder
goals of peace, human rights, and environmental protection have
begun to abound within social-movement and NGO literature, despite the fact that they often remain tangential to other concerns.

Examples of increasing references to globalization on the part of
nongovernmental organizations (NGOs) are easy to find in reports
from the NGO fora of the series of UN conferences held "to review
international agreements in the run up to the millenium."[16] For example, the "women's linkage caucus" formed in preparation for the
September 1995 Beijing conference to increase communication
among activists from all regions of the world, censured "the market
driven global economic paradigm," and advocated "international
labor and employment standards that will protect workers in free
trade zones with adequate employment, health and safety standards"
and "pricing mechanisms, trade policies, fiscal incentives and other
policy instruments that positively affect . . . women small producers'
decisions about efficient and sustainable use of natural resources."[17]
The unofficial women's movement at Beijing also claimed primary
responsibility for insuring that provisions citing the negative effects
of globalization on the environment and economic well-being, and
weaker language regarding its effects on peace, were included in the

final document as barriers to improving the condition of women worldwide.[18] Other UN conferences, including both the UN Social Summit in Copenhagen in March 1995, and Habitat II (the second UN Conference on Human Settlements) in Istanbul in June 1996, were called explicitly to focus on global increases in poverty and consequent social dislocations.[19] The "20/20 compact" proposed at Copenhagen ("a commitment on the part of interested developed and developing country partners to allocate, on average, 20 per cent of overseas development assistance and 20 per cent of the national budget, respectively, to basic social programmes")[20] was in essence a move to extend the concept of the welfare state to the global level. The result of the NGO debates on this proposal at Copenhagen, according to one participant, was that, "whether planned or not, one theme emerged almost everywhere, in different forms and language. Many NGOs described the baleful impact of the globalised economy on their communities; there were constant appeals for the reassertion of 'civil society,' by whatever terms."[21]

Thus there is sporadic evidence that the "problem of globalization" has taken hold as a common integrating force and foe for contemporary social movements. The most significant move to challenge globalization, however, has emerged in the wake of the NAFTA and subsequent WTO (World Trade Organization) debates among movement groups. A constellation of groups and individuals formed in 1994, the International Forum on Globalization (IFG), is attempting a frontal attack on globalization.[22] According to its literature, its "initial goal . . . was simple: Introduce a new concept: *economic globalization* as the central factor affecting people's jobs, communities, and the environment."[23] The IFG thus has articulated a stance that puts forth an analysis of the "problem" that addresses what is "new" about the contemporary era of globalization, forged links between causes, including overt attempts to organization with labor, and developed (or begun to develop) a normative stance that seeks to negate the power of market ideology and promote an alternative.

The IFG's analysis of globalization is straightforward, represents considerable research, and is not particularly unusual, though it might be stated more baldly than most academic analyses.[24] What is of interest is its explicit connection of global market processes to negative effects for the specific goals of the social movements it claims to represent (i.e., sustainability, rights, democracy, and implicitly, "peace"). In essence, the IFG argues that "the world's corporate and political leadership is undertaking a restructuring of global politics and economics that may prove as historically significant as any event since the industrial revolution."[25] What is "new" about contemporary globalization is the virtual deregulation of financial flows along with a push for "freer" trade made more severe by the opening up of cheap labor markets in the formerly Communist societies of Eastern Europe, in the highly populated countries of East and South Asia, and in Latin American nations no longer devastated by civil war. Democracy, human rights, the "natural world," and peace, according to this logic, are threatened on a global scale.

The imperative of "structural adjustment" imposed on countries in the South (primarily by the Northern financial sector through the International Monetary Fund) parallels the ever-increasing threat of firms to move production facilities away from countries in the North due to their high labor costs. The result is self-proclaimed helplessness on the part of governments, the prevention of the development of social welfare policies that would guarantee economic and social rights in the South and the dismantling of the social welfare net in the North. An additional result is a continuing threat to environmental resources, as companies push to relocate in areas in which regulations are lax or nonexistent.[26] For some, these effects of contemporary globalization can be traced to the financial and monetary crises of the 1970s, which led to de facto agreement on the part of corporations (supported by governments) to drive down the costs of production by whatever means necessary. The "crises of the 70s," then, marked the debut of a normative reorientation of governments away from social welfare guarantees and toward supporting the interests of firms that increasingly operated transnationally.[27]

The IFG has attempted to transnationalize itself beyond the Northern and Western hemispheres, with partial success. Its membership represents approximately forty organizations, primarily in the United States, Canada, and the United Kingdom, but also in South and East Asia, South Africa, and Latin America. Moreover, NAFTA and the WTO jolted mainstream environmental group members of the IFG such as the Friends of the Earth and the Sierra Club into making overt attempts to organize with labor in the United States, where the relationship between labor and "progressive" social movements had been in decline since the early 1970s. Thus the IFG represents the most significant contemporary effort to put forth both a transnational and transclass challenge to economic globalization.

The relationship between environmental groups and organized labor is resulting in a broadening of the environmentalists' concept of "sustainability" to incorporate the notion that living wages and health rights are necessary for creating sustainable working conditions and political communities.[28] The IFG's analysis of the problem of globalization sees environmental protection, the promotion of democracy, and human rights as interconnected, and thus promotes linking the causes of "progressive" social movements with the cause of labor.[29] It also continues the focus on "quality of life" issues and internal democratization that formed an essential component of the goals of the "new social movements" of the 1970s and 1980s. For example, activists decry globalization for reorienting the purpose (and thus content) of education exclusively toward increasing market viability. They oppose "the consensus vision" of investment in education and training "as a means for achieving a high-tech future . . . to survive in competitive world markets," with an alternative conceptualization "not just for a narrow vision of the economy, but as a tool for quality of life, a citizen's right, an investment in the community."[30]

Given these understandings of globalization and the interconnection of progressive causes with labor, social-movement activists in the IFG are attempting to create a normative stance that provides a discursive alternative to globalization and reverses the normative power that the faith in free trade and the fear of losing one's competitive position holds across social strata. This attempt at instituting a normative reversal and creating a new conceptual apparatus to compete with that provided by globalization focuses on terms that have demonstrated considerable discursive power for social movements in the recent past. First, the IFG attempts to delegitimize the current order by emphasizing the loss of control over economies and social welfare, on the part of governments (local, state, regional), peoples, and communities. It highlights the inequities resulting from globalization through frequent use of the term "global apartheid."[31] Second, it continues the emphasis on the necessity for "sustainable development" first articulated at the Rio conference, which has become a staple of NGO demands at UN conferences. Although some argue that the term sustainable development has become an overused slogan and a trope for governments, the choice of terminology is important because of its power to suggest a particular normative stance that can go beyond mere sloganeering. The term *global apartheid,* for example, connotes an international economic system that is unjust by definition, one that is comprised of winners (few in number) and losers (the majority), and in which the rules and practices of the system favor the winners and keep the losers in a position of subjugation. Sustainable development combines agreement with the modern faith that progress is possible (through "development"), while implying that current developmental practices are short-run and therefore shortsighted, benefit the few at the expense of the many, and must be reoriented.

The IFG is still in the process of debating and defining the contours of its normative alternative(s). Much of the IFG's normative program thus far, however, focuses on notions of "relocalization." Localizing economic control reasserts the centrality of the concept of "sustainable development" by continuing its insistence on small-scale, "democratic" decisionmaking regarding the production and distribution of goods, but particular articulations of relocalization also go beyond sustainable development on both the normative and material/policy levels.

One articulation, for example, is the concept of "the new protectionism."[32] The "key issue," for its authors, "is to put governments at a local, national and regional level back in control of their economies, and to relocalise and rediversify them."[33] The new protectionism is, in essence, an "international movement towards relocalised economies." The program thus involves controls on imports, exports, capital, and transnational corporations (including a "site here to sell here" policy), all with the purpose of keeping "trade and aid," as well as reinvestment, as local as possible. It also promotes resource taxes to pay for costs associated with the transition to localized production. Despite the emphasis on "the aim of allowing [sic] localities to produce as much of their food, goods and services as they can themselves," the new protectionism's authors insist the program is "neither anti-trade nor autarkic": "Its goal is maximum local trade within diversified sustainable local economies, and minimum long-distance trade; local is used here to mean a part of a country, and regional, a geographic grouping of countries."[34] The new protectionism thus promotes the idea that "protectionism" can be a valuable tool when used in the interests of sustainable development on the local level. In part, it is an attempt to rearticulate the goals of Agenda 21 (from Rio) to provide a more direct challenge to the "free trade/free market" idealization of the contemporary global economy. But it goes beyond previous claims in favor of local control to emphasize local insularity in ways that can easily be labeled autarkic. In the new protectionist construct, not only should localities be *allowed* to produce locally, but "we have got to be as self-reliant as is possible locally. Trade should be local. If you can produce a good and service locally . . . , you should. If you can't get it from the country, go to the region. If you can't get it from the region, then and only then go for long-distance trade."[35]

Militarization/Globalization

The type of normative/discursive contestation of contemporary social, economic, and political practices advanced by the antiglobalization movement at base provides an example of what social movements are able to do most effectively in world politics, that is, delegitimize particular discourses and paths of action in order to legitimize alternatives. Yet the content of normative/discursive challenges to contemporary practices is critical both for the ability of a social movement to legitimize its alternatives and for the shaping of responses to the challenge. Comparing contemporary moves to challenge globalization with attempts earlier in the century to delegitimize militarization and put forth alternatives both highlights the importance of normative contestation and points to problematic aspects of social movements' current discourse on globalization.

The primary, and perhaps only, historical precedents for social movements of various kinds banding together transnationally are the peace movements of the turn of the century, the interwar period, the 1960s, and the 1980s. During each of these periods, coalitions made up of transnational feminist, pacifist, "internationalist," ecology (especially after the 1960s, although an ecological sensibility was present in other movements early in the century), and human-rights movements worked in common to place restraints on states' war-making prerogatives and capacities. Throughout the twentieth century, "peace" activism against war and militarism thus incorporated most other "progressive," "value-oriented" social movements under its wings.

Peace activism points to the importance of normative challenges to entrenched political practices. Peace movements have long worked to delegitimize states' capacities for violence and worked to legitimize alternatives lodged in global international organization.[36] More recently, peace movements' normative stance from the 1960s through its sharpening in the 1980s was capable both of delegitimizing strategies of defense based on nuclear weapons, as Mary Kaldor, E. P. Thompson, and others have argued eloquently, and of articulating discourses of "alternative defense."[37] The wide disjuncture between the notion of "defense" as "protection" and nuclear strategies of annihilation virtually invited delegitimization and begged for alternatives, although even with this inherent lack of credibility, state practices of weapons production and strategy formulation often appeared too entrenched to be overcome. Today, with the former US general in charge of nuclear forces and the former commander of NATO calling for the elimination of existing nuclear arsenals, the notion that war-fighting strategies based on their use could not be called into question seems almost absurd.[38] Yet peace movements during the Cold War had to contend with extremely powerful logics in favor of defense-as-annihilation, making their task of normative contestation quite difficult, and their degree of success in carrying out this task notable.

The "anti-globalization movement," in contrast, is still in its infancy. Nevertheless, it is building a capacity to delegitimize the normative power that aspects of globalization hold in the popular and official consciousness (for example, the necessity of being able to compete in the world marketplace). Widespread malaise about nuclear defense existed during the 1970s and 1980s; widespread unease and uncertainty about economic welfare and the destruction of safety nets exists today, providing a foundation for movement efforts.[39] Today, as movement groups attempt to put together a collective response, even the architects of globalization are worried about its negative effects, and may take steps to stymie a "losers' backlash."[40]

It is, however, unclear if the movement challenging globalization will ever have the breadth of peace movements of the recent past. One major issue involved is the problem of articulating a positive nomenclature to provide an alternative to market capitalism. Earlier in the century, antiwar groups consciously took on the appellation of "peace movement"; but it is unclear what the antiglobalization movement has in common to provide a positive normative foundation. Possibilities are "sustainable development," "local control", and so forth, but local control has normative difficulties, while sustainable development connotes little, explicitly, in the way of connection with "human" rights.

More importantly, however, the normative content of relocalization programs such as the "new protectionism" is problematic. Peace movements, of course, were frequently charged with utopianism and oversimplification, through their advocacy of "solutions" to militarism ranging from unilateral disarmament to multilateral disarmament to regulation and oversight by global international organization. The antiglobalization movement faces normative difficulties that are at least as serious, if not more so. For example, it is one thing to point out the growth of corporate power in generating loss of governmental and individual control in decisions of basic welfare, but quite another to recommend a solution based on a concept of local control that can be criticized as bordering on autarky, despite the protestations of its adherents. Control over decisions of economic well-being are at the heart of the challenge to globalization, as contemporary antiglobalization activists explicitly acknowledge. Nevertheless, an overemphasis on relocalization can easily be dismissed as an antimodern throwback. Its authors recognize the problem, although not directly. Colin Hines, one author of "the new protectionism," tellingly says the following:

> When I'm talking, . . . I love to start by saying "protectionism can be good, protectionism can be good, protectionism can be good." Now, there I watch to see who faints, who puts the sign of the cross. . . . It is so deeply entrenched in . . . most people's psyche, that to protect . . . is somehow bad. But to lay yourself open to the "modern go-go future" is somehow good.[41]

Hines well understands the power of the normative adherence to the free-market ideal, as well as the widespread worry about losing one's "competitive edge." The notion of the new protectionism, like unilateral disarmament, can thus serve an important function, in that it presents a stark alternative to current practices. While the alternative may appear unrealizable or even utopian, its juxtaposition with contemporary practice reveals the latter to be illogical and destructive (for example, nuclear defense based on either MAD (mutual assured destruction) or war-fighting doctrines—or patently unjust—for example, firms "growing the economy" by relocating production and forcing down wages. But the new protectionism ultimately assumes intimate, causal connections between control of well-being, equity among individuals and peoples, and the production and distribution of goods and wealth (i.e., for control to be local, production, investment and trade must also be local) that raise problematic questions for the movement and thus are better disentangled. Supporters of relocalization need to question whether the preaching of across-the-board localization not merely oversimplifies the problems of inequality and poverty associated with globalization, but also glosses over them in its efforts to promote a solution. They also need to revisit more thoroughly the role of state power in staunching and reversing these problems. The issue at stake is whether the contemporary antiglobalization movement will forgo the opportunity to develop the grounds for a sufficiently powerful challenge to globalization's normative headlock.

Social Movements/Civil Society: Problems from the Intersection of Theory and Praxis

Constructing a normative challenge to globalization raises significant issues regarding the relationship between social movements' activities and theorizing about them. First, if the 1970s constituted a critical takeoff period for contemporary forms of global market and financial processes, in that it was marked by economic and fiscal crises that led, in turn, to de facto agreement by firms and governments on the necessity of ongoing measures to drive down production costs, and if, in turn, these measures resulted in the beginning of the end for labor solidarity and the welfare state (where it existed), then there is an interesting parallel with the development of social-movement theory. For the late 1970s and early 1980s was precisely the time when social-movement theory (especially the European, "identity" school of theorizing) began a very influential new trend, based on a strong critique of the capacities of the welfare state. Imbued by the notion of "crisis" in and of the welfare state, theorists of "new social movements" focused on bureaucratic and administrative crises, rather than economic ones. State welfare, labor rights, and social safety nets were believed to be well established, institutionalized, and entrenched. The problem, in the eyes of social-movement theorists, was the ossification of bureaucratic modes of operation that led both to inefficiencies and the inability to address "value-oriented" problems of environmental degradation, self-realization and identity (as in the feminist movement), internal (local) democratization, and peace.[42]

Social-movement theory accompanied its critique of the prototypical European welfare state with another influential move that distinguished "old," "particularistic" social movements, primarily identified with labor and "class," from "new" movements identified with "universalistic" values and goals—most often those of feminism, peace, and environmentalism. The emphasis on internal forms of decisionmaking and democratization in these movements further distinguished them from modes of labor organizing, whose goals were seen to be instrumental and externally oriented rather than internally oriented toward issues of lifestyle, values, and beliefs. The resulting demarcation of "higher-order," universalistic goals and meanings gave rise to the Habermasian notion that in the postwelfare state world, social forces could, somehow, "finish" the Enlightenment project.[43]

Thus theorizing about social movements in the 1970s and 1980s made a double move—from a critique of capitalism to an interest in the "higher goals" of rights, peace, and democracy, and from a focus on "particularistic" movements (that led to the creation of labor syndicalism and policies of social welfare) to movements motivated by "universalistic" values and objectives.[44] Given the considerable overlap between the intellectual leadership of social movements and the intellectuals leading the discussion of social movements, it is a fair question whether the juxtaposition of these theoretical moves, along with the diminishing power of the "old" welfare movements, has abetted the discursive and normative demobilization of social movements over time vis-à-vis the problem of globalization.

Social movements' discursive demobilization vis-à-vis globalization is compounded by the lack of knowledge, or common articulation, of against whom or what any challenge to globalization is targeted. The second interesting problem raised by the intersection of theory and praxis concerns the centrality of challenges to sovereignty. Both international-relations theory and social-movement activists assert various forms of the "decline of sovereignty" thesis as increasingly apt in the post–Cold War world.[45] It is no longer valid, if it ever was, to speak of state sovereignty in rigid terms, and the erosions of sovereign control occasioned by attention to individual human rights, on one hand, and the practices of multinational corporations, on the other, are very real. Yet the decline-of-sovereignty thesis encourages a stance vis-à-vis the state and the world polity that is problematic for any effective normative challenge to globalization.

Again, a comparison with peace movements is instructive. Transnational peace activism during the twentieth century has been clear in its criticisms of the state. State policies, especially those of great powers and superpowers, encouraged militarization and arms races. Given this militarization, and especially the acquisition of ever more destructive forms of weaponry, the state became increasingly unwilling, if not incapable, of protecting its populace adequately and, hence, of fulfilling one quite powerful interpretation of the "social contract." Social movements working for peace reached consensus on the goal of placing constraints on state power, and encouraging a skeptical attitude toward the state and its literally destructive means of providing "security." Constraints were to be provided on the international level—at a minimum by arms limitation and verification agreements and at a maximum by alternative notions of defense and peace. For either a minimum or maximum program to take hold, social movements delegitimized rigid conceptualizations of state sovereignty, legitimized the demobilization of the state's coercive capacities, and encouraged guarantees of controls placed on the state by international mechanisms of oversight.

Thus, for transnational social movements and "global civil society," such as it existed, a critique of state tendencies (toward illogical and dangerous arms races and security strategies) and capacities (as inadequate in and of themselves to reverse dangerous trends) became the norm. The much-talked-about decline of state sovereignty still most often marks the objectives of social movements concerned with the environment, peace, and human rights, in that states are asked to relinquish established practices of economic development, weapons testing, and treatment of subjects. The desire to slough off "the grungy skin of modern statist politics" remains strong.[46] But where the problem of globalization is concerned, this stance vis-à-vis the state, versus that toward the international polity, is thrown into question. Here again, theory meets praxis in an inadequate formulation of the problem and the means to respond to it. "Progressive" social movements (as well as xenophobic ones) are used to promoting solutions that criticize and transcend the state and its capacities, but a return to the state is in all probability necessary to meet the dislocations and poverty generated by the latest round of globalization. For it is not the United Nations, nor in most cases local communities, that can or will provide the social safety net and guarantees to fair remuneration necessary and adequate to social welfare at the turn of the millenium, especially in the likely event that the world falls short of the new protectionist program of localized trade and investment. Thus contemporary social movements must articulate how a return to the state can be possible in an era of sovereign decline. As part of this reconceptualization of state power (or, in other words, figuring out what is to be the "moral capacity of the state"),[47] movements must address the growing belief in state powerlessness vis-à-vis global economic forces.

A final problem for any discursive/normative challenge to globalization on the part of contemporary social movements concerns the amalgam of ideologies that traditionally form part of "progressive" social movements.[48] In each past instance during the century of transnational and transmovement agreement on the issue of "peace," cooperation was made possible by an ideological coalition between "liberal" and "radical/left" or "critical" movement groups. "Liberal" groups' agenda includes individual rights and humanitarian objectives, often paired with an understanding of equality of opportunity that allows many liberals to promote contentious economic ideals such as free trade. "Critical" groups often but do not necessarily identify themselves explicitly with an egalitarian, left-of-center orientation that is skeptical of the capacity of existing political and economic practices and institutions to provide equality, peace, sustainable economic development, and economic and social rights.

It is the existence of this "lib/lab" coalition, beginning in the nineteenth century, that has given rise to the term *civil society* on both the state and global levels. This ideological mix is reflected in attempts to theorize about civil society, from Hegel through Gramsci to the present. Although the specific contexts they were trying to address differed considerably, both Hegel and Gramsci grappled with the role of class and intelligentsia in constituting agents of action to promote the proper modes and ends of life in the public sphere. But Gramsci, and even Hegel despite his grand synthesis, ultimately "resolved" the issue of wherefore civil society by breaking it up into more or less clearly demarcated lines of purpose and function. For Gramsci, the essential components of civil society, whose function is to integrate the state with everyday life, either form part of the hegemonic bloc or demonstrate a counterhegemonic consciousness. Consciousness, not class, ultimately determines one's ability to free oneself of the dominant ideology, overturn the institutional forms of hegemony, create new associational forms, and thereby act in counterhegemonic terms.[49] For Hegel, civil society also plays an integrative, mediating role within and for the state. But the functions of civil society, in Hegel's conceptualization, are best carried out by civil servants, recruited from the bourgeoisie. The working class, in his construct, bears the brunt of inequalities produced by the workings of civil society and the "system of needs," but the associational forms of civil society themselves are inaccessible to workers, and can only mitigate the economic uncertainties suffered by them in the course of their exposure to the vagaries of economic life.[50] Thus, for Gramsci, civil society either integrates liberal ideology or provides a space for critical consciousness to develop, whereas for Hegel, civil society is based upon quasi-modern liberal associational forms whose function is to integrate into the state externally, without genuine participation or representation, those whose interests are most likely to be opposed to such integration. Both presuppose contradictions within society that in effect split liberal forms of consciousness from actual or potential critical ones.

Contemporary theorists of civil society, conversely, most often take for granted the permanence of the lib/lab coalition and attempt to theorize on the basis of it. In the West, twentieth-century experience, again most clearly seen in transnational peace activism, gives rise to an unquestioned acceptance of the coalition, and the issue then becomes how to resolve differences in the context of "plurality" and democratic institutional forms. The stakes involved have shown up more clearly in the East, and formed an inherent component of the problem for Eastern European dissident revivers of civil society as a political concept.[51] Especially after the revolutions of 1989, the problem has become how to reconcile the desire for freedoms on various levels (of access to moneymaking and the market, individual speech, and assembly) with entrenched norms that insure the provision of social welfare.[52]

The attempts of theorists today to come to grips with what "civil society" is and might become represent, in a sense, attempts to understand the possibility of unity between liberal and critical paradigms of governance, notions of economic causality and its effects, and conceptions of moral good. Contemporary debates within and among social movements provide demonstrations of interconnections between paradigms (in rights-based notions of "progress," along with welfare state and labor guarantees) as well as contradictions, seen most vividly in the post–NAFTA/WTO split among movement groups. Cohen and Arato's use of Habermas to put forth a resolution of the contradictions within civil society is perhaps the most serious contemporary theoretical example of such an attempt to reunify paradigms and overcome contradictions.[53] But we might well ask whether such an attempt, theoretical or actual, remains possible given the developing consciousness (as well as material effects) of the "problem of globalization." The eras of peace activism, in which the common foe of social movement groups was *raison d'etat* and the "logic" of power politics, masked the contradictions between paradigms. Today's normative contestation of globalization, however, reveals fissures that are more difficult to bridge.

This criticism of attempts to reunify liberal/critical aspects of civil society differs partially in character from several other contemporary critiques. Richard Falk, for example, recasts the relevant categories of ethical motivation and transformative potential into "modern" versus "postmodern" forms.[54] In other work, he questions whether contemporary liberalism is too "ideologically compact" to accomplish the work of being sufficiently open to either non-Western influences or contemporary criticisms of global economic processes.[55] R. B. J. Walker criticizes the statist nature of most contemporary conceptualizations of civil society, while simultaneously questioning the assumption that one can or should internationalize any essentially Western (or, in the case of Habermas, German) categories.[56] These criticisms all have similarities in that they are dubious of the ability of liberal philosophy and/or economics to provide an adequate basis for meeting contemporary challenges on the global level. But they also point to the constant need for groups critical of the liberal paradigm to broaden their understanding of the bases of critique and alternative possibilities that are grounded in nondominant and/or non-Western social and economic practices.

In a sense, praxis is preceding theory in this domain, as the bourgeois salons of nineteenth-century civil society theorists have already been replaced and complicated by NGOs' unofficial fora at UN conferences, as well as by the increasingly numerous linkages between small, local NGOs working to reverse particular manifestations of "development" and larger, wealthier transnational groups. Activists themselves struggle to cope with the resulting confrontation of practices and beliefs. Instead of salon, some use the metaphor of *bazaar* to connote the "anarchic diversity" with which they must contend, indicating both the breadth of possibility and the sheer diversity of experience that any attempt to globalize civil society must represent.[57] But this confrontation of beliefs and practices also raises the question of whether notions like "sustainable development" can provide a basis for critical reflection and dialogue among activists or whether they easily become tropes that promote the illusion of meaningful action across divides.

This analysis thus suggests the necessity for contemporary social movements to articulate a strategic/normative stance that is clear in its emphasis on the negative role played by market globalization as it seeks to articulate a set of alternatives that is neither romantic nor compromising, and that places questions of labor and livelihood squarely in the center of analysis. The fact that labor and social welfare gains have nowhere been consolidated in any permanent fashion, and that institutions (in the West) guaranteeing social and economic rights that were once thought to be virtually immutable are now under attack where they have not already disintegrated, demonstrates that there is no progressive "order" of goals to be attained by social movements and that skepticism regarding any detachment (in theory or praxis) among objectives is warranted. Yet the discursive and normative content of such a stance is extremely important. The discourse of economic liberalism (and its contemporary globalization variant) is remarkable for its ability to appear both anachronistic, as Carr thought it had already become half a century ago, and irreversible, as contemporary journalists almost daily tell us it is.[58] But its ability to hang on will in part be determined by the presence or lack of challenges that articulate meaningful alternatives that are able to chip away at its still considerable power.

Notes

Earlier versions of this article were presented at the 1996 International Studies Association meeting in San Diego and at the Center for International and Comparative Studies (CICS) at Northwestern University. I am grateful to Helmuth Berking, Jackie Smith, Bruce Cumings, Michael Loriaux, Jeff Winters, Amalia Pallares, Dan Thomas, Audie Klotz, Paul Friesema, William Felice, Nicholas Rengger, and Thomas Warnke for their comments, and to Northwestern University's Center for International and Comparative Studies and the Fulcher Grant Funds for research support.

1. Recent conceptions of "society" on the transnational or global level (that focus on people rather than states) run the gamut of inspiration from Marx and Hegel to Habermas to mainstream liberal IR theory. See Justin Rosenberg, *The Empire of Civil Society* (London: Verso, 1994); Paul Wapner, "Politics beyond the State: Environmental Activism and World Civic Politics," *World Politics*, 47, no. 3 (1995); and Thomas Risse-Kappen, ed., et al., *Bringing Transnational Relations Back In* (Cambridge: Cambridge University Press,

168   *Social Movements and the Problem of Globalization*

1995), respectively. For discussions of the relationship between social move-
ments and civil society on the domestic, transnational, and global levels, see
Millenium (Special Issue: "Social Movements and World Politics") 23, no. 3
(1994), passim; Richard Falk, *On Humane Governance, Toward a New Global
Politics* (University Park: Pennsylvania State University Press, 1995), and Falk,
Explorations at the Edge of Time (Philadelphia: Temple University Press, 1992);
Jean L. Cohen and Andrew Arato, *Civil Society and Political Theory* (Cam-
bridge: MIT Press, 1992); and John A. Hall, ed., *Civil Society, Theory, History,
Comparison* (Cambridge, UK: Polity, 1995).

2. Gill, "The Global Panopticon? The Neoliberal State, Economic Life,
and Democratic Surveillance," *Alternatives* 20 (1995): 1.

3. Thomas L. Friedman, "Revolt of the Wannabees," *New York Times*, February 7, 1996, p. A15.

4. Claire Turenne Sjolander, "Multilateralism, Regionalism, and Unilat-
eralism: International Trade and the Marginalization of the South," in *The
State of the United Nations, 1993: North-South Perspectives*, ACUNS Reports and
Papers no. 5 (1993): 83–84; Philip Cerny, "Globalization and Collective Action," *IO* 49, no. 4 (1995).

5. As Richard Falk points out, one has only to look to the international
political-economy literature of twenty years ago, including the books of
Richard Barnet, especially *Global Reach: The Power of the Multinational Corporations*, with Ronald E. Muller (New York: Simon & Schuster, 1974), or Robert
Gilpin, *U.S. Power and the Multinational Corporation* (New York: Basic Books,
1975). See Falk, note 1, *On Humane Governance*. For recent debates on what is
new (or old) about economic globalization, see Suzanne Berger and Ronald
Dore, eds., *Convergence or Diversity? National Models of Production and Distribution
in a Global Economy* (Ithaca, N.Y.: Cornell University Press, 1996); Andrew Hurrell and Ngaire Woods, "Globalisation and Inequality," *Millenium* 24, no. 3
(1995, special issue on liberalism); John Ruggie, "At Home Abroad, Abroad
at Home: International Liberalisation and Domestic Stability in the New
World Economy," also in *Millenium* 24, no. 3; and Stephen Gill, "Globalisation,
Market Civilisation, and Disciplinary Neoliberalism," ibid.; Richard Barnet and
John Cavanagh, *Global Dreams: Imperial Corporations and the New World Order*
(New York: Simon & Schuster, 1994), and Saskia Sassen, *Losing Control: Sover-
eignty in an Age of Globalization* (New York: Columbia University Press, 1996).

6. On the term *global apartheid* as used by contemporary activists, see
John Cavanagh, "The Crisis of Globalization," comments at the "Teach-In on
Globalization," New York City, Nov. 1995. This usage currently appears to
connote primarily economic segregation, both within and among societies
and states. The term itself, however, is a much older one, referring originally
to the relationship between global racial relations and economic advantage.
See Gernot Kohler, "Global Apartheid," *Alternatives* 4, no. 2 (1978), and
Kohler, "The Three Meanings of Global Apartheid: Empirical, Normative,
and Existential," *Alternatives* 20, no. 3 (1995).

7. Magnusson argues that capitalism's power is rarely understood as the
effect of a social movement, although the evidence easily supports such an
understanding.

> Capitalism has its ideology, its exponents, its true believers. It
> rouses millions of people in its support, generates hundreds of po-
> litical parties, and inspires the most incredible personal sacrifices. It

is a way of life that attracts fierce loyalty, and appears to offer people a means of solving all their problems. . . . In terms of sustained activity, it is hard to think of anything that rivals this effort.

Magnusson, "Social Movements and the Global City," *Millenium* 23, no. 3 (1994): 637.

8. The winter 1985 issue of *Social Research*, with articles by Jean L. Cohen, Charles Tilly, Alain Touraine, Alberto Melucci, Claus Offe, and Klaus Eder represents one of the best collections of theoretical work on the "new social movements." Special issue, "Social Movements," *Social Research* 52, no. 4 (1985).

9. Here there is a problem, although an unavoidable one, of using the term *movements* to denote collective entities, each made up in reality of groups and individuals having many differences between them. Thus I am talking about each movement in somewhat oversimplified terms. Also, I wish to note that I am not attempting to provide an "objective" or single understanding of globalization, which has many facets and interpretations. Rather, my purpose in the following section is to give an outline of particular social movements' understanding and articulation of the "problem" and potential "responses" to it. There are, in fact, interesting debates within movement groups themselves regarding what constitutes an objective analysis of globalization.

10. Tariq Rauf, "A Critique of the Global Approach to Nuclear Nonproliferation," *The State of the United Nations, 1993: North-South Perspectives*, ACUNS Reports and Papers no. 5 (1993): 48.

11. For a discussion of the administration's change in policy, see *Disarmament, New Realities: Disarmament, Peace-building and Global Security*, NGO Committee on Disarmament Conference at the United Nations, New York, April 20–23, 1993.

12. Even the Convention on the Rights of Child employs rather weak language in this regard: "Children have the right to be protected from economic exploitation and from work that threatens their health, education or development. States shall set minimum ages for employment and regulating work conditions, particularly in line with standards set forth by the International Labour Organisation, particularly in the Minimum Age Convention 1973 (no. 138)." Substantive Provisions, 5c.

13. Ronnie D. Lipschutz, "Reconstructing World Politics: The Emergence of Global Civil Society," *Millenium*, 21 (1992); Pamela Chasek, "The Story of the UNCED Process," in Bertram I. Spector, Gunnar Sjostedt, and I. William Zartman, *Negotiating International Regimes: Lessons learned from the United Nations Conference on Environment and Development* (London: Graham & Trotman, 1994).

14. Activists at recent NGO conferences have been quite frank about this split. Comments at plenary session of International Forum on Globalization's "Teach-In," New York City, Nov. 10, 1995; comments by Hilary French, Worldwatch Institute, "We the Peoples" Conference, San Francisco, June 1995.

15. If this is the case, then the major opponent of "progressive" social movements has always been capitalism pure and simple, whether conceptualized as "structure," process, or social movement. My own perspective is that capitalism and its variants in different historical periods have indeed constituted on

170 *Social Movements and the Problem of Globalization*

a consistent basis "a" primary foe for the realization of goals of social justice, although these variants have combined with other "movements" or sets of practices such as militarism in ways that produced internal contradictions and prevent us from assigning them rigid labels or qualities of immutability.

16. "The World Summit for Social Development," Oxfam, UK and Ireland, undated. These conferences include the World Summit for Children (1990), the Earth Summit (1992), the World Conference on Human Rights (1993), the International Conference on Population and Development (1994), the World Summit for Social Development (1995), the Fourth World Conference on Women (1995), and Habitat II (1996).

17. Women's Linkage Caucus Advocacy Priorities for the Draft Platform for Action, March 20, 1995, p. 3.

18. The Platform for Action reaffirms the importance of implementing the environmental standards of Agenda 21 and admits that "the major cause of the continued deterioration of the global environment is the unsustainable pattern of consumption and production, particularly in industrialized countries, which is a matter of grave concern, aggravating poverty and imbalances." Women's Environment and Development Organization, "A Brief Analysis of the UN Fourth World Conference on Women, Beijing Declaration and Platform for Action," New York, 1995.

19. "The Summit . . . is the centrepiece in a series of United Nations gatherings to address pervasive threats to humankind. It is aimed at mounting a global attack on poverty, unemployment and social disintegration." "Consensus Growing on Social Summit," press release, United Nations DPI/1577/Rev.3, September 13, 1994; "The grave deterioration of living conditions the world over has prompted governments [sic] to call upon the United Nations to hold the second United Nations Conference on Human Settlements (Habitat II)," *"The City Summit" Istanbul, 3–14 June, 1996,* Habitat New York Office, United Nations, conference brochure.

20. "The World Summit for Social Development," note 16.

21. Mike Salvaris, "United Nations Copenhagen Social Summit," *Forum,* the Centre for Citizenship and Human Rights, no. 3, August 1995. Oxfam (UK and Ireland) noted in its preparatory materials that "any new institutional framework needs to address the fact that the globalisation of the economy has shifted the burden of protecting people's rights away from national governments and towards private actors, such as transnational organisations." "The World Summit for Social Development," note 16.

22.

The International Forum on Globalization is a new alliance created by sixty activists, scholars, economists, researchers, and writers to stimulate new thinking, joint activity, and public education in response to the rapidly emerging economic and political arrangement called the *global economy.* . . . The International Forum on Globalization advocates equitable, democratic, and ecologically sustainable economics. It is formed in response to the present worldwide drive toward a globalized economic system dominated by supranational corporate trade and banking institutions that are not accountable to democratic processes or national governments.

Undated pamphlet, IFG, San Francisco.

23. "Memo to all public members of IFG from Jerry Mander, Acting Director," December 10, 1996.

24. See Jerry Mander and Edward Goldsmith, eds., *The Case Against the Global Economy* (Sierra Club Books, 1996); and David C. Korten, *When Corporations Rule the World* (Kumarian Press, 1995).

25. IFG pamphlet, note 22, fn.23.

26. This is a summary of IFG activists' arguments, compiled from comments made during the Teach-In on Globalization, by Colin Hines, Maude Barlow, John Cavanagh, and Jerry Mander, New York City, Nov. 1995.

27. Coalition for New Priorities, Debate on Globalization, Chicago, Sept. 1996.

28. "Labor & Environment in the Global Economy: Points of Collaboration," Teach-In on Globalization, note 26.

29. "Peace" now takes a back seat to the interconnection of these other concerns, although the implications for peace are assumed. Mark Ritchie, "Economic, Social, Cultural, and Human Rights: Getting Past the Cold War," Teach-In on Globalization, note 26.

30. Colin Hines, "The New Protectionism: What it is—why it is coming," Nov. 10, 1995, first published in the United Kingdom as "Employment and the Culture of Insecurity: time to protect jobs," Employment Policy Institute, Economic Report 9, no. 5 (June 1995).

31. Cf. note 6.

32. Colin Hines and Tim Lang, *The New Protectionism: Protecting the Future Against Free Trade* (New York: New Press, 1993).

33. Hines, note 30.

34. Ibid.

35. Colin Hines, comments on "Relocalization, Decentralization, Alternatives to Globalization," Teach-In on Globalization, note 26.

36. Cecelia Lynch, "E. H. Carr, International Relations Theory, and the Societal Origins of International Legal Norms," *Millenium* 23, no. 3 (1994).

37. E. P. Thompson, "Ends and Histories," Mary Kaldor, "After the Cold War," and Tair Tairov, "From New Thinking to a Civic Peace," all in Mary Kaldor, ed., *Europe From Below* (New York: Verso, 1991); concerning concepts of "alternative defense," see Thomas R. Rochon, *Mobilizing for Peace, the Antinuclear Movements in Western Europe* (Princeton, N.J.: Princeton University Press, 1988); for a discussion of the variations in reception of social movement alternatives in the Soviet Union, West Germany, and the United States, see Thomas Risse-Kappen, "Ideas do not float freely: transnational coalitions, domestic structures, and the end of the cold war," *IO*, 48, no. 2 (1994).

38. "Generals: Get Rid of Nuclear Weapons," *Chicago Tribune*, December 5, 1996; "The Generals' War," *San Francisco Examiner*, December 6, 1996.

39. Benjamin Page, "Trouble for Workers and the Poor: Economic Globalization and the Reshaping of American Politics," unpublished paper, October 1996.

40. Thomas Friedman, in "Revolt of the Wannabees" (note 3), points out that a recent Davos Forum conference, "the ultimate capitalist convention" that consists of "an annual celebration of globalization," debated the "mounting backlash against its effects, especially in the industrial democracies" that "is threatening a very disruptive impact on economic activity and social stability in many countries."

41. Hines comments, note 35.

42. Thence we have the terms *postmaterial values* and *post-Marxist* approaches. For discussion of these, see Jean L. Cohen, "Strategy or Identity? New Theoretical Paradigms and Contemporary Social Movements," in *Social Research*, note 8; Rochon, note 37; on postmaterial values especially, see Ronald Inglehart, *The Silent Revolution* (Princeton: Princeton University Press, 1977).

43. The "particularistic"/"universalistic" distinction is more complex than it seems at first glance. Peace, environmentalist, and feminist movements, for example, were seen to operate not from a "particularistic" sense of self-interest, but rather from a set of values that went "beyond" self-interest and thus could be promoted, in a sense, for a wider, "universal" good. However, some of the "new" movements, especially feminist movements, emanated from a self-consciously particularistic understanding of identity. The purpose here was to call forth values and norms that would highlight and respect that identity, rather than assume that all would share in it. For discussion and debate on Habermas's "unflinching defense of enlightenment rationality," see Axel Honneth, Thomas McCarthy, Claus Offe, and Albrecht Wellmer, eds., *Philosophical Interventions in the Unfinished Project of Enlightenment* (Cambridge: MIT Press, 1992), quote from preface, p. ix.

44. Here I am speaking primarily about European, "identity" theorizing, although similarities exist with the theoretical concerns of other schools of thought. Since I have been in considerable sympathy with the "new social movement" mode of understanding of what social movements do (i.e., create a semi-autonomous "space" for action that is separate from institutionalized politics; engage in the creation of "new meanings" and norms), this constitutes something of an autocritique.

45. Examples of the debate on the durability and strength of sovereignty in the international relations literature include John G. Ruggie, "Territoriality and Beyond: Problematizing modernity in international relations," *IO* 47, no. 1 (1993); Thomas J. Biersteker and Cynthia Weber, eds., *State Sovereignty as Social Construct* (Cambridge: Cambridge University Press, 1996); Stephen D. Krasner, "Sovereignty: An Institutional Perspective," *Comparative Political Studies* (1988); Janice Thomson and Stephen Krasner, "Global Transactions and the Consolidation of Sovereignty," in Ernst-Otto Czempiel and James N. Rosenau, eds., *Global Changes and Theoretical Challenges: Approaches to World Politics for the 1990s* (Lexington, Mass.: Lexington Books, 1989); and Friedrich Kratochwil, "Sovereignty and All What?" in Chant Chopra, ed., *The Development of International Law* (forthcoming). It is important to note that a current trend in political economy is to emphasize the resistance and importance of the state as a bargainer in the face of global homogenization of national institutions and structures.

46. R. B. J. Walker uses this phrase to describe "the appeal to some supposedly already existing world politics or universal ethics . . . to reveal some essential or potential humanity beneath." Walker, "Social Movements/World Politics," *Millenium* 23, no. 3 (1994): 673.

47. I am indebted to Nicholas Rengger for this term.

48. I use the term *ideology* somewhat gingerly, given the lack of a better alternative, to denote a worldview that incorporates a notion of political causality and some idea of moral good. Ideology in this sense provides an extremely important framework for guiding and shaping action. But in practice it is also fluid, in the sense that people in "real life" tend to adhere to it

grossomodo, while at the same time retaining the ability to question aspects of it that do not "fit" their interpretations of real events, thereby allowing it to evolve with circumstance. Any usage of the term *ideology* should take into account Hannah Arendt's extremely powerful definition and critique of the role of rigidified, more totalizing ideologies that undergird totalitarian systems. For Arendt, ideologies, "isms which to the satisfaction of their adherents can explain everything and every occurrence by deducing it from a single premise," functioned to enable the adherents of Nazi and Stalinist totalitarianism to forgo all space for thought, reflection, and action. *The Origins of Totalitarianism* (New York: Harcourt, Brace & Co., 1975), pp. 468–469.

49. Antonio Gramsci, *Selections from Prison Notebooks*, ed. and trans. by Quintin Hoare and Geofrey Nowell Smith (New York: International Publishers).

50. *Hegel's Philosophy of Right*, T. M. Knox, trans. (New York: Oxford University Press, 1978), pp. 124, 129–134, 145–155; Cohen and Arato, note 1, pp. 97–105.

51. Vladimir Tismaneanu, *Reinventing Politics, Eastern Europe from Stalin to Havel* (New York: Free Press, 1993); Tony Judt, "The Dilemmas of Dissidence: The Politics of Opposition in East-Central Europe," in Ferenc Feher and Andrew Arato, eds., *Crisis and Reform in Eastern Europe* (London: Transaction, 1991), pp. 253–302; Cohen and Arato, note 1, chap. 1.

52. J. K. Galbraith, "Revolt in Our Time: The Triumph of Simplistic Ideology," in Kaldor, ed., note 37, pp. 67–74.

53. Cohen and Arato, note 1, Introduction and chaps. 9, 10.

54. Falk, note 1, *Explorations*.

55. Falk, "Liberalism at the Global Level: The Last of the Independent Commissions?" *Millenium* 24, no. 3: 575–576.

56. Walker, note 46, esp. pp. 682–684.

57. Mike Salvaris, "United Nations Copenhagen Social Summit," *Forum* (Centre for Citizenship and Human Rights), no. 3 (1995).

58. E. H. Carr, *The Twenty Years' Crisis, 1919–1939*, 2d ed. (New York: Harper & Row, 1964); Ruggie reminds us of Carr's views in "At Home Abroad, Abroad at Home," Ruggie, note 45. See also Falk, note 55. Thomas Friedman states that the academic debate on globalization "is beoming one of *the* most important foreign policy debates. "Now, some of these writings are misleading—those that suggest globalization can be stopped. It can't. It's inevitable." "Roll Over Hawks and Doves, The global debate: Who are you?" *New York Times*, Feb. 2, 1997.

[19]

Review of International Studies (1999), 25, 3–28   *Copyright © British International Studies Association*

Civil society at the turn of the millennium: prospects for an alternative world order[1]

ROBERT W. COX

Abstract. The meaning of 'civil society' has evolved considerably since its use in the context of the 18th century European Enlightenment. Then it signified the realm of private interests, in practice the realm of the bourgeoisie, distinct from the state. While one current of thought retains that meaning and its implications, others view civil society rather as the emancipatory activity of social forces distinct from both state and capital. Antonio Gramsci's thought embraced both meanings: civil society was the ground that sustained the hegemony of the bourgeoisie but also that on which an emancipatory counterhegemony could be constructed. Is civil society today in the latter sense, a surrogate for revolution that seems a remote possibility towards the attainment of an alternative social and world order? It is useful to test this proposition by examining the potential for civil society in different parts of the world.

Eric Hobsbawm has written that '[t]he world at the end of the Short Twentieth Century [1914–1991] is in a state of social breakdown rather than revolutionary crisis . . .'[2] The conclusion is hard to avoid. 'Real socialism' has collapsed; the anti-imperialist struggle in the former colonial world has resolved itself into a series of new states seeking a *modus vivendi* in subordination to global capitalism; the Left in Europe is searching uncertainly for an alternative to neoliberal globalization while in the main adapting to it; even the Islamic revolution in Iran is hesitatingly moving towards an adjustment to dominant world economic forces. There is much violence—in the Balkans, central Africa, Algeria, and Ulster—but none of it could be called revolutionary in the sense of promising a transformation of society. Global finance has lurched from the Mexican peso crisis in the 1980s to the Asian crisis in the 1990s, leaving a marginalized Africa almost unnoticed; but while finance dominates and constrains all governments' policies, there is no concerted means of global financial management.

If world politics is in such a condition of turbulent stasis, with little hope of calm but no prospect of fundamental change, the polarization of rich people and poor people is becoming increasingly accentuated throughout the world. There is also evidence that people have become disenchanted with existing forms of politics. In

---

[1] The original version of this article was a paper presented to the Conference on Gramsci, Modernity, and the Twentieth Century, convened by the Fundazione Istituto Gramsci, Rome, in Cagliari, 15–18 April 1997. In revising it, I am most grateful for comments by Yoshikazu Sakamoto, James Mittelman, Masaharu Takashima, Michael Schechter, Timothy Sinclair, Michael Cox and two anonymous readers for the *Review of International Studies*. I am especially indebted to Yoshikazu Sakamoto for directing my attention to the question of civil society in our times. I, of course, alone bear responsibility for the text as it appears here.
[2] Eric Hobsbawm, *The Age of Extremes. A History of the World, 1914–1991* (New York: Pantheon, 1994) p. 459.

these circumstances, many activists and theorists have looked to civil society as the source from which alternative, more equitable forms of society might arise. Is civil society in the late 20th century the surrogate for a revolution that seems unlikely to happen? There is a debate on the Left about this and that is the question behind the revival of interest in civil society.

The concept of civil society has a long history in European and American thought. From that source, it has been exported around the world. In order to explore the transformatory potential of civil society in our time, it is useful to consult some of that history. Antonio Gramsci, drawing upon that tradition, constructed a view of civil society particularly pertinent to the present debate; and he did so at a time when revolutionary transformation still seemed a possibility. I propose to examine the changing meanings of the term 'civil society' over the years, placing these meanings in their historical and contemporary contexts, and then to reflect upon Gramsci's thought as an approach to understanding society and politics that took form in the specific historical context of Italy in the 1920s and 1930s but still has fruitful applicability in the changed world-wide context of the late twentieth century.

Gramsci was not concerned as an abstract theorist with building a system of political analysis that would stand the test of time. He was concerned with changing his world. Any development of his thinking should keep that goal to the fore and should thus both arise from reflection on the condition of the world as it is, and serve as a guide to action designed to change the world so as to improve the lot of humanity in social equity.

Civil society, in Gramsci's thinking, is the realm in which the existing social order is grounded; and it can also be the realm in which a new social order can be founded. His concern with civil society was, first, to understand the strength of the *status quo*, and then to devise a strategy for its transformation. The emancipatory potential of civil society was the object of his thinking. In the *Prison Notebooks*[3], civil society is an elastic concept, having different connotations in different passages. Often civil society appears as a function of the state as in the frequently quoted equation: 'State=political society+civil society, in other words hegemony protected by the armour of coercion' (PN, p. 263). Gramsci honed much of his thought against the philosophy of Benedetto Croce. Croce saw the state, following Hegel, in idealistic terms as the embodiment of ethics.[4] Gramsci, in an historical materialist perspective, understood ethics as emanating from the social and cultural practices that enable historically conditioned human communities to cope with their environment. Croce's ethical state, for Gramsci, becomes ethical through the instrumentality of civil society. There is a dialectic inherent in civil society. In one aspect, the educational and ideological agencies that are sustained ultimately by the state's coercive apparatus shape morals and culture. Yet in another aspect civil society appears to have autonomy and to be more fundamental than the state, indeed to be the basis upon which a state can be founded. Civil society is both shaper and

---

[3] References in the text to the *Prison Notebooks* are taken from Antonio Gramsci, *Selections from the Prison Notebooks* edited and translated by Quintin Hoare and Geoffrey Nowell Smith (New York: International Publishers, 1971), subsequently referred to as PN.

[4] See, e.g., Benedetto Croce, *Politics and Morals* (New York: Philosophical Library, 1945) pp. 22–32, where he described the state as 'the incarnation of the human ethos'.

shaped, an agent of stabilization and reproduction, and a potential agent of transformation.

There is little point in trying to establish a fixed definition of Gramsci's concepts from exegesis of his text. That would negate Gramsci's way of thinking. He thought historically and dialectically, that is to say, his concepts are derived from his perceptions of reality and they serve not only to seize the momentary essence of a changing reality but also to become intellectual tools for fomenting change. Certain basic guidelines are essential in order to discern what Fernand Braudel later called the limits of the possible, the starting point from which strategic planning for social transformation has to begin. The first of these is to know accurately the prevailing relations of social forces. These have material, organizational, and ideological components, together constituting the configuration of an historic bloc.

Yet Gramsci was less concerned with the historic bloc as a stable entity than he was with historical mutations and transformations, and with the emancipatory potential for human agency in history. The concept of civil society in this emancipatory sense designates the combination of forces upon which the support for a new state and a new order can be built. These forces operate in a political and social space, a terrain occupied by different conflicting forces as historical change proceeds—a terrain which is narrowed when there is a close identity between people and their political and social institutions (in Gramsci's terms, when hegemony prevails) but which is widened when this identity is weak.

Any fixed definition of the content of the concept 'civil society' would just freeze a particular moment in history and privilege the relations of social forces then prevailing. Rather than look for clearer definitions, we should try to understand the historical variations that have altered the meanings of the concept in the ongoing dialectic of concept and reality. We should not stop with the world of the 1930s which Gramsci knew but carry on the process into the late 20th century. To continue and develop Gramsci's way of thinking is more true to his purpose than to mummify his text.

The changing meanings of 'civil society'

Writing in the last decade of the 20th century, we must recognize that the European tradition of political thought will now be seen as that of a particular civilization coexisting with others. It can no longer make an uncontested claim to universality, even though the concepts evolved in western discourse have penetrated into all parts of the world through the era of Western dominance. Thus, Western terms may cover realities that are different. To Westerners these terms may obscure these differences by assimilating them to familiar Western meanings. This must be borne in mind in using a term like 'civil society'. We must be alert not only to the surface appearance but also to a non-Western meaning that may be deeply buried. Nevertheless, it is necessary to retrace the concept of civil society to its European roots in the Enlightenment.

Civil society in Enlightenment thought was understood as the realm of particular interests, which in practice then meant the realm of the bourgeoisie. The state ideally embodied universality, the rule of law. The monarch was to be the first servant of the state, bound by and applying the rule of law. An intellectual problem for the Enlightenment was how to explain the necessary compatibility of the two, of the realm of particular interests and the realm of universality. If the state were to embody universality, then civil society must generate universal principles in the ethico-juridical sphere; civil society must be seen as creating the basis of common welfare out of the pursuit of particular interests. Both Hegel and Adam Smith thought they had achieved this reconciliation by in effect refurbishing the Christian doctrine of Providence, in Smith's case as the 'invisible hand' and in Hegel's as the 'ruse of reason'.[5] In its European origins, civil society and the bourgeoisie were synonymous. Civil society signified the self-conscious social group whose influence, if not necessarily its executive power, was expanding.

Karl Marx was, of course, sceptical about the emergence of common good from the pursuit of individual interests. He saw rather that civil society was generating a force within itself that would ultimately destroy or change it: the proletariat. He also cast his regard beyond Europe to sketch an outline of an 'Asiatic mode of production' in which rural villages reproduced themselves *ad infinitum*; and in his analysis of French society of the mid-19th century he discerned a social structure more complex than the bourgeois/proletarian dualism of his capitalist mode of production. If the bourgeoisie was the starting point for civil society, the 19th century opened up the concept to embrace a variety of conflicting social groups and interests.

A particularly significant 19th century addition to the complexity of the concept came from Alexis de Tocqueville's work on American democracy.[6] What impressed Tocqueville was the flourishing of associations, spontaneously formed by people for the achievement of common purposes outside of the state. In the context of American politics, Tocqueville saw this proliferation of associations as a guarantee against a tyranny of the majority that might result from an electoral sweep in an era of populist politics. He drew an analogy to the stabilizing influence he saw in European societies as arising from the existence of secondary bodies inherited from medieval times which acted as a restraint upon monarchic power.

The spirit of voluntary association thus became a significant aspect of the concept of civil society. Civil society is no longer identified with capitalism and the bourgeoisie but now takes on the meaning of a mobilized participant citizenry juxtaposed to dominant economic and state power. For Gramsci, who was concerned with the problem of mobilizing the working class for action in combination with other potential class allies, there was never a pure spontaneity in the construction of social organization but always a combination of leadership and movement from below. His sense of the optimum relationship was to 'stimulate the formation of homogeneous, compact social blocs, which will give birth to their own intellectuals, their own commandos, their own vanguard—who will in turn react upon those blocs in order to develop them . . .' (PN pp. 204–5). Gramsci's historical context was very different from that in which Tocqueville discovered the spirit of association in a society of farmers, artisans, and merchants untrammelled by the class and status

---

[5] Carl Becker, *The Heavenly City of the Eighteenth Century Philosophers* (New Haven, CT: Yale University Press, 1932).
[6] Alexis de Tocqueville, *De la Démocratie en Amérique* 2 vols (Paris: Gallimard, 1951).

inheritance of European societies. To counter the fascist politics of the 1930s, he rejected both 'spontaneity' or 'voluntarism', on one side, and the notion of a revolutionary elite manipulating the masses, on the other.

As counterpoint to the flourishing in America of autonomous voluntary associations outside of the state, 19th century Europe experienced the merger of civil society with the state in the form of corporatism. State leaders, perceiving the disruptive potential of class struggle in industrializing societies, sought to bring employers and organized workers into a consensual relationship with the state for the management of the economy and the support of state political and military goals. Corporatism left those who are relatively powerless in society out of account; but being powerless and unorganized they could hardly be considered part of civil society. The corporatist era began in mid-century with conservative leaders like Disraeli and Bismark and extended into the post-World War II decades in the form of the welfare state. This era is well encapsulated in Gramsci's equation: State= political society+civil society.

The French Revolution left another legacy with implications for civil society: the rejection of anything that would intervene between the state and the citizen. Conceived as a means of liquidating medieval corporations, the principle as embodied in the Le Chapelier law of 1791 was in the early 19th century turned against the formation of trade unions. The same principle was reasserted by the Bolsheviks in the 20th century revolutionary Russian context: all allowable associations under 'real socialism' would have to be part of an all-embracing Party-state. Civil society was denied existence.

Gramsci recognized the weakness inherent in this situation in his juxtaposition of the war of manoeuvre with the war of position when he referred to conditions at the onset of the Bolshevik revolution:

In Russia the state was everything, civil society was primordial and gelatinous; in the West, there was a proper relation between State and civil society, and when the State trembled a sturdy structure of civil society was at once revealed. The State was only an outer ditch, behind which there stood a powerful system of fortresses and earthworks; more or less numerous from one State to the next, it goes without saying—but this precisely necessitated an accurate reconnaissance of each individual country. (PN, p. 238).

The 'proper relation between State and civil society' suggests that the State should rest upon the support of an active, self-conscious and variegated civil society and should, in turn, sustain and promote the development of the constructive forces in that society. The organic intellectual was, for Gramsci, the key link in this process.

This brief review of the use of the term 'civil society' in European and American thought yields broadly two juxtaposed meanings. One shows a 'top-down' process in which the dominant economic forces of capitalism form an intellectual and cultural hegemony which secures acquiescence in the capitalist order among the bulk of the population. The other envisages a 'bottom-up' process led by those strata of the population which are disadvantaged and deprived under the capitalist order who build a counterhegemony that aspires to acquire sufficient acceptance among the population so as to displace the erstwhile hegemonic order. With regard to the latter,

Gramsci insisted that the revolution must occur (in civil society) prior to the revolution (in the form of the state).[7]

Civil society in the late 20th century

Since Gramsci made his analysis, there have been significant changes affecting the relationship of state to civil society and in the development of civil society in different parts of the world. The world crisis of capitalism of the 1970s brought about a reversal of corporatism. Business persuaded governments that recovery of investment and growth from a situation of 'stagflation' required an attack on the power of trade unions and a reduction of state expenditures on social welfare, together with deregulation of capital, goods, and financial markets. As governments acquiesced in this business analysis, trade unions and social-democratic forces were weakened in most economically advanced countries. Protection for the more vulnerable elements in society was cut back; and these elements were implicitly challenged to organize independently of the state both to protest the loss of state support and to compensate for this loss by voluntary initiative and self-help. The collapse of 'real socialism' in the late 1980s seemed to herald a possible rebirth of civil society in those countries where civil society had been eradicated by the Party-state. New independent organizations of protest grew into the political space that was opened

---

[7] There is a current of 'political Marxism' expressed by Ellen Meiskins Wood, *Democracy Against Capitalism. Renewing Historical Materialism* (Cambridge University Press, 1995), which is very critical of the hopes of some people on the Left that civil society will play an emancipatory role. In her view, civil society retains its original identity with the bourgeois order. This originated with the conceptual distinction made in bourgeois ideology between politics and economics, creating the illusion that economics, the realm of civil society, was not an arena of politics, that is to say, of power relations. This mystification of private power has made possible the acceptance and reproduction of the bourgeois social order. She writes: 'It is certainly true that in capitalist society, with its separation of "political" and "economic" spheres, or the state and civil society, coercive public power is centralized and concentrated to a greater degree than ever before, but this simply means that one of the principal functions of "public" coercion by the state is to sustain "private" power in civil society.' (p. 255) Her charge against the current appeal to civil society by the 'new social movements' and postmodernism is that it occludes the reality of class domination and fragments the opposition to the bourgeois order into a variety of distinct struggles for 'identity', thereby perpetuating capitalist domination.

Justin Rosenberg. *The Empire of Civil Society. A Critique of the Realist Theory of International Relations* (London: Verso, 1994) transposes Ellen Wood's reasoning to international relations, arguing that the classical Westphalian concept of state sovereignty and the balance of power mystify the reality of power in the capitalist world order. The 'public' sphere of the state system is paralleled by the 'private' sphere of the global economy; and the state system functions to sustain 'private' power in the latter, the 'empire of civil society'.

'Political Marxism' provides a cogent argument with regard to the 'top-down' meaning of civil society, and in its critique of a postmodernism that indiscriminate deference to identities implies a fragmentation and therefore weakening of opposition to the dominant order. The argument is more questionable in its apparent rejection of the Gramscian 'war of position' as a counterhegemonic strategy for the conquest of civil society and for the transformation of civil society in an emancipatory direction. Two key points in the 'political Marxist' thesis that bear reexamination are: (1) the positing of capitalism as a monolithic 'totalizing' force which excludes the possibility of historicizing capitalism so as to perceive that it is subject to historical change and can take different forms; and (2) the freezing of the concept of 'class' in a 19th and early 20th century form with a two class model juxtaposing bourgeoisie and proletariat which obscures the ways in which changes in production have restructured social relations, especially during recent decades. Both points are discussed below.

by the disruption and uncertainty of political authority. In both cases, the political and social space in which civil society could develop was expanded. Whether or not the opportunity would be realized was a challenge to human agency.

The restructuring of society by economic globalization

The globalization of production is restructuring the world labour force in ways that challenge 19th and early 20th century notions of class structure. Gramsci's keen sense of the strategic importance of building class alliances into a counterhegemonic bloc which could ultimately displace the bourgeoisie—he advocated linking peasantry and petty bourgeois elements with the working class—remains pertinent in today's world. What is relevant today is the strategy of class alliance rather than Gramsci's particular form of alliance derived from his understanding of the class structure of Italy in the 1920s and 1930s. It is problematic today whether the proletariat can still be considered to be a 'fundamental' universal class. Indeed, the very notion of a proletariat as a single class juxtaposed to the bourgeoisie has lost substance in reality even if its ideological persuasiveness retains some impetus.

International production is dividing the world's producers into broadly three categories:

- At the top is a core workforce of highly skilled people *integrated* into the management process. These people take the decisions about what is produced and where and by whom. They carry on research and development; they maintain the productive apparatus; and they staff the administrative frameworks and propagate the ideology of globalization.
- At a second level, this integrated core is flanked by a larger number of supporting workers whose numbers vary with levels of demand for products. Their lesser levels of skill make them more easily disposable and replaceable. These are the *precarious* workers. They are located where business is offered the lowest labour costs, the greatest flexibility in the use of labour, i.e. the least protection of workers' rights in jobs; and the weakest environmental controls. These workers are segmented by ethnicity, religion, gender, and geography, and thus are not easily organized collectively to confront management in a united manner. Transnationalized production has accentuated social fragmentation and environmental degradation.
- The third level comprises those people who are *excluded* from international production. They include the unemployed and many small low-technology enterprises in the richer countries and a large part of the marginalized population in poor countries.

The proportions in this three-fold hierarchical structure (integrated, precarious, and excluded) vary from country to country, but the categories cut across territorial boundaries and the ability of governments to alter the proportions is severely limited by their dependence upon global finance. Precarious employment and exclusion were accentuated by the decline in social expenditures that followed from the capitalist crisis of the 1970s. Economic orthodoxy now focuses on state budget deficits and urges states to further reduce social expenditures.

These tendencies give a new configuration to the material basis of civil society. People who speak of civil society today do not usually have in mind the realm of economic interests as did Hegel and Adam Smith. The distinction common today is between dominant power over society shared by corporations and states, on the one side, and popular forces on the other. 'Civil society' is now usually understood to refer to the realm of autonomous group action distinct from both corporate power and the state. The concept has been appropriated by those who foresee an emancipatory role for civil society. There is thus a marked distinction between the meaning of 'civil society' in the work of 18th and 19th century theorists and the way that term is commonly understood today. In the earlier meaning, civil society is another term for the social power relations deriving from the economy. Gramsci's usage stemmed from that of Hegel and Marx. It differed from Marx's, as Norberto Bobbio has shown, by including the ethical and ideological superstructure and not just the economic base.[8]

The current widely understood usage which excludes dominant power in the state and corporations from the concept of civil society received impetus from the movements of opposition to Stalinist rule in Eastern Europe. They were characterized as a 'rebirth of civil society'[9] Similarly, movements of opposition to authoritarian rule and capitalist dominance in Asian and Latin American countries are commonly perceived as emanations of civil society. So 'civil society' has become the comprehensive term for various ways in which people express collective wills independently of (and often in opposition to) established power, both economic and political.

This current usage has more affinity to Tocqueville than to Hegel, Adam Smith or Marx. But it also has affinity to Gramsci's usage, since Gramsci regarded civil society not only as the realm of hegemony supportive of the capitalist *status quo*, but also as the realm in which cultural change takes place, in which the counter-hegemony of emancipatory forces can be constituted. Civil society is not just an assemblage of actors, i.e. autonomous social groups. It is also the realm of contesting ideas in which the intersubjective meanings upon which people's sense of 'reality' are based can become transformed and new concepts of the natural order of society can emerge.

There is little point in arguing that one usage of the term 'civil society' is correct and the other is wrong. Let us take current identification of civil society with autonomous social forces as a basis for discussion and examine its implications. Even conceived in this more limited way, i.e. without including the powerful economic forces, civil society in the late 20th century, though generally viewed as potentially emancipatory and transformative of the social order, can be seen to reflect the dominance of state and corporate economic power.

In a 'bottom-up' sense, civil society is the realm in which those who are disadvantaged by globalization of the world economy can mount their protests and seek alternatives. This can happen through local community groups that reflect

---

[8] Norberto Bobbio, 'Gramsci and the concept of civil society', in John Keane (ed.), *Civil Society and the State. New European Perspectives* (London and New York: Verso, 1988). The essay was originally published in *Gramsci e la cultura contemporarea: Atti del Convengno Internazionale di Studi Gramsciani*, Rome 1968.

[9] Adam Przeworski, 'Democratic socialism in Poland?', *Studies in Political Economy* 5, spring 1981, pp. 29–54, esp. pp. 37–41.

diversity of cultures and evolving social practices world wide. Looking beyond local grass roots initiatives is the project of a 'civic state', a new form of political authority based upon a participatory democracy.[10] More ambitious still is the vision of a 'global civil society' in which these social movements together constitute a basis for an alternative world order.[11]

In a 'top-down' sense, however, states and corporate interests influence the development of this current version of civil society towards making it an agency for stabilizing the social and political *status quo*. The dominant hegemonic forces penetrate and coopt elements of popular movements. State subsidies to non-governmental organizations (NGOs) incline the latter's objectives towards conformity with established order and thus enhance the legitimacy of the prevailing order. This concords with a concern on the part of many people for survival in existing conditions rather than for transformation of the social order. For many people, clientelism may seem preferable to revolutionary commitment, especially when backed by the force of state and economic power. Moreover, the basic conflicts between rich and poor, powerful and powerless, are reproduced within the sphere of voluntary organizations, whether trade unions or the new social movements.[12]

Global governance

Gramsci's sense that national situations are specific still has validity but now these distinct national situations are much more dependent upon the global economy.[13]

---

[10] I take the term 'civic state' from Yoshikazu Sakamoto, in personal correspondence. See also his article 'Civil society and democratic world order' in Stephen Gill and James H. Mittelman (eds), *Innovation and Transformation in International Studies* (Cambridge: Cambridge University Press, 1997) pp. 207–219.

[11] See, e.g., David Held, *Democracy and the Global Order. From the Modern State to Cosmopolitan Governance* (Stanford: Stanford University Press, 1995). Michael G. Schechter, 'Globalization and civil society', paper presented to the annual meeting of the Academic Council on the United Nations System (ACUNS), San Jose, Costa Rica, June 1997, contains a critical review of literature on 'global civil society'. Even the most optimistic writers regard 'global civic society' in the emancipatory sense as something to be achieved, not as something that already exists. In the 'top-down' hegemonic sense, by contrast, Rosenberg (see footnote 7 above) refers to the 'empire of civil society' as control by global capitalism. In the same sense, but without the Marxist theoretical framework, Susan Strange has written about a 'non-territorial empire' (in 'Toward a theory of transnational empire', E.-O. Czempiel and James N. Rosenau (eds), *Global Changes and Theoretical Challenges. Approaches to World Politics for the 1990s*, Lexington, MA: Lexington Books, 1989).

[12] Laura Macdonald, *Supporting Civil Society. The Political Role of Non-Governmental Organizations in Central America* (Basingstoke: Macmillan, 1997) gives a useful classification of 'ideal types' of NGOs according to their consequences for maintenance or transformation of social and political order. She suggests three types: neo-conservative, liberal-pluralist, and post-Marxist (or Gramscian) (pp. 15–23). With regard to opposition between dominant and subordinate groups within the labour movement, see Robert W. Cox, 'Labor and hegemony' and 'Labor and hegemony: a reply' in Cox with Timothy J. Sinclair, *Approaches to World Order* (Cambridge University Press, 1996).

[13] Bernadette Madeuf and Charles-Albert Michalet, 'A new approach to international economics' *International Social Science Journal* 30: 2 (1978): pp. 253–83, made the distinction between the international economy (understood as flows of goods, payments, and investments across frontiers) and an emerging form of economy in which production was being organized on an integrated basis among entities located in a number of countries. In the English translation of their article, which was written in French, the emerging economy was called the 'world economy', which accords with the French term applied to the process generating it, *mondialisation*. The term 'global economy' is

The territorial distinctness of national economies and societies is penetrated by global and transnational forces. The problem of hegemony is posed at the level of the global political economy as well as at regional, national and local levels. As many analysts of world affairs have suggested, we seem to be moving towards a 'new medievalism' with multiple layers of authority and multiple loyalties.[14]

At the top, there is no identifiable regime of dominance. The new popularity of the term 'global governance' suggests control and orientation in the absence of formally legitimated coercive power. There is something that could be called a nascent global historic bloc consisting of the most powerful corporate economic forces, their allies in government, and the variety of networks that evolve policy guidelines and propagate the ideology of globalization. States now by and large play the role of agencies of the global economy, with the task of adjusting national economic policies and practices to the perceived exigencies of global economic liberalism. This structure of power is sustained from outside the state through a global policy consensus and the influence of global finance over state policy, and from inside the state from those social forces that benefit from globalization (the segment of society that is integrated into the world economy).[15] Competitiveness in the world market has become the ultimate criterion of state policy which justifies the gradual removal of the measures of social protection built up in the era of the welfare state. Neo-liberalism is hegemonic ideologically and in terms of policy. Where ideological and policy hegemony is not sufficient to protect the structure of global governance, then military force is available. The Gulf War was an object lesson in how military force intervenes when a regional power tries to ignore the global hegemony.[16]

This global hegemony has profound consequences for the relationship of political society to civil society. As the state retreats from service and social protection to the public, the public loses confidence in the integrity and competency of the political class. Political corruption is inherent in the transformation of public goods into marketable commodities; a political favour acquires a market value. The loyalty of people to their political institutions becomes more questionable as scepticism and cynicism about the motives and abilities of politicians grows. These tendencies vary among countries. Americans honour the symbols of flag and constitution, but about

commonly used now in English to designate the organization of production and finance on a world scale and 'globalization' as the process generating it. Of course, much of the world's economic activity still goes on outside this global economy, albeit increasingly constrained by and subordinated to the global economy. I reserve the term 'world economy' for the totality of economic activities of which the global economy is the dominant part. The impact of the globalization process on power relations among social forces and states, and in the formation of institutions designed to entrench the global economy or in stimulating resistance to it is the realm of 'global political economy'.

[14] See, for example, Hedley Bull, *The Anarchical Society. A Study of Order in World Politics* (New York: Columbia University Press, 1977) esp. pp. 254–5; also Susan Strange, *The Retreat of the State. The Diffusion of Power in the World Economy* (Cambridge: Cambridge University Press, 1996); and Bertrand Badie and Marie-Claude Smouts, *Le retournement du monde. Sociologie de la scène internationale* (Paris: Presses de la Fondation Nationale des Sciences Politiques & Dalloz, 1992). On this theme of the increasing complexity of world politics and the obsolescence of conventional boundaries and distinctions, see also James N. Rosenau, *Along the Domestic-Foreign Frontier. Exploring Governance in a Turbulent World* (Cambridge: Cambridge University Press, 1997).

[15] See Leo Panitch, 'Rethinking the role of the state', in James H. Mittelman (ed.) *Globalization: Critical Reflections* (Boulder, CO: Lynne Rienner, 1996).

[16] Robert W. Cox, 'Production and security', in Cox with Timothy J. Sinclair, *Approaches to World Order* (Cambridge: Cambridge University Press, 1996), pp. 276–95.

half of them do not bother to vote and most seem to have low expectations of their politicians. Corruption scandals are rife in Europe and Japan, and public hopes for salvation through politics are equally low. Throughout most of the rest of the world, in Asia, Africa and Latin America, people have endured government more than they have felt themselves to be a part of it. At the end of this century, there is a world-wide problem of repairing or building political societies, of constructing a sense of identity between people and political authorities. There is a wide political space between constituted authority and the practical life of people.

Revival of civil society as a response to globalization?

Civil society would be the base upon which a new or reconstructed political authority would have to rest. This was Machiavelli's insight when he advocated the replacement of mercenaries by a citizen militia. There is some evidence of growth in civil society coming about as a reaction to the impact of globalization. In the French strikes of late 1995 and the strikes in South Korea in early 1997, reaction has come through trade union movements, in the French case with broad public support. In Japan and some other Asian countries, there has been a growth of many non-governmental organizations, often of a local self-help kind, and often actively building linkages and mutual help relationships with similar organizations in other countries. In some poor countries of Africa and southeast Asia, community organizations, often led by women, endeavour to meet basic needs on a local level, turning their backs upon states and international economic organizations that are perceived as acting against the people. In central America, the Mayan people have recovered historical initiative through armed revolt in the Mexican state of Chiapas, and the indigenous people of Guatemala have fought a civil war to the point of gaining recognition of their claims. These various instances are indicative of something moving in different societies across the globe towards a new vitality of 'bottom-up' movement in civil society as a counterweight to the hegemonic power structure and ideology. This movement is, however, still relatively weak and uncoordinated. It may contain some of the elements but has certainly not attained the status of a counterhegemonic alliance of forces on the world scale.

Exclusionary populism and the covert world

There is a gap between the retreat of the state and the still small development of civil society. This space, this void, attracts other forces. One is exclusionary populism: various forms of extreme right political movements and xenophobic racism. Social anomie is also a propitious recruiting ground for hermetic religious cults. Another set of forces can be called the covert world, a complex congeries of underground activities, some carried out secretly in the name of states, some criminal.

Exclusionary populism has an ambiguous relationship to established power. Extreme right-wing movements in some European countries (France, Italy, Austria,

Belgium, Norway) have captured fifteen per cent or more of the popular vote in the 1990s, and challenge the conventional right to legitimize them by accepting their support.[17] In the United States, the far right perceives a global conspiracy against the basic principles of American life—especially private property, freedom from government control, and the right to have guns—in which the federal government is collusive.[18] Cults like *Aum Shinrikyo* in Japan, or the Solar Temple in Canada, France and Switzerland, and Heaven's Gate in the United States, pose a nihilistic threat to society; they attract well educated people, an indicator of the extent of alienation, and mobilize them in the service of a doomsday scenario.[19]

The covert world comprises intelligence services, organized crime, terrorist groups, the arms trade, money-laundering banks, and secret societies. There is a certain overlap between right wing extremism and the covert world and also between doomsday cults and the covert world. Right wing terrorists have been suspected of collusion with intelligence services in Italy in several bombings. *Aum Shinrikyo* furthered its doomsday plans, including the sarin gas attack in the Tokyo subway in March 1995, with the help of transnational arms dealers.

The various elements of the covert world have usually been studied one by one. Their activities have often been treated as *faits divers,* the material for spy novels and crime fiction. They have not been considered in their interrelationships as constituting a particular sphere of politics existing between visible government and the people. Yet there are many instances of cooperation as well as of conflict among its component elements.

The covert world penetrates the visible authorities in government and corporations. Its expansion was encouraged by the Cold War when, for instance, *mafia* in Italy and *Yakuza* in Japan acquired a supportive relationship with the political party formations that constituted the bulwark against internal opposition to United States Cold War strategy. Money for electoral politics was channelled through covert agencies to sustain anti-Communist coalitions and to influence electoral outcomes. Covert forces assume a functional relationship with neo-liberal deregulated economies. Covert power substitutes for legitimate authority in a totally unregulated market—contracts are enforced by goons with guns.[20] The high cost of electoral politics encourages clandestine political financing which opens the door to covert influences in national politics.

The political space between constituted authority and the people is the terrain on which civil society can be built. A weak and stunted civil society allows free rein to exclusionary politics and covert powers. An expansive participant civil society makes

---

[17] Ignacio Ramonet, 'Néofascisme', *Le Monde diplomatique*, April 1998.

[18] Mark Rupert. 'Globalisation and contested common sense in the United States', in Stephen Gill and James H. Mittelman (eds), *Innovation and Transformation in International Studies* (Cambridge University Press. 1997). The most extreme manifestation of this tendency is withdrawal from American political society with the formation of private militias and perpetration of terrorist acts like the Oklahoma City bombing.

[19] Yumiko Iida. 'Virtual kingdom and dreams of apocalypse: contemporary Japan mirrored in *Aum Shinrikyo*', paper presented at the 10th annual conference of the Japan Studies Association of Canada, Toronto, October 1997.

[20] The most obvious case today is the role of *mafias* in the Russian economy; but an anecdotal instance relates to Argentina where deregulation has led to increased polarization of rich and poor and former members of the naval intelligence service, notorious torturers during the 'dirty war', have been reemployed by private corporations as 'security' staff. 'Argentine killers find new line of work' by Amaranta Wright, *The Globe and Mail* (Toronto) 28 February 1997.

political authority more accountable and reduces the scope for exclusionary politics and covert activity.

The question of civil society in the late 20th century takes us back to the Machiavellian question of the 16th century: how to form the social basis for a new political authority. Where Machiavelli concluded reluctantly that his contemporaries were too corrupt to do it on their own and looked to the Prince to provide the initiative, Gramsci envisaged the Communist Party as the Modern Prince. At the close of the 20th century, comes the vision of a 'post-modern' collective Prince constructed through a coordinating of popular movements. The feasibility of this project would depend upon a resurgence of civil society.

Gramsci's thought and the making of civil society

Gramsci's starting point for thinking about society, consistent with Marxism, was class structure derived from the relations of production. He referred to 'fundamental' classes (bourgeoisie and proletariat); but other non-fundamental classes, e.g. peasants and some elements of the petty bourgeoisie, had considerable importance as potential allies for the working class in the formation of a counterhegemonic bloc. The consciousness of social groups and their organization for political action was built upon this basic material condition.

Consciousness was not, for Gramsci, a direct derivative of class; it was an historical construction, not an automatically determined condition. There were different levels of consciousness. The lowest form was what Gramsci called 'corporative', the collective self-interest of people in a particular material situation. Corporative consciousness did not challenge the *status quo* in any essential respect; it just looked out for the interest of a particular group. The next higher level was class consciousness; it posed the question of the state. For whom was the state? Class consciousness unified various forms of corporative consciousness, e.g. among different groups of workers or among bourgeois whose specific material interests were in competition with one another, to focus upon the formation of political authority that would advance a concept of society based upon the leading fundamental class, in actuality the bourgeoisie but potentially the working class. Class consciousness accentuated the sense of cleavage necessary to move the dialectic forward. Today, 'class' has become a more ambiguous notion as in common discourse it is mixed with a variety of 'identities' in the formation of consciousness: gender, ethnicity, religion, nationality. Often these identities are subjectively opposed one to another and are open to manipulation by dominant powers in state and economy so as to fragment opposition. The common sentiment among them is a sense of oppression or exclusion. Class, in its generic meaning of social divisions arising from exploitation, can be seen as the substratum of this variety of grievances. But the practical problem remains of forging the links among divergent disadvantaged groups that would bind them together in a counterhegemonic formation.

This challenge leads to what for Gramsci was the highest level of consciousness. Hegemonic consciousness, according to Gramsci, would transcend class consciousness by incorporating interests of the 'non-fundamental' social groups into a vision of society based on one or other of the 'fundamental' classes; and it would make this vision appear to be the 'natural order' of society. Gramsci's particular objective in the 1930s was the formation of a bloc led by the industrial working class in alliance with peasantry and petty bourgeois intellectuals. The questions now, towards the close of the 20th century, are: Who will lead? Who will follow?

This progression in consciousness from corporative through class to hegemonic can be taken as a natural history of civil society. On the basis of the material conditions of production, the potential for collective human action is built upon self-conscious human groups. It is necessary to know when production relations have created the conditions requisite for arousing consciousness and for forming a strategy for change. Not to have these basic conditions would be to fall into idealism and utopianism, leading to failure. Though the formation of class or hegemonic consciousness depends upon the existence of these material conditions, conscious-ness is nevertheless an autonomous force. Ideology and the organization of social forces does not flow automatically from material conditions. The critical agents in the raising of consciousness for Gramsci are the organic intellectuals; they serve to clarify the political thinking of social groups, leading the members of these groups to understand their existing situation in society and how in combination with other social groups they can struggle towards a higher form of society.

Two other Gramscian concepts are relevant to this process of building civil society: the war of position and passive revolution. The war of position is a strategy for the long-term construction of self-conscious social groups into a concerted emancipatory bloc within society. It is only when the war of position has built up a combination of organized social forces strong enough to challenge the dominant power in society that political authority in the state can be effectively challenged and replaced. The war of position is contrasted to the war of manoeuvre which might seize state power before this groundwork of social organization had been built up. To win a state by a war of manoeuvre would constitute a fragile victory, likely to succumb to the entrenched forces of a recalcitrant civil society. Thus, a civil society animated through popular participation is an indispensable basis for durable new political authority.

Passive revolution has a variety of meanings in Gramsci's thought. It represents an abortive or incomplete transformation of society and can take various forms. One is change induced in a society by an external force that attracts internal support from some elements but does not overcome the opposition of other entrenched forces. This can lead to an ambivalent situation of 'revolution/restoration' where neither of the opposed bodies of forces is victorious over the other. Passive revolu-tion can also take the form of a stalled war of position strategy which is strong enough to provoke opposition but not strong enough to overcome it. Furthermore, a strategy on the part of the dominant power gradually to coopt elements of the opposition forces—a strategy known in Italian politics as *trasformismo*—is another form of passive revolution. Yet another form would be emancipatory strategies divorced from the material conditions of the social groups involved, inevitably incurring the illusions of utopianism and idealism. Gramsci cited Tolstoyism and Gandhism in this regard. So passive revolution points to many of the inadequacies and obstacles in the attempted construction of civil society.

Variations in prospects for civil society

The restructuring of production is experienced world-wide in generating the three-fold hierarchy of social relations referred to above: integrated, precarious, and excluded. The proportions, however, differ from society to society. The balance between top-down and bottom-up forces in civil society, and the relative importance of right-wing populism and the covert world, result in distinct types of state/society configurations with different implications for civil society. Tentatively, four different patterns may serve to illustrate the range of conditions and prospects of civil society in the world today. These patterns or types are not intended to be exhaustive in covering the whole world, but they do illustrate some of the significantly different situations and prospects for civil society at the present time.

Evolved capitalism in Europe and America

Evolved capitalism in North America and western Europe constituted the point of impetus for economic globalization. Its influence penetrates to the rest of the world, the impact varying according to the level of material development and the resistance of persisting cultural practices in other regions. Production is being restructured in the form of post-Fordism which brings about the pattern of integrated core workers flanked by precariously linked supporting workers. Global finance exerts a continuing pressure on state budgets to reduce the social expenditures built up during the era of Fordism which gave social legitimacy to capital.

There is an implicit contradiction here between production and finance. Production and the 'real economy' that provides goods and services requires time to develop (research and development and the training of a committed labour force); finance has a synchronic space-oriented perspective directed to short-term returns which can often ignore the time dimension and undermine not only the social legitimacy of capital but also the productive apparatus itself (for example, through predatory buy-outs and asset stripping). In the late 20th century, it is global finance rather than production and the 'real economy' that focuses people's attention on the frailties of the economic order.

Another contradiction is between the real economy and the biosphere. Expansion of consumer demand is the driving force of the global economy. World-wide emulation of the consumption model of North America and western Europe would, however, through resource depletion and environmental destruction, bring ruin to the biosphere—the ultimate feed-back mechanism. To escape this disaster would require shifting the use of labour which is surplus to that required to satisfy the basic needs of society (the labour resource currently employed in arousing and in gratifying the superfluity of consumerism) to investment in social and human services (education, health, care of children and the aged, protection of the environment, and conviviality in social life). This would imply a fundamental change in economic organization and values—a revolution in social practices and in the structure of social power.

A further contradiction is in social relations. A large proportion of jobs are in the precarious category. Downgraded skilled workers in this category are often resentful of immigrants and women who are the other significant groups among the precariously employed. Youth and minorities are prominent among the more or less permanently excluded, a volatile and potentially destabilizing group. There is no longer any such formation as the 'working class' of the early 20th century. A privileged part of that former working class has been absorbed into the integrated category. Other elements are in both precarious and excluded categories; and their material conditions can easily be perceived as generating adversarial relationships between downgraded manual workers, immigrants and women workers. The fragmentation of the old working class, a consequence of post-Fordism reinforced by pressures of global finance towards dismantling of the Fordist-era social safety net, has strengthened capital and weakened and divided labour.

The problem for the organic intellectuals of the Left is how to envisage a strategy that could build from this fragmented situation of subordinate social groups a coherent alternative to economic globalization that would transcend (*Aufhebung* in Hegel's meaning) the contradictions just referred to. These organic intellectuals are now themselves a fragmented lot: trade union leaders, environmentalists, social activists on behalf of the poor and homeless and the unemployed, and promoters of self-help community organizations. They compete for potential clientele with right-wing populists, anti-immigrant racists, and religious cults. All of these various movements are meanwhile developing transnational linkages and organizations.

The covert world (organized crime, the drug trade, and intelligence services) occupies a political space that has, if anything, been enlarged by public disillusionment with conventional politics. The high cost of electoral politics sustains hypocrisy in the political class, who ostensibly respond to public support for campaign finance reform while continuing to rely on occult financial contributions, thus remaining open to occult influences. This, in turn, further erodes public confidence in political leadership.

In Europe, evolved capitalism has two variants. One is the 'pure' hyperliberal form which espouses removal of state intervention in the economy by deregulation and privatization and makes competitiveness in the global market its ultimate criterion. This is the dominant variant. The other is the European tradition of social market or social democratic capitalism which sees the viability and legitimacy of an economy as dependent upon its being embedded in social relations recognized as equitable by the general population.[21] The issue between the two forms of capitalism is being fought out at the level of the European Union in the debate over 'social Europe' and the filling of the 'democratic deficit' in European institutions.

In very general terms, we can think of three constellations of forces: first, the dominant forces in states and markets (corporate management and the political class, surreptitiously sustained by the covert world); second, a heterogeneous category of groups commonly identified as constituting civil society in the emancipatory sense (trade unions and 'new social movements'); and third, right-wing and populist movements and religious cults that compete with the preceding groups for support among the unorganized mass of the people.

In attempts to construct a 'bottom-up' social force, the question arises of compatibility between trade unions and the new social movements, e.g. environmentalism, feminism, anti-poverty movements, and peace movements. The new

---

[21] Michel Albert, *Capitalisme contre capitalisme* (Paris: Seuil, 1991).

social movements have often been suspicious of organized labour, fearing domination by labour's tighter and more hierarchical organization which might not respect the social movements' far more loosely structured and more participatory forms of organization. Moreover, the new movements arise more frequently from problems related to consumption, e.g. poverty and homelessness, rather than, as for unions, from the realm of production. On the other hand, organized labour can sometimes, despite its weakened condition in evolved capitalism, be a catalyst for a more broadly based social movement to confront the established powers in state and corporations. Furthermore, a sustained concertation of social forces, i.e. one that would outlast a particular event or crisis, is hard to achieve among groups with the loose and participatory character of the new movements. Coherence and durability over time would be a necessary condition for having a sustained impact on political parties and thus on the state.

Asian capitalism and the cultural dimension

Japanese capitalism is the prototype of another form of capitalism with a different social context.[22] In its origins, the pre-capitalist social and cultural form provided a foundation for imported Western technology and state sponsorship of industrialization. The result was a Japanese form of corporatism in which the state worked closely with business, and the firm developed on the concept of an extended, if bureaucratized, patriarchal family. Group loyalty contributed to organizational strength; but workers were divided between those integrated with the firm and others with a more casual or remote link to the central production organization (contract or out-sourcing workers). The lifetime employment of the first category corresponded to the impermanence of the second. In this manner, Japanese practice prefigured the pattern that globalization has projected on to the world scale.

This initial Asian pattern coincided with authoritarian political structures. The rapid growth of economies, first in Japan during the post-World War II years, and subsequently in several of the newly industrializing Asian economies (Hong Kong, South Korea, Taiwan and Singapore, followed by the Philippines, Thailand, Indonesia and Malaysia), brought into existence both a large middle class oriented towards consumerism and a more combative working class. In some of these countries, pressures from both of these social forces has resulted in attenuation of authoritarianism.

Japan's political structures show continuity in many respects with pre-war patterns. Democratization was introduced under the auspices of the American occupation authorities. Domestic forces in Japan, reacting against the militaristic state that had brought war and ruin, supported the democratic innovations. These forces continued to urge further democratization when US policy shifted ground to bring Japan into the anti-communist Cold War alliance. Other domestic elements, including those associated with the wartime regime, rallied to the new US anti-

[22] See Shigeto Tsuru, *Japan's Capitalism* (Cambridge: Cambridge University Press, 1993); Chalmers Johnson, *MITI and the Japanese Miracle* (Stanford: Stanford University Press, 1982); and James Fallows, *Looking at the Sun: The Rise of the New East Asian Economic and Political System* (New York: Pantheon, 1994).

communist line.[23] Japan's post-war condition is a case of passive revolution in Gramsci's sense. The revolution/restoration balance remains non-catastrophic because the economic growth priority of Japanese governments during the later Cold War period achieved, at least temporarily, a high degree of depoliticization. The democratizing forces of the post-war years were to a large extent demobilized by the general preoccupation with economic growth.

Japanese society has sufficient cohesion on its own, sustained by the long period of economic growth, so that it has in practice made slight demands upon the state. Whether this would continue through a prolonged period of economic stagnation or recession is an open question. Moreover, some Japanese are concerned that the formerly strong cohesion of family and community may be dissolving as a consequence of modernization leading to more emphasis on individualism as well as consumerism and to a lesser commitment to work and organizational loyalties.[24] The covert world, particularly in the forms of organized crime and political corruption, thrives in Japan as it does also in South Korea and other Asian countries.

Asian scholars point to a distinction among three spheres: state, market, and civil society.[25] They see civil society in Asia as a late and still, relatively to Europe, weak development which has focused on democratization, environmentalism, human rights, the peace movement, and various mutual self-help and internationalist goals. In these respects, civil society has made gains in Japan, South Korea, Taiwan and the Philippines. Private groups (including organized crime) contributed spontaneously and effectively to relief after the Kobe earthquake disaster of 1995, when the state's response proved to be disorganized and ineffective. Indeed, the current emphasis on civil society in Asia could be seen, in its emancipatory aspect, as the transnationalizing of the democratizing and people-based forces of Japan and their effort to atone for Japan's war guilt by building cooperative arrangements with communities in other parts of Asia. There is also a movement towards 'Asianization', or the imagining of a regional Asia-wide community of which Japan is a part, which reflects both the consumerist material values of middle-class economic success and a right-wing aesthetic rejection of 'the West'.[26] Authoritarianism has impeded the democratization movement in Singapore, Malaysia and Indonesia, although many local non-governmental organizations exist in these countries. It is difficult to speak of civil society in China so long as the authoritarianism of the Party-state limits the expression of aggrieved elements, although rapid economic growth and social polarization in coastal China is generating stresses that may be hard to contain.

[23] Yoshikazu Sakamoto, 'The international context of the occupation of Japan', in Robert E. Ward and Yoshikazu Sakamoto (eds), *Democratizing Japan: The Allied Occupation* (Honolulu: University of Hawaii Press, 1987); also Yoshikazu Sakamoto, 'Fifty Years of the Two Japans', typescript, 1995.

[24] Professor Tamotsu Aoki, a cultural anthropologist, Research Center for Advanced Science and Technology, University of Tokyo, at a symposium convened jointly by the International House of Japan and the Friedrich-Ebert-Stiftung, Tokyo, September 26, 1996.

[25] Yoshikazu Sakamoto, Professor emeritus of International Relations, Tokyo University and Young-Ho Kim, Professor at Kyungpook National University, South Korea, at a symposium on Prospects for Civil Society in Asia, International House of Japan, Tokyo, September 24, 1996.

[26] The 'Asianization' idea is presented in Yoichi Funabashi, 'The Asianization of Asia', *Foreign Affairs* 72: 5 (1993). The notion of a regional civil society is discussed in Mitchell Bernard, 'Regions in the global political economy: beyond the local-global divide in the formation of the eastern Asian region', *New Political Economy* 1: 3 (November 1996). For a critical assessment, see Yumiko Iida, 'Fleeing the West, making Asia home: transpositions of otherness in Japanese pan-Asianism, 1905–1930', *Alternatives* 22 (1997), pp. 409–432.

Recent events in South Korea have thrown new light on the condition of civil society. The challenge here has come from the effort of the large South Korean corporations, the *chaebols*, to compete as multinational corporations in the global market. Towards this end they persuaded the government to revert to earlier authoritarian practices by restricting labour rights recently acquired so as to give the *chaebols* more flexibility in hiring and firing. At the same time, the government sought to increase the powers of the intelligence services (Korean CIA). This attempt to revert to authoritarianism and to enlarge the sphere of the covert world provoked a general strike in which the labour movement became united and gained support from students, teachers, and religious organizations. The protest was a direct reaction to globalization.[27]

As in the case of the French strikes of December 1995, the trade unions in South Korea provided the impetus for a response by civil society to state authoritarianism. Change in South Korea may be more authentic than passive, but it does not seem to be oriented towards radical structural transformation, but rather to a more liberal legitimation of political authority. In Japan, trade unions have not been identified with a 'bottom-up' transformation of civil society. They have been more aligned with corporations and the jobs they provide. During the 1970s, environmental protests that resulted in political changes at municipal and regional levels in Japan were led by citizens apart from unions. Union members identified their jobs with corporate interests in maintaining production, while their wives might feel freer to participate in the environmentalist revolt.

Thus in some Asian countries capitalist development has generated the class basis for a development of civil society which is weaker than that of Europe in the face of state and corporate authoritarianism but which has nevertheless made some significant progress in recent years. The social forces involved in this emergent civil society are both middle class (including students, environmentalists, peace activists and feminists) and organized workers. The coherence between middle class and worker elements is problematic. Asia gives a mixed picture of authentic and passive structural change in societies.

State breakdown and predatory capitalism

The prototype for this category is the breakdown of the Soviet Union; but instances of the phenomenon are not limited to the former Soviet bloc. Similar situations have arisen in countries of Latin America affected by the debt crisis. In broad outline, the circumstances leading to this situation are: an economic crisis generated by both internal and external causes leaves an authoritarian state unable to carry out the functions it has assumed; external pressures, welcomed by a politically aware stratum of the population, lead to the establishment of a liberal democratic regime based on electoral politics, but civil society is insufficiently developed to provide a firm basis for the new regime; external pressures then succeed in reducing state powers over the economy in favour of an expansion of market forces; the weakness

---

[27] A series of articles by Philippe Pons in *Le Monde*, 3 January, 15 January, and 16 January, 1997; and by Laurent Carroué, *Le Monde diplomatique*, February 1997.

of institutions to regulate the market and the collapse of state authority open the way for organized crime and political corruption to gain control in both state and market spheres; the general population, struggling for personal survival, becomes politically apathetic and non-participant, while some elements nourish a nostalgic hope for salvation by a charismatic leader. The weakness of civil society is the critical element in this catastrophic cycle.

The domestic cause of the collapse of the Soviet regime stemmed from its failure to make the transition from extensive development, i.e. the addition of more productive capacity of the same kind, to intensive development, i.e. innovating production technology with higher productivity. This was exacerbated by the external pressure to accelerate the arms race which placed an intolerable burden on the economy, preventing the state from maintaining the social services it had instituted as basic citizen rights.[28]

In the eastern and central European countries of the bloc, where the arms burden was less than in the Soviet Union, opposition movements developed openly. In Poland, *Solidarnošc* as a trade union became a rallying point for a broad based opposition to the communist regime; and the Catholic Church had long stood as an alternate pole of loyalty to the state. In East Germany, *Neues Forum* mobilized people into the streets to demonstrate against the authoritarian regime. As noted above, the current scholarly interest in civil society very largely originated in observation of the popular movements in Poland, Czechoslovakia, Hungary and the German Democratic Republic which toppled the communist regimes in these countries after the Soviet Union had signalled it would not or could not support them.

These movements crumbled later after they had achieved their initial purpose of overthrowing established state power. In retrospect, in Gramsci's terms, they may seem more like the phenomena of a war of manoeuvre than of a war of position. Liberal democratic regimes were then established in these countries, encouraged by western politicians and media and welcomed by local citizens. These were cases of passive revolution. In the Soviet Union, change came from the top. In Eastern and Central Europe, civil society played a bigger role. But after the collapse of the communist regimes, those who led the popular revolt did not for long remain as major political forces; and the bureaucratic elites of the former regime became the typical private market elites of post-communism. The solidity and durability of civil society remains questionable.

External support for the new regimes came more in the form of exhortations and technical advice urging 'democracy and market reform' than in large-scale investment and access for trade. It was clear that market reform in the ex-communist sphere had priority in western policy and that democracy was perceived as instrumental towards market economics.

When the erosion of state authority and the absence of effective regulation of the market led to a dramatic growth of mafia control over economic activity, corrupt penetration of the state, and the forging of international criminal links, apologists

---

[28] See various writings of János Kornai, including *Economics of Shortage* (Amsterdam: North-Holland, 1980; and 'Dilemmas of a socialist economy', *Cambridge Journal of Economics*, 4: 2 (1980); also Wlodzimierz Brus and Tadeus Kowalik, 'Socialism and development', *Cambridge Journal of Economics*, 7 (1983); and Robert W. Cox, '"Real socialism" in historical perspective' in Ralph Miliband and Leo Panitch (eds), *Socialist Register 1991* (London: Merlin Press, 1991).

for liberal economics showed their preference for crime over state regulation. They could view it with equanimity as a probably necessary stage of primitive capital accumulation.[29] The collapse of state authority also unleashed sub-national forces of ethnic nationalism which became vehicles for garnering the residues of economic and political power.

Several Latin American countries also fit the model—Mexico and Columbia, for example. The decline of state authority is associated with the imposition of 'structural adjustment' policies advocated with financial leverage by the International Monetary Fund and backed by US pressure. Initially, US policy looked to authoritarian solutions to introduce economic liberalism in Latin America, in the manner of the Pinochet coup in Chile. Subsequently, US policy began to advocate liberal democratic forms of state as being more able to sustain the continuity of a liberal economic regime while allowing for changes of government, making the economy less vulnerable to political coup.[30] This, again, implied passive revolution.

In these societies various forms of popular movements have taken root—trade unions, left wing political parties, and the 'new social movements', as well as the episodic manifestations of 'people power' such as toppled the Marcos regime in the Philippines or 'IMF riots' provoked by rising food and transport prices. There is some evidence that, under the impact of structural adjustment, unions and social action movements have pulled together despite their mutual suspicions of earlier years and have worked to support left wing political parties.[31] However, groups led by social activists have focused more on local demands often obtained by the old patterns of clientelism and compromise with authorities than on the broader aims of change in social and economic structures which are the concern of left wing political parties. These left wing parties have, in turn, been weakened nationally by the hegemony of globalization ideology. Furthermore, promotion of civil society has been coopted by forces behind the propagation of neo-liberal economics as a way of defusing and channelling potential protest.[32] Consequently, civil society, in its dual form of class-based organizations and social activism, has a latent but not very fully realized potential for social and political transformation. The covert world, in the form of organized crime, drug cartels and political corruption, is rife in these countries. The decline of state authority is not matched by a development of civil society.

The most open challenge to the impact of globalization on social and political structures has come from a new type of revolutionary movement, the *Zapatista* rebellion of the Mayan Indians in the southern Mexican state of Chiapas that broke out on New Year's day 1994. This was the day on which the North American Free Trade Area came into effect, which symbolized the anti-globalization message of the

---

[29] László Andor, 'Economic transformation and political stability in East Central Europe', *Security Dialogue*, 27: 2 (June 1996).

[30] See William I. Robinson, *Promoting Polyarchy. Globalization, US Intervention, and Hegemony* (Cambridge: Cambridge University Press, 1996) which contains case studies of the Philippines, Chile, Nicaragua, Haiti, South Africa, and the former Soviet bloc; also William I. Robinson, 'Globalization, the world system, and 'democracy promotion' in US foreign policy', *Theory and Society*, 25 (1996), pp. 615–65.

[31] Judith Adler Hellman, 'The riddle of new social movements: who they are and what they do', in Sandor Halebsky and Richard L. Harris (eds), *Capital, Power, and Inequality in Latin America* (Boulder, CO: Westview Press, 1995).

[32] Laura Macdonald, *Supporting Civil Society*, (see footnote 12 above).

revolt. Indigenous peoples in different parts of the world have proclaimed their distinctness as social formations demanding control of their ancestral lands. The *Zapatistas* have gone beyond this to cultivate international support and attempt to change the Mexican political system. They have sought to transcend both the hierarchical military character of the rebellion in its initial phase and its ethnic base of support in order to become a rallying force in civil society of all forces for democratic change, in other words to create the beginnings of a counterhegemonic bloc.[33]

Africa: civil society versus the state

In Africa there are even more extreme cases of state breakdown and of alienation of people from the state. State structures inherited from colonial regimes had no close relationship to local populations to begin with; yet the state controlled access to any economic activity more substantial than peasant agriculture and petty trading. The political struggle for control of the state was thus a struggle for a share of the economic product of the country, a product divided between foreign investors and the power holders in the state. There has been a history of resistance to this pattern. Some social revolutionary movements and attempts at social democratic experiments have endeavoured to create political authorities that were based on African community life—movements led by Amilcar Cabral in Guinea-Bissau, Samora Machel in Mozambique, and Julius Nyerere in Tanzania, for example. However, obstacles, mainly external in origin, impeded the success of these struggles for a more participant polity.[34] The Cold War came to dominate African politics as both the United States and the Soviet Union chose allies among the power-holders in African states and armed them. This strengthened the tendency towards military rule and towards African states taking the form of kleptocracies—dictators with armed bands that served both as praetorian guards and as gangs who pillaged the population. Mobutu's Zaire was a prime example.

In these circumstances, it is not to be wondered that African people did not readily identify with their rulers. Furthermore, foreign capital proved to be equally hostile to people's welfare. Foreign investors, with the connivance of African states, have damaged the ecology upon which local people depend for their livelihood. The international financial agencies (IMF and World Bank) impose structural adjustment policies that have placed heavy burdens on the populations of these countries.

---

[33] Maurice Najman, 'Le grand virage des zapatistes' in *Le Monde diplomatique*, January 1997. A sketch of the world view of the Zapatistas is to be found in Sous-commandant Marcos, 'La 4e guerre mondiale a commencé', *Le Monde diplomatique*, August 1997.

[34] Amilcar Cabral was a particularly articulate leader who expounded in theory and practice the position that popular participation in revolutionary action and cultural change were essential for African peoples to raise themselves out of imperialist domination. Although the momentum of his movement stalled, following Cabral's assassination by agents of Portuguese colonialism, the historian Basil Davidson thinks that Cabral's success in mobilizing Africans to make their own history has left its impact and example to inspire a renewed movement. See Basil Davidson, *The Search for Africa. History, Culture, Politics* (New York: Random House, 1994, esp. pp. 217–43); and *Unity and Struggle. Speeches and Writings of Amilcar Cabral* (New York and London: Monthly Review, 1979). Cabral's speeches and writing have striking similarity to Gramsci's thought.

In consequence, many Africans have come to see the state and the international institutions as their enemies and have organized in a variety of self-help community groups to confront the daily problems of life, shunning any link to the state. Women have been prominent as initiators and leaders in this movement. An Ethiopian economist has called it 'the silent revolution in Africa'.[35] Similar movements exist in some other poor countries.

This is a form of incipient civil society that has turned its back on the state. The question remains open whether it could develop into a force that would engage with the state to alter the state's character and become the foundation for a new participant form of democracy.[36]

Conclusions

The nature and condition of civil society is very diverse, looked at on a world scale. It is, nevertheless, tempting to look at this diversity through the analytic lens of Gramsci's conceptualization of relations of forces (PN, pp. 180–85). Civil society is itself a field of power relations; and forces in civil society relate, in support or opposition, to powers in state and market.

The first level in Gramsci's relation of forces, is the 'relation of social forces' by which he meant objective relations independent of human will brought about by the level of development of the material forces of production. Through the effect of economic globalization and the passage from Fordism to post-Fordism in the present day world, this has brought about a basic cleavage between, on the one hand, the beneficiaries of globalization or those people who are integrated into the world economy, and on the other hand, those who are disadvantaged within or excluded from the world economy. The latter would include some who, in a precarious way, may become intermittent adjuncts to the world economy and whose

---

[35] Fantu Cheru, *The Silent Revolution in Africa: Debt, Development and Democracy* (Harare and London: Zed/Anvil Press, 1989). Basil Davidson, *The Search for Africa* (see footnote 34 above) has also referred to this phenomenon: 'One finds [in Africa] the striving of countless individuals and collectives towards new types of self-organization—perhaps one should say self-defense—aimed in one way or another at operating outside the bureaucratic centralism of the neocolonial state' (p. 290).

[36] Basil Davidson, 'Africa: the politics of failure', *Socialist Register 1992* edited by Ralph Miliband and Leo Panitch (London: Merlin Press, 1992), envisaged the possibility that more participatory politics in Africa might develop within the framework of market economics, but concluded rather pessimistically: 'How far the developed world of multinational concentrations of power will bring itself to tolerate this devolutionary politics of participation, and its democratic implications, is [a] question to which, at present, we do not have an answer' (p. 225). The fall of the Mobutu regime in Zaire and its replacement by the Democratic Republic of the Congo under Laurent-Désiré Kabila did not really test Davidson's proposition. Kabila's victory was achieved by military means with considerable support from Ugandan and Rwandan military forces. The struggle seemed to take place over the heads of the vast majority of Zaire's population which has evolved techniques of survival in communities that have avoided involvement with the state and the formal economy. Although these elements of autonomous civil society do exist, they have not yet been able to evolve a real politics of participation that could be the foundation for a new state. See e.g. Colette Braeckman, 'Comment le Zaïre fut libéré' *Le Monde diplomatique*, July 1997. In other works, Davidson seems more optimistic about the long range potential for the development of civil society and 'the elaboration of a culture capable of drawing the civilization of the Africans out of the fetters into which it has fallen, and of giving that civilization, in its multitudinous aspects and varieties, a life and meaning appropriate to its present tasks and destiny.' (Basil Davidson, *The Search for Africa*, pp. 261–2 (see footnote 34 above)).

interests may thus waver between hope for more stable affiliation and outright antagonism in despair of achieving it.

This cleavage does not yield anything so clear as the Marxian cleavage along property lines between bourgeoisie and proletariat. The proletariat is divided now between some beneficiaries of globalization and many disadvantaged. The petty bourgeoisie is also divided between some who would identify with the world economy and others who are disadvantaged or excluded in relation to it. Many people would need to be understood more in their relationship to consumption (or the inability to consume adequately) rather than to production—the more or less permanently unemployed, the inhabitants of shanty towns, welfare recipients, and students. The old production-related categories are not entirely superseded; but the scheme of categories of people relevant to the problematic of social change needs to be rethought.

Gramsci's second level, which he called the relation of political forces, addresses the question of consciousness. In today's context, the challenge is to bridge the differences among the variety of groups disadvantaged by globalization so as to bring about a common understanding of the nature and consequences of globalization, and to devise a common strategy towards subordinating the world economy to a regime of social equity. This means building a counterhegemonic historic bloc that could confront the hegemonic formation of globalization in a long term war of position.

Gramsci's strategic concepts are pertinent here, including particularly the role of organic intellectuals. Their task now is to be able to work simultaneously on local, regional and world levels. The obstacles are considerable in that the active or potential opposition to globalization is divided on many issues. There is opposition between manual workers protecting their jobs in environmentally destructive and polluting industries and environmentalists working to stop these industrial practices. Other conflicts arise between manual workers in mature industrial countries who face downgrading through global competition and workers in recently industrializing countries or immigrant workers from poor countries who are perceived to be taking away their jobs. Still other conflicts arise from the claims by indigenous peoples for lands and control of resources that conflict with the aims of mining and forestry corporations and their workers. Also there is the issue between the claims of women's movements for equity in employment and the fears of precariously employed male workers. Organic intellectuals linked to these various groups face a difficult task of transcending the immediate corporative instincts of these groups and the oppositions they engender to other disadvantaged or excluded groups, in order to achieve a commonly shared vision of a desirable and feasible alternative future and a strategy for joint action. They must at the same time do battle with the right wing forces of anti-immigrant racist nationalism, neo-fascism, authoritarian populism, and nihilistic religious cults, which compete for the allegiance of people where social bonds have disintegrated and apathy and alienation has become the norm.

Gramsci's third level in the relation of forces was the relation of military forces, which he divided into two parts: one, the technical military function which we may read as control of the repressive apparatus of a state; and the other, the politico-military, refers to the morale of a population, to the degree of coherence or disintegration among people. In the absence of high morale, struggle against a dominant power over people, whether foreign or domestic, would be improbable. The condition that sustains an oppressive regime, Gramsci wrote, is a 'state of social disintegration of the . . . .people, and the passivity of the majority among them' (PN, p. 183). This, in varying degrees, is the situation characteristic of the populations engulfed by globalization today. To overcome this social disintegration and passivity will require the creation of a vibrant civil society inspired by a strong spirit of solidarity at the community level and, by linkage with other strong communities in other countries, at the transnational or global level. Upon such a basis of participatory democracy new political authorities may in the long run be constructed at national, regional and world levels.

One aspect in developing a vision and strategy is to shift from a predominantly space-oriented and synchronic mode of thinking to a predominantly time-oriented and diachronic or dialectical mode of thinking. Oppositions that are apparently objective in the immediate may be overcome through attacking the structures that ensure the persistence of these oppositions. First among these is the doctrine subscribed to by corporate capital and most governments, and propagated by the intellectuals and media of the status quo, that competitiveness in the world economy is the ultimate criterion of policy. This is the primary form of alienation in the world today—the imagining of a force created by people that stands over them proclaiming that 'there is no alternative'. This contemporary deity will have to be deconstructed to make way for an alternative vision of a world economy regulated in the interest of social equity and non-violent resolution of conflict.

The other important aspect of creating a counterhegemonic bloc is revival of a spirit of solidarity. The crisis of capitalism in the mid 1970s and the subsequent supremacy of the globalization dynamic has not only weakened psychological bonds between people and states but also the level of trust among people themselves and their disposition for collective action. The result is an increase in cynicism, apathy and non-participation of people in politics and social action.[37] Increasingly politics are not about choices concerning the future of society but rather about choices among competing sets of would-be managers of the status quo, many of whom are tainted by corruption and most of whom are professedly incompetent to think of, let alone pursue, an alternative.[38] The political space abandoned by people has been readily taken up by the covert world, which has become functional to the financing of established political systems and is involved in a substantial part of world markets.

Civil society has become the crucial battleground for recovering citizen control of public life. It seems that very little can be accomplished towards fundamental change through the state system as it now exists. That system might be reconstructed on the

---

[37] The American sociologist Robert D. Putnam has suggested that civil society in the United States has lost much of the spirit of association once noted by de Tocqueville as its salient characteristic. He sees this as being replaced by non-participation in group activities and a privatizing or individualizing of leisure time. He calls this a decline of 'social capital' which refers to networks, norms, and social trust that facilitate coordination and cooperation for mutual benefit. See Putnam, 'Bowling alone: America's declining social capital', *Journal of Democracy*, 6: 1 (January 1995). The same author has made a study about social capital in Italy: Putnam with Robert Leonardi and Raffaella Y. Nanetti, *Making Democracy Work. Civic Traditions in Modern Italy* (Princeton: Princeton University Press, 1993).

[38] See, for example, the brilliant essay by Jean-Marie Guéhenno, *La fin de la démocratie* (Paris: Flammarion, 1993).

basis of a reinvigorated civil society which could only come about through a long term war of position. Meanwhile, a two-track strategy for the Left seems appropriate: first, continued participation in electoral politics and industrial action as a means of defensive resistance against the further onslaught of globalization; and secondly, but ultimately more importantly, pursuit of the primary goal of resurrecting a spirit of association in civil society together with a continuing effort by the organic intellectuals of social forces to think through and act towards an alternative social order at local, regional and global levels.

[20]

Oxford Development Studies, Vol. 26, No. 1, 1998

Global Civil Society: Perspectives, Initiatives, Movements

RICHARD FALK

ABSTRACT *This article focuses on the efforts of voluntary associations, rooted in a global consciousness, to address the negative impacts of globalization. In part, this encounter reflects the extent to which globalization has been unfolding in recent years in an ideological climate of neo-liberalism. As a result, there has been steady downward pressure on the social agenda of governments and international institutions. Globalization-from-below represents an overall effort to moderate market logic by reference to the following values embodied in "normative democracy", a view of democracy that takes account of the emergence of global village realities: consent of affected peoples; rule of law in all arenas of decision; human rights; effective modes of participation; accountability; support for public goods to address basic needs; transparency; and non-violence as a principle of public order.*

1. Note on Terminology

The emphasis of this article is upon social forces that respond to the patterns of behavior associated with the phenomena of economic globalization. As a consequence, it seems preferable on balance to frame such activity by reference to "global civil society" rather than to "transnational civil society". Even so the word "society" is definitely problematic at this stage of global social and political evolution, due to absence of boundaries and weakness of social bonds transcending nation, race and gender. Such a difficulty exists whether the reference is to "transnational civil society" or to "global civil society". But the transnational referent tends to root the identity of the actors in the subsoil of national consciousness to an extent that neglects the degree to which the orientation is not one of crossing borders, but of inhabiting and constructing a polity appropriate for the global village. Such a nascent global polity is already partly extant, yet remains mostly emergent. (For helpful conceptual discussion of these issues of conceptual framing, see Wapner, 1996.)

   A similar issue arises with respect to the terminology useful in aggregating the actors. It seems convenient to retain the term non-governmental organizations (NGOs) to designate those actors associated with global civil society because it is accurate and convenient, being so widely used and thus easily recognizable. But it is also somewhat misleading in relation to the fundamental hypothesis of a diminishing ordering capability by the sovereign state and states system. To contrast the actors and action of global civil society with the governments of states, as is done by calling them NGOs, is

Richard Falk, Centre for International Studies, Bendheim Hall, Princeton University, Princeton, NJ 08544, USA.

1360–0818/98/010099–12 © 1998 International Development Centre, Oxford

100   *R. Falk*

to confer a derivative status and to imply the persistence of a superordinate Westphalian world of sovereign states as the only effective constituents of contemporary world order. Until recently this hierarchical dualism was justifiable because the preeminence of the state was an empirical reality, reinforced by the absence of any other significant international actors capable of autonomous action.

To overcome this difficulty of relying upon this somewhat anachronistic statist rhetoric, James Rosenau has proposed an alternative terminology to that of NGOs by calling such entities "sovereignty free actors" (Rosenau, 1990). Besides being obscure, such a substitute terminology is still operating in a Westphalian shadowland in which actor identities are exclusively derived from sovereign actors, namely, states. A comparable problem exists if the reference is to "transnational social forces", although the sense of "transnational" is more flexible and autonomous than "sovereignty free". Another possibility was proposed some years ago by Marc Nerfin (1986), in the form of a framework that recognized the social reality of "the third system" (the first sector being that of states, the second of market forces), from which issued forth civil initiatives of motivated citizens supportive of the global public good.

There is by now a wide and growing literature on "global civil society", especially as related to environmental politics on a global level. (For concise overview see Wapner, 1996; Lipschutz, 1996). For the purposes of this article global civil society refers to the field of action and thought occupied by individual and collective citizen initiatives of a voluntary, non-profit character both within states and transnationally. These initiatives proceed from a global orientation and are responses, in part at least, to certain globalizing tendencies that are perceived to be partially or totally adverse. At present, most of the global provocation is associated directly or indirectly with market forces and the discipline of regional and global capital. As will be made clear, such a critical stance toward economic globalization does not entail an overall repudiation of these developments, but it does seek to regulate adverse effects and correct social injustices.

To focus inquiry further, I also propose to rely upon a distinction that I have used previously: drawing a basic dividing-line between global market forces identified as "globalization-from-above" and a set of oppositional responses in the third system of social activism that is identified as "globalization-from-below" (Falk, 1993, 1995). This distinction may seem unduly polarizing and hierarchical, apparently constructing a dualistic world of good and evil. My intention is neither hierarchical nor moralistic, and there is no illusion that the social forces emanating from the third system are inherently benevolent, while those from the first and second systems are necessarily malevolent. Far from it. One of the arguments of the article is that there are dangerous chauvinistic and extremist societal energies being released by one series of responses to globalization-from-above that are threatening the achievements of the modern secular world that had been based on the normative side of the evolution of an anarchic society of states in the cumulative direction of humane governance. (This normative potential of statism has been most influentially articulated by Hedley Bull, 1977.) To situate the argument, it is important to acknowledge that there are strong positive effects and potentialities arising from the various aspects of globalization-from-above. At the same time, the historic role of globalization-from-below is to challenge and transform the negative features of globalization-from-above, both by providing alternative ideological and political space to that currently occupied by market-oriented and statist outlooks and by offering resistances to the excesses and distortions that can be properly attributed to globalization in its current phase. That is, globalization-from-below is not dogmatically opposed to globalization-from-above, but addresses itself to the avoidance of adverse effects and to providing an overall counterweight to the essentially unchecked influence currently exerted by business and finance on the process of decision at the level of the state and beyond.

2. Deforming Historical Circumstances

The distinctive challenges posed by globalization-from-above have been accentuated by certain defining historical circumstances. Above all, the ending of the Cold War generated an ideological atmosphere in the North supportive of an abandonment of Keynesian approaches to economic policy, and its replacement by a strong version of neo-liberal reliance on private sector autonomy and an economistic approach to social policy, that is, eroding the social compromises between labor and business by way of achieving fiscal austerity, efficient allocation of resources, privatization and international competitiveness. There were other pressures to move in these directions, including a pendulum swing in societal attitudes against "the welfare state" in many states, a generalized distrust of government and public sector approaches to problem-solving, the steadily declining political leverage of organized labor, the waning of industrialism and the waxing of electronics and informatics, an overall disenchantment with ameliorative rhetoric and proposals, and, above all, pressures to neutralize the alleged competitive advantages of countries in the South, especially those in the Asia/Pacific region.

These alleged competitive advantages are associated with the political and economic unevenness of states, and refer especially to cheap skilled labor, minimal regulation and high profit margins that have been supposedly draining jobs and capital away from the North. These differentials have ethically ambiguous consequences, reinforcing neo-liberal rationalizations for harsher economic policy and contributing to chauvinistic backlash politics in the North, while liberating many of the most populous countries in the South from centuries of acute poverty and massive human suffering.

In effect, the material and technological foundation of globalization, based on the possibilities for profitable expansion of business operations without regard to state boundaries, did not necessarily have to be linked to an ideological abandonment of the social agenda and downsizing pressures on public goods, including a disturbing decline in support for mechanisms to protect the global commons and the global public good. Neo-liberal approaches and ideological justifications have been latent in market economies ever since the birth of capitalism during the industrial revolution, but somewhat surprisingly the nastiest features of early capitalism were moderated to varying degrees in the 19th and 20th Centuries in response to the rise of "the dangerous classes", the labor movement, the ordeal of business cycles culminating in The Great Depression, and the adjustments promoted by different versions of "social democracy", and what came to be known in the USA as "liberalism".

Indeed, the recent change in ideological atmosphere can be rapidly understood by the delegitimation of liberalism in the USA since the 1980s, making even those political perspectives of the most socially sensitive leaders in the Democratic Party unwilling any longer to use or accept the liberalism as a label of what came to be derisively called "the L word". What has emerged in this first stage of globalization after the end of the Cold War is a neo-liberal consensus among political élites in the world, powerfully disseminated by a business-oriented and consumerist global media, a power shift that helps explain the economistic orientation of most governments. (For a more historically grounded view of globalization, see Clark, 1997.) In the North, this consensus tends to be justified by reference to the discipline of global capital, or simply by reference to "competitiveness", the struggle for market shares and the virtues of free trade. Such an

102   *R. Falk*

ideological setting is often merged with globalization to make the one indistinguishable from the other.

The evolving perspective of those social forces associated with globalization-from-below is that it remains possible and essential to promote the social agenda while retaining most of the benefits of globalization-from-above (Hirst & Thompson, 1996, 1–17, 170–194). In effect, globalization can be enacted in a variety of governance and fiscal scenarios, including some that are more people-oriented and supportive of global public goods and the goals of the social agenda. The ideological infrastructure of globalization is rather structural, and its reformulation is at the core of the convergent perspectives implied by the emergence of global civil society as the bearer of alternative visions of a more sustainable and compassionate future world order (Falk, 1995). Often this normative convergence is concealed beneath the more particularized banners of human rights, environmental protection, feminism and social justice that have been unfurled within global civil society by issue-oriented social movements that have been transnationally active during the last several decades.

It is also important to acknowledge the limited undertaking of globalization-from-below. It is not able to challenge globalization as such, only to alter the guiding ideas that are shaping enactment. Globalization is too widely accepted and embedded to be reversible in its essential integrative impact. Recent global trends establish the unchallengeable dominance of markets and their integration. In Jeffrey Sachs' words, "...capitalism has now spread to nearly 90% of the world's population, since nearly all parts of the world are now linked through open trade, convertible currencies, flows of foreign investment, and political commitments to private ownership as the engine of economic growth" (Sachs, 1997, p. 11). Sachs points out that only 20 years earlier such conditions pertained to only 20% of the world's population, the rest of humanity being subjected either to command socialist economies or to clumsy Third World efforts to combine capitalism and socialism. Such a shift in so short a time, of course, inevitably produces a fundamental reshaping of the ideas and practices constitutive of world order.

It is this process of economic restructuring according to the logic of markets that establishes the context for globalization-from-below. The strategic question is how can these forces effectively challenge the uneven adverse effects of globalization-from-above as it is currently evolving. These adverse consequences include insufficient attention to environmental protection and resource conservation, failures to offset severe vulnerabilities of social segments, countries and regions that are not currently able to gain sufficient access to the market, and a generalized lack of support for the social agenda and global public goods, including the United Nations (UN), especially in its efforts to coordinate and promote moves to overcome world poverty and to close the gaps that separate rich from poor.

3. Responding to Economic Globalization

There have been varied failed responses to economic globalization, conceived of as the capitalist portion of the world economy. Without entering into an assessment of these failures, it is worth noticing that both Soviet-style socialism and Maoism, especially during the period of the Cultural Revolution, were dramatic efforts to oppose economic globalization that ended in disaster. By contrast, despite the difficulties, the subsequent embrace of the market by China under the rubric of "modernization" and even by Russia (and the former members of the Soviet empire) in the form of the capitalist path have been spectacularly successful. The same is true for many Third World countries that had forged a middle path between socialism and capitalism that made the state a major player in the economy, particularly with respect to public utilities and energy; for most of these countries, as well, the change from a defensive hostility toward the world market to a position of unconditional receptivity has been generally treated as a blessing.

The learning experience at the level of the state has been one of submission to the discipline of global capital as it pertains to the specific conditions of each country. Fashionable ideas of "delinking" and "self-reliance" are in a shambles, perhaps most easily appreciated by the inability of North Korea to feed its population, while its capitalist sibling in South Korea is scaling the peaks of affluence. In effect, the geopolitical managers of the world economy use such policies as a punishment for supposedly deviant states, seeking to legitimize the exclusion under the rubric of "sanctions", a policy often widely criticized in this period because of its cruel effects on the civilian population of the target society. Even Castro's Cuba, for so long an impressive holdout, is relying on standard capitalist approaches to attract foreign investment and open its economy to market forces. Fukuyama's notorious theme about the end of history is partially correct, at least for now, if understood as limited in its application to economic aspects of policy, and not extended to political life (Fukuyama, 1992).

Another direction of response to economic globalization has been negative in the form of backlash politics that looks either at some pre-modern traditional framework as viable and virtuous (as with religious extremists of varying identity, or of indigenous peoples) or ultra-territorialists that seek to keep capital at home and exclude foreigners to the extent possible. These responses, aside from those of indigenous peoples, have a rightist flavor because of their emphasis on the sacred religious or nationalist community of the saved that is at war with an evil "other", being either secularist or outsider. To the extent that such movements have gained control of the state, as in Iran since the Islamic Revolution, or even threatened to do so, as in Algeria since 1992, the results have been dismal: economic deterioration, political repression, and widespread civil strife. Specific causes of these backlash phenomena are related to the failures of globalization and its related secularist outlook, but the correctives proposed have yet to exhibit a capacity to generate an alternative that is capable of either successful economic performance or able to win genuine democratic consent from relevant political communities.

Related to this predominance of market forces is a series of attempts by civil society to avoid the adverse effects of economic globalization. The most effective of these responses have been issue-oriented, often involving local campaigns against a specific project. One notable attempt to enter the domain of transformative politics more generally was made by the green parties in Europe during the 1980s. This green movement often exhibited tactical brilliance in its moves to expose the deficiencies of globalizing trends, especially their dangers to the environment. Its political success was less its ability to mobilize large numbers in support of its causes and programmes, but the extent to which its challenge influenced the whole center of the political spectrum to put the environmental challenge high on its policy agenda. But the green movement's attempt to generalize its identity to provide an alternative leadership for the entire society across the full range of governance or to transnationalize its activities to promote global reform met with frustration and internal controversy that fractured green unity, most vividly in Germany, but elsewhere as well. Those who argued for a new radicalism beyond established political parties within a green framework were dismissed as Utopian dreamers while those who opted for influence within the existing

104   *R. Falk*

framework were often scorned as victims of co-optation or derided as opportunists. The green movement and its political parties have persisted in the 1990s, but as a voice on the margins with neither a credible alternative world view to that provided by globalization nor a sufficiently loyal constituency to pose a threat to the mainstream.

Localism has been another type of response directed at the siting of a nuclear power reactor or dam, mobilizing residents of the area facing displacement and loss of traditional livelihood, and sometimes involving others from the society and beyond, who identify with the poor or nature. These struggles have had some notable successes (Shiva, 1987; Rich, 1994). But these are reactions to symptomatic disorders associated with globalization, and do little more than influence entrepreneurial forces to be more prudent or to make more public relations efforts.

More relevant have been attempts by elements of global civil society to protect the global commons against the more predatory dimensions of globalization. Here Greenpeace has a distinguished record of activist successes, exhibiting an imaginative and courageous willingness to challenge entrenched military and commercial forces by direct action that has had an impact: helping to discourage whaling, protesting against the effort of Shell Oil to dispose of the oil rig Brent Spar in the North Sea, supporting a 50 year moratorium on mineral development in Antarctica and, most memorably, resisting for many years nuclear testing in the Pacific. Rachel Carson's lyrical environmentalism and Jacques Cousteau's extraordinarily intense dedication to saving the oceans suggest the extent to which even single, gifted individuals can exert powerful counter-tendencies to the most destructive sides of an insufficiently regulated market. But these efforts, although plugging some of the holes in the dikes, are not based on either a coherent critique or alternative ideology, and thus operate only at the level of the symptom, while neglecting the disorders embedded in the dynamics of globalization.

Some other efforts to awaken responses have arisen from global civil society on the basis of a more generalized assessment. One of the earliest such initiatives was that promoted by the Club of Rome, a transnational association of individuals prominent in business, science and society that led to the famous study *The Limits to Growth* (Meadows *et al.*, 1972). The argument, tied closely to a sophisticated computer program that was measuring trends in population growth, pollution, resource scarcity and food supply concluded that industrialism as being practised was not sustainable, but was tending toward imminent catastrophe. Around the same time a group of distinguished scientists from various countries working with the British journal, *The Ecologist*, issued their own warning call under the title *Blueprint for Survival* (Goldsmith, 1972). These alarms provoked a debate and led to some adjustments, but the resilience of the world capitalist system was such that no fundamental changes occurred, and the warnings issued as signals soon faded into the cultural noise. Neither a sense of alternative nor a movement of protest and opposition took hold.

The World Order Models Project (WOMP) is illustrative of a somewhat more remote effort to challenge the existing order and find alternatives, through the medium of diagnosis and prescription by a transnational group of independent academicians. The efforts of this group have been confined to the margins of academic reflection on world conditions. Also, until recently, the policy focus and animating preoccupation was centered on war, and then broadened somewhat later to include environmental danger. Although WOMP did produce overall assessments, its background and participants made it less sensitive to the distinctive challenges and contributions of economic globalization (Falk, 1995, 1996, 1997a). As such, its emphasis on war and the war-making sovereign state did not come to terms with either the durability of the state or the need to avoid its *instrumentalization* by global market forces. That is, the principal world order danger is no longer the absolute security claims of the sovereign state, but rather the inability of the state to protect its own citizenry, especially those who are most vulnerable, in relation to the workings of the world economy.

A better connected effort to address overall global issues was attempted by the Commission on Global Governance, as expressed in its main report, *Our Global Neighborhood* (Commission, 1995). This initiative, claiming authority and credibility on the basis of the eminence of its membership drawn from the leading ranks of society, and stressing past or present government service at leadership or ministerial levels, seemed too farsighted for existing power structures and too timid to engage the imagination of the more activist and militant actors in civil society. The Commission report failed to arouse any widespread or sustained interest despite the comprehensiveness and thoughtfulness of its proposals. As an intellectual tool it is also disappointing, failing to clarify the challenge of globalization and the troublesome character of Bretton Woods approaches to world economic policy. As a result, its efforts to anchor an argument for global reform around an argument for "global governance" seemed more likely to consolidate globalization-from-above than to promote a creative equilibrium relying on the balancing contribution of globalization-from-below. In part, this Commission report was unlucky, beginning its efforts in the aftermath of the Gulf War when attention and hopes were centered on the future of the UN and finishing its work at a time when the world organization was widely, if somewhat unfairly, discredited as a result of the outcomes in Somalia, Bosnia and Rwanda. But this was not the fundamental problem, which was more a failure of nerve to address the adverse consequence of globalization, a focus that would have put such a commission on a collision course with adherents of the neo-liberal economistic world picture. Given the claims of "eminence" and "independent funding" that characterize such a commission, it is not to be expected that it would be willing or able to address the structural and ideological deficiencies attributable to the prevailing world order framework. This means that its best efforts confirm pessimism about finding an alternative world picture to that provided by the neo-liberal prism on globalization.

What is being argued, then, is that the challenges posed by economic globalization have not as yet engendered a sufficient response in two connected respects: first, the absence of an ideological posture that is comparably coherent to that being provided by various renditions of neo-liberalism, and that could provide the social forces associated with globalization-from-below with a common theoretical framework, political language and programme; secondly, a clear expression of a critique of globalization-from-above that cuts deeply enough to address the most basic normative challenges associated with poverty, social marginalization and environmental decay, while accepting the emancipatory contributions being made, as well as the unchallengeable persistence of state and market; the political goals of globalization-from-below are thus at once both drastic and reformist.

It is central to realize that the world order outcomes arising from the impact of economic globalization are far from settled, and in no sense pre-determined. The forces of globalization-from-above have taken control of globalization and are pushing it in an economistic direction that considerably instrumentalizes the state on behalf of a set of attitudes and policies: privatization, free trade, fiscal austerity and competitiveness. But there are other options: "sustainable development", "global welfare", "cybernetic libertarianism". The eventual shape of globalization will reflect the play of these diverse perspectives and priorities. The perspectives and priorities of globalization-from-above are being challenged in various ways, but mainly piecemeal. The effort of the final section is to encourage a mobilization of the now disparate forces of globalization-from-below in the direction of greater solidity and political weight. It is my conviction that such mobilization is most likely to occur beneath the banner of democracy, but democracy reformulated in relation to the basic aspirations of peoples everywhere to participate in the processes that are shaping their lives.

The purpose of the next section is mainly to clarify what is meant by "democracy" in relation to the analysis of globalization.

4. Toward Coherence: The Theory and Practice of Normative Democracy

To introduce the idea of "normative democracy" is to offer a proposal for a unifying ideology capable of mobilizing and unifying the disparate social forces that constitute global civil society, and provide the political energy that is associated with globalization-from-below. The specification of normative democracy is influenced strongly by David Held's work on democratic theory and practice, particularly his formulations of "cosmopolitan democracy", but it offers a slightly different terminology so as to emphasize the agency role of global civil society with its range of engagements that go from the local and grassroots to the most encompassing arenas of decision (Archibugi *et al.*, 1995; Held, 1995). Normative democracy also draws upon Walden Bello's call for "substantive democracy", set forth as a more progressive movement alternative to the more limited embrace of constitutional democracy (Bello, 1997). I prefer normative to substantive democracy because of its highlighting of ethical and legal norms, thereby reconnecting politics with moral purpose and values, which calls attention to the moral emptiness of neo-liberalism, consumerism and most forms of secularism. There is also a practical reason: to weaken the political appeal of resurgent organized religion while at the same time acknowledging the relevance of moral purpose and spiritual concerns to the renewal of progressive politics.

Contrary to widespread claims in the West, there is no empirical basis for the argument that economic performance is necessarily tied to constitutional democracy and human rights. Several countries in the Asia/Pacific region, most significantly China, have combined an outstanding macroeconomic record with harsh authoritarian rule. Globalization-from-above is not an assured vehicle for the achievement of Western style constitutional democracy, including the protection of individual and group rights. But democracy, as such, is of the essence of a meaningful form of political action on the part of global civil society, especially to the extent that such action even when revolutionary refrains from and repudiates violent means. In this regard, there is an emergent, as yet implicit, convergence of ends and means on the part of several distinct tendencies in civil society issue-oriented movements; non-violent democracy movements; governments that minimize their links to geopolitical structures. This convergence presents several intriguing opportunities for coalition-building, and greater ideological coherence in the outlook associated with globalization-from-below. Against this background, normative democracy seems like an attractive umbrella for theorizing, not dogmatically, but to exhibit affinities.

Normative democracy adopts comprehensive views of fundamental ideas associated with the secular modern state: security is conceived as extending to environmental protection and to the defense of economic viability (e.g. Mahathir complains about George Soros' financial speculations as jeopardizing Malaysian development successes; *Turkish Daily News*, 1997); human rights are conceived as extending to social and economic rights, as well as to such collective rights as the right to development, the right to peace, the right of self-determination; democracy is conceived as extending beyond constitutional and free, periodic elections to include an array of other assurances that governance is oriented toward human wellbeing and ecological sustainability, and that citizens have access to arenas of decision.

The elements of normative democracy can be enumerated, but their content and behavioral applications will require much amplification in varied specific settings. This enumeration reflects the dominant orientations and outlook of the political actors that make up the constructivist category of "globalization-from-below". It is thus not an enumeration that is a wishlist, but intends to be descriptive and explanatory of an embedded consensus. The elements of this consensus are as follows:

(1) Consent of citizenry: some periodic indication that the permanent population of the relevant community is represented by the institutions of governance, and confers legitimacy through the expression of consent. Elections are the established modalities for territorial communities to confer legitimacy on government, but referenda and rights of petition and recall may be more appropriate for other types of political community, especially those of regional or global scope, while direct democracy may be most meaningful for local political activity; the idea is to be flexible and adaptive.

(2) Rule of law: all modes of governance subject to the discipline of law as a way of imposing effective limits on authority and of assuring some form of checks and balances as between legislative, executive, judicial and administrative processes; also, sensitivity to the normative claims of civil initiatives associated with codes of conduct, conference declarations, societal institutions (for instance, Permanent Peoples Tribunal in Rome).

(3) Human rights: taking account of differing cultural, economic and political settings and priorities, the establishment of mechanisms for the impartial and effective implementation of human rights deriving from global, regional, state and transnational civil sources of authority; human rights are comprehensively conceived as encompassing economic, social and cultural rights, as well as civil and political rights, with a concern for both individual and collective conceptions of rights, emphasizing tolerance toward difference and fundamental community sentiments.

(4) Participation: effective and meaningful modes of participation in the political life of the society, centered upon the processes of government, but extending to all forms of social governance, including workplace and home; participation may be direct or indirect, that is, representational, but it enables the expression of views and influence upon the processes of decision on the basis of an ideal of equality of access; creativity is needed to find methods other than elections by which to ensure progress toward full participation.

(5) Accountability: suitable mechanisms for challenging the exercise of authority by those occupying official positions at the level of the state, but also with respect to the functioning of the market and of international institutions; the ideal of an international criminal court is one mechanism for assuring accountability by those in powerful positions that have been traditionally treated as exempt from the Rule of Law.

(6) Public goods: a restored social agenda that corrects the growing imbalance, varying in seriousness from country to country, between private and public goods in relation to the persistence of poverty amid affluence, pertaining to health, education, housing and basic human needs, but also in relation to support for environmental protection, regulation of economic globalization, innovative cultural activity, infrastructure development for governance at the regional and global

levels. In these regards, a gradual depoliticalization of funding either by reliance on a use or transaction tax imposed on financial flows, global air travel, or some form of reliable and equitable means to fund public goods of local, national, regional, and global scope.

(7) Transparency: an openness with respect to knowledge and information that builds trust between institutions of governance and the citizenry at various levels of social interaction. in effect, establishing the right to know as an aspect of constitutionalism, including a strong bias against public sector secrecy and covert operations, and criminalizes government lies of the sort recently revealed where for years to protect air force spy missions the CIA lied about alleged "UFO sightings"; internationally, transparency is particularly important in relation to military expenditures and arms transfers.

(8) Non-violence: underpinning globalization-from-below and the promotion of substantive democracy is a conditional commitment to non-violent politics and conflict resolution. Such a commitment does not nullify rights of self-defense as protected in international law, strictly and narrowly construed, nor does it necessarily invalidate limited recourse to violence by oppressed peoples; such an ethos of non-violence clearly imposes on governments an obligation to renounce weaponry of mass destruction and the negotiation of phased disarmament arrangements, but also maximum commitments to demilitarizing approaches to peace and security at all levels of social interaction, including peace and security at the level of city and neighborhood; such commitments suggest the rejection of capital punishment as an option of government.

5. Globalization-from-below and the State: A Decisive Battle

Without entering into detailed discussion, it seems that different versions of neo-liberal ideology have exerted a defining influence upon the orientation of political élites governing sovereign states. Of course, there are many variations reflecting conditions and personalities in each particular state and region, but the generalization holds without important exception (Sakamoto, 1994; Falk, 1997b). Even China, despite adherence to the ideology of state socialism, has implemented by state decree, with impressive results, a market-oriented approach to economic policy. The state can remain authoritarian in relation to its citizenry without necessarily jeopardizing its economic performance so long as it adheres, more or less, to the discipline of global capital, thereby achieving competitiveness by reference to costs of production, savings and attraction of capital. In these respects, neo-liberalism as a *global* ideology is purely economistic in character, and does not imply a commitment to democratic governance in even the minimal sense of periodic fair elections.

Globalization-from-below, in addition to a multitude of local struggles, is also a vehicle for the transnational promotion of substantive democracy as a counterweight to neo-liberalism. It provides an alternative, or series of convergent alternatives, that has not yet been posited as a coherent body of theory and practice, but remains the inarticulate common ground of emergent global civil society. Substantive democracy, unlike backlash politics that closes off borders and identities, seeks a politics of reconciliation that maintains much of the openness and dynamism associated with globalization-from-above, while countering its pressures to privatize and marketize the production of public goods. In effect, the quest of substantive democracy is to establish a social equilibrium that takes full account of the realities of globalization in its various aspects. Such a process cannot succeed on a country-by-country basis as the rollback of welfare in Scandinavia suggests, but must proceed within regional and global settings. The state remains the instrument of policy and decision most affecting the lives of peoples, and the primary link to regional and global institutions. The state has been instrumentalized to a considerable degree by the ideology and influences associated with globalization-from-above, resulting in declining support for public goods in an atmosphere of strong sustained economic growth and in polarization of results with incredible wealth for the winners and acute suffering for the losers. An immediate goal of those disparate social forces that constitute globalization-from-below is to reinstrumentalize the state to the extent that it redefines its role as mediating between the logic of capital and the priorities of its peoples, including their short-term and longer term goals.

Evidence of this instrumentalization of the state is present in relation to global conferences on broad policy issues that had been organized under UN auspices, and were making an impact on public consciousness and behavioral standards in the 1990s. These UN conferences increasingly attracted an array of social forces associated with global civil society, and gave rise to a variety of coalitions and oppositions between state, market and militant citizens organized to promote substantive goals (e.g. human rights, environmental protection, economic equity and development). These UN conferences became arenas of political participation that were operating outside the confines of state control, and were regarded as threatening by the established order based on a core coalition between market forces and geopolitical leaders. One effect is to withdraw support for such UN activities, pushing the organization to the sidelines on global policy issues as part of a process of recovering control over its agenda and orientation. Such a reaction represents a setback for globalization-from-below, but it also shows that the social forces that are associated with the promotion of normative democracy can be formidable adversaries.

Such a process of reinstrumentalization could also influence the future role and identity of regional and global mechanisms of governance, especially to the extent of increasing the regulatory mandate directed toward market forces and the normative mandate with respect to the protection of the global commons, the promotion of demilitarization and the overall support for public good.

6. Conclusion

In this paper it is argued that the positive prospects for global civil society depend very much on two interrelated developments: achieving consensus on "normative democracy" as the foundation of coherent theory and practice, and waging a struggle for the outlook and orientation of institutions of governance with respect to the framing of globalization. The state remains the critical focus of this latter struggle, although it is not, even now, a matter of intrinsic opposition between the state as instrument of globalization-from-above and social movements as instrument of globalization-from-below. In many specific settings, coalitions between states and social movements are emergent, as is evident in relation to many questions of environment, development and human rights. It may even come to pass that transnational corporations and banks adopt a longer term view of their own interests, and move to alter the policy content of globalization-from-above to soften the contrast with the preferences of globalization-from-below. It is helpful to remember that such an unanticipated convergence of previously opposed social forces led to the sort of consensus that produced "social democracy" and "the welfare state" over the course of the 19th and 20th centuries. There is evident reason to preclude such convergencies on regional and global levels as

110   *R. Falk*

a way of resolving some of the tensions being caused by the manner in which globalization is *currently* being enacted.

References

Archibugi, D., Held, D. (Eds) (1995) *Cosmopolitan Democracy: An Agenda for a New World Order* (Cambridge, Polity).

Bello, W. (1977) Talk at Bangkok Conference on Alternative Security Systems in the Asia-Pacific, *Focus Asia*, March, pp. 27–30.

Bull, H. (1977) *The Anarchical Society: A Study of Order in World Politics* (New York, Columbia University Press).

Clark, I. (1997) *Globalization and Fragmentation: International Relations in the Twentieth Century* (Oxford, Oxford University Press).

Commission on Global Governance (1995) *Our Global Neighbourhood* (Oxford, Oxford University Press).

Falk, R. (1993) The making of global citizenship, in: J. Brecher, J.B. Childs & J. Cutler (Eds) *Global Visions: Beyond the New World Order* (Boston, MA, South End Press).

Falk, R. (1995) *On Humane Governance: Toward a New Global Politics* (Cambridge, Polity).

Falk, R. (1996) An inquiry into the political economy of world order', *New Political Economy*, 1, pp. 13–26.

Falk, R. (1997) Resisting "Globalization-from-above" through "Globalisation-from-below", *New Political Economy*, 2, pp. 17–24.

Falk, R. (1997b) State of siege: will globalization win out?, *International Affairs*, 73, pp. 123–136.

Fukuyama, F. (1992) *The End of History and the Last Man* (New York, Free Press).

Goldsmith, E., Allen, R., Allaby, M., Davoll, J. & Laurence, S. (1972) *Blueprint for Survival* (Boston, MA, Houghton Mifflin).

Held, D. (1995) *Democracy and the Global Order: From the Modern State to Cosmopolitan Governance* (Cambridge, Polity).

Hirst, P. & Thompson, G. (1996) *Globalization in Question* (Cambridge, Polity).

Lipschutz, R.D. (1996) *Global Civil Society and Global Environmental Governance* (Albany, NY, State University of New York Press).

Turkish Daily News (1997) Malaysia PM Mulls Action Against Speculators, 29 July.

Meadows, D.H., Meadows, D.L. & Randers, J. (1972) *The Limits to Growth* (New York, Universe Books).

Nerfin, M. (1986) Neither prince nor merchant: citizen—an introduction to the third system, *IFDA Dossier 56*, Nov./Dec., pp. 3–29.

Rich, B. (1994) *Mortgaging the Earth: The World Bank Environmental Impoverishment and the Crisis of Development* (Boston, Beacon Press).

Rosenau, J.N. (1990) *Turbulence in World Politics: A Theory of Change and Continuity* (Princeton, NJ, Princeton University Press).

Sachs, J. (1997) New members please apply, *TIME*, 7 July, pp. 11–12.

Sakamoto, Y. (Ed.) (1994) *Global Transformation: Challenges to the State System* (Tokyo, United Nations University Press).

Shiva, V. (1987) People's ecology: the Chipko movement', in: R.B.J. Walker & S.H. Mendlovitz (Eds) *Towards a Just World Peace: Perspectives from Social Movements* (London, Butterworths).

Wapner, P. (1996) The social construction of global governance, *American Political Science Association Annual Meeting*, 28–31 August.

[21]

Human rights, principled issue-networks, and sovereignty in Latin America   Kathryn Sikkink

The human rights issue is an important case study of how understandings of sovereignty currently are being reshaped in the world and of the important role of transnational actors in that process. The doctrine of internationally protected human rights offers one of the most powerful critiques of sovereignty as currently constituted, and the practices of human rights law and human rights foreign policies provide concrete examples of shifting understandings of the scope of sovereignty. In this article, I argue that human rights policies and practices are contributing to a gradual, significant, and probably irreversible transformation of sovereignty in the modern world and that this shift cannot be explained without taking into account the role of transnational nonstate actors.

In the post–World War II period, a human rights movement helped create regional and international human rights regimes. Nongovernmental organizations (NGOs) formed part of a network of organizations working together on behalf of human rights, a network that also included parts of global and regional intergovernmental organizations (IGOs) and private foundations. I refer to this broader set of organizations as an international issue-network.[1]

This research was assisted by an award from the Social Science Research Council of an advanced fellowship in foreign policy studies with the support of a grant from the Ford Foundation, and by the McKnight Land-Grant Professorship at the University of Minnesota. I am grateful to Douglas Chalmers, Raymond Duvall, Margaret Keck, Jeffrey Legro, Ellen Lutz, Thomas Risse-Kappen, Christopher Welna, two anonymous reviewers for *International Organization,* and John S. Odell for their helpful comments on earlier versions of this article and related articles and to Kristina Thalhammer for research assistance.

1. There is a large literature in organization theory on network analysis, some of which is relevant to the case presented here. For an overview of this literature, see Howard Aldrich and David A. Whetten, "Organization-sets, Action-sets, and Networks: Making the Most of Simplicity," in Paul Nystrom and W. Starbuck, eds., *Handbook of Organizational Design* (New York: Oxford University Press, 1981), pp. 385–408. This organization literature occasionally has been applied to international relations. See Christer Jonsson, "Interorganization Theory and International Organization," *International Studies Quarterly* 30 (March 1986), pp. 39–57; and Gayl D. Ness and Steven R. Brechin, "Bridging the Gap: International Organizations as Organizations," *International Organization* 42 (Spring 1988), pp. 245–73. Kamarotos applies network theory to the human

International Organization 47, 3, Summer 1993

These networks differ from other forms of transnational relations, such as epistemic communities or transnationally organized interest groups, in that they are driven primarily by shared values or principled ideas—ideas about what is right and wrong—rather than shared causal ideas or instrumental goals.[2]

This argument will be explored through a comparative study of the impact of international human rights pressures on Argentina and Mexico in the 1970s and 1980s.[3] Both are large countries with traditions of jealously guarding their sovereign prerogatives. Both have had problematic human rights practices, although the Argentine human rights record was much more serious during the period of the so-called dirty war from 1976 to 1980. The international human rights network worked intensively on Argentina, contributing to improved practices by the early 1980s. The network did not focus on Mexico, however, and lower-level but endemic abuses continued throughout the 1980s. Only after the network concentrated international attention on Mexico after 1987 did the Mexican government take moves to improve human rights practices.

Sovereignty and human rights

The debate over human rights is embedded in a more fundamental debate over the changing nature of sovereignty in the modern world. Sovereignty is often seen as a series of claims about the nature and scope of state authority.[4] Claims about sovereignty are forceful, however, because they represent shared understandings and expectations that are constantly reinforced both through the practices of states[5] and the practices of nonstate actors.

---

rights issue but uses much narrower definitions of network and of organizational environment than the research presented here; see Alexander S. Kamarotos, "A View into NGO Networks in Human Rights Activities: NGO Action with Special Reference to the UN Commission on Human Rights and its Sub-commission," paper presented at a convention of the International Political Science Association, Washington, D.C., 10–14 April 1990. Another recent discussion that mentions networks in human rights is Ronnie D. Lipschutz, "Reconstructing World Politics: The Emergence of Global Civil Society," *Millennium: Journal of International Studies* 21 (Winter 1992), pp. 389–420.

2. Judith Goldstein and Robert Keohane classify beliefs into three groups in the introduction to their edited volume, *Ideas and Foreign Policy: Beliefs, Institutions, and Political Change* (Ithaca, N.Y.: Cornell University Press, forthcoming). Ideas that specify criteria for determining whether actions are right or wrong and whether outcomes are just or unjust are called shared principled beliefs. Beliefs about cause–effect relationships are called shared causal beliefs. At a more fundamental level is a third category of ideas about the universe of possibilities for action. Human rights is primarily about a set of shared principled ideas, but to the degree that human rights ideas challenge understandings of sovereignty, they also work at the level of defining possibilities for action. On epistemic communities, see Peter M. Haas, ed., "Knowledge, Power, and International Policy Coordination," special issue, *International Organization* 46 (Winter 1992), pp. 1–390.

3. For a related study that examines the impact of U.S. human rights policy using a two-level game approach, see Lisa Martin and Kathryn Sikkink, "U.S. Policy and Human Rights in Argentina and Guatemala, 1973–1980," in Peter Evans, Harold Jacobson, and Robert Putnam, eds., *Double-edged Diplomacy: International Bargaining and Domestic Politics* (Berkeley: University of California Press, forthcoming).

4. Stephen Krasner, "Westphalia," in Goldstein and Keohane, *Ideas and Foreign Policy.*

5. Wendt stresses that sovereignty is an institution that exists "only in virtue of certain

Traditionally, as stated by the World Court, the doctrine of state sovereignty has meant that the state "is subject to no other state, and has full and exclusive powers within its jurisdiction."[6] Inevitably, international activities to protect human rights contradict a core premise of traditional sovereignty that, as Louis Henkin has put it, "how a state behaved toward its own citizens in its own territory was a matter of domestic jurisdiction, i.e., not any one else's business and therefore not any business for international law."[7] International human rights work presupposes that it is legitimate and necessary for states or nonstate actors to be concerned about the treatment of the inhabitants of other states. The international human rights network seeks to redefine what is essentially within the domestic jurisdiction of states. The question to be addressed here is whether these pressures succeed in changing state understandings and in improving human rights practices. If they do, the meaning of sovereignty has been modified because shared understandings about the scope of state authority and the practices that reflect those understandings are transformed.

Neither the practice nor the doctrine of internal sovereignty has ever been absolute. National political leaders always have faced some international constraints on how they could treat their own subjects. The Treaty of Augsburg and the Peace of Westphalia, for example, limited the discretion of the monarch in controlling the practice of religion of his subjects, and the campaign for the abolition of slavery in the nineteenth century made clear that certain extreme practices would be an object of international concern and action. But until World War II, in the widest range of issues the treatment of subjects remained within the discretion of the state; no important legal doctrine challenged the supremacy of the state's absolute authority within its borders. The moral flaw to internal sovereignty that became glaring during World War II was that if the state itself posed the primary threat to the well-being of citizens, these citizens had nowhere to turn for recourse or protection.

In spite of different languages and approaches, many discussions of sovereignty in international relations share certain characteristics. Most views of sovereignty are so penetrated by state-centric logic that they continue to focus

---

intersubjective understandings and expectations; there is no sovereignty without an other." He argues that sovereignty norms are now so taken for granted, that "it is easy to overlook the extent to which they are both presupposed by and an ongoing artifact of practice." See Alexander Wendt, "Anarchy Is What States Make of It: The Social Construction of Power Politics," *International Organization* 46 (Spring 1992), pp. 391–425. The quotations are drawn from pp. 412–13.

6. This classical definition of sovereignty is given by the World Court in the Wimbledon case, as cited on page 164 of Stanley Hoffmann, "International Systems and International Law," in Richard A. Falk and Saul H. Mendlovitz, eds., *The Strategy of World Order,* vol. 2, *International Law* (New York: World Law Fund, 1966), pp. 134–66.

7. Louis Henkin, *How Nations Behave: Law and Foreign Policy,* 2d ed. (New York: Columbia University Press, 1979), p. 228. Also see James Mayall, *Nationalism and International Society* (Cambridge: Cambridge University Press, 1990), p. 20; and Nancy Newcomb Haanstad, "Compulsory Jurisdiction Over Human Rights and Domestic Jurisdiction," Ph.D. diss., University of Utah, 1984, p. iv.

414 International Organization

almost exclusively on states and the understandings and practices of states as the sole determinant of sovereignty.[8] These views are usually abstract and static. Even theorists critical of standard understandings of sovereignty are so concerned with exposing how the discourse of sovereignty is constructed and maintained that they often ignore the ways in which conceptions of the state are evolving.[9]

If sovereignty is a shared set of understandings and expectations about the authority of the state and is reinforced by practices, then a change in sovereignty will come about by transforming understandings and practices. In this sense, the expansion of human rights law and policy in the postwar period represented a conscious, collective attempt to modify this set of shared understandings and practices. Although the idea of internationally protected human rights was placed on the international agenda when the United Nations (UN) General Assembly adopted the Universal Declaration of Human Rights in 1948, that idea was not initially translated into a modification of sovereignty in practice or to effective protection of human rights. The only exception was in Europe, where the European Convention on Human Rights and the practices of the European human rights system began to have a gradual but profound impact on modifying state sovereignty.[10]

To become effective, the means had to be found to translate the human rights ideals of the declaration and treaties of the postwar period into widely shared understandings and practices. The human rights network helped foster these means in two ways. International organizations developed formal procedures to discuss and investigate human rights situations in member states. But formal procedures are ineffective if not used. The work of NGOs made states' repressive practices more visible and salient, thus forcing states that otherwise would have remained silent to respond. As they became more aware of human rights violations, some states demanded explanations from others. Faced with increased pressures, repressive states tried to provide justifications. In the give-and-take of exposing violations, demanding explanations, providing justifications, and changing practices, states and NGOs gradually questioned traditional understandings of sovereignty and began constructing the elements of a modified sovereignty. When a state recognizes the legitimacy of international interventions on the topic of human rights and changes its domestic

8. See Krasner, "Westphalia"; Kenneth Waltz, *Theory of International Politics* (Reading, Mass.: Addison-Wesley, 1979), pp. 95–96; and F. H. Hinsley, *Sovereignty,* 2d ed. (Cambridge: Cambridge University Press, 1986).

9. See, for example, Wendt, "Anarchy Is What States Make of It"; and Richard Ashley, "Untying the Sovereign State: A Double Reading of the Anarchy Problematique," *Millennium: Journal of International Studies* 17 (Summer 1988), pp. 227–61.

10. Sieghart regards the European Convention on Human Rights as "a substantial retreat from the previously sacred principle of national sovereignty"; see Paul Sieghart, *The Lawful Rights of Mankind: An Introduction to the International Legal Code of Human Rights* (Oxford: Oxford University Press, 1985), pp. 67–68. See also Rosalyn Higgins, "The European Convention on Human Rights," in Theodor Meron, ed., *Human Rights in International Law: Legal and Policy Issues* (Oxford: Clarendon Press, 1984), p. 538.

human rights practices in response to these international pressures, it reconstitutes the relationship between the state, its citizens, and international actors.

To make the argument about the transformation of sovereignty more precise, I will specify a continuum of state actions and declarations that move from reinforcing traditional understandings of the scope of sovereignty to revealing a reconceptualized sovereignty in which a state accepts that gross violations of human rights will no longer be an issue solely within its domestic jurisdiction.

In the human rights realm, this continuum would start with the state denial of the legitimacy and refusal to cooperate with any international human rights pressures or interventions. In the second stage the state would accept the legitimacy of international human rights practices, as evidenced by its statements in international forums, ratification of the relevant human rights treaties, and cooperation with international human rights organizations but not change domestic repressive practices. The passage from denial to lip service may seem insignificant but suggests an important shift in the shared understandings of states that make certain justifications no longer acceptable. The endpoint of the continuum, that is, reconstituted sovereignty, would involve the above recognition of legitimacy and cooperation and also concrete responses to international pressures that change domestic human rights practices. Argentina and Mexico are useful cases to explore changing conceptions of sovereignty, since both have a diplomatic tradition of intransigent defense of the doctrine of internal sovereignty and noninterference. Changes in the understandings and practices of these two states with regard to international human rights pressures serve as an indication of how sovereignty is being reconceptualized.

The human rights issue does not presage an alternative to sovereignty, but it suggests a future model in which understandings of sovereignty are modified in relation to specific issues that are deemed of sufficient importance to the international community to limit the scope of sovereign authority. We can see this modification of sovereignty occurring in other specific issue-areas as well, such as the environment, the delivery of emergency food supplies, and the protection of minorities. As such, human rights is not simply another exception to the rule of sovereignty but part of a significant though circumscribed subset of international issues for which modified understandings of sovereignty are increasingly accepted and practiced.

The international human rights issue-network

An international issue-network comprises a set of organizations, bound by shared values and by dense exchanges of information and services, working internationally on an issue. The diverse entities that make up the international human rights issue-network include parts of IGOs at both the international and regional levels, international NGOs on human rights, domestic NGOs on human rights, and private foundations. Other issue-networks will include a somewhat different array of actors; but international and domestic NGOs play a central role in all issue-networks. They are the most proactive members of the networks, usually initiating actions and pressuring more powerful actors to take positions.

The role of shared values as the basis of the issue-networks helps explain the central involvement of many voluntary NGOs in networks. Activists join NGOs because they believe strongly in the principles of the organizations, not because of any tangible benefits that they receive from membership. Since these organizations survive on donations, voluntary labor, and the dedication of underpaid staff, the NGOs that succeed and thrive are those that have a strong message capable of mobilizing their staff, membership, and public opinion.[11]

The organizations in the network that have been most important for human rights in Latin America include the UN Commission on Human Rights, the Inter-American Commission on Human Rights (IACHR), Amnesty International (AI), Americas Watch, the Washington Office on Latin America, domestic NGOs like the Mothers of the Plaza de Mayo in Argentina and the Academy of Human Rights in Mexico, and the Ford Foundation, as well as foundations based in Europe that fund international and domestic human rights NGOs.

To have a strong network, it must have a certain size and density. In other words, enough actors must exist and be connected in order to speak meaningfully of a network. Much of the history of the emergence of the human rights network is the story of the founding, growth, and linking of the organizations in the network. Groups in a network share values and frequently exchange information and services.[12] The shared values that bind the actors in the human rights network are embodied in international human rights law, especially in the Universal Declaration of Human Rights. This body of law serves to justify actions and provides a common language to make arguments and procedures to advance claims. The flow of information among actors in the network reveals an extremely dense web of interconnections among these groups. In most cases, this flow of information takes place informally through the exchange of reports, telephone calls, and attendance at conferences and meetings. In other cases,

---

11. Mansbridge has made a similar point discussing groups that organized around the Equal Rights Amendment debate in the United States. See Jane J. Mansbridge, *Why We Lost the ERA* (Chicago: University of Chicago Press, 1986), p. 3.

12. Organization theory uses a variety of ways to think about relations among organizations. Mitchell refers to three types of content of relations: (1) communicative content, or the passing of information from one organization to another, (2) exchange content, and (3) normative content. See J. Clyde Mitchell, "Networks, Norms, and Institutions," in Jeremy Boissevain and J. Clyde Mitchell, eds. *Network Analysis* (The Hague: Mouton, 1973), pp. 2–35. To document these linkages, researchers investigate the exchange of resources, communication among staff, friendship or kinship ties, and overlapping boards of directors among organizations. See Aldrich and Whetten, "Organization-sets, Action-sets, and Networks," p. 391.

the connections are formalized, as when NGOs with official consultative status with IGOs present reports to those organizations. A third type of interconnection among the organizations is the flow of funds and services. This is especially the case of relations among foundations and NGOs, but some NGOs also may provide services such as training for other NGOs in the network. As a result of this exchange of information and services, of flows of funds, and of shared norms and goals, the members of the issue-network work together in a constant but informal, uncoordinated, and nonhierarchical manner.

The history of the emergence of international human rights regimes has been discussed at length elsewhere and does not need to be repeated here.[13] What is often missed, however, is how NGOs helped spur state action at each stage in the emergence of the human rights regimes.[14] In two of the main international precursors to the human rights issue—the movement for respect for human rights during armed conflict and the campaign for the abolition of the slave trade and slavery—NGOs brought the issue to public attention and promoted international action.[15] The Red Cross movement spearheaded the activities that created the law of human rights in armed conflict.[16] A group of NGOs, the Anti-slavery League, led the campaign to protect the rights of those held in slavery and eventually to abolish slavery. The league helped persuade states to adopt the 1926 convention outlawing slavery.[17]

Likewise, at the San Francisco conference at which the UN charter was drafted, NGOs played a pivotal role in securing the inclusion of human rights language in the final charter. The initial big power drafts of the UN Charter had hardly mentioned human rights.[18] NGOs representing churches, trade unions, ethnic groups, and peace movements, aided by the delegations of some of the smaller countries, "conducted a lobby in favor of human rights for which there is no parallel in the history of international relations, and which was

13. See Jack Donnelly, *Universal Human Rights in Theory and Practice* (Ithaca, N.Y.: Cornell University Press, 1989), especially the table on pp. 224–25, for a summary of the evolution of human rights regimes and for an explanation of the differences between declaratory and enforcement regimes.

14. For a discussion of the role of NGOs in the building of international action on human rights and U.S. foreign policy, see David Forsythe, *Human Rights and World Politics*, 2d ed. (Lincoln: University of Nebraska Press, 1989), pp. 83–101 and 127–59; and Lars Schoultz, *Human Rights and United States Policy Toward Latin America* (Princeton, N.J.: Princeton University Press, 1981), pp. 74–93, 104–8, and 373–74.

15. David Weissbrodt and Teresa O'Toole, "The Development of International Human Rights Law," in Amnesty International U.S.A. Legal Support Network, ed., *The Universal Declaration of Human Rights, 1948–1988: Human Rights, the United Nations and Amnesty International* (New York: Amnesty International, 1988), pp. 17–33; and Forsythe, *Human Rights and World Politics*, pp. 7–10.

16. For a discussion of the role of the Red Cross in international politics, see David P. Forsythe, *Humanitarian Politics: The International Committee of the Red Cross* (Baltimore, Md.: Johns Hopkins University Press, 1977); and J. D. Armstrong, "The International Committee of the Red Cross and Political Prisoners," *International Organization* 39 (Autumn 1985), pp. 615–42.

17. Forsythe, *Human Rights and World Politics*, pp. 7–9.

18. Jacob Robinson, *Human Rights and Fundamental Freedoms in the Charter of the United Nations* (New York: Institute of Jewish Affairs, 1946), p. 17.

largely responsible for the human rights provisions of the Charter," in John Humphrey's words.[19]

Although nongovernmental actors were central to the campaign against slavery and to the work of including human rights language in the UN Charter, they were not yet issue-networks: there were relatively few actors and there were not the dense and constant flows of information that characterize networks. In the 1970s, as the number of human rights actors increased and these actors consciously developed linkages with each other, the human rights issue-network emerged. Although international human rights norms emerged out of the world reaction to the Holocaust, these norms were subordinated to anticommunism during the period of the cold war. With the advent of détente in the early 1970s, a more permissive environment was created for the consideration of human rights, and the convergence of some shocking cases of human rights abuses, such as in Chile and in Greece, moved world opinion.[20] In reaction to these conditions, all types of human rights organizations in the network increased in the 1970s, with the expansion of NGOs, in particular, giving impetus to the growth of the network as a whole.

International NGOs

Although some human rights organizations have existed for many years, in the 1970s and 1980s human rights NGOs proliferated and increased in diversity (38 in 1950, 72 in 1960, 103 in 1970, 138 in 1980, and 275 in 1990).[21] This explosion of NGOs is indicated not only by the increasing number of organizations but also by the formation of coalitions and communications networks designed to link those groups together.[22] In turn, these international human rights organizations developed strong links to domestic human rights organizations in countries experiencing human rights violations. This growth in

19. John P. Humphrey, *Human Rights and the United Nations: A Great Adventure* (Dobbs Ferry, N.Y.: Transnational Publishers, 1984), p. 13. Also see U.S. Department of State, *The United Nations Conference on International Organization, San Francisco, California, April 25 to June 26, 1945: Selected Documents* (Washington, D.C.: U.S. Government Printing Office, 1946).

20. This discussion on why human rights gained importance in the 1970s is developed further in Kathryn Sikkink, "The Power of Principled Ideas: The Origins and Continuity of Human Rights Policies in the United States and Western Europe," in Goldstein and Keohane, *Ideas and Foreign Policy.*

21. The oldest of human rights organizations, the Anti-slavery Society, was founded in 1839, but most international human rights NGOs have emerged since World War II. For a discussion of NGOs in the area of human rights, see David Weissbrodt, "The Contribution of International Nongovernmental Organizations to the Protection of Human Rights," in Meron, *Human Rights in International Law,* pp. 403–38.

22. Laurie S. Wiseberg and Harry M. Scoble, "Monitoring Human Rights Violations: The Role of Nongovernmental Organizations," in Donald P. Kommers and Gilbert D. Loescher, eds., *Human Rights and American Foreign Policy* (Notre Dame, Ind.: University of Notre Dame Press, 1979), pp. 179–208, and particularly pp. 183–84. These points about the growth and interconnections of international human rights NGOs were also emphasized in interviews with directors and staff of nine key international human rights NGOs.

human rights organizations parallels a more general growth in international NGOs in the postwar period.[23]

Domestic NGOs

As opposed to the international NGOs, which work on human rights violations in other countries, domestic NGOs focus on human rights violations in their home countries. Countries and regions differ dramatically in terms of the number and capability of their domestic human rights organizations. Latin America has more domestic human rights NGOs than do other parts of the Third World. A 1981 directory of organizations concerned with human rights and social justice in the developing world discussed 220 such organizations in Latin America, compared with 145 in Asia and 123 in Africa and the Middle East. An updated listing published in 1990 lists over 550 human rights groups in Latin America. Of all the countries of Latin America and the Caribbean, only Grenada does not have a domestic human rights organization, while some countries have fifty to sixty such groups.[24] An international demonstration effect was at work in Latin America during the 1980s as the work and successes of the original human rights organizations in the region inspired others to follow their example.

IGOs

Prior to 1948, no IGO dedicated to the issue of human rights existed. By 1990, twenty-seven organizations included human rights as a significant part of their work.[25] These international organizations became the arenas where NGOs came together and a focal point for NGO work. The larger international NGOs have UN consultative status. Such status comprises the formal procedure linking IGOs to international NGOs in the issue-network and allows them to participate in the debates and activities of the UN. Both the UN Commission on Human Rights and the Subcommission on the Protection of Minorities,

23. Kjell Skjelsbaek, "The Growth of International Nongovernmental Organization in the Twentieth Century," *International Organization* 25 (Summer 1971), pp. 420–42.

24. The sources for the figures are Human Rights Internet, *Human Rights Directory: Latin America, Africa, and Asia,* eds. Laurie S. Wiseberg and Harry M. Scoble (Washington, D.C.: Human Rights Internet, 1981); and Laurie S. Wiseberg, Guadalupe López, and Sarah Meselson, eds., "Human Rights Directory: Latin America and the Caribbean," special issue, *Human Rights Internet Reporter* 13 (January 1990). By domestic group, I refer to groups operating in their home country. Although the definition used by these directories is broader than in many discussions of human rights groups in Latin America, comparison of the 1981 and 1990 figures gives an idea of the dramatic growth in the Latin American human rights network and the wide range of groups working on diverse human rights issues throughout the region.

25. These figures are based on information coded from Union of International Associations, ed., *Yearbook of International Organizations: 1948* (Brussels: Union of International Associations, 1948); and Union of International Associations, ed., *Yearbook of International Organizations: 1990* (Munich: K. G. Saur, 1990). They include only organizations and exclude treaties, conventions, and declarations also listed in the yearbooks.

which were set up after World War II, became more dynamic in the 1970s under the influence of the new rules and the pressures of international NGOs, the Carter administration, and some European governments.[26] The Human Rights Committee began to function after the International Covenant on Civil and Political Rights came into legal force for adhering states in 1976, providing yet another arena for human rights debate and activism in the UN system.[27]

The IACHR of the Organization of American States (OAS), first established in 1959, was reorganized and strengthened in 1979 when the American Convention on Human Rights entered into force. The reorganized commission was able to play a more important role in the promotion of human rights in the region, especially in its influential 1980 report on human rights in Argentina.[28]

Foundations and funders

A handful of private and public foundations have been active in funding human rights organizations. The most important U.S.-based foundation for Latin America has been the Ford Foundation, but a number of European funders also have played key roles, especially European church foundations.[29] In addition to private foundations, official development assistance agencies in Canada, the Netherlands, Scandinavia, and the United States also have funded human rights NGOs.

Prior to 1975, large U.S. foundations hardly ever funded international human rights work.[30] From 1977 to 1987, U.S. foundation grants for human rights work grew dramatically, in terms of both the total number and, especially, the absolute dollar amounts of grants. The Ford Foundation accounts for much of this change, but a number of other foundations also redirected their giving toward human rights (see Figure 1). Although not reflected in the figure, European foundations also became increasingly con-

---

26. Economic and Social Council resolutions 1235 (passed in 1967) and 1503 (passed in 1970), which authorized the commission to review communications and investigate complaints that appear to reveal a consistent pattern of gross violations of human rights, fundamentally strengthened the UN human rights machinery.

27. The Covenant for Civil and Political Rights and the Covenant for Economic, Social, and Cultural Rights were substantially drafted by 1954 but not approved by the General Assembly and opened for signature until 1966. The two covenants reached the required number of adherents for entry into legal force in 1976.

28. Organization of American States, Inter-American Commission on Human Rights, *Report on the Situation of Human Rights in Argentina* (Washington, D.C.: OAS General Secretariat, 1980).

29. On the Ford Foundation's international work, see Peter D. Bell, "The Ford Foundation as a Transnational Actor," *International Organization* 25 (Summer 1971), pp. 465–78; and Jeffrey M. Puryear, "Higher Education, Development Assistance, and Repressive Regimes," *Studies in Comparative International Development* 17 (Summer 1982), pp. 3–35.

30. The subject of human rights did not appear in the index of major foundation grants in the United States until 1975; see The Foundation Center, *The Foundation Grants Index* (New York: The Foundation Center, 1975). Before this, a few human rights grants were listed under the subjects of civil rights or social sciences, but these comprised a small portion of total international grants.

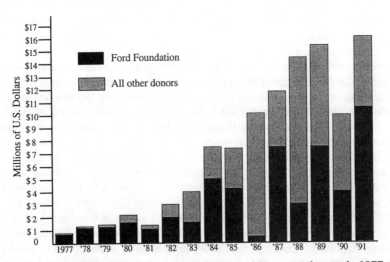

FIGURE 1. *U.S. foundation grants for international human rights work, 1977–91*

Source. The Foundation Center, *The Foundation Grants Index* (New York: The Foundation Center, all editions, 1977–80), and *Dialog,* electronic data base (New York: The Foundation Center, all years, 1981–91). The figures were compiled from all grants listed under the heading of "human rights" and represent the total contributions of U.S.-based foundations for each year indicated.

cerned with human rights.[31] This change in foundation funding helped support the growth in human rights NGOs in the 1970s and 1980s.

Foundations did not create organizations or networks; they only helped to strengthen existing organizations. Foundations are by nature responsive—they fund proposals from functioning organizations but rarely initiate projects themselves. Nevertheless, the move of a handful of foundations into human rights funding helped human rights organizations sustain themselves, institutionalize, and grow.

Networks and governments

What is the relationship of networks to government policy? In most cases, government human rights policy emerged as a response to network pressure and depended fundamentally on network information. For this reason, it is very difficult to separate the independent influences of government policy and network pressures. Networks often work through governments and other powerful actors to achieve their greatest impact. Government policy bodies

31. The *International Foundation Directory* lists fifteen European foundations with human rights as one of their funding priorities. See H. V. Hodson, ed., *The International Foundation Directory 1991,* 5th ed. (London: Europa Publications, 1991).

provide arenas and points of leverage for the work of the network.[32] For example, in the United States, the earliest governmental group to work actively on human rights was the House Subcommittee on International Organizations under the chairmanship of Donald Fraser, later renamed the Subcommittee on Human Rights and International Organizations. Beginning in 1973, this subcommittee held a series of hearings on human rights abuses around the world that put it in contact with many human rights advocates in the network.[33] The primary witnesses providing human rights data and information in these hearings were the representatives of human rights NGOs. In its initial years, the Bureau of Human Rights and Humanitarian Affairs of the U.S. State Department, formed during the Carter administration, maintained close contacts with and sought out the information of NGOs. In European countries, points of influence within the state centered on Ministries of Foreign Affairs and Development Cooperation. In some cases, European governments institutionalized the links with other parts of the network. Both the Dutch and the Norwegian executives, for example, initiated human rights advisory committees, which incorporated NGOs such as AI, ministries, parliamentarians, and scholars.[34]

Often the interactions between the network and bureaucratic groups within governments were mutually reinforcing but not congenial. The U.S. annual human rights reports provide a clear example of that interaction. Because State Department officials did not want to offend foreign officials or undermine other policy goals, their early human rights reports were often weak. However, the State Department reports did serve as a focal point for human rights groups, which were able to create annual public events by issuing responses to the reports.[35] The reports and counterreports attracted press coverage on human rights, and the critiques of the State Department reports held the department up to higher standards in its future reporting. Domestic human rights organizations in repressive countries in turn learned that they could indirectly pressure their governments to change practices by providing information on human rights abuses to human rights officers in U.S. embassies for inclusion in the U.S. annual country-specific reports.

32. This point about network leverage on more powerful actors was first developed by Margaret Keck and is elaborated in further detail in Margaret Keck and Kathryn Sikkink, "International Issue Networks in the Environment and Human Rights," paper presented at the 17th congress of the Latin American Studies Association, Los Angeles, 24–27 September 1992.

33. Interview with John Salzberg, former special consultant on human rights to the U.S. House of Representatives Committee on Foreign Relations, Washington, D.C., April 1991. Although the committee has been less active under subsequent chairpersons, it has continued to hold hearings on human rights abuses in countries around the world.

34. Jan Egeland, *Impotent Superpower–Potent Small State: Potentials and Limitations of Human Rights Objectives in the Foreign Policies of the U.S. and Norway* (Oslo: Norwegian University Press, 1988), p. 193, fn.

35. See, for example, Human Rights Watch and the Lawyers Committee for Human Rights, *Critique: Review of the Department of State's Country Reports on Human Rights Practices for 1987* (New York: Human Rights Watch and the Lawyers Committee for Human Rights, June 1988).

The link to government is simultaneously the most powerful and the least dependable aspect of the work of the issue-network. The effectiveness of the network often depends on engaging support from governments. When network contacts with a government are informal and not institutionalized through NGO advisory committees, changing personnel can block access between the network and the government.

The section above documents dramatic growth in each of the parts of the human rights network in the 1970s and 1980s. This growth alone poses problems to state sovereignty, since each new human rights organization embodies a reconceptualized view of state sovereignty whereby international scrutiny of domestic human rights practices is not only legitimate but also necessary. To demonstrate the impact of the network in practice, however, we need to look at the effectiveness of these pressures in specific cases.

Argentina

Even before the military coup of March 1976, international human rights pressures already influenced the Argentine military's very decision to use the practice of so-called disappearing their perceived political opponents rather than imprisoning them or executing them publicly.[36] The Argentine military believed they had learned from the international reaction to the human rights abuses that occurred after the Chilean coup. When the Chilean military initially executed and imprisoned large numbers of people, the uproar led to the international isolation of the Pinochet regime. The Argentine military decided instead to secretly kidnap, detain, and execute its victims, while denying any knowledge of their whereabouts. By this means, the military hoped to diffuse international condemnation and maintain a moderate international image.[37]

Although this method initially succeeded in muting the international response to the coup, human rights groups eventually were able to document

36. This section draws upon some material from an earlier work; see Martin and Sikkink, "U.S. Policy and Human Rights in Argentina and Guatemala, 1973–1980."

37. Mignone recalls, "One phrase I heard repeatedly in that period from the mouths of Generals, Colonels, Admirals, and Brigadiers was, 'we aren't going to do it like Franco and Pinochet who executed people publicly, because then even the Pope will be asking us not to do it.' " See Emilio Mignone, *Derechos humanos y sociedad: el caso argentino* (Human rights and society: the Argentine case) (Buenos Aires: Ediciones del Pensamiento Nacional and Centro de Estudios Legales y Sociales, 1991), p. 66. This process of perverse learning is also discussed in Claudio Uriarte, *Almirante Cero: Biografía No Autorizada de Emilio Eduardo Massera* (Admiral Zero: The unauthorized biography of Emilio Eduardo Massera) (Buenos Aires: Planeta, 1992), p. 97; and in Carlos H. Acuña and Catalina Smulovitz, "Ajustando las FF.AA. a la Democracia: Exitos, Fracasos, y Ambigüidades de las Experiencias del Cono Sur" (Adjusting the armed forces to democracy: Successes, failures, and ambiguities of the experiences of the southern cone), paper presented at a workshop on human rights, justice, and society in Latin America, organized by the Social Science Research Council, Buenos Aires, 22–24 October 1992, p. 4.

and condemn the new forms of repressive practices. AI and groups staffed by Argentine political exiles first brought the human rights situation in Argentina to world attention after the coup in 1976. To counteract the rising tide of international public criticism, the Argentine junta decided to invite AI for an on-site visit in 1976. In March 1977, on the first anniversary of the military coup, AI published the report on its visit, a well-documented denunciation of the abuses of the regime with emphasis on the problem of the disappeared. AI estimated that the regime had taken six thousand political prisoners, most without charges, and had abducted between two thousand and ten thousand people. The AI report helped demonstrate that the disappearances were part of a concerted government policy by which the military and the police kidnapped perceived opponents, took them to secret detention centers where they tortured, interrogated, and killed them, and secretly disposed of their bodies.[38] When AI won the Nobel Peace Prize later that same year, its reputation was enhanced, further legitimizing its denunciations of the Argentine regime.

In response to increasing dissemination of information on human rights abuses in Argentina, a number of governments, most notably the Carter administration but also the French and Swedish governments, denounced the rights violations of the Argentine junta. Although the Argentine government claimed that such statements constituted unacceptable interventions in their internal affairs and a violation of Argentine sovereignty, the actions of U.S. and European officials indicate that they did not accept Argentine claims. In 1977, the U.S. government reduced the planned level of military aid for Argentina due to human rights abuses. Later, Congress passed a bill eliminating all military assistance to Argentina, which went into effect on 30 September 1978.[39] A number of high-level U.S. delegations met with the junta members during this period to discuss human rights.

Early U.S. action on Argentina was based primarily on the human rights documentation provided by AI and other NGOs, not on information received through the embassy or the State Department.[40] For example, during a 1977 visit, Secretary of State Cyrus Vance carried a list of disappeared people to present to members of the Argentine junta. The list had been prepared by

38. Amnesty International, *Report of an Amnesty International Mission to Argentina* (London: Amnesty International Publications, March 1977).

39. Congressional Research Service, Foreign Affairs and National Defense Division, *Human Rights and U.S. Foreign Assistance: Experiences and Issues in Policy Implementation (1977–1978)*, report prepared for U.S. Senate Committee on Foreign Relations, 96th Congress, 1st sess. (Washington, D.C.: U.S. Government Printing Office, November, 1979), p. 106.

40. After the coup in 1976, Argentine political exiles set up branches of the Argentine Human Rights Commission in Geneva, Mexico City, Paris, Rome, and Washington, D.C. Two of its members testified on human rights abuses in Argentina during hearings in the U.S. House Subcommittee on Human Rights and International Organization in October 1976. See Iain Guest, *Behind the Disappearances: Argentina's Dirty War Against Human Rights and the United Nations* (Philadelphia: University of Pennsylvania Press, 1990), pp. 66–67.

human rights NGOs in the United States.[41] When Assistant Secretary of State for Humanitarian Affairs and Human Rights Patricia Derian met with Admiral Emilio Massera, a member of the Argentine junta, during a visit in 1977, she discussed use of torture by the navy. When Massera denied such practices, Derian told him that she had seen a rudimentary map of a secret detention center in the Navy Mechanical School where the meeting was being held. She asked him whether it was possible that under their feet someone was being tortured. One of Derian's key sources of information was NGOs, especially the families of the disappeared, with whom she met frequently during her visits to Buenos Aires.[42]

By 1977–78, domestic human rights organizations within Argentina began to form and develop significant external contacts. Members of domestic human rights organizations like the Mothers of the Plaza de Mayo, the Grandmothers of the Plaza de Mayo, and the Permanent Assembly for Human Rights traveled frequently to the United States and to Europe, where they met with human rights organizations, talked to the press, and met with parliamentarians and government officials. These groups sought external contacts to publicize the human rights situation, to fund their activities, and to help protect themselves against further repression by their government. They were a crucial link in providing documentation and information to spur the interests and concern of U.S. and European policymakers. Much of the funding for domestic human rights organizations in Argentina came from European and U.S.-based foundations.[43]

If we examine some key events that served to keep the case of Argentine human rights in the minds of U.S. and European policymakers, the impact of these transnational linkages on policy becomes apparent. In 1979, the Argentine authorities released Jacobo Timerman, whose powerful memoir detailing his disappearance and torture by the Argentine military had an important impact on U.S. policymakers.[44] Human rights organizations, members of the U.S. Jewish community, and U.S. journalists helped make Timerman's case a

---

41. Interview with Robert Pastor, former director of Latin American Affairs, National Security Council, 1977–81, Wianno, Mass., 28 June 1990.

42. Testimony given by Patricia Derian to the National Criminal Appeals Court in Buenos Aires during the trials of junta members: "Massera sonrió y me dijo: 'Sabe qué pasó con Poncio Pilatos?' " ("Massera smiled at me and said, 'Do you know what happened to Pontius Pilate?' ") See *Diario del Juicio,* 18 June 1985, p. 3, and Guest, *Behind the Disappearances,* pp. 161–63. Later the report of the Argentine National Commission of the Disappeared confirmed that the Navy Mechanical School was one of the more notorious secret torture and detention centers; see *Nunca Mas: The Report of the Argentine National Commission for the Disappeared* (New York: Farrar Straus Giroux, 1986), pp. 79–84.

43. For example, the Mothers of the Plaza de Mayo received grants from Dutch churches and the Norwegian Parliament, and the Ford Foundation provided funds for the Center for Legal and Social Studies and the Abuelas de la Plaza de Mayo (Grandmothers of the Plaza de Mayo).

44. Jacobo Timerman, *Prisoner Without a Name, Cell Without A Number* (New York: Random House, 1981).

cause célèbre in U.S. policy circles. In 1980, the Nobel Peace Prize was awarded to Argentine human rights activist Adolfo Perez Esquivel. Peace and human rights groups in the United States and Europe helped sponsor Perez Esquivel's speaking tour to the United States exactly at the same time that the OAS was considering the IACHR report on Argentina and the U.S. Congress was considering the end of the arms embargo to Argentina.

The Argentine military government was extremely concerned about international human rights condemnations and pressures. It adopted a series of varying responses to international pressures, each roughly corresponding to a different stage on the continuum of the erosion of sovereignty. They first tried to deny the legitimacy of international concern over human rights in Argentina, to discredit the human rights network by suggesting its members were part of a subversive anti-Argentine campaign, and to mobilize nationalist public opinion against what it defined as interference in internal affairs. When that approach was unable to still international protest, the junta tried to placate international and domestic opposition by cooperating with some parts of the network while at the same time continuing many repressive practices. The third stage involved making concrete improvements in repressive practices in response to international and domestic pressures. Although these stages progressed in a roughly chronological manner, there was continual overlap and backtracking, in part because the Argentine military government was not a unitary actor but a coalition of different factions with different attitudes about the proper response to international pressures.

From 1976 to 1978, the Argentine military pursued the first strategy of denying the legitimacy of international concern over human rights in Argentina. At the same time, it took actions that appear to contradict this strategy, like permitting the visit of the AI mission to Argentina in 1976. The failure of the AI visit, from the military point of view, appeared to reaffirm the strategy of resistance and denial of human rights pressures. This strategy was most obvious at the UN, where the Argentine government tried every means to silence international condemnation in the UN Commission on Human Rights. Ironically the rabidly anticommunist Argentine regime found a diplomatic ally in the Soviet Union, an important trading partner for Argentine wheat, and the two countries worked together to block UN consideration of the Argentine human rights situation.[45] Concerned states circumvented this blockage by creating the UN Working Group on Disappearances in 1980 to draw attention to the practice of disappearances in Argentina and elsewhere in the world. Human rights NGOs contributed to the debates over human rights at the United Nations, providing information, lobbying government delegations, and pursuing joint strategies with sympathetic delegations.

By 1978, however, the Argentine government recognized that the greatest weakness of its regime was the "international variable" and that something had

---

45. Guest, *Behind the Disappearances,* pp. 118–19 and 182–83.

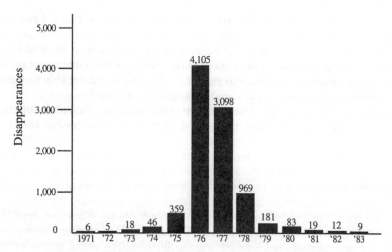

FIGURE 2. *Number of disappearances in Argentina, 1971–83*

Source. Annex to the report *Nunca Mas* (Never again), published by the National Commission on Disappeared People, 1984.

to be done to improve its international image, particularly in the United States and Europe, and to restore military and economic aid flows.[46] To confront this situation, the Argentine government decided to invite the IACHR for an on-site visit to Argentina, in exchange for a U.S. commitment to release Export-Import Bank funds and improve U.S.–Argentine relations.[47] In 1978, the human rights situation in Argentina improved significantly; especially noteworthy was the decline in the practice of involuntary disappearance for which the Argentine regime had gained international notoriety. Figure 2 shows that although the number of disappearances reached a peak in 1976, the practice of disappearance as a tool of state policy was not curtailed until after 1978, when international pressures became more intense and the government began to take the international variable seriously.[48]

The Argentine military government thus moved along the continuum from initial rejection of international human rights interventions to cosmetic

46. *Carta Política,* a news magazine considered to be very close to the military government, commented in August 1978 that international pressures on Argentina continued to increase, citing the examples of the denial of Export–Import Bank credits to Argentina for human rights reasons and the U.S. military aid ban, and concluded that "the principal problem facing the Argentine State has now become the international siege (*cerco internacional*)." See "Cuadro de Situación" (Description of the Situation), *Carta Política,* no. 57, August 1978, p. 8.

47. Interviews with former Vice President Walter Mondale, Minneapolis, Minn., 20 June 1989, and Ricardo Yofre, former political advisor to President Jorge Videla, Buenos Aires, 1 August 1990.

48. See Asamblea Permanente por los Derechos Humanos, *Las Cifras de la Guerra Sucia* (The numbers of the dirty war) (Buenos Aires: Asamblea Permanente por los Derechos Humanos, August 1988), pp. 26–32.

cooperation with the human rights network, and eventually to concrete improvements in its human rights practices in response to international pressures. Once it had invited the Inter-American commission and discovered that the commission could not be co-opted or confused, the government moved to end the practice of disappearance, to release political prisoners, and to restore some semblance of political participation. Full restoration of human rights in Argentina did not come until after the Malvinas/Falklands War and the transition to democracy in 1983, but after 1980 the worst abuses had been curtailed.

Mexico

The political and human rights situation in Mexico was quite different than that in Argentina. Mexico had an elected civilian government that had been under the control of the official political party, the Institutionalized Revolutionary Party (PRI) since the party was formed in 1929. Although massive abuses of the kind that occurred in Argentina after the coup were not the case in Mexico, endemic human rights abuses were common.

The most serious episode of human rights violations in Mexico occurred in October 1968, when army troops opened fire on a peaceful student demonstration in one of the central plazas in Mexico City. The government officially admitted forty-three deaths, but knowledgeable observers suggest that at least three hundred to five hundred people were killed, over two thousand were wounded, and fifteen hundred to two thousand people were taken prisoner.[49]

Surprisingly, the massacre attracted very little international condemnation or attention. The International Olympic Committee, which was to hold the Olympic Games in Mexico City only ten days later, confirmed that the games would go on as planned. Aside from student demonstrations of solidarity in a number of cities, a telegram from PEN Club International protesting the arrest of various authors, and a telegram from a group of French intellectuals, there was no international condemnation of the Mexican government's action.[50] Why did this event, a 1968 version of China's 1989 Tiananmen Square massacre, not inspire an international response? One key part of the answer to this question is that the international human rights network, and the human rights consciousness and practices that it created, did not yet exist in 1968. AI later adopted as prisoners of conscience some of the political prisoners who

49. These figures are taken from Michael C. Meyer and William L. Sherman, *The Course of Mexican History,* 4th ed. (Oxford: Oxford University Press, 1991), p. 669; from Amnesty International, *Annual Report 1968–69* (London: Amnesty International Publications, 1969), p. 12; and from interviews with Mexican human rights activists.

50. Ramón Ramirez, *El Movimiento Estudiantil de Mexico: Julio–Diciembre 1968,* Tomo 2, *Documentos* (The Mexican student movement: July–December 1968, vol. 2, Documents) (Mexico City: Ediciones Era, 1969).

remained in jail after the massacre, but AI was at that time a small organization without the resources to document or report on the massacre or to issue urgent actions, as it would today. Few of the other groups that would later become part of the network even existed. Because there was no credible independent source of human rights information, the Mexican government was able to control information about the event, and the government's low casualty figures were almost universally accepted.[51]

The Mexican government argued that its internal affairs were not legitimate concerns of other countries.[52] The Argentine military used the same argument eight years later; but in 1969, the argument that human rights practices were legitimately within the domestic jurisdiction of a state was much more accepted by the international community than the same argument was in 1977.

Although an episode with violations of this magnitude did not recur in Mexico, human rights abuses in Mexico continued during the 1970s and 1980s. According to Mexican human rights organizations, approximately five hundred people disappeared in Mexico in the 1970s, many in the context of a counterinsurgency campaign.[53] Torture was routinely used to extract confessions from both common and political prisoners, prison conditions were often abysmal, and electoral fraud and press censorship were commonplace.[54] In spite of this record, virtually no international attention was directed to the Mexican human rights situation in the 1970s and early 1980s. The international human rights network had come into existence by the mid-1970s, and yet it did not turn its attention to Mexico. The more serious violations in Central America and the Southern Cone occupied all the attention of the network. The existence of a civilian elected government, Mexico's progressive stance on international human rights (it became, for example, a haven for political refugees from Pinochet's Chile and later a firm critic of human rights violations

---

51. *The New York Times,* the *Washington Post,* and *Newsweek* referred to deaths ranging from twenty to forty-nine people and from approximately one hundred to five hundred wounded, which reflected the government figures. See Paul L. Montgomery, "Deaths Put at 49 in Mexican Clash," *The New York Times,* 4 October 1969, p. A1; Gladys Delmas, "Troops' Show of Force Stuns Mexicans," *Washington Post,* 4 October 1968, p. A3; and "Mexico: Night of Sadness," *Newsweek,* 14 October 1968, pp. 45–48. Because the dead and wounded were taken to the military hospital, which was closed to reporters, it was difficult to get independent estimates of deaths.

52. At the Conference of the Mexico–United States Interparliamentary Group, held five months after the massacre, the chairperson of the Mexican delegation stated: "Mexico affirms that no State has the right to intervene for whatever reason, directly or indirectly, in the affairs of another State." See address by Deputy Luis Farías, chairman of the Mexican Delegation to the Mexico–United States Interparliamentary Group, in *Report of the Ninth Conference of the Mexico–United States Interparliamentary Group, Aguascalientes, Mexico, April 1969* (Washington, D.C.: U.S. Government Printing Office, 1969), p. 8.

53. Committee in Defense of Prisoners, the Persecuted, Disappeared Persons, and Political Exiles, "Diez Años de Lucha por la Libertad" (Ten years of struggle for freedom), as cited in Americas Watch, *Human Rights in Mexico: A Policy of Impunity* (New York: Human Rights Watch, June 1990), p. 35.

54. Americas Watch, *Human Rights in Mexico,* p. 1.

in El Salvador), and the absence of Mexican human rights organizations kept Mexico from becoming a concern of the network.

Mexico had taken a position of firm rhetorical support for the human rights efforts of international organizations and cultivated its image as a defender of human rights. In 1988, the Mexican delegate to the UN Human Rights Commission affirmed, "Our country's adhesion to the most important multilateral human rights instruments entails a permanent double commitment: to preserve their full protection internally, and to contribute to their observance in the world within the judicial framework that the international community has established." He went on to clarify, however, that the UN mandate was to look into only massive and systematic violations of rights where domestic legal recourse is inoperative.[55] Mexico's verbal support for international human rights norms and its acceptance of the international community's role in the supervision of human rights practices were coupled with a failure to address a pattern of domestic human rights violations.

This situation began to change by the late 1980s, when human rights consciousness began to penetrate Mexican civil society. In 1984, only four human rights NGOs existed in Mexico, seven years later there were sixty, and by 1993 there were over two hundred independent human rights monitoring and advocacy NGOs. International attention helped create the political space within which this growth was possible.[56] A key turning point came when a group of prestigious Mexican intellectuals, activists, and politicians set up the Mexican Academy for Human Rights in 1984. The academy focused attention on human rights issues in Mexico, trained human rights practitioners, and fostered research and education on human rights. The academy was explicitly designed as an academic institution rather than an activist group, in hope of opening space for the human rights debate in Mexico without confronting the government on specific issues.[57] The academy received early and strong support from the Ford Foundation, which provided the bulk of its funding during its first five years.[58] The 1985 earthquake in Mexico City gave impetus to the increasing concern with human rights. The discovery of the bodies of several prisoners showing signs of torture during the excavation of the ruins of the headquarters of the office of the Federal District Attorney General stirred national outrage.[59] Second, when the Mexican government was paralyzed in its response to the earthquake, civil society organized and international NGOs

55. "Statement by the Chief of the Mexican Delegation, Mr. Claude Heller, on theme 12 of the agenda in the 44th period of session of the Commission of Human Rights," mimeograph, Commission of Human Rights, Geneva, 8 March 1988 (translation by author).

56. Jonathan Fox and Luis Hernández, "Mexico's Difficult Democracy: Grassroots Movements, NGOs, and Local Government," *Alternatives* 17 (Spring 1992), pp. 184–85; and Human Rights Watch, *Human Rights Watch World Report* (New York: Human Rights Watch, 1993), p. 131.

57. Interview with Rodolfo Stavenhagen, founding member of the Mexican Academy of Human Rights, Buenos Aires, 26 October 1992.

58. This included an initial two-year grant of $150,000 and a follow-up grant of $375,000.

59. Americas Watch, *Human Rights in Mexico*, pp. 9–10.

and funders stepped in to clean up. This collaboration between groups in civil society and international NGOs broke down old assumptions in Mexico that all political activity must be channeled through the state and created new confidence in the capacity of the NGO sector.[60]

A third stage began when the international human rights NGOs first addressed the Mexican human rights situation. With the wave of redemocratization in the hemisphere, human rights had improved in many countries that previously had been targets of the network. The network was now able to turn its attention to the more ambiguous situations of endemic violations of human rights under formally elected governments. The first reports by an international human rights NGO came in 1984 and 1986 when Americas Watch released a report on Mexico's treatment of Guatemalan refugees and AI issued its report on rural violence in Mexico.[61] When AI researchers first visited Mexico, they found no human rights official in the government or human rights NGO to contact. Although the two reports upset the Mexican government because they breached its cultivated image and identity as a defender of human rights, they did not lead to changing government human rights practices.[62]

Human rights practices did not improve until after 1988, when a different domestic and international political context made human rights a more salient issue. The split of the ruling party, PRI, before the 1988 presidential election led to the formation of a potent political challenge from the left in the form of the Party of the Democratic Revolution (PRD) led by Cuauhtémoc Cárdenas. In 1990, Mexico initiated discussions with Canada and the United States over a free trade agreement. Both of these situations made the Mexican government more sensitive to charges of human rights violations.

Americas Watch issued a seminal report on human rights conditions in Mexico in 1990. The introduction to this report begins: "More often than not, Mexico is overlooked when lists of countries that violate internationally recognized human rights are compiled. That this is so is more a testament to the Mexican government's careful cultivation of its pro–human rights image than its care to ensure that individual human rights are respected."[63] The report goes on to document killings, torture, and mistreatment of individuals by the police during criminal investigations; disappearances; election-related violence; violence related to land disputes; abuses directed against independent unions; and violations of freedom of the press—abuses that the report argues have been prevalent for years, and have become an institutionalized part of Mexican society. The Americas Watch report received coverage in the

60. Interviews with Rodolfo Stavenhagen, 26 October 1992, and with Christopher Welna, former program officer, Ford Foundation office for Mexico and Central America, 8 October 1992.
61. See Americas Watch, *Guatemalan Refugees in Mexico: 1980–1984* (New York: Human Rights Watch, September 1984); and Amnesty International, *Mexico: Human Rights in Rural Areas* (London: Amnesty International Publications, 1986), respectively.
62. Interview with Sebastian Brett, Amnesty International researcher on Mexico, 1983–1987, Santiago, Chile, 3 November 1992.
63. Americas Watch, *Human Rights in Mexico*, p. 1.

U.S. and Mexican press and attracted significant attention in Washington, D.C., where the initial negotiations for the free trade agreement were under way.

Until 1990, the U.S. Congress had held no hearings on the general human rights situation in Mexico. Over the years, Congress had expressed concern about the mistreatment of U.S. prisoners held in Mexican prisons but had not broadened its focus to look at Mexico's treatment of its own citizens. Yet in September 1990, only a few months after the Americas Watch report was issued, the Subcommittee on Human Rights and International Organizations and the Subcommittee on Western Hemisphere Affairs of the House of Representatives held hearings on human rights in Mexico. In addition to testimony from the State Department, these two subcommittees heard testimony from AI and Americas Watch.[64]

The IACHR did not consider admissible any Mexican cases until 1989–90, when it took on three Mexican cases. All three cases, brought by members of a major opposition party, the National Action Party (PAN), allege that PRI committed electoral irregularities. In response to these cases, the Mexican government adopted a rigid position that a decision of a domestic electoral body "is not and cannot be subject to international jurisdiction" and that if a "State agreed to submit itself to international jurisdiction with respect to the election of its political bodies, *a State would cease to be sovereign*" and finally that "any conclusion issued by the Commission on the legitimacy of the electoral process . . . would constitute an act of intervention, according to the definition set forth in Article 18 of the Charter."[65]

The IACHR responded to each of these claims, asserting the admissibility of the complaints and the competence of the commission to decide issues related to elections, since the American Convention on Human Rights guarantees the right to vote and be elected. The commission turned to various sources to interpret the claims of the Mexican government about its sovereign rights: the understandings embodied in the human rights treaties, the Mexican government's ratification of these treaties, its failure to express reservations at that point with regard to the issue of elections, and the shared understandings and practices of other states in the region as indicated by their statements or lack thereof. The commission concluded that the Mexican position was unfounded, and it recommended that the Mexican government reform its internal electoral law to make effective the political rights of the convention.[66] This episode

---

64. U.S. Congress, House Committee on Foreign Affairs, *Current Developments in Mexico: Hearing Before the Subcommittees on Human Rights and International Organizations and on Western Hemisphere Affairs of the Committee on Foreign Affairs, 12 September 1990*, 101st Congress, 2d sess. (Washington, D.C.: U.S. Government Printing Office, 1990), pp. 1–97.

65. OAS, *Annual Report of the Inter-American Commission on Human Rights 1989–1990* (Washington, D.C.: OAS General Secretariat, 1990), pp. 103–5, emphasis added.

66. Ibid, pp. 106–23.

underscores the importance of sovereignty as a set of shared understandings and practices and the manner in which the previous actions of a state create precedents that constrain its later actions and statements. In spite of its protestations, the Mexican government is currently reformulating its electoral laws.

In large part as a response to these international network pressures, the Mexican government created the National Commission on Human Rights in June 1990.[67] The Salinas administration was concerned that Mexico might be subject to heightened scrutiny from both the U.S. administration and Congress in the context of future free trade negotiations and subsequent ratification debates.[68] Creating the National Commission on Human Rights served preemptively to defuse the issue by making it appear that the Mexican government had its human rights problem under control.

That Mexico's national commission is a response to international pressure is underscored by the timing of its creation and the fact that its reports are now published simultaneously in Spanish and English and shipped via international express mail to representatives of key U.S. human rights organizations. Three events converged shortly before the creation of the national commission. A leading human rights activist, Norma Corona Sapien, was murdered on 21 May 1990 after spearheading an investigation that concluded that Federal Judicial Police were responsible for earlier killings. In May 1990 as well, the IACHR issued its decision finding Mexico in violation of the OAS American Convention on Human Rights. The final pressure came in early June of that year when Americas Watch issued its own report, *Human Rights in Mexico: A Policy of Impunity,* just days before Salinas and President Bush were scheduled to announce their intention to begin negotiations for a free trade agreement between their countries. Concerned with preempting negative publicity about Mexican human rights practices, four days before the meeting with Bush, President Salinas established the National Human Rights Commission.[69]

Although it was headed by a prestigious Mexican jurist, Dr. Jorge Carpizo, and has a strong presence of members from the Academy of Human Rights, the commission has been criticized for lacking sufficient independence from the government to serve as a watchdog agency. There is some concern that the

67. Jorge Luis Sierra Guzmán, Rafael Ruiz Harrell, and José Barragán, *La Comisión Nacional de Derechos Humanos: Una visión no gubernamental* (The National Human Rights Commission: A nongovernmental view) (Mexico City: Comisión Mexicana de Defensa y Promoción de los Derechos Humanos, 1992), p. 1.

68. According to Dresser, "Foremost among the priorities of Salinas's foreign policy is the avoidance of diplomatic conflicts that might sabotage Mexico's shared economic interests with the U.S." See Denise Dresser, "Mr. Salinas Goes to Washington: Mexican Lobbying in the United States," conference paper no. 62, presented at a research conference entitled "Crossing National Borders: Invasion or Involvement," Columbia University, New York, 6 December 1991, p. 5.

69. Ellen L. Lutz, "Human Rights in Mexico: Cause for Continuing Concern," *Current History* 92 (February 1993), pp. 78–82.

purpose of the commission is to provide a mask for international public opinion.[70] Evidence suggests, however, that in many cases the national commission has been an effective advocate for human rights.[71] Since the formation of the national commission, the government has taken several concrete steps to improve human rights practices. It has taken measures to professionalize the Federal Judicial Police and has approved procedures to prevent the use of evidence from confessions in trials, which had led to routine use of torture during interrogation after arrests.[72] Also, the National Human Rights Commission has investigated and condemned conditions in some of the country's worst prisons.[73]

One alternative explanation for the changes in Mexico is to attribute them to the will of the administration of President Salinas, since all of the changes mentioned occurred after he came to power. Evidence suggests that the Salinas administration, in the absence of human rights pressures, would have been unlikely to have made these changes on its own. For example, shortly after the Salinas administration took office, the mayor of the Federal District (Mexico City) appointed as the director of intelligence services of Mexico City a man with a reputation as a torturer and founder of a death squad, Miguel Nazar Haro. Because the President appoints the mayor, Nazar Haro could not have been named without Salinas's awareness. Yet, it was not until a major campaign was mounted domestically calling for Nazar Haro's resignation that he was given a so-called leave of absence.[74]

There is no doubt, however, that Salinas is extremely sensitive to his country's external image and to the international repercussions of human rights complaints. More than many leaders, Salinas often takes preemptive measures to project the image of his administration's concern with human rights. For example, in late 1992, less than one week before he was to meet with President-elect Bill Clinton, Salinas named Dr. Carpizo, the former Supreme Court Justice who was the president of the National Commission for Human Rights, as his new Attorney General.

The case of Mexico provides three separate historical stages, each of which provides some evidence for the argument presented here. During the first stage, in 1968–69, an episode of serious violations of human rights provoked no international response because the international human rights network did not yet exist. During the second stage, from 1970 to 1988, lower-level endemic

---

70. Emilio Krieger, "Prólogo" (Prologue), in Sierra Guzmán et al., *La Comisión Nacional de Derechos Humanos* (The National Human Rights Commission), p. ix.
71. Lutz discusses the national commission's "hard-hitting recommendations in over 300 cases," many of which included cases that have been the focus of NGOs. See Lutz, "Human Rights in Mexico," p. 80.
72. "Mexico: Human Rights Come to the Fore," *Latin America Update*, vol. 16, no. 1, Washington Office on Latin America, January–April 1991, pp. 1 and 6.
73. Americas Watch, *Prison Conditions in Mexico* (New York: Human Rights Watch, March 1991), p. 46.
74. Mexican Academy for Human Rights, *Boletín* 5 (February 1989), p. 12.

human rights abuses continued. Although the human rights network emerged during this period, it did not turn its attention to Mexico, and there was no condemnation of these practices or substantial change in the human rights situation. In the third stage, from 1988 to 1992, the international human rights network began to focus on Mexico, in collaboration with recently formed domestic human rights groups, and provoked a relatively rapid and forceful response from the Mexican government.[75]

Conclusions

This article has argued that in some cases international human rights pressures contribute to changing understandings about how states should use their sovereign authority over their citizens and to changing specific human rights practices. Although two cases are not sufficient to confirm this argument, the contrast provides substantiation for it and indicates it is worth further study.[76] There are other cases in which the international human rights network has not been effective in changing understandings or practices about human rights: in Latin America (for example, Haiti and Guatemala) and elsewhere (for example, Cambodia and China).[77] The central question then becomes: under what conditions can the international human rights network be effective? The cases here offer some evidence of these conditions.

In both Argentina and Mexico, nongovernmental actors initiated global concern with human rights violations and documented the abuses. Later, when international and regional organizations produced reports, their efforts were aided by earlier reports formulated by NGOs. NGOs also provided the information that served as the basis for governmental human rights policy. Because domestic human rights NGOs are a crucial link in the network, where these groups are absent, as in the case of Mexico initially, international human rights work is severely hampered. Since the human rights network has been strongest in regard to Latin America and to Eastern Europe and the former

75. One recent work gives international pressures little credit for promoting democracy in Mexico. This work was based on research that ended in 1989, however, and was not able to observe and comment on the international pressures and domestic changes in the 1989–92 period that are the basis of the argument presented here. See Lorenzo Meyer, "Mexico: The Exception and the Rule," in Abraham F. Lowenthal, ed., *Exporting Democracy: The United States and Latin America—Case Studies* (Baltimore, Md.: Johns Hopkins University Press, 1991), pp. 93–110.

76. Cases similar to Argentina could be made for some of the other military dictatorships of the Southern Cone, such as Chile and Uruguay. Mexico is unique, both for the lack of attention it received on human rights issues initially and for the rapidity of its response once human rights issues became salient, but there are other cases of semidemocratic governments where targeted international human rights pressures have led to important changes—for example, in the Dominican Republic during the 1978 elections or more recently in Paraguay.

77. Even Guatemala has moved along the continuum from uncompromising rejection of all human rights pressures as illegitimate interferences in sovereignty to a middle position of accepting the legitimacy of international criticism but claiming that it is not responsible and cannot control most of the violence.

Soviet Union, the most forceful human rights work has been directed at violations in these regions.

One possible alternative explanation is that foreign government pressure and domestic political pressure would have been able to change human rights practices without the involvement of the issue-network. What this misses is that foreign governments placed pressure on human rights violators only after nongovernmental actors had identified, documented, and denounced human rights violations and had pressured foreign governments to become involved.

Because of the hidden nature of repression in Argentina and the able and active diplomatic strategies of the Argentine junta, it is unlikely that the true nature of human rights abuses in Argentina would have come to world attention without the detailed documentation and diffusion of information by the human rights network. Unlike the case of Chile, where television crews and embassy officials could attest to the scale of rights violations, the Argentine government's responsibility for the practice of disappearances was revealed only through an intense labor of many parts of the network working collectively. The reports of human rights organizations provided the definitive evidence necessary to mount the international human rights campaign against the Argentine military. Without this information, foreign governments would not have been able to bring diplomatic pressure to bear on the Argentine government. The first strong pressures from foreign governments came almost a year after the coup and after the release of the powerful AI document detailing the Argentine government's responsibility for the practice of disappearances.

The case of Mexico is even clearer because endemic human rights abuses persisted for almost two decades without any pressure or comments from foreign governments. The Mexican case shows the human rights scenario both when the network did not exist and later, before the network turned its attention to a case. When the network did not exist, there was virtually no international response to the 1968 student massacre. When the network existed but did not focus on Mexico, there was no international awareness of the human rights situation in Mexico. It was only after the NGOs within and outside of Mexico began to document human rights abuses and bring them to the attention of the press and policymakers, and only within the context of the free trade negotiations, that the Mexican government made concrete changes to improve its human rights practices.

The existence of the network and a network decision to focus on a particular country are necessary but obviously not sufficient conditions for changing human rights practices. Many argue that human rights pressures would not be effective against strong states that can raise significant costs to the states that pressure them. Network activists admit that they have been less effective against states perceived as too important to the national security interests of superpowers: countries such as China, Israel, Pakistan, Saudi Arabia, and Turkey.[78]

However, supplementing the argument here with a standard international power argument partly misses the point. In Latin America, the countries that have resisted international human rights pressures, such as Haiti and Guatemala, are considerably weaker than such countries as Argentina and Mexico, which have responded to outside pressures. In the realm of human rights, it is the combination of moral pressure and material pressure that leads to change. Transforming state practices has come about as a result of linking principled ideas to material goals: military aid, economic aid, and trade benefits. But significant material pressure may be ineffective when leaders are unconcerned with the normative message. Countries most susceptible to network pressures, which primarily involve providing information to mobilize moral outrage and shame, are those that aspire to form part of the community of nations as a normative community. Pressures are eventually most effective where states have internalized the norms of the human rights regime and resist being characterized as pariahs.

But human rights does not represent a simple dichotomy of norms versus interests. The networks were influential within states because they contributed to a reformulation in the understandings of national interest at times when traditional understandings of sovereignty and national interest were called into question by changing global events. In the process of foreign policymaking, especially during a period of profound global flux, policymakers are often uncertain not only about what constitutes the national interest but also about how it can be promoted.[79] Issue-networks served effectively as carriers of human rights ideas, inserting them into the policy debate at the crucial moments when policymakers were questioning past policy models.

A realist approach to international relations would have trouble accounting for the activities of the network and the adoption and implementation of state human rights policies except by dismissing them as insignificant. Realism offers no convincing explanation for why relatively weak nonstate actors could have an impact on state policy or why states would concern themselves with the internal human rights practices of other states, especially when such concern interferes with the pursuit of other state goals. For example, the U.S. government's pressure on Argentina regarding human rights issues led to Argentine defection from the grain embargo of the Soviet Union. Raising human rights issues with Mexico could potentially undermine the successful

78. Interview with Michael Posner, executive director, Lawyers Committee for Human Rights, New York, 19 March 1992.

79. Theories of epistemic communities also have stressed the importance of these communities to the policy process in conditions of uncertainty. See Peter Haas, "Introduction: Epistemic Communities and International Policy Coordination," *International Organization* 46 (Winter 1992), pp. 1–35, and pp. 12–16 in particular.

completion of the free trade agreement and cooperation with Mexico on antidrug operations. Human rights pressures are not without costs, even in the strategically less important countries of Latin America.

In liberal versions of international relations theory, cooperation results when states and nonstate actors face problems they cannot resolve individually and from which joint gains are possible or mutually undesirable outcomes are avoided. These situations have been characterized as cooperation or coordination games with particular payoff structures.[80] The human rights issue, however, cannot be easily characterized in this way. First, the situation does not fit the standard view of a cooperation or coordination game. In most cases, the internal human rights practices of states can be ignored by other states without causing undesirable economic or security externalities.

In the issue of human rights, it is primarily principled ideas that drive changes and cooperation. We cannot understand why countries, organizations, and individuals are concerned about human rights or why countries respond to human rights pressures without taking into account the role of norms and ideas in international life. Jack Donnelly has argued that such moral interests are no less real than material interests and that a sense of moral interdependence has led to the emergence of human rights regimes.[81]

In this sense, the work here fits into a new literature trying to specify the influence of ideas and normative change on international relations and foreign and domestic policy changes.[82] This literature, however, continues to be vague on how ideas and norms specifically influence international relations. What are the processes and mechanisms through which ideas come to influence state policies and practices? What has been lacking is a means to conceptualize these emerging actors who are contributing to transformed understandings of sovereignty. In the case of human rights, I conclude that the primary movers behind this form of principled international action are international networks. Similar cases could be made for other issue-areas wherein shared values play a

80. See, for example, Arthur A. Stein, "Coordination and Collaboration: Regimes in an Anarchic World," *International Organization* 36 (Spring 1982), pp. 299–324.

81. Donnelly, *Universal Human Rights in Theory and Practice,* pp. 211–12.

82. See, for example, Goldstein and Keohane, *Ideas and Foreign Policy;* Peter A. Hall, ed., *The Political Power of Economic Ideas: Keynesianism Across Nations* (Princeton, N.J.: Princeton University Press, 1989); Kathryn Sikkink, *Ideas and Institutions: Developmentalism in Brazil and Argentina* (Ithaca, N.Y.: Cornell University Press, 1991); Judith Goldstein, "The Impact of Ideas on Trade Policy: The Origins of U.S. Agricultural and Manufacturing Policies," *International Organization* 43 (Winter 1989), pp. 31–71; Judith Goldstein, "Ideas, Institutions, and American Trade Policy," *International Organization* 42 (Winter 1988), pp. 179–217; Ernst B. Haas, *When Knowledge Is Power: Three Models of Change in International Organizations* (Berkeley: University of California Press, 1990); John S. Odell, *U.S. International Monetary Policy: Markets, Power, and Ideas as Sources of Change* (Princeton, N.J.: Princeton University Press, 1982); Michael Shafer, *Deadly Paradigms: The Failure of U.S. Counterinsurgency Policy* (Princeton, N.J.: Princeton University Press, 1988); and Emanuel Adler, *The Power of Ideology: The Quest for Technological Autonomy in Argentina and Brazil* (Berkeley: University of California Press, 1987).

central role, such as the ecological movement or a series of smaller issue-specific movements.[83]

To make the concept of an issue-network more useful, we need to distinguish how it differs from other concepts that could be used to frame the international dimensions of the human rights issue: an international human rights regime, an epistemic community, a transnational human rights social movement, or other forms of transnational relations.[84]

Although the social movement literature has concentrated on social movements within countries, it occasionally refers to international social movements as well.[85] The idea of a social movement, however, with its emphasis on bottom-up citizen protest, fails to portray accurately the range of actors involved in the human rights issues, including foundations and international and regional organizations. We could call the nongovernmental part of the network an international social movement, but the name would not work for the network as a whole.

The regime literature illuminates the emergence of international human rights regimes,[86] but it focuses too exclusively on states and international organizations as the sole "regime makers."[87] The focus on networks complements the regime literature by drawing attention to the role of nongovernmental actors in developing norms and helping to create, monitor, and strengthen some regimes.

By stressing the importance of international interactions of nonstate actors, this article follows in the tradition of earlier work in transnational politics.[88] Interdependence theorists correctly signaled the emergence of multiple channels of contacts among societies and the resultant blurring of domestic politics and international politics.[89] Recent work now seeks to revive the debate on

83. See Keck and Sikkink, "International Issue Networks in the Environment and Human Rights"; and Kathryn Sikkink, "Codes of Conduct for Transnational Corporations: The Case of the WHO/UNICEF Code," *International Organization* 40 (Autumn 1986), pp. 815–40.

84. For an example of an exploration of the human rights issue using both the regime literature and the social movement literature, see Alison Brysk, "From Above and Below: Social Movements, the International System and Human Rights in Argentina," *Comparative Political Studies*, forthcoming.

85. For example, Saul H. Mendlovitz and R. B. J. Walker, eds., *Towards a Just World Peace: Perspectives from Social Movements* (Boston: Butterworths, 1987).

86. See N. G. Onuf and V. Spike Peterson, "Human Rights from an International Regime Perspective," *Journal of International Affairs* 37 (Winter 1984), pp. 329–42; and Jack Donnelly, "International Human Rights: A Regime Analysis," *International Organization* 40 (Summer 1986), pp. 599–642.

87. "International Regimes," special issue, *International Organization* 36 (Spring 1982).

88. Robert Keohane and Joseph Nye, eds., *Transnational Relations and World Politics* (Cambridge, Mass.: Harvard University Press, 1971).

89. Other works now exploring this blurring of domestic and international politics include the following by Douglas A. Chalmers: "The International Dimensions of Political Institutions in Latin America: An Internationalized Approach," paper presented at the annual meeting of the American Political Science Association, Chicago, 3–6 September 1992, pp. 1–35; and "An End to Foreign Policy: The U.S. and Internationalized Politics," conference paper no. 60, presented at a

transnational relations.[90] Although the "new transnationalism" attempts to narrow and make more precise the definitions of transnational relations, the only factors that many of these transnational relations share is that all operate across national borders and all are characterized by purposeful actors, at least one of which is a nonstate agent. What the new transnationalists fail to distinguish, however, is how completely different are the purposes of the different types of transnational relations.

Issue-networks differ from other types of transnational relations in terms of the kinds of ideas and purposes that bind them together. We can identify three main categories of transnational relations, based on the different goals and ideas they embody: (1) transnational relations motivated by *instrumental goals* such as the goal of profit or economic gain, (2) transnational relations motivated by shared *causal ideas* (epistemic communities),[91] and (3) transnational relations motivated by *shared values or principled ideas*—beliefs about what is right or wrong (issue-networks). Each of these subsets of transnational relations has, in turn, a characteristic set of actors. Transnational corporations, global banks, and internationally organized interest groups are characteristic of the first category, groups of scientists or knowledge-based experts characterize epistemic communities, and activist NGOs characterize issue-networks. Human rights has its set of knowledge-based experts—the international lawyers who have defined international human rights law—but in the human rights issue-area, change comes about not through experts exposing the technical complexities but by nongovernmental actors mobilizing shame by disseminating information about government repression.

Sovereignty is not going to disappear. The sovereign state remains the dominant force in protecting and violating human rights. But states are altering their understandings of the scope and limits of sovereign authority. Sovereignty

---

research conference entitled "Crossing National Borders: Invasion or Involvement," Columbia University, New York, 6 December 1991. Another way of theorizing this interpenetration of the domestic and international spheres is the concept of two-level games. See Robert Putnam, "Diplomacy and Domestic Politics: The Logic of Two-Level Games," *International Organization* 42 (Summer 1988), pp. 427–60; and Evans, Jacobson, and Putnam, *Double-Edged Diplomacy.*

90. Thomas Risse-Kappen, "Transnational Relations, Domestic Structures, and International Institutions: A Conceptual Framework," paper presented at the annual meeting of the American Political Science Association, Chicago, 3–6 September 1992.

91. Epistemic communities also share some values, and issue-networks share causal knowledge, but each has a characteristic type of shared idea that defines it and explains the nature of the transnational relations created. Haas has stressed that epistemic communities share both principled and causal ideas, but it is clear from his discussion of the concept, as well as from the cases chosen to illustrate it, that shared causal beliefs under conditions of technical complexity are the hallmarks of the epistemic community. See Haas, "Introduction: Epistemic Communities and International Policy Coordination," p. 18. This fact is recognized by the one essay on epistemic communities in which activist groups play a key role: M. J. Peterson, "Whalers, Cetologists, Environmentalists, and the International Management of Whaling," *International Organization* 46 (Winter 1992), pp. 147–86. Peterson argues that the environmentalist groups concerned with whaling do not qualify as an epistemic community. The tendency of these groups to use the "time honored device of making stark contrasts and dividing the world into 'good guys' and 'bad guys'" is a clear description of action based primarily on principled rather than causal beliefs (pp. 154–55).

is being reconstituted by an accumulation of practices, many as ordinary as writing a letter on behalf of a prisoner of conscience, others as path-breaking as international court decisions against a government for disappearing its citizens. The bulk of issue-network activities can be categorized under the rubric of information or education. Networks attempt to alter state human rights practices primarily by changing the information environment in which state actors work. In most cases this information consisted of documentation and testimony of human rights violations, often described in very personal and graphic terms.

How is it possible that such activities reshape sovereignty? Because sovereignty is a set of intersubjective understandings about the legitimate scope of state authority, reinforced by practices, the mundane activities of the human rights network can accumulate to question the idea that it is nobody else's business how a state treats its subjects. Every report, conference, or letter from the network underscores an alternative understanding: the basic rights of individuals are not the exclusive domain of the state but are a legitimate concern of the international community. The evidence of this new understanding can be found not only in the statements made by states but more importantly in their changing actions. In the cases of both Argentina and Mexico, the states often responded to such pressures by changing their rhetoric and by changing concrete state policies.

I argue here that the concept of principled issue-networks is a useful tool to capture the character of the transnational movements that have shared principled ideas as their defining characteristic. The concept of issue-networks may be useful for understanding actions in issue-areas other than human rights, where principled ideas also influence international relations but gain their strength from their embodiment in transnationally linked organizations and from their ability to transform state understandings. In the realm of human rights the result has been that one of the central principles of international life—sovereignty—is being gradually but significantly reconceptualized. This study suggests that at least in this subset of issues, more attention needs to be paid to the crucial role of issue-networks as the carriers of transformative ideas and to the actors who help create and sustain new international regimes.

[22]

Globalisation and Inequality

Andrew Hurrell and Ngaire Woods

Globalisation has become an important part of the rhetoric of contemporary international relations. It survived the end of the Cold War when many of our other ordering or explanatory concepts did not, and is seemingly endlessly capable of reinvention to describe many different types of change in world politics. The term 'globalisation' is often invoked to describe the process of increasing interdependence and global enmeshment which occurs as money, people, images, values, and ideas flow ever more swiftly and smoothly across national boundaries. It is assumed to be a process driven by technological advance which will lead to a more and more homogeneous and interconnected world. In the new globalised world economy, it is argued, states will cooperate more and international institutions will flourish. All of this draws on the 'liberal interpretation of globalisation'.

Neglected in liberal and other writings about globalisation is one particularly important feature of world politics: inequality. Our concern is not to highlight the discontinuities and unevenness of globalisation, which are often noted, but rather to try to unpack the relationship between globalisation and inequality more carefully.[1] Serious analysis of inequality has been neglected behind a number of rhetorical propositions voiced in loud debates between liberals and their critics. The former argue that globalisation ameliorates inequalities, the latter that globalisation exacerbates inequality.[2] Unanswered are the two fundamental questions which link globalisation and inequality. In the first place: how is the *process* of globalisation influenced by inequalities among states? In the second place: how is the *impact* of globalisation affecting inequalities among states?

This article argues that inequality matters not just on grounds of equity, but is also important for understanding the nature of globalisation and its impact on world politics. Inequalities among states both shape the process of globalisation and are affected by it. In the first part of the article, we examine liberal

---

1. We present a critique which differs from those who argue that neither the impact nor the process of globalisation are as complete or as new as is often asserted. For the latter, see Robert Wade, 'Globalisation and its Limits: the Continuing Economic Importance of Nations and Regions', in Suzanne Berger and Ronald Dore (eds.), *Convergence or Diversity? National Models of Production and Distribution in a Global Economy* (Ithaca, NY: Cornell University Press, forthcoming).

2. For examples of the view that market-driven globalisation exacerbates both political and economic inequalities, see James Petras and Morris Morley (eds.), *US Hegemony under Siege: Class, Politics and Development in Latin America* (London: Verso, 1990), and Barry Gills, Joel Rocamora, and Richard Wilson (eds.), *Low Intensity Democracy: Political Power in the New World Order* (London: Pluto Press, 1993).

© Millennium: Journal of International Studies, 1995. ISSN 0305-8298. Vol. 24, No. 3, pp. 447-470

Millennium

interpretations of globalisation. The term liberal is used to characterise both a market-liberal interpretation of the increasing interconnectedness of world markets, and a broader liberal interpretation of the political and social aspects of globalisation. We start with an examination of this view because its underlying assumptions dominate so much of the literature. Our enquiry both focuses on how and why liberals ignore or downplay inequality, and exposes the unresolved tensions within liberal approaches. This leads us to the second part of the article, in which we present our own reconceptualisation of globalisation, drawing on both an international society view of international relations and a view of the international political economy which emphasises the causes and promulgation of global inequalities. In the third section, we examine four areas which illustrate the linkages between inequality and globalisation: state strength, international institutions, values and norms, and non-state actors.

The Liberal Orthodoxy

Liberalism is a broad church and, as with all churches, has been marked by deep schisms. Yet, three broad propositions, all with deep historical roots, underpin liberal thinking on globalisation and inequality.

In the first place, liberal economists assume that the globalisation of world markets will reduce inequalities among and within states.[3] This strongly optimistic long-run assumption allows liberals to downgrade questions of inequality. The liberal orthodoxy posits a world economy in which a global increase in transactions is driven by technological advance and by self-maximising decisions of private actors. On this view, states and governments are bystanders to globalisation: the real driving forces are markets. Furthermore, the emergence of global markets improves efficiency. In the first place, the free movement of capital and goods across borders produces a more *efficient allocation of resources* around the globe. For example, investment will flow to where it is most profitable to invest it (hence, for example, it flows into developing areas where maximal gains might be made). In the second place, global markets ensure a more *efficient production of goods* in the world economy through the 'gains from trade'. Trade permits countries more effectively to exploit their factor endowments and to gain from specialisation. Furthermore, global investment and the movement of raw materials enhances both effects. Finally, a global world economy with freely exchangeable currencies and open markets ensures an *efficient distribution of goods and services* in a world in which price mechanisms operate globally. There is a real question here as to

---

3. Anne Krueger, 'Global Trade Prospects for the Developing Countries', *The World Economy* (Vol. 15, No. 4, 1992), pp. 457-74; Deepak Lal, *A Liberal International Economic Order: The International Monetary System and Economic Development* (Princeton, NJ: Princeton University International Finance Section, 1980); and John Dunning, *The Globalisation of Business: The Challenge of the 1990s* (London: Routledge, 1993).

whether available evidence endorses the improved efficiencies that the liberals hypothesise. We will pick up this point later, but it is worth noting at this stage that modern economists are questioning these theories by opening up other types of investigation into the causes of growth.[4]

A second observation of the liberal view of globalisation is that it will expand not only global markets but also the associated problems of market imperfections, negative externalities, environmental degradation, and, casting the net still wider, refugees, and humanitarian disasters.[5] As a result, globalisation creates a powerful 'demand' for international institutions and cooperation. Political authorities in the new global economy (be they new, emerging authorities or the governments and states for which they are supposed to substitute) will be forced to resolve common problems and to manage the frictions which arise from increasing interdependence. These insights are well highlighted by the liberals. Greater cooperation has become necessary, even if it is no easier to achieve. The prospects of cooperation are said to be enhanced by the fact that states' autonomy is diminishing, and their capacity to regulate and redistribute resources domestically is increasingly limited. Hence, in many areas, governance and regulation at the international level are becoming ever more important. Although such governance predominantly takes the form of inter-state regimes, both formal and informal regimes between private actors are playing an increasingly significant role.[6]

Third, liberals assume that globalisation will tend, in the long-run, to promote societal convergence built around common recognition of the benefits of markets and liberal democracy, and involving the emergence of global values, issues, and institutions. The liberal interpretation of globalisation suggests that the rise of technology and the enmeshment of world markets is bringing about a decrease in states' power and desire for independence. In the first place, the infrastructure of globalisation (global communications and transport systems) and the rise of new technologies (satellites, computer networks, and so forth) make it increasingly difficult for states to stem flows of information. At the same time, it has become increasingly easy for values, knowledge, and ideas to move across national boundaries. Economically, states must now compete actively for foreign investment and technology in global markets and, in order to do so effectively, they are converging on open-market policies. Politically, preferences for particular types of political organisation and values (free elections, sustainable development, human rights, and the like) are spreading. Hence, liberals explain,

---

4. The literature on endogenous growth is one such investigation. See, for example, Paul M. Romer, 'The Origins of Endogenous Growth', *Journal of Economic Perspectives*(Vol. 8, No. 1, 1994), pp. 3-22.

5. See, for example, Richard N. Cooper, *Economic Policy in an Interdependent World: Essays in World Economics* (Cambridge, MA: MIT Press, 1986), Chapter 11, and Robert O. Keohane, *International Institutions and State Power: Essays in International Relations Theory* (Boulder, CO: Westview Press, 1989), Chapter 5.

6. See generally Stephen D. Krasner (ed.), *International Regimes* (Ithaca, NY: Cornell University Press, 1983).

Millennium

there is an increasing homogenisation of economic policies and political organisation caused by globalisation. 'At least in intellectual terms', write John Williamson and Stephan Haggard, 'we today live in one world rather than three'.[7]

At the core of liberal thinking about globalisation lies a set of assumptions about how and why values, norms, and policy ideas converge. It is worth distinguishing two different processes to which liberals allude. In the first place, the convergence of policies across the globe may be attributed to the rationality of the policies and their proponents.[8] It is assumed that policy-makers are increasingly rational, technocratic, and literate in each particular field, be it, for example, environmental policy or economics. These policy-makers can draw on international links to other like-minded technocrats in other countries or in international institutions. One way in which this process is depicted is—following Peter Haas—in terms of epistemic communities consisting of economists or specialists in a field. Haas defines epistemic communities as 'networks of knowledge based communities with an authoritative claim to policy relevant knowledge within their domain of expertise'.[9] On this view, globalisation is facilitating the emergence of transnational governmental coalitions based on technical understanding of particular issues or sets of problems.

In contrast to emerging transnational technocratic coalitions, a second process of convergence involves the flow of ideas and information across borders as a result of increased societal interdependence. Increased communication and travel have facilitated the diffusion of values, knowledge, and ideas, and have enhanced the ability of like-minded groups to organise across national boundaries. From a liberal perspective, the strength of such groups rests on their ability to articulate a powerful set of human values, to harness the growing sense of a cosmopolitan moral awareness, and to respond to the multiple failures of the state system, both locally and globally. Influence does not derive from narrow economic incentives, nor from power political interests, but rather from ideas and values that are felt directly, if still unevenly, by individual human beings. Here, globalisation is leading not merely to instrumental transnational coalitions but to what some call an 'international civil society', or, better, 'global civil society': the 'emergence of a parallel arrangement of political interaction...focused on the

---

7. John Williamson and Stephan Haggard, 'The Political Conditions for Economic Reform', in Williamson and Haggard (eds.), *The Political Economy of Policy Reform* (Washington, DC: International Institute for Economics, 1994), p. 530. See also Robert H. Bates and Anne O. Krueger (eds.), *Political and Economic Interactions in Economic and Policy Reform* (Oxford: Blackwell, 1993), and Haggard and Steven B. Webb (eds.), *Voting for Reform: Democracy, Political Liberalization and Economic Adjustment* (New York, NY: Oxford University Press for the World Bank, 1994).

8. This view is particularly visible in many of the essays in John Williamson (ed.), *The Political Economy of Policy Reform* (Washington, DC: Institute for International Economics, 1993).

9. Peter M. Haas, 'Introduction: Epistemic Communities and International Policy Coordination', *International Organization* (Vol. 46, No. 1, 1992), pp. 1-36. See also Ernst B. Haas, *When Knowledge is Power: Three Models of Change in International Organizations* (Berkeley, CA: University of California Press, 1989).

self-conscious construction of networks of knowledge and action, by decentred, local actors....'[10]

Together, these processes lead to the progressive enmeshment of other states and cultures within the liberal system. Globalisation and interdependence help ensure the spread of information, values, and ideas that make non-liberal alternatives decreasingly feasible.[11] In part, the driving mechanism has to do with the rational adaptation on the part of policy-makers to a changing structure of external incentives, which in turn leads to processes of genuine learning and to the internalisation of liberal values. However, more generally, this view develops the Kantian notion of a gradual but progressive diffusion of liberal values, partly as a result of liberal economics and increased economic interdependence, partly as a liberal legal order comes to sustain the autonomy of a global civil society, and partly as a result of the successful example set by the multifaceted liberal capitalist system of states. The problem, as we shall see, is that this kind of view drastically underestimates the role that powerful states and institutions have played in offering incentives to, and applying pressures on, other states to alter their policies.

We might summarise the liberal view of globalisation according to the following argument structure:

(1) the increase in transactions across state boundaries is of great significance to the nature of the international system (in terms of *structure*, *process*, and *actors*);

(2) the processes of globalisation have a logic and dynamic of their own, driven by technological change, increasing knowledge, and rational decision-making.

(3) As a result, societies across the world are increasingly linked through *markets* and through an increasingly close-knit *transnational civil society*, rather than through the arena of inter-state competition.

(4) Hence, states will no longer form the only or necessarily most important frameworks of political authority (*cf.*, James Rosenau's picture of an

---

10. Ronnie D. Lipschutz, 'Reconstructing World Politics: The Emergence of Global Civil Society', *Millennium: Journal of International Studies* (Vol. 21, No. 3, 1992), p. 390. See also Richard Falk, 'The Global Promise of Social Movements: Explorations at the Edge of Time', *Alternatives* (Vol. 12, No. 2, 1987), pp. 173-96; *Millennium* Special Issue on Social Movements in World Politics (Vol. 23, No. 3, 1994); and Paul Wapner, 'Politics Beyond the State: Environmental Activism and World Civic Politics', *World Politics* (Vol. 47, No. 3, 1995), pp. 311-40. For an example of the broader revival of interest in transnationalism, see Thomas Risse-Kappen (ed.), *Bringing Transnational Relations Back In: Non-State Actors, Domestic Structures and International Institutions* (Cambridge: Cambridge University Press, 1995).

11. See, for example, Daniel Deudney and G. John Ikenberry, 'The International Sources of Soviet Change', *International Security* (Vol. 16, No. 3, 1991/92), pp. 74-118, and the discussion of these ideas in Fred Halliday, *Rethinking International Relations* (London: Macmillan, 1994), especially Chapter 5.

Millennium

autonomous multi-centric system emerging alongside the long-established system of states[12]).

(5) Thus, there is a growing tension between the reality of a globalising world economy and an anachronistic states-system. This tension may be unsettling, but it does not involve any irreconcilable conflicts or contradictions.

(6) In particular, international institutions will grow as states perceive that their interests are better met in a globalising world economy through institutionalised cooperation.

It would be wrong to suggest that contemporary liberalism takes a naively benign view of the impact of globalisation. Although these core propositions continue to underpin much liberal thought, liberals are neither as inflexible nor as unified as the above outline would suggest. Whilst remaining optimistic in the long-run, problems clearly abound. Thus, although efficiency gains will reduce inequalities both among and within states over time, there are two caveats to be made. Liberals accept that, in the short-run, there will be adjustment costs which might exacerbate inequalities. They also accept that the gains from globalisation will not necessarily be evenly spread: whilst every country stands to make an absolute gain from globalisation, some stand to gain relatively more than others. For some, this points to a positive role that government might play in global markets, tilting the playing field towards their own competitors.[13]

In addition, there are the potentially high costs of *political adjustment*. This is the challenge identified and discussed by Robert Reich:

We are living through a transformation that will rearrange the politics and economics of the coming century. There will be no *national* products or technologies, no national corporations, no national industries. There will be no national economies, at least as we have come to understand that concept. All that will remain rooted within national borders are the people who comprise a nation. Each nation's primary assets will be its citizen's skills and insights. Each nation's primary political task will be to cope with the centrifugal forces of the global economy which tear at the ties binding citizens together—bestowing ever greater wealth on the most skilled and insightful, while consigning the less skilled to a declining standard of living.[14]

The issue of adjustment highlighted by Robert Reich, is taken up by Adrian Wood in his work on the impact of globalisation on unskilled workers in the

---

12. James Rosenau, *Turbulence in World Politics* (New York, NY: Harvester Wheatsheaf, 1990).

13. Laura D'Andrea Tyson, *Who's Bashing Whom? Trade Conflict in High-Technology Industries* (Washington, DC: Institute for International Economics, 1992), and Robert Reich, *The Work of Nations: Preparing Ourselves for 21st-Century Capitalism* (London: Simon and Schuster, 1991).

14. Reich, *op. cit.*, in note 13, p. 3, emphasis in original.

North.[15] Nevertheless, although the market liberal perspective accepts these problems, ultimately it argues that such developments are a necessary part of wealth creation, and can potentially be managed by rational and enlightened state policies.

The important point, however, is not the recognition of these adjustment problems, but rather the failure to acknowledge that deep, unresolved tensions exist within the liberal view of globalisation. The first concerns the role of the state. At one extreme the anti-statist strand of liberalism has reappeared in strident form, rejecting the state as both a rational institution for effective economic management and as the locus of identity in a world characterised by homogenisation and increasingly complex forms of social communication.[16] As Ohmae puts it: '[t]he nation state has become an unnatural, even dysfunctional, unit for organizing human activity and managing economic endeavor in a borderless world. It represents no genuine, shared community of economic interests; it defines no meaningful flows of economic activity'.[17]

Yet, most contemporary liberals accept the need for the state and for institutional reforms.[18] In this dominant liberal discourse there is a good deal of talk of 'reinventing' government and, increasingly, institutions. The important point here is the fundamentally apolitical and technocratic view of what this 'reinvention' entails. On the technocratic view, it is mostly a matter of 'institutional strengthening' and 'capacity building', sometimes with a dose of decentralisation. The state is certainly the problem for market-minded liberals, but it can also become a central part of the solution, if the right policy-mix is chosen. The real problem here lies in reconciling the reduction of the state, undertaken as part of structural adjustment and economic liberalisation, with the new needs for an effective state to provide the necessary infrastructure in the economy.[19] Managed liberalism requires the state to maintain a high degree of political power and authority, while the liberal interpretation of globalisation suggests that states' political power might well be eroding.

---

15. Adrian Wood, *North-South Trade, Employment and Inequality: Changing Fortunes in a Skill-Driven World* (Oxford: Oxford University Press, 1994).

16. In this they follow Karl W. Deutsch, *et al.*, *Political Community and the North Atlantic Area: International Organization in the Light of Historical Experience* (New York, NY: Greenwood, 1957, reprinted 1969). For a more detailed treatment of some of the key themes in this debate, see David Long's article in this issue.

17. Kenichi Ohmae, 'The Rise of the Region State', *Foreign Affairs* (Vol. 72, No. 2, 1993), p. 78. Note how closely his words echo those of Norman Angell writing in 1909: 'the very complexity of the division of labour tends to set up cooperation in groups which might thwart political frontiers, so that the political no longer limits or coincides with the economic'. *The Great Illusion* (London: Heinemann, 1933), p. 157.

18. World Bank, *World Bank Development Report 1994* (Washington, DC: World Bank, 1994), and Inter-American Development Bank (IDB), *Economic and Social Progress in Latin America* (Washington, DC: IDB/Johns Hopkins University Press, 1994).

19. A thoughtful contemplation of this problem is Moisés Naím, *Latin America's Journey to the Market: From Macroeconomic Shocks to Institutional Therapy* (San Francisco, CA: International Center for Economic Growth, 1995).

Millennium

A second problem which remains unresolved in the liberal view is the relationship between different parts of the liberal vision: how to balance economic objectives and market liberalisation with liberal political and social goals. This difficulty has been increasingly visible in, for example, the arguments within the World Bank on how to deal with 'new' issues (such as environmental questions and the promotion of 'good governance'),[20] and in discussions of the impact of structural adjustment on poverty.[21] The dominant response is, once again, to see this as a technical problem, and to deal with it, for example, as an issue of 'sequencing'.[22] Yet, as we will argue below, the tensions run far deeper than this and crucially turn on the choice that exists between the effective management of globalisation on the one hand, and the promotion of such liberal values as participation, representation, and legitimacy on the other.

A third tension within liberalism concerns the differential speeds with which the dynamics of liberal progress work themselves out, and how this should be managed. A common theme of recent liberal writing has been to emphasise the increasing divide between a cohesive, prosperous, and peaceful bloc of liberal states and the instability and chaos of the rest of the world. This cleavage between a Grotian core and a Hobbesian periphery has been characterised in various ways: zones of peace *vs.* zones of turmoil;[23] the OECD as something approaching a giant pluralist security community;[24] the 'West' as a cohesive republican order based on economic growth, democratic governance, and liberal tolerance;[25] and the widening gaps on a global scale 'between publics and governments, between haves and have-nots, between nuclear and non-nuclear power', and so forth.[26] Yet, although new divisions in a globalising world are recognised, insufficient attention is given to the subsequent implications of globalisation either for politics on the 'other side of the divide' (outside of the liberal, integrating zone) or for global inequality.

---

20. See Joan Nelson and Stephanie Eglinton, *Encouraging Democracy: What Role for Conditioned Aid?* (Washington, DC: Overseas Development Council, 1992).
21. This issue was highlighted in the *World Bank Development Report 1990* (Washington, DC: World Bank, 1990).
22. See, for example, Sebastian Edwards, *Macroeconomic Stabilization in Latin America: Recent Experience and Some Sequencing Issues* (Washington, DC: NBER, 1994). For a discussion of other techniques, see Michael Lipton and Jacques Van der Gaag, *Including the Poor* (Washington, DC: World Bank, 1993).
23. Max Singer and Aaron Wildavsky, *The Real World Order: Zones of Peace, Zones of Turmoil* (Chatham, NJ: Chatham House Publishers, 1993).
24. Barry Buzan, *The European Security Order Recast: Scenarios for the Post-Cold War Era* (London: Pinter, 1990).
25. Daniel Deudney and G. John Ikenberry, 'The Logic of the West', *World Policy Journal* (Vol. 10, No. 4, 1993-94), pp. 17-25.
26. James Rosenau and Ernst-Otto Czempiel, *Governance without Government: Order and Change in World Politics* (Cambridge: Cambridge University Press, 1989), Chapter 1.

Redefining Globalisation

The liberal orthodoxy highlights the progressive enmeshment of economies and societies that results from globalisation. It emphasises the powerful international and transnational pressures that both constrain the range of viable state policies and influence the complexion of domestic politics. Neglected, however, in the liberal view is an analysis of the unevenness of the process of globalisation and the importance of the hierarchy among the states and actors which drive this process. The core proposition of our critique of the liberal orthodoxy on globalisation is a simple one: inequality among states matters. We explore this proposition in this section, looking first at the ways in which states are unequal and which types of inequality matter. We then move on to examine how these inequalities shape integration into the world economy, and the emergence of institutions, values, and norms associated with globalisation.

We are especially interested, then, in the two-way relationship between state inequality and globalisation. In order to clarify this relationship, we emphasise two aspects of the process of globalisation. One aspect is directly observable: the increase in transactions and interconnectedness among (especially OECD and selected other) states which is driven by both technological change and political choices. These 'observable' changes obviously affect choices and outcomes in world politics. Firms and governments have to rethink their strategies in a world in which the international arena affects an increasing range of decisions. Yet, tracing out the ways in which increased trans-border transactions, changes in technology, and new forms of economic competition have altered incentive structures does not tell us *how* firms, governments, and other actors will reshape their strategies and objectives. Here, another aspect of globalisation is crucial: the way in which it is 'experienced' and the way that experience is rooted within institutions.[27]

Actors across the globe interpret their choices and constraints in very different ways, and these understandings are embedded in very different kinds of domestic institutions and social structures. As a result, the impact of globalisation is nowhere equal and the simple notion of homogenisation conceals a more complex and ambiguous set of processes. Crucially, globalisation affects the political processes within which actors work. For example, governments dealing with issues such as global investment, the environment, human rights, and, to a lesser extent, democratisation, must now face two new sets of political pressures and constraints. At the international level, states must participate in new sets of negotiations and institutions. Within their own political systems, governments now face pressures from domestic actors, empowered or inspired by the international attention given to these issues. Just as technological change may

---

27. For a related, but distinct, emphasis on the importance of subjective understandings of globalisation, see Roland Robertson, *Globalisation: Social Theory and Global Culture* (London: Sage, 1992). It should, however, be noted that Robertson's approach is different from that adopted in this article.

Millennium

drive domestic firms to push for new types of investment regulation, so too conventions on the environment may fuel domestic interest groups to push for changes in domestic environmental standards. Thus, the 'experienced' aspect of globalisation is important because it enables us to look more closely at these political processes that condition the impact of globalisation, both at the international and domestic levels.

This way of understanding the process of globalisation is crucial to examining the impact of inequality on globalisation and vice-versa. Simply put, globalisation affects regions of the world in different ways. In part, this is due to the unevenness of increased flows and interconnectedness, the spread of technology, trade, and communications which is most heavily concentrated among OECD countries. However, the impact of globalisation is also conditioned by political inequalities, at both the international and domestic levels.

In the international realm, some states will have more power (rooted in military as well as political and economic capacity) to influence outcomes of negotiations and decisions. Hence, 'weaker' states face heavily constrained choices or an agenda which they have little influence in defining. Furthermore, their choices will carry powerful political implications; not just because they submit to the will of larger states over a particular issue, but because, over the longer term, weak states' decisions constrain their future options. For example, when weaker states sign up to a human rights convention, or an intellectual property standard, they face a greater prospect than more powerful states of coercive enforcement. Hence, globalisation affects not just their bargaining power at the time of negotiation, but, more widely, their relative power to make choices in the future.

At the domestic level, too, there are important differences among states and governments. Domestically weak governments face much greater difficulties in getting their constituencies to adapt to the changes or agreements worked out in international negotiations and fora. This is less of a problem if the state has power in the international arena, for it can then change the rules to which it agrees to be bound. However, where weak states enter into international undertakings which they cannot alter, they become not only more vulnerable to international pressures, but more susceptible to domestic political weaknesses. In implementing the necessary policies so as to participate in the new global agreements and economy, they can quickly lose domestic support. Such governments frequently become trapped between the so-called 'imperatives of globalisation' (such as economic liberalisation and subscription to a range of international standards on the environment, human rights, and so forth) and a political constituency which refuses to adapt and increasingly rebels against the government.

Overall, our definition of globalisation requires us, in examining its impact, to look at inequality among states at both the international and domestic levels. We might summarise this definition in the following propositions.

Globalisation and Inequality

(1) The observable face of globalisation is an increase in transactions across state boundaries, in part driven by technological change and increasing knowledge, which are mainly developed in large industrialised countries.

(2) The impact of these observable changes is conditioned by the different experiences that states have of increased interconnectedness, depending on variations in their political and economic capacities.

(3) The new interconnectedness is regulated by rules and institutions formulated and enforced mainly by the most powerful actors in the international political arena (especially states and firms).

(4) The benefits of globalisation flow to those states with the greatest capacity to absorb and adapt to the new types of transactions. This capacity includes the domestic political strength of governments.

(5) Increased linkages between societies are effected not just through markets, but also through issues and ideas which give international voice to non-state actors and empower them to be more active in domestic politics (some would refer to this, perhaps exaggeratedly, as the beginnings of a transnational civil society). These transnational linkages can erode the domestic political strength of the government.

Our definition of globalisation requires us to examine the political forces which shape its emergence and impact, and, in doing so, to reconsider the sources and nature of inequality among states. We need to replace the liberal Kantian image of *progressive enmeshment* with the more complex idea of *coercive socialisation*, involving both a range of external pressures (both state-based and market-based) and a variety of transmission mechanisms between the external and the domestic. In defining globalisation in this way, we bring together strands from several different ways of thinking about international relations. Our attention to inter-state power politics suggests something of a realist starting point, but this is heavily diluted: first, by our concern to explain change; second, by our examination of the role of non-state actors; and, third, by our attention to other dimensions of international relations (such as the role of institutions and values). The different strands of thinking are readily apparent in our definition of the core dimensions of state power which assist in examining inequality: the formal status of states (their degree of formally recognised independence); the territory, population, and natural resources of a state; the domestic strength, efficacy, and viability of a state; the distribution of economic wealth, military, and political power among states; the meta-power to make and change the rules of international relations; and the power and relative status of non-state actors. As we will elaborate below, these dimensions of inequality shape the nature and impact of globalisation, and, in turn, globalisation has highly significant effects on inter-state inequalities.

Millennium

Beyond the Liberal View of Inequality and Globalisation

The liberal view of globalisation, as we have already seen in the first section of this paper, highlights the *formal equality of states* which defines the key set of actors in the global market-place. The liberal view also implicitly recognises the uneven *distribution of economic wealth* among states, since this provides one of the conditions for globalisation: the incentive for capital and production to shift to new areas. However, the other dimensions of state power are virtually ignored in the liberal view. Although the role of *non-state actors* (MNCs, foreign investors, global communications conglomerates, and so forth) is recognised, little attention is paid to the political power of these actors. More fundamentally, liberals do not adequately address the *distribution of political power among states*, the capacity of some to set down rules for others, and the relative *domestic strength and viability of the state*. Yet, these other dimensions of inequality among states are crucial to an understanding of the nature and impact of globalisation. This is most simply highlighted by the coincidence between the unevenness of globalisation on the one hand, and the distribution of military and political power and international rule-making authority (or 'meta-power') among states on the other.

State Strength

Reframing one of the points made above, for large and powerful states (either globally or within a region) globalisation is, at least to some extent, a realm of choice. These states have the power to open or close world or regional markets and have discretion over how fast they wish to develop and exploit technological change. Furthermore, the impact of globalisation, because it is a process they influence, is likely to reinforce their position and their relative power (even if it channels it in new ways). For less powerful states in a region or in the world economy, globalisation is a process which is happening to them and to which they must respond. To some degree, they must choose either to accept the rules of the more powerful or not; although in today's world economy, where relative autarchy is punitive and where there is no alternative centre of power (as provided previously by the USSR), some would argue that they have little choice but to accept the rules.

These propositions, however, do not always reflect reality. There are limits to the control and influence of the large and powerful states, and the above arguments underestimate the importance of path dependence and the extent to which the process of globalisation is shaped by ongoing actions and reactions from both sides. For example, over the past four decades, industrialised countries have exhorted less developed countries to integrate into the world economy and to attract more investment. Yet, in each decade, different types of investment from industrialised countries have produced a backlash and a reassertion of state sovereignty. Hence, in the 1970s, developing countries attempted through the United Nations Conference on Trade and Development (UNCTAD), the United

Globalisation and Inequality

Nations General Assembly, and other fora, to control and limit the activities of multinational corporations which had come to be seen as too powerful and exploitative. In the 1980s, Western international commercial banks became the adversary: accused of punishingly high interest rates and imposing stringent adjustment on debtors. After the debt crises of the 1980s, developing countries pushed for new forms of regulation, control, and replacement of international bank loans. In the early 1990s, the backlash is against capital flows into share and bond markets in developing countries. After the crisis in Mexico in 1994 highlighted the volatility and destabilising effects of such investment, the new call from several different regions is for capital controls, as already put in place in Chile and China.[28]

These different forms of 'backlash' against globalisation highlight that the process is a contested one. Yet, it is not the case that the most powerful states in realist power-political terms always win in such contests. Globalisation, and attempts to control it, are shaped by those with power—derived from all of the sources listed above. East Asia provides a particular example of the varied sources of such power. For, although the recent World Bank study of the 'East Asia miracle' points to these countries' integration into world markets,[29] this interpretation is controversial and wrongly ignores, as several economists have pointed out, other political and economic factors.[30]

The debate about East Asia is a crucial one, because it turns on the extent to which governments of small states might control the nature and impact of globalisation on themselves. Crucial to the East Asian countries' success, most analysts agree, were their domestically strong, efficient, and viable state apparatuses.[31] Hence, we see the importance of distinguishing domestically 'strong' and 'weak' states. However, we must also recall that the internal strength of states in East Asia has in turn been due to the security threat that each country faced in the aftermath of the World War II, their strategic importance during the Cold War, and the economic success that they have enjoyed. So, East Asia highlights both that the categories of domestically 'strong' and 'weak' states are crucial, as well as the fact that these domestic

---

28. Critiques of the various stages of globalisation can be followed in UNCTAD, *Trade and Development Report* (New York, NY: United Nations, annually); through issues of the *Cepal Review* (Santiago: Economic Commission for Latin America); and, in respect of money and finance, in the various papers of the Group of Twenty-Four: *International Monetary and Financial Issues for the Developing Countries* (Geneva: UNCTAD, 1987), and *International Monetary and Financial Issues for the 1990s, Volumes I and II* (Geneva: UNCTAD, 1992).
29. The World Bank, *The East Asian Miracle: Economic Growth and Public Policy* (New York, NY: Oxford University Press, 1993).
30. A good survey is Albert Fishlow, *et al.*, *Miracle or Design?: Lessons from the East Asian Experience* (Washington, DC: Overseas Development Council, 1994).
31. Robert Wade, *Governing the Market* (Princeton, NJ: Princeton University Press, 1990); Alice Amsden, *Asia's Next Giant* (New York, NY: Oxford University Press, 1989); Amsden, 'Taiwan's Economic History: A Case of *Etatisme* and a Challenge to Dependency Theory', *Modern China* (Vol. 5, 1979), pp. 341-79; and Stephen Haggard, *Pathways from the Periphery* (Ithaca, NY: Cornell University Press, 1990).

Millennium

characteristics interplay with the international dimensions of state strength we have listed above. The fact that these are small states which have fairly carefully controlled their integration into the world economy—and continue to do so, as Korea's recent clamp-down on foreign investment displays[32]—suggests that any analysis of the nature and impact of globalisation requires a much more careful consideration of state strength and inequality.

Institutions and the Creation of New Structural Power

As we have mentioned above, globalisation is greatly influenced by international institutions established (or adapted) to facilitate and manage new flows of goods, people, ideas, and values across borders. As the liberals highlight, institutions are important in a globalised world as instruments of common purpose. Yet, liberal institutionalist theory has tended to focus on a narrow range of issues, and has paid too much attention to bargaining processes among states. Thus, going back to *Power and Interdependence*, which largely set the agenda for this scholarship, Keohane and Nye write that they 'sought to integrate realism and liberalism *using a conception of interdependence which focused on bargaining*'.[33] In parallel fashion, there has been a growing literature on the importance of linkages between domestic and international factors. Yet, the influential scholarship sparked by Robert Putnam's two-level game analogy has also focused almost entirely on bargaining and negotiation.[34] Missing from the interdependence and bargaining approaches are questions which, in our view, are central to comprehending the process and the impact of globalisation. These are questions as to what and why particular issues are left off the agenda of inter-state politics, who sets the rules of the bargaining game (meta-rules), and whence come the norms and ideas which are used to define issues and within which bargaining takes place.

Institutions are sites of power or dominance. Indeed, the World Bank's interpretation of East Asia's economic success, mentioned above, provides a case study of the struggle for dominance and control within institutions. As Robert Wade has documented, within the World Bank the interpretation of East Asia's success produced a political battle between Japan and the United States, and resulted in a report, the conclusions of which were markedly tilted so as to support the US-favoured, market-oriented approach to policy.[35] The struggles (and silences) within international institutions can only be understood by recognising that institutions do not emerge solely for utilitarian reasons.

---

32. 'New Curbs Hit South Korean Groups', *Financial Times* (12 October 1995), p. 7.
33. Robert O. Keohane and Joseph S. Nye, *Power and Interdependence*, Second Edition (Glenview, IL: Scott, Foresman and Company, 1989), p. 251, emphasis added.
34. Peter Evans, Harold Jacobson, and Robert Putnam (eds.), *Double-Edged Diplomacy* (Berkeley, CA: University of California Press, 1993).
35. Robert Wade, 'The World Bank and the Art of Paradigm Maintenance: the East Asian Miracle as a Response to Japan's Challenge to the Development Consensus', unpublished paper, University of Sussex, 1995.

Although international institutions ostensibly arise amongst states concerned with solving common problems and promoting overall welfare, in fact they reflect a pattern of structural power which is central to the management of interdependence.[36] On the one hand, states create institutions because they wish to resolve distributional conflicts and relative gains concerns. Yet, in the end, it is powerful states who will shape the agenda, decide who can play the game, define the rules, and enforce outcomes which are favourable to themselves. Thus, globalisation creates new forms of structural power in which institutions play an important role: ultimately, that which powerful states delegate to them. We return to the point made above that globalisation offers powerful states a realm of choice. Most fundamentally, they can choose whether to favour cooperation in multilateral institutions (of which they often determine the internal structure), or to use bilateral negotiations. Indeed, this has been the pattern of US trade policy over the past two decades.[37]

In summary, the balance between state and market in the process of globalisation is itself an expression and reinforcement of political power. It depends on states' decisions to regulate certain aspects of the international economy and not others. Hence, our attention is drawn again to that dimension of inequality which was expressed above as the power to set the rules and to assert rights in the system.[38]

Institutions also play a critical role in the processes by which 'global' liberal values are transmitted and diffused across the system. Indeed, an important feature of the post-Cold War period has been a revival of the question of stronger enforcement: how to give more effective 'teeth' to the norms of international society.[39] Thus, instead of progressive enmeshment and learning, we need also to recognise the role of conditionality and coercion. The spread of conditionality has become a central element of the globalisation of liberalism.

Although defining conditionality is complicated, the core idea is clear enough: both individual states and multilateral institutions attach formal, specific, and institutionalised sets of conditions to the distribution of economic benefits in order to press (mostly) developing countries to adopt particular kinds of domestic policy. The claim to superior knowledge of how developing countries should manage their affairs, and the implicit use of coercion to try to ensure that that

---

36. Stephen D. Krasner, *Structural Conflict: The Third World Against Global Liberalism* (Berkeley, CA: University of California Press, 1985).

37. I.M. Destler, *American Trade Politics*, Second Edition (Washington, DC: Institute for International Economics, 1992), Chapter 3.

38. See Stephen D. Krasner, 'Global Communications and National Power: Life on the Pareto Frontier', *World Politics* (Vol. 43, No. 3, 1991), pp. 336-66.

39. See, for example, Lori Fisler Damrosch (ed.), *Enforcing Restraint: Collective Intervention in Internal Conflicts* (New York, NY: Council on Foreign Relations Press, 1993); Tom Farer (ed.), *Beyond Sovereignty: Collectively Defending Democracy in the Americas* (Baltimore, MD: Johns Hopkins University Press, 1995); and Philippe Schmitter, 'The Influence of the International Context upon the Choice of National Institutions and Policies in Neo-democracies', in Laurence Whitehead (ed.), *The International Dimensions of Democratization: Europe and the Americas* (Oxford: Oxford University Press, forthcoming).

knowledge is acted upon, are, therefore, central to the use of conditionality. Up to the mid-1980s, formal conditionality was mostly limited to IMF-style macro-economic policy conditions.[40] Since then, there has been a very significant expansion within the economic field towards detailed micro-economic reform conditions. There has also been an extension beyond the economic field to include conditions designed to promote good governance, human rights, and democracy; sustainable development; limitations on arms spending; and non-proliferation policies. Here it is important to note, first, the critical move away from conditionality as forming part of a specific economic bargain or contract (as was at least arguably the case with IMF economic conditionality) and towards using conditionality to promote objectives that are wholly unrelated to a specific flow of resources; and second, the entrenchment of political conditionality in the policies of the international financial institutions, and of the OECD development committee.

The trend towards broader and deeper conditionality is not only evident in international institutions. In some ways, conditionality is becoming even more visible at regional levels. It is becoming commonplace for regional groupings to set down formal criteria for admission so that membership of an alliance, economic bloc, or international institution depends on certain kinds of domestic policy. Within regions, the potential levels of coercion rise as the perceived advantages of membership increase. In this respect, the very uneven nature of globalisation is particularly obvious. In both Europe and the Americas, would-be members of existing arrangements (the EU or NAFTA) take their place in a queue. In order to try to move up that queue, aspiring governments attempt to adapt their policies and converge with the required standards. In doing so, however, these future members are taking part in a process which reinforces and perpetuates the power of those who control the conditions and timing of admission. In regions such as the Western Hemisphere, where the distribution of power is already very skewed, this process can easily work to entrench regional hegemony.[41]

Yet, whilst coercion and conditionality are indeed critical features of the ways in which globalisation and liberalism intersect, it is important not to assume that we are dealing simply with external imposition. We need to look very closely at the domestic political processes by which those groups espousing liberal values

40. On economic conditionality, see Tony Killick, *The IMF and Stabilization* (London: St Martin's Press, 1984), and Paul Mosley, Jane Harrigan, and John Toye, *Aid and World Power: The World Bank and Policy-based Lending* (London: Routledge, 1990). The academic literature on non-traditional conditionalities remains thin, but see Nelson and Eglinton, *op. cit.*, in note 20.
41. Andrew Hurrell, 'Regionalism in the Americas', in Hurrell and Louise Fawcett (eds.), *Regionalism in World Politics* (Oxford: Oxford University Press, 1995), pp. 250-82, and Victor Bulmer-Thomas, Nikki Craske, and Mónica Serrano (eds.), *Mexico and the North American Free Trade Agreement: Who Will Benefit?* (London: Macmillan, 1994).

are either able to achieve predominance or else fail to do so.[42] External pressures and inducements are, of course, likely to be important, but so too are the ways in which these external 'signals' are received and interpreted within the subordinate state. Powerful pressures towards liberalisation come up against equally powerful inherited structures and, in the complex process of break-down and adaptation, the result is highly unlikely to conform to a neat 'liberal' model: a liberalising Brazil is very different from a liberalising India, Mexico, or Poland. Indeed, the successful take-up of, say, market-liberal economic policies, may reinforce illiberal patterns of domestic politics or fuel revisionist and assertive foreign policies. Western institutions have seen this effect most clearly in countries such as Algeria, Tunisia, and Turkey, where stringent programmes of economic liberalisation have inadvertently fuelled rejectionist islamic movements.[43] The overall lesson is that powerful homogenising pressures may not, in fact, produce homogeneity: once again, we see that the processes of globalisation are complex and contested.

Conditionality provides a good illustration of the difficulties of reconciling the promotion of economic and political liberalisation within states with the maintenance of a manifestly unequal and illiberal inter-state order and global economic system. On the one hand, the growth of conditionality threatens to lead to ever greater involvement by the industrialised countries and their agencies in the political, social, and economic life of the developing world. This means that an ever greater range of development priorities are determined not by the governments of developing countries, but by external actors. On the other hand, liberal notions of democratic governance are very centrally about making governments more accountable for their policies and representative of their people. Here lies a real contradiction: governments are to be made increasingly accountable for policies and priorities, and yet they have decreasing control or authority over these policies.

Globalisation supposedly facilitates the transmission of liberal values and policies across the world. Yet, because states are politically and economically unequal, whilst some values are 'transmitted', many others are imposed or coerced. The result is sometimes unintended and often contradictory. Economic liberalisation does not always reinforce democracy. Indeed, many argue that 'insulation' from 'populist' pressures is central to the success of economic reform;[44] or that liberalisation skews political power in favour of a small, enriched group. Similarly, in several cases where international institutions

---

42. A case-study detailing the ways in which the domestic processes and international institutions interact is given in Ngaire Woods, 'The Third Arena: The International Financial Institutions and the Politics of Economic Policy-Making in Mexico 1982-1992', paper presented at the *CIDE*, Mexico City, April 1994, and Oxford Social Studies Faculty Senior Seminar, May 1995.

43. See John Darnton, 'Islamic Fundamentalism is on the Rise in Turkey', *International Herald Tribune* (3 March 1995), p. 2, and David Hirst, 'Egypt: Poised between Control and Chaos', *The Guardian* (11 February 1995), p. 15.

44. Stephan Haggard and Robert Kaufman (eds.), *The Politics of Economic Adjustment* (Princeton, NJ: Princeton University Press, 1992).

Millennium

commit themselves to supporting governments which undertake economic liberalisation, they have found themselves supporting governments which, at the same time, show little regard for human or group rights.

Ultimately, although liberals might be expected to be committed to the 'democratisation' of the international system and its institutions (and some are, such as the Commission on Global Governance), in most cases, the dominant liberal discourse in fact assumes high degrees of global management and enforcement.[45] Global management and institutions of enforcement rely upon inequality among states and reproduce and reinforce existing inequalities. Hence, liberals must ultimately choose between effective management of globalisation on the one hand, and values such as participation, representation, and legitimacy on the other. Those who favour 'effectiveness'—and here the economic liberalisers predominate—will very often end up siding with the realists in seeing the positive virtues of inequality and hierarchy.[46] Globalisation, and its management by institutions, is heavily conditioned by inequality among states, as was also shown by our argument about state strength.

Values, Norms, and International Society

One way in which we might explore and elucidate the contradictions mentioned above is by broadening our conception of international society, so as to analyse the impact of globalisation on conventional thinking about international social norms. We have seen that, for some, globalisation involves promoting a *universal* set of values. Stepping back and surveying the impact on international society, one can readily see that the promotion of a particular set of values will in fact reinforce divisions within international society and create different categories of states: those who do share the values and those who do not. This problem opens up an uncomfortable divide for liberals: on one side there is a long Western tradition of doctrines and ideas that rest on principles of exclusiveness, based on being Christian, European, or 'civilised';[47] on the other hand, there is the powerful counter-current in Western thought that has maintained the existence of a universal community of mankind and that has drawn its primary inspiration from the long tradition of natural law.[48]

---

45. Dharam Ghai, 'Social Policy in a Global Context', paper presented at Queen Elizabeth House, 40th Anniversary Conference, 'The Third World after the Cold War'. See also Richard Falk's review article in this issue on *Our Global Neighbourhood: The Report of the Commission on Global Governance* (Oxford: Oxford University Press, 1995).
46. For an important exception, see Daniele Archibugi and David Held (eds.), *Cosmopolitan Democracy* (Cambridge: Polity Press, 1995).
47. This issue was central to the work of Martin Wight and Hedley Bull. For an overview, see Bull, 'The Emergence of a Universal International Society', in Bull and Adam Watson (eds.), *The Expansion of International Society* (Oxford: Oxford University Press, 1984), pp. 117-26.
48. See Joseph Boyle, 'Natural Law and International Ethics', in Terry Nardin and David Mapel (eds.), *Traditions of International Ethics* (Cambridge: Cambridge University Press, 1992), pp. 112-35.

Globalisation and Inequality

Given this division, the pattern of interaction 'across the divide' becomes critical. At one extreme, realist doctrines have often denied all legal and moral rights to those without the power to force respect for their independence.[49] At the other extreme, revolutionist doctrines have insisted on an absolute equality of rights, both as individuals and as communities, and on a duty to assist their liberation, with versions of these ideas developed in both the French and Russian revolutions.[50] In between, liberals have been deeply divided. One strand has argued for a strong (if never quite absolute) respect for pluralism and equality between communities and cultures, and has laid great emphasis on the norms of sovereignty and non-intervention.[51] The other (far more powerful) strand has accorded only conditional or secondary rights to those outside the inner core, and has argued for intervention (or imperialism) to promote the intrinsically superior values of the inner core.[52]

The dominant trend for most of the twentieth century was to move against this exclusivism and exclusion in the name of greater equality. This was exemplified in the struggle for equal sovereignty, for decolonisation, for racial equality, and for economic justice.[53] Moreover, the dominant norms of international society served to provide a degree of protection, for good and ill, to many extremely fragile political entities ('quasi-states' to use Robert Jackson's phrase[54]). The globalisation of liberalism, however, has begun to pull in the opposite direction, and the resulting process of segmentation may well be working towards greater inequality.

In characterising the increasing inequalities in international society, three questions are of the essence: whose rules govern the society, what is the scope of the rules, and how are the rules enforced? The first question—whose rules—requires us to examine the existing structure of power among states. We are thereby returned to the paradox of universalism already alluded to: the successful promotion of 'universal' or 'global' values, even if they are to some degree genuinely shared, will often depend on the willingness of particularly powerful states to promote them. Furthermore, their successful promotion can all too easily work to reinforce the already marked inequality of power and status.

The second question—what is the scope of the rules—points to an area in which international society is undergoing dramatic change. The range of

49. Robert Tucker, *The Inequality of Nations* (New York, NY: Basic Books, 1977).
50. Martin Wight, *International Theory: The Three Traditions* (Leicester: Leicester University Press, 1991).
51. See Andrew Hurrell, 'Vattel: Pluralism and Its Limits', in Ian Clark and Iver Neumann (eds.), *Classical Theories in International Relations* (London: Macmillan, forthcoming). For a powerful contemporary restatement of the pluralist case, see John Rawls, 'The Law of Peoples', in Stephen Shute and Susan Hurley (eds.), *On Human Rights* (New York, NY: Basic Books, 1993), pp. 41-82.
52. On the theoretical underpinning of this view, see Anthony Ellis, 'Utilitarianism and International Ethics', in Nardin and Mapel (eds.), *op. cit.*, in note 48, pp. 158-79.
53. Hedley Bull, *Justice in International Relations, 1983 Hagey Lectures* (Waterloo, ON: University Publications Distribution Service, University of Waterloo, 1984).
54. Robert H. Jackson, *Quasi-States: Sovereignty, International Relations and the Third World* (Cambridge: Cambridge University Press, 1990).

Millennium

objectives that international norms and institutions seek to promote has increased tremendously. This has involved rules that affect the domestic structures and organisation of states, that invest individuals and groups within states with rights and duties, and that seek to embody some notion of a common good (human rights, democratisation, the environment, the construction of more elaborate and intrusive inter-state security orders). The impact on weaker and non-Western states is thus potentially very different from the 'globalisation' of traditional international society, in which the primary goal was minimal coexistence.

The third question which assists us in characterising international society is: how are the new, wider-ranging rules to be enforced? At present, enforcement works through international institutions. These institutions tend to be weak, except where they act as facades for powerful states' actions, or where they are dealing with states which rely upon them for financial assistance (*e.g.*, those states using the resources of the international financial institutions). As strict notions of sovereignty and the norm of non-intervention erode, and as formal schemes of conditionality increase, it has become easier to enforce norms against weaker states. The more powerful target states, however, are able to fend off inclusion (as with China) or to impose 'reverse' conditionalities (as with Malaysia *vs.* Australia and Britain). Furthermore, there is a growing reaction to the imposition of norms in both Asia and in the Middle East, as exemplified by recent controversies over human rights, where official Asian resentment is as much about how human rights are to be implemented as it is over the content of the rights in question.[55] Here, weaker states are reasserting the central defense of state sovereignty, attacking the double standards of powerful states and their conditionalities, and calling for greater democratisation in international institutions.

Contemporary trends suggest that international legitimacy and full membership of international society is increasingly being made conditional on the adoption of certain models of domestic political or economic practice. To some extent, these trends revive an old pattern of hierarchy and superiority. The promotion of 'universal' values and moves towards linking domestic and international legitimacy threaten to re-establish the old pattern of differentiation. Indeed, it is not entirely fanciful to see old, nineteenth-century categories reappearing in the emerging late twentieth-century distinctions between a core zone of liberal states, well-ordered non-liberal societies, and states that have either 'failed' or should be classed as pariahs or outlaws.[56] This prognosis highlights the need for analyses of globalisation to take into account the inequalities which underpin the changing international society.

---

55. See, for example, Bilahari Kausikan, 'Asia's Different Standard', *Foreign Policy* (Vol. 92, 1993), pp. 24-41, and Robert Bartley *et al.*, *Democracy and Capitalism: Asian and American Perspectives* (Singapore: Institute of Southeast Asian Studies, 1993).
56. On the nineteenth-century divisions between civilized, barbarous, and savage humanity, see James Lorimer, *Institutes of the Law of Nations, Volumes I and II* (Edinburgh and London: William Blackwood and Sons, 1883), and Gerrit W. Gong, *The Standard of 'Civilization' in International Society* (Oxford: Clarendon Press, 1984).

Globalisation and Inequality

Transnational Civil Society

Up to this point, we have treated international society as a society of states. Yet, for liberals, globalisation extends the possibilities of global community to a transnational civil society beyond states.[57] The prospect of a transnational civil society is attractive to liberals, who conceive it as enabling and empowering independent self-organised groups to participate politically and to counter the abuses of state power.[58] The use of the word 'society' (and still more 'community') carries with it the idea of some integrated framework of norms and values. Equally, the idea of 'civil society' has long been viewed in liberal thought as something defined in contradistinction to the state and as valuable precisely as a means of checking the power of the state. Confirming this view is the evidence of NGOs which have given voice to the weak and vulnerable and to those who are deemed to be non-members of a particular state or political community, or who fall between the cracks of the state system (*e.g.*, refugees, indigenous peoples, or future generations).

Yet, transnational civil society is itself an arena of power. Relations within transnational civil society, which are not necessarily any more equitable than within the states-system, may work to reinforce and open up new inequalities. In the first place, transnational civil society is pluralistic, encompassing a wide range of social movements, formal political associations, and economic forces and interest groups. It is manifestly wrong to believe that the forces within transnational civil society pull only in one direction. Many actions and actors within transnational civil society are profoundly illiberal and destructive, involving, for example, the privatisation of violence, transnational criminal activity, private trade in weapons, and the increasingly thin line between criminal and social violence. There is a tendency amongst critics of globalisation to take a benign view of transnational civil society and to see 'emerging social forces' as the counterweight both to hegemonic liberal capitalism and to inequalities in the states-system.[59] However, such a black and white image is unhelpful. Transnational civil society can aid the flow of anti-liberal ideas as much as the promotion of justice and equality: religious fundamentalism and Rupert Murdoch are, after all, as much a part of transnational civil society as Amnesty or Greenpeace.

Second, many groups within transnational civil society are the product—direct or indirect—of state action, and cannot be understood outside their relationship

---

57. See Lipschutz, *op. cit.*, in note 10, and Wapner, *op. cit.*, in note 10.
58. Such thinking is reflected in the increasing emphasis placed on NGO-channelled aid by international financial institutions and bilateral donors. These ideas are developed in such works as John Clark, *Democratizing Development: The Role of Voluntary Organisations* (London: Earthscan, 1991), and David Kroten, *Getting to the 21st Century: Voluntary Action and the Global Agenda* (Hartford, CT: Kumarian Press, 1990).
59. See, for example, Joseph A. Camillieri and Jim Falk, *The End of Sovereignty? The Politics of a Shrinking and Fragmenting World* (London: Edward Elgar, 1992), especially Chapter 8; Paul Ekins, *A New World Order: Grassroots Movements for Global Change* (London: Routledge, 1992); and Falk, *op. cit.*, in note 10.

Millennium

to states. Thus, the politics of transnational civil society is centrally about the way in which certain groups emerge and are legitimised (by governments, institutions, or other groups). As we have seen already, assumptions about the transmission of knowledge and ideas across boundaries are often viewed as the diffusion of knowledge through 'epistemic communities'. Yet, this neglects the issue of whose 'scientific knowledge' becomes critical, through what channels, and with what relationship to states and state power.[60] All too often, the links that exist between influential epistemic communities and particular institutions and particular groups within society are left unexamined.

Third, transnational civil society needs to be viewed as a fragmented and contested arena. Thus, we cannot ignore the unequal political voice and influence accorded to different NGOs: in the international context we might compare the effectiveness of Northern as opposed to Southern NGOs. Even more so than with domestic interest groups, there is a real issue of accountability here. This is usually ignored with respect to NGOs, which are often not accountable to any broad grouping or political process.[61] As some aid-giving states try to bypass governments and channel assistance through NGOs, these questions become all the more important.

Conclusion

Globalisation is profoundly affected by inequalities among states, regions, and non-state actors. This fact is underplayed in liberal interpretations of globalisation, which offer a fairly optimistic account of globalisation and which skate far too quickly over four significant problems: the capacity of states to bear the costs of adjustment to globalisation, the need for institutional reform to manage globalisation, the values which are to underpin the new global system, and the complexity and ambiguity of the emerging transnational civil society.

This article has analysed these four problems with the liberal globalisation thesis. Varying *state strength*, it was argued, affects states' capacities to adapt to, and benefit from, globalisation. On the face of it, the powerful benefit, and the less powerful lose out. For this reason, globalisation has always been a contested process, as illustrated by developing countries' attempts to use political power to limit the activities of foreign investors. Yet, some countries, such as those of East Asia, have succeeded in controlling the impact of globalisation on them, in spite of their size and lack of power in the international arena. Here, a crucial factor in their success has been the *domestic* strength of governments. With a high degree of domestic control, East Asian governments have been able effectively to control and adapt to integration in the global economy. It is

---

60. For one example of work that takes this sort of enquiry seriously, see Karen Litfin, 'Framing Science: Precautionary Discourse and the Ozone Treaties', *Millennium* (Vol. 24, No. 2, 1995), pp. 251-77.

61. For a similar challenge, see Hedley Bull, *The Anarchical Society: A Study of Order in World Politics* (London: Macmillan, 1977), pp. 85-86.

Globalisation and Inequality

important to note that domestic strength is itself not just a function of domestic circumstance. East Asia also provides an example of how it is that domestic political strength has been forged as a result of strategic insecurity and, of course, geostrategic position. The insight here is that domestic and international factors interplay in determining a state's capacity to control its insertion into global economic and political processes.

International institutions are put forward by liberals as the solution to new problems and issues which arise from globalisation. They are viewed as fairly neutral, problem-solving organisations. However, we have stressed that institutions are also arenas of power and influence, in which it is usually the powerful who make and break the rules. Here, we emphasised that globalisation plays into existing power-political relations in the international system. The standards of economic and political reform which are emerging both at the international and regional levels are overwhelmingly formulated by a small group of powerful states. Less powerful states are expected to accept these standards as conditions for their entry into intergovernmental institutions, and access to economic and political favour.

The analysis of international institutions is developed in the paper into a broader view of what globalisation in an unequal global system means for *international society*. Here we posed three questions: whose rules govern the society, what is the scope of the rules, and how are the rules enforced? The answers to these questions suggest that globalisation will not lead to the progressive global enmeshment heralded by liberal analysts. Existing inequalities make it more likely that globalisation will lead to an increasingly sharp division between 'core' states, who share in the values and benefits of a global world economy and polity, and 'marginalised' states, some of which are already branded 'failed states'.

Finally, globalisation, it is often claimed, is creating a new *'transnational civil society'*. The growth in non-state economic, political, and social linkages among societies leads some liberal analysts enthusiastically to point to the empowerment of NGOs and the like. The thesis is attractive to supporters of Greenpeace and Amnesty International, but it overlooks the fact that the activities of other non-state actors—such as terrorist groups—are also facilitated by globalisation. There are two further problems with empowering non-state actors in an uncritical way. In the first place, these groups are not necessarily representative, nor politically accountable. It is unclear how we should square enthusiasm for the rise of NGOs and non-state actors with a concern for democracy. In the second place, the rise of such groups—for example, islamic fundamentalist groups in the Middle East—can swiftly erode the order and political stability of often fragile and tenuous, but *elected*, governments.

In summary, the loss of autonomy associated with globalisation falls unevenly. Powerful states are better able to insulate themselves, by adapting domestic state structures to new constraints (and opportunities), dominating the regimes by which interdependence is managed, competing more effectively within global markets, or developing strong enough state structures to control interdependence.

Millennium

Those states that are able to resist 'internationalisation' will emerge as far more powerful than those that fail to do so. Thus, globalisation is a process the nature and impact of which are vastly influenced by inequalities among states; it is also a process which has profound consequences for the equality of states in the future.

Andrew Hurrell is University Lecturer in International Relations and a Fellow of Nuffield College, Oxford University, Oxford, OX1 1NF

Ngaire Woods is a Fellow of University College, Oxford University, Oxford, OX1 4BH

[23]

The End of the Old Order ?
Globalization and the Prospects
for World Order

DAVID HELD AND ANTHONY MCGREW

In reflecting upon the prospects for world order, in the concluding chapter of *The Twenty Years Crisis*, E. H. Carr advised that 'few things are permanent in history; and it would be rash to assume that the territorial unit of power is one of them'.[1] Based upon his observation that world order was being reshaped by the contradictory imperatives of progressive economic integration and a 'recrudescence of disintegrating tendencies', Carr concluded with a confident prediction that 'the concept of sovereignty is likely to become in the future even more blurred and indistinct than it is at present'.[2] Yet his devastating critique of inter-war idealism delivers a powerful rebuff to the hubris of those who seek to construct a new world order on the foundations of nineteenth-century liberal thought. Whilst Carr celebrated the importance of normative and utopian thinking in international relations, he grounded this in a sophisticated appreciation of the routines of power politics and the historical possibilities for international political change. Although a convinced sceptic of the Enlightenment vision of a universal human community and the inevitability of a 'harmony of interests', Carr nevertheless believed that 'it is unlikely that the future units of power will take much account of formal sovereignty'.[3] Indeed, he even went so far as to argue that 'any project of international order which takes these formal units [sovereign states] as its basis seems likely to prove unreal'.[4] In surveying the prospects for world order at the end of the twentieth century, such observations appear remarkably prescient, especially in relation to the contemporary debate concerning globalization and the condition of the modern nation-state.

Any assessment of the prospects for world order must begin with some understanding of how the powerful historical forces of integration and disintegration, which Carr identified over sixty years ago, are articulated today and how they shape modern political life. It is in this context that the current discussion of globalization takes on a special importance. For at the core of this is an inquiry into whether globalization is transforming the nature of modern political community and thus reconstituting the foundations—empirical and normative—of world order. World order, in this context, is understood to embrace more than simply the ordering of relations between states and to include, as Bull conceived it, the ordering of relations

---

[1] E. H. Carr, *The Twenty Years' Crisis 1919–1939* (London, 1981), p. 229.
[2] Ibid., p. 230.
[3] Ibid., p. 231.
[4] Ibid.

between the world's peoples.[5] In the sections that follow, this paper will examine critically the globalization thesis, giving particular attention to what it reveals about the changing conditions of political community and the prospects for world order. This involves an examination of the existing organization, and the future possibilities, of political community as the fundamental building block of world order. The inquiry would be pursued within the spirit of Carr's dictum that 'mature thought combines purpose with observation and analysis'.[6]

Contemporary globalization: what's new?

Globalization refers to an historical process which transforms the spatial organization of social relations and transactions, generating transcontinental or interregional networks of interaction and the exercise of power.[7] It is possible to identify for analytical purposes different historical forms of globalization, from the epoch of world discovery in the early modern period to the present era of the neo-liberal global project. These can be characterized by distinctive spatio-temporal and organizational attributes. Thus to talk of globalization is to acknowledge that, over the *longue durée*, there have been distinctive historical forms of globalization which have been associated with quite different kinds of historical world order. Although contemporary globalization shares much in common with past phases it is nevertheless distinguished by unique spatio-temporal and organizational attributes; that is, by distinctive measures of the extensity, intensity, velocity and impact of global flows, alongside distinctive patterns of institutionalization, modes of contestation, stratification and reproduction. Moreover, since contemporary processes of globalization and regionalization articulate overlapping networks and constellations of power which cut across territorial and political boundaries, they present a unique challenge to a world order designed in accordance with the Westphalian principle of sovereign, exclusive rule over a bounded territory.

Of course, the character and significance of this challenge is hotly debated. For some, referred to here as the hyperglobalizers, these developments lead to the demise of sovereign statehood and undermine a world order constructed upon the basis of Westphalian norms.[8] Amongst those of a more sceptical mind, globalization is conceived as the great myth of our times; accordingly, the proposition that it prefigures the emergence of a new, less state-centric world order is dismissed.[9] By comparison, others argue that contemporary globalization is reconstituting or

---

[5] See H. Bull, *The Anarchical Society* (London, 1977), p. 22.

[6] Carr, *The Twenty Years' Crisis 1919–1939*, p. 20.

[7] For a more extended discussion of this definition, see the Introduction in Held and McGrew, *et al.*, *Global Transformations: Politics, Economics and Culture* (Cambridge, 1999).

[8] See, for instance, K. Ohmae, *The End of the Nation State* (New York, 1995); H. V. Perlmutter, 'On the Rocky Road to the First Global Civilzation', *Human Relations*, 44: 1 (1991), pp. 902–6; J. Gray, *False Dawn* (London, 1998).

[9] On the sceptical position see, for instance, C. Brown, 'International Political Theory and the Idea of World Community', in K. Booth and S. Smith (eds.), *International Relations Theory Today* (Cambridge, 1995), pp. 90–109; S. Krasner, 'Compromising Westphalia', *International Security*, 20: 3 (1995), pp. 115–151; P. Hirst and G. Thompson, *Globalization in Question,* (Cambridge, 1996); P. Hirst, 'The Global Economy—Myths and Realities', *International Affairs,* 73 (3 July, 1997), pp. 409–26.

transforming the power, functions and authority of the nation-state.[10] For these transformationalists, globalization is associated with the emergence of a post-Westphalian world order in which the institutions of sovereign statehood and political community are being reformed and reconstituted. In this post-Westphalian order, there is marked shift towards heterarchy—a divided authority system—in which states seek to share the tasks of governance with a complex array of institutions, public and private, local, regional, transnational and global, representing the emergence of 'overlapping communities of fate'.

This in not the place to review the claims, counter-claims and historical evidence relating to these competing accounts; that has been accomplished elsewhere.[11] Rather the central task is to examine the particular pattern of contemporary globalization in what Carr conceived as the key domains of power—the military, economic and the political.[12] This exercise is a prelude to assessing the central normative, institutional, and intellectual challenges which contemporary patterns of globalization present to the organizing principles of existing world order; namely, sovereign statehood and political community.[13] On the basis of such an assessment a taxonomy of the possible future shapes of world order will be developed.

Military globalization

Over the last century globalization in the military domain has been visible in, amongst other things, the geo-political rivalry and imperialism of the great powers (above all, from the scramble for Africa circa 1890s to the Cold War), the evolution of international alliance systems and international security structures (from the Concert of Europe to the North Atlantic Treaty Organization—NATO), the emergence of a world trade in arms together with the worldwide diffusion of military

[10] See, in particular, A. Giddens, *The Consequences of Modernity* (Cambridge, 1990); D. J. Elkins, *Beyond Sovereignty: Territory and Political Economy in the Twenty First Century* (Toronto, 1995); D. Held, *Democracy and Global Order* (Cambridge, 1995); R. O. Keohane and H. V. Milner (eds.), *Internationalization and Domestic Politics* (Cambridge, 1996); D. Goldblatt, D. Held, *et al.*, 'Economic Globalization and the Nation-state: Shifting Balances of Power', *Alternatives*, 22: 3 (1997), pp. 269–85; B. Jessop, 'Capitalism and its Future: Remarks on Regulation, Government and Governance', *Review of International Political Economy*, 4: 3 (1997), pp. 561–82; M. Mann, 'Has Globalization ended the Rise and Rise of the Nation-state?', *Review of International Political Economy*, 4: 3 (1997), pp. 472–96; J. Rosenau, *Along the Domestic–Foreign Frontier* (Cambridge, 1997).

[11] See Held and McGrew, *et al.*, *Global Transformations*.

[12] See Carr, *The Twenty Years' Crisis 1919–1939*, ch. 8.

[13] The concept of sovereignty lodges a distinctive claim to the rightful exercise of political power over a circumscribed realm. It seeks to specify the political authority within a community which has the right to determine the framework of rules, regulations and policies within a given territory and to govern accordingly. However, in thinking about the impact of globalization upon the modern nation-state, one needs to distinguish the claim to sovereignty—the entitlement to rule over a bounded territory—from state autonomy—the actual power the nation-state possesses to articulate and achieve policy goals independently. In effect, state autonomy refers to the capacity of state representatives, managers and agencies to articulate and pursue their policy preferences even though these may on occasion clash with the dictates of domestic and international social forces and conditions. Moreover, to the extent that modern nation-states are democratic, sovereignty and autonomy are assumed to be embedded within, and congruent with, the territorially organized framework of liberal democratic government: 'the rulers'—elected representatives—are accountable to 'the ruled'—the citizenry—within a delimited territory. There is, in effect, a 'national community of fate', whereby membership of the political community is defined in terms of the peoples within the territorial borders of the nation-state. See Held and McGrew, *et al.*, *Global Transformations*, the Introduction, for a fuller analysis of these terms.

technologies, and the institutionalization of global regimes with jurisdiction over military and security affairs, for example, the international nuclear non-proliferation regime. Indeed, it is possible to argue that all states are now enmeshed, albeit to varying degrees, in a world military order. This world military order is highly stratified, highly institutionalized, and shaped by a relatively autonomous arms dynamic. It is stratified in that there is broadly a first tier (with superpower status), second tier (middle-ranking powers) and third tier (developing military powers); and it is institutionalized in that military–diplomatic and multilateral arrangements define regularized patterns of interaction. Military globalization can be conceived initially as a process which embodies the growing extensity and intensity of military relations amongst the political units of the world system. Understood as such, it reflects both the expanding network of worldwide military ties and relations alongside the impact of key military technological innovations (e.g. steamships to reconnaissance satellites) which, over time, have reconstituted the world into an increasingly unified geo-strategic space. Historically, this process of time–space compression has brought centres of military power into closer proximity and potential conflict, as the capability to project enormous destructive power across vast distances has proliferated. Simultaneously, military decision and reaction times have shrunk with the consequence that permanent military machines, along with their permanent preparation for war, have become an integral feature of modern social life.

With the end of the Cold War the pattern of global military and security relations has been further transformed. In some respects, the structure of world military power at the end of the twentieth century reflects a return to a traditional pattern of multipolar power politics, but, in other respects, especially in relation to the sole military superpower status of the US, it is historically unique. As the Cold War has ended and the foreign military presence of the US and Russia has contracted (by quite spectacular proportions) the reassertion of regional and local patterns of inter-state rivalry has been intense. One consequence of this is the visible tendency towards 'the decentralization of the international security system'—the fragment-ation of the world into relatively discrete (but not entirely self-contained) regional security complexes.[14] This is evident, amongst other cases, in the resurgence of nationalist conflicts and tensions in Europe and the Balkans, in the Indo-Pakistan rivalry in South Asia, and in the rivalry over the South China seas in Southeast Asia. As the overlay of Cold War conflict has been removed, a significant external restraint upon regional conflicts (whose origins often predate even the age of the European empire) has disappeared. In some cases, such as South East Asia, the consequences to date have been relatively benign but in many regions rivalries and tensions have escalated. This 'regionalization' of international security represents an important distinguishing feature of the post-Cold War world military and security order.

One interpretation of this altering military landscape is that the global security and military order is undergoing a process of 'structural bifurcation'; that is, fragmentation into two largely separate systems, each with different standards, rules of conduct and inter-state behaviour.[15] The likely implications and costs of (conven-

---

[14] B. Buzan, *People, States and Fear* (Brighton, 1991), p. 208.
[15] J. M. Goldeier and M. McFail, 'A Tale of Two Worlds: Core and Periphery in the Post-Cold War Era', *International Organization*, 46: 2 (1992), pp. 467–91.

tional or nuclear) war among advanced industrial states, argues Mueller among others, are now so overwhelming that major war has become obsolete: it would be counterproductive either as a mechanism for resolving interstate conflict or as a mechanism for transforming the international status quo.[16] In contradistinction to this, states in the periphery (i.e. states in the developing world) operate within a system in which political instability, militarism and state expansion remain endemic, and in which there is no effective deterrent to war as a rational instrument of state policy. Accordingly, patterns of international military and security relations are diverging radically as the post-Cold War world order becomes increasingly bifurcated.

These processes of fragmentation and regionalization, however, can be counterposed to powerful centripetal forces reinforcing the unified character of the world military order. Four factors in particular deserve mention in this respect:

- First, in most global regions there is a gradual shift taking place towards cooperative defence or cooperative security arrangements. The desire to avoid inter-state conflict, the enormous costs, technological requirements and domestic burdens of defence are together contributing to the historic strengthening, rather than weakening, of multilateral and collective defence arrangements as well as international military cooperation and coordination. The end of the Cold War has not witnessed the demise of NATO, as many predicted in 1990, but rather its expanding role and significance. In many of the world's key regions, multilateral frameworks for security and defence cooperation are beginning to emerge alongside existing bilateral arrangements. These, like the ASEAN Regional Forum (ARF) in Asia–Pacific, may be at a very early stage of development and beset by all kinds of rivalries, but historically they represent a significant institutionalization of military and security relations. Moreover, many of these arrangements are becoming less regionally specific as the US has strengthened its global engagements (e.g. NATO and ARF). At the global level too, the peacekeeping activities of the UN and its more general collective security functions have become more visible, although not necessarily more effective. These developments reflect a realization that, with the end of the Cold War, and against the background of recent military technological change, 'the capacity of the state to defend territorial boundaries against armed attack' may have considerably weakened.[17] Certainly, many states now recognize that national security can no longer be achieved simply through unilateral actions alone.

- Second, the rising density of financial, trade and economic connections between states has expanded the potential vulnerability of most states to political or economic instability in distant parts of the globe. Accordingly, many states, not simply the world's major powers, remain acutely sensitive (if not vulnerable) to security and military developments in other regions. Such sensitivities may be highly selective, and certainly not all parts of the globe are perceived as of comparable strategic importance. Nevertheless, as the 1990 Gulf crisis demonstrated, military developments in strategically critical regions continue to be of global significance. Regionalization and globalization of military/security relations are by no means contradictory processes but may be mutually reinforcing.

- Third, threats to national security are becoming both more diffuse and no longer simply military in character.[18] The proliferation of weapons of mass destruction poses a potential threat to all states. But proliferation is in part a product of the diffusion of industrial and

---

[16] J. Mueller, *Retreat from Doomsday: The Obsolescence of Major War* (New York, 1989).
[17] J. A. Camilleri and J. Falk, *The End of Sovereignty: The Politics of a Shrinking and Fragmented World* (Brighton, 1992), p. 152.
[18] See B. Buzan, O. Waever, *et al.*, *Security: A New Framework for Analysis* (Boulder, CO, 1998).

224   David Held and Anthony McGrew

technological knowledge as well as hardware. Preventing proliferation is thus a classic collective action problem in that it demands world wide action. Similarly, environmental, economic, narcotics, terrorist, cultural, criminal and other threats to national security cannot be resolved solely through either military or national means. Accordingly, there is a continuing demand for global mechanisms of co-ordination and co-operation to deal with the expanding penumbra of security threats.

- Fourth, in the global states system the military security of all nations is significantly influenced by systemic factors. Indeed, the structure of power and the actions of the great powers remain dominant influences upon the military postures of each other and of all other states. At one level this is simply because the great powers set the standards, be it in military technology or force levels, against which all other states ultimately calibrate their defence capability. Thus, US defence policy has more wide-ranging global effects than does that of Kiribati. How the great powers act or react affects the security of all the world's regions.

These points suggest that the contemporary geo-political order, far from simply fragmenting, remains beset by problems of global strategic interconnectedness. The lack of any serious global political and military rivalries of the kind represented by the Cold War, or the New Imperialism of the 1890s, should not be read as a process of military deglobalization. Despite the ending of Cold War rivalry there has not been a detectable return to earlier forms of national military autarky; nor has the world broken up into discrete regional security complexes. Globalization and regionalization in the military domain appear to be mutually reinforcing rather than mutually exclusive processes. Moreover, there are growing (financial, technological, industrial and political) pressures on states to engage in multilateral cooperative efforts to achieve the rationalization of their defence industrial base. This is contributing to the (admittedly slow) de-nationalization of defence industries in most advanced states, and to a globalization of defence production.[19]

The transnationalization of the defence industrial base represents a distinctive new stage in the organization of defence production and procurement akin to (but on a very different scale from) the global restructuring of industrial production.[20] It is also reinforced by the fact that many of the most critical defence technologies are produced in those very civil industrial sectors, such as electronics or optics, which have been subject to increasing globalization. These developments have quite profound, although not necessarily completely novel, implications for the orthodox approach to defence–industrial organization, which traditionally has privileged— alongside national strategies of defence and procurement—the national defence industrial base as the necessary underpinning to an 'autonomous' national defence capability. Both the regionalization and the globalization of the defence–industrial sector compromise such autonomy in a fairly direct way since they make the acquisition (and crucially the use) of arms and weapons systems (not to mention defence industrial policy) potentially subject to the decisions and actions of other authorities or corporations beyond the scope of national jurisdiction.

[19] See R. A. Bitzinger, 'The Globalization of the Arms Industry', *International Security*, 19: 2 (1994), pp. 170–98.

[20] See Bitzinger, ibid.; A. Moravcsik, 'The European Armaments Industry at the Crossroads', *Survival*, 33 (1991), pp. 65–85; H. Wulf and E. Skons, 'The Internationalization of the Arms Industry', *American Annals of Political and Social Science*, 535 (Sept., 1994), pp. 43–57.

In some contexts, however, such regionalization and globalization may be exploited to enhance defence industrial and military autonomy. Sweden, for instance, by engaging in collaborative and licensing arrangements with both American and European aerospace defence contractors, has been able to sustain a highly advanced defence industrial capability which it might otherwise have been unable to support. Japan, too, has reduced its military dependence on the US by exploiting an intensely competitive world market in military technology transfer and licensing. In the realm of defence production and procurement, globalization and regionalization by no means automatically prefigure the demise of a national defence industrial base, but they do alter the strategies and policies which governments have to pursue in order to sustain it as well as the patterns of industrial winners and losers. In the case of European states, the consolidation of 'national champions', through government-supported (but not necessarily initiated) mergers and acquisitions, has complemented the emergence of 'European champions' to compete in the global and regional arms market with their American rivals. Autonomy is, thus, sought through a changing mix of internationalization and nationalization. This in itself represents a significant departure from orthodox notions of military autonomy defined and pursued in essentially national terms.

In the contemporary era of declining defence procurement budgets, the internationalization of defence production provides one solution to the maintenance of a 'national' defence industrial capacity. Accordingly, this is not simply a process which is confined to Europe, or the trans-Atlantic region, where it is most evident, but is a part of a secular trend in defence industrial restructuring.[21] This is largely because, for many big defence companies, 'internationalization is one strategy of consolidation for long-term survival in the market'.[22] Restructuring of the national defence industrial base unfolds alongside a global restructuring of defence production. In varying degrees, all countries engaged in defence production are gradually being touched by these twin developments. As a consequence, in parallel to many political phenomena, the distinction between the 'foreign' and 'domestic' is breaking down. Indeed, the enormous complexity of cross-border intercorporate and production networks involves a 'shift away from traditional, single-country patterns of weapons production towards more transnational development and manufacture of arms'.[23] Global sourcing of defence production, as in the commercial sector, is a growing practice as cost containment becomes more critical. For industrializing states with an indigenous defence production capability, global sourcing remains essential to meeting defence interests.[24] But this is also supplemented by other forms of collaboration, sometimes with the governments of other developing countries or advanced states, in the development or production of 'indigenous' military systems. In the post-Cold War era, the global diffusion of military-technology and defence industrial capacity are becoming closely associated with a transnationalization of defence production.

---

[21] Ibid.

[22] E. Skons, 'Western Europe: Internationalization of the Arms Industry', in H. Wulf (ed.), *Arms Industry Limited* (Oxford 1993), p. 160.

[23] R. A. Bitzinger, *The Globalization of Arms Production: Defense Markets in Transition* (Washington DC, Defense Budget Project, 1993), p. 3.

[24] M. Brzoska and T. Ohlson, 'Arms Production in the Third World', in M. Brzoska and T. Ohlson (eds.), *Arms Production in the Third World* (Oxford, 1986), p. 285.

226   David Held and Anthony McGrew

The spread of both defence industrial capability and military technology is facilitated by the increasingly central role acquired by commercial (civil) technologies (and civil technological innovation) in the development and manufacture of advanced weapons systems. The military technological revolution (MTR) of the late twentieth century is a product of the 'information age'. The same technologies which are revolutionizing aspects of everyday life, from the supermarket checkout to personal communications, are transforming the logistics of war and the modern battlefield which, as the 1991 Gulf War demonstrated, is now 'constructed' as 'a blizzard of electronic blips' rather than simply a 'storm of steel'.[25] Strategic technologies are today largely dual-use technologies. Dual-use technologies, by definition, are commercial technologies and the industries that produce them are considerably more globalized than the defence industrial sector. As a result, most dual-use technologies are intensively traded across the globe whilst the capability to produce them is actively dispersed through the operations of transnational corporations. According to Carus, the result is that an 'increasingly large number of countries have access to many of the technologies needed to exploit the military technological revolution'.[26] This in turn is transforming the stratification of military-technological power within the global system.

Military power has been fundamental to the evolution and the institutional form of the modern sovereign, territorial nation-state. The independent capacity to defend national territorial space by military means is at the heart of the modern conception of the institution of sovereign statehood. But, as discussed here, contemporary military globalization poses quite profound questions about the meaning and practice of state sovereignty and autonomy. For in the contemporary age, the traditionally presumed correspondence between the spatial organization of military power and the territorial nation-state appears to be changing.

The doctrine of national security remains one of the essential defining principles of modern statehood. The autonomous capacity of the modern state to defend the nation against external threats is a crucial (and to some the essential) ingredient of traditional conceptions of sovereignty. For if a state does not have the capacity to secure its territory and protect its people then its very *raison d'être* can be called into question. National security has, therefore, been understood traditionally in primarily military terms as the acquisition, deployment and use of military force to achieve national goals. Without such a capacity the very essence of the institution of modern statehood would be decidedly altered.

Of course, the ideology of modern statehood has not always been replicated in the political practices of states. But in the military domain, above all others, modern states have always sought to maintain their independence. However, in the contemporary era, military globalization and patterns of national enmeshment in the world military order have prompted a serious rethinking about the idea and the practice of national security. Although the discourse of national security dominates political and popular debate about military matters, it acts more as a simplified representation or legitimating device than a reflection of the actual behaviour of states. For many states the strategy for achieving 'national security' has become almost indistinguishable from an international security strategy. This is evident

[25] M. van Creveld, *Technology and War: From 2000 BC to the* Present (New York, 1989), p. 282.
[26] W. S. Carus, 'Military Technology and the Arms Trade', *AAPSS* 535 (Sept. 1994), pp. 163–74.

amongst Western states which collectively constitute a 'security community' within which military force plays no active role in the relations between member states.[27]

Within this 'security community' national defence and the exercise of military force are decided within an institutionalized alliance system (NATO) in which collective discussion and multilateral diplomacy complement existing national mechanisms of security policy. The development and pursuit of national security goals are, therefore, inseparable, in most key respects, from the development and pursuit of alliance security. National security and alliance security can be conceived as mutually constituted.[28] Even for states such as France, which has historically sought to pursue a highly autonomous defence posture, or Sweden, which retains a declared policy of neutrality, post-war national security policy effectively has always been shaped (and in the post-Cold War context increasingly so) by the functioning of this broader 'security community'.[29] Moreover, for the United States, membership of NATO represents an historic shift in national security posture away from autarky, isolationism, and the avoidance of external military commitments.[30] For the US, along with other members of the Western 'security community', the practice of cooperative security is redefining the traditional agenda of national security.

The widening agenda of security, combined with the institutionalization of cooperative defence (and security) and the global regulation of military power, through arms control and other regimes, has contributed to a broadening of defence and security politics. The notion that the politics of defence and security issues are coterminous with national political space is belied by such diverse phenomena as the existence of global campaigns to ban landmines or to establish an International Criminal Court for crimes against humanity, and defence contractors within NATO and Europe lobbying for changes in defence industrial policy or government regulations on both sides of the Atlantic or in the East. Political activity focused on 'national security' matters is no longer simply a domestic affair. Accordingly, there can be little doubt that contemporary military globalization has significant implications for the sovereignty, autonomy and politics of modern states. Although states are differentially enmeshed in the world military order and retain differential capacities to mediate military globalization, the institution of modern sovereign statehood is subject to powerful transformative forces. This thesis is also supported by a consideration of global economic processes.

Economic globalization

Today all countries are engaged in international trade and nearly all trade significant proportions of their national income. Around twenty per cent of world output is traded and a much larger proportion is potentially subject to international com-

[27] K. Deutsch and S. A. Burrell, *Political Community and the North Atlantic Area* (Princeton, 1957).
[28] See S. Weber, 'Shaping the Postwar Balance of Power: Multilateralism in NATO', in J. G. Ruggie (ed.), *Multilateralism Matters* (New York, 1993), pp. 233–92.
[29] See, in particular, R. H. Ullman, 'The Covert French Connection', *Foreign Policy* 75: 3 (1989), pp. 3–33; Commission on Neutrality Policy, *Had There Been a War—Preparations for the Reception of Military Assistance 1949–69* (Stockholm, Statens offenliga utredningar, 1994).
[30] This point is emphasized by Ruggie; see J. G. Ruggie, *Winning the Peace: America and World Order in the New Era* (New York, 1996), p. 43.

petition: trade has now reached unprecedented levels, both absolutely and in proportion to world output. If, in the past, trade sometimes formed an enclave largely isolated from the rest of the national economy, it is now an integral part of the structure of national production in all modern states.[31]

The historical evidence, at both the world and country levels, shows higher levels of trade today than ever before, including during the classical Gold Standard period. The post-war growth of trade, at rates above those previously recorded, has been related to a liberalization of international trade relations that is unprecedented in the modern epoch. The contemporary world trading system is defined by both an intensive network of trading relations embracing virtually all economies and evolving global markets for many goods and some services. This shift towards global markets has been facilitated by the existence of worldwide transport and communications infrastructures, the promotion of global trade liberalization through the institutionalization of a world trade system, and the internationalization of production. National markets are increasingly enmeshed with one another as intra-industry trade has expanded and global competition transcends national borders, impacting directly on local economies. In these respects individual firms are confronted by a potential global marketplace whilst they simultaneously face direct competition from foreign firms in their own domestic markets. The stratification of the global trading system also reflects these developments as a new international division of labour emerges associated with the evolution of global markets. To talk of North and South is to misrepresent contemporary patterns of stratification in respect of trade. For whilst a hierarchy of trading power remains, the North–South geographical divide has given way to a more complex structure of trade relations. Despite the historical concentration of trade amongst OECD states, global trade patterns have shifted during the contemporary era such that North and South, in this context, are becoming increasingly empty categories.[32] The composition of global trade is shifting too as trade in services becomes more intense. In all these respects, the world trading system is undergoing a profound transformation. An extensive and intensive network of trading relations operates, creating the conditions for functioning global markets, the domestic impacts of which extend well beyond the traded sector into the economy as a whole. While institutionalized trading arrangements have evolved, they have tended to reinforce the trend towards freer trade—as the evolution of the World Trade Organization (WTO) indicates.

From its inception the nation-state has used protection to raise revenues, manage balance of payments difficulties and promote domestic industry. By the late twentieth century institutional constraints, as well as economic costs, have severely limited the scope for national protectionism. Today, not only tariffs and quota restrictions, but also policies supporting domestic industry and even domestic laws with respect to business competition and safety standards, are subject to growing international scrutiny and regulation. In addition, the historical experience of achieving economic development through protection, though mixed, is now a much-diminished policy option, as the East Asian crisis of 1997–8 demonstrated.

---

[31] For more detailed statistical evidence on all aspects of economic globalization discussed here, see Held and McGrew, et al, Global Transformations, chs. 3–5. We would like to acknowledge our debt to our co-author, Jonathan Perraton, for helping clarify many of the points made in the section below.

[32] See A. Hoogvelt, Globalisation and the Postcolonial World: The New Political Economy of Development (London, 1997).

Autarchy, or 'delinking', too is off the political agenda. Recent enthusiasm for human capital policies—education and training—reflects not only academic and political interest in the potential of these measures for ameliorating some of the adverse consequences of global free trade, but also concerted pressures to foreclose other policy options. In these respects, the contemporary globalization of trade has transformed state autonomy and induced shifts in state policy. Furthermore, the global regulation of trade, by bodies such as the WTO, implies a significant renegotiation of the Westphalian notion of state sovereignty.

The explosive growth of global financial activity since the 1980s and the complexity of global financial markets has also transformed the management of national economies. Whilst global financial markets play a key role in the world-wide allocation of capital, they do so in a manner which has significant implications for national autonomy. Contemporary global finance is marked by both high intensity and relatively high volatility in exchange rates, interest rates and other financial asset prices. As a result, national macroeconomic policy is vulnerable to changes in global financial conditions. Speculative flows can have immediate and dramatic domestic economic consequences, as evident in the aftermath of the East Asian currency turmoil of 1997. Contemporary financial globalization has altered the costs and benefits associated with different national macroeconomic policy options, and has made some options—for example, pursuing expansionary demand management without due regard to exchange rate consequences—prohibitively expensive. These shifting costs and benefits, moreover, vary between countries and over time in a manner that is not entirely predictable. Besides these policy impacts, contemporary patterns of financial globalization also have significant institutional, distributional and structural consequences for nation-states.

Cross-border financial flows transform systemic risk in-so-far as financial difficulties faced by a single or several institutions in one country can have a major knock-on effect on the rest of the global financial sector. This was evident in the East Asian financial crisis of 1997 as the collapse of the Thai currency rippled through foreign exchange markets leading to precipitate falls in currency values across the region and affecting currency values in other emerging markets. Stock markets too were affected by the rush of short-term capital flows out of these economies. In a 'wired world' high levels of enmeshment between national markets mean that disturbances in one very rapidly spill over into others.

The existence of systemic risks produces contradictory imperatives. On the one hand, the desire on behalf of financial institutions, both public and private, to avoid a major international financial crisis produces a demand for more extensive and more intensive international regulation of world finance. Thus, in the wake of the 1997 East Asian financial crisis, the annual IMF/World Bank summit meeting in 1998 agreed to more effective international surveillance mechanisms and greater transparency in the release of financial information in an attempt to prevent such a crisis in the future. On the other hand, it is not in the interests of any state or financial institution to abide by more stringent regulatory standards than its potential competitors. The consequence is that regulatory instruments to manage systemic risks often fall far short of those necessary to deal with them effectively. The absence of any substantive attempts, following the East Asian crisis, to regulate short-term capital flows at an international level is indicative of this problem. Given the volatile nature of global financial markets, and the instantaneous diffusion of financial information between the world's major financial centres, systemic risks continue to pose a permanent threat to the functioning of the entire global financial system which no government by itself can either resolve or insulate its economy from.

The increased salience of systemic risk is, in addition, strongly associated with a structural shift in the balance of power between governments (and international agencies) and markets—more accurately, between public and private authority in the global financial system.[33] Although there is a tendency to exaggerate the power of global financial markets, ignoring the centrality of state power in sustaining their effective operation (especially in times of crisis), there is much compelling evidence to suggest that contemporary financial globalization is a market, rather than a state, driven phenomenon. Reinforced by financial liberalization, the shift towards markets and private financial institutions as the 'authoritative actors' in the global financial system poses serious questions about the nature of state power and economic sovereignty. As Germain observes, 'states have allowed private monetary agents, organized through markets, to dominate the decisions of who is granted access to credit (finance) and on what terms. The international organization of credit has been transformed . . . from a quasi-public to a nearly fully private one'.[34] In this new context the autonomy and even sovereignty of states become, in certain respects, problematic.

Compared with the era of the classical Gold Standard, or that of Bretton Woods, contemporary financial globalization has many distinctive attributes. Chief amongst these is the sheer magnitude, complexity and speed of financial transactions and flows. More currencies, more diverse and complex financial assets are traded more frequently, at greater speed, and in substantially greater volumes than in any previous historical epoch. The sheer magnitude of capital movements, relative to either global or national output and trade, is unique. All this relies upon a highly institutionalized infrastructure such that 24 hour real-time cross-border financial trading constitutes an evolving global financial market which generates significant systemic risks. Contemporary financial globalization represents a distinctive new stage in the organization and management of credit and money in the world economy; it is transforming the conditions under which the immediate and long-term prosperity of states and peoples across the globe is determined.

Aside from global finance, perhaps the commonest image of economic globalization is that of the multinational corporation (MNC): huge corporate empires which straddle the globe with annual turnovers matching the entire GNP of many nations. In 1996 there were 44,000 MNCs worldwide with 280,000 foreign subsidiaries and global sales of almost $7trillion.[35] Today, transnational production 'outweighs exports as the dominant mode of servicing foreign markets'.[36] A small number of MNCs dominate world markets for oil, minerals, foods and other agricultural products, whilst a hundred or so play a leading role in the globalization of manufacturing production and services. Together, the 100 largest MNCs control about 20

[33] See, for instance, A. Walters, *World Power and World Money* (Brighton, 1993); R. Germain, *The International Organization of Credit* (Cambridge, 1997); L. W. Pauly, *Who Elected the Bankers?* (New York, 1997).
[34] Germain, ibid., p. 163.
[35] UNCTAD, *1997 World Investment Report* (Geneva, 1997), p. 1.
[36] Ibid.

per cent of global foreign assets, employ 6 million workers worldwide, and account for almost 30 per cent of total world sales of all MNCs.[37] But the growth of MNCs does not tell the whole story about the globalization of production. Advances in communications technology and the infrastructural conditions which have facilitated the evolution of global financial markets and global trade have also contributed to an internationalization of production amongst small- and medium-sized enterprises (SMEs), at least within the most advanced economies in the world. SMEs are being integrated into production and distribution networks in which the manufacturing or distribution of goods and services is globalized.

By comparison with earlier epochs of business globalization, the contemporary phase is both more extensive and intensive as measured in terms of FDI, numbers and size of MNCs, subsidiaries, etc. Production capacity is now dispersed among an unprecedented number of countries across the globe. Whilst there has been a significant expansion of international production in the last three decades it has also become more institutionalized, as strategic alliances, sub-contracting, joint ventures and other forms of contractual arrangements regularize inter-firm networks and arrangements. Such arrangements have been facilitated by the liberalization of controls on FDI, capital movements and other restrictive measures on financial flows. In some respects, this is a return to the more 'open' investment climate of the turn of the century, although freed from the constraints of imperial priorities and policies. This freedom from imperial constraint is reflected in changing patterns of stratification as more FDI flows to NIEs and developing countries, in the organization of global production which is encouraging a new global division of labour, and in the internationalization of business within developing countries which is becoming a more visible feature of the global political economy.

MNCs are the linchpins of the contemporary world economy. Around 44,000 MNCs account for 25–33 per cent of world output and 70 per cent of world trade.[38] Despite regional concentrations of production, transnational business networks span the three core regions of the world economy, linking the fortunes of disparate communities and nations in complex webs of interconnectedness. MNCs are not simply 'national firms with international operations', nor are they 'footloose corporations', which wander the globe in search of maximum profits. Rather, MNCs play a much more central role in the operation of the world economy than in the past and they figure prominently in organizing extensive and intensive transnational networks of coordinated production and distribution that are historically unique. MNCs and global production networks are critical to the organization, location and distribution of productive power in the contemporary world economy.

Despite some obvious continuities with the past, such as the lasting traces of imperial ties on European FDI and MNCs, the contemporary globalization of business and production has transformed 'what goods and services are produced, how, where and by whom'.[39] Of course, multinational production still only accounts for a minority of total world production. Nevertheless, its growing significance has profound implications for the economic autonomy and sovereignty of nation-states,

---

[37] Ibid., p. 8.
[38] See S. Strange, *The Retreat of the State* (Cambridge, 1996); J. Perraton, *et al.*, 'The Globalization of Economic Activity', *New Political Economy*, 2: 2 (1997), pp. 257–77 and UNCTAD, ibid.
[39] Strange, ibid., p. 44.

although this is mediated by national patterns of enmeshment in global production networks.

Political globalization

Economic globalization has not occurred in a political vacuum, although it is too often interpreted as if it has. Alongside processes of global economic transformation there have been parallel but distinct political changes, referred to here as 'political globalization', by which we understand the shifting reach of political power, authority and forms of rule. The distinctive historical form of this in the contemporary period is captured by the notion of 'global politics'—the increasingly extensive or 'stretched' form of political relations and political activity. Political decisions and actions in one part of the world can rapidly acquire world-wide ramifications. Sites of political action and/or decision-making can become linked through rapid communications into complex networks of decision-making and political interaction. Associated with this 'stretching' is a frequent 'deepening' impact of global political processes such that, unlike in ancient or modern empires, 'action at a distance' permeates with greater intensity the social conditions and cognitive worlds of specific places or policy communities. As a consequence, developments at the global level—whether economic, social or environmental—can frequently acquire almost instantaneous local consequences and vice versa.

The idea of 'global politics' challenges the traditional distinctions between the domestic/international, inside/outside, territorial/non-territorial politics, as embedded in conventional conceptions of 'the political'.[40] It also highlights the richness and complexity of the interconnections which transcend states and societies in the global order. Although governments and states remain, of course, powerful actors, they now share the global arena with an array of other agencies and organizations.[41] The state is confronted by an enormous number of intergovernmental organizations (IGOs), international agencies and regimes which operate across different spatial reaches, and by quasi-supranational institutions, like the European Union. Non-state actors or transnational bodies, such as multinational corporations, transnational pressure groups, transnational professional associations, social movements and so on, also participate intensively in global politics. So too do many subnational actors and national pressure groups, whose activities often spill over into the international arena. Global politics today, moreover, is anchored not just in traditional geopolitical concerns, but also in a large diversity of economic, social and ecological questions. Pollution, drugs, human rights and terrorism are amongst an increasing number of transnational policy issues which cut across territorial jurisdictions and existing political alignments, and which require international co-operation for their effective resolution. Defence and security issues no longer dominate the global agenda or even the political agendas of many national govern-

---

[40] See R. B. J. Walker, *Inside/Outside* (Cambridge, 1994).
[41] For a detailed explication of this point, with supporting documentary evidence, see Held and McGrew, *et al.*, *Global Transformations*, chs. 1, 2, and 8.

ments. These developments, accordingly, challenge the conventional Westphalian (and realist) principles of world political order.

Nations, peoples and organizations are linked by many new forms of communication and media which range in and across borders. The revolution in microelectronics, in information technology and in computers has established virtually instantaneous world-wide links which, when combined with the technologies of the telephone, television, cable, satellite and jet transportation, have dramatically altered the nature of political communication. These new forms of communication enable individuals and groups to 'overcome' geographical boundaries which once might have prevented contact; and they create access to a range of social and political experiences with which the individual or group may never have had an opportunity to engage directly.[42] The intimate connection between 'physical setting', 'social situation' and politics which has distinguished most political associations from premodern to modern times has been ruptured; the new communication systems create new experiences, new modes of understanding and new frames of political reference independently of direct contact with particular peoples or issues. At the same time, unequal access to these new modes of communication has created novel patterns of political inclusion and exclusion in global politics.

The development of new communication systems generates a world in which the particularities of place and individuality are constantly represented and reinterpreted by regional and global communication networks. But the relevance of these systems goes far beyond this, for they are fundamental to the possibility of organizing political action and exercising political power across vast distances.[43] For example, the expansion of international and transnational organizations, the extension of international rules and legal mechanisms—their construction and monitoring—have all received an impetus from the new communication systems and all depend on them as a means to further their aims. The present era of global politics marks a shift towards a system of multilayered global and regional governance. Although it by no means replaces the sedimentation of political rule into state structures, this system is marked by the internationalization and transnationalization of politics, the development of regional and global organizations and institutions, and the emergence of regional and global law.

States are increasingly enmeshed in novel forms of international legal and juridical regimes. As Crawford and Marks remark, 'international law, with its enlarging normative scope, extending writ and growing institutionalization, exemplifies the phenomenon of globalization'.[44] Increasingly aspects of international law are acquiring a cosmopolitan form. By cosmopolitan law, or global law, or global humanitarian law, is meant here a domain of law different in kind from the law of states and the law made between one state and another for the mutual enhancement of their geopolitical interests. Cosmopolitan law refers to those elements of law—albeit created by states—which create powers and constraints, and rights and duties, which transcend the claims of nation-states and which have farreaching national consequences. Elements of such laws define and seek to protect

---

[42] See A. Giddens, *Modernity and Self-Identity* (Cambridge, 1991), pp. 84–5.
[43] See R. Deibert, *Parchment, Printing and Hypermedia* (New York, 1997).
[44] See J. Crawford and S. Marks, 'The Global Democracy Deficit. An Essay in International Law and its Limits', in D. Archibugi, D. Held and M. Köhler (eds.), *Re-imagining Political Community* (Cambridge, 1998), p. 82.

basic humanitarian values which can come into conflict, and sometimes contradiction, with national laws. These values set down basic standards or boundaries which no political agent, whether a representative of a government or state, should, in principle, be able to cross.[45]

Human rights regimes and human rights law, for example, sit uneasily with the idea of accepting state sovereignty alone as the sole principle for the organization of relations within and between political communities. They can be thought of as an element of an emerging cosmopolitan legal framework, along with the law of war, the law governing war crimes and environmental law (for example, the Convention on the Law of the Sea and elements of the Rio Declaration on Environment and Development). Together, these domains of law constitute a developing set of standards and constraints which bear upon and qualify the notion of an untrammelled principle of state sovereignty. While commitment to these standards often remains weak, they signal a change affecting the concept of legitimate state power. For the rules of war, laws governing crimes against humanity, the innovations in legal thinking concerning the use of resources and human rights regimes all mark out a shift in the direction of the subject and scope of international law. Opinion has shifted against the doctrine that international law must be a law 'between states only and exclusively'. At issue is the emergence of a vast body of rules, quasi-rules and legal changes which are beginning to alter the basis of coexistence and cooperation in the global order. The legal innovations referred to challenge the idea that the supreme normative principle of the political organization of humankind can and should remain simply that of sovereign statehood. Most recently, proposals put forward for the establishment of an International Criminal Court add further testimony to the gradual shift toward a 'universal constitutional order'.[46] The new legal frameworks aim to curtail and to delimit state sovereignty, and set basic standards and values for the treatment of all, during war and peace. Of course, this body of law is by no means subscribed to systematically; but it points to the development of a post-Westphalian order—setting down a new regulatory framework for the conduct of relations among political communities.

At the end of the second millennium, political communities and civilizations can no longer be characterized simply as 'discrete worlds'; they are enmeshed and entrenched in complex structures of overlapping forces, relations and movements. Clearly, these are often structured by inequality and hierarchy. But even the most powerful among them—including, the most powerful nation-states—do not remain unaffected by the changing conditions and processes of regional and global entrenchment. A few points can be emphasized to clarify further the changing relations between political globalization and modern nation-states. All indicate an increase in the extensiveness, intensity, velocity and impact of political globalization, and all suggest important questions about the evolving character of the democratic political community in particular.

---

[45] See Held, *Democracy and Global Order*, chs. 5–6.
[46] See J. Crawford, 'Prospects for an International Criminal Court', in M. D. A. Freeman and R. Halson (eds.), *Current Legal Problems 1995*, 48, pt. 2, collected papers (Oxford, 1995); J. Dugard, 'Obstacles in the way of an International Criminal Court', *Cambridge Law Journal*, 56 (1997); M. Weller, 'The Reality of the Emerging Universal Constitutional Order: Putting the Pieces Together', *Cambridge Review of International Affairs* (Winter/Spring, 1997).

Today the locus of effective political power can no longer be assumed to be national governments—effective power is shared and bartered by diverse forces and agencies at national, regional and international levels. Furthermore, the idea of a political community of fate—of a self-determining collectivity—can no longer meaningfully be located within the boundaries of a single nation-state alone. Some of the most fundamental forces and processes which determine the nature of life-chances within and across political communities are now beyond the reach of individual nation-states. The late twentieth century political world is marked by a significant series of new types of 'boundary problem'. In the past, of course, nation-states principally resolved their differences over boundary matters by pursuing reasons of state backed by diplomatic initiatives and, ultimately, by coercive means. But this power logic is singularly inadequate and inappropriate to resolve the many complex issues, from economic regulation to resource depletion and environmental degradation, which engender—at seemingly ever greater speeds –an intermeshing of 'national fortunes'. In a world where powerful states make decisions not just for their peoples but for others as well, and where transnational actors and forces cut across the boundaries of national communities in diverse ways, the questions of who should be accountable to whom, and on what basis, do not easily resolve themselves. Political space for the development and pursuit of effective government and the accountability of power is no longer coterminous with a delimited political territory. Contemporary forms of political globalization involve a complex deterritorialization and re-territorialization of political authority.[47]

Giving a shape to prospective world orders

Virtually all nation-states have gradually become enmeshed in and functionally part of a larger pattern of global transformations and global flows.[48] Transnational networks and relations have developed across virtually all areas of human activity. Goods, capital, people, knowledge, communications and weapons, as well as crime, pollutants, fashions and beliefs, rapidly move across territorial boundaries . Far from this being a world of 'discrete civilizations', or simply an international society of states, it has become a fundamentally interconnected global order, marked by intense patterns of interaction as well as by evident structures of power, hierarchy and unevenness.

Contemporary globalization is associated with a transformation of state power as the roles and functions of states are re-articulated, reconstituted and re-embedded at the intersection of globalizing and regionalizing networks and systems. The meta-phors of the loss, diminution or erosion of state power can misrepresent this recon-figuration. Indeed, such a language involves a failure to conceptualize adequately the nature of power and its complex manifestations since it represents a crude zero-sum view of power. The latter conception is particularly unhelpful in attempting to understand the apparently contradictory position of states under conditions of contemporary globalization. For whilst globalization is engendering, for instance, a

---

[47] See, in particular, J. Rosenau, *Along the Domestic–Foreign Frontier* (Cambridge, 1997).
[48] T. Nierop, *Systems and Regions in Global Politics* (London, 1994), p. 171.

reconfiguration of state–market relations in the economic domain, states and international public authorities are deeply implicated in this very process. Economic globalization by no means necessarily translates into a diminution of state power; rather, it is transforming the conditions under which state power is exercised. In other domains, such as the military, states have adopted a more activist posture, whilst in the political domain they have been central to the explosive growth and institutionalization of regional and global governance. These are not developments which can be explained convincingly in the language of the decline, erosion or loss of state power *per se*. For such metaphors (mistakenly) presume that state power was much greater in previous epochs; and, as Mann reminds us, on almost every conceivable measure states, especially in the developed world, are far more powerful than their antecedents.[49] But so too are the demands placed upon them. The apparent simultaneous weakening and expansion of the power of states under conditions of contemporary globalization is symptomatic of an underlying structural transformation. This is nowhere so evident as in respect of state sovereignty and autonomy, which constitute the very ideological foundations of the modern state.

There are many good reasons for doubting the theoretical and empirical basis of claims that states are being eclipsed by contemporary patterns of globalization. The position taken in this article is critical both of hyperglobalizers and of sceptics. We would emphasize that while regional and global interaction networks are strengthening, they have multiple and variable impacts across diverse locales. Moreover, it is not part of our argument that national sovereignty today, even in regions with intensive overlapping and divided authority structures, has been wholly subverted— such a view would radically misstate our position. But it is part of our argument that there are significant areas and regions marked by criss-crossing loyalties, conflicting interpretations of human rights and duties, interconnected legal and authority structures, etc., which displace notions of sovereignty as an illimitable, indivisible and exclusive form of public power. Patterns of regional and global change are transforming the nature and context of political action, creating a system of multiple power centres and overlapping spheres of authority.

Neither the sovereignty nor the autonomy of states is simply diminished by such processes. Indeed, any assessment of the cumulative impacts of globalization must acknowledge their highly differentiated character since particular types of impact— whether decisional, institutional, distributional or structural—are not experienced uniformly by all states. Globalization is by no means an homogenizing force. The impact of globalization is mediated significantly by a state's position in global political, military and economic hierarchies; its domestic economic and political structures; the institutional pattern of domestic politics; and specific government as well as societal strategies for contesting, managing or ameliorating globalizing imperatives.[50] The ongoing transformation of the Westphalian regime of sovereignty and autonomy has differential consequences for different states.

Whilst for many hyperglobalizers contemporary globalization is associated with new limits to politics and the erosion of state power, the argument developed here is critical of such political fatalism. For contemporary globalization has not only

---

[49] See Mann, 'Has Globalization Ended the Rise and Rise of the Nation-state?'.
[50] See A. Hurrell and N. Woods, 'Globalization and Inequality', *Millennium*, 24:3 (1995), pp. 447–70; R. O. Keohane and H. V. Milner (eds.), *Internationalization and Domestic Politics* (Cambridge, 1996); Jessop, 'Capitalism and its Future'; Mann, 'Has Globalization Ended the Rise and Rise of the Nation-state?'.

triggered or reinforced the significant politicization of a growing array of issue-areas, it has also been accompanied by an extraordinary growth of institutionalized arenas and networks of political mobilization, surveillance, decision-making and regulatory activity which transcend national political jurisdictions. This has expanded enormously the capacity for, and scope of, political activity and the exercise of political authority. In this respect, globalization is not, nor has it ever been, beyond regulation and control. Globalization does not prefigure the 'end of politics' so much as its continuation by new means. Yet, this is not to overlook the profound intellectual, institutional and normative challenge which it presents to the existing organization of political communities.

At the heart of this lies a growth in transborder political issues and problems which erode clearcut distinctions between domestic and foreign affairs, internal political issues and external questions, the sovereign concerns of the nation-state and international considerations. In all major areas of government policy, the enmeshment of national political communities in regional and global processes involves them in intensive issues of transboundary coordination and control. Political space for the development and pursuit of effective government and the accountability of political power is no longer coterminous with a delimited national territory. The growth of transboundary problems creates what was earlier referred to as 'overlapping communities of fate'; that is, a state of affairs in which the fortune and prospects of individual political communities are increasingly bound together.[51] Political communities are locked into a diversity of processes and structures which range in and through them, linking and fragmenting them into complex constellations. Moreover, national communities themselves by no means make and determine decisions and policies exclusively for themselves when they decide on such issues as the regulation of sexuality, health and the environment; national governments by no means simply determine what is right or appropriate exclusively for their own citizens.

These issues are most apparent in Europe, where the development of the European Union has created intensive discussion about the future of sovereignty and autonomy within individual nation-states. But the issues are important not just for Europe and the West, but for countries in other parts of the world, for example, Japan and South Korea. These countries must recognize new emerging problems, for instance, problems concerning AIDS, migration and new challenges to peace, security and economic prosperity, which spill over the boundaries of nation-states. In addition, the communities of East Asia are developing within the context of growing interconnectedness across the world's major regions. This interconnectedness is marked in a whole range of areas from the environment, human rights, trade and finance, to issues of international crime. There are emerging overlapping communities of fate generating common problems within and across the East Asian region. In other words, East Asia, as recent developments have demonstrated, is necessarily part of a more global order and is locked into a diversity of sites of power which shape and determine its collective fortunes.

The idea of government or of the state, democratic or otherwise, can no longer be simply defended as an idea suitable to a particular closed political community or nation-state. The system of national political communities persists of course; but it

---

[51] See Held, *Democracy and the Global Order*; *Models of Democracy*, second edition (Cambridge, 1996); and Archibugi, Held and Köhler, *Re-imagining Political Community*.

is articulated and re-articulated today with complex economic, organizational, administrative, legal and cultural processes and structures which limit and check its efficacy. If these processes and structures are not acknowledged and brought into the political process they will tend to bypass or circumvent the traditional mechanisms of political accountability and regulation. In other words, we must recognize that political power is being repositioned, recontextualized and, to a degree, transformed by the growing importance of other less territorially based power systems. Political power is now sandwiched in more complex power systems which have become more salient over time relative to state power.

Accordingly, we are compelled to recognize that the extensity, intensity and impact of a broad range of issues (economic, political or environmental) raise questions about where those issues are most appropriately addressed. If the most powerful geo-political forces are not to settle many pressing matters simply in terms of their own objectives and by virtue of their power, then existing institutions and mechanisms of accountability need to be reconsidered. Such a reconsideration is an essential part of political inquiry, as Carr understood it. Political analysis, he wrote, 'must be based on a recognition of the interdependence of theory and practice, which can be attained only through a combination of utopia and reality'.[52] Thus, he always sought to link substantive inquiry into power with normative reflection on its desirable form. Pursuing this dual focus, we explore below recent approaches to the reconsideration of the proper nature and form of political power in the face of contemporary globalization. Indeed, it is possible to identify four leading schools of thought—the neo-liberal, liberal-reformist, radical and cosmopolitan—which together contribute a taxonomy of prospective world orders.

For the advocates of a neo-liberal world order, globalization today defines a new epoch in human history in which 'traditional nation-states have become unnatural, even impossible business units in a global economy'.[53] Such a view privileges an economic logic and affirms the emergence of a single global market alongside the principle of global competition as the harbingers of human progress. The neo-liberals celebrate the fact that economic globalization is bringing about a denationalization of economies through the establishment of transnational networks of production, trade and finance. In this 'borderless' economy, national governments are relegated to little more than transmission belts for global market forces. As Strange interprets this view, 'where states were once the masters of markets, now it is the market, which, on many critical issues, is the master over the governments of states... the declining authority of states is reflected in a growing diffusion of authority to other institutions and associations, and to local and regional bodies'.[54]

For the elites and 'knowledge workers' in this new global economy tacit transnational 'class' allegiances have evolved, cemented by an ideological attachment to a neo-liberal economic orthodoxy. Even amongst the marginalized and dispossessed the world-wide diffusion of a consumerist ideology also imposes a new sense of identity, displacing traditional cultures and ways of life. The global spread of Western liberal democracy further reinforces the sense of an emerging civilization defined by universal standards of economic and political organization. This civilization is replete with mechanisms of global governance, whether it be the IMF

---

[52] Carr, *The Twenty Years' Crisis*, p. 13. See also his remarks on realism and utopianism on p. 10.
[53] Ohmae, *The End of the Nation State*, p. 5.
[54] Strange, *The Retreat of the State*, p. 4.

or the disciplines of the world market, such that states and peoples are increasingly the subjects of a plurality of new public and private, global and regional, authorities. Accordingly, globalization is considered by many neo-liberals as the harbinger of the first truly 'global civilization'.[55] This represents a radically new world order; one which its advocates argue prefigures the demise of the nation-state and the liberation of peoples to pursue their interests unencumbered from the dictates of the stifling bureaucracy and the power politics of states. Economic power and political power, in this view, are becoming effectively denationalized and diffused such that nation-states are increasingly becoming 'a transitional mode of organization for managing economic affairs'.[56] For neo-liberals this is to be welcomed since it represents nothing less than the fundamental reconfiguration of world order to fit with the aspirations of peoples rather than states.

Rooted in what Carr referred to as the 'harmony of interests' between states—as opposed to a world shaped by global competition and global markets—liberal-reformism considers that political necessity will bring about a more cooperative world order. Avoiding global ecological crisis and managing the pervasive social, economic and political dislocation arising from contemporary processes of economic globalization 'will require the articulation of a collaborative ethos based upon the principles of consultation, transparency, and accountability. . . . There is no alternative to working together and using collective power to create a better world'.[57] In key respects, liberal-reformism is a normative theory which seeks to recast elements of world order. In essence, its contemporary advocates, such as the Commission on Global Governance, aim to construct a more democratic world in which states are more accountable to peoples. In late 1995 the Commission published its report, *Our Global Neighbourhood*.[58] The report recognizes the profound political impact of globalization: 'The shortening of distance, the multiplying of links, the deepening of interdependence: all these factors, and their interplay, have been transforming the world into a neighbourhood'.[59]

To achieve a more secure, just and democratic world order the report proposes a multifaceted strategy of international institutional reform and the nurturing of a new global civic ethic. Central to its proposals is a reformed United Nations system buttressed by the strengthening, or creation, of regional forms of international governance, such as the EU. Through the establishment of a Peoples' Assembly and a Forum of [Global] Civil Society, both associated with the UN General Assembly, the world's peoples are to be represented directly and indirectly in the institutions of global governance. Moreover, the Commission proposes that individuals and groups be given a right of petition to the UN through a Council of Petitions, which will recommend action to the appropriate agency. Combined with the deeper entrenchment of a common set of global rights and responsibilities the aim is to strengthen notions of global citizenship. An Economic Security Council is proposed to coordinate global economic governance, making it more open and accountable. Democratic forms of governance within states are to be nurtured and strengthened through international support mechanisms whilst the principles of sovereignty and

[55] See Perlmutter, 'On the Rocky Road to the First Global Civilization'.
[56] Ohmae, *The End of the Nation State*, p. 149.
[57] Commission of Global Governance, *Our Global Neighbourhood* (Oxford, 1995), pp. 2 and 5.
[58] Ibid.
[59] Ibid., p. 43.

240   David Held and Anthony McGrew

non-intervention are to be adapted 'in ways that recognize the need to balance the rights of states with the rights of people, and the interests of nations with the interests of the global neighbourhood'.[60] Binding all these reforms together is a commitment to the nurturing of a new global civic ethic based upon 'core values that all humanity could uphold: respect for life, liberty, justice and equity, mutual respect, caring, and integrity',[61] central to this global civic ethic is the principle of participation in governance at all levels from the local to the global.

Richard Falk has referred to the Commission as the 'last of the great liberal commissions'.[62] Given their faith in progress and human rationality, liberal-reformists, since the last century, have argued that creating a peaceful and democratic world order is far from a utopian project but, on the contrary, a necessity in a world of growing interdependence. As a normative theory of world order, it is concerned with how to reform the system of states with the aim of abolishing power politics and war. In the twentieth century, liberal-reformist ideology has played a critical role in the design of international institutions, specifically under US hegemony, in the aftermath of both the First and Second world wars. The creation of the League of Nations, and a 'world safe for democracy', was effused with such ideology, as was the establishment of the UN system. In the context of the post-Cold War New World Order, liberal-reformist ideas have acquired renewed vitality but have been adapted to fit 'new times'. Whilst still remaining faithful to the liberal political ideal—'to subject the rule of arbitrary power . . . to the rule of law within global society'[63]—contemporary thinking, as reflected in the Commission's report, is decidedly reformist rather than radical. Reformist in this context refers to incremental adaptation of the institutions and practices of world order, as opposed to their reconstruction. As expressed by Keohane, this is a normative vision of 'voluntary pluralism under conditions of maximum transparency'—a harking back to Woodrow Wilson's notion of open covenants openly arrived at.[64] It is reformist also in the sense that it gives 'peoples' a voice in global governance whilst not challenging the primacy of states and the most powerful states at that. Thus, the accountability and legitimacy of institutions of global governance are ensured 'not only by chains of official responsibility but by the requirement of transparency. Official actions, negotiated amongst state representatives in international organizations, will be subject to scrutiny by transnational networks'.[65]

While liberal-reformism emphasizes the necessary adaptation of core organizations in the existing world order, contemporary advocates of the 'radical project' stress the creation of *alternative* mechanisms of governance based upon civic republican principles: that is, inclusive, deliberative and self-governing communities in which the public good is to the fore.[66] The 'radical republican project' is concerned to establish the necessary conditions which will empower people to take control of

[60] Ibid., p. 337.
[61] Ibid., p. 336.
[62] R. Falk, 'Liberalism at the Global Level: The Last of the Independent Commissions?', *Millennium*, 24: 3 (1995), pp. 563–78.
[63] Commission on Global Governance, *Our Global Neighbourghood*, p. 5.
[64] R. Keohane, 'International Institutions: Can Interdependence Work?', *Foreign Policy* (Spring, 1998), pp. 82–96.
[65] Ibid.
[66] cf. Burnheim, *Is Democracy Possible?* (Cambridge, 1985); R. B. J. Walker, *One World, Many Worlds* (Boulder, CO., 1988); R. Falk, *On Humane Governance* (Cambridge, 1995).

their own lives and to create communities based upon ideas of equality, the common good, and harmony with the natural environment. For many radical republicans the agents of change are to be found in existing (critical) social movements, such as the environmental, women's and peace movements, which challenge the authority of states and international agencies as well as orthodox definitions of the 'political'. Through a politics of resistance and empowerment these new social movements are conceived as playing a crucial role in creating a new world order in a manner similar to the role of the (old) social movements, such as organized labour, in the struggle for national democracy. These new social movements are engaged in mobilizing transnational communities of resistance and solidarity against impending global ecological, economic and security crises. Underlying these projects is an attachment to the achievement of social and economic equality, the establishment of the neces- sary conditions for self-development, and the creation of self-governing political structures. Encouraging and developing in citizens a sense of simultaneous belonging to overlapping (local and global) communities is central to the politics of new social movements as well as to the search for new models and forms of social, political and economic organization consonant with the republican principle of self-government. The radical republican model is a 'bottom up' vision of civilizing world order. It represents a normative theory of 'humane governance' which is grounded in the existence of a multiplicity of 'communities of fate' and social movements, as opposed to the individualism and appeals to rational self-interest of neo-liberalism and liberal-reformism.

The cosmopolitan project, finally, attempts to specify the principles and the institutional arrangements for making accountable those sites and forms of power which presently operate beyond the scope of democratic control.[67] It argues that in the millennium ahead each citizen of a state will have to learn to become a 'cosmopolitan citizen' as well: that is, a person capable of mediating between national traditions, communities of fate and alternative forms of life. Citizenship in a democratic polity of the future, it is argued, is likely to involve a growing mediating role: a role which encompasses dialogue with the traditions and discourses of others with the aim of expanding the horizons of one's own framework of meaning and prejudice, and increasing the scope of mutual understanding. Political agents who can 'reason from the point-of-view of others' will be better equipped to resolve, and resolve fairly, the new and challenging transboundary issues and processes that create overlapping communities of fate. In addition, the cosmopolitan project contends that, if many contemporary forms of power are to become accountable and if many of the complex issues that effect us all—locally, nationally, regionally and globally—are to be democratically regulated, people will have to have access to, and membership in, *diverse* political communities. Put differently, a democratic political community for the new millennium necessarily describes a world where citizens enjoy multiple citizenships. Faced with overlapping communities of fate they need to be not only citizens of their own communities, but also of the wider regions in which they live, and of the wider global order. Institutions will certainly need to develop that reflect the multiple issues, questions and problems that link people together regardless of the particular nation-states in which they were born or brought up.

---

[67] See Held, *Democracy and the Global Order*; A. Linklater, *The Transformation of Political Community* (Cambridge, 1998); Archibugi, Held and Köhler, *Re-imagining Political Community*.

With this in mind, advocates of the cosmopolitan position maintain that the reform of world order needs to be rethought as a 'double-sided process'. By a double-sided process—or process of double democratization—is meant not just the deepening of democracy within a national community, involving the democratization of states and civil societies over time, but also the extension of democratic forms and processes across territorial borders. Democracy for the new millennium must allow cosmopolitan citizens to gain access to, mediate between, and render accountable, the social, economic and political processes and flows which cut across and transform their traditional community boundaries. The core of this project involves re-conceiving legitimate political activity in a manner which disconnects it from its traditional anchor in fixed borders and delimited territories and, instead, articulates it as an attribute of basic democratic arrangements or basic democratic law which can, in principle, be entrenched and drawn upon in diverse self-regulating associations—from cities and subnational regions, to nation-states, regions and wider global networks. It is clear that the process of disconnection has already begun as political authority and legitimate forms of governance are diffused 'below', 'above' and 'alongside' the nation-state. But the cosmopolitan project is in favour of a radical extension of this process so long as it is circumscribed and delimited by a commitment to a far-reaching cluster of democratic rights and duties. It proposes a series of short- and long-term measures in the conviction that, through a process of progressive, incremental change, geo-political forces will come to be socialized into democratic agencies and practices.[68]

Conclusion

It has been argued that the contemporary historical phase of globalization is transforming the very foundations of world order by reconstituting traditional forms of sovereign statehood, political community and international political relations. But these transformative processes are neither historically inevitable nor by any means fully secure. As a result, the contemporary world order is best understood as a highly complex, contested and interconnected order in which the interstate system is increasingly embedded within evolving regional and global political networks. The latter are the basis in and through which political authority and mechanisms of governance are being articulated and re-articulated. To refer to the contemporary world order as a complex, contested, interconnected order is to acknowledge the 'messy appearances' which define global politics at the turn of the new millennium. Globalization involves a shift away from a purely state-centric politics to a new more complex form of multilayered global governance. There are multiple, overlapping political processes at work at the present historical conjuncture.

In reflecting upon the inter-war years, Carr argued that the real lesson of this epoch of international crisis was 'the final and irrevocable breakdown of the conditions which made the nineteenth-century order possible'.[69] To seek to restore that order was, in Carr's judgement, a useless project. Yet, in certain respects, that

---

[68] See Held, ibid., pt. III.
[69] Carr, *The Twenty Years Crisis*, p. 237.

was precisely what many of the architects of the post-war order sought to achieve and in so doing unleashed a new, distinctive phase of globalization. At the close of the twentieth century there are strong reasons for believing that, under conditions of contemporary globalization, the old states order can never be fully restored or effectively realized. Paradoxically, the idealism of the contemporary epoch tends to be most in evidence amongst those strands of international political analysis which conceive of world order as an expression of eternal truths—whether couched in terms of power politics or of the market—but which have yet to come to terms with the transformative impacts of contemporary globalization. Today, in Carr's words, 'the old order cannot be restored, and a drastic change of outlook is unavoidable'.[70] Such changes of outlook are clearly delineated in the contest between neo-liberalism, liberal-reformism, radicalism and cosmopolitanism. Globalization is not, as some suggest, narrowing or foreclosing political discussion; on the contrary, it is reilluminating and reinvigorating the contemporary political terrain.

[70] Ibid.

[24]

Justice unbound? Globalization, states and the transformation of the social bond

RICHARD DEVETAK AND RICHARD HIGGOTT*

'The political problem of mankind is to combine these things: economic efficiency, social justice and individual liberty.' John Maynard Keynes noted in *Essays in persuasion* (1931).

Globalization has become the most over used and under specified term in the international 'policy sciences since the end of the Cold War. It is a term that is not going to go away. More recently, globalization has come to be associated with financial collapse and economic turmoil but our ability to satisfy Keynes' three requirements under conditions of globalization is as remote now as at the time he was writing. Neither markets nor the extant structures of governance appear capable of providing for all three conditions at once. Globalization has improved economic efficiency and it has provided enhanced individual liberty for many; but in its failure to ensure social justice on a global scale, it also inhibits liberty for many more.

Even leading globalizers—proponents of continued global economic liberalization occupying positions of influence in either the public or private domain—now concede that in the failure to deliver a more just global economic order, globalization may hold within it the seeds of its own demise. As James Wolfenson, President of the World Bank, noted '… [i]f we do not have greater equity and social justice, there will be no political stability and without political stability no amount of money put together in financial packages will give us financial stability'.[1] His words, even if they appear to invert justice and stability as 'means' and 'ends', are a sign of the times in the international financial institutions.

Conventional accounts of justice suppose the presence of a stable political society, community or state as the site where justice can be instituted or realized. Moreover, conventional accounts, whether domestic or global, have also assumed a Westphalian cartography of clear lines and stable identities and a settled, stable social bond. In so doing conventional theories—essentially liberal individualist theory (and indeed liberal democracy more generally)—have limited our ability to think about political action beyond the territorial state.

---

* The authors would like to thank Robin Hodess of the Carnegie Council for Ethics and International Affairs for her contribution to this paper.

[1] Address to the Board of Governors of the Bank (October 1998).

Richard Devetak and Richard Higgott

But what if the territorial boundaries of politics are becoming unbundled and a stable social bond deteriorates. Must a conception of justice relinquish its Westphalian coordinates? These are not merely questions for the political philosopher. In a time when the very fabric of the social bond is constantly being rewoven by globalization, they cast massive shadows for those making policy.

There are no settled social bonds in an age of globalization; the Westphalian 'givens' of justice no longer pertain. The forces and pressures of modernity and globalization, as time and space compress, render the idea of a stable social bond improbable. If this is the case, how are we to think about justice? When the social bond is undergoing change or modification as a consequence of globalizing pressures how can justice be conceptualized, let alone realized? Can there be justice in a world where that bond is constantly being disrupted, renegotiated and transformed by globalization? What are the distributive responsibilities under conditions of globaliztion, if any, of states? What should be the role of the international institutions in influencing the redistribution of wealth and resources on a global scale?

These are serious normative questions about governance. In the absence of institutions of governance capable of addressing these questions, justice (no matter how loosely defined) is unlikely to prevail. This paper suggests we need to begin to think about the relationship between globalization, governance *and* justice. To date, the question of 'justice'—a central question of academic political philosophy as practised within the context of the bounded sovereignty of the nation state—is underdeveloped as a subject of study under conditions of globalization. Similarly, the study of globalization—especially when understood as economic liberalization and integration on a global scale—has been equally blind to 'justice' questions. This should come as no surprise. The struggle to separate normative and analytical enterprises has long been common practice in the social sciences. Indeed, it has been for a long time the hallmark of 'appropriate' scholarly endeavour. But such is the impact of globalization that we need to consider how we can traverse this artificial divide. Nowhere is this more important than at the interface of the processes of globalization and our understanding of what constitutes the prospects for creating a just international order at the end of the second millennium.

This article is in three sections. Section one looks at the changing role of the state under conditions of globalization. It explains how assumptions made about the social bond—almost exclusively conceived in terms of sovereignty—are changing. It considers the specific challenges to the embedded liberal compromise that did so much to solidify the social bond in welfare states in the post-Second World War era. Section two charts the rise of some new global (non-state) actors, that are now contesting with states over the policy agendas emanating from globalization. The argument is twofold. First, strain on the social bond within states is giving rise to a search for newer forms of organization that transcend the sovereign state. We thus need to rethink how we understand the public domain on a global, as opposed to a national, level.

Justice unbound?

Second, limited and flawed as the activities of non-state actors (especially NGOs and global social movements (GSMs)) are in the global public domain, they represent an important, evolving, alternative voice in the discourse of globalization to that of the semi-official, neo-liberal orthodoxy on globalization. Moreover, the voice of the NGO and the GSM is the one serious voice that aspires, rhetorically at least, to the development of a 'justice-based' dialogue beyond the level of the sovereign state.

Section three draws the strands of the first two sections together. It suggests that we have an analytical deficit occasioned by the failure of economic liberalism to assess the threat to its legitimacy emanating from its theoretical and practical myopia towards the *political* and *cultural* dynamics at work under globalization— the key sources of resistance to economic globalization. Neo-liberalism, with its emphasis on global commercialization, has forgotten why societal and democratic governmental structures were developed over the centuries.

Thus, the conclusion to the article exhorts us to remember that states have important practical assets and normative theoretical roles. They are not mere passive actors in the face of globalization and justice. Difficult as it would be even if we could conceive of structures of global governance that might deliver it, justice will prove even more elusive in the absence of such political structures under conditions of economic globalization. The prospects of a satisfactory synthesis of the imperatives of a liberal economic theory of globalization, a normative political theory of the global sphere and a new form of social bond to compensate for the decline of the social bond within the contours of the sovereign state are deemed to be slight.

Sovereignty and modern political life

The sovereign state is the primary subject of modern international relations. Indeed, it has been the exclusive legitimate subject of international relations in the Westphalian system; the highest point of decision and authority. Since the middle of the seventeenth century the sovereign form of state has become hegemonic by a process of eliminating alternative forms of governance.[2] The modern state achieved a particular resolution of the social bond hinged on the idea that political life is, or ought to be, governed according to the principle of sovereignty. The concept of sovereignty concentrated social, economic and political life around a single site of governance.

This conception of politics dates back to the legitimation crisis of the late sixteenth and early seventeenth centuries. Thomas Hobbes saw the political purpose of the sovereign state as the establishment of order based on mutual relations of protection and obedience.[3] The sovereign acted as the provider of security and the citizen in turn offered allegiance and obedience. This account

---

[2] Hendrik Spruyt, *The sovereign state and its competitors* (Princeton, NJ: Princeton University Press, 1994).
[3] Thomas Hobbes, *Leviathan* (Harmondsworth: Penguin, 1968).

Richard Devetak and Richard Higgott

emphasized sovereignty as the centre of authority, the origin of law and the source of individual and collective security. Citizens were bound together, whether for reasons of liberty or security, by their subjection to a common ruler and a common law. This basic structure of governance forged a social bond among citizens and between citizens and the state.

The institution of state sovereignty brought with it a spatial resolution which distinguished between the domesticated interior and the anarchical exterior. In general terms, inside and outside came to stand for a series of binary oppositions that defined the limits of political possibility.[4] Inside came to embody the possibility of peace, order, security and justice; outside, the absence of what is achieved internally: war, anarchy, insecurity and injustice. Where sovereignty is present governance is possible; where it is absent governance is precluded. Modern political life is predicated on an exclusionary political space ruled by a single, supreme centre of decision-making claiming to represent and govern a political community. In recent interpretations sovereignty has been understood as a constitutive political practice, one which has the effect of defining the social bond in terms of unity, exclusivity and boundedness and by the state's monopolization of authority, territory and community.[5]

A further crucial function performed by the sovereign state, of particular concern in this article, has been the management of the national economy. Historically there have been competing accounts of how states should govern their economies, especially over the manner and extent to which governments should intervene in and regulate economic activity. Yet historically, and despite many important ideological and normative differences, there has been a tendency within the dominant liberal tradition to treat national economies as discrete systems of social organization more or less delimited by the state's territorial boundaries. Economies are conceived as largely self-contained, self-regulating systems of exchange and production. This was as true for economic liberals such as Adam Smith and David Ricardo as it was for economic nationalists and mercantilists such as Friedrich List and Alexander Hamilton. This is not to suggest that such thinkers were blind to the fact that economic activity commonly spilled over national frontiers, but that they treated national economies as self-contained units in the international market.

The economy served the community of the state in which it was embedded; its functions and benefits were defined via the interests of a given political society. That states monopolized the right to tax within their boundaries enhanced the correlation of the economy with the state's boundaries. One of the general functions of the state therefore was to govern the economy in such a way as to promote the wealth and welfare of the community. Liberals focused on the market mechanism as the surest and most efficient means of ensuring the liberty, security and prosperity of both individuals and the community; non-

---

[4] R. B. J. Walker, *Inside/outside: international relations as political theory* (Cambridge: Cambridge University Press, 1993).
[5] Andrew Linklater, *The transformation of political community* (Cambridge: Polity, 1998).

Justice unbound?

liberal approaches tended to emphasize the need for regulation and manipulation of economic activity in order to satisfy the social needs of the community.

In short, a purpose of the sovereign state in modern political life was to stabilize the social bond. It did so by resolving questions of governance around the principle of sovereignty. Structures and practices of governance were established with direct correspondence between authority, territory, community and economy. It is in this context that justice has conventionally been conceived. Justice, no matter how defined, depended on a settled, stable social bond. Outside of a settled social bond justice was thought to be unlikely if not impossible. The sovereign state was thus a precondition for justice. However it is defined—whether as security from injury, as most natural law thinkers understood it, or as the distribution of rights and duties, as liberals tend to define it—justice has generally been circumscribed by the territorial limits of the sovereign state. The boundaries of justice were thought to be coextensive with the legal-territorial jurisdiction and economic reach of the sovereign polity.

But that was then. The sovereign state is a historical product that emerged in a particular time to resolve social, economic and political problems. With the passage of time, and the changed milieu in which states exist, it is no longer axiomatic that the sovereign state is practical or adequate as a means of *comprehensively* organizing modern political life and especially providing the array of public goods normally associated with the late twentieth-century welfare state. In the following section we survey the manner in which some of the trends associated with economic globalization have begun to unravel the distinctive resolution of the social bond achieved by the sovereign state, and in particular the welfare state. Increasingly, the sovereign state is seen as out of kilter with the times as globalization radically transforms time–space relations and alters the traditional coordinates of social and political life.

Globalization and embedded liberalism

Material changes associated with economic globalization—especially the processes of liberalization, deregulation and integration of the global economy in the domains of production, exchange and finance—are affecting the ability of the sovereign state to stabilize the social bond. Even if we reject the more extreme postmodern readings of sovereignty under globalization, several normative questions are raised by this destabilization. As the coordinates of modern social and political life alter, states—the traditional Westphalian site of authority—are supplemented, outflanked and sometimes overrun by competing sources of authority. Alternative sources of power and authority arising from globalization place pressure on the capacity of the state to deliver welfare provisions and, in turn, transform the social bond.

To be specific, the urge for free markets and small government has created asymmetries in the relationship between the global economy and the national state that have undermined the post-Second World War embedded liberal

487

Richard Devetak and Richard Higgott

compromise.[6] According to John Ruggie, the liberal international order was predicated on measures taken concurrently to ensure domestic order and to domesticate the international economy.[7] Consequently, the modern welfare state was the product of both domestic and international forces. States were the sites of trade-off, charged with cushioning domestic society against external pressures and transnational forces. But globalization has changed this and one as yet unexplored implication of Ruggie's early analysis is that it focuses attention on a reconfiguration of the social bond as a result of changes emanating from the processes of adjustment in the division of political space between the domestic and international policy domains. Domestic and international politics became embedded and intertwined in the same global system—the post-Second World War liberal order.

States are thus crucial in shaping the social bonds which exist at any given time and in any given space. They alter the relationship not just between insiders and outsiders, but between citizens and the state. However, as domestic and foreign economic policy issues become increasingly blurred, as the domestic economy becomes increasingly detached from the sovereign state, and as economic deregulation and denationalization continue, it is more difficult for states to manage the domestic–international trade-off in a way that satisfies competing demands on it. It becomes more difficult for states to sustain the trade-offs managed in the Bretton Woods, embedded liberal, era.

Globalization makes it harder for governments to provide the compensatory mechanisms that could underwrite social cohesion in the face of change in employment structures. As it has become more difficult to tax capital, the burden shifts to labour, making it more difficult to run welfare states.[8] Policy-makers may be wising up to this problem but a felt need to avoid socially disintegrative activities has not been joined by a clear policy understanding of how to minimize dislocation in the face of the tensions inherent in the structural imperatives of economic liberalization and where economic compensation alone may not be sufficient. In the closing days of the twentieth century, the internationalization of trade and finance may be sound economic theory, but it is also contentious political practice. When pursued in combination, free markets and the reduction of, or failure to, introduce compensatory domestic welfare is a potent cocktail leading to radical responses from the dispossessed.[9]

An economist's response to this dilemma—that liberalization enhances aggregate welfare—might well be correct, but it does not solve the *political problem*. It might be good economic theory but it is poor political theory. While some objections to liberalization are indeed 'protectionism' by another name, not all

[6] John G. Ruggie, 'At home abroad, abroad at home: international liberalisation and domestic stability in the new world economy', *Millennium: Journal of International Studies* 24: 3, 1995, pp. 507–26.

[7] John G. Ruggie, 'International regimes, transactions and change: embedded liberalism in the post war economic order', *International Organisation* 36: 2, 1982.

[8] Daniel Rodrik, *Has globalization gone too far?* (Washington, DC: Institute for International Economic Affairs, 1997).

[9] Vincent Cable, *The world's new fissures: the politics of identity* (London: Demos, 1994).

Justice unbound?

objections can be categorized in this manner. Moreover, even where compensatory mechanisms might be adequate, the destruction of domestic social arrangements can have deleterious outcomes of its own. If nationalist responses are to be avoided then public policy must distinguish between protectionism and legitimate concerns. Securing domestic political support for the continued liberalization of the global economy requires more than just the assertion of its economic virtue. It also requires political legitimation.

Thus the question facing political theorists and policy analysts alike is: can the embedded liberal compromise (maximizing the positive and mitigating the negative effects of international liberalization) be maintained, or repaired even? This is now a much wider question than when first formulated by Ruggie. Under conditions of globalization, the question must now be addressed not only within, but also beyond the boundaries of the state. Sovereignty as the organizing principle of international relations is undergoing a more dramatic rethink than at any time since its inception. In an era of globalization—accompanied by assumptions about the reduced effectiveness of states—policy-makers and analysts set greater store by the need to enhance the problem-solving capabilities of various international regimes in the resolution of conflict and the institutionalization of cooperation. But the contours of this rethink are still primarily linked to enhancing the effectiveness and efficiency of international regimes.

The language of globalization, especially in its neo-liberal guise, is about the managerialist capacity of the modern state. But it has failed to recognize the manner in which the internationalization of governance can also exacerbate the 'democratic deficit.' States are not only problem solvers; their policy elites are also strategic actors with interests of, and for, themselves. Collective action problem-solving in international relations is couched in terms of effective governance. It is rarely posed as a question of responsible or accountable government, let alone justice While these latter questions may be the big normative questions of political theory, it is the political theory of the bounded sovereign state. For most of the world's population, the extant institutions of global governance—especially the financial ones—are not seen to deliver justice.

Questions of global redistributive justice, accountability and democracy receive scant attention from within the mainstream of political philosophy and a political theory of global governance is in its infancy. Extant political theories of justice and representative governance assume the presence of sovereignty. In an era of a fraying social bond at the state level and the absence of alternative focuses of identity at the global level, the prospects of securing systems of efficiency, let alone accountability, seem slim. For realist scholars and practitioners of international relations this is unsurprising. They assume the absence of altruism. Force and power—not global dialogue about the prospects for community and democracy, *pace* the work of the cosmopolitan political theorists such as Linklater and Held[10]—are the driving forces of international relations.

[10] Linklater, *The transformation of political community*; David Held, *Democracy and the global order* (Cambridge: Polity, 1995).

Richard Devetak and Richard Higgott

Yet there is a paradox. The language of democracy and justice takes on a more important rhetorical role in a global context at the same time as globalization attenuates the hold of democratic communities over the policy-making process within the territorial state. As the nation-state as a vehicle for democratic engagement becomes problematic, the clamour for democratic engagement at the global level becomes stronger. But these are not stable processes. Attention to the importance of normative questions of governance and state practice as exercises in accountability, democratic enhancement and what we might call justice-generation, must catch up with our understanding of governance as exercises in effectiveness and efficiency. There are a number of ways to do this. One route, explored in section two, is to extend the public policy discourse on the nature of market–state relations to include other actors from civil society.

Global governance and the transformation of the public sphere

The modern social bond was conceived in terms of the concentration of authority, territory and community around the notion of sovereignty. Moreover, this political resolution was intimately tied to a notion of a corresponding economic space. But for 130 years—since the marginalist revolution—economic analysis has become separated from the study of politics and society. It is only with a recognition of globalization that civil society, along with the market and the state, has become an increasingly significant third leg of an analytical triangle without which our ability to reconstruct, or create, social solidarity, trust and political legitimacy is limited.[11] There is still a reluctance in much of the policy community to recognize the manner in which markets are socio-political constructions whose functioning (and legitimacy) depends on their possessing wide and deep support within civil society.

If sovereignty bestowed upon modern political life an organizational form premised on boundedness and exclusion, globalization is unpacking this form of organization. Under globalization—especially with the emergence of a new international division of labour underwritten by the increased, indeed largely unrestrainable, mobility of capital and technology—our understanding of political and economic space has changed. This section examines transformations in the public sphere brought about by the emergence of new actors under globalization, especially the increasing role of NGOs, the rise of multilateralism and an emerging emphasis on civil society in an interwoven triangular relationship with the state and the market. But if non-state actors are now influential agents of change in a number of key policy areas of international relations, we are less sure of the degree to which this influence is 'unscripted' or if it represents a coherent process of expanded international diplomacy 'appropriate' to globalization.

---

[11] Richard Higgott, 'Economics, politics and (international) political economy: the need for a balanced diet in an era of globalisation', *New Political Economy* 4: 1, 1999, pp. 23–36.

Justice unbound?

The public sphere, at least in its Kantian sense, is where 'private' individuals come together as free and equal participants in an informed discussion of matters affecting the common welfare of the community. Its emergence as a critical reaction to the absolutist state in the eighteenth century was driven by a sense that society could and should press its demands upon the abstract, impersonal, modern state. The public sphere functions as a zone where civil society can engage with and scrutinize the state's exercise of power and authority.[12] In performing the important legitimation function within the modern state, the public sphere is integral to the formation and transformation of the social bond. For a public sphere to be genuinely open it must be inclusive: any citizen who stands to be affected by decisions reached in discussion must be allowed to bring their perspective to bear and freely express their viewpoint.

Normally, the public sphere has been confined to individual states. Today, with the arrival of electronic communication technologies and other means by which time and space are compressed, it is possible to conceive of a transnational or global public sphere; that is, a public sphere which interacts and functions on the plane of global social relations. We survey below some of the ways in which the interaction between states and non-state actors now find expression in the global sphere

Transforming the global public sphere? Civil society and NGOs

Theoretically, one of the functions performed by non-state actors is to hold states and inter-governmental organizations to account. In much the same way that domestic civil society expresses itself via the public sphere, new social movements and NGOs are attempting to voice their concerns in a global public sphere. While remaining outside the official realm of the institutions of states and international organizations, they seek to establish the interests and rights of those generally excluded from discussion.

As embryonic as this global public sphere may be, it is possible to see the contours of an evolving arena where social movements, non-state actors and 'global citizens' join with states and international organizations in a dialogue over the exercise of power and authority across the globe. The emergence of the global public sphere, albeit partial, has an impact on the social bond by modifying the citizen's relationship to their own state, to citizens of other states, and to international organizations. The development of a global public sphere loosens the social bond traditionally defined by the sovereign state.

Global civil society has come to represent a domain that traverses the boundaries of the sovereign state, albeit in a range of contested ways. For some, global civil society is but a substitute for revolution forgone; it is merely the domain of the new managerial class, the habitat of 'Davos Man'. For others, it can be the source from which a more just society might develop in an era when

---

[12] Jurgen Habermas, *The theory of communicative action: the critique of functionalist reason* (London: Heinemann, 1989).

Richard Devetak and Richard Higgott

disillusionment with the ability of traditional forms of politics to deliver justice has never been higher. But is it legitimate to develop the concept of civil society beyond its origins in nineteenth-century European political thought? Is it permissible to extrapolate from civil to global civil society? We think so.

In contrast to its earlier correspondence with the bourgeoisie under the development of capitalism, Robert Cox calls for a 'bottom up' understanding of civil society in which:

[C]ivil society is the realm in which those who are disadvantaged by globalization of the world economy can mount their protests and seek alternatives...More ambitious still is the vision of a 'global civil society' in which these social movements together constitute a basis for an alternative world order. In a 'top down' sense ... states and corporate interests...[would make it]...an agency for stabilizing the social and political *status quo*...and thus enhance the legitimacy of the prevailing order.[13]

In such a theoretical formulation, NGOs, GSMs and other kinds of transnational associations become the principal actors in the reconstruction of political authority at the global level. Transnational associations bring together politically, culturally and territorially diverse organizations and individuals to advance a common agenda on one or another issue of global import. In empirical terms, the growth of NGOs has been dramatic. The number of international NGOs (defined as operating in more than three countries) was estimated to be in excess of 20,000 in 1994;[14] NGOs can facilitate cross-national policy transfer and modify policy processes; trans-national networks of NGOs are vehicles to empower domestic NGOs on a range of issue at the global level.

But increasingly prominent as they may be, it remains to be seen whether NGOs and GSMs are agents for building a post-Westphalian global civil society and reconstructing a new social bond at the end of the twentieth century. The behaviour of NGOs is invariably normative, prescriptive, increasingly inter-nationalized, highly politicized and at times very effective.[15] NGOs try to universalize a given value and their growing influence is revolutionizing the relationship between 'old' and 'new' forms of multilateralism. The old multi-lateralism is constituted by the top-down activities of the existing structures of international institutional governance (IMF, World Bank and WTO). The new multilateralism represents the attempt by social movements to build 'a system of global governance from the bottom up'.[16]

The preferred strategy of the old multilateralism of the international insti-tutions is to extend their remit *geographically* (wider institutional membership),

---

[13] Robert Cox, 'Civil society at the turn of the millennium: prospects for an alternative world order', *Review of International Studies* 25: 1, 1999, pp. 10–11.

[14] *Handbook of international organisations* (Brussels: Union of International Associations, 1994).

[15] Margaret E. Keck and Katherine Sikkink, *Actors beyond borders: advocacy networks in international politics*, (Ithaca, NY: Cornell University Press, 1998).

[16] Robert Cox, ed., *The new realism: perspectives on multilateral and world order* (Basingstoke: Macmillan, 1997), p. xxxvii.

Justice unbound?

functionally (deeper coverage of issues) and *inclusively* (by the co-option and socialization of recalcitrant actors into the dominant neo-liberal market mode). By contrast, the new multilateralism of the GSMs (especially NGOs in developing countries) tries to change prevailing organizing assumptions of the contemporary global order and thus alter policy outcomes. While multilateralism is not imperialism, a working assumption of many NGOs is that many existing institutions are instruments, if not of US hegemony, then at least of an OECD ideological dominance of the existing world economic order.

Whatever their agendas, the ability of social movements to affect decision-making in international fora rubs up against the processes of globalization. Throughout the 1990s, social movement resistance to 'free trade' related issues has invariably been characterized as protectionist or globophobic. This is certainly the case with the environmental movement, where demands for sustainable development imply a form of 'fettered development' to counter the deregulating tendencies of globalization. It is also the case in the domain of human rights, where NGOs attempt to strengthen labour rights generally (women's and children's rights in particular) in the face of MNCs' location decisions based on factors such as cheap labour costs. Much current NGO activity can be captured under a broad, if ill-defined agenda to secure 'justice for those disadvantaged by globalization'.

NGOs articulate a view of globalization—emphasizing privatization, deregulation and market conforming adjustment—as antithetical to their aims of securing human rights and environmental protection. NGOs represent alternative discourses to those reflected in the positions of those who gain most from the advance of globalization. Opposition to globalization has become an integrating feature of much of the literature of 'internationalized' NGOs.[17] Nowhere is this better illustrated than in the opposition to the North Atlantic Free Trade Agreement in the late 1980s and early 1990s, in resistance to the agendas of the WTO and the OECD initiative on a Multilateral Agreement on Investment in late 1990s. This interest in how to alter (resist) globalization represents a shift in the *modus operandi* of NGOs—from the field to the corridors of power. In many policy domains they have become the discursive opposition.

Traditional agents—such as the established policy communities holding office in the major industrial countries and the inter-governmental financial institutions—are only just beginning to recognize the significance of NGOs and GSMs. At times, established actors appear to lack the skills to deal in anything other than a resistive or combative fashion with these groups. But governments are learning that they must secure their support or, at the very least, neutralize their opposition. And the ability to secure a balance between wider consultation and accountability on the one hand and an ability to resist the pressures of lobby groups on the other is still underdeveloped. Nowhere is this better illustrated than in the ambiguity of the international economic institutions towards

[17] Cecilia Lynch, 'Social movements and the problem of globalisation', *Alternatives* 23: 2, 1998, pp. 149–73.

Richard Devetak and Richard Higgott

interaction with bodies purporting to be acting on behalf of one or another group within 'civil society'. This is certainly the case at the IMF, WTO and, albeit to a lesser extent, at the World Bank. While there is now quite a long history of engaging NGOs on the ground in developing countries at the World Bank, extending this engagement to the decision-making processes in Washington is still largely resisted.

In short, the elite driven nature of the neo-liberal globalization project is under challenge. The internationalization of NGOs, enhanced by new technologies, allows them to address governmental policy from outside, as well as from within, the state. They represent, or at least purport to represent, interests that are conventionally excluded from decision-making processes. As such, they are vehicles for the advancement of strong normative ideas in global civil society. NGOs and other similar, mission-driven, agents are increasingly important actors in contemporary international politics and governance. Securing a peaceful and constructive *modus operandi* with non-state actors will be a major exercise for state actors in the global policy community in the twenty-first century.

The rise and rise of the NGO: keeping a sense of perspective

Some NGOs are now global agents or players of influence, as the 1997 award of the Nobel Peace Prize for the campaign to ban landmines and the role of NGOs in the defeat of the Multilateral Agreements on Investments (MAI) attests.[18] NGOs are clearly capable of setting agendas and changing international policy on important issues. But the age of innocence is over. NGOs are in many ways the victims of their own success. Longer standing actors in international relations— state and intergovernmental organisation policy making elites—now treat them much more seriously.

At present there is a discrepancy between the demands of NGOs for rights (to be heard and to influence policy) and an acceptance of certain obligations or duties that may be attendant on these rights (especially the duty to reflect truthfully the position of one's antagonists). While a balance may come with time, to date only minimal efforts to inculcate a 'rights–duties' balance within the larger NGO families have been made.[19] If NGOs and other non-state actors are to become legitimate agents of acceptable structures of global governance in an era of globalization they will have to develop transparent, accountable and participatory systems of decision-making of exactly the kind they expect to see in national governments, multinational corporations and international organizations.

Speaking the language of 'opposition', their discourse reflects a greater commitment to questions of justice, accountability and democracy. But there are limits to the degree of support and acceptance their agendas are likely to secure. For example, despite the economic crisis that began in East Asia, the

[18] P. J. Simmons, 'Learning to live with NGOs', *Foreign Policy* 111, 1998, pp. 82–97.
[19] Leon Gordenker and Thomas G. Weiss, 'NGO participation in the global policy process', *Third World Quarterly* 16: 3, 1995, pp. 543–55.

Justice unbound?

power of the free market ideal remains strong, and support for interference in the interests of redistributive justice is unlikely to replace the market ideal in the corridors of public power and private wealth. Moreover, not all opponents of the worst effects of globalization are necessarily protectionists or opponents of economic liberalization *per se*. Educated populations are capable of disaggregating the various elements of liberalization. Survey data suggests greater support for trade liberalization than for financial deregulation.[20] Much social movement interest in the 'new protectionism'—a return to 'localization'—is an over-simplified rhetorical position that lacks the intellectual power to counter the logic of liberalization.

Globalization, justice and the state

That the activity and influence of NGOs has increased in international relations is in little doubt. It is naive, however, to universalize the NGO experience. States still propose and dispose of international agreements and NGOs still—as in their involvement in the activities of the international institutions—need governmental sponsorship, or at least governmental acquiescence, to secure influence.

Polarization, social disintegration and the re-emergence (often violent) of identity politics are visible outcomes of the inequalities between globalization's winners and losers. They raises several questions that will become increasingly important if we are to create a more just world order. Will we have: i) enough food for growing populations? ii) enough energy for growing economies? iii) a sustainable physical environment to inhabit? iv) global institutions to manage these issues, preserve the peace, prevent burgeoning civic unrest and political–military dislocation within the developing world and in relations between the developed and the developing worlds?

Economists tell us that the key elements of globalization—the greater economic integration of the international economy and the revolution in communications and technology—are, of themselves, neutral and have the potential to solve these problems. In theory maybe, but it is not axiomatic that the tension between economic growth and environmental sustainability will be contained. Making the world's population more secure depends on how this tension is managed. This is the governance question. Governance—the means by which societies deliver collective goods and minimize collective bads—is as important today as it ever was and states remain central to this process. But there is a deficit in the relationship between the *de facto* market led processes of economic liberalization and integration and the *de jure* state generated mechanisms that underwrite the international fora for the delivery of collective goods.

Thus, the efficacy of the major international institutions remains a key normative and policy question for the twenty-first century. Will they remain vehicles for the pursuit of state interests, as traditionally defined in realist understandings

[20] *The Economist*, 2 January 1999.

Richard Devetak and Richard Higgott

of international organization? Or, can they evolve into sites to accommodate multiple demands and interests of public and private and state and non-state actors throughout the widening policy communities and civil societies of states? These are normative and analytical questions, yet they cast long policy shadows. The contest between the 'multilateralism from above' and the 'multilateralism from below' is just beginning.

State policy elites may be conscious of their own diminished sovereignty but also of the accompanying need to control the 'public bads' that emanate from the effects of technology on cultures and eco-systems and the international order; especially the spread of drugs, crime, terrorism, disease and pollution. For sovereignty erosion to be acceptable, it must occur via collective action in an issue-specific, not generalized, manner. 'Sovereignty pooling' will have to be volunteered out of a recognition that self-interest is sometimes advanced collectively, not individually.

How likely is this when the major factor explaining inter-state cooperation is still *domestic actor preferences*?[21] Despite impeccable normative arguments in favour of collective action problem-solving, prospects for regular successful international cooperation among states must not be exaggerated. The desired basic goods for a 'just' global era—economic regulation, environmental security, the containment of organized crime and terrorism, and the enhancement of welfare—will not be provided on a state by state basis. They must be provided collectively.

If the limitations of inter-state cooperation are to be overcome, greater use will have to be made of innovative approaches to governance arising from the information revolution. Technology can strengthen the governance capacities of both state and civil society. Information technologies offer opportunities for private sector supplementation of the governance functions of states. Public/ private provision of collective goods must not be seen as an either/or policy option. Private sector actors, from both the corporate world and civil society, will continue to be more significant in inter-governmental negotiation processes as issue-linked coalitions operate across borders to set agendas and enforce compliance.

In addition to the 'how' question in the international institutional management of those global forces that have a major impact on societies, this article has also asked an important normative question. What are the prospects for supra-national institutional forms of regulation that guarantee some kind of fairness? Justice in a global context—we have tried to suggest—is an underdeveloped, but emerging issue. The normative agenda for international relations will not go away. But for justice to have meaning in an era of globalization, governance will have to be exercised at a global level. As yet, however, the institutions of global governance are ill-equipped to cope with such issues.

---

[21] Helen Milner, *Interests, institutions and information: domestic politics and international relations* (Princeton, NJ: Princeton University Press, 1997).

Justice unbound?

Moreover, we live in a culture of moral hazard in which, to provide but the most obvious example, the speculative operation of the international capital markets is underwritten by the sacrifices of ordinary members of society, especially in the developing world. The era of instant global capital mobility is seen by many of the world's population, and not just in the developing world, as a time of heightened and permanent insecurity. There may be movement in the international financial institutions, but unless something is done to mitigate the prospects of events such as the East Asia currency crises reoccurring, the lesson the majority of the world's population will draw is that even a reformed system, let alone the system as it is currently constituted, will be unable to deliver anything approaching an acceptably just or equitable world order.

In this respect, economic liberalization holds within it the seeds of its own downfall. Intellectual and evidentiary arguments for liberalization and open markets as superior generators of wealth have been won, or should have been. But rapid aggregate increases in global wealth and production have been accompanied by a corresponding naivety as to the political and social effects of these processes on the civil polities of developed and developing societies alike. As the politics of the East Asia crises demonstrated, theoretical parsimony blinds modern liberal economic theory and current market practices to the complex and combative politics that constitutes the downside of economic liberalization. Sound rationalist economic logic of its own is not sufficient to contain the backlash against globalization.[22]

Conclusion

For many in the developed world, liberalization has become an end in itself with little or no consideration given to its effect on prevailing social norms and values within societies and polities. Consequently, the consensus over how society is organized within the spatial jurisdiction of nation-states is strained and the continued process of liberalization is threatened. Globalization is unravelling the social bond. The policy remedies for maintaining the cohesion of communities at the disposal of state agents are curtailed, although not eliminated. Some governments attempt to 'depoliticize'—that is place at one remove—the state's responsibility for the effects of globalization on its citizenry. Yet it is the practice of politics that creates the structures of communities.[23] As such, it will make the role of state institutions much more important in the next decade than has been assumed throughout the neo-liberal era when the retreat of the state was deemed axiomatic.[24] States have assets and capabilities; they are not merely passive or reactive actors.

---

[22] See Richard Higgott, 'Economic crisis in East Asia: a case study in the international politics of resentment', *New Political Economy* 3: 3, 1998, pp. 333–56.
[23] Bernard Crick, *In defence of politics* (London: Penguin, 1962), p. 24.
[24] Susan Strange, *The retreat of the state* (Cambridge: Cambridge University Press, 1996).

Richard Devetak and Richard Higgott

But these assets have to be put to better use, domestically and internationally, if economic liberalization is to allow for the more effective provision of public goods. How to strike the appropriate balance between domestic socio-political imperatives and a normative commitment to an open liberal economic order remains the central policy question for the next century. Globalization is clearly an issue in need of sophisticated technical economic analysis, but it is also in need of analysis that is normative and ethical. First best, economically efficient solutions may not always be politically feasible, or indeed socially desirable, and most economic analysis has to date studiously ignored those socio-political and cultural conditions that, often more than economic explanation, will condition the prospects of continued liberalization.

Following from this analytical and theoretical deficit, the practical question facing policy-makers in the early twenty-first century will be how to develop appropriate international institutions; and 'appropriate' does not mean simply 'effective'. Attempts to implement collective policies through the international institutions will lack legitimacy if there is no shared normative commitment to the virtue of a given policy. International institutions must secure converging policy positions by agreement and willing harmonization, not by force. There must be provision, where necessary, for political communities to exercise an exit option on a particular issue where it is thought that this issue threatens the fibre of their (national) identity. This is not to offer a free riders' charter in the contemporary global economy, but to call for tolerance and an acceptance of difference rarely displayed under a neo-liberal orthodoxy in the closing stages of the twentieth century.[25] Without such tolerance the prospects for the development of some kind of social bond conducive to the development of a minimum conception of global justice cannot be envisaged.

[25] Stephen Gill, 'Globalisation, market civilisation and disciplinary neo-liberalism', *Millennium: Journal of International Studies* 24: 3, 1995, pp. 399–423.

Name Index